Harvard East Asian Series 72

DEUS DESTROYED

The East Asian Research Center at
Harvard University administers projects
designed to further scholarly understanding
of China, Korea, Japan, and adjacent areas.

DEUS DESTROYED

The Image of Christianity
in Early Modern Japan

GEORGE ELISON

HARVARD UNIVERSITY PRESS

CAMBRIDGE MASSACHUSETTS

1973

FILIS

GVLIELMO ANTONIOQVE

VT VITAM ATQVE IMAGINEM

PATRVORVM PATRIS

GVLIELMI ANTONIIQVE

AC

VIRI DOCTISSIMI

GEORGII ELISONAE

REFERANT

GEORGIVS IVNIOR

DEDICAT

Acknowledgments

WORKS of supererogation cannot be enumerated singly. All those on whose labors I drew can therefore not be acknowledged in this brief space. But they will surely pardon me; for it was not ill will that relegated some to footnotes.

I should like to mention first of all my teachers at Harvard University. Professor Donald Shively was my *Doktorvater* and Professor Edwin Reischauer the sponsor at my admission to academic grace. I wish to express here my gratitude for their kindness and assistance, which at times clearly went beyond the call of duty. I thank Professor Albert Craig for his careful and stimulating critique of the initial draft of this book. And I recall with fondness my days of study with Professors Howard Hibbett and Itasaka Gen, who impressed the humanistic stamp on my image of Japanese culture.

In the course of composition I imposed heavily on my friends. Peter Frost, now a member of the faculty of Williams College, helped to set my studies in motion during the early stages of my research in Japan, and has been most accommodating throughout. Extensive parts of this book reflect the suggestions of Bruce Spiegelberg of Franklin and Marshall College, who has the sharpest eye for solecisms of anyone I know. George Macklin Wilson of Indiana University has probably as sharp an eye for organizational flaws. To his day-by-day commentary, delivered over the course of a very hot summer, the final product owes much of its measure of coherence.

The first of this book's elements to be completed was the translation of Fabian Fucan's *Ha Daiusu*, which I did in 1961, when I held a fellowship from the Ford Foundation. Since then I have been the beneficiary of several other grants and research appointments. The translations were finished and much of the study's groundwork was laid down during the two years 1962–1964, when assistance from the Foreign Area Fellowship Program enabled me to come to Japan. An appointment as Research Associate at the Asian Studies Research Institute of Indiana University in 1969 gave me the opportunity to reconsider what was by then a semifinal manuscript; and it was substantially redrawn in the summer of 1970, when I was Research Fellow of the East Asian Research Center at Harvard. I am very grateful to those who contributed to my stay at these two institutions, and particularly to their directors, Professor Denis Sinor and Professor John King Fairbank.

The book was finished while I was again in Japan, working on a project which inspired the addition of a chapter, although at first it seemed unrelated to the topic of the early Christian mission and its relics. Chapter 8—which I have subtitled "Epitaph to an Encounter"—owes its entire concept and a good part of its material to my current study of another encounter between Japan and the West, the Meiji Restoration. That most complex of problems has taken me into far wider fields than I originally envisioned, and this is probably only my first of several opportunities to acknowledge the project's source of support, the National Endowment for the Humanities.

I owe a special debt of gratitude to Professor Motoyama Yukihiko. His helpfulness has made my most recent term of study in Kyoto not merely pleasant but possible in the first place. By his recommendation I became a Research Associate at Kyoto University, where he teaches. Moreover, he graciously permitted me the use of his study, where I have worked for the past half-year. These facilities were important, and the completion of this book would have been far delayed without them. Above all, however, I value Professor Motoyama's constant good humor, friendly solicitude, and expert counsel.

Finally, I wish to express my profound appreciation to my wife, the former Nakabayashi Toshiko of Kyoto, who helped me infinitely, and not only in translations from the Spanish. Her knowledge of the detail of history surpasses that of many scholars. To our two sons this book is dedicated.

Unzen   20 July 1971

Chronology

ix

1581   —*firm guidelines for a Japanese mission policy are set down by Valignano*
1582   —**Honnōji Affair: Akechi Mitsuhide attacks and kills Nobunaga**
(21 June; Tenshō 10/6/2)
—**Battle of Yamazaki: Toyotomi Hideyoshi eliminates Akechi and
begins his rise to hegemony over Japan** (2 July; Tenshō 10/6/13)
—*150,000 Christians in Japan*
1584   —the Shimazu destroy Ryūzōji Takanobu at Okitanawate and rise to pre-eminence in Kyushu
1585   —Tokugawa Ieyasu sends hostages to Hideyoshi, concluding a peace agreement (January); Hideyoshi defeats the Shingon sectarians of Negoro (April) and Chōsogabe Motochika of Tosa (July)
1586   —*Vice-Provincial Coelho requests Hideyoshi's intervention against the Shimazu and promises Christian support in his invasion plans* (Osaka Audience; 4 May); Hideyoshi orders Shimazu Yoshihisa to make peace in Kyushu (19 May)
1587   —the Shimazu forces occupy Funai in Bungo (January)
—Hideyoshi sets out from Osaka to invade Kyushu (April)
—Shimazu Yoshihisa capitulates to Hideyoshi (June)
—**Hideyoshi issues decrees restricting the practice of Christianity**
(23 July; Tenshō 15/6/18) **and expelling the missionaries from Japan**
(24 July; Tenshō 15/6/19)
1590   —*Valignano arrives in Japan on his second visit* (to 1592)
—**Hideyoshi defeats the Hōjō of Odawara and is supreme in Japan**
(12 August; Tenshō 18/7/13)
1591   —suppression of the rebellion of Kokonoe Masazane in Mutsu: all Japan is reunified under Hideyoshi's hegemony
1592   —Hideyoshi's armies invade Korea
1593   —*Spanish Franciscans are permitted to remain in Japan: the Jesuit mission monopoly is broken*
1596   —the Spanish galleon *San Felipe* is wrecked on Shikoku and its cargo confiscated; *the Jesuit-Franciscan quarrel exacerbates the situation*
1597   —**martyrdom of the Twenty-Six Saints of Japan: first instance of bloody persecution of Christianity** (5 February; Keichō 1/12/19)
1598   —*Valignano arrives in Japan on his third visit* (to 1603)
—**death of Hideyoshi** (18 September; Keichō 3/8/18); the Japanese armies are withdrawn from Korea
1599   —Tokugawa Ieyasu permits the Franciscans to settle in Edo
1600   —the first Dutch ship (*Liefde*) arrives in Japan
—*the Jesuits resume their public mission in Kyoto*
—**Battle of Sekigahara: Tokugawa Ieyasu becomes the paramount power in Japan** (21 October; Keichō 5/9/15)
1601   —*the first two Japanese are ordained to the priesthood*
1603   —**Ieyasu acquires the title of shogun: establishment of the Tokugawa Bakufu** (24 March; Keichō 8/2/12)
—*the Dominicans begin mission activities in Japan*
1605   —Ieyasu passes on the shogunal title to his son Hidetada, retiring to Sunpu
—*Fabian Fucan writes the* MYŌTEI MONDŌ
1609   —the Dutch establish a trading factory at Hirado
—*222,000 Christians under the care of the Society of Jesus in Japan*
1612   —*the Bakufu issues decrees prohibiting Christianity and takes steps against the mission in its immediate domains*

1613   —the English establish a trading factory at Hirado (bankruptcy 1623)

1614   —**Statement on the Expulsion of the Bateren: beginning of the general persecution** (1 February; Keichō 18/12/23)
—Osaka Winter Campaign (November; armistice 19 January 1615)

1615   —**fall of Osaka Castle, death of Toyotomi Hideyori, and end of Hideyoshi's heritage** (4 June; Keichō 20/5/8)

1616   —**death of Ieyasu** (1 June; Genna 2/4/17)
—the Bakufu restricts foreign trade to Nagasaki and Hirado (September)

1620   —*Fabian Fucan writes the* HA DAIUSU

1622   —*the Great Martyrdom in Nagasaki*

1623   —Hidetada passes on the shogunal title to his son Iemitsu (August)
—*the Great Martyrdom in Edo* (December)

1633   —Sakoku Edict I severely restricts Japanese trade and travel overseas, and prohibits the return of Japanese who had settled abroad (7 April; Kan'ei 10/2/28)
—*apostasy of the Jesuit Mission Superior Christovão Ferreira* (October)

1634   —Sakoku Edict II (23 June; Kan'ei 11/5/28)

1635   —Sakoku Edict III puts an end to Japanese shipping overseas, and prohibits under pain of death any Japanese travel abroad (12 July; Kan'ei 12/5/28)

1636   —Sakoku Edict IV (22 June; Kan'ei 13/5/19)
—the Portuguese traders are restricted to the artificial island of Deshima in Nagasaki harbor
—*Christovão Ferreira writes the* KENGIROKU

1637   —*martyrdom of Marcello Mastrilli* (October)
—**Shimabara Rebellion** (11 December; Kan'ei 14/10/25——12 April 1638; Kan'ei 15/2/28)

1639   —**final Sakoku edict: end of the Portuguese trade and of all Japanese traffic with Catholic lands** (4 August; Kan'ei 16/7/5)
—*composition of the* KIRISHITAN MONOGATARI (September)

1640   —*the office of the inquisition* (shūmon-aratame yaku) *is established by the Bakufu, and Inoue Chikugo no Kami appointed its first incumbent*
—execution of the Macao embassy in Nagasaki: 61 merchants and seamen are put to death (August)

1641   —the Dutch trading factory is transferred from Hirado to Deshima

1642   —*landing and immediate capture* (August) *of the First Rubino Group of Jesuits* (martyred March 1643)

1643   —*capture* (June) *and apostasy* (October) *of the Second Rubino Group*

1647   —a Portuguese embassy is blockaded in Nagasaki harbor and forced to depart unreceived

1662   —*publication of Suzuki Shōsan's* HA KIRISHITAN

1685   —failure of the last Portuguese attempt to re-establish relations with Japan

1708   —*Giovanni Battista Sidotti, the last Christian missionary to break the seals of Sakoku, is captured off Kyushu* (death in prison 1714)

Contents

Translations

DEUS DESTROYED

Introduction

THE "Christian Century" of
Japan extends from 1549 to 1639, from the arrival of Saint
Francis Xavier to the Tokugawa interdiction of all traffic with
Catholic lands. The century falls short of a hundred years, the
religion failed in its evangelical aims. Paradoxically, the significance of this *entr'acte* is not in the triumph of Christianity but
in the effect of its defeat. The Christian intrusion left few
Christian traces; it was but the exotic element in an already
gaudy period of Japanese history. But upon the "Christian
Century" follow more than two centuries of Sakoku, the Closed
Country. The Christian aberration would be a mere interlude
were it not for its causal relation to the Sakoku policy. The
total rejection of Christianity helps to define an era.

Christianity was introduced into Japan at a time when that
country's mediaeval order was in its final convulsions. The
missionaries viewed a tumbling body politic. But beneath the
surface of a country rent by war developed institutional changes
which gave form to Japanese history's Early Modern period.
The broad terms which define this concept of comparative
history for Europe apply as well to Japan: secularization of the
tenor of life and rationalization of political authority. In the
Japanese interpretation, the ethos and the doctrine of Christianity
clashed with these.

Japanese thought held no preconception corresponding to the
Christian predicate. The Japanese critic found the notion of an
omnipotent personal deity specious, its consequence disastrous.
The foreign religion could be accused of otherworldliness; for
the Christians removed the justification of human action from
the social sphere to an extraterrestrial locus. The Christian
dictate of a supernal loyalty pre-empted loyalty to a secular
sovereign. Philosophy, ethics, and politics rejected the Christian
claim that the One God existed and acted to determine the
moral order.

These judgments the artificers of Early Modern Japan took into
account and applied to the fabric of policy. The negative verdict
was prosecuted unremittingly under the Tokugawa Bakufu: the

I

stigmatization of all internal traces of Christianity is one of the most prominent motifs in the history of the shogunate's establishment and initial development. This measure could not be effective unless external Christian influences were denied entry. And contacts with the outside world were cut.

Tokugawa Japan is a culture under isolation. The brief Azuchi-Momoyama age, which preceded it, appears flamboyantly cosmopolitan by contrast. But the anti-Christian verdict had already been weighed, passed, and partially implemented by the immediate predecessors of the Tokugawa. Direct antecedents of the shogunate's policy are found along the course which Toyotomi Hideyoshi (in his own fashion a champion of external contacts and foreign ventures) set in reorganizing Japan. And the seeming friend of the foreigners, Oda Nobunaga, in his steps against Buddhist sects first set in motion the machinery which his successors were to operate so efficiently against the Christians. To check centrifugal tendencies was the common interest of the hegemons; and they worked to eliminate potential poles of disaffection. The required corollaries of their labors were the suppression of Christianity and the land's nearly total seclusion. The dictates of internal policy were the principal causes of Christianity's doom.

The acceptance of Christianity in Japan was a peculiar phenomenon of the disjointed polity of Sengoku, the Country at War, and the factors which had made it possible were nullified in the Tokugawa realm of political equilibrium and an established intellectual orthodoxy. The rejection of Christianity was a necessary characteristic of this Japanese version of the state as a work of art, whose dynamic tensions were held in bounds by the cordons of Sakoku. The political organism of the Tokugawa—the *bakuhan* system—was in many ways a remarkable structure. Its most notable aspect was, of course, its endurance as a régime of peace for over two hundred years. But the stability was posited upon a subtle arrangement of countervailing forces. The structure's architects were primarily intent, at the time when they formulated the Sakoku policy, that nothing should disturb the balance of what yet seemed a perilously organized realm. They viewed with the gravest suspicion the Christians' loyalty to foreign masters, and refused to distinguish between spiritual and temporal allegiance. Indeed, in the case of certain daimyo of Sengoku Japan, that distinction is difficult to draw even today.

One of them, Ōmura Sumitada, had even ceded the authority over Nagasaki and the neighboring portion of his domain to the Jesuit Order.

The Tokugawa policy-makers extended the principle of distrust into a sweeping generality. The causes of Sakoku were complex, but a nurtured stage of alarm at Christianity as the external threat was prime matter in the policy's justification. And Sakoku became the sum total of the shogunate's approach to foreign affairs.

The conclusive proscription in the final Sakoku Edict of 1639 of all vessels of the Christian contagion was forced by the shock of the Shimabara Uprising of 1637–38. Although even hostile sources attribute the origins of the outbreak to the harsh taxation levied by a lord who was inordinately greedy, the rising did possess an incontrovertibly Christian taint. The peasants were spurred on by quasi-messianic hopes; the blazon of their leader, Amakusa Shirō Tokisada, was "LOVVADᵒ SEIA O SÂCTISSIMᵒ SACRAMENTO."[1] In their inspection of the emblems of the Shimabara Uprising, the leaders of the newly established Tokugawa régime could review the other major crisis in the securing of their dominance over Japan. When quelling the vestigial challenge of Toyotomi Hideyori's party in the Osaka Campaigns of 1614 and 1615, they saw the ranks of their adversaries swelled by Christian rōnin with "so many crosses, *Jesus* and *Santiagos* on the flags, tents, and other martial insignia which the Japanese use in their encampments, that this must needs have made Ieyasu sick to his stomach."[2]

The Tokugawa indeed felt that Christianity was a disease which infected their subjects with disloyalty. Their effort to extirpate Christianity inspired certain of the measures of social control which were such significant features of their system. Forced registry of all the land's people in Buddhist temples made of Buddhism an instrument applied to the elimination of religious heterodoxy. Groups of collective responsibility—the five-family neighborhood associations, *goningumi*—were utilized to arrest the Christian peril. The suspiciousness of the Tokugawa officials, and the thoroughness of their control measures, reached a hysterical pitch akin to that of their Spanish contemporaries (or of those petty bureaucrats of modern Germany) who were bent on enforcing "racial purity." Entry into almost any sort of service occupation involved the prior attestation that the person was not a Christian. For instance, a whore's initial contract required such a formula; for officialdom was most concerned that the lady's customers not be contaminated.[3]

The governmental measures were fortified by an artfully composed image of Christianity as the pernicious faith, *jashūmon*. The theme was developed by literary hacks, but also by adroit intellectual figures, by the Japanese Buddhist, but also by the renegade European Jesuit. Grotesqueries dominated the orchestration of propaganda directed at the plebeian. But the niveau of other tracts was substantially higher. The range of rejection is represented in the works included below; the acid-toned picture is best viewed directly, as its authors developed it.

The image has many aspects, its study a multiple interest; there are various approaches to it. The initial encounter between Christianity and Japan is an important chapter in the history of religion and has often been treated as such. But a further excursion into missiology is not the purpose of this book. The context of international history has provided the frame for other writers, who have emphasized (and sometimes exaggerated) the benefits for Japan of the contact of cultures and accordingly have been forced to view Sakoku as a tragedy. Such assumptions, however, tend to be overly subjective and are at best of doubtful value. The factors of Japanese institutional history are the most important in the analysis of Christianity's impact: the stimulus to the development of the Tokugawa polity and policy was considerable. But the avenue of intellectual and cultural history is the most interesting, because the connection with the institutional realm is so apparent.

In discussing the Tokugawa system one assumes that this body politic, while being the result of evolutionary processes, was also in many respects an artificial structure. Its components were carefully articulated at various levels: there was design and choice in the construction. And Neo-Confucianism was the society's intellectual matrix.[4]

The Neo-Confucian philosophy was not new to Japan; but in the Early Modern period it ceased being the private province of littérateurs and the academic field of Zen monks, and was transferred into the public domain. Its standards were consciously applied to the shaping of policy, and were eventually internalized in the society. The universal East Asian ideology fitted the particular ends of Japan: the Tokugawa hierarchy was founded upon it; Japanese values were further patterned by it. The Japanese leadership relied on a Chinese system—there was, after all, a measure of cosmopolitanism in a country which had chosen isolation. The artificiality of the Tokugawa structure is illustrated nicely by this Sakoku paradox. The paradox, however, would have been stretched beyond tolerance by the inclusion of the totally alien Christian ideology.

The principal ideological battle of Sengoku and the early Tokugawa period was fought over the varying interpretations of the concept of *Tenmei*, Heaven's Mandate, or *Tentō*, Heaven's Way. Indeed, Kitajima Masamoto has suggested that the prime service of Chu Hsi scholars to the Bakufu was the subjugation of the mediaeval *Weltanschauung* embodied in this concept.[5] The Sengoku notion of Heaven's Mandate as resident in the *virtù* of the victorious—the successful as Heaven's minion—had a revolutionary character, justifying *gekokujō*, the feudal subordinates' overthrow of superiors. *Virtù* and *fortuna* infused the consciousness of Sengoku princes no less than that of Machiavelli's models: the contemporary literature is full of appeals to *Tentō* upon the assumption of power, and such phrases as "Heaven wills it!" The reference to chance or individual prowess obviously could not be used for permanent legitimation. But the unifiers of Japan not only did not commit the sins which Machiavelli excoriated, they improved even upon that master's political rationality.

Tokugawa Ieyasu conquered the empire on horseback, but he ruled it by books. The shogunate's ideologues refined the concept of Heaven's Mandate and transformed the Sengoku warriors' slogan into an abstraction which governed the Tokugawa realm of peace. *Tentō* was given a moral context by the application of Sung Neo-Confucian theories, and its potentially explosive charge was thereby disarmed.

According to those theories, Heaven's Way was the order of nature, and the natural order inhered also in the social realm; the virtue of harmony, not the spirit of discontent, was what man obtained from Heaven. Adherence to status was the supreme duty (*taigi meibun*), and the constancy of eminent rules of behavior the essential moral imperative. The Way of government was nothing but the realization of natural norms.

In their own fashion, the Christians had also tried to make a positive value of Heaven's Way. They set *Tentō* identical with

Deus and attempted to abstract the entire complex of human duties toward Him; but the equation proved anachronistic and exceedingly perilous.[6] The most withering blast leveled at Christianity by its most incisive critic, Fabian Fucan, arose out of this ideological nexus.

That acerbic apostate Fabian, in the Seventh Step of his 1620 tract *Deus Destroyed* (*Ha Daiusu*), exhausts himself in denouncing the potentially revolutionary use of nothing less than the First Commandment. The critic manipulates the text of the Commandment in his zeal to accuse his former coreligionists of divided loyalties. Christianity does not accord with the supreme duty of fulfilling one's role in society. "What greater iniquity than this?"[7]

The period's double-edged reaction to Christianity has its ideal representative in the person of Fabian Fucan, the Japanese Jesuit reverted to Buddhism. He incorporates all forms of the Japanese response to Christian claims. In 1605, while still in the fold of the Society of Jesus, he had written the highly sophisticated *Myōtei Dialogue* (*Myōtei mondō*) to exalt the Christian religion. But his subsequent *Deus Destroyed* is the very anthology and seedbed of anti-Christian polemics. Its translation is an integral part of this study, which borrows its title from Fabian's tract.

A different form of apostasy from Fabian's was that of the Portuguese Padre Christovão Ferreira, sometime Jesuit Mission Superior turned Bakufu spy and thrall of the inquisitors who had by torture forced him to convert. His magnum opus is *Deceit Disclosed* (*Kengiroku*; 1636), an informer's tome. Ferreira contributed his Jesuitical expertise to offer his new masters an exposition of Christian doctrine and its First Commandment as "the root of rebellion and the inception of reign's overthrow."[8] It is of jarred images that the Bakufu authorities composed their official picture. For that reason Ferreira's distorting mirror, although but weakly framed by intellect, is of exemplary value to a study of Christianity in Early Modern Japan.

The ideological basis for the social stratification and duty-orientation which characterized the Tokugawa rationalizing effort was derived from Neo-Confucianism. But the anti-Christian combatants were catholic in the search of sources for their arguments. Fabian's *Deus Destroyed* comprehends in its counters to Christianity all the major East Asian systems of thought: Confucianism, Taoism, Buddhism. But the invocation of the native Japanese tradition is also strikingly pervasive. There is hardly one anti-Christian statement in the vast literature of edicts, tracts, and popular narratives which fails to include the sentence, "Japan is the Land of the Gods." The chapbooks titillated their readers with the story that on the day of the first Padre's arrival sixty-six pine trees in the precincts of the Sumiyoshi Shrine had fallen.[9] Even the least sophisticated could not fail to grasp this symbol of the Christian threat to the native religion and to the traditional polity of Japan, a land of sixty-six provinces.

The literary rejection of Christianity finds its degenerate form in the chapbook. The image presented is gross, but seduces the vulgar. The prototype of a voluminous genre, and our exemplar, is the *Kirishitan monogatari* of 1639. Its tone is mixed: literary crudities accompany serious Buddhist homilies, and fantastic stories of Christian practices that reek of evil are followed by a moderate account of the Shimabara Uprising. The strident inconsistencies of style support the assumption that the anonymous author was actually an anonymous collective. In any case the cliché is cast from a collective cultural mold.

The aftermath of the Shimabara Uprising saw yet another exemplary tract contributing to the image of Christianity in Early Modern Japan. In 1642 the advocate of "ferocious Zen," Suzuki Shōsan, appeared in Amakusa to found Buddhist temples and preach anti-Christian sermons in that heartland of the peasant rebellion. In each temple he left a copy of *Christians Countered* (*Ha Kirishitan*), providing spiritual support to the political efforts of his brother Suzuki Saburō-Kurō Shigenari, who in 1641 had been appointed the first magistrate of the newly absorbed Bakufu domain of Amakusa.[10] Shōsan's pamphlet outlines the Buddhist philosophical pattern which the Christians had sought to construe as void and bereft of reliability.

The intellectual collision of Christianity and Buddhism in Early Modern Japan has been called by Ienaga Saburō an epochal event in the history of thought.[11] And the anti-Christian influence of leading Buddhist figures is readily discernible in politics. Shōtai of the Shōkokuji composed Hideyoshi's celebrated Letter to the Viceroy of the Indies (1591). And Konchiin Sūden in 1614 worked through an entire night to draft the Statement on the Expulsion of the Padres at the requirement of Ieyasu.[12] But it would be a mistake to assume that the results obtained for Buddhism—official establishment and the forced addition of parishioners—had a revivifying effect. In the Tokugawa period the Buddhist spirit stagnated.

The sometime Buddhist Fujiwara Seika, who was the first Chu Hsi scholar to exert a strong influence on Ieyasu, summed up his motives for leaving the cloister in the laconic statement: "All is reality in human ethics . . . Why then should the sage flee the world of men?" Seika further determined: "To rule the land and keep the people content . . . the Buddha's frame of mind is welcome."[13] These Confucian sentiments express much of the shogunate's attitude toward religion. The otherworldly Buddhist direction was an approved opiate for the masses, but no such beneficial effect offset the declared evil of Christian otherworldliness. Indeed, what possible application could the ethic of pietism expressed in that glory of the Jesuit mission press, the *Imitatio Christi* of Thomas à Kempis, have to the value system of Tokugawa Japan? Significantly enough, the Japanese edition of 1596 was titled *CONTEMPTVS mundi jenbu* (Contempt of the world; complete).[14] "YO VO ITOI, IESV CHRIStono gocŏxeqiuo manabi tatematçuru——To despise the world and imitate the merits of Jesus Christ" was hardly a popular slogan in the eyes of the Tokugawa leaders, or of the ideologues in their employ.

On every count Christianity was found wanting. The rejection of Christianity colored the general view of Western culture. The self-defeating nature of this rejection may best be seen in the chief pillar of Neo-Confucianism and member of the shogunate's brain trust, the combative Hayashi Razan himself. His 1606 disputation with the still-Christian Fabian Fucan, recounted in his *Anti-Jesuit* (*Hai Yaso*), is an attack upon the newfangleness of the Southern Barbarians, their prismatic lenses and their conceits about the roundness of the earth. Razan should have spared himself the sneers. In this exchange the traditionalist was the victim, not the victor.

It would be altogether facile to state that the opinions of Razan and his congeners amounted to nothing more than a sectarian and malevolent rationale, the sophistical lead toward the brutal final solution of the Christian problem. It would likewise be altogether simple to romanticize the Christian missionaries as the bearers of a new and exciting culture to Japan. But what exactly would be the role of that familiar dramatic figure, the Jesuit philosopher, in such a juxtaposition?

Orthodoxy is a demanding mistress. The Christian position was fixed by the need to adhere to it. The discourse which resulted was not free but from the outset polemically determined. The stand was doctrinal, not intellectual. The adversary followed suit. This form of debate necessitates the total negation of value in the opinion of the other party. And that in turn practically invites a sharp recoil.

The Christian argument exhausted itself in the metaphysics of grandiose theological claims. The eventual native reaction—the result of unfamiliarity with this sort of religious panache—was the vilification of anything Christian. It is true that for a time, in certain circumscribed areas, the Christians and their message were tolerated and even encouraged. The reasons varied according to the personage and the conditions; but they are aptly summarized in Inoue Mitsusada's curt remark: "The attitude of the Japanese rulers towards Western civilization was such that they accepted it only insofar as it served to strengthen their power."[15] In the end Christianity could not prevail. It was incompatible with the ideologies of Early Modern Japan. It was incongruous with the aims of Early Modern reconstruction. Moreover, in several notable instances the acts of its servants were plainly destructive.

The Christian triumphalism had manifested itself in the wreckage of all the native religious symbols that stood in its way. It was not difficult for the clever political technician to seize upon this evidence and construe it as a threat to the Japanese entity. Propaganda played its part: the populace shuddered over the un-Japanese activities. The Christians were banned and eradicated. Ferocious persecution added a grim chapter to the Christian martyrology.[16] There was a tragic end to what had started as an optimistic venture.

The attitude of the missionaries' entry into Japan had been penetrant. The most perceptive, such as the Jesuit *Visitator* Alexandro Valignano, had succeeded in developing at least a formal method of accommodation to the Japanese setting. But what was the sum of their cultural contribution? The missionaries' choice of the material to be introduced was contingent upon its concordance with the absolute truth that was preached. The news they bore was trimmed to fit the place rather more than the time. Intellectual purity was sacrificed to the exigencies of the mission. The Jesuits were familiar with the post-Renaissance sources and could, while the opportunity was given them, have done more with them had they felt it wise. But the rich world of philosophical analogy was, in their eyes, one that hid grave dangers. To be sure, they did work hard to establish a synthesis. Their catechetical works are in some cases impressive presentations of orthodoxy adapted to Japanese conditions. And yet their ethical amalgam, much too particular a formula, was in the end not viable. It did not help their cause that the scheme of mission activity involved entanglements in areas affecting sovereignty. The political ventures appeared necessary at the outset but in the outcome proved fatal.

But for a historical moment upon the entry of Christianity there was a degree of acceptance, and that process of entry and the problems of acceptance are the preliminaries to the Japanese rejection of Christianity.

PART I

Problems in the Acceptance of Christianity in Japan

Das ist nicht ein weltlich Stechen,
Keine Eisenwaffe blitzet—
Eine Lanze ist das Wort,
Das scholastisch scharf gespitzet.

*

This is not a wordly tourney,
And no iron weapon glitters—
A lance is the word that's pointed
With scholastically sharp wit.

Heinrich Heine
Romanzero, III
"Disputation"

Chapter 1

Attitudes of Entry:
The Jesuit Approach to
the Japanese Setting

MANY WORDS have been written and many phrases spent in comparing the process of Christianity's introduction into sixteenth-century Japan with the initial progress of the Christian movement in the classical West. The missionaries of Japan in the midst of their adversities constantly took solace in the parallels between their situation and that of the Primitive Church. They did not refer as frequently to the intrinsic differences. But those differences constituted a formidable obstacle to the spread of their religion in Japan.

The history of the two missionary periods does manifest many similarities which stem from the basic problem of gaining entry into an alien world. But it is undoubtedly true that concepts at the root of Christianity were more foreign to the Japanese civilization than they had been to a cultural sphere already suffused with the spread of Near Eastern religious thought and possessing philosophical preconceptions which were amenable to Christianity. In Japan the conditioning factors were lacking; the points of resemblance with Buddhism were ephemeral and delusory; the first missionaries had no foundations to build on. And beyond the problem of preconditions lay that of the religion's own character. The messengers of the gospel looked back upon an uninterrupted tradition of a millennium and a half. And yet what they preached was in many respects not the same as the faith of the apostles.

The purity of the Primitive Church was in its simplicity. Complex dogmatic standards had not yet been developed in Christianity's first century of existence; sophistication was not the hallmark of the apostolic age. The faith of the era which had witnessed the moment of salvation could be spread effectively by enthusiasts who did not require strict training. But by the sixteenth century all that was no longer the case. The Catholic Church had become a highly sophisticated religious organization with an extensive and finely developed philosophical basis, authoritatively defined dogma, and a comprehensive system of juridical controls. The initial Catholic venture into Japan coincided in time with the initial vehemence of the Counter Reformation in Europe and with the Tridentine effort at a purified orthodoxy. The religion preached in Japan was so complex that without a compromise of standards it could not be spread by untrained enthusiasts, even if the country had been disposed to accept untrained enthusiasm. The purity of this Church was disciplinary.

It was therefore fortunate for the Church that the Jesuit Order was its primary agent in the mission field of Japan. This was the only organization with sufficient discipline, versatility, combativeness, and sheer intellectual ability to preach the faith in such a difficult area. But no amount of mastery of the subtleties of creed, no measure of rhetoric skill in their exposition, no weight of unity of purpose could make up for the lack of numbers of missionary personnel which plagued the Church in Japan throughout the "Christian Century." The field was too wide, and the problems too many. The apparent solution was to train the Japanese Church to grow on its own. Yet the Society of Jesus felt that it had to nurse the seedling carefully before leaving it to its development. The Society knew that its European manpower was insufficient; but it could not, or would not, embark on an immediate program of training a substantial number of Japanese missionaries. The Jesuits did not appreciate fully the temper of the host country, and altogether too long misjudged the character of its inhabitants. Too wary of hasty remedies to the manpower quandary, they left themselves exposed to a multitude of other problems. Christianity from its very inception in Japan was living on borrowed time.

When Saint Francis Xavier, the mission's founder, landed in Japan, he thought that he had come upon the ideal climate. His oft-quoted letter from Kagoshima brims with optimism: "The people we have met so far is the best that has until now been discovered; and it seems to me that among heathen peoples no other will be found to surpass the Japanese."[1] This report having reached Goa, Jesuit circles in Portuguese India soon abounded with enthusiasm for Japan, a "white" nation and fully capable of apprehending reason, a veritable mission Eldorado. Jesuits who actually went there found their initial enthusiasm dampened considerably by the experience of vast difficulty in adjusting to the high culture which was so thoroughly different from any they had previously encountered. In some, an unsatisfactory explanation of native forms of life gave rise to pessimism concerning the Japanese national character.

Were the Japanese inherently too proud? And insincere? And therefore intractable? Padre Francisco Cabral thought so; and he, in the critical formative period between the years 1570 and 1581, was the Mission Superior of Japan. For Cabral it was *a priori* to be assumed that in the process of mission activity the Japanese would have to adapt themselves to the Portuguese Jesuits and not vice versa. Of course not every Jesuit in Japan had such a frame of thought; for that matter, not every one was psychologically as much a product of the Portuguese knightly caste as was Cabral, *hombre criado del Rei, fidalgo y muy fidalgo.*[2] But Cabral was the Superior and the policy maker. His attitudes were reflected in the entire mission endeavor.

A critical instance was Cabral's treatment of those few who had been permitted to join the Jesuit ranks as Irmãos (the Iruman of Japanese sources). The Father Superior viewed the Japanese Brothers as second-class Jesuits; and they were given no opportunity to rise. It was a matter of policy to humble them and at times to malign them with rough language—in order to keep them subject to discipline. They were not given Latin or Portuguese lessons—so that they would not be in a position to reveal the secrets of the Society. Not treated as proper sons of the Society, the Japanese did not always behave as such. It is not surprising that some of them did not persevere as enthusiastic recruiters but instead turned into tellers of most unedifying tales about life in the cloister. That inequities and discontents prevailed in Jesuit purlieus long after Cabral's tenure in office is clear: Fabian Fucan's case of desertion for the stated reasons of mistreatment and failure to obtain promotion to the priesthood is the best known; but there were also quite a few others who dropped by the wayside. Fabian's rationale ought not to be taken at face value; but there is no need to rely on him alone. The missionaries' own words offer ample evidence of their bias.

The direct connection may be lacking; yet it is not un-profitable, by way of illustration, to juxtapose certain of Cabral's statements with utterances made by Fabian. In 1596 Cabral (who by this time had become the Jesuit Provincial of Goa) wrote the polemic:

If one does not cease and desist admitting Japanese into the Society . . . that will be the reason for the collapse of the Society, nay! of Christianity, in Japan, and it will later hardly prove possible to find a remedy . . . I have seen no other nation as conceited, covetous, inconstant, and insincere as the Japanese . . . Among the Japanese it is considered a matter of honor and wisdom not to disclose the inner self, to prevent anyone's reading therein. They are trained to this from childhood; they are educated to be inscrutable and false.

Besides—he continued—they are by nature too inclined to learn-ing and to novelties; unless they are tightly controlled, they might in their pride revolt, and a schism might result. "What will the Japanese Irmãos do once they have studied and stand on the same level with Europeans in knowledge!" And there-fore, "I could not see my way clear to accept more than seven or eight Irmãos. But I only admitted them as *dōjuku*"—to which is to be added that *dōjuku* were, in effect, the workhorses of the Society without actually belonging to it as members, acting as preachers and translators while yet being subjected to the humiliations of menials.[3]

So much for the Japanese national character. But what of the Europeans? In the *Ha Daiusu* of 1620 Fabian (by this date a renegade of several years' standing) countered:[4] "The devil himself could not measure up to them in arrogance! Could it be their inborn national character? . . . Because of their arrogance they do not even consider the Japanese to be human. And the Japanese, considering this outrageous, in their turn do not tender courtesy with sincerity." The stresses of acculturation were evidently much too punishing for some.

To correct the malpractices of Cabral's mission method— or rather for the first time to apply a real method to the mission of Japan—was the principal task faced by Padre Alexandro Valignano. When Valignano, the *Visitator* of the Jesuit Indian Province for the General of the Society, landed in Japan on 25 July 1579, he found not the ideal pastorage but rather a mismanaged field beset with problems. Too great a proportion of Japanese converts had come to baptism with questionable motivation. Pressure from daimyo intent on profit from Portuguese ships had forced the populations of some areas of Kyushu wholesale into the arms of the Portuguese missionaries. The harvest had been great in quantity, but there was reason to doubt the quality of the fruit. The disquieting situation had been aggravated by Cabral's failure to adapt methods to circumstances, and particularly by his refusal to avail himself of the pool of native manpower. The Mission Superior had genuine misgivings about his new Christians and lamented their shallow foundations in the faith. Hence he refused to train Japanese to be missionaries in their own right, thereby foreclosing his converts' access to a true familiarity with the tradition he wished to impose on them.

Valignano was scandalized by Cabral's mode of procedure. Unless the unequal treatment of Japanese were stopped (the *Visitator* soon perceived), it would surely cause the collapse of the Society, nay! of all Christianity, in Japan. Valignano saw in Cabral's ministry no reason beyond Cabral's personal will, which was in turn governed by prejudices.[5] The Society's constitutions were not being observed. No colleges had been founded. No concerted effort had been made to teach the Japanese language to the Europeans. The grammar was considered unteachable to start with. The conversational pattern, it had been decided, could not be mastered. After six years in Japan the missionary might at best assimilate enough of it to hear confessions. Fifteen years of residence in the country were held to be the minimum in order to obtain enough facility to preach to Christians; never a thought was given, according to Valignano, to the possibility that Europeans could ever learn enough to preach effectively to pagans.[6] And yet there had been no attempt to make full use of Japanese, without whom the culture could not be penetrated.

What was the essential problem, and what the solution? The Jesuits had aimed for Eldorado but landed in the antipodes; there was no foothold to be had without an inversion of past attitudes. How difficult it was to perform that headstand is apparent from a look at Padre Luis Frois' attempt at cultural analysis, a treatise he composed in 1585 on *Contradictions and Differences of Custom Between the People of Europe and This Province of Japan.*[7] This is a booklet of amazing banality, in which everything Japanese—from the man's head to the horse's tail—is made to appear the precise opposite of its European counterpart. The author's nostalgia for Europe after an absence of thirty-seven years is understandable, and his depiction of the Japanese topsy-turvydom is not without value. There was a lesson to be drawn from this sort of view. It took the keen mind of Valignano to apply that lesson.

Valignano started from the proposition that the cultures of Europe and Japan differed in essence. Hence it followed that men who came from Europe to work in Japan had not merely to adapt themselves to local circumstances and customs but "like children begin to learn again" all the essentials of behavior.[8] The Japanese, on the other hand, could not collaborate effectively or become full members of the Society unless they were in-doctrinated properly in the essentials of the faith. Both the Europeans and the Japanese required formal institutions which would train the ones in demeanor, the others in doctrine, and all in a universal discipline.

Within one and a half years after the *Visitator's* arrival an impressive complex of such institutions had sprung into existence. There were two preparatory seminaries for the noble youth of Japan and a college in which European aspirants were receiving an introduction into their alien mission field. But the most important—because most immediately promising remedy—of the schools was the Jesuit novitiate of Usuki in Bungo, which was formally opened on Christmas Eve of 1580.[9] Six Portuguese were enrolled in this house of probation, but the critical element was the presence of six Japanese. So important did Valignano consider the novitiate that he allotted to himself the role of first Master of Novices, and for two months (with Frois acting as Japanese interpreter) concentrated upon tutoring the pro-bationers. Here was set the departure point for the training of a native Jesuit clergy. It is regrettable that concrete plans for such a solution had not been made nine or ten years previously. Had a junior seminary been founded by Cabral, the novitiate of 1580 might have had sixteen or twenty-six Japanese students rather than the six who did enter.

In one very important respect Valignano's solution may be accounted a compromise: in the final analysis, the burden of adaptation remained on the Japanese. A mutilated text which was rediscovered as recently as 1960 at Evora in Portugal, in the lining of a decrepit Japanese folding screen, sheds much light upon this point. It is called *Iruman kokoroe no koto* (Instructions for Irmãos), and apparently contains notes of lectures given at the Usuki novitiate by Valignano himself. (An alternative suggestion holds that the provenance is the seminary of Azuchi, and Padre Organtino Gnecchi-Soldo the lecturer.) [10] A close reading of the text reveals that for the instructor the acceptance of Japanese into the Society was a step which had to be taken but involved a risk. The departure from Cabral's position was by no means unconditional.

There is here the same preoccupation with Japanese duplicity: the text practically spells out the more recent cliché, "You can't tell what they're really thinking." This Japanese "double-heartedness" (*nijū naru kokoro*, admonished with the biblical citation, "ve dupplici corde et labijs coleretis")[11] is the root of falsehoods, plots, vexations, and disagreements. There is no coming together of minds. The conflict between the Padres and their Japanese charges is fed by frustrations. Ultimately, it is born out of the disagreement concerning the best way to nourish the Japanese in the faith. The final enemy of mutual understanding is that "the Japanese feel no sense of obligation toward the ecclesia (*on mo shirazu*) and act in an overbearing manner, without charity*** To see [this], every Padre's heart is filled with unbearable sorrow . . . Even though [the Padres] exhaust themselves in cordiality, this has no effect, for [the Japanese] have no love for the ecclesia and in everything they do they take the part of other Japanese, and this is their guiding principle. The honor and the property of the ecclesia they look upon as though these were matters of no personal concern to them. Not only do they have no interest in the power and position of the ecclesia, they even say that the church practices are bad . . . They do not teach their country's language and practices to the *Europeans*."[12] The lectures constitute an exhortation: while the Padres, granted, must change their modes of behavior, the Japanese must change their entire attitude. The Jesuits did have confidence that the bad points of the Japanese character could be vanquished by education. But this was not without its difficulties: it required the type of submission which some Japanese could not bear. Again one might adduce the example of Fabian Fucan—who in answering the implied question, "Why can't Japanese become priests?," makes the dangerous suggestion: "It's because the Southern Barbarians feel that in their designs against Japan they will find the natives partial, after all, to the interests of their native land. You can be sure of that!"[13]

It would of course be unfair to carp overmuch at the imperfections of Valignano's method. For it is true that his perception led, by way of an enrichment of the Christian missionary life, to developments of considerable significance to Japanese cultural history. His insistence caused the creation of an entire genre of literature: Valignano is the spiritual father of *Kirishitan bungaku*. And he also made a substantial material contribution to the culture of the host country. The introduction of the movable type printing press into Japan may be dated 1590, the occasion being Valignano's second visit. The motive of the publishing venture was duplex: instruction in the Japanese language for the missionaries, propaganda of the faith among the Japanese. The literature eventually produced by the mission press included not only devotional tracts and the rather quaint intrusion of Aesop into Japan but also works of monumental importance for the study of contemporary Japanese linguistics, such as the *VOCABVLARIO DA LINGOA DE IAPAM com adeclaração em Portugues* (Nagasaki, 1603–1604) and the exhaustive *ARTE DA LINGOA DE IAPAM* of Padre João Rodriguez Tçuzzu (Nagasaki, 1604–1608).[14] The translations of European works such as the *Imitatio Christi* can only be called superb, and prove that language at least formed no barrier to spiritual transmission.

Such developments were far from the vision of a Cabral, who considered the Japanese language unlearnable, accordingly saw no need to develop a method for its study, and drew the consequences for himself. Valignano caustically commented on Cabral's joust with the language: "Indeed, the thirteen years during which he was Japan Superior went by without his learning more of it than a few barbarous beginnings for most essential usage."[15] Assuming that linguistic facility is a key to cultural familiarity and empathy, Cabral's attitude seems akin to a self-induced blindness. But it would be more accurate to say that his very sense of high purpose obscured his powers of reflection and made him unbending and unteachable. He was without doubt a dedicated missionary, but his outlook was Gothic, fundamentalist, and closed to experimentation; one might label him more monk than Jesuit. Valignano was not a whit less orthodox, but he was a modern. The Italian, unlike the Portuguese, was pliable, perspicacious, above all a politician.

Cabral's impatience with Japanese standards drove him to open frustration and to rash and intolerant statements. The *Visitator*'s sting was on occasion quite as sharp, but no prejudice diverted him from practicality. His analyses of Japanese conditions were in some instances gloomy and pessimistic, but he did not permit vexations to overcome him. Valignano faced realistically the problem which broke Cabral—insufficient motivation and performance among Japan's new Christians. Of course there were many who came to baptism without the right disposition, but there were also many who brought correct conceptions to the sacrament. In any case, all could be made into good Christians if they were given proper instruction. The converts, however, could not be instructed if there were no facilities available, and if they had for teachers and shepherds men who did not understand their flock and were in turn not understood. An expansion of the mission field was desirable, but not the type of unbounded proselytizing which for lack of manpower would be cursory and would register nothing but a waste of time, finance, and energy. It was above all necessary to face up to the realities of the Japanese setting.

One point seemed obvious: The history of Christianity in Japan was inseparably tied to the fates of the Country at War. The position of the Church was never secure because it was dependent upon the protection of personalities whose own security was never ensured in the panorama of constant contention. The only hope was in a widespread base. It was essential to gain influence among as many daimyo as possible: otherwise, the fruits of year-long labor could with one blow be destroyed entirely, disaster following upon a single political reverse. Nothing illustrates this concern better than the plaint of Cabral upon the crushing defeat suffered by the Jesuits' protector, Ōtomo Sōrin of Bungo, at the hands of the Shimazu (Battle of Mimigawa, or Mimizugawa, December 1578). The somber Spanish perfectly reproduces the sense of tragedy:[16]

Pero quiso Dios N. Señor, o para probar la fé deste buen Rey o por sus altos y ocultos juizios, darle un desbarate y pérdida en una guerra que traya contra otro Rey, en la qual dizen que perdió quarenta mil hombres, y él se uvo de acoger uyendo. Y de aquí sucedió que se levantaron contra él los más de los señores de los otros reinos suyos, y hasta en su proprio reino de Bungo uvo muchos alevantamientos y revueltas y aun hasta agora no son acabadas del todo, en las quales los Nuestros que allá residen no an padecido pocos trabajos.

—But it pleased Our Lord God, either for the sake of testing the faith of this good King or on account of His lofty and mysterious judgments, to bestow upon him destruction and defeat in a war he was waging against another King, in which they say he lost forty thousand men, and he had to seek safety in flight. And hence it came to pass that most of the lords in his other kingdoms rose against him, and even unto his own main kingdom of Bungo there were many uprisings and revolts and are to this day not entirely extinguished, wherein Our people that reside there have suffered not little of tribulations.

The daimyo was not a bulwark never failing, and the Ōtomo demonstrate why. The rise and fall of this house is an excellent (although, in the final analysis, negative) illustrative case of the development of the daimyo institution.[17] Its genealogies claim descent from Minamoto no Yoritomo; and, indeed, it is established that the Ōtomo were *shugo* (military governors) in Bungo from the days of the Kamakura shogunate. The family's progress to the position of *shugo daimyō* accords with the standard pattern as also with the limitations of the model: the Ashikaga shogunate invested the Ōtomo with jurisdictional authority over several provinces in Kyushu and even with the title of *Kyūshū Tandai*, the shogunal Deputy over the island; but from the start there were significant gaps between nominal jurisdiction and actual authority. By the sixteenth century the shogunal legality was at best a tawdry embellishment, an added fillip to power. Only those who bridged the gaps by lines of vassalage held taut could succeed in the world of Sengoku. The ancient *shugo daimyō* family of Ōtomo strove to succeed and for a time manifested a dazzling rise. But it failed just as Sengoku came to an end.

Ōtomo Sōrin Yoshishige (1530–1587) had in 1550 succeeded his murdered father Yoshiaki as lord of Bungo; he was the twenty-first of his lineage, and in his day the fortunes of his house attained their apogee. In the course of campaigns against the Mōri, Ryūzōji, Akizuki, and Tachibana he extended his influence into Buzen, Chikuzen, Chikugo, Hizen, and Higo as well, and became the seeming master over half of Kyushu. His power also encompassed much of Hyūga and reached across to part of Iyo in Shikoku. The armies which debouched upon Mimigawa were in the chronicles called the seven-province host— *Ōtomo shichikakoku no zei*—of the Ōtomo.

But the huge power complex Sōrin built was weak in its foundations. The Ōtomo mode of operation remained traditional even as the rival daimyo were reforming their organizational base. The bonds of extended vassalage were never drawn taut. The centrifugal tendency inherent in the retainers' military groupings could only partially be redirected because too many of their mediaeval privileges were left intact.[18] The collaterals (*shoke* or, in the Ōtomo parlance, *dōmonshū*) had from the beginnings of the house's history in Bungo shown a pronounced independence; families such as the Shiga and Tawara, which are often mentioned in Western sources of Sōrin's period, were close to being their own masters. The same is true of many of the *kunishū* and *shinsanshū* (old local families and newly absorbed vassals): some of these nominal retainers, such as the Aso and Kikuchi of Higo, were in fact *sengoku daimyō* themselves. Even the most meritorious of vassals could drift straight out of the daimyo's sphere of influence and attract others with him: such was the case with Hekki Akitsura, who conquered the Tachibana on Sōrin's behalf, moved into the defeated family's castle and took over its name, and thereafter retained at best a sentimental allegiance to the Ōtomo.[19] The House of Ōtomo was large but brittle. Sōrin's involvement with Christianity did nothing to cement it.

Sōrin's friendship with the Christian missionaries dated back to 1551, when he received Saint Francis Xavier with much sign of favor. He saw the Jesuit mission of Bungo through several crises caused by popular animosity, and was in various ways a benefactor of the Padres. His beneficence was quite possibly motivated by commercial considerations. On the other hand, the contemporary Jesuit historian Luis Frois assigns to him statements implying recognition that his measure of success in Sengoku was attributable to the intervention of Deus: "It has been thirteen years since the Padres first came to my dominions. Before that I was poor and had only Bungo; and now I have five of the most prosperous kingdoms of Japan in my possession."[20] Frois and the other Christian writers in general heroize Sōrin.

At Christmastime 1575 Sōrin had his second son baptized; this boy of fourteen was named Sebastião.[21] In 1578 followed Sōrin's break with his wife, the "perverse Jezebel," due at least in part to her anti-Christian orientation. And finally, on 28 August 1578, Cabral baptized Sōrin himself, with the name

Francisco; thus Sōrin consummated his long flirtation with the missionaries. In a sense, his acceptance of Christianity marked the apex of Christian proselytizing activity in Japan: he was the most prominent Japanese to be converted, and in his person all Kyushu seemed within the compass of missionary ambitions. But a scant thirteen weeks after his baptism there followed the disaster of Mimigawa.

The Japanese chronicles draw the Ōtomo defeat into an intimate association with Sōrin's conversion to Christianity and his atrocious conduct against the Buddhas and the gods, which caused strange and bloody omens to appear.[22] Hekki Akitsura in a letter sent from his Tachibana domain to leading Ōtomo vassals stated flatly, "There is nothing but perversion in your land," lamented the internal disturbances, and attributed them largely to the introduction of the "Indian sect" and the widespread destruction of native shrines.[23] The Tokugawa period moralist Yamaga Sokō also condemned Sōrin for his infatuation with Christianity and his profligacy, but perhaps even more for his strategic blundering.[24] It may be significant to note that while his troops were wading across the ravines of Mimigawa in the face of the enemy, Sōrin himself was nowhere near the site. The likes of Fabian Fucan were to see his fall from glory as well-deserved punishment sent down by the Buddhas and gods.

Mais où sont les neiges d'antan? In a brilliant demonstration of the *ubi sunt* technique, Fabian in *Ha Daiusu* draws a moral precisely opposite to that of Frois on the matter of success in Sengoku[25]—

Look! Look at Ōtomo Sōrin of Bungo. In the days when Sōrin was still devoted to the Buddhas and gods he brandished his power over all of Kyushu and the glory of his name spread throughout the Four Seas. But after he entered the ranks of Deus the fortunes of war suddenly turned against him. With his eldest son Yoshimune he fell over Hyūga to fight the Shimazu, suffered a crushing defeat at Mimigawa, and had to flee home deserted by all and in desperate straits. After that his house gradually fell to ruin; so prosperous, so flourishing for many generations, the family is practically extinct today. Are any offspring left, or not?—such is the sad state of the house at present.

After Mimigawa, Sōrin was hard-pressed to retain a measure of order in Bungo itself, while losing the outlying territories.

There were tumults among the Ōtomo vassals, renewed anti-Christian pressures in Bungo, and a turn to Buddhism in the heart of Sōrin's son Yoshimune: sutras once again were chanted in the daimyo residence.[26] In the last months of 1586 the Shimazu armies flooded over Bungo; the Ōtomo were saved only by Toyotomi Hideyoshi's invasion of Kyushu, which took place in 1587 with prominent Christian daimyo taking part. Yoshimune was at last baptized in April of that year, but proved unworthy of his new name, Constantinho, and reverted to an anti-Christian position when Hideyoshi issued his Expulsion Edict that same July. Christian sources condemn Yoshimune as craven and cowardly. Hideyoshi concurred in that judgment, in 1593 confiscating his Bungo fief for his cowardice: Yoshimune's performance in the Taikō's Korean expedition had been a dangerous fiasco. In the climactic year 1600 Yoshimune postured as a supporter of the anti-Tokugawa forces, but fell afoul of Kuroda Josui (Dom Simeão) and was defeated with his small band in Bungo two days before the Battle of Sekigahara even took place.[27] Kuroda spared Yoshimune's life and supposedly reconciled him with the Church. He died in exile in 1605, a symbol of the failure of a policy.

Ever since the days of Xavier the Jesuits had worked from the top down: first to gain firm establishment in the courts of princes was their policy in Japan as in Europe. There were risks and vagaries in this mode of procedure, but also successes. It was indeed a cardinal success for the Church in Japan when Jesuits gained the favor of Oda Nobunaga. Oda was at the time in question clearly the rising power in Japan. In 1568 he had embraced Ashikaga Yoshiaki and installed him in the shogunate, occupying Kyoto. The area of the Capital was not only of great strategic value but also the source of great prestige to him who held it. When Oda Nobunaga at Easter 1569 granted two interviews to Frois, he was acting as no mere daimyo but as a significant figure indeed. The mystique of this prince was backed by power and rested upon institutional innovation. His modes of operation (and perhaps most of all his approach to religion) would have won him Machiavelli's approval. As it happens, he found the Christians useful.

Oda's picturesque meeting with Frois on the bridge of the Nijō Castle was followed by the issuance of patents allowing the Padre to maintain a mission residence in Kyoto.[28] A few months later, Frois and the redoubtable mountebank (*biwa hōshî*) Irmão Lourenço appeared at Gifu, the first Jesuits to be received by Nobunaga at his own residence. The success of this audience exceeded all expectations: it concluded with the spectacle of Oda with his own hands serving a meal to the bedazzled Frois. From the experience Frois drew a moral concerning mission method among the Japanese:[29] "One must strive to obtain and hold first the favor of the kings, princes, and lords who rule over the land, so that it is apparent to all and that all may see what love, respect, and reputation the preachers of Holy Gospel enjoy. For without these means (speaking in terms of human power) little or no fruit will be reaped among them, but quite the contrary."

The intercourse with intelligent, energetic men who promised to spread his fame abroad may have flattered Oda; and his own intelligence and curiosity were fed by the converse with representatives of a new culture. Indeed, the best portrayals of Oda that have been passed down to the present day come from Jesuit pens, particularly that of Frois, and were designed for the European audience; the sixteenth-century European conception of the hero was much more dramatic and multicolored than that which flowed from the single-dimensional Japanese perspective. On the other hand, the Southern Barbarian brand of exoticism, *Nanbanryū*, was to become *de rigueur* among the fashionable of Azuchi-Momoyama. But that does not yet reach the heart of the matter. Nobunaga's encouragement of the Padres is explainable as a reaction of his avowed hate of Buddhist institutions and a side effect of his effort to extinguish their threat forever.

The interview at the Nijō Castle is, to Frois, primarily significant for Nobunaga's anti-Buddhist pronunciamento. The *mise en scène* is worthy of kabuki: the hero robed in tigerskin, the cringing bonzes, the grandiose arm gesture, the diatribe delivered in distorted voice—"Not like you are those deceivers over there who delude the populace, false and lying and swollen with pride and with arrogance. Many times have I been willed to kill and exterminate them all. But in order to avoid stirring up the people, and because I have pity on them, I leave them alone though they disgust me."[30] Frois also quotes Nobunaga as saying to Cabral, in a 1571 interview at Gifu, "I can well see how those who tread a crooked path hate your religion." And that, applied to the Buddhist clergy, is no doubt a more accurate rendition of Nobunaga's sentiments than another statement attributed to the same occasion: "I swear to you . . . that there is no difference between my heart's feelings and the Padres' doctrine."[31] The man who savaged the True Pure Land sectarians and destroyed the Osaka Honganji, who put to fire and sword the Tendai monasteries of Mount Hiei and threatened the Shingon monks of Kōyasan with the same fate, *ipso facto* shared a great many of the sentiments of his Jesuit friends. But did he *ipso facto* further Christianity?

Hopes for the conversion of Oda were entirely groundless.[32] There was also little reason for rejoicing at the fact that this putative supporter was subjecting more and more provinces to his central control. The work of the mission would have been easier in a country unified under a ruler who was well-disposed toward Christianity. But by the same token, an anti-Christian ruler in a unified country could more easily conduct a general persecution, as the Tokugawa were to prove with a vengeance. Nobunaga's destruction of obstreperous Buddhist sectarians was motivated by political considerations. His successor, Hideyoshi, turned the identical rationale against other religionists, and justified his Expulsion Edict of 1587 with the unsavory comparison of Christians and True Pure Land adherents; his sense of irony was perhaps more acute than even his political instinct.

None of the lords who did convert had a standing even remotely comparable to Nobunaga's; in the case of some, weakness was the apparent reason for conversion. Less than the purest of motives seems to have worked in Ōmura Sumitada, a minor daimyo of Kyushu, whom the Jesuits Cosme de Torres and Luis de Almeida tried to make Christian "by stirring his hopes that the China Ship would come to his harbors."[33] Ōmura was at the time swaying perilously upon the balance of extinction or survival as *sengoku daimyō*, and he grasped at the promise of European support. In 1563 he accepted Christianity, and by 1579 there were in his domain forty churches and fifty or sixty thousand Christians. Whatever his motives had been as Sumitada, as Dom Bartolomeu he became a true and invaluable pillar of the Church. To his efforts on behalf of the mission a subsequent chapter is devoted.

A similar instance was the domain of Arima in the Takaku region of Kyushu. In 1563 the daimyo Yoshisada gave permission to conduct missions in his territory because he hoped to attract the Portuguese China Ship to Kuchinotsu. The hopes did not materialize, and there were initially no great numbers of baptisms in Arima. But Yoshisada himself was baptized on Palm Sunday of 1576, becoming a Christian at Padre Gaspar Coelho's suggestion that he might require aid against his enemy Ryūzōji. Between 8 April and 24 September 1576, Almeida and the freshly arrived Padre Alonso Gonçalez baptized eight thousand persons; Cabral estimated the total for the year at 15,000.[34] There was, naturally enough, no question of thorough instruction for this mass of new Christians. When Yoshisada died in January 1577, his successor, Harunobu, reversed the Arima policy and turned persecutor. Mass apostasy followed. By 1578 the Church in Arima had all but vanished.

In the face of military crisis, Arima again reversed the field.[35] Pressed by the powerful Ryūzōji Takanobu and by enemies within, and in expectation of succor from Ōmura and from the Jesuits (which latter arrived in the form of consignments of lead and saltpetre for his besieged fort), Harunobu was baptized in March 1580, taking the name Protasio and giving Valignano assurances which led to the foundation of the famed Jesuit seminary of Arima. Military assistance caused Arima to become solidly Christian territory; and it is difficult to avoid the suspicion that Valignano had acted with charity aforethought, and had purchased the six hundred ducats' worth of supplies from the China Ship of 1579 with the specific intent of luring Harunobu.[36]

The Battle of Mimigawa notwithstanding, the Christian population of Bungo increased after Ōtomo Sōrin's baptism, to number ten thousand by 1580. Sōrin's motives were not as overt as the others'. Portuguese ships had only a few times called at his ports, and it is tempting to judge that he converted in purest sincerity after observing for almost thirty years the efforts and the effects of Christianity in his domains. Yet it must also be pointed out that he received special consideration in trading with the Europeans. Valignano himself testified that King Francisco of Bungo favored Cabral's mission because through Cabral's mediation "he had always found many advantages from the ship of the Portuguese."[37]

All too keen was the Great Ship's attraction for the *Kirishitan daimyō* of Kyushu. More remote, and aclinic to this magnet, were the lords of the Kansai. In them could work with far less obstruction the new religion's strong moral force. Christianity was a clearcut faith, without any compromise. Even the Zen Sect of Buddhism lacked such a direct authoritative character. This stringency may serve to explain Christianity's appeal among men of a warrior's temperament. But the exclusive loyalty which the new faith demanded put it on a collision course with the established religions of Japan. Its dogmatism meant that it could not be tolerated even by essentially tolerant and syncretist Buddhism.

After the unavoidable initial misunderstandings, the Christian counterstroke at Buddhism was redirected and refined: its intellectual point was honed to rapier sharpness, and the edge of moral judgment cut perhaps even more painfully. The missionaries condemned the Buddhist religion's effect on Japanese morals, attempted to override that effect, and sought to construct their own ethical synthesis with Japan. Much of the Buddhist establishment had sunk to a sad state at the end of Sengoku; and that fact made penetration by the Jesuits easier than it might otherwise have been. They were, moreover, correct in stating that the Buddhist sectarianism and lack of a unified doctrine facilitated the introduction and spread of the rigorous Christian faith.[38] But it was an illusion to believe that Christianity, with the human means at its disposal, could vanquish a religion which was so many-sided in its foundations in Japan, and which had so much helped to shape the country's culture. Nor was it correct to assume that Christianity, with the superhuman ideal which was its aim, could transcend the earthly commonplaces of Japanese history.

Chapter 2

The Christian Attempt at an
Ethical Synthesis:
The Misunderstandings and the Appeal

𝕴N THE reign of Mikado Go-Nara no In . . . a Southern Barbarian trading vessel came to our shores. From this ship for the first time emerged an unnamable creature, somewhat similar in shape to a human being, but looking rather more like a long-nosed goblin or the giant demon Mikoshi Nyūdō. Upon close interrogation it was discovered that this was a being called Bateren.

The length of his nose was the first thing which attracted attention: it was like a conch shell (though without its surface warts) attached by suction to his face. His eyes were as large as spectacles, and their insides were yellow. His head was small. On his hands and feet he had long claws. His height exceeded seven feet, and he was black all over; only his nose was red. His teeth were longer than the teeth of a horse. His hair was mouse-grey in color, and over his brow was a shaved spot in the outline of a winebowl turned over. What he said could not be understood at all: his voice was like the screech of an owl.[1]

Thus the *Kirishitan monogatari* of 1639 in its very first paragraphs establishes its theme. The trickery of description immediately fixed in the reader's mind the image of perniciousness approaching: the burlesque Bateren landed, and menace hovered in the air. This alien apparition was altogether unnatural—the primitive consumer of the chapbook could shiver contentedly in his xenophobia.

But even a sympathetic account of the arrival of the first Padre reveals in the Japanese observer a measure of puzzlement. The image was, after all, a jarring one:

One of the things which amazes me most and which causes me to be strengthened in my faith is considering at times the marvellous

and astonishing fashion in which Our Lord God spread His Holy
Law in this area of Miyako. I say this because I know the pride
and vain conceit of the Japanese, of whom I am one by race and
character. I see how great, how mighty, and how all-encompassing
are the strength and power of the bonzes, what respect the populace
accords them, how deeply founded among all is the regard for their
teachings. I see the family relationships which tie them to the nobility
and the lords of Japan, their money income, their pomp, their pos-
sessions. I see so many splendid temples built for the bonzes by the
people out of their high esteem and out of their desire for salvation—
influenced as they are by the cleverness of the bonzes' speech and
easy promises of salvation, to free them of guilt and let them commit
as many disgusting things and sins as they desire in sensual lust and
the laws of the flesh, stifling the people's every pang of conscience
with their devilish treacheries and casuistries.

Even a great scholar arriving in dignity and pomp from China,
the classical source of learning and prestige, must surely fail
now in any attempt to introduce a novel religion; yet the
reminiscence concerned a far less imposing sort of intruder.

And now Our Lord God comes to shame us in our pride and sends
us in Miyako a foreign Padre whose language, dress, tradition, and
customs were so ridiculous in our eyes that when we saw him in
those first beginnings he served us to no other purpose but to give
us occasion to laugh at him, mock him, and ridicule him. We did
not know where he was from, whether he had fallen from the sky or
grown out of the earth. And he seemed to us so much a man lacking
entirely the qualities necessary to make us form a different opinion
of his matters.

Frois tells us that this speech affected him so much that he
attempted to write it down verbatim for the edification of his
brethren in India, as soon as the speaker finished his peroration.
The speaker was Sanga Hōki no Kami, given the name Sancho
in baptism.[2] The immediate subject was Padre Gaspar Vilela
and the beginnings of the Church in the area of the Capital.
But in a wider sense Dom Sancho Sanga was speaking of the
faith's beginnings any place in Japan, of strange men in black
robes preaching a doctrine steeped in ludicrous paradoxes in
Amakusa, Bungo, Chikuzen, Yamaguchi—of Cosme de Torres or
Luis de Almeida or Francis Xavier himself, or any of the others.
In every locality, misunderstandings stood in the way of conversions. The best keynote to this problem may be a brief
discussion of the acts of the Apostle of Japan and Saint Paul of

the Indies, the indefatigable—if not always infallible—Saint Francis Xavier.

Xavier landed in Kagoshima on 15 August 1549, on the auspicious day of the Assumption of the Blessed Virgin Mary.[3] He did not come entirely unprepared, for he had a native informant. In December 1547 he had met at Malacca a Japanese named Yajirō, who had fled his native Satsuma on board a Portuguese ship, having killed a man.[4] In the relationship between this adventurer and the saint we may perhaps detect a quest for spiritual consolation on Yajirō's part, and certainly a considerable venturesomeness on the part of Xavier also.

In May 1548 Yajirō was baptized at Goa with the name Paulo de Santa Fê. He had learned the Portuguese language quickly, and had absorbed most eagerly the Christian message. We are told, for instance, that after twice hearing the explanation of Saint Matthew's Gospel he knew it by heart, chapter and verse.[5] Such indications of this neophyte's aptitude and zeal encouraged the Jesuits in their expectations of success among his countrymen.[6] Indeed, they regarded Yajirō as a most valuable agent in the catechetization of Japan. Upon his return there, he would be employed as a translator. But even while still in Goa he provided indispensable intelligence concerning Japanese religion and society. That being the missionaries' assumption, it was unfortunate that Paulo de Santa Fê was not an educated man, did not know Chinese characters, could therefore not read Buddhist scriptures, and therefore could not know well even the exoteric doctrines of Buddhism, let alone the esotericism of Shingon, the sect to which he apparently had once belonged. Xavier had an intimation of the problem quite early, writing from Cochin on 2 February 1549: "The religions of the Japanese are handed down in certain recondite letters unknown to the vulgar, such as among us are the Latin. On which account Paul, an uneducated man (*homo idiota*) and quite plainly unschooled in such manner of books, states that he is not equipped to give evidence on the religions of his native land."[7] Nevertheless, Xavier had to depend upon Yajirō.

Yajirō passed on to his mentors only the most elementary concepts of Buddhism, and these in a conditioned state: in the process of transmission there occurred adjustments to Christian ideas. What the Jesuits gathered from him concerning other Japanese religious forms also seems to have been chaff. In effect, he gave the missionaries a dangerously simplified conception of the doctrinal opposition they would face in Japan. His most striking disservice was his account of Shingon.

According to Yajirō, the Japanese believed in one personal God who punished the evil and rewarded the good, the creator of all things, adored in a trinity surrounded by saints (one easily recognizes in this latter fancy a trace of the typical mandala representation). This Lord of All and God Creator was in Japan called Dainichi. Upon this point rests a most curious result. The dynamic force of perfect wisdom illuminating the universe—Dainichi of the Diamond Realm—was by the un-tutored layman identified with the personal omnipotence and wisdom of the Christian God, Deus. Yajirō told Xavier the Japanese appellation of the Buddha Mahāvairocana by way of translating the Christian concept "God." And thus it was that Xavier upon landing in Japan commenced his missionary activity there by preaching Dainichi.[8]

Xavier's use of the term Dainichi was based on his general desire to utilize existing native terms in order to make the new teachings more easily understood and acceptable. Such a practice, however, involved a grave risk. The danger was that old beliefs would remain tied to the adopted terminology, being submerged under the surface of the new creed rather than erased. In that case Christianity could never be pure in the convert's mental makeup. Luis de Almeida gives an interesting account of a personal experience which illustrates precisely this point.[9] Almeida in January 1562 was the first missionary since Xavier's departure to visit Ichiku in Satsuma, which had a community of fifteen Christians remaining. As he began to speak about Dios—for by this time the missionaries had switched to the use of unmistakably orthodox terms in Japan, preferring to burden the language with neologisms rather than the convert with illusions—he was surprised by the question: "Is this Dios of whom you speak the same as Dainichi? Because Padre Mestre Francisco preached to us that Dainichi is God and Him we should adore." One can easily picture Almeida's embarrassment.

It is not difficult to see why some Japanese listeners could mistake the Christianity preached by Xavier for just another sub-sect of Buddhism. To give one example from Frois:[10] In 1551, during his second visit to Yamaguchi, Xavier in a discussion with Shingon priests spoke of God as "pure substance, separate from all elements—powerful, wise, and good, without beginning or end." To the Buddhists this meant that "the contents of the law confessed by the Padre were one and the same with their own." Xavier, however, was suspicious, and after reflecting for some days decided to establish whether there actually was any agreement. Upon receiving unsatisfactory responses on the Trinity and on the Incarnation and Passion of Christ, Xavier ordered his companion, Irmão João Fernandes, to go into the streets and tell the people never to adore Dainichi again but rather to consider him an invention of the devil. The Shingon bonzes, Frois states, from then on ceased to associate with Xavier. Xavier, for his part, ceased to use the name of Dainichi for God.[11]

It is apparent that the complications just described were in the main caused by a lack of familiarity with the language. That Xavier himself spoke little Japanese is quite clear. João Fernandes, although barely acquainted with the language himself, had to be utilized as translator when Xavier left Yajirō behind in Kagoshima. Sometimes Fernandes preached himself. Nothing illustrates better the pathetic and yet indubitably heroic aspect of that early missionary period than the picture drawn by Frois: While Fernandes preached, Xavier "stood by his side and in his soul prayed for the success of the Brother's sermon and for the listeners."[12] In numbers, the success of the saint's effort appears to have been slim. In Satsuma, he and his companions baptized no more than 150 people; in Hirado he claimed 100 converts; in Yamaguchi there were about 500.[13] This was not a period of mass baptisms. Xavier's converts must indeed have been sincerely affected by his message to become Christian at a time egregiously marked by missteps and misconceptions, and to persevere in the faith even when deprived of spiritual ministrants.

It is interesting to view Xavier's experiences in the light of later happenings in the Japanese mission. For instance, he was foiled in catechetical work in Satsuma by Shimazu Takahisa's prohibition of baptisms; the prohibition had been issued because of Takahisa's disappointment at the failure of the Portuguese ship to call at one of his ports in 1550—the nao had gone to Hirado instead.[14] Xavier, a practical man, departed Kagoshima to go preach in Hirado. A lesson could also be drawn from Xavier's visit to Kyoto to see the "O, the supreme king of all Japan."[15] Poor and withdrawn in a rundown palace as the Emperor may have been, he was nevertheless not available for an audience to a shabbily dressed foreigner who bore no gifts beyond a spiritual message. One is tempted to smile at Xavier's naïveté in this expedition. But his devotion and heroism in the face of staggering vexations and harassments on the journey are profoundly impressive. And he did manifest a high degree of perceptiveness, in principle if not in the estimate of actual historical conditions. This early attempt to obtain legality for the mission undertaking was a guide for later Jesuits, who were to succeed for a time in gaining the approbation of lords even more paramount than the Emperor. In any event, Xavier himself learned a good lesson. On the occasion of his second visit to Yamaguchi, he called on the daimyo, Ōuchi Yoshitaka, with great pomp, in an impressive costume, and bearing exotic presents: a large clock, a three-muzzle musket, brocade, mirrors, spectacles.[16] The result was placards in the streets, permitting baptisms in Yoshitaka's domain. Similar success was achieved at the court of Ōtomo Sōrin, Xavier initiating the relationship which in the course of thirty years was to prove so valuable to the Christian cause.

Xavier's greatest contribution to the later progress of the Japanese mission was, however, not the indication of perils and gains in political associations but rather his pioneer work in the doctrinal foundations of a mission method. The most striking feature of Xavier's teaching in Japan is his uncompromising emphasis on moral issues. In Hakata, and in Yamaguchi, in front of Yoshitaka himself, he preaches fearlessly against the sin of sodomy. His particular concern is with three sins, with which the Japanese appear to him especially cursed—denial of the True God, sodomy, abortion and infanticide. His teaching generally is based upon sermons on sin and its consequences.[17] It may be said that this is a basic emphasis, common perhaps to all religions. But the ramifications of the Catholic doctrine of sin were far-reaching and had for Japan a peculiar significance. In teaching that humanity's affliction with concupiscence is the result of the punishment meted out to man's first ancestors for their original sin, the Catholic missionaries at the same time could not fail to stress the power of a personal Creator with an all-encompassing interest in His creations. In teaching eternal reward or eternal punishment, Catholicism could not do without the doctrine of a personal immortal soul to which God grants sufficient grace to make it capable of salvation. It was clear to

Xavier that in preaching this faith it was necessary to dispel the illusions of similarity which existed between popular Buddhism and Christianity. According to Frois, the instructions which Xavier set down for the Japanese mission included the following step-by-step catechetical procedure:[18]

—proof of the existence of a personal and infinite Creator of a finite world;

—proof of a personal soul which lives on after its separation from the body, and of the difference of this immortal human soul from the mortal soul of other sentient beings;

—explanation of problems the potential converts may have concerning natural phenomena;

—a logical refutation of the potential convert's particular sect;

—indications of the mystery of the Trinity;

—tales of the creation, and of the sins of Lucifer and Adam and their fall from grace;

—explanations of the arrival of the Savior and the new opportunity given to man by His Passion, Death, and Resurrection;

—indoctrination concerning the Last Judgment, the reward of Heaven, and the eternal punishment of Hell;

—sermons on the Ten Commandments as definite guides to the good life, and on the sacrament of penance as a special God-given grace;

—assertion of the exclusive loyalty owed the Church;

—finally, after an explanation of the sacrament's significance, admission to baptism.

Xavier, in this program, was attacking the Japanese religious tradition all along the line. And he stated further that after much research he had been forced to conclude that Japan had never before heard of Deus or of Christ. The Religion of Deus was what he was preaching since his second stay in Yamaguchi. This was no new sect, this was a new religion; and it rejected all taint of Dainichi. The bonzes, seizing upon the term "Deus," maligned the new faith as *dai uso*, the great lie.[19]

To counter Buddhist aspersions, the assistance of men trained in Buddhism was an absolute necessity. The Jesuits saw very early that if they expected any success at all in apologetics they needed to recruit people more adept than their previous informant, Yajirō. Xavier recognized that one of the most important converts made by him in Yamaguchi was a former Buddhist priest blessed with a critical spirit and held in high repute as a scholar because he had studied for many years at the Ashikaga Gakkō, mediaeval Japan's famous institution of higher learning (which Xavier calls "huniversidade de Bandou").[20] This was no doubt a very valuable convert; and he was not the only such. Padre Baltasar Gago, for example, in his work in Hirado in 1555 considered Paul Kyozen, a former Zen priest, an indispensable companion.[21] Later (1574), Padre Coelho was not above paying about three tael in silver to a Christian to attempt the conversion—"as if by his own initiative"—of his brother, a Buddhist priest: "for he knew the character of the bonzes and how to deal with them in smooth fashion."[22] There is no need to multiply examples. One might merely note that the origins of Fabian Fucan, the Jesuits' ablest Japanese apologist, also appear to have been in a Buddhist temple. (But so was his end. Orthodoxy reclaimed him, and in his last years he was to make his mark as Japan's ablest anti-Jesuit polemicist.)

The intelligent use of well-versed native informants is one of the most notable features of the method followed by the *Visitator* Alexandro Valignano. He recognized that the force of Japanese religion could not be attenuated unless it was first appreciated. Only expert guidance could make possible the approach through the multiple barriers of misunderstanding to the heart of the objective. How well Valignano himself understood and applied the lesson is demonstrated in his own masterful work of apologetics, *CATECHISMVS CHRISTIANAE FIDEI*.[23]

Only three copies of the published Latin text are extant. It is therefore all the more fortunate that the same *byōbu* screen in which was discovered the aforementioned *Iruman kokoroe no koto* should also have disclosed the existence, although in mutilated form, of a Japanese version of the *CATECHISMVS*. Valignano seems to have drafted his work in Bungo in November and December 1580, and the Japanese version was either contemporaneous with the original or was written down soon after.

Valignano's concept was ambitious. He aimed at an incisive analysis of the main points of Japanese religion and an apposite exposition of Christian verities. It is likely that he intended to make revisions later: the news of the book's publication in Lisbon caught him by surprise.[24] But the work as it stands is nevertheless impressively erudite. This erudition is of great credit to Valignano himself, but it is also a reflection of the talents of his collaborators. His principal informant on Buddhism was the physician and man of letters, Yōhōken Paulo, whom the *Visitator* accepted into the Society as an Irmão at precisely the time of the catechism's composition (he had already been a *dōjuku* for over fifteen years).[25] An additional tutor may have been the sometime holder of the title of Zen *chōrō*, Ōtomo Sōrin himself.[26] And Luis Frois probably acted as the translator for Valignano, who understood little Japanese.

The Japanese version of the *CATECHISMVS* and the other manuscript fragments found in the Evora *byōbu* are the oldest extant texts produced by the Christian mission in the native language, with one exception. That exception, however, is merely a collection of routine letters compiled *c.* 1568, and its Christian characteristics are incidental; it may at best have served as an epistolary primer, and hence has been provisionally titled *Kirishitan ōrai*.[27] Valignano's catechism, on the other hand, is a systematic and highly sophisticated work, one which could be used both as a handbook for Padres and as a textbook in the Jesuits' Japanese schools. The subsequent catechisms of the *Doctrina Christam* type, applied to the instruction of simple laymen, did not attain the same level. Only Fabian Fucan's *Myōtei mondō* is in a truly comparable category. Fabian's work is much sharper than Valignano's, but of course it was composed in 1605 and thus postdates the *CATECHISMVS* by some two dozen years; nor is it free of indebtedness to Valignano.

Valignano's is a book of two parts. The first contains eight chapters which aim to demonstrate the "mendacity, frauds, contrivances, & fables" of the Japanese sects so that the truth of Christianity might be the better understood. The second proceeds to an exposition of that "true, & right law of living," developed in four chapters.[28] The first part is the more interesting, for it is curious to see what central idea of Buddhism Valignano was able to grasp out of the welter of sects he was attempting to confute. The whole picture of Jesuit attitudes toward their adversaries is thereby put into focus.

Valignano begins by discussing what he deems the most fundamental of all religious problems: the question of God as creator, preserver, and judge of all things. All nations, declares the *Visitator*, recognize a primary source of existence, although they do not agree—and, indeed, diligently dispute—on questions concerning this original principle's nature, the manner in which it informs all things in the universe with being, and the ultimate destination of man in his relationship with this primary source.[29] Japanese religion also speaks of these problems—but there are so many sects, and their teachings lack unity. It is therefore difficult to discover their actual meaning or essential doctrine, especially since a given sect may not be consistent with itself much of the time. But concepts at the root of Buddhism, whatever the sect, all come together in a single knot. The basis of the teaching is the principle *gonjitsu*, which combines two elements: truth and the semblance of truth.[30] This double standard of doctrine involves two levels of knowledge and exposition.

The lower, *gonkyō*, is religious food for the masses, a sort of provisional set of salvation teachings for the uneducated. The plebs believes in the personal Buddhas Shaka and Amida, in the reward of Buddhahood and a glittering paradise for a life of furthering the Law, and in a sextuple hell with sextuple tortures for those who disregard the Buddhist teachings.[31] The various sects offer various interpretations of these beliefs; but only simple, deluded fools adhere to this exoteric doctrine. Valignano for the time being dismisses *gonkyō* as rank absurdity and extravagant contradiction.

He spends more time explaining the higher level, *jikkyō*. This is religious knowledge secreted by the initiated who teach it only within their own circle of adepts, disdain external expression, and direct themselves entirely to an introspective discipline. There does exist, according to them, an original principle of all things, which is contained in all things. The inmost "heart" of man as well as the inmost signification within all things is identical with this principle called *isshin* and returns to it after its own dissolution. This principle is one with all eternity, bereft of increase or decrease, without shape or form; it is free of the burden of making decisions and exists in highest serenity, peace, and tranquillity. The different sects call it by different names.[32] But they all agree on its immanence and its absolute lack of interest in the things of this world. Men who in this world arrive at a perfect understanding of this principle become its sharers. Those who do not realize it wander through a series of existences without peace; but they too are eventually absorbed into the eternal principle.

Valignano in discussing the question "of the active force, nature *sive* substance of this principle" is personifying too much;

there is too much of the Western logician's stamp on his exegesis of *jikkyō*. That the pattern of presuppositions governing the problem did not coincide for the European and the East Asian can be seen in the most casual comparison of Valignano's work with Fabian's *Ha Daiusu* or Shōsan's *Ha Kirishitan*. There is no need to discuss Valignano's method at length here: it is based upon familiar scholastic arguments. A brief indication of the orthodox Catholic position which he represents will suffice.[33] The "First Principle," since it is perfect, must be all act, have knowledge of all things in the world, and participate in the world as the ultimate determinant of all that happens. All existing things are its creations; each possesses its own substance, derived from but not shared with the Creator. The "First Principle" informs all things with being without forming part of their being: God is "in" all effected things because He is their efficient cause (as the sun is "in" all those inferior bodies to which it gives light), but He is not one of their constituent principles. All living things do not possess the same vital principle. Only in man does the soul exist as a personal and responsible spiritual substance which is the basis of his physical life and yet is immortal. If man's soul does not resist Divine Grace during this life, its acts can merit justification in the personal and permanent judgment which it must undergo upon its separation from its bodily encumbrance. The judgment is rendered by the personal Creator in His functioning as the source of all justice. Perfection can only be attained in Heaven, after that judgment, and full participation in the Divine Mystery is never possible in a finite world.

This is the type of argumentation which Fabian mocked in the *Ha Daiusu*: "𝕯 possesses wisdom and discrimination, and therefore surpasses Thusness, you claim. The very idea! . . . I can't help laughing out loud! The Pure Undisturbed Absolute is something you fools can never understand."* Valignano's discussion of *jikkyō* may be worthy of an Aquinas. But it is

---

*In the original of *Ha Daiusu*, the Gothic 𝕯 is used as a hieroglyph for Deus, the Christian God. The intrusion of the solitary Western letter into the Japanese-character text is not merely exotic: in the anti-Christian tract, it produces the effect of alienation; in works extolling Christianity, where a similar practice occurs, it serves the related purposes of letter-perfect orthodoxy and taboo. I have retained the usage in order to approximate its suggestiveness. Wherever 𝕯 appears in this book, it is to be read "Deus."

wise to keep in mind the mournful warning of Cosme de Torres: Zen priests ask questions which even Thomas and Scotus could not answer to their satisfaction.[34]

Valignano's discussion of *gonkyō* is not so determined or methodical; in its intentions, however, it is no less crushing. A speculative rejection of the existence of Buddhas and Shinto deities, of a sensual paradise, of a transmigration of souls and of the sharing of the Buddha-nature is followed by attacks on the real consequences of Japanese forms of religion as Valignano saw them.[35] Valignano's line of argumentation (as Xavier's thirty years before) manifests a strong moral slant. At the feet of the Buddhas and gods he lays the blame for evil conditions of life in the Japan of his day. He attacks idolatry, he attacks widespread sodomy, he attacks the lack of sacredness in human life (as evidenced especially by abortion or infanticide and by *seppuku*), and he attacks the weak ethical basis of the religious persuasions which had the firmest hold over the minds of the populace at large, Amidism and Nichirenism. A mere "Forengequio" suffices to forgive ever so many sins and crimes without contrition or reparation! These flaws and perversions have brought upon Japan the punishment of God: war, pestilence, and famine.[36]

On all sides they are pulled asunder by wars, torment each other with continuous carnage: by famine, pestilence, and six hundred other troubles and miseries are burdened: tremble constantly at some pernicious conspiracy arising: promiscuously defraud and deceive each other in turn, with artifice, fraud, and stratagem everywhere dominant: the servitor does not keep faith with his master: men's pacts and treaties are violated: in such a fashion that there is perceived among them no sense of duty, and of compassion none, nor of charity: inasmuch as they often kill themselves: and others butcher their fellows with total impunity: sons slay their parents, unmindful of duty: in short, so many species of crimes and execrable perfidies are regnant among them that it may clearly be gathered of what sort are Japanese laws and sects, that they permit suchlike to rest unpunished, nay! even encouraged.—

. . . vndiq bellis diuexantur, continuis se se coedibus enecant: fame, peste, & alijs sexcentis aerūnis, & miserijs praemuntur: exitiosis subinde ortis coniurationibus trepidant: se se inuicem defraudant, & passim decipiunt, vbique doli, fraudes, & insidiae dominantur: seruus hero fidem non seruat: hominum pacta, & foedera violantur: itaut inter eos nulla pietas, misericordia nulla, nulla caritas esse videatur:

siquidẽ saepe ipsi seipsos interimunt: & alij alios impunè trucidant:
filij suos parentes impiè necant: denique tot criminum, execrandorumq
scelerum genera regnant, vt aptertè colligatur, quales sint Iaponienses
leges, & sectae, vt quae talia impunè permittunt, imò etiam probant.

The pessimism drips through the Erasmian accents.

A positive demonstration of the attractions of Christianity
follows the denunciations of Japanese Buddhas, gods, and customs.
Again, it must be emphasized that Valignano's approach is based
preponderantly upon moral considerations. Book Two of the
catechism is devoted to the standards of the Christian life. The
Ten Commandments are stressed as guides; and here Valignano
constantly takes into account problems specific to Japan.[37]

The explanation of the Fourth Commandment strives for
concord with the Japanese feudal ethic: kō (or rather its corre-
spondent in the Commandment) melds with chū, and grave indeed
is this dictate of loyalty due the lords—"if need be, we must
even spill our blood for them, and part with life itself, so
that we may preserve their life, honor, supremacy, and sway,
absolutely alien to all treachery and conspiracy against them,
and to rebellion." The predicate is founded on the hierarchic
conception: kings, princes, and the rest to whose authority we
are subject administer justice on earth in God's stead, loco Dei
in terris; hence they must be obeyed in everything that they
order. There is, of course, the unavoidable disclaimer: the
obligation is contingent upon the lords' own avoidance of conflict
with "right reason, & divine laws."[38] This reservation was to
prove fatal.

The Fifth Commandment, Valignano states, is not directed
against just war but rather against homicide on personal whim,
against suicide and infanticide. Discussions of the Sixth Commandment treat the indissolubility of marriage, but take into
account also the Pauline Privilege, which enables a Christian to
cast aside a spouse who persists in idolatry. After the comprehensive
instruction on the Commandments, the CATECHISMVS closes
with homilies on the power of the sacraments, the resurrection
of the dead and the Last Judgment, and the glories of Paradise
and torments of Hell.

Valignano's catechism draws on and gives form to the whole
series of apologetical experiences of thirty years. Doctrinal disputation had been almost a daily occurrence for the Jesuits since
the days when Francis Xavier in Kagoshima sought out Buddhist

monks in their cloisters without prior invitation. It was easy
enough to attack Buddhism and confound its protagonists by
the use of dialectics foreign to them. Indeed, the *Historia de Japam*
of Frois is full of stories of bonzes skulking away from the
scene of dispute in great frustration. The style is reminiscent of
gospel accounts of Christ destroying the arguments of the
Pharisees: "And since they knew no answer to it, they all arose
covered with shame and confusion, and went away without
saying a single word in answer."[39] But confusion and frustration
were one thing, and persuasion was another.

It was necessary to persuade the Buddhist that Christianity's
personal and positive formulations were preferable to his own
impersonal and negative dialectics. The struggle had to be without compromise and based on the purest orthodoxy: the enemy
was one in whom there resided a certain familiarity. It is
interesting to observe the form which recognition took in
Valignano.[40] After making the assertion that the great temporal
success of Buddhist priests in Japan rests squarely upon their
facile promises of salvation, he pontificates rather inelegantly
on the bonzes' claim:

Even though humans commit as many sins as they wish, if only
they invoke [the Buddha's] name, saying *Namu Amida but*—which is
to say, *sanctissimo Amida fotoque*—with faith and hope in him and the
merits of his accomplishment, or if they mention the name *Meo*—
which is a scripture wherein are comprised all the secrets of *Xaca*
—then by this they will be rendered immaculate and purged of all
their sins by the virtue and merit of these *fotoques*, without any
necessity to perform other penance or to involve themselves in other
works, for thereby injury would be done to the penances and works
which [the Buddhas] performed for the salvation of mankind. So
much that they hold precisely the doctrine which the devil, father of
both, taught to Luther.

There follows the moral directed at Europe: "Hence might
the wretched heretics of our times well take occasion to recognize
their blindness, becoming confounded by their own doctrine,
persuaded by the knowledge that this very same doctrine has
been bestowed by the devil through his ministers upon Japanese
heathendom. Nothing is changed except the name of the person
in whom they believe and trust, the same effect being created
among the heretics as obtains amidst these heathen: for these
as much as the others are sunk in total carnality and obscenity,

divided in divers sects, and living therefore in great confusion of belief and in continuous wars." The notion of a Kamakura Reformation is a conceit of modern historians of religion; but Valignano was in the sixteenth century already aware of the thematic analogies between Japanese and European Protestantism. From this universalist vision flowed the requisite axioms.

The appeal of authoritativeness could be applied to Japan no less than it was in Europe. Division was the hallmark of the Japanese political scene. The positive attraction of Catholic Christianity for Japan was to be in the provision of unity and the stress on sanctifying works of loyalty. Thus would be redressed one of the principal faults which Valignano found in the Japanese character:[41]

There is little fidelity among them for their lords, against whom they rebel whenever it suits them, forming league with their opponents, or into lords transforming themselves. Tergiversating to become friends, shortly after they turn again to rebellion as the situation demands, losing thereby none of their honor. It follows thence that none or very few are secure in their lands, and that there abound the permutations and wars which we witness, that are accompanied by so many deaths and betrayals of kinsmen and friends; for without them the lords could not obtain that to which they aspire. And the principal root of this evil is that they are all not as before subject to the *Dayri*, who was their natural and true sovereign; since they rose against him, rendering Japan divided among so many lords who are neither natural nor legitimate, therefore continue the everlasting wars among them, for each endeavors to acquire for himself as much territory as he can. And in truth vassalage in Japan is so lax and so different from that in Europe, and lordship and the lords' authority of such a different manner from ours, that there is no need to marvel at the many treasons and uprisings which prevail among them, for which the bonzes are not the least culpable, being commonly the principal abettors and procurers of these uprisings, so that they themselves may thrive.

This vivid portrayal of the Sengoku condition is accurate enough: the cracked and disrupted surface of the body politic was all that the observer on the spot could perceive. Contemporary accounts of this sort have been passed down in abundance from the pens both of European and Japanese reporters, and have led many modern historians to cleave to the notion that *gekokujō*—a melée of treasons—was the period's sum and signification. Only the analytical ingenuity of other scholars, such as John Hall, has made it apparent that a new order was seeded within the disruption. Valignano, of course, did not dwell in the luxury of the historian's hindsight. When he wrote his tirade he had before his eyes the disintegrating Ōtomo realm and a Kyushu splitting at the seams. And yet he did more than photograph chaos. He and his fellow missionaries also groped for an answer and tried to interpose their own solution. Their efforts struck a responsive chord.

Success in Sengoku devolved upon those who could rationalize force and authority. Indeed—as Valignano correctly observed— the form of vassalage was the key question. The model daimyo of John Hall's thesis emerged fortified from the Sengoku carnage because they were able to bind their vassals with the direct chains of a command relationship and because they operated from compact and therefore extensible bases of military and economic power. But organizational technique was surely not the whole of the answer. There is also the ideological dimension to consider; and in it Christianity had its potential place. The daimyo who applied new modes to rise above the crumbling old order could utilize the new religion as a rationalizing force, to sweep away the relics of the *ancien régime* in his domain. Christianity represented a double attraction: ethical to the *bushi*, the leading class of Japan; and salvationist to the masses. In religious uniformity some daimyo saw an alluringly powerful bond over the domain's entire populace.[42]

Of what relevance was Christianity to the *bushi*? It promised the resurrection of authority; that was a major part of its appeal. Its definite teaching concerning the personal relationship between God and man bore a strong psychological impact. The strict moral postulates of this relationship could fuse with the samurai cadre of values. Men who sought a religious basis for ethics could easily become convinced that the Christian foundation was stronger than that of their accustomed beliefs. Was it so strange for a Takayama Zusho turned Dom Dario to berate his non-Christian retainers: "What service can a man render who is not Christian? And what merit can he have therein? Or how can one trust a man who neither knows nor fears God? For that reason I say I do not consider him a man who is not Christian, much less do I want to have any dealings with him or be served by him."[43] The claims of exclusive and unquestioning feudal loyalty could be justified by an uncompromising religious dressing. The step to Christianity was not a large or an illogical one for a samurai of the Sengoku era. Perhaps it may even be argued that a deep desire for personal security in a secular order bolstered by transcendent ethical dictates was responsible for Christianity's appeal to the nonmilitary populace. The Buddhist Law had clearly reached its Age of Decline in a time when asuras prowled the earth.

The appeal to the samurai may well have been fortified by its particular formulation at the hands of the Jesuit Order. The Society of Jesus was by its founder Ignatius Loyola organized in a perfect mold of religious and military discipline. The definition of Max Weber aptly describes the activating force of this elite group:[44]

> The content of discipline is nothing but the consistently rationalized, methodically trained and exact execution of the received order, in which all personal criticism is unconditionally suspended and the actor is unswervingly and exclusively set for carrying out the command. In addition, this conduct under orders is uniform. Its quality as the communal action of a *mass* organization conditions the specific effects of such uniformity. Those who obey are not necessarily a simultaneously obedient or an especially large mass, nor are they necessarily united in a specific locality. What is decisive for discipline is that the obedience of a plurality of men is rationally uniform.

Not only did these eucharistic warriors offer to the Japanese their expositions of the articles of a new creed: they presented also the vigorous example of fortitude and made a preachment of the uncompromising practical application of a thoroughgoing moral code. The exaltation of the self-sacrificing ideal and the stress on a moral code marked by the lack of compromise were the points of coincidence in the appeals of *bushidō* and of the Christianity propounded by the Jesuits. But the Jesuits did their work *ad maiorem Dei gloriam*, for the greater glory of God. The locus of Christian morality must be in God as the *summum bonum*, the absolute form of the highest good; whereas the traditional focus of Japanese morality was in *chū*, the loyalty owed to political authority, and in *kō*, the filial piety due to family. The synthesis toward which the missionaries worked was never fully persuasive. The supernal, extraterrestrial locus of Christian loyalty was the point of severest collision between Christianity and the Japanese tradition.

The religious sanction was given to *chū* in a whole series of

Christian devotional and instructional tracts. Prescripts of loyalty were based upon the boundless majesty of Deus and the accordant boundless honor due Him. Luis de Granada's *GVIA DO PECADOR* (The Sinner's Guide; Nagasaki, 1599) elaborates:[45]

Even the reverence owed men is deep according to the height of their augustness. And similarly, it is meet to worship 𝕯 boundlessly, and to be filled with boundless awe of Him, than Whom there is no higher in exaltation. Be mindful of this! You must know that if there is in the heart of man boundless submission, reverence, awe, then it must without any reserve be offered up to Him.

Be sure you understand from what has been said above that you must love and worship the Lord, submit to Him, and serve Him. If you do not acknowledge with love the merit of His deep compassion, what can you then love? If you are not filled with awe at His majesty, what can you then fear? If you do not serve this Lord, into whose service can you then be taken? And therefore, since the limits of the volition of man are in the [quest for] good in all things, how then is it possible to know not the Lord, Who is thus possessed in plenitude of all good and all virtue? . . . No matter how reasonable it is here in the present to serve a man, however great his majesty, when compared with the reason of serving 𝕯 it is as though one were speaking under a different sun. That is because the degree of excellence bestowed upon a created being, when likened to the majesty and merit of 𝕯, cannot even be termed majesty or merit. In like manner, now to consider offence, it is impossible to speak of an offence against a created being and align it with one committed against the Creator.

Deus is the *summum bonum,* and the source of order in the universe. To adore and to serve Him (with an eye to Paradise) is the highest good attainable to man, and the highest duty. The *FIDES NO DŌXI* (Guide to the Faith; Amakusa, 1592) put it in language easily accessible to the samurai:[46] "It is of absolute necessity that a general who has received a castle to keep for his lord be determined rather to cast away his life than capitulate immediately the enemy comes to lay siege to the place. In the same manner, it is of absolute necessity that a Christian rather cast away his life than worship Buddhas or gods."

An epitome of that famous compendium of *bushi* virtues, the *Taiheiki,* was one of the publications of the Jesuit mission press. It therefore seems all the more natural to find the language of certain accounts of Christian moral example reminiscent of the

Taiheiki style. An illustration from the *SANCTOS NO GOSAGVEO* (Acts of the Saints; Kazusa, 1591) might be cited.[47] In the passage Saint Clement is admonished by his mother to prepare for martyrdom:

A man born to a house of bow and horse deems it his honor to have his corpse rot exposed to the sun of the fields for the sake of his lord. He keeps his constant code to fulfil his fate in the face of danger. How much the more should you, a soldier in the army of the Lord 𝄃, cast away your life for the sake of this Lord! Is not that a greater loyalty? Especially since this Lord has already preceded you and has given His life for our sake! A soldier is disgraced as long as he lives if he withdraws to the rear guard, grudging to give his life. Prepare therefore, and do not grudge your life.

Deus is the *summum bonum*, and the source of order in the universe. Only the man who offers up fullest faith and loyalty to Deus can approximate the zenith of goodness. If need be, he must offer the supreme sacrifice, to reap his reward in Paradise. Only the adherence to rules emanating from the wellspring will ensure order for the world. The temporal lords of this earth are but God's delegates: the loyalty due them is but derivative. While it is true that the retainer owes absolute allegiance to his sovereign, it is no less true that this loyalty is transcended by a higher duty. If the temporal lord interferes with the exercise of Christian faith or morality, or even prohibits it, such interference must be regarded as denial of the *summum bonum* and interpreted as wicked disregard of Deus' will. If suasions fail there remain two forms of action. One is martyrdom, the palm of Christian fortitude. The other is the refusal of fealty. The "absolute allegiance" to a temporal sovereign is cancelled out by the greater loyalty, the higher duty, by the other absolute. Out of such Christian dictums followed the formulation of Hideyoshi and the Tokugawa: The Christian Heaven's Mandate implies the right to revolt.

The point is: What were the limits of loyalty? Professor Ebisawa Arimichi states: "The self-sacrificing loyalty and fidelity preached by the Christians . . . was based in the Ultimate Good, Absolute Justice. Directed it may have been at the lord to whom immediate vassalage was owed; but its ultimate exercise was in the sacrifice of the self for the sake of justice and benefit in the wide sense—what was thought to be of paramount value for society and for the nation as a whole."[48] Therein lay the danger. Whose interpretation of the highest good was the valid one? Was it that of the ministers of Deus, the Bateren? And what did that imply for the Early Modern state and for the realm undergoing secularization?

It would not be without profit, in examining these questions, to observe with some attention to detail the near-fatal triangle of Oda Nobunaga, Araki Murashige, and Takayama Ukon, with Padre Organtino Gnecchi-Soldo SJ as bisector. The events take place in the late autumn of 1578.

Nobunaga's plans "to overspread the Empire with military might"— Tenka fubu, the slogan he flaunted on his seal—had not reached fruition. In 1575, in a model demonstration of modern warfare, his musketry had annihilated the Takeda at Nagashino; three months later he wrested Echizen from the grasp of the True Pure Land sectarians; in 1577 he put down the revolt of Matsunaga Hisahide in Yamato. His control of the vital area of Kyoto thus appeared secure on several fronts. But there remained a particularly odious thorn in his side: the Ishiyama Honganji of Osaka, which the True Pure Land Sect under the leadership of Kennyo Kōsa had made into a near-impregnable fortress. The Honganji received much succor from Mōri Terumoto, at the time Oda's most dangerous enemy; not even a monstrous iron-clad built by Oda (which Organtino visited and admired in Sakai) could prevent fully the flow of supplies brought to the Honganji sectarians (monto) by the Mōri fleet. To confront Mōri, Oda had sent Hideyoshi on his Chūgoku campaign toward the end of 1577; but the campaign was not progressing with the requisite speed.

At this juncture of events—in the month of November 1578— Araki Murashige of Settsu suddenly turned against Nobunaga to take the side of the Honganji and Mōri. This was a severe threat to Nobunaga's hold over the area of the Capital: the crucial glacis of Settsu would now be denied him. Especially critical was the position of Takatsuki, equidistant from Kyoto and Osaka, and the key to success or failure for both Nobunaga and Murashige. The castle of Takatsuki was held for Araki by Takayama Ukon and his father Takayama Zusho—Dom Justo and Dom Dario, stalwart Christians. To settle the matter Nobunaga summoned Padre Organtino into his presence.

Nobunaga, with much pathos and a tearful countenance (if

one may trust the melodramatic account of Frois[49]), and with great effusions of praise for Christianity and for the rare gifts of Takayama Ukon, impressed upon Organtino "that if Vcondono agreed to cast in his lot with him and be his friend, he would favor the Law of God in whatsoever the Padre demanded of him." Organtino was dumbfounded by this harangue and by Nobunaga's unseemly passion: "for it seemed as if he was all the while moaning and sobbing." But the Jesuit retained enough wit to strike a balance: "In case Vcondono became Nobunanga's friend, there would follow an extraordinary Conversion in Japan; and in case he did not agree, there would be no avoiding a cruel persecution."

The initial suasions of Organtino were rejected by the Takayama, at the special insistence of Ukon's father Dom Dario. There resulted further pourparlers, Organtino shuttling danger-ously between Nobunaga's camp and Takatsuki.[50] The result is adequately reported in the *Nobunaga kōki*:[51]

> But the castellan of Takatsuki, Takayama Ukon, was a Deus sectarian (*Daiusu monto*). Lord Nobunaga devised a plan, and summoned the Bateren to him. At this time he [asked the Bateren] to contrive that Takayama should tender allegiance to him. If this happened, the adherents of the Bateren would be allowed without constraint to build [temples] wherever they wished. And he uttered his intent, if [the Bateren] did not accept, to exterminate the religion. To be sure, the Bateren accepted. Sakuma Uemon, Hashiba Chikuzen, Kunaikyō Hōin, and Ōtsu Denjūrō accompanying him on his way, the Bateren went across to Takatsuki, and performed there all sorts of moral suasions. Of course, Takayama had left hostages [with Araki], but counting not the little birds in the bush, he realized the import of the big bird at hand—to preserve and make prosper [his own brand of] Buddhism. For this reason he handed over the castle of Takatsuki. Takayama himself is a *shami* novice of the Bateren, as report has it; and he accepted the demands. Lord Nobunaga's rejoicing was not in minor key.

Organtino had pointed out the path of higher duty to Ukon. But the bisecting of a triangle of forces involves the irremediable severing of one of the angles. It is only fair to point out that it was an untenable position in which Organtino found himself, that Ukon made a tortured compromise decision while transfixed by the dilemma's horns,[52] that the immediate result—Nobunaga's favor—was highly desirable for the Christian endeavor in Japan. But was the end result so favorable? Ominously present in the list of those who accompanied Organtino to Takatsuki is a certain Hashiba Chikuzen, later to become famous as Toyotomi Hideyoshi. What was played here before his eyes was a tragedy of the collapse of *chū* in face of the greater loyalty. And of *kō*: Ukon's father was to the end impervious to the schemes to play the castle into Nobunaga's hands. Ukon's party-takers had to use stratagem and stealth to ensure themselves of the castle, behind Dario's back, at night. Ukon was in Nobunaga's camp by the time Dario realized what the game was.

The son's letter—written "in very good style, and with words full of great respect and reverence, that he always had" for his father—apprised Dario of the situation.[53]

And Dario was struck with astonishment, and as one in blank consternation and beside himself, he leapt up in great and precipitate fury, and rushed straight for the donjon, and finding it locked called in grand choler for his old retainers and fidalgos that were inside, but none answered him for none wanted to be involved with him, who was the father of Vcondono their lord. And he made himself thence, and circled all the bulwarks, and all around the fortress; and, finding everything locked, seized in his hands a *nanguinata* (halberd), and with an uncommon and to him very alien fury and violence began to wave it about, [rushing] hither and thither, through all the fortress court-yards, calling for his men, without there being anyone that would present himself to him . . . Dario now finding himself without any force in [the fortress], called for the Gatekeepers, that they should open for him; and there being none that would assist him, since he was a man of much strength and great stature, he lunged at one of the gates (and that the stoutest of all) and opened it with his own powers— which the Padre saw later, and it appeared impossible that it could be opened by human strength. And leaving the donjon, and finding the other gates locked, he set to singular hewing about with his poniard, bursting gates and cleaving irons and breaking open pathways for him-self, which was a matter of great amazement for those that saw it later.

He proceeded to Arioka, to report to Araki and to save his hostages, "and was upon arrival praised by all for his determin-ation." But the plot in which Dario played this *aragoto* interlude remains to this present day in Japan a familiar Sengoku story of Christian duplicity.[54]

Was Christianity a religion which fostered foul political games? As is so often the case, the best apologia against the aspersion is in Fabian Fucan's *Myōtei Dialogue*. Subsequently the bitterest anti-Christian, he provides here the most clever Christian rationale, and the brilliant exposition is all the more effective for its obvious stamp of Jesuitry. The sapient Yūtei is here expostulating to her marionette, the noble lady Myōshū:

The claim that the land is put at peace by virtue of the gods' power is without foundation. Even more unreasonable yet is the claim that it is put at peace by the majesty of Buddha's Law. That is because Buddhism, in the final analysis, is a doctrine which preaches the absolute void, and considers good and evil undifferentiated, perniciousness and righteousness the same. How can the claim that our mind is of void and that there is no master over punishment or bliss be construed into a basis of peace! Quite the contrary: here is the origin of revolt and perturbation.

Let us look at the proof. I have heard that in Cathay also—wasn't it about the seventh or eighth year after the accession of Emperor Ming of the Later Han?—when Buddhism was first introduced from the Westland and began its spread through society, there afterward was continuous disturbance in the empire, and the sovereigns who succeeded did not last long on the throne.[55] This is what the Han Confucians censure so severely. Especially remarkable is the case of Emperor Wu of Liang. He turned his back on Confucianism and became a devotee of Buddhism. He built temples and made Buddhist priests his companions. Some three times he abandoned his worldly self and became a drudge of the monks. And in the end, we are told, he was put under siege by Hou Ching and finished by starving at T'ai-ch'eng. So that's the sort of benefit one gets from Buddhism! Or are we to call this too the way to universal peace? Then what else shall we designate, what else abominate as the root of rebellion?!

Shaka had not yet been born in the reigns of Yao, Shun, Yü, T'ang, Wen, and Wu. Of Buddha's Law no one had yet heard the words "Buddha" or "Law." And still, when you come right down to it, there is no report either in Cathay or in Our Empire of a time when the Royal Sway was as blessed with felicity as it was then. The superior treated his inferior with compassion; and since the sovereigns acted as sovereigns, the subjects also acted as subjects; the inferior honored his superior. The hearts of men were gentle, and that is because the "men of Yao and Shun patterned their hearts on the hearts of Yao and Shun."[56] They conceded to each other their ricefield partitions, and did not stoop to quarrels. And thus the land was prosperous and the people wealthy, and there was no one to strike the Drum of Plaints. Now this is what I call an example of a well-ordered realm! Both Japanese and Chinese may rightly call this the mirror of Royal Sway of felicity. To say that without Buddha's Law the Royal Sway is forsaken, and that without reverence for Shinto the land cannot be safe is the verbiage of people who know nothing. My advice to you is: don't believe a word of it!

I don't have to tell you about the Affairs of Shōhei and Tengyō. But let us dwell upon Hogen and Heiji.[57] At that time there had been heard in Our Empire not even the syllable "ki" of "Kirishitan"; but Buddhism and Shinto were especially in flower. And the Empire was in uproar, the Royal Sway was held for trifles, warrior subjects showed no submission to the Court. From that time on, beginning with the wars between the houses of Minamoto and Taira, steeped in pride, through the Shōkyū Disturbance,[58] all the way down to our times, you will find in the histories nothing but: assault upon one place, battle at another. About more recent events, you can hear from men advanced in years: the rout of such-and-such a year, the uprising of another; here a conflagration, there a demolition. That's all you'll hear. Peace by benefit of the Buddhas and gods, indeed! What period in our country's history can be designated that? Because of the worship of the pernicious Buddhas and gods Japan has been cursed with the punishment of Heaven, so that military conflict has proliferated here more than in any other land; that's the one thing I'm sure of.

At any rate, unless all of Japan turns Kirishitan, it cannot be perfectly put to order. That is because the Kirishitan teaching is to worship the Lord 𝕯, and then to love and honor one's master, from the bottom of one's heart, and to serve him: from the Emperor and Shogun on down to each and every lord below. Day and night our faith exhorts us to this . . . If all of Japan turned Kirishitan the land would be in tumult and the Royal Sway abandoned—upon what reasoning rest these assertions? In the Kirishitan countries there is no Buddha's Law; but the Royal Sway flourishes there and its virtue abounds and fills the Four Seas.

"True, true is what you say; quite clearly true"—is the response of Myōshū.

The dream of an *universitas Christiana* flickered before the eyes of Fabian in Japan. It was a well-known fact that in Christian lands for more than one thousand years there had been neither war nor rebellion.[59]

Chapter 3

The Accommodative Method:
The Jesuit Mission Policy and
Cultural Contribution

HERE was a definite appeal in the Christian message. But the appeal could never be universal. The message was diffused only in limited areas of Japan. Not all of those whom it reached were amenable to it. The country's political development was not favorable to the Christian cause. In any event, the resources at the disposal of the missionaries were inadequate. The eventual doom of their endeavor was caused by forces beyond their own control; but internal problems also gravely impeded the Jesuits' effort. And these can be summed up in two words, finance and manpower.

No truly satisfactory remedy existed for the problem of finance. The Church in Japan could not support its own mission undertaking because it was never secure enough to plan acquisitions of income-producing property; and contributions from its Japanese supporters could never be sufficient because they were not sufficiently prosperous themselves. The Jesuits found a provisional solution to their financial troubles in the Portuguese China Ship; but that does not concern us at the moment. What does concern us is the fact that the Jesuits at a critical point did not act effectively to reduce their manpower problem. It is difficult to avoid blaming Padre Francisco Cabral for a delay of ten years in the formulation of a farsighted mission method in Japan.

At first sight it seems unfair to question Cabral's capacity. In 1570, when he arrived in Japan, there were in the country some twenty or thirty thousand Christians.[1] By 1579, the year of the *Visitator* Valignano's arrival, the number had quadrupled, and may have reached 130,000.[2] In nine years of activity as Superior of the Japan mission, Cabral had registered the extremely impressive increase of as many as 100,000 Christian souls. But the very rapidity of this expansion raised further problems. The Church in Japan was constituted of raw material. There had not been time to refine the quality of this Christianity. Only one generation had passed since Xavier's advent and mission. The Japanese were "new Christians," and the connotations of the phrase were not necessarily good. The question was: Could they be trusted?

In the final analysis, the answer was no. To be sure, Cabral stated that it was necessary to admit Japanese into the Society and give instruction in the Japanese language to European Jesuits. In a conference held at Kuchinotsu in 1576 he stressed the need of a college and of a novitiate with strong language instruction.[3] His suggestions in regard to a Japanese mission method would therefore seem to have anticipated some of Valignano's most constructive measures. Indeed, Valignano, while still in India, observed rather dubiously what he considered Cabral's undue enthusiasm for Japan.[4] But Cabral's were only paper plans.

Cabral made not a few bad mistakes in judgment, and his main fault was a failure to fit himself into the modes of the mission country. The Roman behaved as though he were in Rome, and the narrow view distorted his sense of purpose. Actions immaterial in themselves achieve significance in such a context. One example is Cabral's stand on the question of dress for the Jesuits in Japan. Prior to his arrival they had worn silk robes, in accordance with the local custom of men of their standing and vocation. Cabral, in the interests of apostolic poverty and of discipline, insisted that only the Jesuit blackrobe could be worn. And the Japanese genre scene was enriched by the intrusion of yet more exotica.

The eminent Jesuit historian J. F. Schütte observes that the twin presuppositions which governed Cabral's mission method were "a pessimistic judgment concerning the Japanese character" and "stress on the primacy of supernatural mission resources (the poverty and humility of apostolic life, the power of the Cross, the reliance upon God . . .)," and it would certainly appear that this estimate is correct.[5] But what were the consequences of Cabral's attitude? In precisely that period when Christianity in Japan was growing by numerical leaps and bounds, Cabral with an astonishing lack of foresight refused to take the step which would ensure its corresponding growth in quality: a vigorous program of training Japanese for the priesthood. The superior of the Weberian status group feared the compromising of the group's discipline.

Cabral may have wondered why Japanese found it hard to adjust to him. But perhaps he merely made one of his customary remarks: "But, of course, that's a Japanese for you!" or "After all, they are blacks and their customs are barbarous!"[6] The hostile attitude was reciprocated. There was widespread demoralization among the Japanese workers of the Society and discontent among Japanese converts. The daimyo Arima Harunobu and Ōmura Sumitada told Valignano that they had never come away from a visit to a Jesuit residence without a feeling of dissatisfaction at the constant tactlessness prevailing there. Ōtomo Sōrin alone remained a great friend of Cabral's. But that, according to Valignano, was due to Cabral's good offices for Sōrin with the Portuguese traders; and even Sōrin found it hard to bear the insulting behavior. Other Christians told the *Visitator* that no teachings could have persuaded them to convert had they known while still pagan of the things which went on in the residences of the Padres.[7] Cabral's crude rigorism offended commoners, samurai, and lords alike. And this was the situation in a new mission country and a land where Christianity's very existence depended on the good will of the daimyo.

Valignano ordered a complete reversal of approach. Everywhere in every possible way everything was to be done in the Japanese fashion and with Japanese ceremony; and this was a matter of principle. The measures ordained by the *Visitator* constituted a remarkable surrender of Europe to Japan. By giving up the external line the Jesuits hoped to capture the internal.

Valignano provides the rationale in his *Sumario de las Cosas de Japón* (composed in 1583 as a synthesis of the experiences of his first visit to Japan): "The Japanese manner of life is so strange . . . that those who live among them, if they wish to accomplish anything, must accommodate themselves to their ways." If the missionaries fail to keep the Japanese statutes of custom, they will either cause their hosts "affront and injury (which they will not suffer)," or themselves suffer debasement and their Christian religion disdain. "And thus is lost the reputation of our law jointly with its fruit." For this reason Valignano urges upon the Padres three major rules of behavior.

The first is that they live immaculately, maintaining themselves im-maculate as concerns their residence, and its furnishings, and their food, their clothing and that of the others of the residence, and in everything else connected with the residence; preserving in every-thing immaculateness according to the usage of Japan.[8]

Valignano takes account not only of the legendary Japanese cleanliness, a model for Europe, but also of the native passion for decorum. "*The second thing they have to maintain is politeness in their behavior*, acting very well-bred and behaving with courtesy."[9] And the third thing the Padres have to aim for is dignity and authoritative bearing—*la tercera cosa que han de guardar es la autoridad*. Not the least of the reasons for this norm of behavior was:

Our Lord does not assist with the miracles He performed for the Primitive Church, and inner virtue is not recognized as such in Japan. And the bonzes have much advantage over us in their exterior bearing, in what even appears in the eyes of men to be virtue—their exterior modesty and composure, their manner of not showing any passion to the outside, and their appearance of docility, kindness, and good breeding. If we—and we are strangers here and preach to them so rigorous a law—do not attempt to acquire some credit in these three points, then we and our law will forever remain in a position of much abasement in Japan.[10]

Here Valignano points to his resolution of problems debated in the Jesuits' Japan Consultation at Nagasaki at the end of 1581. This was the final of three formal meetings which he convened during his first visit to Japan in order to set down a concerted mission program. The others were held at Usuki in October 1580 and Azuchi in July 1581; the *Visitator* made certain to confer with his subordinates in each of the three main mission areas. After the particular discussions, he was able to make general and binding determinations. Especially interesting is the Japan Consultation's resolve on Question XVIII of the agenda: "Is it appropriate to observe in everything the customs and cer-emonies used by the bonzes?"[11] The answer was in the affirmative. Accommodation was totally necessary—*es del todo necesario que nos acomodemos*.

Question XVIII further stated the desirability "that there be made by the Japanese themselves a compendium and sure manual of the customs and good breeding which we have to observe, among ourselves as also toward outsiders, of the manner which

the bonzes use, so that we all should keep one mode of behavior and not wander, as until now, sometimes ignorant of
what we are doing or what we should do." Of course, it was
not necessary to observe in everything all the ceremonies of the
bonzes; Christians could hardly find applicable the entire Buddhist
sacerdotal routine. But the Jesuits had to play a role similar
in its forms to that of the native religious, in order to mask
their own alien character. Familiarity would perhaps result in
assimilation.

Valignano himself wrote the necessary manual of etiquette;
and he charged the superiors of the mission with the enforcement of the essential rules it contained. These *Advertimentos e
Avisos acerca dos Costumes e Catangues de Jappão* were composed
(apparently at the insistence and with the assistance of Ōtomo
Sōrin) in Bungo in late 1581.[12] A citation of the chapter
headings will give an idea of the contents of the treatise:

1. Of the measures which have to be taken to gain and preserve
authority in dealing with the Japanese.
2. Of the measures which have to be taken to win the confidence
of Christians.
3. Of the courtesies which the Padres and Irmãos have to follow
with outsiders.
4. Of the manner to be used in proffering or accepting wine and
relishes.
5. Of the manner of behavior to be used by the Padres and Irmãos
among themselves, and to the others of the residence.
6. Of the measures which have to be taken in entertaining Ambassadors or other persons of standing, and of the invitations and presents
which are to be tendered.
7. Of the measures which have to be taken in building our residences
and churches in Japan.

Every one of these questions is treated in the most painstaking
manner. Meticulous observance of rank is stressed, and of the
courtesies appropriate to it. Dignity, reserve, and self-control
are urged. The *prima facie* necessity is a thoroughly Japanese way
of life. And the high value placed on considerations of status
also makes evident the need of a rather grand style.

The Jesuits are to live in residences of Japanese architecture,
the veranda overlooking a well-ordered garden. "In large cities
where there is concourse of great lords, and in places where
reside *yakata*" are to be provided immaculate and well-decorated

zashiki for such lords' special use (with an adjoining toilet, to be kept "immaculate and for the sole use of the aforesaid lords"). The contemporary craze for the tea ceremony required that a tea pavilion also be set apart, "with a cubicle containing a chest in which are kept all the implements pertaining to pledges of wine; and a brazier must also be there, with its companion shelf cabinet, such as would serve for the preparation on the spot of some broth or hors d'oeuvres or other such things."[13]

The Japanese mode is to be observed in eating. Even when by themselves, the missionaries are always to eat Japanese foods at low Japanese tables. Question XVII of the Japan Consultation exhaustively treats the topic, and Valignano's resolution reveals the full measure of his perspicacity and thoroughness. He is reluctant to omit even the most banal of details. That the assiduity was not misplaced was to be proved in 1587, when (perhaps because subordinates had failed to observe the *Visitator's* injunctions) Hideyoshi cited the Southern Barbarian slaughter of useful household beasts to explain his decision to banish the Padres. The meticulous care which Valignano devotes to the dietary problem therefore deserves some detailed attention:[14]

Making allowance for human frailty, and with consideration for the many reasons which therefore influence me, it appeared fit to me to ordain the following measures:

1. The first is that henceforth there shall be kept in none of our residences (whether in Christian or in pagan territory) either pigs or goats; nor shall cows be slaughtered; neither shall their hides be exposed for sale or cured; and there shall be no other suchlike practices which are filthy and abominable in the eyes of the Japanese. By this is not meant to say that the keeping of chickens and ducks is prohibited; provided that they be enclosed in a place set apart, so that they do not run about the residence.

2. The second measure is that in territories either of Christians or of pagans where the eating of pork and beef or other foods prepared in our manner has not been introduced among them, such shall not henceforth be introduced, unless they be very pure foods by which they will not be taken aback—to wit: bread, sugar pastry, preserves, olives, and things of such nature. And when lords are invited where the custom of offering them food in our manner has not been introduced, it shall not be introduced . . .

3. The third measure is that in territories where due to intercourse with the Portuguese the eating of pork and beef is not found so

strange, as in the territories of Nagasaki, of Kuchinotsu, and of Bungo, suchlike foods may at times be eaten in our residences; provided that they accord with Japanese usage, and that scraps and bones are not let fall upon the table, and that there be no such large slices as might appear grotesque to the Japanese. And the soup made of beef is to be put in plates and not in [lacquer] bowls, so that the cups and soupbowls be free of smell when Japanese afterward eat in our residences.

4. The fourth measure is that the ordinary food of the Padres and Irmãos must be rice and soup with two types of side-dish prepared in the Japanese manner, with a dessert of fruit or other such. They may help themselves to seconds of rice or soup—that is to say, those who eat are to be given as much as they desire—and at the proper time the winecup shall be passed. But both in the serving and in the eating, the order and custom of Japan shall be observed.

5. The fifth measure is that although the ordinary food in the residences must be of this manner, nevertheless consideration is to be given to those who may be indisposed or ill or who according to the judgment of the Superiors for special reasons require something prepared in our manner . . .

6. The sixth is that I request and require all my dearest Padres and Irmãos who are now and who hereafter will be in Japan, that they do as much as they should to win control over themselves, accommodating themselves in everything to the foods used in Japan and the manner of eating; since it is very important—for many reasons which I know by experience—to the service of Our Lord and to the success of our endeavor in Japan that we win control over ourselves in this matter, becoming accustomed to their food. They should not weaken and be easily overcome by initial repugnance at these [foods] or by the notion that they might be excused, that their stomachs cannot bear such foods; rather, they should with virtue and charity vanquish this repugnance. For experience has shown to me personally and to many others that, determined to control ourselves, we can achieve in this matter more than we had considered, and that our nature in a few short days accommodates itself to that which man wants, when he is determined to do it.

But because we do not all share the same stomach and the same good health, each shall act according to the precept of the Apostle: "Is qui manducat, non manducantem non spernat, et qui non manducat, manducantem non judicet."

Valignano's striving for perfect accommodation appears extremely impressive. Nevertheless, it is wise to recall what has been said above in connection with the *Iruman kokoroe no koto*:

Jesuit indoctrination exhorted the Europeans to change their modes of behavior, but demanded that the Japanese change their entire attitude. "It is of ultimate importance that Europeans, when they cross over to Japan, abandon their original habits and customs and learn Japanese habits and customs."[15] To make everyone behave like Portuguese is far from being the Jesuits' intent. Nay!, for it is their intent to advance Japanese customs. The Japanese should refrain from imitating the Southern Barbarian manner—this is detrimental to (the Church's interests in?) Japan and is prohibited. But accompanying this advice are continuous attacks upon Japanese habits as contrary to natural law. The major emphasis of the lectures reproduced in *Iruman kokoroe no koto* is on the creation in Japanese aspirants of the moral makeup fit for a Jesuit. Ultimately, the question concerned the purity of the Japanese background. Again: external show of virtue is the Japanese manner; duplicity they hold to be the better part of wisdom. No faith is kept between parent and child, between man and wife. Even among those who have dwelt in the ecclesia for more than twenty years there are many in whose double hearts lurk dark thoughts. For that reason it has been very difficult to admit Japanese into the Church. But now there is a program to make them into true children of the ecclesia: "From each *anima* these foul"—Japanese—"habits are to be extirpated."[16]

The problem of adaptation was discussed in near-identical form in all three mission consultations which Valignano held: Usuki, Azuchi, Nagasaki. The Usuki Consultation of October 1580 served as the point of inspiration of Valignano's manual of etiquette.[17] The Azuchi Consultation of July 1581 saw Padre Organtino "stand in the first line of support for every point of the question of accommodation."[18] Organtino was also the premier advocate of a native clergy. It may therefore seem odd— assuming that Ebisawa was correct when he identified Organtino as the source of the *Iruman kokoroe no koto*—to find the pessimistic estimate of Japanese character emanating from him; it appears contrary to the spirit of Valignano's *Advertimentos*, of which he was a prime supporter. The extravagant statements seem stranger yet if we accept that Valignano himself made them. But there is no need to wonder. The Jesuit measures of accommodation were conceived pragmatically and had a highly formalistic character. The compromise with Japan did not involve the sacrifice of inner essentials.

A striking illustration of the formalism is to be found in the first chapter of the *Advertimentos*. Here Valignano shows himself willing to learn from the mortal enemy, the bonzes, and at least on the surface to imitate them, in order to gain authority. In formulating a clear outward classification of ranks for the Jesuits of the Japan mission, he takes over the levels of ceremonial listing from the Zen Sect. "It seems fit that the Padres and Irmãos, who are the bonzes of the Christian religion (*os bomzos da relegião christãa*), should place themselves at the same level at least on which stand the bonzes of the Zen Sect, which is held in Japan to be the principal of all." Accordingly, the Japan Superior should be ranked the same as the Superior of the Nanzenji, that sect's most honored position. The Superiors of the three major areas of the Japan mission should be considered equal to the abbots of the Five Monasteries of Kyoto (simco *Choros/chōrō* de *Gosan*). The other Padres should hold ranks corresponding to the *chōrō* or *tōdō* of other, less important temples. Elder Irmãos should be comparable to Zen *shuso*, and novices to *zōsu*. The Jesuits' own *dōjuku* should occupy the position which *jisha* maintain in Zen temples.[19] There follows a detailed description of the exterior forms of life in a Zen cloister, to be adapted to Christian needs. And always the most exquisite care is lavished on punctilio.[20] It was a far cry from the days of Cabral.

The new stress on ceremonial propriety was, of course, only one part of Valignano's program. His effort was directed toward the establishment of a truly viable position for the Church in Japan, and he recognized that structural obstacles would remain even after the psychological blocks were removed. His solution may be seen in outline as early as December 1579, in the extensive reports he wrote for the General of the Society; and a tentative formalization is visible in the preliminary consultation he held in July or August 1580 at Nagasaki with Padres Cabral, Coelho, Mexia, and the newly ordained Luis de Almeida.[21] Three main groups of questions can be detected. The problem of ecclesiastical organization is not of prime interest to us, and that of Church politics and trade is a topic in itself. Valignano's main concern and major contribution dealt with the third complex of questions, those bearing upon the inner growth of the Church in Japan. The answers are of some importance to the cultural history of Japan, and their prime significance is in the field of education.

Was the Church to attempt continued expansion, or should it merely work to consolidate what it had gained? Was there to be a buildup of a native secular clergy? Or were Japanese to be admitted into the Jesuit Order as full-fledged members? If so, were they to be admitted for preparation to the Jesuit priesthood? And what was to be their training? Was Latin to be taught them? And sciences as well? Were formal institutions of learning to be opened for Japanese? Was the treatment accorded Japanese to be the same as that to which Westerners were subjected?

Arguments against further expansion centered upon the fear that the available manpower did not suffice to care for the souls of new Christians. As of December 1579 there were in Japan up to 130,000 Christians, and all of 55 members of the Jesuit Order—only 23 of them priests. Expansion would take men away from incepted missions and thus thin out even more the quality of the Faith in Japan. The internal discipline of the Order would break down. Financial insolvency, already chronic, would become unbearable. Of course, according to one of the most elementary theological precepts, it was a grave and cruel dereliction not to spread Christianity among the heathen: however weakly instructed, the baptized were capable of salvation, whereas pagans were not. Furthermore, without an expansion of the Christian area the newly gained flock could not be expected to remain constant: the susceptibility to non-Christian pressures was too great and could be reduced only by the conversion of entire provinces. An exceedingly grave practical reason was the basis of the decision to continue expanding: because of the constant turmoil and war in Japan, the Church's sole chance of security was in a wide diffusion. But all that required more missionaries.

Valignano wrote this estimate of the situation in December 1579, early in his stay in Japan; but by the end of his visit he had not changed it. His decisions presupposed an orderly, continued spread of Christianity; but there was no hope of obtaining from Europe or India enough priests to guarantee such an advance. In any case, Japan's Church to be strong had to be staffed by Japanese. To gain and to train recruits for a native clergy, a program of Christian education had to be instituted in Japan. Its base, according to Valignano's plans, was to be in three preparatory schools (*seminarios*), one to be located in each of the three main mission areas of Shimo, Miyako, and Bungo. Initially, most of the teaching cadre would be Europeans, who would in turn require a strong program of language instruction; grammars and dictionaries of Japanese had to be provided for that purpose. The systematized linguistic studies which were the byproducts of this missionary scheme remain even in the present day invaluable to the scholar.

The plans were soon translated into action.[22] Construction of the first *seminario* was begun in Arima in the early summer of 1580, when the newly converted Dom Protasio Arima Harunobu put the site of a Buddhist monastery at the Jesuits' disposal. Instruction began in October, with twenty-two students —all from noble families—actually present.[23] The seminary of Azuchi, which was built with the assistance of all the Christian lords of the Kansai on a plot of land provided by Oda Nobunaga in the vicinity of his splendid castle, also began its operations in the same autumn, although it was not festively dedicated until the following Easter. By October 1580 there were enrolled twenty-two students, not all as yet actually in attendance.[24] The seminary planned for Bungo was never to be built because of the collapse of the protecting power.[25] The educational structure was never completed, due to circumstances beyond the Jesuits' control. But it is also important to note that there were purposeful limitations in its very blueprint.

Extravagant claims have been made for the Jesuits' educational contribution to Japan. For instance, Professor Ebisawa Arimichi asserts that during the Tenshō period (1573–1593) there were two hundred Christian primary schools in Western Japan alone. He further tells us that these schools taught a curriculum including Portuguese, arithmetic, music, painting, and drama. He attributes great value in particular to the system's penetration down to the masses of the unlettered common people, who thus for the first time gained access to letters, innovative ideas, and scientific knowledge.[26] But the number of institutions he cites seems posited upon the mere count of Christian churches and chapels in that period, and his lesson plan upon wishful thinking.

Some simple catechetical training must have gone on at each Christian center. But such elementary indoctrination is not tantamount to formal schooling. Although Valignano vaguely and casually mentions in the *Sumario* that primary schools should be founded at each Jesuit residence (*en nuestras casas*, "houses" and not "churches"),[27] the wish was not to be realized. One such school was founded in 1604, adjunct to the *collegio* in Nagasaki. Another came into existence in 1607 at the Jesuit parish of Saint James in the same city. But these are the only two which J. F. Schütte SJ—the ultimate authority in such matters—lists in the latest and monumental product of his exhaustive researches into the history of the Society of Jesus in Japan.[28]

It should not be lightly assumed that the Jesuits neglected the common people. But their generally elitist attitude toward education is well known; and the practicalities of their mission method required an aristocratic orientation in Japan. Valignano's *Regimen for the Seminaries of Japan* (dated 28 June 1580) spells out the original concept: formal education is confined by design to the upper levels of society, *gente nobre e honrrada*, those with access to their lord's chambers. The *Sumario* of 1583 reiterates this elitism.[29] The exclusive nature of the schools is manifest in yet another sense. Valignano did not plan an expansive curriculum; indeed, in some respects it was consciously restrictive.

The *Sumario* asserts that the main thing is training in virtue and in good habits, and decrees:

Because in Japan there is no knowledge of any of our authors or of our books, and because these contain many things which the Japanese should not by any means find out . . . it would seem meet and necessary to compose for the Japanese special books in all the sciences, in which would be taught simply the gist of the matters at hand and the pure truths, well-founded and with their proofs, without referring to other divers and dangerous opinions . . . for it is not necessary for them to know any of these things, because knowledge would cause them much damage and no profit.

Too much knowledge would only pervert the Japanese, especially if there were introduced from the West opinions tending to agree with those of their sects. Heresies would then proliferate. Therefore neither Aristotle nor Cicero should be taught, and to avoid them would be easy; for they had no prior authority in Japan, and the Japanese were not apt ever to hear of them from other sources.

Valignano clearly thought it best to preserve the illusion that the European tradition was exclusively Christian. The children should learn their Latin from a tender age, but not from the pagan poets. They should rather be provided with books which solidly teach "virtue and the Christian religion and to abominate vice." Upon this rock the *Visitator* planned to build his seminaries.

These schools were meant to shape the minds of a select group of young people. Practical reasons dictated that students who were not expected to remain in the Society should also be taken into the seminaries: they would later become knights and lords, and pillars of the Church. But the main purpose of the institutions was to care for the development of preachers, pastors, and eventually bishops for the Church of Japan, and to ensure at the same time the growth of the Jesuit Order in Japan. The end result of the educational program would be the synthesis of Christian theology and philosophy with Japanese spirit and culture. The means to that end were in the combination of "scientific" instruction and moral-theological training. The Jesuit pedagogy had a tinge of the spirit of Christian humanism. But the Christianity prevailed over the humanism; the dangerous thought of the Renaissance was kept from entry; Erasmus, after all, was on the Index. The sciences (not for nothing did Valignano accentuate "*las ciencias* VERDADERAS," the *true* sciences) meant philosophy and theology. The natural sciences did not figure in the lesson plans, nor were they necessary to the concept. The *Visitator*'s ideas on education were subsumed in his concern for the preparation of native missionary manpower. Doctrinal purity was the aim, dogmatic rigidity the root of the method. The spirit of the Counter Reformation had reached Japan.

The students were to be introduced to the Western pattern of thought very selectively. Valignano set down the guidelines in the *Regimen for the Seminaries of Japan*.[30] It will be noted that this educator frowned not only on Aristotle but mistrusted even the Doctors of the Church:

After they have apprehended Latin, those who have the ability shall learn other sciences, especially cases of conscience; and when time and experience demonstrate that it is fit to teach them philosophy and theology, they shall be taught them. But one should avoid—especially in matters touching upon our Faith and the immortality of the soul—to teach them the diversities of opinion which exist among the Doctors, and the controversies and opinions of the heretics; one should only teach them true and solid doctrine, so that they know in philosophy as in theology [only] the truths held in common and accepted by the Church. One should avoid reading Aristotle to them, or other authors from whom they would learn perplexities and diversities of opinion, and the errors held by the others, whether they be ancients or moderns; which, if they were known, would be of no use to this people—which is so new in the Faith and so bereft of knowledge—and could have many damning effects. And therefore one should either compose for them a pamphlet (*livro corrente*) containing in sum the common doctrine without other controversies, or one should lecture to them from some other already existing compendium or summa, such as that of Vigerio or Denys the Carthusian, or some other such. And in this matter I gravely charge the conscience of the Superiors as of the masters [in the seminaries], that they do nothing to the contrary, at least until Christianity is more expanded in Japan and with a better fundament in matters of our Faith; for with a contrary course many grave and damning inconveniences could accrue.

The hothouse which the *Visitator* envisioned would later—when the mission press was instituted—be built with Thomas à Kempis and Luis de Granada as its main pillars. Several other doctrinal and devotional manuals were published; and the schools could of course utilize the catechism which Valignano himself had composed. The textbooks were a major concern. The *Visitator* vested great expectations in his alumni. He was eager to provide them with the proper materials in order to ensure their "progress in virtue and the Latin language," and he made certain to minimize delays. The printing press brought from Europe at his behest was used while still at the way station of Macao to produce a book designed especially for the students of the Japanese seminaries. This was Valignano's own adaptation of a celebrated Jesuit handbook of moral training: *CHRISTIANI PVERI INSTITVTIO, ADOLESCENTIAEQVE perfugium* (The Education of a Christian Youth, and Adolescent's Refuge) by Padre João Bonifacio.[31] The contents nicely mark out the degree of cosmopolitanism which the seminaries were to be permitted.

This "Adolescent's Refuge" is a parade of examples of virtuous conduct, prudence, and chastity. The Bible predominates. The exhortations from Scripture and from the Church Fathers—most notably Jerome, Ambrose, and John Chrysostom—are accompanied by Valignano's multiple additions of edifying stories designed to appeal particularly to the Japanese consumer. But the text is also replete with allusions to classical events and figures and contains citations from classical authors, especially Cicero. Caesar is present as well; Xenophon's *Cyropaedia* is also invoked.

The uplifting effect is the principal aim; but, true to the *Visitator's* intent, the book also exposes its student to much good rhetoric.

In the end the ancients could not be banned from the schools altogether. Quite apart from the well-known Japanese edition of Aesop, and the *Visitator's* initial doubts to the contrary, Cicero's orations had apparently been printed as early as 1592, and Virgil probably in 1600; no copies are extant, but the evidence seems conclusive.[32] Indeed, one should deem it strange if Cicero had not abused the patience of Japanese seminarians, if Virgil had not found his way from the shores of Troy, a fugitive fated to drift to Japan. Since the inception of Jesuit education down to the present day those two have remained the principal drill-masters of Latin in the Society's secondary schools.

From the preparatory seminaries those who aspired to become Jesuits were to advance to institutions of a higher level. Pro-bationary aspirants were first to spend two years at a novitiate and then progress to a *collegio* to receive training in philosophy and theology. The history of the College of Saint Paul, which was opened in 1580 at Funai in Bungo, offers another illus-tration of the contrast between the active character of Valignano and Cabral's negativity.[33]

On 5 September 1571 Cabral (at this date still in the mood of initial optimism) had written to the General of the Society, Francisco de Borja, of the necessity of a Jesuit college in Japan.[34] On 22 June 1576 Cabral had received from India the *Visitator's* letter concerning questions of education: "Of what type should the college be which is to be established? . . . Should a novitiate be established as well, and instruction be started in the humanities and in moral theology?" The Kuchinotsu Consultation, which was held to answer these questions, agreed on the necessity of a college; the location was to be in Bungo, under the wing of Ōtomo Sōrin.[35] In 1576–77 Sōrin himself recommended to Cabral the opening of a *collegio* near Usuki. In 1578 Sōrin's son Yoshimune assigned to the missionaries "a very large site for the College" in a spot about a half-league distant from Usuki, "taking it from one of the principal lords, & from some bonzes that also held share of it, satisfying them with other sufficient stipend. The location is maritime, with a very beautiful beach, & a spring of the best water to be found in this land. And the prince had us told that when construction began, he would come there in person with many lords to work at it."[36] But nothing was done.

Valignano landed in Japan on 25 July 1579, and first arrived in Bungo on 14 September 1580. By 20 October a novitiate was in the process of organization in Usuki, and the college, which Valignano decided to locate in Funai, was in operation.[37] The first students of the college were eight Europeans; accordingly, the initial emphasis was on training in the Japanese language. The instructor was Irmão Yōhōken Paulo, and success was considerable: we are told that conversational proficiency was attained in two years. From 1583 on, the entry of Japanese, former novices of Usuki, necessitated the beginning of instruction in Latin. Formal lectures in philosophy began in the same year, and advanced theological training in 1585.[38] The beginnings were not bereft of promise.

In 1580 were created in Japan the first formal institutions for the training of missionary recruits in the spirit of the Church and of the Society of Jesus. Heretofore, Japanese taken into the Society had received only a private introduction into its inner discipline and into the material which they were to pass on to their compatriots. Now, the Order might with good confidence expect that its Japanese helpers would get a proper indoctrination. The highly trained preachers who were needed in order to spread a pure and uncorrupted faith might be forthcoming. The Jesuits could have stronger hopes of directing their message not only at a wider audience but also within the circles which determined the cultural direction of Japan. And that was not yet the sum of the *Visitator*'s vision. Valignano dreamed of an institution with the authority to grant academic degrees—a Jesuit University of Kyoto—with courses in the humanities, political philosophy, and law.[39] But that was not to be.

Had Cabral acted promptly, the number of Jesuit recruits would have been larger. "Had the great organizer [Valignano] had his way regarding the three preparatory schools which he had planned, he would soon have had an annual graduation list of 100."[40] So comments Hubert Cieslik; but concern with the eventual number and its consequences verges on idle speculation. Political circumstances soon brought on the inevitable failure. The Azuchi seminary went up in smoke together with Nobunaga's castle town when that hegemon met his violent end in 1582. Nor was Bungo a safe haven for the missionaries, due to the growth of Shimazu power at the expense of the Ōtomo and to the hostile attitude of Yoshimune. As early as 1584 Sōrin advised the Jesuits to move novitiate and philosophate out of Bungo. At the beginning of December 1586 the Shimazu forces occupied Usuki, and Frois frantically hastened to Shimonoseki and begged Kuroda Josui (Dom Simeão) to save the collegians of Funai. Kuroda sent a ship, and the college was transferred to Yamaguchi in the first days of 1587.[41] It was the fateful year of Hideyoshi's Expulsion Edict.

Hideyoshi's move upset Valignano's grand design. The Jesuits managed to keep several of their schools in operation: the Arima *seminario* and the Order's novitiate and college survived until the general persecution of 1614. Expansion, however, was no longer possible. The University of Kyoto never opened its gates to receive the laymen whose leadership would have leavened the Japanese world of letters with the disciplines of Christian education. After Hideyoshi had passed from the scene, and before Ieyasu had had the time to formulate his own anti-Christian program, another institution of higher learning did open to serve the Church in Japan, although—in Cieslik's words— "considerably later than intended and in a different and more modest way than its first planner had dreamt it."[42]

In September 1601 the Bishop of Japan,[43] Luis de Cerqueira SJ, ordained the first two Japanese priests. They were Sebastião Kimura SJ and Luis Niabara SJ; and Cerqueira wrote to the Jesuit Provincial of Portugal that Japanese Christians "could not restrain their tears as they thanked God for having chosen those of their own people to the sublime dignity of the priesthood."[44] In that same year of 1601 was established a formal center of higher theological studies, the diocesan priests' seminary of Nagasaki (*seminario de clerigos*). A half-century, and a world of possibilities, had passed since Xavier's optimistic message to Loyola:[45] "Because the land of Japan is much disposed for the self-perpetuation of Christianity among [its people], all the efforts spent here are well-employed, and so I live in great hope that your holy charity will send saintly men from abroad to Japan. And that is because among all the lands discovered in these parts, the people of Japan alone is [capable] of the self-perpetuation of Christianity; although it shall require the greatest of labors."

The labor required to make possible the Japanese self-perpetuation of Christianity had been performed too late; therefore it cannot be labeled the maximum effort in the sense of

Xavier's letter. Japanese Christianity was left with woefully understaffed cadres of leadership when its moment of crisis came. In 1614 the Nagasaki diocesan seminary fell victim to Bakufu suppression. Graduated from the institution in the thirteen years of its existence were seven Japanese secular priests. Cerqueira also ordained eight Japanese Jesuits; but one of these (Mancio Itō) died in 1612, four years after his ordination. In short, when the general persecution broke out in 1614 there were in the country only fourteen native priests. Father Cieslik would have us look not at the small number but rather at the triumph of the principle that an indigenous clergy was desirable, possible, and necessary.[46] That the effort had been made at all was due to Alexandro Valignano's vision. The *Visitator* established the principle for Japan.

He expressed it in his usual pragmatic terms. Not only were the Japanese fit for admission to the priesthood and into the Society of Jesus; there were overwhelming reasons for admitting them. They did not lack the "nobility, capacity, prudence, authoritative bearing, and all the other requisite qualities." More to the point, they were indispensable to the mission endeavor. They alone were fully conversant with Japanese customs; they alone were fully familiar with their country's traditional scholarship and modes of expression; they alone fully fitted in. Besides— the *Visitator* predicted—"the Society will never set firm roots in Japanese soil nor obtain the income or advantageous means for its sustenance unless it be through the mediation of Japanese Irmãos"; for only Japanese could build the requisite bridges of trust between the Society and their own compatriots, and utilize family connections to secure the endowment of Christian institutions, "the same way as do the bonzes."[47] The *dōjuku* who had heretofore assisted the Padres had performed better than could have been expected (especially since they had received no formal training). Isolated scandals notwithstanding, there were no grounds for complaint about the Japanese collaborants' behavior: correct conduct presupposed correct treatment.

Valignano admitted that the greatest internal difficulty in conducting the Japanese enterprise was the "preservation of unity of spirit among the Japanese Irmãos and *dōjuku* and our Europeans; failing in this point, which is the fundament of the entire fabric, the Society of this Province shall without doubt in a short time cast itself into perdition." For that reason he cautioned the Superiors to operate with "much solicitude and vigilance and much dexterity and prudence" in governing both their Japanese and European charges.[48]

The difficulty was so great because the national characters seemed so different. The difference did not appear accidental to Valignano but substantial: *intrínseca y natural por ser como fundada en la naturaleza.* The Japanese mode of reasoning (mental) and of sensation (corporal) were as different from the European as was Japanese judgment on practical matters and on incidentals— food, song and music, taste and odor. The Japanese seemed inscrutable even to this acute observer: they showed no agitation even when they were highly offended; they were "very covert in their hearts." By contrast, the Europeans were hasty, choleric, and frank. Surely there was need for adjustments.

The *Sumario*'s thesis did not depart from the utterance of the Japan Consultation: the Europeans must accommodate themselves to the Japanese. The guideline was set through five points: Japanese members of the Society to be treated as equals of the Europeans; gentleness, love, tact, and reason to govern the treatment of Japanese in the Society; mutual respect for each other's customs, ceremonies, and feelings; adoption of Japanese modes of behavior by the Europeans; mortification of the taste buds and adoption of Japanese foods. Still, one has the feeling that the form predominates over the substance.[49]

Valignano had no fear of a dearth of vocations among the Japanese, paradoxically enough being reassured by the land's superabundance of bonzes with their multiplicity of congregations. Nor was there fear of a lack of perseverance in Japanese aspirants to religion: once they shaved their heads, they deemed themselves obliged to remain in the cloister forever. And finally there came from Valignano's pen this effusion of praise:

If we are to speak of the requisite capacity in virtues and letters, then I frankly do not know how there could among men be found a better. For the Japanese by nature make it a point to be masters of their passions, agreeable, docile, prudent and very circumspect, and modest and serious beyond measure. They are much given to ceremony. They are great endurers of hunger and cold and inured to rigors and personal maltreatment (even the kings and great lords glory in this), and are sublimely forbearing in the loss of their estates and in persecutions, without taking recourse to murmur and resentment; and in all this, and even unto death, they demonstrate a most noble and valiant heart and soul.

In this quality they surpass the Europeans—Valignano declared—doing naturally what Westerners must first acquire with the cost of much effort. Much the same can be said about their capacity for learning:

> Even though the Latin language is so new to them, and though such difficulties reside in the conversion of our art [of speaking] into their language, because of the contrarity in sentence [order] and because of the lack of terminology . . . they are of their nature so quick, ingenious, and so absorptive and studious that it is cause for wonder, for even the children stay at their studies for three or four hours, as if they were grown men, without budging from the seat; and we have seen in our own experience how in the seminaries they learn in a short time—together with learning to read and write Japanese, which is a very difficult thing—to read Latin and translate it into Japanese, and many of them also to play musical instruments and to sing.

Once they are provided with the proper textbooks—he continued—they will surely be seen to absorb as much as Europeans in the same time, or even in less.[50]

And how to treat these paragons of virtue and of learning? By an art Jesuitical: *modo suave*, the manner of pliant affability mixed with resolute firmness.

> One must always talk to them peaceably and courteously, even when assigning them penitence or reprehending them, much on guard against speaking with ill-bred words and in choler . . . for they do not suffer injurious words spoken in choler and impetuousness . . . But ordinarily when they are being reprehended they must be convinced by reasoning; one must sway them with a sort of piteous disappointment and earnest endearment (*hablándoles con una manera de sentimiento y encarecimiento*), so that they feel ashamed and abashed (*corridos y avergonzados*) at falling into the faults for which they are reprehended, and so that they feel addressed with love and grieving concern, such as a father uses with his son . . . For when one does it in this manner, then the Japanese yield immediately and improve immeasurably.

There is not a trace of empathy in the fatherly statements: they are preoccupied with what is politic. It is clever counsel. Patronizing treatment, however, necessarily humbles.

Nor did Valignano fail to insert some words of caution: "One must also be much on guard against revealing that he has a bad opinion of them and against displaying distrust of them; for they are by nature punctilious about their honor, and one would thus lose them . . . And it is necessary to maintain vigilance and caution with them, yet doing this in such a manner that they do not notice that one distrusts them, only that the Superiors endeavor to maintain the good order and discipline of the Irmãos and of the residence." That certain reluctance to extend complete trust to the Japanese is always lingering, gnawing. One may with good reason wonder whether the Japanese in fact did "not notice," as the *Visitator* hoped they would not—notwithstanding the repeated insistence that the Europeans eat *à la Japonaise* and in every way behave "purely and honorably in conformity with the custom of Japan." And it is cause for melancholy to see Valignano warn the Superiors against disclosing any inner distrust of the Japanese, and then turn immediately to urge those same Superiors above all to persuade these same Japanese to be always communicative and openhearted.[51]

Beyond the problem of personality rested the question of morality; and Valignano was a penetrating critic of Japanese mores. An example is his appraisal of one of the more picturesque "strange customs of the Japanese."[52] One of the bad qualities of this nation, he observes, is that—

They are very cruel and quick to kill, because for the most insignificant reason they kill their subjects, and they do not think more of cutting a man down the middle than if it were a dog; so much that many of them, when they can do it without danger to themselves, in encountering some poor individual will split him in half, for no better reason than to test how their swords cut. And in their wars they plague and destroy the population by fire and flow of blood, without sparing even the temples of their idols; and they even go so far as to kill themselves with the greatest of ease, slashing themselves in the guts, whether it be for sake of vexation or to avoid capture at the hands of their enemies. And what is most cruel and contrary to the order of nature, the very mothers often kill their children, either while still in the womb by taking something to induce abortion, or after birth in suffocating them by trampling on the throat; and that only to avoid the bother of bringing them up, or with the excuse of poverty and inability to support so many children. Not a little guilt in this matter accrues also to the bonzes: for in trying to cover up the perversities they practice with their nuns they have invented this evil, which is propagated by way of many bonzes' now proffering herbs and medicines to all who request them for the purpose of inducing abortion.

The parting shot at the bonzes may be superfluous. And Xavier had already pointed to abortion or infanticide as one of the principal sins of the Japanese, to be followed by a series of other missionaries who drew attention to this problem before Valignano. But the problem was indeed critical. Professor Okada Akio has discussed it within the general thesis: the traditional Japanese concept of morality admits a low valuation of human life (*seimei no keishi*).[53]

This disregard of the value of human life represented a formalization of actions and mores originating in the cruel circumstances which ruled life in the Sengoku period. In the two centuries between 1400 and 1600 Japan passed from a régime of authority to a régime of power and then emerged again as a régime of authority. Sengoku was the transitional stage of this historical process. The Ōnin War exposed the political bankruptcy of the Ashikaga shogunate; and in the hundred years after its outbreak in 1467 new lines of the exercise of power were drawn across Japan. These lines were increasingly taut and often crossed each other. With the entire country swept up in war, and principalities to be either gained or lost, brutality more than ever displaced mercy: efficiency in the new art of warfare dictated that. The essential Sengoku condition is perhaps best expressed in the words attributed to the famous general Asakura Sōteki Norikage: "The warrior doesn't care if he's called a dog or a beast; the main thing is winning."[54]

A murderous sentiment pervaded the consciousness of the *sengoku bushi*, and was to be transferred into the period of the Pax Tokugawae in an idealized form. The prevalent manifestations of that form in *bushi* were the "beautiful act of suicide"—disembowelment, or *seppuku*; and *junshi*, following the lord unto death—and the practices of vendetta (*katakiuchi*), assistance at suicide (*kaishaku*), and the proof of a new sword (*tameshigiri*). A low valuation of human life was an inescapable part of the developing notion of the warrior's absolute, inviolable, self-immolating duty to his lord. This ideal was to be firmly established for the samurai by such Tokugawa thinkers as Yamaga Sokō, who sought for the peacetime warriors a categorical *raison d'être*. But a rudimentary definition had been achieved in the later stages of Sengoku by daimyo who asserted direct control over their vassals and attributed a moral significance to the tightened relationship between lord and retainer. A multitude of examples might be chosen, but a brief citation from the "house laws" of Takeda Shingen will suffice. "To serve the lord *yakata* means to have no rebellious thought in all eternity." And: "Though the lord act not as a lord, the servant must never fail to act as a servant."[55]

The lack of compromise involved the complete abandonment of certain dicta of conventional morality. The Buddhist prohibition against killing, for instance, was anything but universally observed. The cynic will of course remark that this prohibition was widely ignored long before Sengoku; it is significant nonetheless to note that the Sengoku warrior had lost all concept of criminality in the taking of life. It may be somewhat anticipatory to mention in this context the *Hagakure* (the famous codex of *bushidō*, completed in 1716), which was to raise the intensity of the self-immolating ideal almost to the level of a farce in which a narrow loyalty supersedes all dictates of morality and even the greatest models of valor.[56] The point is that the intensification was born out of practical necessity in the Sengoku cataclysm. And the harsh facts of life in Sengoku were not hidden from missionary eyes.[57]

Suicide was for the warrior the rational expedient when confronting the demise of his entire family after a lost battle or on account of a faulted lord. Yet suicide went counter to the basic Christian precept that life is a gift from the Creator. Christian indoctrination on this point was effective, at least in some cases. The best example of one who acted according to it is Dom Agostinho, that same Konishi Yukinaga over whose fate Fabian Fucan gloated: "He joined the atrocious rebellion of Mitsunari; but he wound up dragged down the avenue to the execution ground and was beheaded. One and all, his relations were eradicated; he left no survivors."[58]

Dom Agostinho had the misfortune of choosing cooperation with Ishida Mitsunari after Hideyoshi's death, becoming one of the guiding spirits of the anti-Ieyasu party. After the defeat of the Western Army at Sekigahara, he wandered about for days in the mountain wilderness, agonizing over the decision whether or not to "slash himself in the guts." His Christian beliefs won out over his concept of *bushi* morality; and he was executed together with Mitsunari on the riverbank in Kyoto. Mitsunari—so goes the popular story, unhistorical as it may be—at his end the very image of the Sengoku general, refused the favor of a thirst-quenching persimmon, claiming it was bad for his phlegm. The *Kirishitan daimyō* Yukinaga begged for the favor of a priest confessor to salve his soul. This Ieyasu refused him; nevertheless, his end was holy. His last words were "Jesus Maria."[59]

The manifestations of disregard for the value of human life among the common people took the form of abortion and infanticide. The practice was a consequence of the prevailing poverty and lack of food in a land which was devastated by warfare, and was, to start with—in the words of Valignano— "sterile and mountainous, and generally speaking one of the most sterile and poor that exist in the entire Orient."[60] The missionaries condemned the practice, to the point of refusing Christian burial to women who died in the attempt at abortion.[61] Moral instruction on the requisite love of children was made vivid by the presentation of religious plays with themes such as the judgment of Solomon.[62] But the missionaries went beyond mere preachment and made concrete attempts to ameliorate the situation. Luis de Almeida established an infant refuge in Funai as early as 1555. It was the very first Christian institution of social action in Japan.[63]

The Jesuit concern was also directed at the proper upbringing of children. One of the reasons why Valignano thought seminaries necessary was because in his view Japanese parents were far too permissive, and the children "brought up so spoiled and unrestrained (*se crían tan viciosos y libres*)" that "there are none other than ourselves who could instruct them"—especially, he added ingenuously, "after we have expelled the bonzes from their lands."[64] It might not be altogether amiss to remark, in concluding this brief discussion of works of Christian charity, that Valignano's concern for the children was not totally disinterested. These are the last words of his *Sumario de las Cosas de Japón*:[65]

It appears that it would be a very good thing to take in such children as are commonly killed by their mothers; for thus, apart from saving many souls and preventing many sins, the Church would gain many servitors, because they would be put under the obligation that at least up to the age of thirty they must serve the Church. And the same could be achieved with girls, giving them to some Christian Japanese women with the same obligation of service up to the age of thirty. And although this appears to depart from our constitutions, still there are none in Japan who will do it if we do not do it ourselves; and among all this new Christianity it is necessary to commence with many things which are not precisely appropriate to us, in order to introduce them and bequest them, in time, to the Japanese.

One can hardly avoid a double take at this grand gesture.

Little escaped Valignano's eyes, but they lingered especially upon the area of the Capital. He understood the great importance of Kyoto as the center of culture and prestige in Japan. Propaganda motives made him desire to measure the authority of Christianity against that of Buddhism in this very nest of the bonzes. And practicality dictated an emphasis on mission activity in the Kansai. "The lords who are in the parts of Shimo, and even those of Bungo, always have their eyes fixed upon their own interests," and pressure the Jesuits to pilot the Portuguese ships to their harbors; slack is their Christianity, and that of the parts of Miyako much better.[66] The *Visitator* also noted the importance of Sakai—"not only a large city and inhabited by many rich merchants, but also free like a republic, always possessing great privileges and freedoms"—and found it incomprehensible that no Jesuit residence had been established there.[67] He visualized the Kansai as a great center of activity from which the rays of Christianity would spread all over Japan; and he did send missionaries on exploratory expeditions farther than any had been before. Frois and the Japanese Irmão Cosme Takai went to Echizen to visit Dom Dario Takayama in his place of exile and to call upon Shibata Katsuie, who showed himself not uninterested in obtaining the spectacle of the Portuguese carrack for his harbor.[68] Padre Gregorio de Cespedes and the Japanese Irmão Paulo of Amakusa went to Mino to call on Oda Nobutada in Gifu, and on to Owari.[69] Another Japanese Irmão went to visit Hideyoshi, who was at the time (1581) occupied in Harima.[70]

The *Visitator* concerned himself minutely with the problems of ministration to the countryside, as his *Regimen for the Padres who are in the Residences of Japan* reveals.[71] ("Out in the villages they must have with them little, low confessional stools, comfortable to the Japanese.") A set of rules for the uniformity of liturgical practice details the mode of accommodation to traditional festivals: they should be celebrated, and coated with a Christian meaning.[72] The Japanese New Year should be met with High Mass. There is no objection to Bon Festival dances; but the missionaries should strive to do away with the companion pagan superstitions, such as the invocation of the name of Buddha in *nenbutsu* canticles. Valignano even looked into the evils of Japanese usury. In each of the three main mission areas he desired the establishment of credit associations to keep Christians out of the grasp of loan sharks charging 70 or 80 percent interest. *Mutuum date nihil inde sperantes!* Valignano's suggested Christian rate was 10 percent.[73]

The structure which Valignano sketched he wanted to remain unchallenged by competitors. Japan was to be a mission of the Society of Jesus alone. The *Visitator* elaborated the reasons "why it is ill suited for other religious orders to move into Japan" in Chapter IX of his monumental *Sumario*.[74] The influx of other religious orders he feared quite frankly as a destructive threat to the picture of perfect Christian unity presented to Japan. *Una sancta catholica et apostolica ecclesia* was much better represented by one holy universal and apostolic order than by a monkish rabble whose intrusion would create a Christian correspondence to the Buddhist Babel.

Each order had its own conventions. Valignano particularly feared the jarring note which the advent of a motley of mendicant monks would deliver to the superbly attuned Jesuit image. The Jesuit masquerading as Zen *chōrō* could ill admit fraternity with the barefoot Franciscan beggar. The virtue of apostolic poverty is little honored in Japanese eyes, sibilates the suave Valignano. The mission method which had been painstakingly constructed after years of bitter experience would be imperiled by mendicant missteps. There would be no way of avoiding dissension and quarrel. For these reasons it appeared to Valignano "extremely pernicious and baneful for Japan that any other type of religious outside of ourselves come here." Other orders do not know the actualities of Japan; but, hearing of "the abundant fruit which our people reap here, and of the honor and name which the Society gains thereby, divers religious who are in the Port of China [Macao] and in the Luzon [Islands] and in India greatly desire to move into Japan, especially because where they are the people are of little capacity; and from New Spain many are moved by this desire to come to Japan. And therefore it would appear well to me to obtain an order from His Majesty and a Bull from His Holiness" to prevent them from coming.[75]

Valignano's desire to maintain a Jesuit monopoly in the Japan mission was given formidable support by the General of the

Society of Jesus. Gregory XIII on 28 January 1585 granted his papal brief to that effect. The Viceroy of the Indies, Duarte de Menezes, twice in the year 1586 issued in the name of King Philip *Provisions* which in some paragraphs reproduce literally the text of Valignano's objections.[76] But Sixtus V, who succeeded to the papacy in April 1585, was himself a former Vicar General of the Franciscan Order and cooperated with the mendicants, who no longer felt themselves bound by Gregory's injunction.[77] The embargo was finally broken in 1593, when Fray Pedro Bautista OFM arrived in Japan with three confrères, in the role of ambassador from the Spanish governor of Manila, and was received with much apparent friendliness by Hideyoshi. Hideyoshi's motives were probably commercial; but he did permit the Franciscans to remain in Kyoto, where they soon began to missionize with great (and to Jesuit eyes quite unseemly) zeal and lack of discretion.

A notorious *odium theologicum* obtained in Japan between Jesuits and mendicant friars from the date of the first confrontation. The first recorded visit of a Franciscan to Japan occurred in 1584, when the ship of Fray Juan Pobre de Sanlucar de Barrameda was driven off course on a voyage from the Philippines to Macao.[78] The friar stayed at Hirado for two months and was lodged in the Jesuit residence there; but even this passing visit left the Jesuit Vice-Provincial Gaspar Coelho somewhat ill at ease.[79] The bile built up in the years that followed. In 1621, in the midst of persecution and in the most hideous circumstances, the Jesuit Padre Baeça—with informers and constables at his heels, and forced to change hiding places constantly—used a rare opportunity to write to an intimate friend by taking the time to complain:[80]

> These friars of ours, though there be but few, are all spent in pamphleteering against us (*todo he papeladas contra nos*) and brassily meddle in our Christianity. All they want is to usurp them into their confraternities (*cumis/kumi*). Not for them is to venture into all the kingdoms of Japan that there are, for the sake of baptism and the making of Christians; but they are all for intrusion into that for which we labored so many years, at the cost of lives, of exertions, of Padres, of Irmãos, and of a thousand outpourings of bloody sweat. Now here are stouthearted men for you!—everything to unmake the Society and make their own *cumis*, without going among pagans for the making of new Christianity. God help us!—for there is much

schism in Japan for this reason. If each possessed his own body of Christianity, then all might be governed in peace; but many masters in one house mean total discord. And not only do they usurp our Christianity, on top of that they malign us.

The *Visitator*'s fears had not been misplaced.

On 25 July 1579 Valignano had arrived in a Japan where Catholic missions were in the hands of Cabral, the stiff director of a perilously unsteady body of charges. Valignano left on 20 February 1582. Japan's missions were now a Jesuit Vice-Province, and Padre Gaspar Coelho, it was hoped, would be a more pliant guardian of a field which boasted institutions Cabral had not thought possible. The 150,000 Japanese Christians[81] could well look forward to great things from members of their own nation who were preparing to become missionaries on an equal basis, at last, with the Europeans. There was a Jesuit college in Funai, a novitiate in Usuki, seminaries in Arima and Azuchi. There were in existence ten Jesuit residences and some two hundred churches. According to the *annua* of 15 February, thirty European priests were engaged in the care of souls, assisted by forty-five Irmãos and novices; almost twenty of the latter number were Japanese.[82] *Dōjuku* and other servitors brought the total of missionary personnel up to almost five hundred. Planned were the University of Kyoto, a language institute for Ōmura, a seminary for adolescents in Bungo, and large residences in Sakai, Gifu, Hakata, and Kagoshima. Christianity seemed to bask in the approbation—and even protection—of the powerful Oda Nobunaga. Would the institution flourish?

On 9 March 1582 Valignano stepped off his ship in Macao to hear the news of the personal union of the crowns of Portugal and Spain. The eventual consequences of this union for the Church of Japan may be considered epiphenomenal: the storm would have broken over it anyway. The intelligence of distant European affairs was, in Japan, material only for political pretexts. But the pretexts would be calamitous. Valignano sensed the impending crisis:[83]

Until now many of the lords of Japan have been very suspicious of us, that we are engaged in machinations of evil in Japan, and that if they permitted their kingdoms to become Christian, then we might later rebel with them for the king who maintains us in Japan; and they have been unable to persuade themselves that the kings [of Europe] go to such great expenditure unless it be with the intent to turn it to profit later by the seizure of land. Many lords have many times stated this quite clearly, for this is one of the things in which the bonzes propagandize against us. Now that they know about the union of the kingdoms of Castile and of Portugal, should there move into Japan other religious orders which are strange to them, then this suspicion would be greatly augmented among them and might move them to contrive some foul game against us and against the Christians.

It was a remarkably accurate prophecy.

In the gloom of the pre-dawn hours of the twenty-first day of June 1582, Akechi Mitsuhide, a general who had received Oda Nobunaga's orders to set out with his troops on an expedition to Western Japan, instead took his more than ten thousand men by stealth to surround the Honnōji Temple in Kyoto, where his lord Nobunaga was staying. It was an attack which achieved marvellous surprise.

Nobunaga had only some seventy attendants with him. His armed retinue of two thousand had been left with his son Nobutada at the Myōkakuji Temple. His purpose in coming to the Honnōji was not that of the warrior but rather that of the connoisseur of the major *elegantiae* of the age, the tea ceremony and the various *objets d'art* appurtenant to it. He had invited famous teamen and court nobles to attend at a sumptuous display of his precious utensils—a list of the most valuable thirty-eight exists to the present, dated the day prior to the disaster. Nobunaga's tea party proved a very expensive diversion. He entertained his guests late into the night with talk of his dreams of the past and designs for the future, until the irruption of Akechi's soldiers ended the pleasantries. All accounts agree that Nobunaga put on a magnificent show of personal bravery, shooting off arrows and then spearing his enemies as the burning temple fell in and crashed down upon him. But there was no hope of escape. He died at the age of forty-eight, a young man still. Ambitious plans were before him, but he did not live to see their completion. His tea utensils perished with him.[84]

The Jesuits, whose Temple of Southern Barbarians was only a city block away from the Honnōji, describe his end picturesquely and with a sense of drama. Frois' tone is the proper one for the downfall of the great but unworthy, half-mournful and half-satisfied: "For sake of the fire being so great it is unknown in what manner he died: what we know is that of him who made all tremble not only at his voice but at his mere name there remained not a strand of hair, nor bone, nor anything but be turned to dust and ashes; wherefor there be of him on earth no vestige."[85]

And further, in the tones of a universal moral:[86]

In such a miserable and wretched manner did he come to his end who imagined that there was no one, on earth nor even in Heaven, that would predominate over him; withal it cannot be denied that Nobunaga was a distinguished man, and of very rare talents, illustrious and famous Captain, and one who governed the Tenca with great prudence. Aquechi, who also pretended to pride and vainglory of no lesser degree, forgetful of his proper principles, fell prey to a hapless and wretched fate. And although in the eyes of men they appeared as exalted as the cedars of Lebanon, after the briefest passage of time there could be found no trace of their potency, but rather they were, in one instant, descended into Hell. And although the portrait of life's brevity and of the sheer velocity of its course is such, and so frequent, in Japan as to cause in men a strange wonderment and astonishment, nevertheless the continuous use of these variations and transmutations relaxes their powers of reflection, so that with fleeting forgetfulness they pass over all these images of death.

The Honnōji Affair was the end of Nobunaga and also of the chance of an Oda domination over Japan; but it did not end the train of events which Nobunaga's activity had set into motion. The task at hand was the restructuring of the polity. It has been argued that without Nobunaga's part in the clean sweep of the shards of mediaeval institutions the apparent chaos and disarray prevalent since the Ōnin War would have continued. If that is a valid estimate, then indeed Japan owes much to Nobunaga, and he even assumes the proportions of a historical necessity. Certainly, the outline of the organizational pattern which his successors completed was clearly present on a supralocal level in Nobunaga's day. What that meant for the Jesuits they did not at the time perceive. But to that pattern no accommodation was possible. The successors would rank the Christian presence with the relics of the disturbed mediaeval era. Frois had dubbed Nobunaga "Rey Assuero"[87]—and Ahasver was followed by kings even more wicked and scourges ever more dreadful.

In the aftermath of the Honnōji Affair that same Hashiba Chikuzen who had been witness to the Takayama-Organtino intrigue inherited Oda's place as the dominant power in Japan. So grandiose was the sweep of his ambitions that certain of his grave measures, paradoxically enough, were made to appear incidental and even whimsical. Political pretexts were, in his hands, to lead to bloody persecution of the Catholic Church in Japan. The instrument of fate in this tragedy (some dramatists say) was the pilot of a Spanish ship, who averred that His Catholic Majesty's mode of military conquest made use of a missionary fifth column.[88] Valignano was proved correct. Franciscans figured prominently in the mystery play.

Chapter 4

The Donation of Bartolomeu:

A Jesuit Colony in Nagasaki

THE WRITER of history is a tragedian in a theatre of the absurd. Airy speculation is not the most tantalizing aspect of his study. Nothing frustrates more than the sight of dynamic hopes moving toward an inevitably disastrous end. The historian can see what the actors of the historical drama could at best suspect. History's basis is hindsight; but hindsight is also history's absurdity.

The Christian play of politics in Early Modern Japan is an excellent example of such a foredoomed venture. The structure of Christianity in Japan was demolished before it had survived a hundred years. Christianity's heroes had labored to fill holes in a foundation which never was very solid; and such men as Cabral are to be condemned only for the neglect which made the process of dissolution under pressure faster and easier. Hideyoshi and the Tokugawa persecuted Christianity because it was an external force and one engaged in political intrigue. Neither indictment could be left unprosecuted, and both were perfectly true. Christianity played a political game because political patronage was the basis of its very existence in Japan. Its success was linked firmly to the success of Portuguese trade efforts because the China Ship—the *nao*—was the vehicle of its financial support. It is difficult to see what other means could have kept the Church afloat in Japan, for it had not had enough time to grow into a Japanese institution.

Experience had seemed to indicate that working from the top down, through the lord to the people, was the only way to establish a relatively secure position for the Church. Bungo is an illustrative case. By 1557 the Jesuits had founded there a hospital with two divisions, one of which was for lepers.[1] The intention was most charitable, and the medical success quite gratifying; but the results of charity were not what the Padres had hoped. The hospital was popular among the very poor; but persons of quality were reluctant to associate with missionaries who left themselves open to contamination with the most dreadful afflictions. There were few significant baptisms. The situation only changed markedly when the second son of Ōtomo Sōrin was baptized at Christmas 1575. The attraction of a member of the land's ruling house into the Church meant also the attraction of many other young samurai. Christianity had before been *outré*; the new Dom Sebastião made it fashionable. What did it profit, then, to dream about the works of apostolic charity and the poverty of the Primitive Church if acknowledgment by the daimyo was the only truly meaningful acknowledgment? Well might the Padres sigh that the Lord God did not assist with miracles. In reality, there were no better missionaries than the feudal lords. The daimyo's requirement was excellent persuasion for even the most hesitant candidates for Christianity.

To build upon the favor of the feudal lord was, however, a mission method which all too often turned out to have that lord's material interests for its foundation. Again and again this fact was made clear; but it was a fact that had to be lived with. The Portuguese China Ship acted as a magnet to a whole catalogue of Kyushu daimyo. The missionaries made use of its powers of attraction.

Their reports comment upon the expediency quite matter-of-factly. Frois, for instance, wrote under the date 1563: "It was a sign of the grace of Divine Providence that the traffic and trade between the Japanese and the Chinese in their junks and *somas* had stopped. Instead, only the one yearly China Ship came with the Portuguese and their wares; and because of this very favorable opportunities arose for our purpose, which is the conversion of souls."[2] It was the obvious observation. The Ming government had placed severe restrictions upon Chinese voyages abroad. That did nothing to diminish the Japanese desire for Chinese silk, which only the Portuguese now brought in quantity. The lords of Kyushu, the natural terminus of the mainland trade, were eager to obtain for their domains the commerce and the resultant increase of their own economic and military power. They were convinced that the Portuguese Catholic Padres could dictate to the Portuguese Catholic traders what harbors to go to, and were willing to support Catholic missionary activity as their part of the bargain. The Jesuits, in turn, took advantage of the opportunity. The principle was set down in black and white in Valignano's *Regimen for the Superior of the parts of Shimo* of 1582: "When the [Vice-Provincial] is absent, the area Superior may write to the Portuguese ships and tell them his opinion (*avisando*) at which harbors they should call. Consideration must be given to the benefit of the traders, to the service of God, and to the advancement of Japanese Christianity, but none to personal predilection."[3]

The case which best illustrates the interaction of religion, politics, and finance in the Japanese mission is Ōmura. "Great were the gates which Our Lord opened up in those days for the conversion of Japan."[4] The utterances of the missionaries fascinatingly describe the manner of the gates' opening. The account of Frois, for instance, is nothing if not explicit:[5]

Padre Cosme de Torres took it much to heart to see how time passed without there appearing on the horizon a mission to which he could devote the rest of his life. Driven by this holy zeal, he sent the Irmão Luiz de Almeida . . . to see whether there might not be some means to make one of the lords of the Shimo into a Christian, by stirring his hopes that the China Ship . . . would come to his harbors, were he to have suitable such. For in these things Irmão Luiz de Almeida had extraordinary skill and talent. [Almeida, it might be interjected, was a man of many talents: preacher, physician, and before his entry into the Society in 1556 a merchant of great repute in the Indies. The four or five thousand cruzados which he brought with him constituted the capital with which the Jesuits founded their share of the Japan trade.[6]] Already in the year 61, when the ship of Fernão de Souza came to Hirado . . . Almeida had secretly gone there, and had agreed with the pilot of the ship, Domingos Ribeiro by name, and with a Christian from the city of Miyako named Konoye Bartholomeo . . . that they should in deepest secrecy . . . look over and make soundings of a harbor belonging to Ōmuradono, Yokoseura by name. If they were to find it satisfactory for the ship to put in there, then Bartholomeo, being a Japanese and from Miyako, should begin with his inducements to Ōmuradono, that he should turn Christian and permit the preaching of the Law of God in his land; for great spiritual and material profits would accrue to him therefrom.

The secret soundings of Yokoseura revealed that the harbor was deep enough. There now began discreet soundings of Ōmura Sumitada's willingness. The response they obtained was not unfavorable. Padre Cosme de Torres was notified and, to ascertain himself of the compact, he sent yet another Japanese convert to Sumitada. To hear Frois tell it, Ōmura promised high dividends: "to build churches and grant stipends, and the harbor of Yokoseura itself he would give to the Church, so that a large Christian community might arise there, in the houses whereof the Portuguese traders would find sure shelter for themselves and their merchandise; and if the Portuguese would only come to said harbor he would for ten years' duration free them of all taxes; and he made many other offers."

On 12 July 1562 Almeida with the *dōjuku* Damião arrived in Yokoseura to conduct final negotiations. And we now take up the text of Valignano himself:[7]

> Upon arriving in . . . Yocoxeura, they discovered that a ship of the Portuguese had entered there, not wanting to put into Firando [Hirado] because of the admonition (*aviso*) it had from the Padres. At this they rejoiced in the extreme. And immediately on the next day they went to visit Omurandono . . .by whom they were well received, finding him very happy at the entry of this ship into his harbor.
>
> And getting down to the business for which they had come, in conformance with the draft which the said lord had written for the Padre, in a short few days they concluded this agreement: that Omurandono gave that harbor to the Padres with all the lands and laborers that were within a certain distance of its surroundings, in such a manner that half remained for the said lord and half for the Padres; that they should build their church there, and all who remained in that port to be made Christians; and finally that the Padres could make Christian all those who wished to be converted in his territories.

Hence were the Jesuits nonplussed to see that no sooner had the Irmão and his companion departed newly won Yokoseura, a Portuguese carrack and its companion junk entered antagonist Hirado, "a thing of such evil turn for the honor of God and the good of Christianity," as Valignano sourly comments. The Matsuura daimyo of Hirado was chronically anti-Christian, and given to violent provocations even of the Portuguese merchants.[8] The Jesuits had no compunction about machinating against him. This time all was managed to the Padres' satisfaction. The *nao* was brought round to Yokoseura. It was viable encouragement for Ōmura Sumitada.

Sumitada was baptized in the middle of June 1563, taking the name Bartolomeu. The fruits of conversion were soon forthcoming. For the party of the first part: on Assumption Day 1563, there were to be found at anchor in Yokoseura the Great Ship of Dom Pero da Guerra, the galleon of Francisco Castão, and the large Siam junk of Gonçalo Vaz de Carvalho.[9] For the party of the second, there was the symbolic action described by Frois:[10]

As Dom Bartholomeo had gone off to the wars, it so happened that he passed on the way an idol, Marishi-ten ... by name, which is their god of battles. When they pass it, they bow and pay reverence to it; and the pagans who are on horseback dismount in sign of their respect. Now the idol had over it a cockerel. As the *tono* came there with his squadron he had his men stop and he ordered them to take the idol and burn it together with the whole temple; and he took the cockerel and gave it a blow with the sword, saying thereto, "O how many times have you betrayed me!" And after everything had been burnt down, he had a very beautiful cross erected on the same spot, and after he and his men had paid very deep reverence to it, they continued on their way to the wars.

What prompted this turn of the soul? Perhaps a brief discussion of the history of the House of Ōmura will provide the answer.

The roots of the Ōmura family in the Sonogi region of Kyushu are traceable back to the end of the tenth century.[11] By the Kamakura period the house was well established in the area, and was absorbed into the ranks of the shogunate's housemen (*gokenin*). What transformations it underwent during the breakup of central authority in the succeeding centuries is unclear, and a focus on the Ōmura is not obtained until the late fifteenth century, when the main line of the family attempted to establish itself as *sengoku daimyō*. The emergence was accompanied by long and weary labor pains, and at first the result seemed paltry.

The visitor to the area will observe that the topography is not of the type which would further domanial consolidation: Ōmura Bay practically splits Sonogi into two; and the landscape of coves and inlets, islands, and mountains seems designed for the proliferation of diverse petty interests. Indeed, in the Middle Ages local landholders did proliferate here. The West Sonogi Peninsula was the scene of the rise of families bearing such names as Kozasa, Fukuda, and Nagasaki. And the eastern portion of Sonogi, which fronted upon the spheres of activity of a series of powerful daimyo, was destined to become the very cockpit of Sengoku contention.

The sixteenth Lord of the House, Sumiyoshi, in 1474 fled all the way to an island in the Tsushima Straits after being defeated by the Arima. He returned in 1480 and was able to re-establish and even extend his authority.[12] The consolidation, however, proceeded in the pattern of the enfeoffment of branch families, who turned out to be the ones that flourished. When Sumitada succeeded as the eighteenth lord, the direct holdings of the daimyo himself encompassed but a few villages.

Sumitada's accession itself created problems. He was the second son of Arima Haruzumi and was adopted by Ōmura Sumisaki, whose own son—the bastard Takaaki—was thereby displaced, being adopted in turn into the locally prominent house of Gotō. Hence arose endless vexations: the family was split, and the attempt to establish the daimyo's direct authority rendered exceedingly difficult. In his dealings with the foreigners Sumitada therefore consistently operated from a weak position. He was contained on unsolid ground; one of his very few assets was the maritime location of his territory; his need for an external line of support coincided with the foreigners' need for an internal base; and he played partners. The reason why Sumitada was so anxious to assure himself of the presence of the Portuguese was his hope that the encouragement of foreign trade would gain for him the means for the assertion of his authority as daimyo; in fact, it would not be farfetched to say that this was for him the only possible insurance. To make doubly certain he himself turned Christian.

The eventual monopoly of the Portuguese trade was not an unmixed blessing, for it invited more trouble with the neighboring daimyo, who were as eager for the profits as was Sumitada. Each incursion by the Matsuura, Saigō, Gotō, Arima—and especially the very powerful Ryūzōji—further exacerbated the internal tensions of the loose Ōmura vassalage structure; in West Sonogi there was continuous party-taking with the Ryūzōji. Sumitada's losses, as will shortly be seen, drove him to ever more extraordinary measures.

The house could not continue to survive on its own resources, and the Southern Barbarians could at best tide it over a gap. In the final analysis, it was Hideyoshi's 1587 invasion of Kyushu that saved it. Hideyoshi confirmed the house as the holder of a unified fief; the Ōmura daimyo was protected under the umbrella of the Taikō's national policy. At the same time, his former props, the Bateren, were uprooted; but he no longer needed them (later, when the time came, the Ōmura daimyo turned into a persecutor of Christianity just as he had been a destroyer of Buddhist idols before). Hideyoshi's final blessing upon the Ōmura was his Korean venture: the disparate forces of the entire fief had to be mobilized for the Taikō, and that guaranteed direct military allegiance. After his return from the wars, Fukuda Kanechika moved into the Ōmura castle town; the Kozasa and a whole series of other families in West Sonogi were dispossessed.[13] The puny *sengoku daimyō* was recast into a lord of the Early Modern mold: local military landholding was eliminated, the *bushi* class separated from the peasantry, and in 1599 a cadastral survey was for the first time conducted throughout the fief.

The House of Ōmura was a late developer; but one must give it credit. The weakling survived when a large number of its stronger fellows went under. The Ōmura *han* would last out the Tokugawa era. Of course none of this later fortune could be predicted in Yokoseura in 1563. When the Jesuits embraced Sumitada they were taking a very risky gamble indeed.

Yokoseura may with little exaggeration be termed the very first explicitly ceded Treaty Port in East Asia; but it did not long flourish. Frois notes ominously: "This rich flow in the work of conversion bothered the Enemy, and he feared what he had to expect for the future. And therefore he secretly stirred in the hearts of some close relatives of Dom Bartholomeo a dangerous conspiracy against him and the Padres."[14] In this rebellion of 1563 Yokoseura was turned into a heap of ashes, Frois and Torres wound up hostages held by Japanese merchants against delivery of goods on Portuguese ships, and the newly converted Dom Bartolomeu seemed at the end of his fortunes. It took some three years for him to recover, and for the Padres to return to Ōmura. In 1566, when he had lost Sonogi Castle ("without which there remained for him almost no human hope"), he was able to recover and hold the place when the Portuguese supplied him with weapons.[15]

The encouragement continued, at rates of *quid pro quo*. In 1574, four Portuguese ships came to the Ōmura domain to help Dom Bartolomeu against the forces of Saigō Sumitaka of

Isahaya.[16] This contribution to success in war and the blandishments of Padre Gaspar Coelho now combined to move Dom Bartolomeu to the forced Christianization of all his subjects. Pagans were directed to accept baptism or leave the land. Buddhist temples were either turned into churches or destroyed; their priests were swayed to turn Christian by promises to leave them their stipends.[17] On 13 September 1575 Cabral reported twenty thousand new Christians in the Ōmura territory; in this number were included the former bonzes of fifty or sixty monasteries.[18] And Frois was to write piously: "And so it came to pass through the boundless goodness of God, out of whose mercy all good flows, that after the destruction of the pagodas and temples all of [Ōmura's] vassals, numbering sixty thousand souls, became Christians, and in this present year of 1585 . . . there were in all his lands 87 churches, where Mass was read and Our Lord God glorified."[19]

The conversion of his entire populace to Christianity was, however, not the greatest effort of Dom Bartolomeu Ōmura for the cause of Jesus or of the Jesuits in Japan. The "Donation of Bartolomeu"—the cession to the Society of Nagasaki and Mogi in 1580—seems an example of unsurpassed zeal. The arrangement was one of mutual advantage.

Sumitada's actions must be considered within the context of the ferocious struggle for paramountcy in Kyushu waged by three major powers: Ōtomo Sōrin, Ryūzōji Takanobu, and the Shimazu (Takahisa and Yoshihisa).[20] Ōmura was a minor pawn in this panorama of contention; thus was his existence all the more threatened, and his measure of security dependent upon near-backbreaking contortionist feats. Hence resulted his lobbying with the Jesuits, whose influence with the Portuguese traders provided him with indispensable external sustenance. Dom Bartolomeu survived by virtue of being the Jesuits' client.

Ōmura's harbor of Yokoseura was destroyed in 1563, the year of his conversion, by the rebellion of Gotō Takaaki. But beginning with the year 1565 (with the sole exception of 1567) Portuguese ships consistently called at other harbors of the Ōmura domain, initially at Fukuda. From 1571 onward, the recognized terminal point of the Great Ship from Macao was the magnificent harbor of Nagasaki.[21] The cession of Nagasaki was a formalization of that same spirit which earlier had created the arrangement in favor of traders and missionaries at the ill-fated Yokoseura.

The name of Nagasaki first enters the forefront of attention in 1569. This was a year in which the Sengoku pattern of march and countermarch extensively crisscrossed the north of Kyushu. Ōtomo Sōrin campaigned against Ryūzōji, who appeared to capitulate but secretly saw fit to ask for assistance from the powerful Mōri daimyo of Yamaguchi across the straits. The response of Mōri Motonari was to dispatch seventy thousand men under Kikkawa Motoharu and Kobayakawa Takakage to confront Sōrin in Kyushu; but Sōrin used Ōuchi Teruhiro, a scion of the dispossessed masters of Yamaguchi, to threaten the dangerously denuded Mōri stronghold. The Mōri army had to be withdrawn from Kyushu; and the assorted feudatories of Kyushu, who had in large part favored Mōri, now faced the prospect of Sōrin's vengeance. It was the intervention of Cosme de Torres and Luis de Almeida with their protector, the "good King of Bungo," which on this occasion saved the *Kirishitan daimyō* Dom Bartolomeu Ōmura.[22] Torres had initiated the pourparlers in the town of Ōmura, but the terrified Sumitada insisted that the Padre's safety would better be served in Nagasaki, and Torres took the advice.

Nagasaki in 1569 was an unprepossessing village (*logar inculto*) of some 1500 souls, all baptized in the course of the year.[23] In 1570, Padre Belchior de Figueiredo, with a Portuguese pilot, made soundings of the coast there; the harbor of Fukuda had been found unsuitable, and the missionaries wanted to fix upon a safe port for the *nao* while yet remaining within the Ōmura domain.[24] Here the Jesuits settled many Japanese Christians who had been expelled from various hostile territories and had since wandered to whatever spot the *nao* chose for an anchorage each year: Nagasaki was to become a permanent place of refuge. But the natural advantages of the spot did not include full security. Nagasaki was menaced by Gotō Takaaki, Saigō Sumitaka of Isahaya, and Fukahori Sumikata, all individuals with intimate family connections to the house of Ōmura, and all intent upon foiling Dom Bartolomeu's alliance with the foreigners —all therefore turned henchmen of Ryūzōji. At one point, when the Ōmura vassal Nagasaki Jinzaemon Sumikage (Dom Bernardo) already considered the struggle lost and advised the Portuguese to take to the woods, the Christians, urged on by Padre Gaspar

Coelho, proceeded to fortify the spit of land containing the Jesuit residence with a wood palisade and a ditch. "Thus the place which today is Nagasaki became a fortress."[25]

In the late seventies Ryūzōji made gestures to invade the Ōmura domain from the north; and Fukahori in 1578 and 1579 repeatedly attacked Nagasaki. In the end the attacks failed. But the Great Ship of Leonel de Brito, on account of the threat to its security, in 1579 went to Kuchinotsu in the Arima domain. The interruption of the steady traffic to his harbor must have been a severe shock to Dom Bartolomeu. And the pressure mounted again from Ryūzōji. In 1580 Ōmura with a whole train of relatives and servitors went to Saga to swear fealty to Takanobu.[26] The Jesuits feared a Sinigaglia, but Ryūzōji saved a demonstration of his Borgian traits for another unfortunate. Ōmura returned safely, in an escape which Coelho viewed as miraculous. Some time later Kamachi Shigenami of Yanagawa, invited by Ryūzōji on a similar errand and at the same time as Sumitada, was killed with his entire family for being so trusting.[27]

The desperate nature of the situation in which Ōmura found himself in 1579 and 1580 will explain the appearance of urgency with which he tried to assure himself of the advent of the *nao* of 1580 to Nagasaki and of a secure position with the Jesuits. Hence the "Donation of Bartolomeu."[28]

The Japanese text of the document is unfortunately not extant. The measure of Ōmura's largesse must therefore be reconstructed from a Spanish version (preserved in the Jesuit archives in Rome, the text apparently somewhat condensed), and from Valignano's explanations of the donation's purport. A translation of the Spanish text follows.[29]

> This is the substance of the donation which Don Bartholomeu, Lord of Omura, made of the two places Mongui and Nagasaqui.
>
> Don Bartholomeu, lord of Omura, and his son Sancho. With respect for the many things which we owe to the Padres of the Society, I make the free donation for always to the said Society and to its P[e] Visitador of the settlement of Nangasaqui, with all the terrains and arable lands which are within its confines, without any exception; and thus I hand over from now on the possession thereof. And thus the said Padres of the Society may put as captain over the said place whomsoever they please, and remove him from his charge: and to whomever they should select I give the faculty, that he may kill and

exercise all the justice necessary for the good government of the land and for the chastisement of those that should break the laws thereof.

I also give up and hand over for always that which the ship of the Portuguese is wont to pay for the time that it spends in the said port, reserving for myself the tariff dues of this and all other ships that may arrive at the said port, which I shall have collected by my officials; who shall not intrude into any matter touching upon the [exercise of] justice or upon the government of the said place.

And in the same manner I hand over for always to the Padres the localities of Mongui, with all the terrains and arable lands which appertain thereto. And in pledge that there never shall be any change in the said donation, but that it shall be valid in perpetuity, I have made this charter, signed by me and by my son Sancho, on the twenty-seventh of the 4th moon of the eighth year of Tenxo [9 June 1580].

Don Bartholomeu
Don Sancho.   /

Donation of Don Bartholomeu, lord of Omura.
By the 1st route.
For the eyes of Our Father [General].
From the Visitador of India.

Ōmura's donation amounted to the surrender of judicial sovereignty in Nagasaki and Mogi: the Society of Jesus was explicitly assured legislative authority. The Jesuits assumed the responsibility "to kill and exercise all the justice necessary." For members of a religious order acceptance of such faculties was, to say the least, irregular. News of the donation was certain to evoke the greatest astonishment in Rome, and Valignano (as Schütte points out[30]) was well aware of that.

What considerations moved Ōmura to cede this invaluable portion of his domain to the Jesuits? What reasons moved the Jesuits to accept? Valignano attempted to provide an exposition in a letter he wrote to the General of the Society on 15 August 1580.[31] He cautioned: "Let not judgment be made according to the ideas held abroad, because such judgment will be in error." According to Valignano, the negotiations were almost a year in duration, and the initiative was Ōmura's: when the *Visitator*, after landing in Japan, called on Ōmura, Dom Bartholomeu "pleaded with great insistence" that the Church take possession of Nagasaki. It was not, for Ōmura, a question of gratitude to the Padres but rather of well-considered self-interest, stated in three reasons. "The first—he said—was because I greatly fear that Ryūzōji (who is a pagan with domain in Hizen) will ask me for this harbor, for he craves it mightily. If I hand it over to him, I will lose the anchorage fees which the Portuguese ships pay me and which I need for my finance. If I refuse, I have reason to fear a terrible war. On the other hand, if I make the cession to the Church, the gain will be mine and Ryūzōji will no longer demand it." The second reason was that the Portuguese were not bound to one specific harbor (as, indeed, had been proved in 1579); but if Nagasaki became Jesuit territory, it was a certainty that the *nao* would not go elsewhere, and Bartolomeu would be assured a steady flow of income. The third reason was life insurance for himself: "for in case of necessity I will have a place of refuge," under the shadow, presumably, of Portuguese guns.

But the Jesuits would also derive substantial advantage. Extended deliberation led the Padres (with the exception of one or two) to the conclusion that acceptance was "useful and necessary."[32] The first reason was that Ryūzōji menaced not merely Ōmura but the entire Church of Kyushu; if he obtained Nagasaki, he gained also the financing to "prosecute with much reinforcement the war against Don Francisco of Bungo." Second, Nagasaki was a potential place of refuge not only for Ōmura's person but also for other Japanese Christians. Third, Nagasaki would offer "a secure place of safeguard" for the persons of the missionaries and for the entire mission endeavor. Fourth was the financial reason. In its ultimate development it meant that Ōmura ceded the anchorage fees (the Portuguese paid between 700 and 1000 ducats for the duration of stay) while retaining tariffs paid by Japanese merchants. The Jesuits were to divide the substantial infusion of funds into three parts: for harbor improvements and fortifications; for gifts to daimyo; for the maintenance of their residences in Ōmura. The fifth and final reason for acceptance was that the city would be an excellent see for the future Bishop of Japan.

Valignano's letter of 15 August 1580 speaks in terms of actual acceptance of authority already accomplished. On the part of Ōmura the donation was unconditional. On the part of Valignano there was one condition: that he would be able to give up possession again at any time. The consideration was of political contingency, and of the fact that Nagasaki's prosperity was posited upon the continued commerce of the *nao*.

Valignano took care to point out: "As far as justice is concerned, which each lord exercises according to the custom of Japan, we have arranged that it be administered by headmen or captains called *Yakunin*; but Don Bartolomé has tempered the rigor of the laws that are to be observed." For the Jesuits this was a crucial question. Acceptance of the two harbors under the conditions stated in Ōmura's conveyance of cession was hardly tenable from the standpoint of canon law. Territorial possession would involve the exercise of the power over life and death, and that of itself was inappropriate. Moreover, Japanese legal practices differed so much from the European that it seemed impossible to meet the Christian standard of justice on their basis. The very existence of a systematized code of laws was not apparent in the Sengoku shambles. The Jesuits would have to create one.

The *Visitator* sought recourse in expedients. Criminals were to be handed over to the secular arm. The Ōmura suzerainty was to be preserved: the Jesuits would appoint a *yakunin* for each of Nagasaki and Mogi, but his authority in office as judicial executor was explicitly derived from Ōmura's residual sovereignty. Schütte puts heavy emphasis upon the legalities of the Jesuits' tenure: in order that the *yakunin* "could exercise their office with justice, the missionaries caused Dom Bartolomeu to promulgate for both harbor areas *a new judicial code oriented to the Christian conception of ius naturale and positivum*—a memorable date in the legal history of Japan."[33] This did not completely eliminate the difficulty. The missionaries distanced themselves from the laws' execution; but they were still involved in their formulation. Valignano, the *Doctor Iuris utriusque*, even stated proudly that the Christian daimyo actively sought the advice of Jesuits on account of their legal erudition. The *Visitator* asked the General to obtain from the Pope a brief which would absolve the Padres of the formal irregularity of the involvement in capital jurisdiction. And a further adjustment of the rules was required: the Pope should extend to the Jesuits the specific authority to engage in civil and criminal jurisdiction in Nagasaki and Mogi.

The General of the Society obtained the requested permission from Gregory XIII and informed Valignano of the disposition in a letter dated 26 November 1583. A formal brief was never obtained: the death of the Pope on 10 April 1585 interfered.[34]

By then the matter was hardly of pressing urgency. In 1584, after crushing Ryūzōji, the Shimazu forces had occupied Nagasaki. And in 1587 the super-power Toyotomi Hideyoshi intruded into the Kyushu arena. The expedition had been solicited by Ōtomo Sōrin. But it set at naught the ambitions of the protégés of that "good King of Bungo" in regard to Nagasaki, which was absorbed into Hideyoshi's immediate domain. It surely is not unreasonable to suspect that those very ambitions contributed to Hideyoshi's decision to ban the Padres from the land.

What Valignano had envisioned for Nagasaki was nothing less than the establishment of a military colony, in which native Christians would assist a hard core of Portuguese. In the *Regimen for the Japan Superior* (24 June 1580, fifteen days after Bartolomeu signed the donation document) he wrote—to cite Schütte's paraphrase—as follows:[35]

For the welfare and preservation of Christianity the fortification of the two harbors taken over by the Church, Nagasaki and Mogi, is of great importance. Both should accordingly be protected with forts and equipped with munitions, weapons, and artillery for defence: not only Nagasaki, the harbor of the *nao*, but also Mogi, which covers the Christian areas of the Shimo, Ōmura and Arima . . . In the first year [the Superior] should spend on the defence installations as much as necessary. Thereafter, 150 ducats out of the anchorage fees of the Portuguese should be applied to this purpose. Both fortresses are to be armed in a manner to withstand any attack. In order to secure Nagasaki even more, as many married Portuguese are to be settled there as will find accommodations in the town. In case of siege these will be taken into the fort and will reinforce it. The Superiors are to take care that the inhabitants increase, and that they are equipped with all necessary weaponry.

By the end of 1581 the Church domain of Nagasaki had been surrounded with a solid clay wall and with bastions.[36] What further work was done is unclear. An extensive *Apologia in which are answered divers calumnies written against the Padres of the Society of Jesus of Japan and of China*, which Valignano wrote in 1598, makes light of the question of the extent of armament:[37]

And because in that port the merchants of Japan gathered to buy the goods of the Portuguese, which during the time they spent there they stored in the houses of the natives, and because they ran much peril with all the continuous wars and the many pirates of that time: therefore did the people of that town determine, with D. Bartolomé's command and the Padres' counsel, to dig some ditches through those parts where the spit joins the land, with some very frail and tiny earthworks (quite ill-constructed), in order to obtain in this manner security from the thieves of the sea and from any soldiers that might stray from the wars and launch some assault upon the town, coveting the goods. And there never was any other fortress in said town, nor a garrison of people other than from that same town, nor other munitions and armaments but two middling falconets with three or four guncradles, which the viceroys had sent for presents to D. Bartolomé, who kept them more for representation than for anything else.

And Valignano further ridicules any possible aspersion of provocation in Jesuit policy:

If D. Bartolomé gave to the Padres what he did give them in the harbor of Nagasaki, reserving for himself the domination and the tariffs on commerce . . . it was done primarily because it appeared good to him and was profitable and no damage could result to him therefrom; for the Padres and the entire town and harbor of Nagasaki remained as obedient and subject to him as ever, and they neither had the power to act contrary to him nor was there any peril that they would do so . . . It was nothing but gratitude to the Padres [that inspired him], and the beginning of compliance in some manner with the obligation he had, in conformance with the teaching of Saint Paul, to support the ministry of the Gospel in his land . . . But if by any chance he had imagined that we might have the intention to deliver that town over to the kings of Spain and that we planned that there should be a fortress there with a garrison of Castilians—would he have been content with that and deemed it good? . . . Or are the Japanese lords peradventure so slight of perception? Or do they hold the preservation of their states to such small account that they do not reflect upon what could befall them if they kept foreign soldiers and designed to build garrisoned fortresses in their lands? Or are they so little warlike that they would allow their land to be taken over by a few Castilian soldiers as was Peru and New Spain?

The Japanese sources which pretend to discuss the historical origins of the Nagasaki cession had different kinds of aspersions to contend with. Valignano, in the contemporary report to the General of the Society as in the retrospective *Apologia*, wants to accentuate the positive: the initiative is Ōmura's here, and Jesuit acceptance was meant to let Christian justice prevail. The chroniclers of Ōmura, in accounts composed more than a century after the event, at a time when the repression of Christianity was a key national policy, desired self-justification. Their *han* had at one time ceded a piece of Japanese land to the pernicious foreigners. It was necessary to purge, as much as possible, the Ōmura reputation of this unsavory nuance of collaboration with the *jashūmon*. They attempt to make light of the question of the surrender of authority.

The historical circumstances related in *Ōmura-ke hiroku* (Confidential records of the house of Ōmura)[38] are identical with those found in the Jesuit accounts—Ōmura is pressed by Ryūzōji and by his own relations (presumably by Gotō, Saigō, and Fukahori). But the intimation is infinitely different: he agrees only *in extremis*, and the initiative is the Jesuits'. And there is not the trace of a surrender of sovereignty, only an arrangement with respect to income.

During the Tenshō period, Lord Sumitada had aggression committed against him by Ryūzōji Takanobu; and even his relations turned against him, so that he was beleaguered by enemies on four sides. Even the intrepid and ingenious Lord Sumitada, faced as he was by a dearth of military resources and by the difficulty of self-dependent success, in order to obtain cannon, muskets, gunpowder, gold and silver, and funds for rice, to construct castle walls, to prepare weaponry, and to facilitate defence against external enemies, for a time took party with this group and assented to the proposals of the Jesus [sectarians]. He borrowed one hundred *kanme* of silver, applying to the repayment the yearly income of the villages of Nagasaki and the neighboring Yamazato, Urakami, and Fuchi.

The account of the *Nagasaki shi* (Nagasaki chronicle)[39] is more directly ominous. Here it is no longer a question of Jesuit initiative but rather that of Jesuitical pressures.

These barbarians were by nature rapacious and burdened with no morality, but possessed rather of wicked contrivance. On the surface they came to trade; but inwardly they cherished the scheme to usurp the lands of other nations. To various people they gave gold, silver, and treasure, thus burdening them with a debt of gratitude. Or, seeing in the foul trickery of magic an instrument wherewith to impress the foolish, they led them on into their pernicious Kirishitan doctrine; for these reasons those converted into that religion were extremely numerous. In the surfeit of the wicked zeal impinged upon them, they destroyed the shrines of the gods and the temples of the Buddhas without sparing even one; and moreover in the area of Nagasaki they built Kirishitan temples. And also they asked that the city [of Nagasaki and adjoining] towns, villages, and hamlets be turned into temple domain; but [Ōmura Sumitada] Risen did not agree. Then they contrived all sorts of difficulties [for him] and exhausted themselves in artifice. And therefore Risen perforce countenanced their plans and gave over this area to those sectarians.

If the Japanese sources contain any measure of accuracy, then the first sentence of Dom Bartolomeu's charter is more than a conventional formula of courtesy. "With respect for the many things which we owe to the Padres" should then be translated "with respect to our great debt" rather than interpreted according to the words of Valignano's *Apologia*: "in recognition of the great benefit which he had received from God through the mediation of the Padres, in the illumination of the Faith as in the profit which his lands had from the *nao*."[40] But it is difficult to believe that Valignano in official—and confidential—correspondence with the General of the Society would have wilfully suppressed information. The *Visitator*'s function was accurate inspection and report. His various missives demonstrate that he can scarcely be termed reticent in discussing controversial aspects of his decisions. Hence it would appear that financial dealings with Ōmura did not form the direct causal antecedent of the donation.[41]

In all likelihood it was not any single factor but rather the total accumulation of involvement with the Jesuits that finally resulted in Ōmura's cession of Nagasaki. The pressure of financial indebtedness was perhaps a part of his decision, but not the precise immediate cause which the Japanese sources would have it be. The question of initiative is not easily settled. It may have appeared to be Ōmura's (even to Ōmura himself), but the initial suggestion may well have been the Jesuits', and the responsibility certainly was equally shared. In the final analysis the arrangement proved damaging to the Jesuits. Whatever the causes and the development of their tenure may have been, the effect was to create the impression of a threat-in-being on the soil of Japan. Hideyoshi settled the matter.

In order to appreciate fully the Jesuits' position, we must recognize that their traditional manipulation of the *nao* was to them a very necessary activity. Their absorption of sovereignty over Nagasaki may be explained as the manifestation of a desire to have a formal voice in the regulation of Portuguese commerce with Japan. How important that was to the Society is obvious from a raw statistic. Valignano in the *Sumario* of 1583 estimated[42] that the Jesuit Order's minimum financial requirement in Japan was "ten or twelve thousand cruzados each year." Five to six thousand of this sum were yearly realized in profits from the *nao*, "in which ordinarily venture for the Padres ten or twelve thousand ducats of capital employed in silk." It was quite literally a floating investment.

By 1582 the Jesuits were supporting in Japan some five hundred mission personnel and their residences. The institutional improvements caused by Valignano had been very costly. The lean and hungry style of Cabral may have been satisfied with the ordinary five or six thousand of annual gain from the *nao*; but the seminaries, the novitiate, and the college founded by Valignano had doubled the cost, "so that in the somewhat less than three years which I spent there . . . the expenses amounted to more than thirty-two thousand ducats." In the future new construction of churches and residences would be required. But few materials were furnished by Christian lords: many of them needed financial assistance themselves. Rich presents were necessary in order to obtain and maintain the favor of leading Japanese figures. Travel expenses for missionaries took substantial sums; so did charity work. Valignano reflected on the problem:

> Actually I am confounded and astonished whenever I consider how great the expenses are, and I cannot persuade myself otherwise than that it was God who augmented our funds in this expenditure, doing the same as He did with the five loaves of bread and the two fishes; for in order to sustain all this machinery we have to this day nothing but the trade of the China Ship.

Japan itself could not supply the money. The Faith was still new. The people was poor. The mission method of operating from the top down did not eliminate the serious weakness: even the most prosperous supporters of the Church were not prosperous enough to support it. Bungo was big. But its *yakata* was not rich. The system of feudal distribution of income in sixteenth-century Japan, according to Valignano, kept the greatest of daimyo in permanent need of money, and his subordinate samurai in genteel penury.[43]

For that matter, up to the date of Valignano's writing few of the more significant Japanese personages had become Christian. Arima, Ōmura, and Amakusa might even be listed as (financial) liabilities, being as they were "in continuous wars pressed now by Ryūzōji and now by other lords." The solitary Christian *yakata*, Ōtomo Sōrin of Bungo, lived in retirement and with diminished estate; besides, the Ōtomo power had sunk deep indeed from the zenith it had reached before Mimigawa. The Christian "King of Tosa," Ichijō Kanesada (Dom Paulo),[44] deprived of his domain, led an ephemeral existence on a small island by the sufferance of the usurper Chōsogabe Motochika; he sought assistance—spiritual, for he was beyond temporal aid, and Valignano states that the Padres had abandoned all hope of him—from the Jesuits. In the Kansai were stalwarts such as Takayama Ukon; but in general the "many caballeros and fidalgos" of those parts could not be regarded as dependable sources of contributions. In sum, the financial straits of Christianity in Japan could not be ameliorated until "entire kingdoms be made Christian, and the great lords of Miyako and their parts." Christianity was new in Japan; hence any analogy with Buddhist institutions was ill-applied. The prosperity of Buddhist temples was founded in a past which was dim indeed to the *Visitator*— "when Japan was in flower, very prosperous, with one king only," who granted to the bonzes rich incomes and built for them monasteries, universities, and other great edifices. Of course, the bonzes were natives. "And we are strangers and unknown to them and it is no small grace of Our Lord that they receive us in their lands." That the Jesuits were suffered at all Valignano regarded with charming frankness as something supernatural.

Valignano had concerned himself with securing the financial position of the Jesuits in Japan even before he himself had reached the country: during his stay in Macao in 1578 he concluded with the trust of Macao merchants the agreement which gave the Jesuits a fixed share in the silk shipped to Japan.[45] From Nagasaki in December 1579 he sent very precise financial information to the General of the Society.[46] At the conclusion of his stay in Japan his concern had not waned.

An entire chapter of the *Sumario* is devoted to the discussion "Of the great danger in which Japan is placed unless income is provided and of the fruit which is lost for lack of it."[47] The disquisition is written in the most urgent tones. At the outset the *Visitator* confesses that he lives "in perpetual anxiety and much anguish" on account of the financial uncertainties of the Japanese enterprise. As stated so often before, there was no remedy but the trade in silk.

Successive Generals of the Society had looked with disfavor upon that trade.[48] Francisco de Borja had in 1567 written to the Provincial of India to express his discontent with it. Eberhard Merkurian had flatly prohibited it. Claudio Aquaviva, acting on Valignano's appeal, on 10 February 1582 finally gave a temporary dispensation for it, guided by the dictum of Pope Gregory XIII, "istud non est mercatura, sed opus charitatis"; the dispensation was confirmed on 25 November 1583. Valignano himself readily admitted that it was "very inconvenient for our profession" to engage in it—although he added immediately that "necessity and charity have made it licit." All the Padres who discussed the matter in the Japan Consultation expressed their disgust with it.[49]

Valignano was dispassionate in the analysis of its short-comings. Not only was it unseemly; it was insufficient. The costs of the mission were greater than the profit derived from it. And the investment could not be increased: the China Ship carried 500,000 ducats' worth for the merchants of Macao, who would not consent to the diminution of the space available to them. Finally, there was no overlooking the un-certainties and perils of the trade. "The seas from China to Japan are most tempestuous, and in these eight years two ships have already been lost with all their capital." The *Visitator* might well have added that one of the ships he had in mind (the *nao* of 1573) had carried with it to the bottom of the Amakusa Sea his predecessor in office, Gonçalo Alvarez, and four confrères.[50]

Adding to the problem was the fact that "many times there is a dearth of silk, so that it is impossible to send the entire amount that is sent customarily, and therefore the gain is diminished." For two consecutive years during Valignano's stay this situation had come about. The planned profit did not materialize, and the Jesuits had to dip into their reserve capital. The effect may be summarized in the following table, con-tracted from the account of the *Sumario*:

Total capital at Valignano's arrival	30,000 ducats
— loss of planned profit during stay	6,000
— extraordinary expenses for new construction	4,000
Remainder of capital at Valignano's departure	20,000
— usual investment in the China Ship	12,000
Balance (reserve)	8,000 ducats

If the *nao* were lost at sea, the reserve would have to be utilized for running expenses. Balance at the end of the year: zero. Further investment in the China Ship: impossible. Collapse.

The *Visitator* did not envision any possibility of the sort of temporary relief which might tide the Padres over a crisis. "To hope for it from the Viceroy of India—thanks a lot! He has nothing to give. And moreover, the round trip between Japan and India takes three years, during which time the Padres would already be dead of pure starvation, without having any means of sustenance in their houses. And that follows all the more if one were forced to go look for remedy in Portugal."[51]

Acute anxiety affected Valignano's activities, and for a time threatened to paralyze his ability to make decisions. In February 1582 the *nao* was about to leave Nagasaki. Only "after a thousand consultations and still in perplexity until the day of embarkation"—Valignano states—"did I finally decide to return to India; for it appeared to me that it would be tempting God to wait another year in Japan." What he feared very nearly happened. The larger of the two ships of 1582 was lost, and with it sank eight thousand ducats of capital and some four thousand of expected profit. There remained four thousand ducats invested in the other ship; but whether that had arrived safely in Japan Valignano still did not know at the time of his departure from Macao. In the emergency he was able to raise six thousand in contributions in Macao; and from Malacca, his next stop, he was able to send another three thousand ducats.[52] But if yet another ship were lost!

Valignano directed the desperate cry for help to all of Europe: His Holiness the Pope, His Majesty of Spain and Portugal, the cardinals, and all the other Christian princes.[53] If the Pope could dispense his liberality upon a single seminary or college in Rome to the extent of ten thousand ducats a year, he could certainly

do the same and more for Japan, to assist in its total conversion. The *Visitator* promised absolute or near-absolute success
within thirty years. If the Pope were unwilling—closes the chapter
—then certainly the King of Spain would not fail.

PART II

Forms of the Rejection
of Christianity in Japan

Welcher recht hat, weiß ich nicht—
Doch es will mich schier bedünken,
Daß der Rabbi und der Mönch,
Daß sie alle beide stinken.

*

Who is right, I do not know—
But I'm much inclined to think
That the rabbi and the monk,
That the both of them do stink.

Heinrich Heine
Romanzero, III
"Disputation"

Chapter 5

Hideyoshi and the

Sectarians

O̶N THE eighth day of April, 1587, Toyotomi Hideyoshi set out from Osaka on his Kyushu Expedition. This campaign was to result in the attainment of one of Hideyoshi's major strategic objectives, the subjugation of southwestern Japan under his reorganizing will. Hashiba Chikuzen had immeasurably grown in prominence since the Jesuits first encountered him in Oda Nobunaga's entourage.

In 1582 Nobunaga died in the flames of the Honnōji, and Hideyoshi in a swift stroke eliminated the inept incendiary, Akechi Mitsuhide, and his "Three Day Empire." In the following year he vanquished a very dangerous rival, Shibata Katsuie. By 1585, after inconclusive campaigning, he had achieved a rapprochement with the "premier bowsman of the eastern seacoast," Tokugawa Ieyasu. In that same year Hideyoshi defeated the powerful Shingon sectarians of Negoro and ravaged their mountain, and, turning his attention to Shikoku, forced the capitulation of Chōsogabe Motochika. He had obtained the highest of court ranks: in 1585 that of Regent, *kanpaku*; and *daijō daijin*, Grand Chancellor of State, in January 1587.[1] Although some of his most ambitious ventures were still before him, he seemed to his contemporary observers (among whom some of the most hopeful were Jesuits) to have attained unparalleled heights of power and glory.

As the Kyushu Expedition got under way, the Christian missionaries could rejoice in the fact that some of their spiritual charges shared in that glory as the Taikō's intimate cohorts. Their prize quadriga consisted of Konishi Yukinaga (Dom Agostinho), Gamō Ujisato (Dom Leão), Kuroda Josui (Dom Simeão), and—last but to Jesuit eyes not ever least—Dom Justo Takayama Ukon. And there was even more cause for missionary optimism. In the years immediately prior to 1587 the movement to baptism among the worthies of Hideyoshi's entourage appeared to become high fashion. So much *en vogue* had Christianity become in Osaka that the Jesuit letters stop mentioning names of prominent converts and merely say "many"; and Organtino even asserts that some of these courtiers told him, "There is none of the nobility that would not turn Christian."[2] Was it, under the circumstances, so farfetched to view the Kyushu Expedition as departing under the sign of the cross?

"Here in Osaka," states Padre Antonio Prenestino, "I saw the departure of the *kanpaku*, and although there was much to see I nonetheless found the greatest comfort at the [sight of the] Christians, who marched in the most beautiful order among the companies of unbelievers, some with the cross in their armorial bearings and on the helmet, others on the flag, and others again on the tunic." Prenestino was also present in Akashi to witness the departure of Takayama Ukon and his men. He describes the "dramatic sight" with much concentration upon the instructional and symbolic:

Almost all confessed themselves and, insofar as they were worthy, took Holy Communion for a spiritual parting cup . . . On their flags and pennants they wore the sign of the cross, and some also had on their dress the cross and other insignia of the Passion . . . The morning when Ukondono set out all came to the church to pray. And he begged the Padres to come for a moment, see his men, and give them their blessing. That was without a doubt a wonderful sight; but I took a special pleasure in noticing how some of them . . . wore their large and beautiful rosaries about the neck over the armor . . . In such a manner did this celebrated knight of Christ go off to the war.[3]

The ostensible purpose of Hideyoshi's expedition (a point most gratifying to the Padres) was to deliver Ōtomo Sōrin from his enemy, and Arima Harunobu from his incubus, Shimazu Yoshihisa. Kyushu daimyo had made approaches to Hideyoshi as early as 1584. Hideyoshi, for his part, had as early as 1585 (Tenshō 13/10/2) sent Shimazu a command to make peace with Ōtomo. The *kanpaku* brandished his new title as representative of the imperial will; but Yoshihisa rejected as preposterous the very notion of "a house of unblemished lineage since the days of Prince Minamoto no Yoritomo" countenancing the bluster of a parvenu.[4] The Shimazu might well have rested in their false sense of security while Hideyoshi was occupied elsewhere.

But by January 1587, when the Shimazu northward advance reached its crest with the capture of Usuki and Funai, the two principal towns of Bungo, the Taikō's hands were no longer tied; nor could he tolerate the further buildup of this power which now held almost all of Kyushu. His intervention was massive. The Shimazu were humiliated. On 14 June the Taikō from his headquarters at Taiheiji in Satsuma reported to his consort that the previous day Yoshihisa himself had appeared, with head shaven, to plead for his life.[5] That mucn was granted him, and retention of the two provinces Satsuma and Ōsumi as well. The Ōtomo, Arima, and Ōmura were saved, after a fashion. In the distribution of fiefs to recognize meritorious service Christian daimyo fared well. And yet the end result of the Kyushu Expedition was to be far from the Padres' expectations. After having seemingly coddled them while the campaign was in preparation, the Taikō, now the expedition was concluded, turned on them with an edict of expulsion.

Hideyoshi had appeared to Jesuit eyes as munificent with his favors as he was magnificent in his displays of splendor; and they were not sparing of accounts to describe how they shared in his bounty. On April First, 1586, for instance (a singularly appropriate date), the Taikō suddenly appeared at the Jesuit establishment in Osaka and repaid the Padres' improvised hospitality with the following tribute:

"Well do I know that the padres are better than the Bonze of Vozàca; for you maintain a different purity of life, & the filth in which he is so absorbed, & all the other Bonzes, is not your practice . . . I am pleased by everything this law of yours preaches, & I feel no other obstacle to becoming Christian than its prohibition against keeping many wives. If you stretched a point for me there, I would turn Christian myself."[6]

Perhaps the Padres were dazzled by this prospect, although its only base was vain banter; but, master logicians that they were, they should have recognized the danger of the first proposition. A contrast is impossible without an implicit comparison. Kennyo Kōsa, the Bonze of Osaka, had been master over a tightly organized corpus of militant sectarians. The defiance which his temple fortress of Ishiyama Honganji had offered Oda lasted over ten years, to say nothing of the omnipresent provincial risings (*Ikkō ikki*) conducted by True Pure Land groupings. The parallel between Christians and Honganji *monto* would in 1587 be adduced by Hideyoshi as the prime explanation of his decision to ban the Padres from Japan.

The Jesuit Vice-Provincial Coelho unwittingly gave direct evidence to support the suspicion that Christian religious authority could and would dictate secular interventions of organized force. In a most undiplomatic interview conducted for him by Frois, his chosen interpreter, he assured the Taikō of his best efforts to deliver the support of all the Christian lords of Kyushu in the campaign Hideyoshi was then planning. On the surface auspicious, the famous Osaka audience of 4 May 1586 was (according to the Jesuits' own later accounts) the first step toward their impending calamity.[7]

Coelho arrived at Osaka Castle with a train of over thirty: Padres Frois, Organtino, Cespedes, and Damião Marin; Irmão Lourenço and three other Irmãos; and a covey of Osaka seminarians. Hideyoshi's Christian secretary, Ai Gozaemon (Dom Simão), and Yakuin Zensō, the hegemon's crony and the missionaries' *bête noire*, conducted the Jesuits into the presence. The requisite initial formalities concluded, the Taikō dismissed his paladins with the exception of Ukon, and beckoned the Christian group into his immediate proximity. An intimate discussion ensued.

The conversation is made difficult to reconstruct by the vast divergence in substance and detail of the accounts of Frois and Organtino, eyewitnesses and sole providers of primary material. Frois discusses the audience in the *annua* of 4 October 1586; Organtino's report is dated 10 October 1589. While taking due note of the historian's first rule, to rely upon the most nearly contemporary source, one might nevertheless place the major portion of his trust in the report of Organtino, as Matsuda Kiichi does for persuasive reasons. Although Organtino's letter was written after the expulsion edict (*viz.*, after the tyrant had revealed his true self), and therefore is probably burdened with subjective postpositions, it was a confidential report to the General of the Society. Frois' account, on the other hand, is pious propaganda meant for publication throughout Europe. As such it distorts or suppresses what might prove unedifying, and concentrates upon detailing an image suggesting that the word and the servants of God held a great attraction for the exotic mighty. Frois, it should be remembered, was a consistent adherent of the mission method which sought first to capture the hearts and the courts of princes.

Not a jot of mistrust enters Frois' paean on the Taikō's cordiality; not a single discordant note mars the harmony of the whole. In Hideyoshi's demeanor he saw no trace of dissimulation. The conversation, according to its translator, was initiated by Hideyoshi's profuse repetitions of praise on the Padres' self-sacrificing and profit-bearing mission to Japan. The Taikō supposedly continued his harangue with an account of his rise from obscurity to the highest position in the land; his sole purpose now was to transmit this tale of glory to posterity. He would pacify all Japan, and thereafter devote all his effort to the subjugation of Korea and of Great Ming. To that purpose "he asked no other aid of the padres but that we should negotiate for him two well-equipped great ships," with expert pilots. Actually, it was not his intent to occupy China, only to submit it to his will; and once that was accomplished, he would build Christian churches everywhere in China, order all Chinese to turn Christian, and then himself return to Japan. Japan itself (the half of it or even the major portion) would, he envisioned, in the future be converted to Christianity.

And that, according to Frois, was not yet the end of Hideyoshi's splendiferous promises. The Taikō regaled the missionaries with a highly personalized tour of his pleasure dome and, between wonders, with talk such as this: "The port of Nagasaki he would leave to the Church; and he had no objection to giving the Padres a signed guarantee of this. But that must wait until the country's affairs had been settled completely and he had obtained hostages from the various *tono*. For, he said, the impression must be created that he advanced the suggestion himself, rather than acting at the Padres' request; so that the lords of Hizen would not entertain ill humor over the matter." Whatever Hideyoshi may actually have said, Frois' report shows at least that thought of Nagasaki was not distant from the Taikō's mind as he set his plans for Kyushu. But Frois did not properly evaluate Hideyoshi. This prince was lion and fox combined; of his diplomatic tricks the Jesuits would have been aware had they fully mastered their Machiavelli.

That Coelho had not seems abundantly clear. Organtino's account indicates that the Vice-Provincial was unaware of some of the most elementary maxims: to deal from reality and not from self-serving illusion, to cast an accurate estimate of the adversary, not to connive at inviting a potential enemy into vital terrain. In this report to the General of the Society, the blame for a reckless initiative is placed squarely on the shoulders of Coelho.

Being aware of Coelho's intention to invite Hideyoshi into Kyushu, and knowing full well that the *kanpaku* had the greatest disgust for priests' involvement in military affairs, Organtino (according to his own account) thought to prevent the conversation from turning to such topics, and asked to act as interpreter. Coelho, however, refused this request. After Frois had in a few words expressed the Jesuits' gratitude for the favor which Hideyoshi had heretofore shown, he turned the conversation to the matter of Kyushu and requested the *kanpaku*'s military intervention, promising the Vice-Provincial's best efforts to put all the Christian lords of Kyushu on Hideyoshi's side. As the conversation advanced, Hideyoshi also intimated that he planned an expedition against China, and Coelho's response was to volunteer the suggestion that he would arrange with the Portuguese for two Great Ships to be put at the *kanpaku*'s disposal toward that end. Organtino again attempted to turn the conversation to other matters, to no effect. All of Ukon's strenuous efforts to divert the untimely effusions also failed on account of the stubbornness with which Frois stuck to his topic. After the audience—we learn from Organtino—Hideyoshi's secretary Ai Simão stated that he himself and other Christian lords were dissatisfied with the conduct of the interview, and that he feared the results would be unfortunate.[8]

That the Jesuits had their military adventurist faction is all too well established. Gaspar Coelho was one of its members. In 1584 he had addressed to the Spaniards in the Philippines a plea for the dispatch of "four ships laden with men, artillery, and food . . . to succor the Christians of Japan that are pressed by the heathen," and specifically to save Ōmura from Ryūzōji; and he seems to have continued with similar pleas in the succeeding years.[9] At precisely the time of Coelho's arrival in Sakai (April 1586) Padre Alonso Sanchez SJ was in Manila submitting his project for the conquest of China, of which C. R. Boxer has to say: "This report has to be read to be believed."[10] The Padre, "a person of very holy life, much learning, prudence, and excellent judgment" (as he was touted to Philip II) envisioned that the modest objective would be obtained easily enough, with a motley force of Spaniards, Filipinos, and Japanese auxiliaries conducted by "the fathers of the Society of Jesus, who are to act as guides." It would be interesting to know whether Coelho was aware of the project (or, better yet, Hideyoshi). The figment of an armada of Iberian ships crammed with Japanese sailing off to conquer China had achieved all too extraordinary proportions. The union of the crowns of seemingly invincible Spain and of Portugal, providing an ineluctable promise—or rather temptation—of power, was for the Jesuits and their Japanese Christianity to prove a most unholy alliance. That, however, is anticipating matters by ten years: in 1597 the question of external machinations would bring about bloody persecution at the hands of Hideyoshi. The events of 1587, however, had best be explained in the context of Hideyoshi's internal policy.

The preliminaries are quite familiar. In the first week of July Hideyoshi, having accepted the surrender of Shimazu Yoshihisa, returned to his headquarters near Hakata. Here he was visited by Coelho, who came from Nagasaki aboard his *fusta* to congratulate the Taikō on his victory and to ask for a plot of land for a church in Hakata, which was granted. This *fusta* seems to have been a boat of some two or three hundred tons, and was armed with artillery.[11] Why Coelho thought he needed the vessel at all, and the display of guns, is obscure;[12] but it did draw the attention of Hideyoshi, who spotted it as he was crossing Hakata Bay on 15 July, came aboard, and admired the equipment. Another Southern Barbarian ship was not too far for him to admire, the uncommonly large carrack of Domingos Monteiro which lay at Hirado. The Taikō requested Coelho to have it brought round to Hakata, so he might feast his eyes on it. On 24 July 1587 Capitão Monteiro appeared with his regrets: Hakata was not a suitable harbor. Hideyoshi to all appearance was satisfied with the explanations of navigational difficulty, and dismissed Monteiro and his chaperon Coelho with every sign of favor. And on that same date he issued the following edict:[13]

ORDAINED

Item.   Japan is the Land of the Gods. Diffusion here from the
[1]   Kirishitan Country of a pernicious doctrine is most undesirable.

Item.   To approach the people of our provinces and districts and,
[2]   making them into [Kirishitan] sectarians, cause them to destroy
        the shrines of the gods and the temples of the Buddhas is a
        thing unheard of in previous ages. Provinces, districts, estates,
        and stipends are granted in fief contingent upon the incumbent's
        observance of the laws of the *Tenka* and attention to their
        intent in all matters. But to corrupt and stir up the lower
        classes is outrageous.

Item.   It is the judgment [of the lord of the *Tenka*] that since the
[3]   Bateren by means of their clever doctrine amass parishioners
        as they please, the aforementioned violation of the Buddhist Law
        in these Precincts of the Sun has resulted. That being outrageous,
        the Bateren can hardly be allowed to remain on Japanese soil.
        Within twenty days they must make their preparations and
        return to their country. Should there during this time appear
        among the lower classes villains who make unwarranted accu-
        sations against the Bateren, this shall be considered criminal.

Item.   The purpose of the Black Ships is trade, and that is a different
[4]   matter. As years and months pass, trade may be carried on in
        all sort of articles.

Item.   From now on all those who do not disturb Buddhism (merchants
[5]   as a matter of course, and all others as well) may freely travel
        from the Kirishitan Country and return. Act accordingly.

Text as above. Tenshō 15/6/19.   [24 July 1587]

The edict struck the Padres like a bolt from the blue. Their
subsequent reports agonize over the possible reasons for such
sudden displeasure after so many demonstrations of favor. Frois
gives the dramatic depiction of a blow which totally lacked
any sensible motive, an abrupt and unpremeditated turn of
fancy.[14] And he projects the image of Hideyoshi as a capricious
tyrant, surrounded by venomous advisers such as the pander
Yakuin Zensō, who fawned on the Padres when they seemed to
bask in his master's favor, and covertly held his bile, awaiting the
right opportunity. The racy anecdote of the tyrant's frustrated
lusting after Christian maidens completed a picture long familiar
from the Levant: the pagan potentate was exposed as satyr. The
Padres' accounts are subjective vindications of Christian innocence
outraged by the Oriental despot.

Hideyoshi's decision did not spring out of a megalomanic
whim, or drunkenness, or annoyance at amorous ardor foiled.
It was not caused by chagrin at Coelho's failure to present

him the *fusta* or pilot the *nao* to Hakata for his inspection. It was only an apparent bolt from the blue; the storm had long been brewing. What seemed a wild *volte face* was instead a rational political decision. Perhaps there had been need, prior to the conquest of Kyushu, for dissimulation. But the matter of Kyushu being settled, July 1587 was from Hideyoshi's stand-point a good and proper time to act. The expulsion of the Bateren was not of itself a xenophobic measure. It was part of Hideyoshi's program for the restructuring of Japan under central authority. It cannot be overemphasized that the step was essentially a matter of internal policy. As such it forms a matured antecedent to the Tokugawa construction, Sakoku. This ante-cedent role (the ordinance not being enforced as to the point of expulsion) is the major historical significance of Hideyoshi's decree. The Taikō was intent on establishing a basic principle: his reorganization of Japan was meant to be comprehensive, and therefore could not exempt the Padres or ignore their own arrogations of authority. The Padres not only had pretensions to a moral dictate over certain important objects of his scheme of political subordination; they even postured as a quasi-sovereign power on a portion of Japanese soil. Their enclave was the commercially valuable port area of Nagasaki. That fact fitted the Taikō's fiscal purposes no less than his demonstrational intentions. He specifically exempted the Portuguese traders from his anti-Christian directive; in action which followed forthwith, he absorbed their *entrepôt* Nagasaki into his own immediate domain. He neatly excised the interference in commerce of the brokers in religious authority. There was nothing ill-considered in the Taikō's decree.

The decree itself is not the most interesting document of those days. Its chief stress was directed at external (Jesuit and Portuguese) consumption. More elaborate is a Notice addressed to the internal audience. And here Hideyoshi's motivation appears crystal clear.[15]

NOTICE

Item.   The matter of [becoming] a sectarian of the Bateren shall be
[1]   the free choice of the individual concerned.

Item.   That enfeoffed recipients of provinces, districts, and estates
[2]   should force peasants registered in [Buddhist] temples, and others
         of their tenantry, against their will into the ranks of the Bateren
         sectarians is unreasonable beyond words and is outrageous.

Item.   Provinces and stipends are granted in fief with tenure limited to
[3]   the incumbent. The recipient may change; but the peasants do
          not change. In case of unreasonable demands exerted upon any
          point, the recipient will be held in contumely. Act accordingly.

Item.   Persons holding above 200 *chō*, 2 or 3 thousand *kan*, may become
[4]   [sectarians of the] Bateren upon obtaining official permission,
          acceding to the pleasure [of the lord of the *Tenka*].

Item.   Persons drawing stipends below the aforementioned: in the
[5]   matter of choice among the Eight Sects or Nine Sects, the head
          of the house shall decide as he pleases, for himself only.

Item.   The Bateren sectarians, it has come to the attention [of the lord
[6]   of the *Tenka*], are even more given to conjurations with
          external elements than the Ikkō Sect. The Ikkō Sect established
          temple precincts in the provinces and districts and did not pay
          the yearly dues to their enfeoffed recipients. Moreover, they
          made the entire Province of Kaga into [Ikkō] sectarians, chased
          out Togashi, the lord of the province, delivered the stipends
          over to bonzes of the Ikkō Sect, and, beyond that, even took
          over Echizen. That this was harmful to the *Tenka* is the
          undisguisable truth.

Item.   The bonzes of the Ikkō sectarians had temples built in every
[7]   cove and inlet. Though they have been pardoned, they no
          longer regulate matters in their temple precincts in the same
          manner as before.

Item.   That daimyo in possession of provinces and districts or of
[8]   estates should force their retainers into the ranks of the Bateren
          sectarians is even more undesirable by far than the Honganji
          sectarians' establishment of temple precincts, and is bound to be
          of great harm to the *Tenka*. These individuals of no discretion
          shall be subject to chastisement.

Item.   Bateren sectarians by their free choice, [insofar as they] are of
[9]   the lower classes, shall be unmolested, this being a matter of
          Eight Sects or Nine Sects.

Item.   The sale of Japanese to China, South Barbary, and Korea is
[10]   outrageous.
          Add: In Japan trade in human beings is prohibited.

Item.   Trade and slaughter of cattle and horses for use as food shall
[11]   also be considered criminal.

The above items shall rest under strict prohibition. Any transgressor
shall immediately be put to severe punishment.

Tenshō 15/6/18.   [23 July 1587]

VERMILION SEAL

Item 1 is far from being a guarantee of religious freedom. It is rather a prohibition of forced conversions; and that, elaborated into a general assertion of central authority's control over the actions of feudal subordinates, is one of the two major themes of Hideyoshi's memorandum. The other is the invidious analogy between Christians and Honganji *monto*. The two themes are interconnected within the context of Hideyoshi's policy of consequent control of all the land's population. This policy included most prominently the regulation of the peasantry, the disarmament of the *kokujin* class of quasi-independent samurai, and the drawing of direct lines of authority to daimyo (an institution eventually to develop into the famous type of "potted plants," displaceable agents of a bureaucratized system in the governance of domains autonomous but subject to confiscation). Hideyoshi's fear was that the continuation of Christian influence would perpetuate a force cutting across his lines of rationalization. In such a context the comparison of Christianity with the Ikkō Sect was the most dangerous that could be made.

The "temple precincts" (*jinai*) mentioned repeatedly in Hideyoshi's Notice were not merely the precincts of religious edifices. As Inoue Toshio has pointed out, powerful temples of the True Pure Land Sect were practically indistinguishable from military fortresses.[16] The typical temple of the Jōdo Shinshū was located in the midst of moats and other fortifications; and the township that grew up with it possessed the characteristics not of the temple town (*monzen-machi*) but of the emergent castle town (*jōkamachi*). Such temple precincts were the visible provincial manifestations of a power that cannot be ignored in discussing the history of Sengoku Japan: the religious monarchy (*hōō-koku*, as Inoue calls it) of the Honganji. Hideyoshi did not have to go far afield from Hakata to find a Christian analogue: Nagasaki, as we have seen, had in 1580 been made over into *jiryō*, temple/Church domain. And we shall shortly discover that a further type of religiously influenced exercise of authority could be found in the case of one of Hideyoshi's own vassals. It is no accident that concomitant with Hideyoshi's Notice was the dispossession of Takayama Ukon.

The keynote of Hideyoshi's comparison was in the implied similarity of the soteriology, and its social implications, of Shinshū and of Christianity. Valignano, the theologian, had damned Pure Land as Lutheran. But Hideyoshi, the practitioner of power, was insensible of European theological subtleties. To him, both religions derived their dominance over believers' minds from a salvationist *sola fide* approach. The Ikkō adherents found their justification in the boundless compassion of Amida, the Christians in the boundless mercy of Deus; Faith was Truth. The religious consciousness extended into political and organizational motivation. "To maintain and protect the True Law is nothing else but to follow reason and conscience."[17] The Shinshū priests had developed this predicate into an ideology which tightly knitted together the cells of their adherents. It would be an interesting topic of further research to investigate whether or not Hideyoshi's analogy had a detailed basis of truth: was Christian communal activity indeed indebted, in imitation of structure or in utilization of precedent, to Ikkō techniques? The Christian confraternity perhaps shared more with the Pure Land village organization than its Japanese name, *kumi*.[18] But the potential detailed analogy pales before the significance of Hideyoshi's actual general formulation. It is therefore important to have a view of the Ikkō side of the background.

The establishment of Ikkō Sect groupings (*kyōdan*) was a late mediaeval phenomenon which accompanied the breakup of the *shōen* system of land tenure. It proceeded concomitant with the early stages of development of the daimyo institution (the centrifugal drift of *shugo* and *jitō*) and with the transformation of the yeoman (*myōshu*) class into samurai. The absentee landowner, aristocrat or temple of the old sects, was reduced to impotence by the interposition of independent provincial military forces. The missionized peasantry of extensive areas preferred the prestige-based authority of Honganji priests to the authority of *shugo daimyō*, which was ultimately derived from shogunal legality but required force for its implementation. The original essence of Ikkō groupings was peasant organization rationalized by the religious motive. The eventual transformation of the sixteenth century was into a coordinate mass, worthy of being called a religious monarchy, with an elaborate hierarchy in which countless house chapels (*dōjō*) formed the base of response to calls of action emanating from the sect's leader, the Honganji *hossu*. His authority was in part magical: it could be traced beyond even the sect's founder Shinran, of whom the *hossu* was direct successor; he was the representative on earth of Amida, whose aureole of boundless light was the sole incandescence perceived by the faithful. But the bonzes regnant over temple precincts utilized the aura of mastery over the life to come in the extension of secular power. The temple of itself was at the same time religious and secular lord; that is the most significant aspect of this form of domination. At every level of the hierarchy an analogous temporal and military function could be found for sacerdotal and parishioner roles. The peasant level (*hyakushō-bun*) was succeeded by *samurai-bun* and *daimyō-bun* at the apex. The Honganji itself was daimyo over entire provinces.[19]

In tracing the progress of the daimyo institution, Professor John Hall distinguishes between four ideal types:[20] the *shugo daimyō*, who emerged in the middle of the fourteenth century and lost their predominance by the end of the fifteenth; the *sengoku daimyō*, who represented the most notable form from the end of the fifteenth century until the eighth decade of the sixteenth; the *shokuhō daimyō*, who rose during the hegemony of Nobunaga and Hideyoshi and lasted into the early seventeenth century; and the *kinsei daimyō*, the final development, characteristic of the Tokugawa era and matured by the end of the seventeenth century. The nomenclature is essentially a device of periodization, although it is well founded in distinctions of modal character. One or two sub-categories based on distinctions of substance might be added to the schematic table. The *Kirishitan daimyō* element, although perceptible, had perhaps too infinitesimal a half-life to be considered significant. No so the religious daimyo as such. And of these *shūkyō daimyō* the active provincial complex of the Honganji is the outstanding example.

The political, social, and military activities of the Ikkō sectarians found their expression in *ikki*, organized manifestations of strength. *Ikki* is conventionally translated "uprising," but that convention does not fit this context. "Uprising" is a word containing a double bias—spontaneous and revolutionary. The *Ikkō ikki* cannot properly be accounted either. They were directed, they possessed strong internal organizational ties, and their coalescence proceeded parallel to the development of the *sengoku* and *shokuhō daimyō*, with whom they competed and by the latter of whom they were crushed.

The most important evolutionary forms taken by *Ikkō ikki* were: resistance to taxation; usurpation of taxes and of terrain; military struggle against *shugo* and against other sects; intervention in the struggles of military groupings; overt emergence into the position of territorial rule. Control at the lowest level rested in the hands of *osa-byakushō*, village prominences in whose houses the *dōjō* were typically located. Enforcement combined the dual sanctions of excommunication and formal ostracism (*mura hachibu*). Collection of the skeletal remains of direct dues formerly transmitted to *shōen* holders continued in the form of local taxes for the Honganji organization. Thus was the influence of *shugo* excluded; and the rise of the *kokujin* class was kept well within bounds, that latent energy being transfused into the Honganji kinetic. A formidable combination resulted. "What greatly hindered the daimyo management of their province domains was the fact that the external influence of the Honganji, utilizing the glow of Mida's aureole, controlled [*kokujin*] and *osa-byakushō* alike."[21] That describes precisely what Hideyoshi meant in Item 6 of his Notice; and he made explicit reference to the most notorious case, the displacement by Honganji *monto* of the *shugo* family of Kaga, the Togashi.

The power of the Ikkō Sect in the provinces along the Sea of Japan was founded by Rennyo, the eighth *hossu*, who was in 1465 forced to flee Kyoto by the soldier monks of Mount Hiei. His place of refuge was Echizen, whence spread his work of organizing the *monto* in the entire area. Rennyo himself disclaimed any ambitions of territorial possession. But the very fact of the organization of *ikki* necessitated the absorption of territory. The takeover of the Province of Kaga by the *monto* proceeded in that fashion. The sectarians intervened in the conflict between factions of the Togashi family (a byproduct of the general conflagration of the Ōnin War). The long struggle culminated in 1488, when Togashi Masachika committed suicide in a castle under attack by the *monto*. By the last decade of the fifteenth century, Kaga was simply called peasant-held, *hyakushō-mochi*.[22]

The *monto* became a truly formidable political force after the middle of the sixteenth century. Hardly a year passed in the chronology of the sixties and seventies without mention of *Ikkō ikki*; the major daimyo were forced into violent confrontations with the sectarians. The Mikawa *ikki* of 1563–64 was the first serious crisis in the career of the Tokugawa shogunate's future founder, the young Ieyasu, who was hard put to suppress the threat because some of his most trusted vassals abandoned him for Amida. But the most prominent target of the sectarians, and their most ruthless opponent, was Oda Nobunaga. The Honganji *hossu*, Kennyo Kōsa, flung down the gauntlet in 1570, forming a coalition with Nobunaga's enemies Miyoshi, Rokkaku, Asakura, and Asai, and ordering the *monto* to rise in arms throughout Nobunaga's domains. Of the *ikki* which resulted, the hardest to overcome was that of Ise Nagashima: here in the Kiso River Delta the *monto* fought a guerrilla war and were not suppressed until October 1574, when Nobunaga cordoned them off from the seaside and starved them out. Twenty thousand, we are told, were herded into palisades and burnt alive.[23] In the spring of 1574, Echizen had become an *ikki*-held province, Asakura Kageakira going the way of Togashi Masachika of Kaga; the Honganji appointed its own *shugo*. The sectarians' sway did not last more than a year and a half. After defeating Takeda Katsuyori at Nagashino in the end of June 1575, Nobunaga was free to move against the *ikki* of Echizen, and could by mid-September report that the sectarians' stronghold of Fuchū was "so littered with corpses that there seemed no empty space left: a good show! Today I intend to search out the *monto* in every mountain and valley, and kill them all." When they rose again in Echizen the next year, Nobunaga's vassal Maeda Toshiie crucified or boiled alive some thousand prisoners. Also in this year of 1576 occurred the famous Echizen "sword hunt" of Shibata Katsuie, early instance of a pattern to be expanded into national policy by Hideyoshi; thus was the province finally set in order. The religious monarchy was not eliminated until 1580, when Kennyo and his reluctant son Kyōnyo surrendered the Ishiyama Honganji to Oda. In that same year the remnants of *monto* resistance in Kaga were liquidated.

And this was the history to which Hideyoshi alluded when he made the statement: "The Bateren sectarians . . . are even more given to conjurations with external elements than the Ikkō Sect." Was this estimate accurate? The question is not truly relevant. What was more important was not the actuality but rather Hideyoshi's suspicion of it. One of the factors of modernity in Early Modern Japan was that in it there was no place for sectarians of any sort.

In this context also one might invoke the hackneyed pasquil—

> Oda mixed the flour and Hashiba baked
> The Empire Cookie.
> Sitting back relaxed, who ate it?—
> Tokugawa.

The precedents for the regulation of subversive or suspect religious groupings reach back, replete with martyrdoms, to the first of the "Three Heroes." Sakoku, to the extent that the notion implies concomitant internal cordons, was not a Tokugawa invention. The policy was undergoing maturation at the very time when external contacts appeared most flourishing.

The Padres did not perceive the broad scope of Hideyoshi's motivation. Their reporting of the case is flawed. Not only did Frois fix his attention upon incidentals; there is reason enough to say that he did not write down the whole truth. He did not mention the very important Notice, although he had many words for the expulsion edict, which followed it by a day. It is hardly likely that Frois (who had been on the scene with Coelho) was still not aware of the memorandum's existence when he drafted his effusive reports on the matter. But mention of the Notice would have deprived the drama of its surprise. On the part of Hideyoshi, the lapse of one day in issuing the two decrees perhaps was purposeful: perhaps the Taikō meant to give his vassals time to fall into line before he moved against the Padres. When Hideyoshi, during the night of July 24th, sent Ai Gozaemon with a list of inquisitions to awaken Coelho and take him ashore from the *fusta*, the Japanese had already for a day been cognizant of the Taikō's disposition. "The only ones who did not know were Coelho and Frois, the two of them still drunk with the impressions of welcome" received from Hideyoshi in Osaka and in his Kyushu headquarters.[24] Ai Gozaemon was that night probably Dom Simão no longer, and most of the important Christian vassals of Hideyoshi who were present there had probably abjured Christianity already, if only on the surface.[25] The striking exception was Takayama Ukon. The *chevalier sans peur et sans reproche* thrice denied his master, choosing to remain loyal to Christ.[26]

There is a dearth of Japanese sources which would explicitly clarify what incited Hideyoshi to action. But it is interesting to note that one significant account, written apparently by one of the Taikō's intimates, after lingering on the shocking details of Southern Barbarian perfidy, concludes with the figure of Takayama Ukon in perfect focus:[27]

The Bateren, thinking the time ripe, with all sort and manner of treasures heaped mountain high, worked all the more in concocting stratagems to make their sect flourish. In Gotō, Hirado, Nagasaki, and in other places, they had already subverted the rulers with the abundance that came there with every Southern Barbarian ship's arrival. Not only did they drag the members of the various sects into their own pernicious doctrine; even beyond that, they bought up several hundred Japanese (man or woman regardless) for the Black Ships, where they were taken with iron shackles on arms and legs, and thrust down into the bottom hold, with tortures exceeding those of hell. Moreover they bought up cattle and horses, flayed them alive, and ate them, using their hands, the bonzes together with their disciples. There was no propriety preserved between parent and child, elder and younger brother; so that, as report has it, it was as if this world were transformed into the Realm of Beasts.

What is seen is oft imitated. And so the Japanese of those parts, having learned in every particular the manner of the foreigners, sold their children, sold their parents, and sold their wives. Reports of this, one after the other, reached the ear of authority. And [the Taikō] thought it obvious that, if the aforesaid sect were tolerated, Japan would soon turn into a pit of heresy, with Buddha's Law and Royal Sway both thereupon discarded. This he lamented. In his infinite grace, mercy, and compassion he formulated a remedy. Already he issued a decree to ban the Bateren bonzes from Our Empire. But then there was Takayama Ukon no Suke. From the first he had himself honored and believed that religion; even beyond that, he had most unreasonably made the people of his fief, priests as well as laymen, to join that sect. Being informed of this, the Taikō chased that minion of the disciples of perdition, the aforesaid Ukon no Suke, out of his fief. And, truly, in building the firm base for the flourish of Buddha's Law and Royal Sway, and for the Empire's good order, how could anything surpass this?

On the same topic the Jesuit source has to say :[28]

After the *kanpaku* had made his decision to break with the Padres and Christians, he sent a message to Ukondono, the brunt of which was that the Christian law be of the devil and diffusing much in Japan, especially among noted warriors and the first lords; and that he knew that one of the reasons therefor was Ukon's influencing such personages. This greatly displeased him, for there prevailed among Christians the sort of mystery-bound and close concord which was not equaled even among brothers; and he was worried that they would somehow stir trouble for the *Tenka*, that is to say, the monarchy of Japan. He also knew how Ukon had made the people of Takatsuki and of recent also of Akashi into Christians, how he had destroyed their temples and burnt their idols. This be outrageous all, and contrary to reason.

The facts were not to be disputed. Ukon had been influential in persuading such prominent individuals as Gamō Ujisato and Kuroda Josui to accept baptism; and that Hideyoshi was concerned about the number of such conversions was the nearly unanimous agreement of Jesuits on the scene. Moreover, Ukon himself "considered it his *tegara* (by which is meant to say, 'praiseworthy exploit') that he hade made the people of Takatsuki and Akashi Christian." This exploit had not been accomplished without destructiveness.

The career of the *Kirishitan daimyō* Dom Justo Takayama Ukon (1552?–1615) is a revealing vignette of Sengoku history.[29] The chapbook of the Tokugawa period, *Kirishitan monogatari*, attributes to him and his father, Takayama Hida no Kami Zusho (Dom Dario), a crucial role in the introduction of Christianity into Japan; and the survival of the Church in the Kyoto area during the critical early period of the 1560's is indeed attributable in large measure to the indefatigable zeal of Dario.

The popular narrative deliberately, but correctly, associates the two Takayama with Matsunaga Danjō Hisahide, one of the stock villains of Japanese history, who for the major part of the decade in question was the power to be reckoned with in the Home Provinces.[30] Jesuit commentators portray Matsunaga as a fanatical adherent of the Nichiren Sect and a sworn enemy of Christianity, full of anti-missionary devices which were foiled only by external intervention.[31] In particular, he appears as the ceaseless tormentor of Gaspar Vilela, the first Padre after Xavier to arrive in Kyoto (1559). He does seem to have granted a patent of privileges to Vilela in the summer of 1560,[32] but he was instrumental in the Padre's short banishment from the Capital in August of that same year, and aimed at another ban in May 1563. It was on this latter occasion that Takayama Hida no Kami entered the picture of Christianity in Japan. At the time Takayama was in Matsunaga's service, holding the fortress of Sawa in Yamato for him.

Initially, Hida no Kami was anti-Christian: Frois writes that he advised Matsunaga to investigate Vilela's new religion for statements contrary to the Buddhas and gods, and to have the Padre's head if such were found.[33] The scholars and dignitaries of the Kyoto establishment, Yūki Yamashiro no Kami Shinsai and Kiyohara Geki Ekata, joined Takayama in the inquisition.[34] A marvellous bouleversement followed: the three were converted to Christianity. Matsunaga was gracious enough to receive Vilela in audience, and the Padre returned in triumph to Kyoto, to remain there until July 1565, when Matsunaga (his grace being a transient quality) connived at an Imperial Edict to banish the Jesuits.[35] Hida no Kami was baptized at Sawa in 1564, and his whole family—including Ukon—received the sacrament with him.[36]

In 1565 Matsunaga destroyed the Ashikaga shogun Yoshiteru, but soon thereafter found himself at war with the party of his accomplice Miyoshi Yoshitsugu. A year or two into the fighting Sawa fell, and its castellan, Dario Takayama, had to flee. He next emerges into view in 1568, in the train of Oda Nobunaga's victorious entry into Kyoto: Oda had embraced Ashikaga Yoshiaki and installed him as shogun; and Takayama's old friend Wada Koremasa, who had performed valuable services for Yoshiaki, had taken Dom Dario into his own employ. Wada's influence with the new power-holders was considerable, as was Dom Dario's with Wada; and this line of intercession made possible the missionaries' return to the Capital. Through Wada, Dom Dario obtained for Frois the two celebrated Easter 1569 interviews with Nobunaga, and the mission of the Kyoto area was thereby for the first time put on a firm footing.

By 1571 Wada's position in Settsu had involved him in clashes with the rising daimyo Araki Murashige. One of his most exposed forts, which was captained by Dom Dario, became the prime object of Murashige's attack. Responding to Takayama's urgent plea for reinforcements, Wada Koremasa himself hastened to the relief, but he was ambushed by an overwhelming force and was killed.[37] The Church had lost a powerful supporter; but through his demise the way to the top was opened for even more ardent protectors. Koremasa's son Korenaga succeeded to the Wada domain and its main castle, Takatsuki. Dom Dario Takayama assumed the role of principal adviser to the young man, and Takayama Ukon (Dom Justo) was about to take the first steps in his own right onto the stage of history. And this our Sengoku hero did "in the standard manner"—as the essayist Aida Yūji points out—"by killing his lord."[38]

The background of the tawdry episode which gained for the Takayama the castle of Takatsuki and their 20,000-*koku* fief is fairly clear. Frois, the master of an exciting and tutored prose style, casts parts to actors and arranges the scenario to fit the stage of a truly theatrical *coup de main*; but his account matches that of the Japanese source, *Intoku Taiheiki*, surprisingly well, so that there is little cause to doubt the essential accuracy of his description. The letter he wrote to Cabral on 20 April 1573 was composed a scant eight days after the event, and the vivid narrative testifies to the immediacy and force of the impression.

According to Frois, Korenaga—the unworthy son of a great father—had killed his uncle and plotted also to do away with his other guardians, the Takayama. They were apprised of the scheme, however, and immediately sought out Araki, whose advice was to kill before being killed; he would assist them with troops and, after the successful outcome, would reward them by confirming them in the Takatsuki domain. The Takayama thereupon seized the initiative. Followed by fourteen or fifteen of their own samurai, they called upon Korenaga (who had a like number with him) in his chambers. What ensued seems to have been a *danmari* action scene right out of the kabuki, with the candle going out at the start and the two sides blindly slashing away at friend and foe alike in the darkness. From the confusion emerged Ukon with several serious wounds, and Korenaga with a wound that was fatal.

After this intrigue the Takayama held Takatsuki in direct vassalage from Araki Murashige, and had thus taken a distinct step forward; but during Oda Nobunaga's campaign against Murashige in the late autumn of 1578 Ukon, as has been described in a previous chapter, played the castle into the hands of Nobunaga and then passed into his service. Perhaps the notion of Sengoku as a melée of treasons is after all useful.

When Hideyoshi moved into Settsu in 1582 on his way to avenge Nobunaga's death, Ukon lost no time in appearing before the Taikō, bringing his son as hostage.[39] He was rewarded with the joint command of the vanguard of horse at the Battle of Yamazaki, and performed meritoriously, although the apodictic statement of his biographer Laures, "Ukon conquers Akechi," does seem a trifle grotesque.[40]

Yamazaki was not the only climactic battle in which Ukon is supposed to have played a key role. He was, for instance, part of Hideyoshi's advance guard at Shizu ga Take in 1583, and does not appear in a particularly heroic light in that series of violent skirmishes, which ended with the elimination of Shibata Katsuie.[41] But neither does he deserve the reputation of cowardice which has been imputed to him by some. Certain

Tokugawa period chronicles consciously denigrate him on account of his Christianity, and several of the more recent Japanese historians have followed that lead. Aida Yūji in a book titled *The Loser's Condition* stamps Ukon as a real loser. But Aida seriously underestimates Ukon. He was first and foremost a ruthless *sengoku daimyō*, and one to be reckoned with. Unfortunately for him, his star could never develop to the first magnitude, being already eclipsed at the moment of birth by infinitely more powerful luminaries.

Contemporary Jesuits laud Ukon as the very incarnation of the ideal of the sublime life, the mirror of chivalry, the relentless agent of the Hound of Heaven. The transplantation of a European cliché into Japan is interesting enough. But the hyperbole is cultivated into the twentieth century by Laures, whose encomiad seems the unwitting parody of the Baroque historian of missions. Laures' book is meant to fortify the case for Ukon's sainthood.[42] But which category of saints would Ukon enter? Johan Huizinga distinguishes between two types: "the men of fiery speech and energetic action, like Ignatius Loyola, Francis Xavier . . . and the men absorbed in tranquil rapture." And he continues with the observation: "It would not be unreasonable to compare to the romanticism of chivalry, as an element of medieval thought, a romanticism of saintliness, in the sense of a tendency to give the colours of fancy and the accents of enthusiasm to an ideal form of virtue and of duty. It is remarkable that this romanticism of saintliness always aims far more at miracles and excesses of humility and of asceticism, than at brilliant achievements in the service of religious policy."[43] The depiction of Takayama Ukon, from the pens both of his Christian contemporaries and of his modern panegyrists, glitters with all the colors of the romantic conception. And yet he was a martyr to his own sense of service to policy. I would classify him with the ferocious saints, along with his spiritual masters Loyola and Xavier.

One need only consider his actions at Takatsuki and Akashi, even through the lenses of a profoundly sympathetic Laures. Takatsuki immediately before Nobunaga's death had a population of some 25,000 souls. In the incomplete decade of Takayama tenure, 18,000 of these had become Christian. Laures advances these statistics as proof that there had been in Takatsuki no forced conversions—else the entirety would have been Christian! And there follows a further example of the missiologist's logic:

"When Ukon after the subjugation of Araki sought to make his entire land Christian, not a few bonzes were apparently also baptized, for the sources report the destruction of a great number of temples or their conversion into churches. But [the bonzes] could have made their decision quite freely." Enforcement of the peculiar type of freedom intensified once Ukon had assured himself of Hideyoshi's favor after Yamazaki: he told the bonzes to submit or be harried out of the land. The mere threat seems to have sufficed. All the Buddhist priests, some one hundred in number, submitted to baptism; their temples were ripped down or made over into churches.[44] Continuous baptisms were accompanied by continuous destruction. The picture is not especially attractive.

In 1585 Hideyoshi transferred Ukon to a new fief at Akashi, with an increase of income to 60,000 koku. It is clear that the transfer was made within Hideyoshi's general policy of the redistribution of fiefs, which that year reached notable proportions as the Taikō attempted to make a clear demonstration of a new order, major subordination rather than coalition.[45] But it is interesting to speculate on the circumstances of Ukon's particular case. Perhaps Hideyoshi wanted to move Ukon away from his firmly rooted platform of authority rationalized by the religious uniformity of the populace, and into alien ground. If so, then the Taikō was to be disappointed. Ukon continued his holy indiscretions in Akashi. The very news of his imminent arrival sent the Akashi bonzes into a frenzy: carrying their sacred images with them, they took boat for Osaka to plead intercession of Hideyoshi's mother. Hideyoshi let Ukon do his will, and the Buddhist statues wound up as firewood. The first move, the Jesuits take care to point out, had been the bonzes'; and Ukon felt no constraint in putting upon them the onus of the perturbation of his new fief. The bonzes were not allowed to return to Akashi; but the Padres moved in.[46] The work of conversion was interrupted only by the Kyushu Expedition, from which Ukon did not return. Ukon had operated according to the principle: he who is not with me is against me. Hideyoshi applied the same formula to him. Fief and favor lost due to Christian fortitude, Ukon found refuge with Konishi Yukinaga on Shōdoshima and in Higo. In 1588 he went to Kanazawa and was able to obtain service with the Maeda. There he remained until the issuance of another expulsion edict, one more rigidly enforced, that of Ieyasu in 1614. He died in exile in Manila.

Est rara avis in terris—this is the characterization made of Ukon by Padre Gregorio de Cespedes.[47] At the same time removed from earthly concerns and yet a man of infinite charm; a man of thorough and pure conviction radiating upon all who came into his proximity; in regard to his faith, an uncompromising nature—discretion resting upon the razor's edge of rectitude; total commitment to the higher duty; this last trait, when coupled with the secular power of a *sengoku daimyō*, potentially dangerous. Hideyoshi, who valued Ukon's talents as general and teaman,[48] could not in the end remain insensitive to the intolerant cast of his striving for perfection. Quite clearly the interests of Ukon were not in the first line those of acceding in all to the Taikō's pleasure. As a legionary of the servants of Christ, Ukon became in the end simply a case study in the justification of purge.

Hideyoshi's aspersions against the Padres were not fashioned out of whole cloth, although the hostile narrative quoted above is a good example of the twists to which a bit of truth can be subjected by a convinced propagandist. The Padres were not guilty of conniving at the Portuguese slave trade, which seems to have been substantial. But the other points quoted at them by Hideyoshi were verifiable examples of the disturbance of the internal order. Coelho's apology that the destruction of temples and shrines was the initiative of Japanese believers was altogether too feeble: the Padres made their flock do it, and did it themselves, and relished it.[49] Efforts at formal accommodation notwithstanding, the Jesuits were engaged in wholesale destruction of the Japanese tradition.

When was the limit of tolerance reached? The diffusion of a new religion was permissible in Japan as long as the case was one of attraction to a concordant system of faith and ethics. The introduction of a foreign element was possible to the extent that it did not interfere with the dominant internal secular interests. The forced alienation from tradition was not tolerable. Exclusive claims of loyalty to an external element involved a secular clash.

The precedent of Japan's adoption of a foreign religion—Buddhism—was obvious, and one of great antiquity. But the Christian parallel diverged into a zone of contrasts. Buddhism, as Christianity also, had been confronted by the vehement initial resistance of those involved in the administration of native (Shinto) rites and directly threatened in their vested interest. But the process of entry was eased for Buddhism by its accidental instrumentality and inherent pliability. Buddhism was utilized by the founders of Imperial autocracy in Asuka and Nara Japan to rationalize their quasi-cosmic assumptions of power. In contrast, the other-worldly Christian justification of secular power was at best irrelevant to men like Hideyoshi and Ieyasu, who created their own world, or was suspect to them, and was not countenanced by them. Buddhism readily submitted to adaptation: its syncretistic character reacted with Shinto to form theological colloids. Catholicism was uncompromising: in that lay part of its attraction, but also the essence of its threat. The activities of its zealots were too destructive of the national tradition to be ignored by those who were recasting the national polity. There remained only the ultimate divergence. Could the intrusion of Christianity be accounted a prelude to invasion by Christian powers? Did "conjurations with external elements" transcend the borders of Japan? The important factor in the dilation of the idea of the Christian threat was—to reiterate—not the element of actuality but rather that of suspicion and its propagandistic orchestration, *ad captandum vulgus*. The Christian side itself provided the plausible rationale for the destruction of Christianity; and the ostensible reasons at times may justify the political decision far more persuasively than the facts behind it. If there were pretexts to be utilized, so much the better. Once the pretexts were fully in hand, the external cordons would be drawn; the curtain would close on the "Christian Century."

In 1587 was set only the point of departure for Sakoku. Hideyoshi had not yet fixed upon the notion of a fifth column of Padres, for dearth of proof or lack of conviction that this sort of propaganda was desirable.[50] Before he left Kyushu, he issued (Frois reports) a series of anti-Christian ordinances; but these may all be considered measures of internal policy. Flags displaying crosses were to be eliminated from military camps and vessels, rosaries and relics seized; the "Church domain" of Nagasaki, Mogi, and Urakami was to be confiscated; the fortifications of Nagasaki were to be razed, the forts of Arima and Ōmura destroyed—the symbolic was the target as well as the strategic.

The Jesuit reaction was confused. Coelho initially feared the worst: his messages to Nagasaki to salvage whatever possible and hide all Christian maidens induced in that city a doomsday atmosphere. Bribes saved the churches of Nagasaki from destruction. But those of Ōmura were not saved, nor were those of Osaka, Kyoto, and Sakai. And yet the totality of the edict of expulsion was not enforced. Coelho begged of Hideyoshi a delay in departure, with the transparent excuse that the *nao* could not take so many passengers. No Padres and no Irmãos left permanently when Capitão Monteiro set sail in October 1587; three Irmãos were sent to Macao for the purpose of ordination, but that was all. After a grave consultation held at Takushima off Hirado, the Padres dispersed to Christian territories within Japan, some—such as Organtino in Dom Agostinho Konishi's Shōdoshima—*in solitudinibus errantes, in montibus et speluncis et in cavernis terrae*, as Valignano was to say with the words of the Apostle.[51] Daft Coelho in the meantime brewed the plan to take up arms, stand a siege in Nagasaki, and wait for aid from abroad.[52]

Wholly unaware of Japanese thunderbolts, the *Visitator* Alexandro Valignano on 13 April 1588 took ship from Goa, shepherding on board four samurai youths on their way back from Kyushu Christianity's famed "Tenshō Embassy" to Europe. Valignano was taking the occasion to act as return ambassador of European Christianity to Japan, with diplomatic credentials from His Catholic Majesty's Viceroy of India, Dom Duarte de Menezes. The presents which the youths had accumulated on their grand tour were to be diverted to Hideyoshi, in appreciation of his great and continuing favor (which had caused Coelho, years previously, to solicit the embassy). After a voyage of some four months the ship landed in Macao, and Valignano knew that the Taikō's grace had not continued. And there was a further draught of wormwood at the arrival in Macao of Padre Belchior de Moura, whom Coelho in February 1589 sent abroad as the emissary of his schemes.

Valignano states that he was thoroughly nonplussed by Coelho's concoction of "such temerity and exceedingly dangerous fancy." Not only was the plan impossible, imprudent, and improper, "it was so immensely ill-advised and indiscreet that I lose my composure every time I chance to recall it." Not only Padres and Japanese Irmãos but also a great number of their terrified believers had knowledge of Coelho's figment. "It is a marvel that none of it reached the ear of the *kanpaku*." When Valignano finally arrived in Nagasaki (21 July 1590), he reports, he immediately ordered the weapons and other matériel stockpiled by Coelho to be sold in deepest secrecy; the artillery ammunition was loaded onto the *nao* for disposal in Macao. Coelho had died on 7 May 1590. "Had I met him while he was still alive"—states the *Visitator*—"I would have punished him severely; for all was contrary to the orders and to the policy of the Society."[53]

But the popular image of perniciousness was made out of the assertion that plans not unlike Coelho's were in fact the policy of the Society of Jesus in Japan. Might one not label the standard bogey Bateren of the *Kirishitan monogatari* genre a caricature of the Coelho type?

The anti-Christian literature of the Tokugawa period is a cacophony on the theme of European imperialist designs confluent with missionary activity. One of its most interesting players—a captious cymbalist—is the renegade Jesuit Christovão Ferreira. In the *Kengiroku* of 1636 he smacks papal pretension and expansionist thievery by way of a denunciation of the Seventh Commandment:[54]

The Seventh Article sets down as law: "You shall not steal." Nevertheless, in spreading the gospel of the Kirishitan religion it is a matter of course to tear away and usurp country after country. *Nova Hispania* (this is the name of a country), *Luzon* (ditto), *India* (ditto), and others have been torn away and taken over by *Europe* (South Barbary) . . . Spreading the gospel always proceeds this way. Fifty [!] years ago the emperors of two countries called *Portugal* and *Castela* designed to construct Black Ships, dispatch men, search out yet unknown countries, open routes thereto, and do commerce. When the *pappa* (that is to say, the head of the Kirishitan religion, the representative of *Jesus Christus*) heard of this plan, he divided the routes of navigation into two. And here is the message he dispatched to the aforementioned two emperors: "Your plans, of course, are of great benefit to the wealth and reputation of your countries, and to the spread of the faith. However, it appertains to my position to determine the directions to which those who spread the faith are dispatched. The emperor of *Portugal* to the east, the emperor of *Castela* to the west: thus dispatch your men and spread the faith! And if at any time you should tear away and take over some lands, any place, treat them as you please." Thus the *pappa* determined; and accordingly men of those two countries crossed the seas to the several directions, tore away and took over many places with no trouble, and thus they continue to act this way. Is this not theft by religion?

The routes arbitrated by Pope Alexander VI in the Treaty of Tordesillas of 1494 were to converge upon Japan in the late sixteenth century. For the Portuguese, Japan represented the extremity of eastward advance along the route of carracks which rounded the Cape of Good Hope and proceeded by way of Goa and Malacca to Macao and then the terminus of Nagasaki. For the Castilians, Japan was a locus in tangential proximity to the pole of their westward expansion which, having crossed the Atlantic to Mexico, spanned also the Pacific to the Philippines; the Manila Galleon on its way back to Acapulco skirted the Japanese coast. Hideyoshi's Japan was within the intersect of the two spheres of influence.

Iberian rivalries were in fullest acrimony transplanted to this soil. Spaniards encroached upon Portuguese prerogatives after the union of the two crowns in the person of Philip Habsburg. Indeed, there were some who maintained—leaning on Pope Alexander's decision—that Japan was a sort of Far West and therefore appertained to the Crown of Castile. Yet another historical curiosity is the sight of Portuguese loyalists in Japan disclaiming at the court of Hideyoshi the legality of the Spanish Philip's accession, to break a lance for Dom Antonio, Prior of Crato, a bastard of the Portuguese House of Avis.[55]

One of the conditions to which Philip agreed at his accession was to keep strictly separate the administrations of the Spanish and Portuguese overseas territories and interests. This capitulation involved not only the political and economic levels, but also the religious: the Portuguese *padroado* of missions and the Spanish *patronazgo* were to be kept distinct. There was constant Spanish erosion of these demarcations. Valignano, as we have seen in a previous chapter, had worked mightily to keep Spanish friars out of Japan; but he was not successful, despite his use of papal brief and viceregal injunction. The Franciscans who arrived in 1593 from Manila as ambassadors to Hideyoshi remained in Kyoto as missionaries. The expulsion edict of 1587 had not been revoked; the Jesuits, who since had achieved a tenuous *modus vivendi* with the Taikō, did not flout it. But the Franciscans, no sooner ensconced, were—as Boxer inimitably puts it—

behaving generally as if they were in Rome rather than in a country where the letter if not the spirit of the law expressly prohibited the practice of Christianity. The Jesuits and such local Japanese officials as were friendly to Christianity were naturally aghast at this intemperate zeal. They more than once remonstrated with the friars over their reckless behavior, advising them to tread delicately like Agag, and to dress as Buddhist priests as the Jesuits did. The infatuated friars not only laughed these warnings to scorn, but boasted that they basked in the sunshine of Hideyoshi's favor, accusing the Jesuits of cowardice for going about their work in disguise.[56]

Boxer, with considerable relish, pursues the theme of Friars Minor possessed by a plebeian sort of hubris and heading toward certain (disaster of?) martyrdom, a fate presaged by the wreck of the Manila Galleon *San Felipe* on the shores of Tosa and consummated in Nagasaki on 5 February 1597.

Boxer's treatment of the relations between Jesuits and friars in Japan is sympathetic to the Jesuit and Portuguese point of view, to the disadvantage of the Franciscan and Spanish. It is difficult to establish a balance. It is indisputable that members of the two orders were in Japan (to use a Japanese turn of phrase) dog and monkey to each other. But it is nearly impossible to determine what causal relationship existed between the monkish quarrels and Hideyoshi's move to bloody persecution. The martyrdom was heroic but its background humiliating. The actuality of events is hidden in a morass of aspersions, counter-claims, and philippics.

Matsuda Kiichi, collating sources in his usual highly scrupulous manner, has established the following sequence of events:[57]

1596

19.X.	*San Felipe* adrift in the sandbanks off Urado Bay in Shikoku;
20.X.	*San Felipe* sits fast on a reef;
24.X.	Captain Matias Landecho's emissaries leave Urado for Kyoto (these include the Franciscans Juan Pobre and Felipe de las Casas);
27.X.	Hideyoshi's agent Mashita Uemon no Jō Nagamori issues orders to various neighboring provinces for ship's carpenters and other craftsmen to organize the transfer of confiscated goods from the *San Felipe*; the Chōsogabe of Tosa issue similar orders;
29.X.	the resident Franciscan Pedro Bautista from Osaka sends
(30.X.?)	Landecho a letter assuaging his worries;
1.XI.	Dom Pedro Martins SJ, the Bishop of Japan, leaves Nagasaki for Kyoto;
12.XI.	Mashita Nagamori arrives in Urado;
14.XI.	Bishop Martins arrives in Kyoto;

16.XI.   Hideyoshi receives Martins in audience at Fushimi;
30.XI.   Mashita arrives in Fushimi to report to the Taikō;
7.XII.   Bishop Martins departs Kyoto;
8.XII.   Day of the Immaculate Conception; the Franciscan residence
           in Kyoto is surrounded by guards.

So far, so good. These facts are independent of prejudiced twists
of interpretation and are derived from immediate sources. But it
would be rash to disagree with Matsuda's judgment that any
further attempts to fix responsibility for Hideyoshi's action would
represent mere guesswork.

Jesuits heaped the blame for the confiscation of the Spanish
galleon and for the ensuing persecution upon Franciscan excess of
missionary zeal, ineptness in diplomacy, and wild-eyed insistence
upon empty legality. Franciscans attributed the tragedy to a
Jesuitical plot. At the bottom of the antagonism (as Hubert
Cieslik SJ takes care to point out) were not doctrinal disputes
but an exacerbated nationalism. Even the most severe Jesuit
opponents of the Franciscans, such as Bishop Martins and Padre
Jeronymo de Angelis, "wrote time and again that all problems
would be solved if only Portuguese Franciscans came to Japan."[58]
On the other hand, there were among the Jesuits of Japan
Spaniards, such as Vice-Provincial Pedro Gomez and Padre
Pedro Morejón, who welcomed their Franciscan compatriots
into the country. But no sooner had the Portuguese Bishop
Martins arrived in Nagasaki (14 August 1596) than he reversed
the approach of Gomez. Armed with ecclesiastical and secular
injunctions, he threatened the Spanish friars with canonical
punishment for their intrusion. Bishop Martins caused the
antagonisms to explode into the open.

The Bishop presents the Jesuit version of this *cause célèbre* with
absolute assurance: "I certify that the cause and occasion of the
friars' death . . . they themselves brought about by their mode
of procedure in the work of conversion, and that is the truth."[59]
And he further details the background of the tyrant's fatal impulse
in terms which make assurance double sure:[60]

As Christianity was enjoying such tranquillity [in Japan], it was
unsettled by the outbreak of this 2nd persecution, on account of the
Spanish ship which was on its way from Manila to New Spain and
was cast ashore by a tempest in these lands of Japan; for when
Cambaco [Hideyoshi] decided to seize its cargo, the major pretext
he used to cloak this tyrannical crime and act of brigandage was to

state that the Spaniards on this ship had come for no good purpose but rather as spies and conquistadors, toward that end taking along friars and monks. These would first produce Christians [among the populace] and then, with the Christians once there, the land would be taken over, as was done (he said) in other parts. And that is what a Spaniard told in Urando, the port of Tossa, to [Mashita Uemon no Jō], who had asked him how [his countrymen] had conquered lands as distant from their own as Peru and New Spain. Hence [Hideyoshi] leapt to the conclusion that the friars of St. Francis, who had been in Meaco near unto three years, should also be taken for spies. And also, certain pagans who were his intimates denounced them for making Christians, contrary to his edict; so that he ordered the friars killed, as well as some of their Christians for having accepted the laws the friars preached to them.

The most factitious aspect of the problem is the testimony concerning a fifth column of friars. That missionary activity was only a prelude to invasion was a form of aspersion current in Japan decades before the *San Felipe* incident. But the Jesuit side of the story weighs heavily upon a particular Spanish indiscretion as direct cause of Hideyoshi's decision. The Jesuit/Portuguese focus is on the figure of a Spaniard on board the galleon—the ship's pilot, Francisco de Olandía—who, in his ire at the confiscation of the cargo, attempted to impress the *bugyō* Mashita with tales of the Spanish design for world conquest and its efficient vanguard, Spanish friars. When Mashita reported this news, Hideyoshi broke out in wrath against the friars and passed the sentence of death upon them and their Christians. And here we have yet another instance of sudden lycanthropy.

The Franciscan/Spanish accounts blame Portuguese for spreading about slanders of Spanish thefts by religion, and claim that such intelligence was sent to Mashita from Kyoto before his interview with the pilot took place. "And so the pilot is blamed for no reason at all, because he is blameless," states the Franciscan Juan Pobre de Zamora. Then he records Mashita's lurid conversation with several Spaniards on what amounted to highly subversive and disloyal Portuguese denials of Spanish legitimacy. Mashita, it seems, was not uninterested in cabbages and kings: "Well, then, who is this don Antonio, and why did the King don Phelipe turn him out of the kingdom, and for what reason does [Philip] make war against England and the Grand Turk?" Well might the Spaniards marvel at hearing "such strange questions."[61]

Martins indignantly rejected all allegations that Portuguese had turned informers on the Spaniards, certifying that no Portuguese were in Kyoto at the time in question, early November 1596.[62] But could it be that the Bishop's assurance was false? Matsuda Kiichi claims that João Rodriguez Tçuzzu had at that time been in Kyoto and Fushimi, attempting to arrange an audience with Hideyoshi for Martins, and that Padre Organtino (not a Portuguese, but a sympathizer) was there also.[63] The assertion seems incorrect, at least in the instance of Rodriguez. At a formal process convened by the Jesuits in Nagasaki in the late summer of 1597 a whole series of witnesses swore that neither he nor any Portuguese was in Kyoto, Fushimi, Osaka, or neighboring parts when the galleon's emissaries arrived there; and there is further evidence to suggest that he was absent.[64] Whether his absence precludes the presence of others potentially inimical to Spain is, of course, a different problem. Nor was the mere confiscation of the ship the key question.

On balance it seems not at all unlikely that Portuguese and Jesuits, attempting to protect their trade and mission monopoly, resorted to stories of Castilian piracy and usurpation. The interloper had to be branded as such before the third party—a more difficult task if allegiance to the same king were admitted. Hence the shade of Dom Antonio may well have entered upon the stage: the Portuguese were to be totally dissociated from denouncable Spanish designs. The Taikō and his servitor Mashita—to borrow again the words of Fray Juan Pobre—"could not possibly have known of such matters unless the Portuguese had in fact produced the information." The disavowals repeated at length by Bishop Martins are not convincing.

It is highly probable that there was (as Matsuda Kiichi insists) a connection between the movements of Martins and Mashita and the Taikō's decision to do away with the friars. Perhaps Hideyoshi made his decision after being assured by Martins that action against the Spanish missionaries would not imperil the continuation of his profitable trade with the Portuguese. Perhaps he took the step to persecution under the influence of disturbing reports from Mashita, who had entrapped the Spanish castaways of Urado in damaging statements. Only one thing may be said with certainty: the Taikō's manner of dealing with the *San Felipe* incident signals yet another stage in the formation of the Sakoku policy. The major constituents of the anti-Christian aspect of Sakoku were complete in 1597 with the apotheosis of the Twenty-Six Saints of Japan.[65]

The *Kirishitan monogatari* of 1639 reports on this antecedent of Tokugawa measures in scandalmongering tones. A group of Iruman concoct a (not further specified) plot. News of their criminal activity leaks out, and Hideyoshi determines to slash at the Kirishitans' very roots. Twenty-five of the culprits have their ears and noses slit, are placed in tumbrils, dragged through the Capital, and transported to Nagasaki.

Along the way they were constantly looking for a miracle from Deus, gazing up at the sky, peering across the mountains—but there wasn't even a dewdrop of a miracle, and their faces became drawn with fright and disappointment. They were crucified at Nagasaki. For a while a guard was posted at the site; but then the bodies rotted on the crosses. Their bones and skulls were stolen by other believers, and afterwards the crosses, too, were whittled down to toothpicks. These relics were used as amulets, and what is more (so report has it), were later bartered at high prices.

Christian sources present rather the picture of a truly blessed, indefatigable, and even joyous progress to a "hill like Calvary." Indeed, a substantial cult developed subsequently about this first of many Golgothas for the Church of Japan. But for the historian the important point is that 1597 marks the end of the first half of the "Christian Century." Although it is true that Japanese Christianity for a while thereafter enjoyed tranquillity and even prosperity (its first persecutor Hideyoshi dead the following year, and Ieyasu, the next lord of the *Tenka*, not turning wolf until a decade and a half later), it was like a Great Ship sailing in the eye of a typhoon, its problem after 1597 no longer that of acceptance but of survival.

What were the blasts which followed Hideyoshi's political thunderbolts? The second half of the "Christian Century" was marked by the increasing ravages of persecution. An ideological platform was built for the rejection of Christianity, and the image of perniciousness erected upon it. Propagandists trucking hyperbole attempted to mobilize the common populace against the Christian peril. But the prevalence of shoddy pop art need not obscure the presence of sophisticated, although at times malicious, academic discourse. The most significant actor of the intellectual confrontation was the religious turncoat Fabian Fucan.

His career spanned the two halves of the "Christian Century." A highly talented Christian apologist, he was also nonpareil critic; to him we now turn our attention.

Chapter 6

Pilgrim's Progress:
Fabian Fucan

$\mathfrak{F}$ABIAN FUCAN is a name unavoidably associated with disputations.

The image of disputatiousness is firmly drawn by the authors who have at one time or another commented upon him, and who have given him his modicum of immortality in the Japanese tradition. Hayashi Razan in the *Hai Yaso*—the record of an interview which took place in 1606—depicts him as an arrogant, irascible, and withal not very clever discussant of such substantial things as the Great Ultimate. The anonymous authors of the *Kirishitan monogatari* genre make him the central figure of their narratives' structure, a bad loser of somewhat vulgar encounters with Buddhological experts. And Akutagawa Ryūnosuke in one of his "Kirishitan Stories" makes Fabian debate Lucifer incarnate, with results quite foreseeable.[1]

Of Fabian's twin *chefs d'oeuvre*, one—the *Myōtei mondō* of 1605—is a dialogue between two ladies, who illustrate to their own satisfaction the verities of the Christian faith, exalting them against the base falsehoods of Buddhism, Confucianism, and Shinto. The other major work—the *Ha Daiusu* of 1620—attempts to go about the task of destroying wickedness and demonstrating truth in quite a contrary fashion: here it is the Christian adversary who suffers demolition at the hands of a Fabian armed with every device that traditional East Asian systems of thought could supply. The sum of his two major treatises makes the author into a disputator against himself. Since the works are equally brilliant, it is an interesting battle of wits. He had—it is obvious—quite a checkered career.

Fabian was a double apostate. His own words on the matter are as follows:

I joined [the Kirishitan] creed at an early age; diligently, I studied its teachings and pursued its practices. Due to my stupidity, however, I was long unable to realize that this was a perverse and cursed faith. Thus fruitlessly I spent twenty years and more! Then one day I clearly perceived that the words of the adherents of Deus were very clever and appeared almost reasonable—but in their teaching there was little truth. So I left their company.[2]

The self-justification bears a tone of disappointment with Jesuitry. But it does not ring quite true. The words of the Padres of the Society of Jesus may, to the Japanese of the Momoyama period, have borne only the semblance of truth, but Fabian himself was their principal purveyor in intellectual circles. And it was purest sophistry to turn about, as Fabian did in *Ha Daiusu*, and use the very same arguments once marshaled in support of the Christian position to prove the contrary when the time so dictated. The caprioles were dazzling: in some cases, classical quotations applied in the *Myōtei mondō* by way of an apologia for the Christian posture in Japan were utilized in *Ha Daiusu* in discussions of the same points, to reinforce the current aspersions. The tracks of Fabian the Christian were covered by Fabian's *Doppelgänger*. As Fujita Kankai has demonstrated in a very plausible thesis, Fabian obtained in the *Kirishitan monogatari* of 1639 a double apotheosis.[3] The erratic Fabian who figures in the pages of that narrative as "a Zen monk originally and then turned renegade," the zealot whose "eyes kept turning round and round, and his mouth also . . . with a flood of words like swift-running water, and never a hitch"—this is undoubtedly the historical Fabian Fucan, in a description which flatters him very little. But his partner in diatribe, the ascetic "Devotee of the Way named Hakuō Koji" is merely the historical Fabian's *alter ego*. The *Kirishitan monogatari* may state that Hakuō had "realized the identity of all elements. Rapt in Zen Concentration and Meditation, his body clouded by drifts of incense smoke, he looked quite like a mystic sage. And the eloquence of this disciple of Buddha would have baffled even the matchless Furuna!"[4] But Hakuō still is the image of that same Fabian, grown old, apostate, and from a certain standpoint wise.

This pilgrim's progress has few ascertainable facts which could serve as markings. His provenance is an unresolved question. It would, of course, be folly to credit the descriptive detail of the *Kirishitan monogatari* genre. On the other hand, Fabian is the recurrent *jitsuaku* figure of the genre's *dramatis personae*, and the pervasiveness of the traditional accounts does lend some support to the assumption that the general sketch of his background is not totally inaccurate.

In the *Nanbanji kōhaiki* (The rise and fall of the Temple of Southern Barbarians), a work of the early eighteenth century, Fabian appears as one of three converts who, "possessing wisdom and cleverness, became disciples of the Bateren and were put to the task of indoctrinating ignorant fools."[5] He is here "a native of the country of Kaga, who as a priest of the Zen Sect took the name Eshun. This priest, suffering leprosy, his body eaten away by sores so that bloody pus dripped from it and there were boils all over, could no longer perform his priestly duties in converse with people. His parents were poor and could not afford to give him treatment; so he became a beggar and came to Kyoto." In his miserable place of refuge he is found by minions of the Temple of Southern Barbarians, and in a few months recuperates totally under the expert ministrations of two foreign Iruman. In repayment of the immense debt of gratitude, he becomes a devotee of the Kirishitan faith, pledging to exert himself to the ultimate for his new religion. The missionaries rejoice in the new convert's capabilities, and give him the name Baian—a Fabian corrupted.

The scabrous depiction of Fabian's motive for conversion is a literary device. Deprecation of a candidate for Christianity is here combined with capitalization on the exotic effect: the scabby cured by the quasi-magical and put to its service; abhorrence neatly mixed with fascination for the plebeian audience. Fabian's two fellow converts are, of course, also grotesquely afflicted: one with the pox, the other with a harelip; both scooped up by the Kirishitans' scouts from underneath the Tōji floor. Other narratives of the same genre give the same conventionalized account, with the same description of motive.[6] The chapbooks' purpose was the perpetuation of the image of Christianity as the pernicious faith, and their general character was designed to serve this purpose among a low-level readership. Accordingly, their contents present much that is fantastic, cut just enough with the factual to make the whole appear plausible. It is difficult in this case to disentangle the embellishments from the facts. One feels comfortable only with the postulate that Fabian, before he became a Christian and a Jesuit, was a Buddhist monk. There are Jesuit sources which list his name under the variants "Unquio Fabian" and "Vnguio fabiam"; and "Unkyo," "Ungyo," or "Ungyō" do suggest a certain Zen flavor.[7] But the best testimony to Fabian's experience of a Buddhist monastery schooling is, of course, his own writings. Both the *Myōtei mondō* and *Ha Daiusu* offer ample evidence of intimate and profound familiarity with traditional learning. Fabian's range of allusion and citation from Chinese classics and Buddhist texts is quite astonishing. He could hardly have picked up this knowledge under Jesuit tutelage. Rather, the missionaries must indeed have rejoiced in the expertise which Fabian brought with him. He was not the first Buddhist monk to be recruited into the ranks of the Society of Jesus and its helpers in Japan; but for a good while he may have been the most useful.

Fabian entered the Society in 1586 as an Irmão; that much may be stated with a measure of certainty. A codex of the Ajuda Library in Portugal includes in its list of Irmãos accepted in Japan a "Fabian de Goquinay," received that year at the *seminario* of Osaka.[8] "Unquio Fabian de la ciudad de Miaco" figures under the rubric *Scholastici Japonenses in Theol. et aliis studiis* in a Jesuit catalogue cited by Louis Delplace; the entry is for the year 1592, and gives Fabian's age as twenty-seven, his tenure in the Society as six years.[9] And Doi Tadao has published a *Roll of the houses and residences which the comp!ˀ has in the Vice province of Japan in this month of November of the year 92*: here we find "Jrᵒ Vnguio fabiam" as master of the Japanese language in the *collegio* of Amakusa. The added notation states: "knows some Latin."[10]

To this year of 1592 dates Fabian's first major effort on behalf of the Society's endeavor in Japan, the compilation of *FEIQE NO MONOGATARI*, the Jesuit version of the *Heike*.[11] The book bears the explanatory title: "simplified into the popular tongue for the sake of those desirous of learning the language and history of Japan." In the prefatory notes Fabian reproduces his mentor's instructions on the form of the task: "Now do you not make this *Heike* too bookish but copy it out in the form of a conversation between two people, with grammatic particles to suit . . . I wish you to eschew not only the floscules and curlicues of language but also the enumeration of official ranks and the attachment—so much a custom in this country!— of multiple names to one and the same person . . . Such practices serve but to disturb the gist of the matter." The stylistic effect was not the principal consideration in the minds of missionaries intent on rapid acquisition of the cultural tools necessary for their endeavor. The editor, however, was quite conscious of the problem inherent in his assignment.

"Fucan Fabian" signed his preface on 10 December 1592, after repeated protestations that the results of his editorship were conditioned by the necessity of simplification. "I prostrate myself"—he says—"and I beg: Learned and virtuous gentlemen, read this book and extend to me your sympathies. And do not ridicule my short measure of talent!" This was not merely an expression of editorial modesty or of fraudulent concern. The Amakusa *FEIQE* is a curious mélange: the classic *Heike monogatari* is here somewhat vulgarized. Although Fabian states that he attempted as much as possible not to change the original wording, there are very few passages in his version which are identical or nearly identical with their correspondents in texts considered as standard. The net effect is akin to that of Shakespeare read by way of Lamb.

This is not the place to embark upon detailed textual comparisons. And it would be too much of a *tour de force* to suggest that the initial passage establishes the tone of the entire work in both instances. Still, one might do with a brief citation.

The first lines of the *Heike monogatari* are the most famous lines of Japanese literature. The first words of the *FEIQE NO MONOGATARI* are not so memorable. The samurai Uma no Jō abruptly demands to hear about the Heike. The minstrel Kiichi Kengyō as abruptly begins *in medias res*:[12]

VManojô.	Qĕgueônobŏ, Feiqe no yuraiga qiqitai fodoni, ara ara riacu xite vo catari are.
QIICHI.	Yasui coto de gozaru: vôcata catari maraxôzu. Mazzu Feiqemonogatari no caqifajime niua vogori uo qiuame, fito uomo fito to vomouanu yŏ naru mono ua yagate forobita to yŭ xôjeqi ni, Taitŏ, Nippon ni voite vogori uo qiuameta fitobito no fateta yŏdai uo catçu mŏxite cara, sate Rocufara no nhŭdŏ Saqi no Danjŏ daijin Qiyomori cô to mŏxita fito no guiôgui no fufŏna coto uo noxeta mono de gozaru. Sate sono Qiyomori no xenzo ua . . .

* * *

Uma no Jō.   Kengyō no Bō, I want to hear about the Heike. So tell me about them! Be brief, summarize.

Kiichi.   An easy thing to do: I shall give you a general account. First of all, at the beginning of the Heike Monogatari, in evidence of the fact that the likes of those who do not consider other men as human in the end did perish, the exemplary tale is told of the end of men that were steeped in pride, in Great T'ang as in Japan. Now after that comes the story of the atrocious conduct of a man called the Lay Monk of Rokuhara, the Former Chancellor of the Realm, Lord Kiyomori. Now the ancestors of this Kiyomori were . . .

Fabian's beginning is hardly the perfect lyric of the standard text. But in the end the effect proves by no means unpleasant. Fabian's version of the *Heike monogatari* is, of course, not the best basis for a judgment of his style: his effort here is directed toward an instructional simplification, and the narrative is derivative. But the effectiveness of the whole is considerable, and the book's value unquestionable. It is a good representation of the standard conversational language of the day, and of great use in its study.[13]

In all his works Fabian demonstrates command of a vigorous (some would say, of a ripe) style. In his polemics he is not sparing with expletives: desiccation is not for him. Hayashi Razan found his *Myōtei mondō* "patched together in the most plebeian Japanese." But it is needless to point out that Razan himself was hardly a master of Japanese prose; it was the snobbish addict of *kanbun* who criticized Fabian for lack of elegance. Elegance, however, need not be synonymous with excellence, and Fabian's Japanese is excellent. In an era which saw the production of no prose masterpieces, he might well rank as principal exponent of a Momoyama style in literature: a trifle vulgar perhaps, but highly colorful nonetheless.

Two other books are bound together with Fabian's FEIQE NO MONOGATARI. To represent Asia alongside the Japanese historical romance there are the sinitic Golden Words of the *Qincuxǔ*, a culling of Confucian maxims, poetic citations, and Zen aphorisms which the Jesuit Superior's imprimatur calls "Morales Sentenças." This material is clearly homiletic; indeed— as Yoshida Sumio observes—"it could be safely assumed that missionaries learning these sentences by heart, could quote them in their sermons and on other occasions to impress their hearers."[14] And also, to represent Europe, there is included nothing less than a selection of the Fables of Aesop.[15] The combination is interesting: the Asian classic and the European side by side, *catçúua cotoba qeicono tame, catçúua yono tocuno tame*—on the one hand for language practice, on the other hand for society's profit. Little did it matter that Aesop was, after all, a heathen: the Jesuit intention apparently was to obtain, through the amusing little stories, an entrée for moral example among the curious and fashionable of Momoyama. It is an unsettled question just who was the compiler of these companion pieces. Doi Tadao is inclined to think that it was not Fabian but rather his fellow instructor of Japanese at the Amakusa college, Irmão Cosme Takai.[16] It seems profitless to question this judgment. It might only be pointed out that Aesop was translated from a Latin version and that the previously cited November 1592 catalogue states expressly that Cosme knew no language outside of Japanese, but that Fabian knew some Latin. At any rate, it is certain that Fabian was a valued collaborator in the creation of a Japanese corpus of Christian devotional literature and in the Jesuit contributions to the study of Early Modern Japanese. He may have had a hand in the compilation of any or all of the dozen-odd other Japanese works extant from the production of the mission press of Amakusa and Nagasaki in the decade after the *FEIQE* was published. But this period of his life does constitute a lacuna. Nothing certain is known of him until he is found debating Razan in Kyoto, more than thirteen years after he completed work on his *FEIQE*.

The Jesuits' activity in the Capital, which after Hideyoshi's expulsion edict of 1587 had been conducted in the shadows or under the threat of actual persecution, was again given official sanction soon after Ieyasu's great victory of October 1600. That very year the Jesuits had astutely established a presence in Kamigyō, the city's northern quarter and its "most noble . . . for the Dairi dwells here, as do many other nobles and the most important people of Miaco." Before much time had passed, a church had been joined to this residence, and by 1605 a splendid church (worthy successor to the Nanbanji destroyed in 1588) had also been built in Shimogyō, the southern quarter of the Capital.[17] The Kyoto mission was resurrected with a flourish, and clearly required the best of personnel. The Jesuits' most learned and articulate Japanese apologist—a man in command of eloquent if not always elegant Japanese—would be a decided asset in this cultural center of Japan, and was assigned there. The year of Fabian's return to the Miyako area is unclear, although there is some reason to suspect his presence there by 1603. The general assumption that the *Myōtei mondō* of 1605 was produced in Kyoto seems quite reasonable.

"Jr. fabiaõ" is registered as a member of the Jesuit establishment of Shimogyō in a *Catalogue of the Houses which the Comp.ⁱ has in Japan *** of 1606.*[18] This year is relatively bountiful of reports of his activities. The relation sent by Vice-Provincial Francisco Pasio to the General of the Society on 18 October 1606 speaks of the funeral of an eminent noblewoman of Kyoto (the daughter of Maria Kyōgoku and niece of Hideyoshi's consort Yodogimi); the pompous Christian funeral caused a general scandal in the Capital and a furious Buddhist reaction, complete with appeals to Ieyasu. Significantly enough, the stirring sermon was preached by our hero, extolled in the letter as "the Japanese Irmão Fabian, who is very well versed in the doctrines of Japan, so that there is no bonze who could surpass him, nor any that would dare dispute with him."[19]

A former bonze was Fabian's most eminent adversary in debate that year. Hayashi Dōshun (better known as Razan) was not quite twenty-three years old at the time of the encounter, but all the more aware of his own talents: he was already becoming known as a prepositor of Sung Neo-Confucianism, and rivaling his teacher Fujiwara Seika as an interpreter of Chu Hsi. One gets the impression from reading Razan's account of the occasion (the *Hai Yaso*, of which a complete translation follows) that he was merely indulging in a little slumming, at the insistence of Matsunaga Teitoku, his Virgil. But he had done his homework: he came prepared to discuss the outlandish theories of Matteo Ricci. The following interchange resulted:[20]

HAI YASO
(The Anti-Jesuit)

On the fifteenth day of the sixth month of Keichō *hinoe uma* Dōshun and Nobuzumi, at the suggestion of Shōyū and not by their own intention, called on the Jesuit Mr. Fucan. Fucan had the chief gatekeeper (Fucan's attendant) show the three into a room which was filled with the adherents of that sect. They took their seats.

After the usual comments about the weather, Dōshun inquired about the portrait of Deus, asking Fucan to explain it. The response was evasive: Fucan evidently feared the exposure of his shallowness and did not elaborate.

Again, seeing their circular map, Dōshun said: "Does it not have a top and a bottom?"

Fucan said: "Mid-earth being the bottom, above the earth is heaven; and underneath the earth is heaven as well. Our country has sent ships to voyage upon the ocean. The East's extremity is West; the West's extremity is East. From this we know that the earth is round."

Dōshun said: "This reasoning is impossible. How could there be a heaven underneath the earth! An inspection of the myriad phenomena reveals that all have an up and a down. To say that there is no up and down is ignorance of reason. Furthermore: On the ocean there are winds and waves, and ships heading west may actually go north or south or even east, the men on board not recognizing the direction, thinking the while that they are going west. To say from this that the West's extremity is East is impossible. If the ship were heading east—meaning by that an actual course north or south or, inescapably, west—then to say from this that the East's extremity is West is impossible. And furthermore: In the final analysis, you are unaware of the principle that all things have an up and a down, and so assert that mid-earth is the bottom and make earth's shape be round. I cannot help lamenting this delusion! Chu Hsi states that half of heaven rotates about earth's bottom, but you are unacquainted with this."

Now Fucan said: "There is a North and a South, but no East or West."

Dōshun said: "Once North and South are affirmed, how can there be no East and West?"

I-hsing or Shen Kua. Evidently they spied celestial sphere method in Great Ming and secretly made an imitation, that is all. Laughable!
I-hsing or Shen Kua. Evidently they spied a celestial globe in Great Ming and secretly made an imitation, that is all..Laughable!

I also saw a triangular thing, in form like a crystal. If one covers his eye with it and looks at something, the object will appear five-colored. Evidently it is because it has the angles that the colors appear. And I saw an eyeglass with the surface convex and the reverse even. If one looks through it at something, the one object will divide and appear as multiple objects. Evidently it is like that because the surface side is uneven. At any rate, it is impossible with the best of will to count all such clever and marvellous implements for the dazzlement of the common people. The *Wang chih* states: "Who deludes the populace by constructing strange devices and strange implements shall be killed." How appropriate these words![21]

I also saw a book composed by Fucan, the *Myōtei mondō*, and had Fucan read from it. That book presents the two nuns Myōshū and Yūtei, who put questions to each other and answer them. Now they discuss the Buddhists (beside the Ten Sects adding Ikkō and Nichiren, making twelve sects) and now they talk about Confucianism and Shinto; not one thing worth looking at. All of it is patched together in the most plebeian Japanese: wild, hysteric imprecations and abuse— hearing it is like confronting a passing swarm of gnats and gadflies. How could one take it seriously! Nevertheless, how could one tolerate this offence of contempt for the sages!—if one put up with that, what would remain insufferable? And if the book is used to delude the foolish and the common, the gravity of the offence increases all the more. Nothing like burning the book! For if it remains in existence one will be passing down derision for a thousand years of posterity.

Dōshun inquired: "Matteo Ricci (the Jesuit) states that heaven and earth, the spirits, and man's soul have a beginning but no end. I do not believe this. If there is a beginning, then there is an end. No beginning and no end: this is possible. To have a beginning and to have no end: this is impossible. But is any further specific proof necessary?"

Fucan could not answer.

Dōshun said: "God created heaven and earth and the myriad things, etc. etc. But who is it that created God?"

Fucan said: "God has no beginning and no end."

Heaven and earth are termed creations; God is termed without beginning and without end. Such evasions may be exposed without debate.

Dōshun said: "Principle (*li*) and God: is one first and the other after?"

Fucan said: "God is Substance (*t'i*). Principle is Function (*yung*). Substance is first, and Principle is after."

Dōshun pointed to a utensil before their eyes and said: "The utensil is Substance. What gives rise to the utensil's construction is Principle. And accordingly Principle is first and God is after."

Fucan did not understand, and said: "The lamp is Substance. The light is Principle."

Dōshun said: "What gives rise to the fire's being a lamp is Principle. The light is not Principle. One simply calls it light."

Fucan still failed to understand, and said: "The locus of origin of the will to produce the utensil is posited as Principle. But before the will arises, in the original uncogitated and unwilled state, Substance exists. And accordingly Substance is first, and Principle is after."

Dōshun said: "Unallowable! We are not discussing the uncogitated and unwilled state, but only Principle and God. In the uncogitated and unwilled state, Principle exists and subsists."

Shōyū smiled and said: "The questions are sublime, the answers ridiculous. His lack of comprehension is truly lamentable."

Dōshun had something to do, and stood up to leave. At this moment, rain poured down and there was a terrific blast of thunder.

Fucan was extremely dissatisfied, and said: "The so-called Great Ultimate of the Confucians cannot measure up to God. God is not within the range of understanding of youngsters like you. But I understand the Great Ultimate perfectly."

Nobuzumi said: "You are mad and arrogant. The Great Ultimate is not something you can ever understand."

Fucan was offended, and shut his mouth.

Dōshun now sat down again and said: "This thing called logical reasoning generally means that if one side does not gain the advantage, then advantage must necessarily be with the other. If one contends determined to win, then the colors of rage and the airs of jealousy appear upon the countenance. That is the beginning of ruin to your disposition. Control this tendency!"

By now the skies had cleared, and they took their departure. Fucan accompanied them to the gate, and saw them off politely.

In addition:

The Jesuits claim that underneath the earth as well is heaven. If one were to dig through the earth and get to the bottom, and look and see, one would peer upon the sky as if viewing it mirrored in a well. If one were to drop a stone down this excavation, then it would come to rest in the middle of the earth, without a movement up or down. Now this is proof that the earth is located in the middle of heaven.

But I say: As I inspect the bounds of heaven and earth, I find not one thing which does not have an up and a down. But they take the middle and make it be the bottom: how then could they ever know the principle that each and every thing has an up and a down! If there were somebody who asked where the falling stone stops, I would certainly answer only that it falls where it falls. How could there be such a thing as movement neither up nor down!

In addition:
The Jesuits claim that heaven is round and the earth also round. But I state: There is motion and there is quiescence; there is squareness and roundness. All things are thus, and heaven and earth extraordinarily so. Moving things are round, and quiescent things square: their Principle is like this. But if it were as they say, then how could there be squareness and roundness, motion and quiescence? Nevertheless, it is not easy to persuade a man unless he listens quietly and understands and there is a meeting of minds.

It is moot to find an example here, as Mr. Ebisawa has done, of a clear juxtaposition: on one hand, the obscurantist Neo-Confucian, his "rationalism" pre-scientific, his theses unpenetrating and filled with contradictions, his bag of arguments empty at the bottom; on the other, the Christian emissary of modern tidings from the West, his logic conclusive, his spirit anti-traditional.[22] Of course, Fabian scores points on geography. But in the end the confrontation between Razan and Fabian merely illustrates to perfection the incompatibility of two patterns of thought, each with bulwarks of presuppositions which seem unshakable to its adherent, who proceeds to develop his argumentation along lines of logic *a priori* incontrovertible. The quandary is very clear in the final words of Razan's essay. Not easy, indeed, to persuade a man who is not open to understanding! There was no meeting of minds. Herein lay the tragedy of the confrontation between Christianity and Early Modern Japan. The true significance of the figure of Fabian and the peculiar interest evoked by his image is in the fact that he combines in his person both poles of reference and proves that in Early Modern Japan the West's extremity could never be East.

Unfortunately there is available no Christian libretto of this operatic encounter between Fabian and Razan. But the Jesuit *annua* for 1606 describes a parallel disputation.[23] The events discussed take place in Kyoto, and there is little doubt of the unnamed protagonist's identity. We know him by his fixed epithet: our Irmão is "more profoundly familiar with Buddhist scripture" than his Buddhist adversary. The letter regales its European audience with a petty farce in which Fabian, taking care to utilize Buddhist terms, demolishes the most eminent master of the Hokke Sect. The bonze loses control of his words, thoughts, and all his senses. The end of the scene finds him unable to stand up, his nose practically touching the floor, a cloud of bitter anxiety about his forehead, as a Christian youth does a little jig of joy to the words: "Heh! Master, that was the wrong way to do battle! . . . Take my advice, go get yourself some better arms, come back with a more solid shield!" One has the curious sensation of reading the *Kirishitan monogatari* all over again, but in reversed letters. And in the jeers of advice to the cringing bonze is also the hollow echo of Razan's parting shot at an offended Fabian, on contentiousness, colors of rage, and airs of jealousy. The significance of such japes lies in the fact that they illustrate once again the unbridgeable gulf between attitudes: each side is dogmatically convinced of its righteousness, and victory always appertains to its own.

The year 1607 sees Fabian listed in the catalogues both of February and October as attached to the Jesuit residence of Miyako.[24] This year he traveled in the company of the Vice-Provincial Francisco Pasio and of João Rodriguez Tçuzzu to call on the retired Ieyasu in Sunpu and on the Second Shogun, Hidetada, at Edo; and he seems to have had the experience of similar audiences before.[25] But this is the last time we see him figure as *persona grata* in Jesuit accounts. The next mention of his name in an available Jesuit letter occurs on 20 March 1616, when P. Jeronymo Rodriguez writes to the General of the Society:[26] "Our Father will already have been informed there of the case of Fabião, how he left the Company, apostatizing from the Religion [*i.e.*, Jesuit Order]; and it appears also that he has done the same from the Faith." It is somewhat surprising to see that the Vice-Provincial was not yet certain whether the former Irmão had abandoned Christianity together with his allegiance to the Society of Jesus; for he notes that Fabian "now is here in Nangasaqui" and complains that although he is still (technically) under the obligation of his religious vows "we cannot do anything to him, for in this land even when we are at liberty we do not possess *vim coactivam*." The status of our Christian was shadowy. We shall shortly see that this may have had special reasons.

By March 1621 there was no longer any room for uncertainty, and Joanbaptista de Baeça wrote from Nagasaki:[27] "The apostate Fabian is here and is on the verge of death. He has written a book replete with heresies and blasphemies." The book, of course, was *Ha Daiusu*. The persecution was raging in Nagasaki. And Fabian (who had in the meantime also been active in Edo) had returned to this spot to plague his former confrères. Apparently not for long. If Baeça's prediction can at all be trusted, then we may write his dates as 1565?–1621.[28]

What made Fabian turn his back on the Jesuits, abandon his Christian faith, and write his notorious treatise? His stated reason for becoming a renegade has already been adduced in the context of the general discussion of Jesuit attitudes toward their Japanese charges. He took his departure—he says—out of resentment at maltreatment and frustration at the Jesuits' refusal to admit him to the priesthood.[29] Fabian's disappointment appears natural in view of his long and incontrovertibly meritorious service as an Irmão. But there seems to have been yet another, complementary reason for his desertion.

The most interesting single piece of information concerning Fabian to come from a Jesuit pen is the letter written by Padre Mattheus de Couros to the General of the Society of Jesus and dated 15 March 1621, the day prior to Baeça's missive.[30] Not only does this letter reveal how sharp was the sting of *Ha Daiusu*, it also alludes to the background of the book's composition; most important, it lays open a critical date in Fabian's career. Couros' words are:

In the meantime there has been no change in the temporal estate of Japan. The xogun continues to rule in great peace, nor does there appear to be anyone likely to risk some new sally.

The persecution of Christianity goes on, nor do we have any human hope that it will end so soon, for it is based principally upon reasons of state, as the xõgun and his Governors in their hearts cleave to the notion that the law of God is a design and device for the conquest of kingdoms, although—so as not to reveal that they fear us—they proffer other complaints to the exterior. Now since this theme is of itself so hate-provoking, Gonrocu the President of Nagasaqui perceived that this way he could most easily topple the Christians, and this last time that he came back from the Court he brought with him the Apostate Fabiam. It will be thirteen years ago that [Fabiam], who was at the time our Irmão, fled the Compỹ with one of the several devout women who lived a common life in a House adjoining ours in Miyaco, and soon thereafter he abandoned the faith of Christ. And he always stood by [Murayama] Tóan in the suit that he had against Feizo, in which that same Tóan also falsely accused us of various things, aiming to destroy us in Japan.

In the past months this Fabiam came out with a tract against the law of God, called Sattaixu, in which he aspires to persuade the Japanese that [this law] is false and sham and that our intent in its promulgation is nought else but to subjugate and usurp these king-doms.[31] And in order that Our Father [General] see what this miserable wretch has written I have translated this same tract as faithfully as I could into the Portuguese language, and I had two P^{es} who are the best interpreters that we have today in Japan check my rendition with the Japanese original itself: Now I send it via two routes, by way of the Philippines together with this [letter]: and also I shall send it to Macao to My Lord Bishop, and to the P^{e} Visit^{or}

As soon as I learned that it began circulating in Nagasaqui, I ordered that all the Confraternities in which the Christians of this place are distributed be warned that no one be allowed either to read it or keep it, and I collected several copies that were being disseminated; but since I have already been informed by letter from the Cami [Kansai] that there was talk about it there, it is probable that this pestilence of Hell is also proliferating, like poison ivy [?], in those parts. And although almost all the doubts which the Apostate raises as arguments against our Holy faith also are touched on and resolved in special tracts that have been composed and published by our people in Japan, such as the Compendium of P^{e} Pero Gomez which the Dojucus are lectured on after they have perfected their Latin;[32] nevertheless I have charged the P^{es} my Consultants, and others, that they should write anew something that could be presented concerning these [doubts], so that we would put forth an entirely new tract against this [work of the Apostate's].—

In the light of this letter (the censorious comments about *Ha Daiusu* apart) Fabian appears as the anticipator of a very modern dilemma. The case of the religious who transgresses his vows—particularly those of celibacy—and abandons his vocation is a problem which in recent years has confronted the Catholic Church with ever greater frequency and seriousness. The lost sheep is even in these days condemned by some as a Judas; in Fabian's day the opprobrium was at least as severe. But for him the dilemma was perhaps not very difficult to escape: the factor of resentment assisted. He had not been made a priest; why then should he remain celibate and subject to the monastic rigors? Of course, certain scars of the psychological trauma remained. For more than twenty years he had wielded his talents with exemplary skill on behalf of the Society. This effort had remained fruitless. At the end of his life he mustered his redoubtable intellectual and rhetoric resources to produce a denunciation of what his previous career had stood for.

Deus Destroyed—the *Ha Daiusu* of 1620—has been described by the eminent critic Ebisawa Arimichi as a vengeful, offensive diatribe pure and simple.[33] An even more eminent critic, Shinmura Izuru, at one time intimated that the book, while purporting to be a confutation of Christianity, was actually a covert attempt to present in the only allowable form Christianity's doctrines.[34] This latter notion is rather too fanciful. But neither is Ebisawa's deprecation precisely fair. Very few people like an apostate, and Professor Ebisawa perhaps less than most. Accordingly, he damns Fabian for seizing the chance to pour out his rancor at the very time when Christians were being subjected to relentless persecution, for assuming a meretriciously threatening attitude, and for publishing *Deus Destroyed*. But the exact circumstances of the book's publication are yet unknown. In what sense did the atmosphere of 1620 represent a "good chance" to get back at the Christians? *Deus Destroyed* in a very marked way displays the traces of a defensive treatise. Perhaps that was Fabian's measure of self-perception: there were many recantations to be made.

There was, to start with, the authorship of the *Myōtei mondō* to live down. It was no mere accident that Fabian stated in the introduction to *Ha Daiusu*, in 1620: "So I left their company. Some fifteen years have passed since: every morning I have lamented my desertion of the Great Holy True Law; every evening I have grieved over my adherence to the crooked path of the barbarians."[35] The fifteen years take us back to 1605, the date of composition of the *Myōtei mondō*: and Fabian was very anxious to imply that he had done nothing untoward since. But in 1606 Razan, in a general way, had deemed him and his fellow deluders of the populace worthy of execution. In the same year of 1606 Fabian had preached at a funeral which was associated with uproar; and his disputation with the priest of the Lotus Sect had also caused a considerable stir in the Capital. His reputation was clearly scandalous, and no less persistent— the popular *Kirishitan monogatari* genre contains ample testimony to the long life of the odious image. In short, it may well be that Fabian, instead of threatening in the midst of persecution, felt himself to be one of the threatened. *Ha Daiusu* thus appears as a detailed recantation of past errors, and a chance for Fabian to prove his loyalty. The tones of direct address to the shogun, and the obloquies on the subject of Ōkubo Iwami no Kami, would seem to support this assumption. *Ha Daiusu* in some aspects of its structure takes the form of direct repudiation of *Myōtei mondō*. In this sense the rather double-meaning utterance of 1620 achieves a deeper significance: "I had a friend who remonstrated with me, saying, 'If you have made a mistake, do not be afraid of admitting the fact and amending your ways.'" The phrase was perhaps not merely the trite Confucian maxim[36] it appears to be.

Fabian's moratorium—not of fifteen but of twelve years since desertion—had come to an end. It was time to undo the damage once wrought, by dissecting (his own) "cursed teachings into little pieces to proffer to my august audience." The rhetoric of the text's climactic Seventh Step appears to be directly addressed to the shogun Hidetada, subjugator of perfidy and promoter of merit, perspicacious of ear and eye, sagacious in mind and will. The turn of irony becomes complete as one considers the account which states that Fabian during his visit to Sunpu in 1607 saw presented to Ieyasu's and Hidetada's intimate, Honda Kōzuke, his book on Christian doctrine, supposedly written especially for the occasion but quite obviously the *Myōtei mondō*.[37] Or is there more poignancy in the statement of a martyred contemporary that Fabian's anti-Christian book was indeed written expressly for the eyes of the shogun?

In the Archives of the Dominican Province of the Most Holy Rosary in Manila is a manuscript volume on the History of the Church in Japan. The author is Jacinto Orfanel OP, a friar who was burnt at the stake in Nagasaki during the Great Martyrdom of 1622. And there, inserted as an afterthought into the context of an apologia for that same Murayama Tōan about whom Padre de Couros had complained, is the following text:[38]

There is another very substantial piece of testimony in favor of Toan, that of a certain Fabian Apostate from the faith (who was in Yedo when they killed him, and knew his affairs very well) in a booklet which he has now put out against Christianity, replete with heresies and blasphemies against God and His infinite goodness and providence. Since he was not rooted in studies and wanted to penetrate and scrutinize the [Divine] Majesty he found himself in the dark.

Now it may be assumed furthermore that he who is the most abject in confessing his inability to comprehend God is in fact the most learned and the very one who fathoms Him best; for that Divine Substance infinitely exceeds our natural powers of comprehension, nor would He be God if any created intellect were to reach Him. But that fool of a Fabian, ignorant of this principle which is evident in philosophy, wanted to measure the measureless, find an end point to that which does not possess one, and to speak with his perverse tongue of Him Who is ineffable; and for all that he fell aslant and even into heresy, and reverted to the idols whom he could measure in the palm of his hand, thus fulfilling his desires. He also says in his book many things about the religious, and one of them is that they keep the Christians under deception; and also that Tocuã, disobeying on their account the laws of the emperor, was the cause of the death of his father and brothers. And although this one's testimony—for his being what he is—is of no value, nevertheless if it had not been so he would not have dared to write it, because Gonrocu and Feizo were sure to see it, at whose instance the book was produced, in order to send it to the emperor. And before him lies had to be avoided all the more; for no one is better acquainted with the matter than he who had him killed. And so what I make of all this is that one at least of the causes, and perhaps the principal one, of his death was on account of the faith.

This added leaf of text has the nub of an interesting question concerning Fabian. What was his role in yet another scandal? Murayama Tōan, with whom Fabian is again associated here, was one of the period's more notorious personages. Tōan's suit against "Feizo"—Suetsugu Heizō—was no ordinary matter; neither was an ordinary man; the resonance of the episode was extraordinary and spread as far as Europe.

Couros asserts that Fabian always stood by Tōan; Orfanel states that Fabian knew Tōan's affairs very well and testified to his persistence in the faith. In this association there was the stuff of yet another renunciation on the part of Fabian. And hidden within it is perhaps also the answer to Jeronymo Rodriguez' lack of certainty whether or not Fabian in 1616 could still be considered Christian.

The actualities of the Murayama Tōan Affair are as difficult to determine as those surrounding the galleon *San Felipe*, and for much the same reasons. To the Jesuits Tōan was anathema, *este hombre diabólico*.[39] The Dominicans defended him as one of the most stalwart pillars and buttresses that upheld the Christian cause in its hour of peril.[40] The truth is sunk deep in the morass of recriminations. What makes it almost impossible to grasp is the fact that Tōan was in every sense of the word a lubricious figure.

The pedantic scribbler Richard Cocks, chief of that bankrupt venture, the English Factory in Japan, sized him up as "the richest man in Japon, and com up of base parentage by his subtil and craftie wyt."[41] Another merchant, the Spaniard Bernardino de Avila Girón, made a similar estimate of a man who rose to great riches and power by his ready intelligence, great industriousness, and clever business sense.[42] The Jesuits regretfully attributed the causes of his initial rise to themselves.[43]

Indeed, Antonio Murayama owed much to the Jesuits. A lucky interview with Hideyoshi gave him the prestige he needed to come to prominence in Nagasaki.[44] But it was the intercession of João Rodriguez Tçuzzu with Ieyasu that enabled him to solidify his position and ultimately to become magistrate (*daikan*) of Nagasaki.[45] The concord lasted until the notorious incident of the carrack *Nossa Senhora da Graça*. Her captain André Pessoa on Epiphany Day 1610 blew up this vessel rather than see her taken by a Japanese flotilla; the Jesuits accounted Tōan the principal instigator of the plot to seize the ship, and it does seem that he further enriched himself with the plunder.[46] This affair caused the parting of the ways between Tōan and the Jesuits (quite literally for Rodriguez, who was that same year forced to leave Japan). Their mutual hate mounted thereafter. The Jesuits viewed Tōan as their greatest adversary in Japan and the root of all their troubles: "apostate" was one of their milder words for him. What galled them most was that Tōan entered into what they deemed an unholy compact with the Dominicans.[47]

It is fortunate for the historian that there was on the scene a neutral observer—Avila Girón—who depicted the depraved streak in Tōan's character but also bore witness to his return to righteousness. According to Avila, Tōan was so corrupted by his riches and power that he became a reckless voluptuary, spent money like water on women (in return being infected with the chancres), lived "like a Turk in his harem," and eradicated entire families in order to obtain yet another victim for his debaucheries. Because this style of life could scarcely be called Christian— comments the Spaniard—"there were those who thought that it would be an easy thing to make him abandon the faith."[48]

But when the first waves of the General Persecution of 1614 approached Nagasaki there occurred in Tōan a great change.

The *bugyō* Hasegawa Sahyōe's letter concerning the expulsion of the missionaries, the destruction of their churches, and the requirement to reconvert their flock was delivered to Tōan at the beginning of May 1614. What followed was an extraordinary burst of fervor on the part of the Nagasaki Christians. The whole city was swept up in a series of expiatory processions and demonstrations of willingness to martyrdom.[49] In a procession of more than three thousand flagellants which departed from the Church of Saint Dominic on 19 May could also be seen Tōan and his children. The leaders of this procession were all friars; Tōan was by the side of the Augustinian prior. The next day Tōan participated alongside his son, the diocesan curate Francisco, in a similar devotional march from the Church of Saint Augustine. But in the description of the Jesuits' procession—could it be due to the author's inadvertence?—Murayama Tōan is conspicuously absent. Christianity was no longer a Jesuit monopoly. And Tōan was a new man, at least according to Avila Girón, who sighs in astonishment: he bore a heavy cross on his shoulders, and down his back streamed blood.[50]

These great outpourings of religious emotion could not fail to alarm the Bakufu. The city appeared to be in open revolt; and the *daikan*'s prominent role among the Christian penitents could scarcely do anything but destroy his position. Tōan seems to have tried to recoup by a series of desperate ploys. The expedition he fitted out at his own cost in 1616 to invade Taiwan was probably an attempt to save himself from the shogunate's ire by the opening of a new sphere for Japan's prosperity.[51] When his thirteen ships were blown to the winds, he ventured an embassy to the Ming to seek trade, but this also met failure. And before all that—although Cocks wrote that Tōan's Formosan fleet actually meant to head for the Ryūkyūs "to look for Fidaia Samme"[52]—he had attempted to cover his bets by sending succor to that very same Hideyori Sama in Osaka Castle; his son, the priest Francisco, perished when the castle fell to the Bakufu armies in 1615. That became the cardinal factor of his doom. What his rival Heizō could not accomplish by denouncing him for financial misfeasance and wanton murders he obtained by branding him an enemy of the state.

Suetsugu Heizō João came from a family of Christians baptized (according to Heizō's own claim) by Saint Francis Xavier him-self.[53] His father, Suetsugu Kōzen Cosme, was a famous merchant with interests in Hakata, Sakai, and Nagasaki, so that Heizō was originally better established than Tōan; the successes of the newly risen must have rankled. Like Tōan, he was active in the Japanese Southeast Asian trade, and the general sweep of his ambitions was also similar to Tōan's. What resulted was a bourgeois tragedy: the two principal citizens of Nagasaki engaged in a venomous contest for position, profit, and power. Heizō had evidently laid his ground with great care, "equipping himself with papers and proofs for ten or twelve years" before he presented his accusations that Tōan had habitually embezzled Bakufu income.[54]

The affair burst into the open in the first weeks of 1618, and the dates of its progress can be followed in the gossip which Cocks entered into his diary.[55] In January he refers to Heizō's quarrel with "Tuan Dono, the rich (as they terme hym) . . . whome this man hath gotten a sentence against, and utterly undon Tuan." In June he receives a letter from Nagasaki to the effect that Heizō had accused Tōan of "murthering 17 or 18 Japons without law or justice" but been told to concern himself more with the living than with the dead: so then he "apeached Twan and his children as Christians and maintayners of Jesuistes and fryres." And in August he reports that Tōan has lost, all his goods being confiscated and "his lyfe at Emperours pleasure."

The "Jesuistes" would have found it bitter irony to see Tōan described as their maintainer; they intimated darkly that the "fryres" had incited him into plots against them.[56] The Dominicans, on the other hand, believed that the Jesuits had abetted Heizō's intrigue with their counsel and money. What aroused the suspicions of the friars most was that after Heizō's victory all properties connected with Christian churches in Nagasaki—except the Jesuits'—were parceled out, and that Heizō himself took over the site of the Church of Saint Dominic, building his house with the stones of the church and "emplacing himself where we used to keep the Most Holy Sacrament."[57] The Jesuits gathered affidavits to prove that they had had nothing to do with Heizō, Tōan, or Hideyori's last stand. And they stated that Tōan in a last attempt to clear himself supplied the Bakufu with a suspiciously edited list of hidden priests: "while knowing very well that in Japan and in Nagasaki there were friars—his intimates—and Japanese secular priests, he denounced none of them but only those of the Society."[58] The near-contemporary Jesuit historian Daniello Bartoli names the two authors of the list, and one of them is Fabian.[59]

Murayama Tōan was banished to "an island which lies adjacent to Yendo." In March 1619 his eldest son, André Tokuan, was seized for concealing missionaries; on 18 November he was martyred in Nagasaki. The Dominican accounts put the son's martyrdom into a direct causal relationship with the father's death. Tōan was decapitated in Edo on 1 December 1619. His son Juan Shūan, the Formosan venturer, met with the same punishment. Two other sons, Pedro and Paulo, also were executed in Kyoto.[60]

This sort of family history would seem ideally suited for inclusion in the *ubi sunt* section of Fabian's *Ha Daiusu*. And yet, Fray Orfanel's elaborate statement to the contrary, the names Tōan and Tokuan are to be found nowhere in the extant text, which has a preface signed on 19 February 1620. It is difficult to believe that Orfanel was mistaken in his review of the book. Perhaps the author made improvements in another version which he circulated later; or possibly there were different editions for Nagasaki and for other regions. What seems quite certain is that there could be no profit for Fabian in the public rehearsal of his involvement with a man who had so recently been executed for crimes against the state. Indeed, the timing of the book suggests that it was meant to erase the stains of that association. If nothing else had compromised Fabian after his defection from the Jesuits, the alliance with Murayama Tōan must have. At the critical moment—perhaps, as Orfanel suggests, under direct pressure from Heizō and the *Nagasaki Bugyō* Hasegawa Gonroku —he fell away from Tōan, becoming in effect a triple apostate.

There remains one very interesting question: Could it be possible that Fabian was, after he left the Society of Jesus, more of a rōnin than a reprobate? Of course, the sole index for such a speculation is Jeronymo Rodriguez' cryptic note: "it appears" (in 1616) that he has abandoned the faith. And yet he did dwell for a time in Murayama Tōan's demimonde: his patron, excoriated by the Jesuits (as Fabian was), was by the Dominicans praised to the heavens (as Fabian, however, never was). "He hated the Jesuits, to whom he owed all; and since he saw that certain persons come from the Philippines were not well disposed in their favor, he made common cause with them."[61] In this sentence Pierre F. X. de Charlevoix SJ summarizes Murayama Tōan's motivations. But the words might apply as well to Tōan's instrument, a Fabian hiding in some not-quite-Christian limbo.

In 1620, when he made his final renunciation, Fabian took care to cast himself in a righteous role. In fact, the penultimate passage of *Ha Daiusu* has him play the unlikely part of victim of persecution at the hands of Christians and of their villainous supporters. The giant shadow is cast here of Ōkubo Iwami, in his lifetime a valued tool of Ieyasu, but dead these seven years and posthumously convicted of pecuniary malfeasance on a grand scale. The scandal had been colossal.[62] Ōkubo's fortune was confiscated, his seven sons forced to commit suicide, and his close associates subjected to severe punishments. The affair was rationalized by the very convenient discovery under the floor of his mansion (in a black lacquer box further contained in a stone locker) of the proverbial list of conspirators in a plot to take over the country. The canard that the powerful Ōkubo Chōan had been a secret Christian appears to have been given widespread currency. Unfortunately, there is no historical evidence which would clarify its origins. But the unsavory aura was there for the utilization. One might venture the suggestion that Fabian invoked the association for the purpose of insinuating a red herring across the trail which led back to his apostasy from Christianity. Who would serve better as persecutor of a scrupulous returnee to Buddhism than the scandalous Chōan (a surrogate for Tōan?) and his wicked subordinates! Ōkubo Iwami was a splendid straw man for the kicking, especially since the very mention of his name would suggest the memory of a subversive plot, even specifically a Christian conspiracy, but one far away from the home ground.

And, in the final analysis, the question of a Christian conspiracy was the crux. Each of Fabian's treatises is preoccupied with discussions of Christian compatibility with the Japanese setting in a time of political transformation. It was the development of the image of the Christian peril which Fabian tried so assiduously to counteract in the *Myōtei mondō*. The construction of his argument is not at all unsophisticated: Deus, the Christian God, emerges here as Daimyo of daimyos, and sempiternal peace and order reign over all the lands where His law is honored.

The dialogue concentrates almost exclusively upon the establishment of the claim of paramountcy for the One Lord, creator and determinant of all that is.

The Lord is One. All good and all quality are vested in Him. He is *spiritualis substantia, sapientissimus, misericordissimus*, and *justissimus*. He is *omnipotens*, the Lord self-sufficient in all things.[63] All other explanations of cosmogony and all other attempts to rationalize the ultimate aspirations of humanity pale into insignificance before the eminent dominance of Deus' *fiat*. Buddhism in the final analysis resolves itself into void, and the Buddha is a vacuity. The hidden sense of Shinto resolves itself as Yin-Yang speculation, and the gods are simple representations of natural forces, names for the insentient *materia prima*. The Great Ultimate which Confucianism posits is ultimately void.

To the Christian Fabian, all the traditional East Asian systems of thought were thoroughly baseless. He viewed the "void" as simple non-ens, something which does not exist (*kū wa tadachi ni mu ni shite naki mono nareba*),[64] and thus by definition a point of no reliance. Prayers addressed to an expedient pantheon are sham, for there is no one to respond to them, as the various sects' adepts know only too well. No miracles can be expected from *kaji* incantations; there is no merit in the sacrificial flames of the *goma*.[65] Shaka and Hachiman are dead men, not to be mentioned in the same breath with Deus.[66] Oaths and pledges of allegiance sworn on baseless Buddhas and gods are by dint of logic baseless. The only substantial oath is the one sworn on the substantial Lord Deus.[67] It is only the Christian servitor of the God of all majesty and justice that can fully serve order under heaven.

The Lord of All cannot be bereft of mind and wisdom, as is the Buddhist Thusness: lack of intellection can at best lead to incognizant combinations. He must be possessed of wisdom and quality to be the source of creation.[68] The key point in the debate, to the Christian Fabian, is the assumption that religion at its core requires a personalization. This is the proposition out of which all further understanding flows:

There is no true Lord outside of the one ㊉ taught by the Kirishitan religion. But what manner of Lord is the one called ㊉? He is the Creator of Heaven and Earth and of the myriad phenomena. If you only understand the truth that the existence of this heaven and earth and of the myriad phenomena is inconceivable without the existence of the one Creator, endowed with all good and all quality, then you will have understood that this is 𝕯, Who is the true Lord.[69]

Myōtei mondō exhausts itself in establishing this argument. *Ha Daiusu* is a thoroughgoing attempt to refute it.

Myōtei mondō is a book of three parts. The first, a confutation of Buddhism, is no longer extant, although a skeletal set of notes on it is available, discovered by Anesaki Masaharu and published under the provisional title *Buppō no shidai ryaku nukigaki* (An account of Buddhism: abbreviated extract).[70] The second part is subdivided into two sections, each of seven dialogue interchanges: *Judō no koto* (On Confucianism) and *Shintō no koto* (On Shinto). The third and concluding part is an exposition of Christian verities, consisting of a brief introductory outline, four statements of propositions, and an apologia. There is a postscript to explain the book's purpose.[71]

The organizational correspondence of *Ha Daiusu* and the concluding expository volume of *Myōtei mondō* is very precise. The sequence of argumentation is identical: the seven steps of *Deus Destroyed* are point-by-point rejections of the dialogue's propositions, and "An Evening's Conversation" forms a parallel to the prior defense against "Various Points of Doubt Concerning the Kirishitan Teachings." There is widespread identity of wording. Hence it is impossible to avoid the conclusion that *Ha Daiusu* is a formal retraction of *Myōtei mondō*. The ideological somersault landed Fabian in a familiar niche of history. He prefigured a much later syndrome of Japanese intellectuals: *tenkō*, defection under pressure.

The purport of the *Myōtei Dialogue* is threefold:

1. to assert the logical necessity of the one Creator, personal wellspring of all in the universe, vis à vis the Buddhist, Confucian, and Taoist void non-ens;

2. to demythologize Buddhism and Shinto;

3. to demonstrate the superiority of the Christian morality of responsibility derived from an extraterrestrial locus.

The effort of *Deus Destroyed* is exactly the opposite:

1. to assert the logical primacy of immanent, apersonal explanations of the source of .order in the universe, vis à vis a wilful Deus;

2. to demythologize Christianity;

3. to demonstrate the antinomy, in the feudal restructuring of

Japanese society, of the Christian dependence upon the extra-terrestrial sphere of justification.

The notion that *Deus Destroyed* is defensive in character is reinforced by the observation of care taken by Fabian in the organization: Always the reverse! The arrays of arguments and analogies presented in Volume III of *Myōtei mondō* are followed in straight lines of opposite impact in *Ha Daiusu*. Concluding anecdote mirrors concluding anecdote: the virtuous, totally altruistic Padres of *Myōtei mondō* are rambunctious, grasping, and vile in *Ha Daiusu*.[72] *Deus Destroyed* is a self-refutation.

The conscious nature of this detailed recantation is readily perceptible on the very surface of the text. For example, what the adherents of Deus claim in the Second Step of *Deus Destroyed* is a paraphrase of what Fabian's surrogate Yūtei had claimed in the *Myōtei Dialogue*'s chapter on *anima rationalis*.[73] But, whatever overt identification with *Myōtei mondō* Fabian assumed in *Ha Daiusu*, it was with doubting Myōshū than with Yūtei, who had all the Christian answers. The duplication of images already present in the dialogue is, in the counter, hardly an example of indolent repetitiousness but rather that of the conscious use of an ingenious eyeglass to produce a refraction.

Myōshū's moot queries, once transposed into *Ha Daiusu*, turn into evidently proven anti-Christian rejoinders. One instance is the following statement from the dialogue, which later forms the substance of the counters of the First and Second Steps:[74]

All things in heaven and earth have two aspects: object and principle. Object may be defined by use of the analogy: Willows are green, flowers are red, and that is their external appearance; pines are straight, bushes are crooked, and that is the body which appertains to them. By principle is meant the internal nature which inheres, although smashing to pieces the trees and looking one can see neither green nor red. And therefore object is associated with the state of specific character, and principle is equivalent to the nature. Accordingly, if one describes these two by way of an analogy: The water in a bamboo pipe is the principle nature. But this water, solidifying, has turned into snow or ice—now think of this as the state of specific character. Snow or ice are distinctions of the object state; but, melting, they are but the same water in a valley stream. In similar manner, there are provisional distinctions in the object state of the myriad elements: birds are not beasts, and grasses are not trees. But when the object state is destroyed, all returns to the same principle nature. And this is also called the True State of the One Thusness, without distinctions.

In Confucianism they also posit two categories: nature and material force. There are no distinctions in the nature; but with respect to material force there are four levels—the true, the penetrant, the slanted, and the clogged. And therefore, according to the extent of their combination, what results may be human, but mayhap also a horse or a cow. That there are differences of dull or sharp among humans is not caused by differences in the nature but by distinctions in the endowment of material force. The humanity of Yao and Shun and the rapacity of Chih and Ch'iao were not because their natures were distinct but because their endowments of material force were different. How could there be an individual and differentiated nature for each and every thing! Because there is the one nature it is said, without regard to the external object state, that of their nature heaven and earth have the same root, the myriad things the same substance.

In *Myōtei mondō*, this argument is set up for the express purpose of being knocked down. In *Ha Daiusu*, the identical point becomes unassailable. The willows and flowers are the same, and the water that flows is dissimilar only in specific character: in *Ha Daiusu*, the object is determined by its receptacle.[75] And the recantation is completed with the invidious snort apropos of the Christian argumentation: "So much China-man's gibberish it is, crooked twaddle to dupe idle fools!" If Fabian the philosopher had not scored, then certainly the rhetorician had.

There are many other examples of the contrapuntal relation-ship between the two books. Consider the words of Yūtei in the dialogue:[76]

After Adam and Eve had broken the law (as I have just described), their lot was as follows. They saw the misery and adversity that would redound upon their descendants. They reflected upon the extent of the offence they had committed in turning against 𝕯. Facing the heavens and prostrate upon the ground; repentance flaring up eight thousand times to rack the body and rend the mind; shame, self-abasement, contrition, and penitence deep in their hearts; sunk in the bed of a river of tears—thus they prayed to 𝕯. "Forgive this sin! Save us in the life to come, and our children down to their last descendants, all those who shall repent of their sins!" And 𝕯, with the will of universal mercy and universal compassion, [bestowed upon mankind] His grace, to give them dispensation of their suffering and to grant them bliss.

What "the adherents of Deus claim" in the Fifth Step of *Deus Destroyed* is a simple expansion of this passage. But the "counter to reply" contains a remarkable flashback. The flood of tears and the eight-thousand-fold repentance recur here, although they had not appeared in the immediately preceding segment of claim. It is as if Fabian had been writing the rejoinders of *Deus Destroyed* with the pages of the *Myōtei Dialogue* spread open before him.

What was in this manner copied, inverted, retracted could also be falsified. The crucial instance of such purposeful manipulation occurs in the citation of the First Commandment.

The *Myōtei Dialogue*'s wording is:[77] "Goittai no 𝕯 o taisetsu ni uyamai tatematsurubeshi.— — You shall hold the one 𝕯 dear and Him shall you worship." But *Deus Destroyed* has: "𝕯 goittai o *banji ni koe* taisetsu ni uyamai tatematsurubeshi.— — You shall hold the one 𝕯 dear *above all things* and him shall you worship." The statement that God is to be held dear "above all things" hardly is inconsistent with Christian doctrine. And yet this additional stress of *Deus Destroyed* scarcely is accidental: it serves Fabian as the foundation for the entire polemic of the Seventh Step. Put to Fabian's use, the added words make for a guarantee of ulterior loyalty on the part of Christians and signify an exhortation to rebellion.

The intentional nature of the manipulation becomes apparent upon inspection of other contemporary versions of the Ten Commandments. Let us take as an example the standard catechism, *DOCTRINA*, which was published at the Amakusa *collegio* in 1592, when Fabian was teaching Japanese there, working on the *FEIQE* but undoubtedly being consulted at the same time on the composition of other texts. Fabian's wording in *Ha Daiusu* differs slightly from that Christian Doctrine's in several Commandments (as, indeed, subsequent versions of the *DOCTRINA* were to differ slightly among each other). But the departure from standard is significant only in the case of the First Commandment, where *DOCTRINA* reads: "Dai ichi, go ittai no Deus uo vyamai, tattomi tatematçurubexi.— — One. You shall adore the one Deus and Him shall you worship." The fact is that Fabian's phrasing is analogous to *DOCTRINA*'s on a somewhat different matter. The standard Christian summary of the decalogue is in the two precepts: "Fitotçu niua, tada go ittai no Deus uo *banji ni coyete*, go taixet ni vyamaitatematçurubexi. Futatçu niua, vaga mi no gotoqu, Proximo uo vomoye toyŭ coto core nari.— — First of all, you shall hold the one Deus dear *above all things* and Him shall you worship. Second, love your neighbor as yourself."[78] Fabian, a catechist for more than twenty years, was certainly familiar with the proper terminology of basic catechism items. He edited to suit his own purpose. The extra emphasis would have great rhetorical impact when applied to the basic and initial, in the numerical listing the first of *mandamentos*. The focus of *Deus Destroyed* is very precisely fixed upon the First Commandment. Citation of the summary "great commandment in the law" in its proper place, after a detailed exegesis of the decalogue, would have diffused the depth of field and weakened Fabian's major point. The insertion was a well-contrived thrust.

The apostate foisted upon his former coreligionists the burden of defense against the infinitely damaging assertion: the Christian theory of Heaven's Will implies the right to revolt. Furthermore: not only are Christian loyalties divided by the First Commandment's emphasis upon an exclusive and extraterrestrial locus of loyalty; the whole structure of morality is subverted by stress of a higher duty. Whereas the *Myōtei Dialogue* had utilized the Fourth Commandment as a base for the coordination of social precepts, the later work rejected that attempt as adherence to the dictate of filial piety for mere form's sake, and superseded, at any rate, by the atrocious First.

The first *mandamento* urges disobedience to the orders of sovereign or father if compliance would mean denial of 𝕯's will; it entreats one to hold life itself cheap in such a situation. In this precept lurks the intention to subvert and usurp the country, to extinguish Buddha's Law and Royal Sway. Quick, quick! Put this gang in stocks and shackles! . . . But the adherents of Deus, without even fearing that their lives be cut, will not change their religion. How horrible, how awful it is! And whence did this flagrant wickedness arise? One look will show that its origin is in the first *mandamento*: "You shall hold 𝕯 dear above all things and him shall you worship." The spread of such a cursed doctrine is completely the working of the devil.[79]

These are words spoken with the frenetic zeal of one absolutely intent on proving his relentless orthodoxy.

The essential element of the intellectual confrontation between Christianity and Early Modern Japan is readily visible in the content of Fabian's two treatises. Around the functioning of Deus, the active personal source of all, revolved the entire argument of *Myōtei mondō*. Around the functioning of apersonal, subsistent, immanent organizational forces in the universe was constructed the precise rejoinder of *Ha Daiusu*. To use Fabian's own terminology, the two books differ only in object, not in principle.

Which is the superior work? The question is largely irrelevant. If pressed to make a judgment, one might lean to the side of *Ha Daiusu*, on account of the later work's tighter rhetoric.

Ha Daiusu is a consistently picturesque diatribe. *Myōtei mondō* is a highly pedantic tractate. Its discussion of Confucianism, for instance, amounts to a dazzling citation of indubitable authorities. Chu Hsi, Chang Tsai, Ch'eng I, Shao Yung . . . all the coryphées of the Sung Confucian learning parade across Fabian's stage.[80] As a demonstration of intellectual niveau this was unquestionably most effective: yes, indeed, the Christians in Japan also had a competent *jusha* in their ranks. But Fabian shared the fault of all who overindulge in quotation: his argumentation is dry because it is not thoroughly explicit. "On Confucianism" is not truly persuasive because the author merely cited authorities (at times indulging in overlong, obvious, and repetitive exegeses), and tacked on tails of rejoinder without taking issue with his opponents' intentions. In the process Fabian departed from his forte. The brilliant touch of petulance would predominate if only the pedantry were not so perfunctory.

Fabian's failure to come to firm grips with the Confucian adversary did, of course, also have its positive reasons. In one sense the adversary was an ally: "The Confucians hate both the doctrines of [Buddhism] and of Taoism extremely, calling them doctrines of the void non-ens and of quiescent extinction."[81] This was by no means an unimportant tactical consideration, being what made debate with the emergent orthodoxy at all possible; 1605 was a remarkably early date to recognize the significance which the Confucian pattern would bear for Japan. Fabian hastened to add that of the East Asian systems of thought Confucianism was *facile princeps*, and to some extent even sympathetic to Christianity.

Doctrines such as the Confucian are called *natural*; the parts which tend to stress preservation of the Five Constant Virtues of humanity, righteousness, propriety, wisdom, and faith are praised even in the Kirishitan teaching. But the Confucians regard Heaven and Earth, Yin and Yang, as the Great Ultimate and the Way of Heaven and do not speak of their Creator; they claim that men, beasts, grasses and trees differ only to the point of material force and its manifestant tangible matter, their nature being undifferentiated. Now these are properly termed delusions! Speaking in terms of the three doctrines, there is much profit in Confucianism. "The three doctrines are one." So they say, but two—of Shaka and of Tao—are too outrageous for words.

But neither did Confucianism measure up to the Kirishitan teaching.

The point of departure for the discussion "On Confucianism" is the rejection of the Buddhist dialectic—*zen'aku funi, jashō ichinyo*; good and evil undifferentiated, pernicious and true resolved as one.[82] Buddhism had been condemned as heretical and suicidal for its reliance upon the ultimate void. But from the Christian standpoint a similar criticism could be applied to Confucianism; along this line proceeded Fabian's argument.

What is the Way of Heaven? It is the Great Ultimate. And whence does the Great Ultimate emanate? Adduced are the *Lao Tzu* and the *Changes* to assert that the Confucian view is that of generation out of nothingness. The Tao is the Great Tao of vacuity and nonexistence; and yet, out of this state of nonexistence of one single thing, it gave birth to the One (*viz.*, the Great Ultimate), and the One gave birth to the two (*i.e.*, the Great Ultimate divided into Yin and Yang). "Accordingly, the Confucians say that the Tao produced the One. They posit the distinct separate existence of this Tao antecedent to the Great Ultimate. The Great Ultimate, and Ultimateless; the Ultimateless and the Great Ultimate!—this is their view. In the final analysis, the Great Ultimate is their basis; accordingly, they say that this Great Ultimate is the state before the Yin and Yang divided."[83]

Fabian makes his statement and, typically enough, immediately resorts to analogy by way of rejoinder. A box of medicines unopened is the Great Ultimate. The cover is separated from the box: the Yin and Yang divide. The medicines are mixed: the Yin and Yang combine. But—

Since Yin and Yang are bereft of mind and bereft of wisdom, they cannot of themselves possess the functions of combination and separation. As in the aforesaid analogy of the box containing medicines . . . how can it be opened without a man possessed of wisdom and discrimination! In the state when that Great Ultimate was bereft of mind and volition, with Yin and Yang combined . . . how could they be opened without a [personal] opener?[84]

An entity without mind, will, and cognition cannot function constructively of itself. Even the medicines (not too difficult to combine) do not form compounds of themselves; how much the less can the Four Elements produce even one bamboo! *QED*: "Then to call Yin and Yang the Way of Heaven and the well-spring which produces the myriad things . . . is impossible."

Fabian could not rid himself of the necessity to make a sequential argument and was unwilling to see that his putative adversary was speaking not of lineal causative descent but of concomitant categories of function and subsistence in a natural process. At time's it seems almost as if the mere addition of the one antecedent Creator at the apex of a temporally organized listing—(1) Deus; (2) Heaven and Earth/Yin and Yang; (3) spiritual forces—would ratify the entire set of Confucian notions and somehow lend them validity. Fabian almost makes that very statement:

Motion is Yang, positive spirit (*shen*); quiescence is Yin, and is negative spirit (*kuei*). These are not spiritual beings apart from Yin and Yang. But who is it that effectuates the Yin and Yang which constitute the wellspring of these spirits? What is said in the Kirishitan [teaching] about the existence of the one Creator of this Heaven and Earth, Yin and Yang—is not that the truth?[85]

Of course, as Joseph Needham has pointed out,[86] there could be for the Neo-Confucian no question of such a governing apex: the theistic preconception which dominated the sources of the Christian Fabian's thought did not exist in Chinese philosophy. What Fabian had to contend with was Chu Hsi's perfectly naturalistic definition of the universe. In the Sung Neo-Confucian conception, the world was a single organism; hence, no single part of it could have the attribute of permanent control of the whole. The Great Ultimate "was a recognition of immanent power informing the wholeness of the universe, and present everywhere within it," to be discussed as a "kind of organisation centre." In the ultimate analysis the organizing pattern is identical with the organism. Successive levels of *li* define the integrative pattern of the universe. This pattern is by no means un-differentiated: wholes at one level are parts of the next. The crucial distinction is one of determining order vis à vis generative cause. The Great Ultimate is resolution in harmony. In that sense does Chu Hsi say: "The Great Ultimate is nothing other than principle [*li*]," continuing, "Fundamentally there is only one

Great Ultimate, yet each of the myriad things has been endowed with it and each in itself possesses the Great Ultimate in its entirety."[87] Needham is persuasive in suggesting that Chu Hsi endeavored to establish the concept of organizing pattern in a pristine form, cleansed of accretions (specifically of Buddhist origin) of the transcendent notion. The universe is organic: order (*li*) and matter-energy (*ch'i*) interpenetrate to form it. "In the world of Li and Chhi there was no *Chu-Tsai* whatsoever."[88] But this Supreme Director in a supernatural sense was of vital importance to the Christian Fabian.

Hence the exquisite care of the *Myōtei mondō* to reduce the basis of Neo-Confucian definitions to a statement of non-ens. The rejection of the notion of an ordered universe as immanently perfect organism with microcosmic elements containing the organizational force of the macrocosm is for Fabian unavoidable. His essential concern is to prove the ultimate identity of Neo-Confucian teaching with the Buddhist proposition, already destroyed, of the lack of independent reality in phenomena and with the consciousness-only basis of Buddhist speculation. Fabian's studied amalgamation of terminology is what drew the ire of the Neo-Confucian Hayashi Razan. For an example of the Fabianesque form of attack one might consider in some detail the *Myōtei Dialogue*'s discussion of the well-known Diagram of the Great Ultimate by Shao Yung.[89]

Myōshū presents a description of the diagram in circular form; and the concentration is immediately established on the "round empty space in the middle"—hence all things were born and hither they return again. "That things are produced is but the natural process of the Way of Heaven, and this is beyond dispute."

Yūtei, however, does find room for disputation. Again analogy reigns. And by an implicit extension of the analogies—Yūtei abhorring a vacuum—the round empty space must soon enough be filled.

The empty space in the middle is the coordinate pivot[90] of the Great Tao, like unto the central ridgepole of a house with all the wood gathered in toward it. The North Star of heaven has all the others grouped about it; the imperial rank is the culmination of a country, all the people paying obeisance to it. The ancient sages established organs [of society] in accordance with heaven: these are the organs of the Great Median of Perfect Right. The sixty-four emblems emanate from the center: no point of pattern (*li*) that is not established thereby; no power that is not endowed therein; no thing that is not concordant thereto; no material element that is therewith unpenetrated. From the empty middle, six reduplications are produced: these are the emblems. If one adds six reduplications there will be 4096 emblems, and with yet other reduplications outward one reaches an infinite number.

The inexhaustible number of emblems signifies the boundless extent of the natural order: the Great Ultimate of perfect order is contained within each thing; none that are not endowed with boundless perfection. The stone, for example, contains its Great Ultimate. But break it: and there is a Great Ultimate in each chip.

Aah! This Great Ultimate indeed should not be sought afar. One instant of volition arising in the human mind: this already is a miniature Great Ultimate, and is endowed with boundless perfection. Volition upon volition, all is thus; human after human, all are thus. The Hundred Families every day function in this manner, but are unaware of the fact. Therefore Heaven and Earth and the myriad things are in reality only the cognition of the human mind. The Confucians' so-called microcosm and the Buddhists' so-called in-carnation (*niku zōka*): these are precisely what is meant by this . . . Needless to say, Confucianism also in the final analysis is one with Buddhism. And I hear that the same is true of the Taoists' doctrine. "The three doctrines are one" is the long-tested saying, and it is quite true . . . What Lao Tzu said about "the Tao gave birth to the One," the natural state of the void non-ens—is that not pointing to what the Buddhists call the Dharma-World of Empty Void (*kokū hokkai*)?

Great Ultimate, Thusness, the Great Tao—these are to Fabian perfectly interchangeable terms: a mandarin orange by any other name is still a tangerine.[91] The disingenuous confusion had served its purpose. The void in the vortex could now be filled. "Without the existence of a Creator endowed with wisdom and the power of consideration not even a dustspeck element can come into being. How much the less can this heaven and earth, man and material things, of themselves and naturally come into existence out of the void non-ens!" Of course, Fabian had chosen to ignore the cardinal Neo-Confucian disclaimer. The Great Ultimate could not properly be held identical to *śūnyatā*, as Chu Hsi had pointed out: "The Great Ultimate contains all principles of the Five Agents and yin and yang.

It is not an empty thing. If it were a void, it would approach the Buddhist theory of dharma-nature."[92] But Fabian had a great proclivity for such identifications.

Needless to say, in *Ha Daiusu* Fabian restored the empty space at the epicenter. The later work, for all its catholicity, is predominantly Buddhist. But, significantly enough, here also a hypersyncretist tendency prevails in terminology, Buddhist, Taoist, and Confucian united to show unnecessary the prime mover and creator.[93] Fabian was never one to mark a precise registration when the massive volley would better serve his attack.

The *Dialogue*'s further elaborations "On Confucianism" continue the stress on the unacceptability of naturalistic explanations of cosmic and human activity. The complex of quotations is, to be sure, extremely impressive, as is their manipulation. Thus, for instance, Chu Hsi's glosses on Su Shih's commentary on the *Changes* (*Tsa hsüeh-pien: Su-shih I chieh*)[94] are adduced to demonstrate that Confucians do not recognize the existence of a soul or of a hereafter. Their "ancestor worship" is but ceremonial directed toward Heaven and Earth, Yin and Yang, which are the beginning and end of all humans and things, their origin and locus of dissolution. When man dies, according to the Confucians, the heavenly aspect of his spirit (*hun*) returns to Heaven and the earthly aspect (*p'o*) to Earth; that is all.[95] Belief in the process of natural dissolution naturally excludes the possibility of belief in the immortal soul. To the Christian Fabian the inadequacy of such a position seemed obvious: no permanent recompense vested in a personal soul meant no basis of moral responsibility, and there was simply no essential distinction between things. Even the most praiseworthy element in Confucianism, the stress on virtuous humane behavior, foundered upon this precipitous void. Well might the Confucians speak of the Nature and of Illustrious Virtue (Fabian cites *Shang shu*, *Odes*, *Mencius*, and *Great Learning*); in the final analysis, delusion reigned over Confucianism, for it knew not the True Creator.

"On Confucianism" terminates with a clever elision. Myōshū admits the need of "the one Creator, possessed of wisdom and quality," and asks: "May not the one they call P'an-ku Wang be called the Lord of Heaven and Earth?" To this Yūtei responds with persiflage:

It is immediately clear that P'an-ku is not someone who created heaven and earth . . . He merely popped out, a chicken, from an egg.

Only the "cockadoodledo!" is missing from this account. Of course, the gap is somewhat filled by the statement that he reigned 84,000 years. My, what a long life! Needless to say, all this is so absurd that no true Confucian will mention anything of the sort. And it is quite similar to stories about the Age of the Gods in Japan. Don't believe everything you read in books![96]

Thus is the point of transfer made to the discussion "On Shinto." Chickens (and other such) figure here as well: the lengthy initial quotation from the *Nihongi* immediately makes it obvious that the Shinto genealogy of the gods and the generation account are derived from Chinese sources. What follows is a witheringly effective *reductio ad absurdum* of the Shinto mythology. In this section of *Myōtei mondō* Fabian demonstrates a brilliant talent for the salacious.

Myōshū responds to the enumeration of gods' names with a pompous proto-nationalist statement:[97]

First of all—as people say customarily—this country is called Our Empire, First of the Three Countries, for it surpasses even India and Cathay. And that is because the Realm of the Sun (small country though it may be), rendering worship to Kuni-tokotachi no Mikoto as the first, is as you have just said where Izanagi no Mikoto and Izanami no Mikoto opened up heaven and earth. Those beginnings stem from this country. And therefore Japan is called the Land of the Gods: here the gods are hallowed and worshipped as the Lords of Heaven and Earth. Generally speaking, all things take their beginning from something small: that explains why our country is smaller than others. Out of the froth which fell from the churning spear and congealed to form Awaji Island, India and China also took their beginnings; or so I've heard. This country is called Dainippon-koku, the Country of the Great Sun's Origin. When the two gods of Yin and Yang lowering the spear churned the ocean there appeared floating above the tide the letters *dai nichi*, great sun. And because the froth from the spear fell and congealed thereupon to form the islands, one terms them Dainippon-koku; such is the explanation. At any rate, I believe that this country is the beginning of the Three Countries and takes its issue from Kuni-tokotachi no Mikoto.

Shinto is a profound mystery to the naïve traditionalist. Not so to the cosmopolitan Yūtei, who implies that it really is somewhat vulgar to take things on faith. There is nothing mysterious about Shinto, and anyone who can tell black from white can understand it: its recondite element is merely a paraphrase of Confucian Yin-Yang theories, and only the ignorant

will find astonishing the statement that all of Shinto has already
been discussed by Chinese authorities. In this context, Fabian is
a firm believer in the famous dictum of Chang Tsai: *"Kuei-shen
che erh-ch'i chih liang-neng yeh*—the negative and positive spiritual
forces are the spontaneous activity of the two material forces."[98]
The *kami* of Shinto, set to equal the *shen* of Confucianism, are
by the Christian reduced to substantial nothingness with the
implicit application of Chu Hsi's exegesis of the phrase: "Coming
and going, and contraction and expansion, are all natural according to principle, without any manipulation or deliberate arrangement. Hence they are called spontaneous activities."

There was in the world of spontaneous expansion and contraction no room for a Creator: in fact, by citation of source
Fabian proved that Shinto deities with Kuni-tokotachi no Mikoto
as the first were even in the *Nihongi* held to be subsequent to
the creation of the universe.[99] The gods' names can be explained
in perfectly naturalistic fashion. Further: the shallow and vulgar
character of Shinto is apparent in the mere consideration of the
sequence of deities as translation of stages in the process of
sexual generation:

> Kuni-tokotachi no Mikoto signifies the intercourse between father
> and mother. The father's sperm entering and gathering absorbed in the
> mother's womb is Kuni-sazuchi no Mikoto. The stage of motion inside
> the womb is the Virtue of Fire—Toyokunnu no Mikoto. The stage
> of hardening within the womb is called Uijini and Suijini. The stages
> of birth and growth to adulthood, and the formation of a family—
> Ōtonoji no Mikoto, Ōtomabe no Mikoto. Well, then: when after a
> while one becomes father or mother, and has children, this signifies
> Izanagi no Mikoto and Izanami no Mikoto, so that our body, as it is,
> equals the Seven Gods of Heaven. This conception is the true notion
> of Shinto.[100]

In point of fact, states Fabian, all Shinto accounts of the beginning of the lands of the earth represent an intent analogous to
that of *gonkyō*, the expedient doctrine of Buddhism.

Fabian's response, couched in intimate tones, is a true master-
piece of the art of the disingenuous. Fabian is sophisticated
enough to operate on two levels: deeming unworthy a frontal
attack upon the myth, he states that the surface tale is only an
expedient and delves into the symbolism which overlies the
secreted base. He has pointed out repeatedly that Shinto represents
merely a crenellated restatement of Confucian speculation. He has

discredited as vacuous the original form; now he ridicules the crenellations. His technique is exceedingly clever: taking advantage of the obvious phallic symbolism of the creation myth, he plays upon the sexual connotations to highly purposeful extent, and arrives at total denudation of Shinto beliefs. Observe Yūtei, the perfect confidante, on the Shinto account of land's origin:[101]

Now, just think for a moment. If there were no hidden meaning in all this . . . wouldn't it be idiotic? . . . First of all, what the story of the spear dangled downward has for its hidden meaning is so embarrassing that even intimates such as you and I cannot talk about it, so I won't discuss it. What is the spear? And what the drippings? You can easily guess. And about the letters *dai nichi*—again, this points to the human body. A person lying down with arms and legs outspread: this is the shape of the letters *dai nichi* 大 日. Now this again is something I need not discuss in detail.

And, after further such expostulations, there comes the reply of Myōshū:

How right you are, how right! . . . If one takes the statements of Shinto at face value, they are absurd. When one hears the hidden meaning, one is embarrassed . . . How foolish of me! I really did think that this country in fact was born as issue from Izanami and Izanagi.

Fabian was to reach a stylistic acme of sorts in his banter about this primal pair.

In all his work Fabian demonstrates all the affectations of the intended virtuoso. Akutagawa's Lucifer accused our incontinent Irmão of the deadly sin of pride; and, paradoxically enough, the dictates of *Sancta Obedientia* to which the Jesuit Fabian had committed himself demanded on his part a certain intellectual arrogance, *ad maiorem Dei gloriam*. But the acrid flair of his Japanese was his own. His style is best described as theatrical, both in its rhythm and in its choice of words. This impression is stronger in *Ha Daiusu* than in *Myōtei mondō*. Some semblance of gentility had to be preserved in the *Dialogue*: the conventions of the tract's framework, a conversation between two ladies, somewhat cramped Fabian's style. *Deus Destroyed* therefore is the more lively book to read; but the *Myōtei Dialogue* is not without its illustrative points. In *Deus Destroyed* Fabian proves a superb technician of the scathing invective; but in the *Myōtei Dialogue* he is no less a technician of sarcasm. Remarkable are the lapses into outright ribaldry.

Quite unrestrained by monastic decorum is Fabian's gloss on the *Nihongi* account of the birth of Japan with all its seas and its mountains, grasses and trees, as issue from Izanami and Izanagi: "My, what a bodacious womb! And the body which contained such an immense womb . . . where did it find room to squat before it gave birth to the land?"[102] And there is further progress to explicitly lewd suggestions: What is the sword of Susanoo? What the jewel of Amaterasu? Why all the gnashing of teeth in their converse? Why the fierceness of breath? One could hardly be more obvious.

Are these examples of the rational, the critical spirit which Professor Ebisawa finds so praiseworthy in the *Myōtei mondō*?[103] Is the realization of the phallic nature of the Shinto imagery to signify modernity? Fabian does manifest here a type of sophistication, and yet he is at his least attractive. His method ascends (descends) the scales from false coyness to a snide and snickering tone to the lewd and then the gross. In short, his discussion of Shinto reaches a level undignified enough to annoy even the neutral-minded. Perhaps the scatological climax of the disputation scene in *Kirishitan monogatari* is an echo of the *Myōtei Dialogue*'s irreverent banter with the native deities: as Fabian offers to pollute the most sacred shrines of the Japanese tradition, so does Hakuō undertake to pollute the Virgin Mary.[104]

"On Shinto" had begun with a promising progression of thought, the explanation of Shinto on a quasi-Confucian basis. But the end effect of this section of the *Dialogue* is that of a burlesque. This impression contributes in large measure to the total estimate of the book. The character of the zealot is even more pronounced in the *Myōtei Dialogue* than in *Deus Destroyed*. *Myōtei mondō* is the more offensive tract of the two.

The *abbé* Humbertclaude, who published a French translation of *Myōtei mondō* in the rampantly nationalist Tokyo of 1938–39, discreetly omitted the entire section "On Shinto."[105] What was until recently the standard edition of the *Dialogue* (Nihon Koten Zenshū, 1927) made certain to purge at least the supreme blasphemy. Empty spaces now remain where explicit denials of Shinto sacrosanctities once resided:[106]

Since it is perfectly clear that the sun is simply the sun and not Amaterasu Ōmikami, then it must follow that what is called Amaterasu Ōmikami **** [does not exist] . . . The sun is called Amaterasu Ōmikami, progeny of Izanami and Izanagi, but since that is not so,

*** [there is nothing] that should be called Amaterasu Ōmikami. In that case, you can be sure that what is called Ise Daimyōjin also ****** [is of no substance]. ******* [There is no reason] also for the Grand Shrines of Ise to exist, since Amaterasu Ōmikami, the deity they enshrine, is *** [nonexistent].

All the more poignant is the irony of the fact that the sole surviving copy of the *Myōtei Dialogue* was found preserved for posterity in the library of the Grand Shrines of Ise.

So much for the Age of the Gods. "But there is also the Age of Men, with this god and that god and all sorts of gods in it. What do you make of it?"[107] The Christian Fabian did not make much of the innumerable local deities, shrines, and mausolea, mentioning in detail only Hachiman Daibosatsu and Tenman Tenjin. This selectivity was consistent with the purpose of *Myōtei mondō*: Fabian was not primarily interested in attacking the Shinto cult but rather in establishing the necessity of a Creator—hence the preoccupation with the progenitor deities. Again, there is precise duplication, in the oblique, in *Ha Daiusu*. The enumeration of the Gods of Heaven stresses Kuni-tokotachi no Mikoto, "the lord who always rises to the land's government," this time seen as "a god before even one human existed, before heaven and earth were opened up"; the authority of the Sage Confucius is cited to hallow the gods. Again, the only Shinto deities invoked outside the progenitors are Hachiman and Tenman. But whereas in *Myōtei mondō* they were merely posthumously deified humans, in *Ha Daiusu* their humanity is merely surface appearance: the *kami* are manifestations of the Buddhas. *Honji suijaku*—original substance manifests traces. The gods' humanity, in the later work, is the demonstration of their boundless concern for men. But what of Jesus Christus? Thus proceeded Fabian's verbal *auto da fé*, relentless but not heroic.

A similar attempt at recantation may in part be reconstructed with respect to Buddhism. Some portions of *Ha Daiusu* seem suited for contrast with the putative fragments of the first volume of *Myōtei mondō*, the discovery of Professor Anesaki.[108] The comparison must be extremely cautious: criticism based on a text of unestablished authorship is perhaps the historian's prime error.[109] The very form of the available text—it is not cast in dialogue but the (rest of) *Myōtei mondō* is—leads one to assume that it is a reader's abstract *of* a subsequently lost treatise, truncated to suit the scribe's interests, rather than Fabian's preliminary draft *for* a treatise.

Anesaki labels the initial segment *Buppō sōron*, general discussion of Buddhism. It is indeed very fragmented, and not at all in keeping with Fabian's customarily careful, pedantic introductory statements; and it must be pointed out emphatically that the leaps of logic and grotesque formulations are also uncharacteristic —Fabian may have been a sophist and even a soritist, but not a shoddy one. *Buppō sōron* is in its present state a highly perverted description of the basic Mahayanist doctrine of the triune Buddha-body, *trikāya*. One might cite the initial passage:

> What is Buddhism? Mida, Shaka, Dainichi is it. Said three Buddhas are called the Three Bodies: Law, Recompensed, Accommodated. This, then, refers to the mind of human beings. The human mind possesses three spiritual qualities: covetousness, anger, stupidity. To consider these three one by one: Stupidity is the state of no volition and no mind, called the Buddha of the Law Body; this is called Dainichi Nyorai. Next, covetousness—the state of desiring what is in fact harmful, called the Buddha of the Recompensed Body; this is called Amida Nyorai. Next, anger—the state of rage aroused and rancor accumulated, called the Buddha of the Accommodated Body; this is called Shaka Nyorai. These are all vested in the mind of human beings. Outside of these there are also such as Kannon and Yakushi; but neither do these exist apart from the human body.

Something of the sort may indeed have been distillable out of Fabian's original compound. The counters of the First Step of *Deus Destroyed* would in that case achieve an extrapolated significance as specific disclaimers of the *Myōtei Dialogue*. But the lost First Volume of *Myōtei mondō* seems to manifest traces even beyond Fabian's own work. The initial harangue of the Iruman in the *Kirishitan monogatari* disputation scene extols Deus, "the Buddha who opened up heaven and earth," to the detriment of "Shaka! Amida!—how could they be Buddhas!"[110] And there are certain striking parallelisms in the textual matter of Suzuki Shōsan's *Ha Kirishitan* and segments 6, 10, and 12 of *Buppō no shidai ryaku nukigaki*.

The Christian Fabian in the *Myōtei Dialogue* of 1605 postulated the all-consuming need of a personal Creator: all of natural history was the direct emanation of His will, His wisdom, and His all-powerful properties. Fabian's attack on traditional East Asian systems of thought was not at all temperate; he thus left his flank open to thrusts by such proponents of orthodoxy as the Hayashi brothers—"You are mad and arrogant. The Great Ultimate is not something you can ever understand." By 1620 the Buddhist Fabian had presumably reached a ripe understanding; and he raises in his reader a faint ironic memory when he rails in *Deus Destroyed* at the Christians—"I can't help laughing out loud! The Pure Undisturbed Absolute is something you fools can never understand."[111] Fabian had switched his views to the belief that a personal creator is a creator with an ego, that a prime mover with a will is a wilful prime mover, that a God with personal qualities must *ipso facto* be limited by their antipodes. The obvious had been replaced by its diametrically opposite obvious. In one tract Fabian flayed his opponents with the same arguments he had scorned and rejected in the other.

The Bakumatsu resurrector of Fabian, that combative monk of the Chion'in, Kiyū Dōnin, found great value in *Deus Destroyed*.[112] "It seems that the author had studied the Religion of Jesus, had apprehended that all of it was rank perversion, and, turning on it, had attacked it. Though his style is not very refined, he carries his arguments with vigor and facility, and indeed he cannot be budged. Borrowing their own halberd, he hews at their buckler, and he soon has these disciples of wickedness tongue-tied." And he endowed Fabian's book with a great topicality: "Of late the disciples of wickedness have reappeared, violating our prohibitions and breaking our regulations. Their treacheries number in the hundreds, and there is no place where they have not penetrated. Officials and common people quarrel, assaulting each other with empty words; thus it is impossible to devise clever counteraction." With these words Kiyū Dōnin admonished "men of purposeful conviction and of righteous mind" to follow Fabian's example. And the postscript to his edition stated: "Fabian's *Deus Destroyed* ably dissects the heart of their contention; it can be termed a golden gouge scraping their very membranes." The pious opponents of foreign intrusion never suspected the existence of the *Myōtei Dialogue*.

Of late the most prolific historian of the "Christian Century" in Japan, Professor Ebisawa Arimichi, has found no value in *Deus Destroyed*, labeling it superficial and concerned merely with side angles and trivialities. He has, however, eulogized the *Myōtei Dialogue*:[113]

The rational and critical spirit evidenced in the *Myōtei Dialogue*, together with the splendid intellectual contents of the book, must be called a shining monument in the history of Early Modern Japanese thought. The Azuchi-Momoyama period is the period of Japanese intellectual history with the smallest number of works worthy of attention. But it is quite correct to say that the *Myōtei Dialogue* is the most notable book of the period.

It is quite incorrect to make such an analysis. "The adherents of Deus claim"—"To counter, I reply." The *Myōtei Dialogue* and *Deus Destroyed* are really very much the same book. To cite *The Concise Oxford Dictionary*'s definition of the fencing term "counter"—"Circular parry in which hand retains same position while point describes a circle."

Chapter 7

The Final Solution

𝒜ND EVEN among the Kirishitans the *predestinados* (by that is meant to say, the elect for the afterlife) are elected and chosen by Deus from all eternity without beginning or end, and they are saved; but the remainder from among the same religion, called *reprobos* (by that is meant to say, the abominated for the afterlife) fall down into *Inferno*. Thus they teach. Is this to be called the wellspring of mercy and compassion? And moreover, the *predestinados* are saved no matter what evil they commit; and the *reprobos* fall down into hell no matter how they strive toward good.

These are words taken from *Deceit Disclosed*, a tract composed by the apostate Padre Christovão Ferreira, sometime Mission Superior of Japan, after his fall.[1] For a former Jesuit, this was a perversely Jansenist (if not Supralapsarian) interpretation of Christian doctrine.

The dramatic potential of the passage is obvious. The novelist Endō Shūsaku takes it for Ferreira's agonized recognition of himself as reprobate.[2] If that notion be true, the paradox is intensified. Ferreira saw himself doomed. But his former confrères, who had formally expelled the renegade from the Society of Jesus, in one vital point remained optimists concerning him and maintained the typical Jesuit position that a spark of Divine Grace exists even in the worst of sinners, and might by his revived will to salvation be fanned into a thoroughly purging fire. Ferreira's defection had shocked the Society, whose enemies made the most of it. But groups of Jesuits, one after the other, attempted to penetrate Japan for Ferreira's sake, prepared (they thought) to confront certain torture in order to save his soul and by the blood of martyrdom to wash away the stain of his original sin. Indeed, for the Jesuits he was predestined to be saved: eagerly grasping at uncertain information, they accepted and embellished the story that Ferreira in his old age recanted his apostasy and died for the greater glory of God.

The stories of Ferreira's reconversion have little substance. More solid is the image of Meakashi Chūan, Chūan the Spy, the professional cognomen which naturally attached itself to the name he adopted after his apostasy, Sawano Chūan. Chūan—or Joan, or Syovan—moves specter-like through the pages of contemporary Japanese and Dutch accounts until they record his death in November 1650.[3] The appellations differ, but the function remains the same. There is nothing in these sources to indicate that he was less than a faithful servant of the Bakufu in performing the tasks allotted to him, which were those of interpreter, informant, and inquisitor's cur in the roundup of Christians.

Ferreira had turned apostate only after bearing for five hours the fiendish torture of *anatsurushi*, suspension in the pit. But martyrdom, for the Mission Superior of the Church under persecution, was the final *raison d'être*, and failure to live the ideal—or, rather, die for it—the ultimate psychological shock. Once the rejection of the missionary's self had been extracted from him, he became the very model of susceptibility to thought reform, and was used by his expert manipulators as a tool to strike and cleave at the identities of others. Missionaries who had risked breaking the hermetic seals of Sakoku, and those captured after years of clandestine activity, were confronted with Ferreira and his taunts. His active participation in the grilling of his fellows increasingly fanned the flames of his inner guilt.

The technique used upon Ferreira in seventeenth-century Japan was meant to obtain results similar to those which Robert Lifton analyzes in subjects of "brainwashing" in twentieth-century China:[4]

The series of denunciations of friends and colleagues . . . [increased] their feelings of guilt and shame, it put them in the position of subverting the structures of their own lives. They were, in effect, being made to renounce the people, the organizations, and the standards of behavior which had formed the matrix of their previous existence. They were being forced to betray—not so much their friends and colleagues, as a vital core of themselves . . . But the more of one's self one is led to betray, the greater is one's involvement with his captors; for by these means they make contact with whatever similar tendencies already exist within the prisoner himself—with the doubts, antagonisms, and ambivalences which each of us carries beneath the surface of his loyalties. This bond of betrayal between prisoner and environment may develop to the point where it seems to him to be all he has to grasp; turning back becomes ever more difficult.

Ferreira was in the hands of masters of the art. There is no reason to believe that he was, at the end, unpersuaded.

Ferreira figures at the center of a series of juxtapositions in which the variable is martyrdom. He was himself, while still a subterranean, the author of profuse reports on the martyrdom of Christian heroes. His—the Superior's—own apostasy after five hours of torture is in stark contrast to the perseverance of the seven priests and novices subjected to *anatsurushi* together with him, one of whom is said to have borne the agony into the ninth day before expiring.[5] It seems more than probable that the highly imaginative account of the martyrdom of Padre Marcello Mastrilli, who had smuggled himself into Japan with the idea of confronting Ferreira, was spread about to counteract the un-edifying image of his apostasy. Ferreira—the trusted Portuguese—was the one who tempted the sometime Jesuit rōnin Pedro Casui Kibe, whose independence had once drawn invidious comments on Japanese character from his masters in the Society, but who in the end proved faithful to the ideal. And, finally, Ferreira helped to obtain the apostasy of an entire group of Jesuit venturers to Japan (the so-called Second Rubino Group), who were thus destroyed by the very man they had intended to save; one of these, Giuseppe Chiara, became as Okamoto San'emon a renegade second in fame only to Sawano Chūan.

Ferreira himself was lackey to another apostate, Inoue Chikugo no Kami Masashige, who was in turn the major tool of the Bakufu in administering the policy of extermination. Inoue Chikugo was the ideal inquisitor, demonic because intellectual. The former Christian knew the truth of the cliché: the blood of martyrs is the seed of Christians. The clumsiness of the torture that kills was not for him. "This is the great realization of Inoue, and the goal before his eyes: he would destroy the impression that the Christian religion is insuperable. Therefore he wants not martyrs but apostates. Apostates better than martyrs attest the impotence of a religion, especially when these apostates have been apostles of the faith and priests."[6] This end Inoue pursued by ruthlessly sophisticated means. The interplay of the mentalities of persecutor and persecuted produced another series of juxtapositions, in which the variable is apostasy. An inspection of Ferreira's career within this nexus is one view of the Tokugawa final solution of the Christian problem.

Christovão Ferreira was born in 1580 in the vicinity of Torres

Vedras in Portugal, and entered the Society of Jesus in 1596 at Coimbra. In 1600 he set sail for the Indies and was directed to proceed to the Japan Mission.[7] He is listed in a Jesuit catalogue for 1603 as present in Macao, at the end of his third year of theological studies; by 1609 he was a priest, and seems to have crossed over to Japan in 1610 or the year after. The catalogue for 1613 has him assistant superior of the Jesuit residence in Kyoto; and after the expulsion edict of 1614 he remained underground in that area. In 1617 he made the final vows of a Jesuit.[8] That year he seems to have traveled throughout the Kansai and perhaps even to Shikoku, administering the sacraments in the midst of great dangers;[9] and in the autumn he had made his way to Nagasaki.[10] In 1620 he visited Hirado, an angel heaven-sent (so Pagés has it) to the long-deprived Christians: he heard some 1300 confessions, while walking the beach nights, to escape discovery.[11] A catalogue of September 1620 accounted his ability superior, his knowledge of Japanese excellent; he was the *Procurator* of the Society in Japan.[12]

On 4 December 1623 the newly acceded Third Shogun, Iemitsu, gruesomely demonstrated his intent to pursue the policy of persecution by having fifty Christians burnt at the stake in Edo. The report of this great martyrdom was compiled "with a view to an eventual process of canonization" by the Miyako Superior, Christovão Ferreira.[13] His further accounts of martyrdoms include a 41-page manuscript (preserved in Lisbon) on the 1627 Shimabara persecution.[14] But most affecting is Ferreira's detailed description, in the *annua* dated 22 March 1632, of the acts of faith of the Japanese Padre Antonio Ishida SJ.[15]

Ishida suffered under Takenaka Uneme, the *Nagasaki Bugyō* whose term of office (1626–1633) was unmatched for anti-Christian horrors.[16] The Bakufu authorities seem to have shuddered at his various other atrocities: adjudged malfeasant, he had the sentence of death passed on him in 1634. But to him the persecutors of Christianity owed an important innovation in method: the inception of the stress on apostasy to implement the policy dates from his time. The arrested sectarians were no longer to be merely killed; they would first be cajoled and pressured. If promises failed to sway, then abuse and torture might force abandonment of the faith. And the inquisitor's method very prominently included attempts at intellectual persuasion. Potential models of Christian fortitude were at all costs to be turned into actual displays of corruptibility.

This method Takenaka followed step by step with Antonio Ishida. Ishida was arrested on 5 November 1629 and was—according to a letter he smuggled out of prison[17]—at first treated by the *bugyō* with a sort of false *bonhomie*. The initial process culminated in queries by scholars in a well-attended disputation before the inquisitor. Dismissing as idiotic their demands that he adopt a Japanese religion, Ishida was thrown into the Ōmura prison, to rot there until in November 1631 he was called again before Takenaka Uneme.

Uneme again tried to break down the Padre by scholarly argument, enlisting to this end the Confucian Saitō Gonnai. Ferreira's report makes it appear that the Confucian thought to establish equations rather than cancellations: the Great Ultimate was set identical to Deus.[18] But on the Padre's scale the differences outweighed the areas of coincidence. The Confucian came back with the crucial demand: the Padre should subordinate the dictates of his reason to the orders of his sovereign; his primary duty was to demonstrate adherence to the Shogun's authority, and he might well continue to believe what he pleased in his heart. The Jesuit rejected the casuistic compromise. For Ishida, as for the author of this report in 1632, the only possible path was that of the higher duty. Ishida's loyalist response was that the Shogun's demands could have no force whatsoever when they were contrary to God's commandments. The debate lasted a day and a night, until Saitō deemed continuation useless. There remained only the ancient diabolical temptation—that of the riches of this world. Withstanding it, the Padre was damned by his captors to the Hells of Unzen.

"Unzen Spa," states *The Official Guide* of the modern Japanese government's Tourist Industry Bureau, "is an ideal summer resort, being situated 2,400 ft. above sea level amid splendid scenery, and with the additional attraction of a plentiful supply of hot mineral water of great efficacy in many diseases . . . The area contains more than 30 sulfataras and fumaroles, the water from which overflows into a pond, which is in a constant state of tumult. Everywhere in the area are beds and mounds of whitish earth, from which rise dense clouds of steam, and the paths are bordered with streams stained many colors by the chemicals in the water. Rheumatism and skin disease are two of the ailments for which this water is beneficial."[19] The tourist industry's admiring customers are at best but dimly aware of the ideal summer resort's special past uses.

This was a terrestrial paradise in the sense of Hieronymus Bosch, and the scene of a great inquest of Christians. The pond that is in a constant state of tumult was to the anguished prisoner one "of which the very sight sufficed to cause a faint," unless the help of God prevent it.[20] The filthy bubbling of the fumaroles, the stenches of the sulfataras, the stained streams and brimstoned, lifeless earth; amidst dense clouds of steam, fiends ladling precise measures of the efficacious waters to scald the naked and bound victims—surely the psychological torture was at least the equal of the physical. One who had survived the combined ordeal could properly say, "Je fis de Macabré la dance."[21]

Ferreira tells us that Ishida, while in Unzen, managed to reconvert several apostates, and that his moral example impressed hardened pagans. Unable to break him, the inquisitors brought him back to Nagasaki on 5 January 1632. Ferreira's account closes with words of defiance for the tyrant's plans and lauds upon the heroism of the Church Militant.[22]

Ishida was burnt at the stake in Nagasaki on 3 September 1632, together with five other priests. The martyrology records their last words: "Viva la fè de Christo!"[23]

Ferreira, the author of the report of his subordinate's suffering, was captured on 24 September 1633. On the 18th of October he apostatized. He was at the time the Vice-Provincial of the Society in Japan and the administrator of the Japanese Diocese.[24]

Within three years he had put the seal on his apostasy: the date on which the "Chief Bateren of Japan and Macao, Christovão Ferreira, reformed in religion and turned an adherent of Zen, Chūan set his hand to" the *Kengiroku* translates to 29 September 1636. On 2 November 1636 in Macao, the *Visitator* Manoel Dias and nine other Jesuits, having accumulated sufficient proof of his fall, pronounced the canonical ban on the apostate and signed the formal document of his expulsion from the Society.[25] By September 1637, Ferreira was far anough advanced in thought reform to appear as interrogator at the martyrdom of the Dominican friar Antonio Gonçalez in Nagasaki;[26] and in the summer of 1639 he was called to Edo to assist at the inquisition of Pedro Casui Kibe. The torture of suspension in the pit is the dominant image in the background of Ferreira's career as Sawano Chūan.

The *anatsurushi* was a consummate torture. The victim was trussed upside down, the head pendulous in a pit filled with excreta. Tight bonds about the body impeded the free flow of blood to the brain. By way of precaution, the temple was slit to provide a vent; else cerebral hemorrhage would bring the procedure to too rapid an end. The toxic gases from the pit's putrescence induced a partial anaesthesia, so that the period of suffering could be prolonged. The inquisitors wanted the victim to hang in the balance between overpowering pain and release-bringing death; and the *anatsurushi* enabled them to utilize that most minute of intervals. The only salvation for the victim was, as he felt himself bursting, to signal his apostasy. The hand was left unbound for that purpose.

The efficacy of the torture was established by Ferreira's lapse. Thereafter it would become the mainstay of the inquisition process. The master of its application was Inoue Chikugo.

The *Tokugawa jikki* (True record of the Tokugawa) in the entry for Manji 3 (1660)/7/9 gives his capsule biography as follows:[27]

Inoue Chikugo no Kami Masashige, holder of Takaoka in the Province of Shimōsa, was according to his request relieved of official duties, and as a lay monk took the name Yūsan . . . This Masashige is the fourth son of the late Han'emon no Jō Kiyohide, and since Keichō 13 (1608) served Taitokuin-den [Hidetada], with a stipend of 200 *hyō* of storehouse rice. In Genna 4 (1618) he was granted 500 *koku*, and in Genna 9 (1623) this was increased to 1000 *koku*. In Kan'ei 2 (1625) he was appointed inspector (*metsuke*) and again had his stipend increased, to 2000 *koku*. On Kan'ei 4 (1627)/9/1 he was permitted to wear as blazon the letter "5," and on 12/29 of the same year was ennobled, with the title Chikugo no Kami. On Kan'ei 9 (1632)/10/3 he was granted his fief. When the office of inspector general (*ōmetsuke*) was first established on 12/17 of that year, he was selected and took up service in that post (at the time it was called *sōmetsuke*, general inspector). On Kan'ei 17 (1640)/6/12 he was granted a domain of 10,000 *koku* in Shimōsa. This year he went down to the Land of Tsukushi to conduct an inquisition into the Westerners' Jesus Doctrine . . . On Kan'ei 20 (1643)/5/23 his fief was increased again, by 3000 *koku*. On Manji 1/interc. 12/8 (30 January 1659) he resigned his post, and was today relieved of official duties.

The record goes on to say that he died in his seventy-seventh year, on Manji 4/2/27 (27 March 1661).

His is another instance of the banality of evil. His origins are obscure. He seems to have been initially a vassal of the *Kirishitan daimyō* Dom Leão Gamō Ujisato; and it is not unreasonable to assume that to turn Christian was part of that service.[28] Inoue Chikugo is a case study of the emergence and rise of the bureaucrat type in the Tokugawa Bakufu. It is likely that he advanced by being part of the clique of Matsudaira Nobutsuna, the famous Chie Izu; and Clever Izu was one of the principal molders of the final cast of Sakoku. Whatever the case may be, the advancement from an insignificant 200 *hyō* to 13,000 *koku* and daimyo status, while not truly extraordinary, is noteworthy. In the eyes of the shogunate's policy-makers Inoue Chikugo clearly was a man of merit.

A parvenu and an apostate, Inoue Chikugo was doubly zealous. The first recorded instance of his specific involvement with the Christian problem is the *Tokugawa jikki* entry for Kan'ei 15 (1638)/1/3: "*Ōmetsuke* Inoue Chikugo no Kami Masashige, invested emissary to Shimabara, was bestowed an Aoe sword, and was summoned into the Presence for an audience."[29] The occasion of Inoue's mission was the peasant rising of Shimabara, which had broken out two months previously. There were distinct Christian overtones to this manifestation of popular discontent.

Twenty-four years after the issuance of Ieyasu's expulsion edict, and fourteen after Iemitsu's grisly demonstration of intent to extirpate heretical pravity, the Bakufu was shocked by the realization that the *jashūmon* had enough vitality left to provide the spiritual impulse to a peasant rebellion. To quell the *ikki*, the Bakufu had to muster over a hundred thousand men from sixteen of its feudatory houses. This was the sole instance of such a major mobilization in two and a half centuries of the Pax Tokugawae, from the fall of Osaka Castle in 1615 to the Bakumatsu period. The rebels were not easily crushed, despite the overwhelming force that besieged them: the representatives of various daimyo interests constantly squabbled, and there was widespread lawlessness perpetrated by rōnin in the army camp.[30] *Ōmetsuke* Inoue Chikugo was meant to inspect the irregularities of the situation.

In subsequent years his responsibilities in this geographic area increased. The *Tokugawa jikki* records for Kan'ei 17/6/12 (30 July 1640): "*Ōmetsuke* Inoue Chikugo no Kami Masashige was granted an additional 6,000 *koku*, being raised to 10,000 *koku*. Each year he is to be dispatched to Nagasaki and attend to the management of that area."[31] The date of this entry should be kept in mind to understand the nature of the affairs Inoue was meant to manage.

On Kan'ei 16/7/5 (4 August 1639), taking specific reference to "the insurrection and foul plot of the sectarian rabble" of Shimabara, and accusing the Portuguese of the continued smuggling of missionaries in their ships, the Bakufu had declared: "For the reasons stated herein, the traffic of galliots shall henceforward be terminated. Accordingly, in case some do cross over [to Japan], the vessel shall be broken up and those who ventured on it shall immediately be executed by decapitation." This was the final Sakoku Edict.[32]

To the Portuguese of Macao, the end of their trade with Japan meant the ruin of their city; they resolved upon the bravura of an appeal. The embassy arrived in Nagasaki on 6 July 1640 and was confined on Deshima. Not only did the Bakufu want no part of them; it decided to demonstrate in the most rigorous fashion that it meant precisely what it promised in its decree. On the 4th of August Nagasaki was the scene of a martyrdom of merchants. Sixty-one of the venturers were beheaded; thirteen were spared to bear the tidings to Macao.[33] The "Christian Century" was over.

The careful initial distinction between missionary activity and commercial—a ban on the former, encouragement of the latter—was in the end not maintained. The prophylactic seal was meant to exclude Portuguese and Spaniards, who were considered virulently Christian beyond remedy. The subsequent development of Sakoku meant that, for all practical purposes, only Dutch and Chinese were to be allowed entry into Japan (there was also the occasional Korean embassy). But they were tolerated only under the condition that they keep their hands clean of the Catholic stain. Memoranda addressed to the Chinese and Dutch traders were attached to the decree of 1639, warning against giving passage to crypto-missionaries. And the *Tokugawa jikki* has for the sixth month of Kan'ei 17 (1640):[34]

Ōmetsuke Inoue Chikugo no Kami Masashige was ordered to caution the Chinese merchants:

In recent years there have been instances of those who used the cover of the Macao trade to venture by ship to Nagasaki with the secret intent to spread the pernicious creed of the Lord of Heaven and thus to delude the populace. This was immediately detected by the perspicacious and valiant government, which instituted stringent proscriptions. If worshippers of this pernicious creed were discovered, punishment was extended unto their relations. Nevertheless, Bateren continued being hidden in Macao vessels and brought over to delude our populace. For that reason, last year an even more stringent prohibition was issued and traffic from Macao was stopped altogether, with the injunction that any ship coming again would be completely demolished and its passengers killed. And yet the barbarians transgressed our country's prohibition and under the false pretence of presenting their side of the matter came again. Once again they dispatched ambassadors to the port of Nagasaki. Seventy of the gang were arrested and their heads put on exhibition; the ship and its various implements were broken up and sunk to the bottom of the sea. This is something you have seen before your very eyes. From now and ever after you must observe our proscriptions: thus, when the boats ply back and forth, there will be mutual profit.

Now that those who came from Macao have met their punishment the prohibition of the Jesuits is ever more stringent: that they should come is not permissible. And yet the possibility cannot be excluded that the barbarians in their surfeit of zeal to disseminate their accursed doctrine will hide within your ships, the ministers of monstrosity and preachers of perdition venturing secretly across to work deceit upon the populace. They may arrive with shaved heads or unshaven, dressed in Chinese robes or affecting our country's costume—but where will they hide their cat's eyes and protruding noses, their red hair and shrike's tongues! And moreover, it is also intolerable to give passage to natives of our country who, having traveled to that land, have been initiated into their monstrosities. It may occur that natives of that land be brought over falsely documented as our countrymen or identified as men of Ming. Anything of the sort will mean that all on board that ship, the old and the young, will be executed and the ship burnt and sunk . . .

Take care to observe the official proscriptions of our country; do not be taken in by the barbarians! It has also come to our attention that the barbarian savages seduce you with bribes and that you secretly bring them over hidden in the bottoms of your ships and let them off upon our shores; and then you falsely claim to be innocent of any knowledge of their advent. If by any chance such should occur, then an immediate denunciation to the *bugyō* office will merit a reward quite in excess of their bribes. But if the matter remain hidden and unreported, then the offenders shall certainly be bound over according to the law of the land and shall be subject to capital punishment.

The author of the instructions that Inoue Chikugo was ordered to transmit to the Ming merchants was none other than Hayashi Razan. The parvenu Inoue had graduated to travel in the best of intellectual circles. And the intellectual pope of Tokugawa Japan, author of other similar missives, had not forgotten his anti-Jesuit encounter of 1606 and cultivated the acquaintance of the inquisitor.[35] The brotherhood of purpose (if not total affinity of mind) is quite symbolic.

The search for Christians within Japan was intensified and systematized after the Shimabara Uprising. One major step of the Bakufu was to renew instructions to the daimyo for a strict winnowing of their populations. Another was the establishment of an organ in Edo to coordinate the pursuit throughout Japan of the anti-Christian policy. The office of the *shūmon-aratame yaku* (the name translates very well as Inquisitor) was instituted in the sixth month of Kan'ei 17, the month of the Macao embassy's martyrdom.[36] Inoue Chikugo was the first incumbent. The constituents of the final solution were now complete.

The expanded dragnet reached into previously neglected areas. To it between 1638 and 1640 fell victim all the missionaries who had remained active in Northern Japan.[37] Inoue scored a major coup by obtaining the apostasy of several who had been examined by Iemitsu himself. *Kirishito-ki*, the records of the *shūmon-aratame yaku*, describe this inquest as follows:[38]

During the reign of Taiyūin-sama [Iemitsu], after the fall of the castle of the Shimabara *ikki*, the Bateren Juan, Martinho Ichizaemon, and Ki[be] Pedro were brought captured from Sendai. They were taken four times before the Tribunal (*hyōjōsho*), but were not penetrated by the scrutiny. Thereupon, [the Shogun] having proceeded to the suburban residence of Sanuki no Kami, the three Bateren were summoned and [the Shogun] questioned them on the doctrines of their religion; Takuan, Yagyū Tajima no Kami, and others were present. After two or three days, Nakane Iki no Kami was sent as emissary to order Chikugo no Kami not to send the aforementioned three before the Tribunal, but that Chikugo no Kami by himself should conduct the scrutiny.

The aforementioned three Bateren were for ten days examined at the place of Chikugo no Kami concerning the Kirishitan Doctrine. After ten days Chikugo no Kami sent a retainer into their prison to submit them to the torture. Juan of the Society and Martinho Ichizaemon were made to apostatize and to invoke the name of Buddha.

They were then taken to Chikugo's place and left in custody there for a year or two, until both died of disease.

Ki[be] Pedro did not apostatize, and was killed by suspension. That was because until then he remained unregenerate. Two *dōjuku* were suspended in the same pit with Kibe; Kibe kept encouraging the *dōjuku* and therefore was killed. After Kibe had expired the two *dōjuku* apostatized. Accordingly, they were raised out of the pit and sent to prison, where they remained alive for a long time.

This interrogation of the Sendai missionaries Giovanni Battista Porro, Martinho Shikimi Ichizaemon, and Pedro Casui Kibe took place in the summer of 1639. The presence of the Zen master Takuan and the "metaphysician of the sword," Yagyū Tajima no Kami, makes this at least as notable a literary gathering as that of Fabian, the Hayashi brothers, and the poet Matsunaga Teitoku in the *Anti-Jesuit* disputation of 1606. The duo of Inoue Chikugo and Sawano Chūan is clearly established here: Ferreira, with his own brand of encouragement, took part in the operation, only to flee (according to Pagés) before Casui's criticism.[39]

That Ferreira should have been confronted with Kibe is particularly ironic. Pedro Casui Kibe had been one of the Jesuit candidates who followed their masters to Macao in 1614. But in the tight Jesuit establishment of Macao old anti-Japanese animosities again came to the fore. Closely regimented, and frustrated by an increasingly restrictive process of selectivity which barred their way to the priesthood, the more adventurous among the Japanese decided to strike out on their own and seek the satisfaction of their ambition in Rome. The Jesuits were confronted with a revolt of the acolytes. One of these recalcitrants was Kibe.

In a letter dated 16 September 1618 the *Visitator* Francisco Vieira sent the alarm to Rome:[40]

To be a priest is in Japan considered a matter of honor and of profit. But these are new believers; self-conceit is their inborn nature; they are faddists addicted to novelties. And therefore, should they return to Japan as priests and, separated from priests of the Society, draw close again to their pagan relatives and friends, falling into apostasy and schism, then such a state of affairs would mean great damage to the faithful of Japan. This sort of thing has already happened in the instance of the several that were novices or catechists or priests' assistants and left the Society. In view of these facts it will be of ultimate importance to give absolutely no assistance toward the priesthood to those that venture to Rome and various other parts of Europe, and even though they know some Latin or possess other good qualities . . . On this occasion I should like to caution Your Reverence: The Padres in Rome should not prove uncritical and rash in demonstrating good will toward any of these vagabonds that may appear in those parts without letters from some Superior, but with contrivance of a hundred or a thousand lies. That is because they will but take a hundred or a thousand missteps immediately they return here with the power and the glory of the priesthood gained.

Fabian Fucan would have relished sight of this letter.

Obstacles notwithstanding, Pedro Casui Kibe made his way to Rome to gain the power and the glory. It was a fantastic journey. He seems to have traveled by way of Goa to Ormuz, and then through Persia to Palestine to view Jerusalem. In 1620 he reached Rome and in November of that year was ordained a priest and admitted into the Society of Jesus.

Kibe took ship back to the Indies in the fleet which left Lisbon in March 1623. His adventures before he finally managed to return to Japan are too multifarious to mention.[41] His voyages were along the most tortuous of routes (he criss-crossed the periphery of Southeast Asia) and filled with countless hazards, among which a leap overboard to escape capture by the Dutch seems the least hair-raising. In 1630, by way of the Philippines, he attained his objective and—after yet another shipwreck— landed in Satsuma disguised as a merchant. For almost nine years he escaped detection. This was indeed one who might have sent Sawano Chūan scurrying: his pilgrimage to Rome and back had far eclipsed Ferreira's dead end journey to Japan.

The image of Kibe remains real because his contemporaries did not distort it. The contrast with Ferreira is feasible. But another contrasting image, that of Marcello Mastrilli SJ, is the product of the perfervid Baroque imagination.[42]

The Neapolitan Mastrilli (the traditional account has it), cured of a severe wound by the intercession of Francis Xavier, there- after sees himself as his heavenly patron's surrogate. In Rome he venerates Xavier's severed right arm, a relic sent there at the special insistence of the Jesuit General. In Madrid he draws the homage of King Philip IV for his tales of miraculous recovery and readiness for martyrdom. In Goa the tomb of Xavier is opened for him. In Macao he is foiled in his ambition to cross to Japan by the merchants' smallhearted reluctance to risk their lives on his account. He proceeds to Manila. Crowds flock to hear him. The governor promises support for his scheme to act as Xavier's own ambassador, but first retains him as chaplain of a campaign against the Moros.[43] Mastrilli bids the troops bear the portrait of Xavier instead of a flag; iron bounces off him as he leads the Spaniards in battle against the infidel. The governor begs for his continued services; but Mastrilli, ever faithful to his heaven-sent mission, refuses and sets out for Japan. The ship is wrecked on the coast of Taiwan; Mastrilli's sign of the cross becalms the seas.

In the summer of 1637 he succeeds in smuggling himself into Japan and lands in Hyūga. He plans to retrace Xavier's steps, go to the emperor, and prove to him the truth of Christianity. He is discovered. The soldiers sent to arrest him would rather adore him. Mastrilli himself beckons them to bind him. The earth quakes.

Guarded by two hundred, he arrives in Nagasaki; an aureole glows about his head. The Bakufu officials, pagan skeptics, ask him how Xavier, dead these many years, could send anyone as emissary. Mastrilli offers as proof the story of his own Neapolitan resurrection. The minions of the law profess great admiration for his tale. Only their fear of their sovereign's wrath causes them to put Mastrilli to the torture; and they submit him to the test by water. In return, Mastrilli proposes to cure all the shogun's ills by the infusion of some powdered relics of Xavier. And he promises miracles by the display of Xavier's portrait. When red-hot tongs are applied to his genitals he merely complains of his tormentors' lack of a sense of shame. Again, he is subjected to the water torture. That night, enraptured in a dream, he floats depended in midair, and a mysterious light streams down from heaven unto the place of his incarceration.

He is led to the execution ground, an iron with sharp nails thrust inside his mouth to keep him from preaching. When the gag is removed he thanks the *bugyō* for his martyrdom. He is suspended in the pit and remains there in a trance for four days. To the prying executioners he responds: "I need nothing. I am in Paradise." No blood flows from him. An angel descends from heaven into Mastrilli's pit to wipe his brow and comfort him.[44] The executioners despair of his end: the next day being an idol's festival, they decide upon a hurried decapitation.

Mastrilli prays to Xavier. The first blow of the sword fails even to inflict a scratch, the second pricks him slightly. The tremulous executioner lets drop his instrument. The martyr tells him to go about his business; only then is he able to take Mastrilli's life. At the instant of death the earth quakes throughout the land. The sun darkens above the *bugyō* residence.

One of the more sardonic measures employed by the inquisitors to confirm their captives' apostasy was to make them acknowledge that Mastrilli's aureole, which had beckoned them to Japan, was a false light. The records of the *shūmon-aratame yaku* contain the following item:[45]

When Marcello was suspended in the pit at Nagasaki (Baba Saburōzaemon having ordered the *yoriki* and *dōshin* to suspend him on the execution ground), he died in agony, screaming and wailing in the pit. All sorts of lies were fabricated about this: That Saburōzaemon, the *yoriki*, and the *dōshin* had cowered before him, mouths frozen speechless; that when Marcello was pulled out of the pit to be beheaded the sword broke; that darkness engulfed the Nagasaki guardhouse; that it had thundered and that the earth did quake. These tales were concocted at the temple of Macao and were spread abroad in Kirishitan lands. Juan, Pedro, Francisco, Alonzo, and Joseph took these lies for truth and taking six Iruman and *dōjuku* with them [ventured to Japan], to be captured off the coast of Chikuzen, brought to Nagasaki, and imprisoned. The four Bateren and the *dōjuku*, taken in by suchlike farfetched fraud and therefore come to Japan, are the worst of fools, extraordinary fools even for foreigners! Accordingly, such redounds to the glory of Japan—who is there that would dispute this? If anyone call this a lie, then San'emon, the Iruman Juan, and the others should be called on to confess the truth.

The names enumerated here are those of members of the so-called Second Rubino Group: the Cantonese *dōjuku* Juan, and the Padres Pedro Marquez, Francisco Cassola, Alonzo de Arroyo, and Giuseppe Chiara, who were captured on 27 June 1643, together with their companions, four other *dōjuku* and one Japanese Irmão. One month later they were taken from Nagasaki to Edo and there subjected to the attentions of Inoue Chikugo no Kami. The inquisitor proved triumphant. All ten apostatized. Only Arroyo later revoked his apostasy.

The purpose of the venture to Japan organized by Padre Antonio Rubino had been, states Pagés, the reconversion of Ferreira.[46] The missionaries came divided into two groups, both of which encountered their objective. The first, composed of the

Visitator Rubino himself, four other Jesuit Padres, and four *dōjuku*, landed in a small island off Satsuma in August 1642 and was captured several days later and taken to Nagasaki. Ferreira was the interpreter at their interrogation. The report has it that he was forced to withdraw by the victims' harsh words.[47] The First Rubino Group endured seven months of tortures interspersed with medical ministrations designed to keep their potential for cooperation alive. On 17 March 1643 they were suspended in the pit. The diary of the Dutch *comptoir* of Nagasaki tells us that five of them remained alive into the 25th.

The Dutch also provide primary sources concerning Ferreira's attachment to the Second Rubino Group. On 27 July 1643 their Nagasaki diary records the departure of the captives for Edo;[48] the apostate Joan is to go along so that he can put it to the Edo authorities "that the Pope considers it his prerogative to dethrone non-Catholic kings. He is to give past and present examples therefor, and recount the history of Queen Elizabeth of England and other facts, and prove that the Pope does not have the authority to do such. This especially is a point that much affects the Japanese authorities."

As it happened, there were Dutch eyewitnesses at the Jesuits' inquest in Edo, and the grim account of what they saw is transmitted to posterity in the *Atlas Japannensis* of Arnoldus Montanus. The occasion was not altogether fortuitous. A group of ten sailors from a ship that set sail from Batavia "to discover by the East of *Japan* the Northern Coasts of *Tartary*" had landed for provisions in an inlet in the North of Japan (far from Nagasaki, the sole permissible landfall) and were taken prisoner, to be brought before Inoue Chikugo for interrogation.[49] The inquisitor angled for Dutch self-incrimination by less than subtle procedure. Terrified to start with, and continuously being "ask'd also . . . if they were not *Roman Catholicks*," the sailors were further intimidated by Inoue's display of "Iron Hand-cuffs, Fetters, Chains, and other Instruments for Torture." Dismissals were followed by sudden summons; at the sessions "Inovii Sicungodonne" kept in his entourage several apostate priests, proofs of his previous rank triumphs. Themselves subjected to the tightest interrogation on their mission, the Dutch were finally put before the sight of actual torture. They were spectators at several performances of Inoue's Grand Guignol until in late September "Sicungodonne . . . signifi'd, that the imprison'd

Jesuits and *Japanners*, not being able to endure the exquisite Tortures, had deny'd Christianity."

The climactic séance took place on 20 October 1643 before a distinguished assembly: the *tairō* Sakai Sanuki no Kami was present, as was Matsudaira Izu no Kami; the inquisitors' thrall, "the Renegado Priest *Siovan*" had the lead monologue.[50]

The Dutch were "commanded to sit down on Mats by four *Jesuits*, who look'd exceeding pitifully; their Eyes and Cheeks strangely fallen in; their Hands black and blew; and their whole Bodies sadly misus'd and macerated by Torture." The Jesuits confided to the Dutch Company's interpreters that only the insufferable torments forced them to apostasy.

The inquisitor poured acid upon their wounds: "O despairing Jesuits! What Confidence can you repose in your God, who hath so shamelessly forsaken you? Is he the Creator and Governor of all Things? Why doth he not release you from your Troubles, by which your Bodies seem rather to be Anatomies than Living Creatures? Cannot the *Japan* Emperor do with you whatever he pleases, without asking leave of the *Christian* God?" But the apostates at this point still clung to their previous matrix and answered courageously that "when a tortur'd Person is not sensible of his Pain, the Soul being rapt with Heavenly Contemplations," his consolation is "that these Temporal Torments last no longer than Life." The *rōjū* could not understand such recidivism.

The *Japan* Council not well experienc'd in the *Romish* Religion, wanted Questions to ask them, and therefore call'd for *Syovan* the Apostate Priest, who was there ready for that purpose. So soon as he saw the *Jesuits*, he look'd very fiercely upon them, notwithstanding he had formerly been of their Order, and in a scoffing manner said,

"Now fie upon you *Jesuits*, that make this World in an Uproar. How you vapor of your God and Salvation? Are none sav'd but *Jesuits*, or those that embrace your Opinion? In what consists your Interest in Heaven? Is it because you privately dissemble with, and defraud all Princes; and gathering, hoard up the Worlds Treasure? Had you remained still in your usual Pleasures, the *Japan* Prisons had not harbor'd such a crue of Antichrists; nay, *Japan* had never shed so much Blood: for thousands, by your Delusions, were taken from their Worship of the ancient Gods *Amida*, *Xaca*, and *Canon*, and embrac'd the *Christian* Religion, for which they suffer'd the cruellest Deaths. Was it under a pretence to win Souls? Why did you then carry so

many Tun of Gold yearly out of *Japan*? And why did you plot to
bring *Japan* under the Subjection of the *Spanish* Tyrant, and so to
order all things according to your pleasure? But now, what is the
Power of the *Christian* God? Look upon your miserable Bodies; can
he not help you? Where then is he Omnipotent? Will he not help
you? Where is his Mercy? O foolish thought of Salvation! You are
distracted to continue thus in your stubborn humor, imagining to
receive great Rewards from God, and great Esteem of your Successors,
in suffering wilfully your Bodies to be thus tormented. I ask once
again, Why doth not your God help you? Certainly your Life is not
in your Hands, but in the Emperors of Japan, who when he pleaseth
can punish and torture you more than ever he hath done yet."

This the *Hollanders* understood very well, because *Syovan* spoke with
a loud Voice; and they also were us'd to his Stile, by reason of
their conversation with him in their Inn. But whilst *Syovan* rail'd thus
at the *Jesuits*, he seem'd exceedingly to please two of the *Japan* Council,
Sackay Sammoccysame, and *Matsodairo Ysossama*, with his Discourse, and
chiefly when he spoke of *Amida* and *Xaca*.

The Dutch later heard from the attendants of their hostel that
two of the Romish priests had revoked their apostasy. Ferreira,
who was ready to make the trip back to Nagasaki, had to be
retained in Edo on their account. He was needed: the Jesuits
were to be put again to the torture.[51]

The account reproduced by Montanus is fully persuasive.
The *Kirishito-ki* testifies to the accurate description of procedure:
the points of its Document XI, "Arguments which Chikugo no
Kami put to the Bateren in order to awaken doubts in them,
inextricably convince them, and cause them to apostatize," have
at their core the proof of Deus' ineffectuality by the abandonment
of his own.[52] The "Arguments" borrow information and
terminology from Fabian Fucan's tract, and from Ferreira's. But
the standard previous polemic is by Inoue channeled into a
horrid new dimension. The theologian in his study would
dismiss the "Arguments" as crude and unworthy. But in the
victim of torture the processes of intellection are racked, distorted,
and destroyed. What compounds *Angst* is what persuades. The
infernal physical torture is here the tangent of a sphere of
spiritual agonies. Unknowingly, the Inquisitor had lit upon the
weak point of the Christian psyche, the sense of a tormenting
Divine Wrath.

The religious sufferer's microcosm, Luther tells us, seems at
times of fear of justification reduced to ashes. "Then God

appears horrifyingly angry and with him, the whole creation. There can be no flight, no consolation, neither within nor without, but all is accusation. Then he laments, 'I am cast away from thy face: Lord accuse me not in thy Wrath.' In this moment, marvellous to relate, the soul cannot believe it can ever be redeemed, but that it is suffering a punishment not yet complete . . . and left only with the naked longing for help, and terrifying trembling, but it knows not whence help can come. This is the soul stretched out with Christ, so that all his bones can be numbered, nor is there any corner not filled with the most bitter bitterness, horror, fear, dolour, but all these things seem eternal."[53]

When the body is in fact stretched upon the torture rack, and the sarcous tissues infused with waves of excruciating pain, and well-aimed mockery of God's mercy removes from the weakened spirit the notion of identity with Christ, then for some the moment comes when the tangent dips and the bubble of purposefulness is punctured, and there is a religious void. The True State turns into No State, and the Ultimate Reality leads to apostasy.

The combination with *anatsurushi* made Inoue's "Arguments" persuasive. The haunting presence of Ferreira beckoned toward a nihilist escape. The sufferer was saved from the negating sense of isolation by an identity with the damned.

I have stated above that Ferreira's *Kengiroku* is an informer's tome weakly framed by intellect.[54] But now the exemplary value of the tract becomes apparent: the inquisitors who "wanted Questions to ask" their victims needed a textbook of terminology. The lack of a systematic exposition would seem to be more a reflection of their requirements than an indication of the author's lack of care. Ferreira did not himself write the volume; he compiled themes on suggested items of interest. It is established that he did not write Japanese but instead used "barbarian characters"—romanization—to set down his essays, which had to be transcribed.[55] His editors trimmed to fit. The only thing that need further be said about *Deceit Disclosed* is that it is by nature remarkably similar to Document XIII of *Kirishito-ki*, "An outline of the religion,"[56] the author of which should be sought among the apostates of the Second Rubino Group. The *Kengiroku* and the outline bear the same stamp of the pressure of the inquisitors' demand for technical information.

Information on Christianity and its diffusion in Japan is one part of the contents of *Kirishito-ki*. But the most significant portions of this manual are those which deal with the methods of the *shūmon-aratame yaku*. The greater part of the documents was compiled during the early years of tenure of the second Inquisitor, Hōjō Awa no Kami Ujinaga, who succeeded Inoue in 1658.

Inoue departed the office in circumstances that were less than glorious. His prosecution of the anti-Christian policy had for almost twenty years seemed successful. But the seed had not really been extirpated: in 1657, 608 Christians were discovered in Ōmura; 411 of these proved unregenerate and were executed. The incident may well have contributed to Inoue's resignation.[57]

The *Kirishito-ki* is Inoue's monument, and in the main represents his effort to initiate Hōjō Awa into his duties. The documents were meant strictly for internal use, and not for propaganda. As Cieslik and Voss point out, this unquestionable measure of authenticity greatly increases their value for the historian. The purpose and procedures of the inquisition are herein revealed in all their grim sobriety and downright terrifying banality. The meticulous nature of the process is best illustrated in Document VII of the compendium, which deserves quotation *in extenso*:[58]

To Keep in Mind in the Religious Scrutiny

1. At first the religionists when questioned whether they were Kirishitans would hide nothing at all, responding that they were Kirishitans. But these days they hide their religion as they can.

2. Old wives and women when made to tread upon the image (*fumie*) of Deus get agitated and red in the face; they cast off their headdress; their breath comes in rough gasps; sweat pours from them. And, according to the individual, there are reportedly women who venerate the *fumie*, but in a way to remain unobserved.

3. During the religious scrutiny the native province and the place of extended residence are to be inquired into, for reasons of consideration whether it be a province where Bateren have not wandered or one which they have visited and where their religion is diffused.

4. They engrave sword pommels with tiny *imagem* or put *imagem* and Bateren bones, ashes, and suchlike inside their pillows, inside pottery and incense boxes, or into medicinal salve. All of this has happened, so pay attention.

5. The Kirishitan religion prohibits suicide. But during what they call *jejum* they reduce their meals and when they do eat they eat but little, eating moreover just enough of radish, turnip, or the sort to keep

alive. Gradually the body weakens and they expire. This has happened; but they persuade their *consciencia* that it is not suicide, for they die even while taking food to themselves. And thus they die.

6. When one used to sentence them to death by suspension, or to the fire, the Bateren kept right on being shipped to Japan. But afterward, when one made them apostatize and assume a Japanese religion, when they were made to stay in Kobinata[59] and given wives, when ten rations were given to each Bateren and a *kan* of silver, when they were subjected to close questioning on various topics and to the torture when they failed to respond—since this mode of procedure was adopted, the religionists have become few.

The wooden horse is good for such by way of torture.[60] But when someone without the proper understanding is assigned as supervisor and, deeming the progress of the torture hopeless, increases its severity, then they merely die. Or they get ill, so that the torture cannot be continued. At any rate, the torture must be conducted in such a way that they do not die, and that is an order.

There are various pluses and minuses in the conduct of the torture by suspension, the mild way and the severe. Reportedly there have been occasions when scruples arose over the possibility that an innocent person has been suspended in the pit or trussed. On the other hand, it has often happened when the suspension was undertaken at the execution ground that the outcaste executioners (*eta*) got bored with it and killed the prisoner. Use prudence in the matter!

7. It has happened that Bateren during the scrutiny by indirection proselytized and in various ways tricked even the *bugyō* and, of course, his retainers as well. During the very scrutiny! Keep this in mind.

8. As they are being taken to the torture, they try in various ways to gauge the mind of the one come to supervise it; and when they think it is a supervisor with some mercy and compassion, they attempt to arouse an increase of this mercy and compassion.

9. In the Kirishitan religion there is glory.[61] So they claim, but when one has them queried under torture, or in the pit—"What sort is this your glory? Let's see you produce it!"—then, since what they claim is false, nothing extraordinary happens at all.

10. When the Bateren, Iruman, *dōjuku*, and their religionists apostatized they were pressed as hard as possible to adopt a new religion. They were made to join the Zen or the Pure Land Sect and to attend a temple, enrolled as parishioners. The Bateren and Iruman were also given wives. Moreover, when they relapsed they were not treated as Kirishitans but rather as common pickpockets and thieves, and were sentenced to decapitation. Two or three *dōjuku* and religionists had their heads chopped off in Kobinata, and in prison some fifty or sixty.

11. Formerly when Bateren were executed their bones and ashes were secretly distributed to various parts. The bones and ashes of outstanding religionists were also gathered up. Quite a long time ago the bones and ashes of those who died *martyr* in Japan were even shipped to foreign parts.

12. To date there have been no Kirishitans among the [Buddhist] monks, but there have been some turned *yamabushi*.

13. In every particular during the inquest the *bugyō* is to take care that the religionists in prison or in the pit know he speaks no falsehood and does not alter what he has once said. Otherwise they will mistrust the *bugyō* and will be reluctant to speak out, in informing upon their relations as in their own apostasy. This must be made clear down to the lowest grade of those charged with the scrutiny.

14. It will be an obstacle to the scrutiny if the *bugyō* or his retainers and officials should gain among the Kirishitans the reputation of merciful and compassionate *bugyō* and officials. But it is much worse yet on those grounds unreasonably to torment them with increased severity. One must very carefully strive to appreciate the religion's mentality.

If during the inquest they should desire to climb off the wooden horse and urinate as the need arises, or to have a smoke, there is some profit in acceding to their wishes. But also, according to the occasion and the person, it may be wise not to let them come down too often.

15. If the husband is Kirishitan, so is the wife. If the child is Kirishitan, so is the parent. If father and mother are Kirishitan, so are the children. Generally speaking, seven or eight out of ten will be Kirishitan.

Korean Kirishitans, once converted, are deeply dedicated, the men and the women. Especially the women, once persuaded, are deeply dedicated.

16. Here is how the scrutiny should be conducted: On the first day one listens to the general drift of what they have to say, and on the second and third day also only listens to what they say. Only after acknowledging their testimony does one put points of doubt to them. It is bad to get involved in disputations and sudden assaults with doubts until one has with a cordial manner listened to their piece. The religionists love to end up in hammerheaded arguments. But when a debate is waged on the afterlife—for which neither side possesses proofs—and it all does wind up in a hammerheaded disputation, and the bystanders get the impression that the *bugyō* is in the wrong, and even his retainers get to thinking that there is some reason to this Kirishitan doctrine—now that is the worst of all.

The pernicious Kirishitan doctrine preaches naught but a myriad lies to delude the people. Unless one strives for conclusive reason, to make the people understand the pravity, the retainers down to the lowest rank of those involved in the scrutiny will deem [the Kirishitan doctrine] admirable.

17. The Bateren teach their Kirishitan religionists about the scrutiny that the *bugyō* is a man of wisdom and the ability to distinguish right from wrong; but when he undertakes the religious scrutiny his wisdom is beclouded and his eloquence paralyzed. But the religionists, though they be neither eloquent nor intelligent, will for the glory and through the special grace of God develop wisdom and clearest intelligence. Thus they teach, and the religionists size up their situation according to this teaching.

Then there are those who, even at the moment of confrontation with their informer at the *bugyō* office, set their clothes in order and in an ever so polite a manner show their respect for the *bugyō* and refrain from bad words even toward the informer. That is because they have been taught that when the time comes for them to ascend into heaven they will first be called before the *bugyō*. They feel no hate even toward the one who has informed against them. For they are taught that if they should consider him their enemy, then the road to heaven would be barred to them.

18. Among the territorial lords there are those whose prosecution of Kirishitans is conducted well, and those who do it badly. They hide in provinces where the religious prosecution is badly conceived. Since in that case they find it easy to blend into the populace, in such provinces there unfailingly are Kirishitans.

The greatest care must be exercised during the test in the parish temple. Even the priests are fooled. Heretofore the Kirishitans have not had their corpses cremated. They have put the cadaver into a tub in the home and, placing inside the tub a *cruz* made of planks, they have tied up the top of the tub tightly and buried it in the ground. It is true that in places with a dearth of firewood the Buddhists also use interment; but one must be wary in such places also. Discovery of a Kirishitan has sometimes resulted when a corpse was exhumed and the tub's inside scrutinized.

There are provinces where peasants, townsmen, and artisans are made to take a Japanese and a Southern Barbarian oath[62] and to register in a temple, and after that are left alone with no test for another year or two. To such negligent places Kirishitans unfailingly come to hide. The instances are many.

Inoue had cynically stated that "it is bad to take a liking to torture and to depend upon it," and he had insisted that "one must carefully consider the criminal's mentality."[63] But the intrusions into the criminal's mentality were made possible only by the ultimate reliance upon torture. The jarring switch from the soft and pliable manner to the harsh and threatening was in the classical interrogator's mode. The assaults with Fabianesque rhetoric further took advantage of disoriented minds. And finally the pedant demanded something in writing. The consummation of the dismal self-betrayal was the signed confession. This is the sum of Inoue's intellectuality.

Inoue Chikugo was an intellectual in the same sense as was Adolf Eichmann. His diabolism was that of the farceur drawn to the query of cadavers. His method was quite successful. What is more, it strikes one as being quite modern.

Are there redeeming qualities to Inoue's dreary Faust? Curiously enough, Ferreira has some slight claim to a medical reputation, and he was the Western informant in the compilation of a Japanese tract on astronomy. Ebisawa Arimichi, whose magnum opus is a study of the lineage of the Southern Barbarian Learning, and who takes infinite pains to establish a distinction between "Southern Barbarian" studies and "Dutch," views him as a major figure in the continuation of the former.[64] Ferreira was, after all, a Southern Barbarian.

But he was not a medical specialist. As Ebisawa himself points out, the Society of Jesus had prohibited its members' engagement in medical training. News of this proscription had reached Japan in 1560 and forced Almeida to turn over his Funai hospital to Japanese. Francisco Pasio had in 1612 reiterated the prohibition.[65] The chance for Ferreira to become familiar with medicine came only after his apostasy. That he did dabble in such studies is clear; but his experience was under Dutch auspices. The diary of the *comptoir* of Nagasaki in the year 1648 registers a whole series of his visits toward this end. On 12 July, for instance, the apostate Portuguese missionary Joan appears to inquire about medicines. On 26 July he comes to watch an operation on one of Inoue Chikugo's servants, who had for three years been plagued with an open wound in his leg—"so that if need be he could learn to perform the cure himself." Finally, on 26 October, he brings in deepest secrecy a horn of the beast *eenhorn*; but a pharmacist from the Dutch ship happened to be present, and Chūan was surprised to hear that what he actually had in hand was the horn of a rhinoceros, not of a unicorn.[66]

Ferreira passed on the arcane knowledge revealed to him by the

Dutch to a group of disciples, some of whom were to become physicians in official employ. The notes he compiled remain extant under several titles. For instance, the library of the Kyoto University Faculty of Medicine contains a manuscript purporting to be Chūan's "Secret Transmission of the Southern Barbarian Style of Surgery."[67] When published in a more elaborate edition in 1696 and again in 1705, the transmission had shed the suspect Southern Barbarian association and bore the name *Oranda-ryū geka shinan* (Introduction into the Dutch style of surgery); no attribution of authorship was made. The first paragraph reads: "In the Five Parts of the human body there are four types of blood called *Humours*. These are: first, *Sanguis*; second, *Cholera*; third, *Phlegma*; fourth, *Melancholia*."[68] The work, as can readily be surmised, is an exposition of the humoral theory. It contains prescriptions for the treatment of various wounds and ailments, and comprises also a pharmacopoeia and a glossary of technical terms.

Ferreira's familiarity with other branches of learning scarcely exceeded his smattering of knowledge in medicine. His training in astronomy, for example, does not seem to have gone beyond the general orientation given all Jesuit novices. But yet another ironic aspect of the career of this apostate is that he did succeed in justifying what the still-Christian Fabian had tried, and failed, to demonstrate to Hayashi Razan—the pre-eminence of certain basic aspects of Western science.

Chūan acted as the Western informant in the compilation of a tract completed with rebuttals by Mukai Genshō, *Kenkon bensetsu* (Debate on astronomy). According to Mukai's Preface, two or three years after the 1643 arrival and capture of a group of Padres, Inoue Chikugo ordered Chūan to translate an astronomy book which one of them had brought:[69] thus the propositions which Genshō was called to criticize were first put down in a sort of Japanese. Ferreira left the text in Roman letters, which were inaccessible to all but a very few; in 1656, acting on the behest of the *Nagasaki Bugyō*, the translator Nishi Kichibei and Genshō collaborated to transcribe it into the native writing system. Which one of the Padres of the Second Rubino Group bore the book with him is unclear; neither is the original author established.[70] Ferreira may have added his own interpolations.

Genshō's itemized critiques of Southern Barbarian learning are not blessed with internal consistency. He roundly condemns barbarian science for its lack of a metaphysical base and for its general deviltry.[71] And yet in sum—no matter how reluctantly— he admits the superiority of Western astronomy and geography. He continues to emphasize the sinister aspect of Southern Barbarian science; for all that, he constantly and frantically searches for classical Eastern precedents which would demolish European claims to originality.[72]

The religious bond (or religious bias) of Western science seems to him obvious. He intimates that the foreigners must be expert in geography to enable the King of South Barbary by the use of foul methods and pernicious doctrines to encapture the world. Only after a series of imprecations against barbarian false views, extravagant inventions, fantastic teachings, and extremities of monstrous trickery does Genshō acknowledge that the earth is round. If nothing else, the Kenkon bensetsu demonstrates the tortured nature of the orthodox manqué striving to remain loyal to the Chu Hsi tradition while having to affirm the verity of barbarian observations.[73]

Ferreira's own introductory statement is dated to correspond to 1650. Mukai's Preface states that Chūan died before he had the opportunity to put a title to the tract.[74]

Thus finished our Renaissance man, after a life of engagement in Philosophy and Medicine (und leider auch Theologie), and even a form of Jurisprudence.

Ferreira's confrères treated him in Baroque fashion. The reputation of the Society was refurbished by use of a series of reports which in 1653 and 1654 by devious routes (via a Japanese mandarin of Tonkin!) reached the ears of Jesuit superiors.[75] According to these stories, Ferreira after long years of infidelity was seized by remorse, and returned to the True Faith. Betrayed by a servant to whom he had taught the Christian doctrine— or, alternatively, betraying himself by his loud addresses to God —he was taken from his sickbed and dragged before the bugyō.

Delplace cites the 1655 annua of Padre João Nuñes from Macao:[76]

Ferreira was 74 years old when the Lord deigned to take consideration of the prayers and tears of the Society and of the blood of our martyrs: He bestowed upon the old man a sickness which made him take note of the approaching eternity, and he was heard to say with a great feeling of pain: "O God! O Lord! Is it possible that I abandoned the faith out of fear of losing a transient life? O Father of Mercies! *erravi sicut ovis quae periit.* Give strength to this body enfeebled by age, so that I may suffer and confess my faith and my love for Thee!"

The news is transmitted to the *bugyō*, who has him interrogated. Ferreira's witness is: "In truth, I am in anguish, for I have sinned against the True God of Heaven and Earth; nothing afflicts me as much as the fact that I abandoned Him for fear of death."— "He is in delirium," comment the laughing tormentors. Ferreira's response is: "No, I have my entire presence of mind."

The Jesuits' probabilist impulses moved them to report: He was three days in the pit, and died a martyr.[77]

Chapter 8

The Effects of Propaganda:
Epitaph to an Encounter

$\mathbf{P}$ ROPAGANDA wears many faces. The deliberate manipulation of symbols affects the thought and value patterns of the audience it reaches, but over the long run also reduces the perceptiveness of the propagandists. The anti-Christian propaganda of the Tokugawa period is a good illustrative case. A mixture of faith and fear, analytical conviction and irrational assumption, brought it into use and sustained it. Some of the period's most eminent intellectual figures eventually fell into its trap.

The social value of this propaganda to the Tokugawa system is obvious. The Christians were execrated: loyalty and obligation to the Tokugawa, who had choked off the barbarians' threat, thereby came into focus. The diversion of anxieties to the outside reinforced the factors of homogeneity which were already strong within Japan. The Tokugawa realm under Sakoku became a single organism: the particular elements which it contained were fused into a social whole. The shut-in populace was malleable. Anti-Christian propaganda assisted in the integration of its allegiances.

Interestingly enough, the word "propaganda" seems to derive from the name of a committee of the Roman curia, the Sancta Congregatio de Propaganda Fide. This Holy Congregation for the Propagation of the Faith came into existence in the early seventeenth century and was charged with the coordination of Catholic mission activities. "Hence"—Bruce L. Smith comments —"to many Catholics the word may have, at least when referring to ecclesiastical utterances, a responsible and respectable connotation that it lacks in many other contexts."[1] Indeed, religious propaganda is always defined as salutary elucidation by its agents and their positive reactors. The counterpropagandist who strives to demolish that claim can achieve his ends by a *reductio ad absurdum*; but when his audience is plebeian and untutored, it may be more effective to sow fear and abhorrence. The dread of alien designs and practices was the emotion invoked by the Tokugawa period's persuaders.

The Kirishitan Bateren with his flapping bat wings, cunning red eyes, and grasping bear claws became the principal scare symbol of Sakoku. Close behind him was the seduced Christian believer, who lashed himself in his religious blindness and besmirched himself with blood. Blood, brocade, and gold are the constant images of the popular anti-Christian literature. The Bateren dazzle with their exotic finery, and they buy allegiance. But the end result is death.

The vehicle of this message to the lower classes was the profuse genre of popular narratives of the *Kirishitan monogatari* type. They were indeed very popular. A standard bibliography lists 113 items in the category, and that list is by no means exhaustive.[2] In the libraries of the Kyoto area alone several dozen variants may be inspected. The chapbooks were mostly passed down in manuscript, were copied and recopied, and evidently consumed with great fascination. The pages are well-thumbed, begrimed with much handling, and dotted with ink stains. The effort to reach the semiliterate is apparent: some texts go to great lengths to spell out their meaning, providing not only the *kana* reading for the simplest compounds but also an even simpler equivalent word.[3]

Within the Closed Country consciousness there existed a nerve center which craved exposure to the exotic element and could be reached by pleasure-giving shocks with the bizarre. The *Kirishitan monogatari* genre filled the need in an officially sanctioned manner. Here the barbarian perfidy was stripped of its cloak, deceit disclosed, and truth revealed triumphant; and all this was done with a bewildering simplicity. A random admixture of stories of the digestive tract made the vulgar chortle. There is no need to speculate about the extent of official inspiration behind the genre. The novels were popular because they were inherently interesting. The Christians' outlandish wickedness was all the more fascinating because it was proscribed. Why not enjoy it at a distance?

The *Kirishitan monogatari* was published in 1639, the year of the final Sakoku Edict, and was the first to bear all the essential hallmarks of the genre.[4] It was reprinted in 1665 under the title *Kirishitan taiji monogatari* (Tale of the quelling of Kirishitans). Illustrations accompanied the text of this edition, and the result was a perfect example of pop art. Yet the printed prototype does not seem to have been disseminated as widely as its handwritten successors. Perhaps, for all its fantasies, it was too factually oriented. The first of the novels was also the most restrained because it was still rooted in history, as may be surmised from the date of composition. The eighteenth-century works had lost even that feeble root.

Variants of the *Kirishitan shūmon raichō jikki* (A true account of the Kirishitan religion's advent to Our Empire) seem to have been the farthest spread. What distinguishes one of them from another is merely the relative quantity of inventive detail lavished on describing the antecedents of the Southern Barbarian plot and locating the Kirishitan Country, the lair of the bogey-man Urugan Bateren. Sometimes the copyist took umbrage at the overly great inventiveness: the geographical extravagances flew in the face of what he knew from other sources. For instance, a copy of the *Kirishitan raichōki* dated 1761 contains a rather skeptical epilogue. And the compiler of the *Nanbanji kōhaiki* (The rise and fall of the Temple of Southern Barbarians; early eighteenth century?) deleted the overture dealing with the Great King Kōshinpi's country altogether, stating that he doubted its existence; for it was not to be found in Nishikawa Joken's atlas.[5]

Books of the *Raichō jikki* subcategory as a rule begin with an outline of Kōshinpi's plot to subjugate Japan by religious means, and his efforts to enlist Urugan Bateren and Furaten Bateren as his agents. These two adepts dwell in the far-off land of Yaso (Jesus), where they practice an art called Hisōjiyō (Philosophia) and by the application of its dark secrets have attained perfect mastery over nature.[6] After declining thrice, they agree to become accomplices in the imperial conspiracy; and it is decided that Urugan should go first in order to spy out the prospects of success.

Urugan arrives in Japan; sixty-six pine trees in the Sumiyoshi Shrine fall. What renders his mission feasible is the fact that Oda Nobunaga is in power in Japan; for this is a dark and evil ruler who takes delight in wrecking Buddhist temples and the shrines of the gods. Not only does Oda build the Temple of Southern Barbarians for Urugan, he orders him to invite others from his home country. At this news there is great rejoicing in Emperor Kōshinpi's world. Furaten then crosses over to abet Urugan's devices; and with him come the Iruman Gerigori and Yariisu.

The coven is now complete, and we may identify as its members Padre Organtino, the Fratres of the mendicant orders in a collective anonym, Gregorio de Cespedes, and Luis de Almeida. (Later on the inspector Furukomu—Valignano—arrives, and brings other Bateren and Iruman with him.[7]) They go about their work in the most insidious fashion.

Unlike Buddhist monks, they do not accept alms from their parishioners but rather hand out gold and silver freely. More-over, they concentrate upon the scurvy. "They sent out men to search throughout the Capital and its outskirts, in wayside chapels in the hills and plains, and even underneath bridges. They gathered in outcasts and beggars and others with diseases and afflictions, had them take a bath and cleanse the body, and gave them clothing, succor, shelter, and care. Yesterday's beggar today dressed in cloth of Cathay." We may infer that these are far from commendable deeds. The Bateren attract to them-selves the base rabble. What else is this but rank subversion?

The ignorant are tricked and beg to have their souls cured as well as their bodies. They first must learn the mantra "Shigo Shōten Haraizō Zensu Maro." After seven days of constant repetition of this formula they are admitted into the holy of holies. All are dazzled by its splendors and are con-verted. The Bateren then teach them to flagellate themselves. *Exeunt omnes*, hands dripping blood.[8]

This will suffice for an initial taste. One might merely list some of the other, familiar *dramatis personae*: Takayama Ukon, Konishi Yukinaga (some variants add Ōkubo Chōan), and—most familiar of all—the sometime Zen priest Fabian. This leprous beggar turns into the cleverest of Kirishitan zealots. The dis-putation is, of course, his greatest scene. Mummed up in gorgeous finery, he works on an old woman through whom he hopes to ensnare Hideyoshi. We know that he cannot succeed, despite all of his sacrilegious tricks; his nemesis Hakuō is there to foil him. As Fabian flees in disgrace, so must all Kirishitans: those who do not admit defeat are found out and eradicated. Hideyoshi chastises them when they overdo their magic in his presence. The Tokugawa complete the pious task: Japan is freed of Kirishitans. Our authors do not fail to note that the Shimabara rebels tried to ban the righteous hosts opposing them with the mantra "Santa Mariya, Santa Mariya."

The books' evident popularity is an index of their success. No doubt they achieved the objective of manipulating many minds. They presented a prefabricated argument. They are not good literature. But merely to condemn them as primitive, and "bad" because they served the "feudal" purpose would be too simple a judgment. They are of genuine use in a comparative study of propaganda techniques, and that is their great value to the historian.

Consider a brief representative section of the *Nanbanji kōhaiki*, where Fabian and his two fellow outcasts are inducted into the Kirishitan mysteries. Out of a surfeit of joy at gaining such valuable converts, the Bateren teach them their magic. And there, within the precincts of the Temple of Southern Barbarians, a towel is turned into a horse, a handful of dust thrown in the air becomes a flock of birds, flowers bloom upon a withered tree, from clumps of mud jewels emerge, a Bateren floats in midair or disappears into the ground, suddenly summons forth black clouds and makes rain or snow fall at his will.[9] How distant is all this from Marcello Mastrilli's story?

Or take the reverse example. The *Kirishitan monogatari* contains a chapter titled "How the followers of the Kirishitan religion were inserted in straw sacks."[10] The topic is a persecution which took place in the Kyoto area in 1614, so that some of the account's readers in 1639 must have still remembered the events described. The writer must therefore mix fact and burlesque in just the proper measures; and he comes up with the story of a droll and even good-natured happening. The Kirishitans are wrapped in two sacks each, snug like bugs in self-spun casings, squirming little. For a while they keep blabbing, "Zensumaru, Zensumaru." But as mealtime approaches they get hungry and their stomachs start growling. So they fall away from their religion, and are sent home "to the sound of much laughter." At first sight we assume this to be an ordinary fable and are inclined to doubt its historicity.

But then we turn to Avila Girón's account of the same incident and find a scene of terror:[11]

This is what was done this year in Meaco and Oçaca to the men
and the women. They were inserted into straw sacks (such as are used
for rice), with only the neck sticking out, and were left pilloried
on the streets and in the public places. The husbands were torn from
their wives and the mothers from their children. And they were
exposed naked to public scorn. The men had their hands tied behind
their backs. And the women had their thighs thrust apart: and then
with tongs and hooks they pried into their private parts . . . Most of
the Christians endured these tortures and other such torments, even the
tender, chaste, and pure women bearing them with stouthearted
fortitude. But that there should have been several apostates is hardly
surprising.

With the poltroonery stripped away, the *Kirishitan monogatari* is
no longer amusing.

The subsequent chapbooks do not include the detail of martyrdoms or mass persecutions, and only mention them in passing.
A century of the Tokugawa peace had intervened, and even the
dressed-up picture of oppressive measures would have been
inconsistent with the desired image of humane government. One
event, however, was not forgotten. The chapbooks invariably
refer to the Shimabara Rebellion of 1637–38. A huge literature
of military romances grew up about it. Some of these, such
as the *Kinka keiranshō*, melt together the *Raichō jikki* and the
record of the peasant war.[12] None doubt that the pernicious
faith stirred up the peasants. And yet, when we examine the
rebels' associations with Christianity we find ourselves in a
deepening shadow zone.

Every one of the Tokugawa analysts of the Christian peril
was concerned with the question of the religion's role in paving
the way for conquistadors from abroad. But in the mind of
every one it was also clear that the paramount danger was not
external conquest but rather internal subversion. The proof
seemed evident from the Shimabara Uprising. The Tokugawa
leadership could with little effort define the rebellion as Christian-
inspired. This definition was indubitably one of the critical
determinants of the Sakoku policy. And yet it may be argued
that this most manifest of Kirishitan revolutionary acts was, from
the standpoint of the Christian teaching, quite heterodox and
that the rebels, far from being guided by the Christian ideology,
were men who were desperate because they were spiritually
rootless.

The eschatology of the Shimabara Uprising was the common fantastic delusion of the poor, exploited, and downtrodden. Their movement may be termed an eruption of social chiliasm. The Tokugawa, needless to say, were not familiar with the history of peasant revolts in mediaeval Europe. The modern student, however, will have little difficulty in recognizing the type.[13]

No visitor to the Amakusa-Shimabara area can fail to be impressed by the evidence of the pains which the problem of agricultural survival required. The landscape is extremely beautiful but obviously infertile. The rice paddies have over the centuries been terraced up to the very tops of steep hills; the crop they give is meager. It takes very little imagination to reconstruct the implications of that setting for its seventeenth-century inhabitants, especially if one considers the extortions they had to suffer.

The *Kirishitan monogatari* states about Matsukura Katsuie, the lord of Shimabara: "In a domain designed to yield 60,000 *koku* of rice he made his own survey, arbitrarily setting the yield at 120,000 *koku* and taking from the peasants fifty or sixty percent of this estimate, being inordinately greedy . . . How could they sustain life itself under those circumstances!"[14] It will be noted that, according to this report, the peasants were forced to deliver up as much as their land was supposed to produce, or even more. As if that were not enough, Matsukura devised still more and yet unheard-of levies: there were taxes on windows and on shelves, on hibachi and tatami; there was a head tax on each newborn child and a "hole" tax on everyone who died and was buried.[15] In cases of evasion or abscondence, "the wife and children were held hostage and put to the ordeal by water. Or they were made to wear *mino* straw capes and these were set on fire. The victims writhed and tossed themselves about in agony, and this was fun to watch and called the Mino Dance."[16] Under these circumstances one did not need to be a Christian to revolt.

Shimabara, of course, had been solidly Christian since the days when the Arima governed it; five Jesuits were working there as late as 1632.[17] Amakusa had as old a Christian tradition, one which dated back to Almeida's visit in 1566. By 1592 there were twenty-three thousand Christians on the islands.[18] After 1614 they were forced by increasingly severe control measures to reconvert or go underground, but their faith had not been quenched completely. What may be even more important is that Amakusa had for eleven years been under the control of Konishi Yukinaga. The Konishi rule was finished when Yukinaga met disaster at Sekigahara in 1600; but when the Terazawa gained possession of the islands in 1603, they also inherited the presence of large numbers of Dom Agostinho's rōnin. The Terazawa daimyo, true to the Early Modern pattern, attempted to carry through the separation of the samurai and the peasant status, and in the process annulled whatever privileges Konishi's former vassals had retained. An additional pool of discontent was created. The ingredients for an *ikki* were present, in Amakusa as in Shimabara. A residual Christianity activated them. But it was no longer the Christianity of the missionaries.

The population of Shimabara had been subjected to active propaganda efforts designed to make them revert since 1613, when the Jōdo priest Banzuii Chiyo was dispatched to the area by Ieyasu and "began to strew about the seed of Amida's accursed sect and try to seduce the Christians . . . who had drunk Holy Gospel with their mother's milk."[19] Although this seed initially fell on barren ground, the efforts of propaganda combined with the measures of persecution in the long run could not but succeed. Indeed, Japanese sources speak of mass apostasy in the time of Katsuie's father, Shigemasa, who for a time was lenient towards Christians but took heed of the shogunate's warning to be more stringent. By 1628, states one report, "all of the peasants of the Matsukura domain had expressed their reform in religion."[20] But these sources also complain that the fire lived on in apparently dead coal: the *Korobi Kirishitan* (those who had fallen away) relapsed, what had been eradicated grew again, the extinct was resurrected. And in 1637 it flared up in rebellion.

There is a series of paradoxes involved. The daimyo requires a formal adherence to Buddhism. But even the formality means the betrayal of Deus. The missionaries' propaganda has maintained that martyrdom is the only way to meet the final test. But some of the missionaries have themselves apostatized; at any rate, none are any longer present to give guidance. The lapse from Christian orthodoxy is the only way to preserve Christianity. But those who reject martyrdom and tread the sacred image are no longer Christian. The orthodox resistance is passive, or rather a reproduction of the Passion. But the grievances are too severe to be resolved by such submissiveness. The combined weight of the paradoxes broke down the Christian propaganda's effect. The exhortations to martyrdom and sainthood could not be followed.[21]

The peasants of Shimabara and Amakusa were goaded beyond the breaking point by extortions and famines. They did not seek the sainted status of martyr; what they wanted was to survive on this earth. Therefore they sought to establish on this earth a chiliast paradise. The structure of the missionaries' Christianity had been dissolved by the persecution.[22] For a decade and more the guise of apostasy had masked the peasants' own structure. The daimyo's prong stripped off that cloak and made their religion reveal itself as a millenarian dream. The peasants little knew that their action could never recertify them as Christians: for the Church which they had once left had always associated the active rebel with heresy.

Peasant messianism was the raw stuff of the rebellion. Rōnin discontent gave it sinew. The leader, Amakusa Shirō Tokisada, was the son of a Konishi rōnin, and there were many such among the stalwarts of the fighting. But the organizing force was clearly religious. Prophecies and portents abounded. One of the Kirishitans' circulars declared: "An angel was sent as messenger and the instructions he transmitted must therefore be passed on to the villagers. The sixty-six provinces of Japan will all be Kirishitan, of that there is no doubt. Anyone who does doubt, the Lord Deus with His own feet will kick him down into Inferno; make sure this point is understood. And the august personage named Lord Shirō who has these days appeared in Ōyano of Amakusa is an angel from Heaven."[23] Another circular drew attention to the fate of a village magistrate who "was killed today because he was an enemy of the Lord Deus" and then cited the instructions received from an angel "to slay all village magistrates and heathen bonzes without sparing even one; for judgment day is at hand for all Japan."[24]

Even after the purview of their dream had been reduced to the circuit of Hara Castle, the peasants and the rōnin desperadoes continued to shoot at their besiegers messages such as this: "Heaven and earth have one root, the myriad things one substance. Among all sentient beings there is no such distinction as noble and base."[25] This is what John Ball had taught his English peasants, and far from what the missionaries had taught their Japanese Christians.

The rebellion ended in great slaughter, as such rebellions always have. But in our day the Kirishitans of Amakusa have been resurrected with a vengeance. Five bridges bind the islands with Kyushu and convey a growing stream of tourists. Cruciform road signs post the "Kirishitan Route." Hondo, the main town, boasts a Kirishitan-kan. For sale at this museum are the usual trinkets, and also figurines of the islands' famed heroes: Almeida, Terazawa, and Amakusa Shirō put on the bill with great impartiality. A statue of Shirō pointing heavenward stands before the building, and inside is a fantasy portrait depicting him as he summons forth a dove from heaven. Artistic conceits have made him appear as a pure and saintly youth. In actuality he probably was a far earthier figure. His historical image would seem to resemble an angel less than one of the miracle-working mediaeval peasant leaders, such as Hans Beheim, the Piper of Niklashausen, or (if one looks for knightly lineage) Janko von Wirsberg, the latter-day Taborite.[26] Of course, all such analogies must stop short. The Japanese, as many of the missionaries pointed out, were after all "new Christians." This meant that their chiliast vision also had to be infinitely more naïve than that of old world heresies. The rebels may have satanized their adversaries. But in a world ruled by anti-Christians there was no need to imagine an Antichrist.

To place Amakusa Shirō in his proper dimension one need not view him as an explicit social revolutionary or define the rebellion which he led as a peasant cataclysm in Marxian terms. The point is that such pseudo-prophets have throughout Christian history had not only the sword directed against them but also anathema. The latter the Shimabara rebels avoided, for the Tokugawa realm was not subject to the Universal Church. Nevertheless, Shirō Tokisada and his fellows were spiritually twice beyond the pale.

Hara Castle fell on Kan'ei 15/2/28 (12 April 1638). The rebels were exterminated. Women and children were not spared. The number of the Kirishitans who perished is said to have totaled 37,000. Matsukura Katsuie was deprived of his Shimabara domain and ordered exiled. In August 1638 he had the sentence of death passed on him. None other than Inoue Chikugo transmitted the message.[27] Terazawa Katataka was deprived of the Amakusa islands, but unlike Matsukura he was spared his life. Nine years later he committed suicide.

Immediately after the *ikki* had been suppressed, the shogunate's special commissioner Matsudaira Izu no Kami Nobutsuna crossed over to the Amakusa islands to undertake an on-the-spot inspection.[28] Chie Izu's cleverness was proverbial; and he directed it at the exterior world as well as the interior. He recommended the erection of coastal lookout stations for spying the possible approach of Christians from abroad. And the inquisition of the Kirishitans within was intensified as a result of his travels. Amakusa seems to have been overrun by officials determined that there should remain no villager who had failed to abjure Christianity.

The intimidation was not entirely successful. Large numbers were merely driven deeper underground and continued to practice their Kirishitan faith in secret. But time was on the side of the shogunate. As memories of orthodoxy receded farther, the faith of those who were deprived of expert pastors was transformed into a folk religion in which the Christian element was explicitly magical. The incantation of incomprehensible pseudo-Latin or pseudo-Portuguese formulas became the hallmark of the cult, along with the veneration of cruciform images and other such symbols concealed and absorbed within Buddhist icons. The major tenets of Christianity assumed a thoroughly legendary coloration.[29] The amuletic practices and the counter-magic directed against Buddhist sacramentals are said to have persisted in Amakusa well into the modern era.[30] Although they have died out there, they continue in widespread locales of Nagasaki Prefecture even today. On the island of Ikitsuki off Hirado, in the Sotome area of the Western Sonogi Peninsula, and throughout the Gotō island group there are major concentrations of *Kakure* (crypto-) Kirishitans.

The durability of their faith may be attributed to the inherent religious attraction of hermeticism as well as to the familial and tutelary ties of the cult's perpetuation. The solidarity of the true believers could only be intensified by generations of successful dissimulation and withstood duress. Any research into the sociology of this religion is, of course, made extremely difficult by its secret nature.[31] The *Kakure* learned well the lesson to be distrustful of anybody who was not one of them. A single careless instant could destroy them. In 1805, for example, it was discovered that some peasants in the village of Imatomi—not very far from the former site of the Jesuits' Amakusa *collegio*,

Kawachiura—had killed a cow, offered up its meat on the altar of their "Buddha," and then eaten it. Such an act was, of course, unthinkable to genuine Buddhists. In the ensuing investigation three other nearby villages were involved and more than five thousand Kirishitans rounded up.[32] In two of those villages, Ōe and Sakitsu, there now stand Roman Catholic churches; for the surviving *Kakure* of this area returned to orthodoxy in the 1870s and 1880s. But the tradition had for too long been bludgeoned, and by that time not many Kirishitans remained. The total number of Catholics on the Amakusa islands today barely exceeds one thousand. History has endowed other islands with different characteristics. On Ikitsuki, for instance, the few hundred Catholics are outnumbered more than tenfold by those who preserve the *Kakure* practice.[33] The heritage of the Tokugawa yet remains.

Inoue Chikugo was more correct than even he suspected when he stated that Kirishitans "hide in provinces where the religious prosecution is badly conceived."[34] The fish slipped through the inquisition's nets in the backwaters of Ikitsuki and Gotō. In the heartland of the peasant *ikki* the Bakufu tried to be more careful. The shogunate's efforts after the rebellion to reintegrate Amakusa into the Japanese social order were undertaken on two fronts. The first was political: the island fief was assigned to Yamazaki Ieharu in 1638, but a scant three years later was absorbed into immediate shogunal domain.[35] Suzuki Shigenari, who had served at Hara Castle in the capacity of a commander of musketeers, was appointed the domain's administrative officer (*daikan*). When Shigenari's brother Shōsan in 1642 followed his call to the islands, the second—spiritual—front was opened in earnest. In this Zen monk the Kirishitans had a formidable adversary and an opponent who gave no quarter.

It is impossible to escape the military image in discussing Shōsan: it recurs over and over again in his own statements; he never forgot it himself nor did he let his audience ever forget it. He came from a family of those legendary stalwarts of the Tokugawa, the Mikawa samurai. In 1600, at the age of twenty-one, he fought at Sekigahara in the contingent of Honda Sado no Kami; he was again to be found in the fighting ranks during the Osaka Winter Campaign of 1614; and he was in at the kill during the next year's Summer Campaign as a member of the advance guard of the shogun Hidetada.[36]

Even during his samurai career Shōsan had made himself known as a combative Buddhist and had actively sought the company of Buddhist priests.[37] In 1620 he himself entered religion. This late date of conversion is significant. Shōsan was not trained in Buddhism from an early age, and he never dwelt for any length of time in a large or famous temple. Nor was he ever properly ordained or made to submit to the discipline of a specific school, although he associated himself with the Sōtō branch of Zen. His disciples had to contend with the aspersion that their master's unconventional manner was "evident heresy" (*tennen no gedō*).[38] They countered that Shōsan did not require another's assistance: he was enlightened directly, by inspecting his own nature. What he saw there could only have been impressive. His self-confidence was immense. He washed his mouth with water he himself had polluted: it was pure enough for him.[39] He could not be bothered by criticisms that he had broken monastic convention. Throughout his life he was an overt and outspoken laicist. He denounced bitterly the Buddhist establishment of his day and disdained the Japanese Zen masters.[40] His chief fame reposes in his preachments on functional virtue in the secular walks of life. What is it then that led him to become a monk?

Perhaps he left the world because the world of 1620 no longer held much that was familiar or attractive. In the Tokugawa realm of peace there was no place for the old warhorse. Nostalgia for the life of the army camp fills Shōsan's utterances. They are easily mistaken for the statements of another disgruntled Mikawa warrior, Ōkubo Hikozaemon, whose heart also leapt at the trumpet's first bray. Ōkubo loved the solitary charge and despised the latter-day *bushi* who "trembled in the hips" and wielded the abacus better than the sword; he is the hero of military romances and moralistic *kōdan* tales, but modern historians use him as an example of atavism.[41] Shōsan, on the other hand, has been made out to be a forerunner of modernity or even of capitalism.[42]

Such a notion is far off the mark. Neither his attitude nor his manner changed after he turned to the Zen life. His Buddhism was molded by his samurai temperament: the in-pouring of *bushidō* was so heavy and is so readily identifiable that it might almost be labeled the substance which underlies the religious form. Shōsan does not apply Buddhist standards to the samurai as much as he transplants the samurai ideal of action into Buddhism. The samurai experience is the key element of his spiritual composition.

His favorite images are brusque, intimidating, and relentless. He patterns himself on the Niō, those glowering twin guardians of the Buddhist Law. To make certain that the model is understood, he strikes the pose of one or the other of the pair: "A," who snarls, and "Un," who gnashes his teeth, are for him the alpha and omega of religious practice. He admires the tense, wrenching power of the Twelve Divine Generals and of the warrior deity Bishamon, who mercilessly treads the demon.[43] He identifies with the livid, fierce, and fiery Fudō. His way to Zen is to fix the eyes, grit the teeth, clench the fists, tense the bow (all this he acts out in front of the inquirer), and to attack evil.[44] Discipline yourself and destroy your self, apply the diamond-hard rigidity of the Niō and Fudō, be on guard twenty-six hours a day—this is Shōsan's counsel. When evil challenges, then, "Kill! Kill! Kill this instant! Else you fly like an arrow to hell."[45]

Shōsan's teaching has been called the "intrepid" (yūmyō) Zen, but the adjective pales before the actual ferocity of the teacher's example. The violent shock is his constant technique. For instance: A Shingon monk comes to discuss Buddhism with him, and Shōsan tells him not to quibble but merely be prepared to die. The monk professes a lack of concern with the matter. Shōsan turns livid and roars: "I'll kill you right now! Will you die like it's nothing?" (The monk tests Shōsan no farther.) Another time he bellows a samurai awake in the middle of the night: "How would you like a spear stuck at your breast?"[46] As the muskets bang away and the lances are leveled at the ready, as the armies raise the fearsome battle cry—that, according to Shōsan, is when the samurai does zazen.[47]

Shōsan's dicta bristle with spears, swords, bows, and arrows. He wants to exterminate the hosts of demons, crush the castles of delusion, mow down the enemies that bar the way to enlightenment. Such statements recur with monotonous regularity in his works and in the collections of anecdotes about him. One wonders at times what the point of the lance is.

Shock treatment has been for ages one of the standard methods of Zen. But the character of Shōsan's practice seems to me vastly different from that of the patriarchs he disavowed.

Shōsan was not principally concerned with breaking down the chains of conceptual logic. His was an obsessive projection of his own critical experience. He continued acting out his military past throughout his Zen career, and he wanted those who sought his guidance to act it out also. And he was most impatient with laxity.

One of his callers in sharing reminiscences of the Osaka Campaigns states: "Now that was good zazen." Shōsan asks him whether he still applies that same determination, and berates him for a bad samurai when the answer is no.[48] As far as Shōsan himself was concerned, there was no doubt. Years after the event he was still mentally in the Osaka Castle moat, glowering up at the walls, gnashing his teeth, resolved to die. He was forever telling everyone within earshot to shape up, buck up, firm up. He would have made a good top sergeant in any man's army.

Such qualities of mind do not make for a great thinker. Indeed, Shōsan's construction of Buddhism is simplistic; but that is not meant to imply that it is unprincipled. When Shōsan states that feudal service equals religious practice (*hōkō sunawachi shugyō nari*) and that the samurai better than the priest is equipped to fulfil the religious ideal, because the warrior's mind is firmly set, because he is prepared always, and because he does not grudge his life, the phrasing is quite similar to what we encountered in the Christians' *FIDES NO DŌXI* and *SANCTOS NO GOSAGVEO*, and the spirit not all that different from Loyola's.[49] But the direction is precisely the opposite. No one can accuse Shōsan of otherworldliness. He is all practice. He aims for the here and now, and not at all for the other life; in fact, he counsels against that latter aim. This counsel is firmly grounded in Buddhist doctrine: to sever attachment to the Wheel of Life and transcend the borders of life-and-death means to extinguish the self. The reiteration of the basic precept of no-self (*muga*) is the sum of Shōsan's teaching. The ideal remains the samurai who serves his lord unhesitatingly. But the dictate can be applied to other walks of life as well. And, of course, it is brought to bear upon Christianity. The brunt of *Ha Kirishitan* is its exposition.

It is no accident that the tract's most effective chapter should be one in which Shōsan treats the origin of the common ill of Christians and all unenlightened fools: "To cleave to the notion that the self, this dream and phantasm, is real" is the cause of all error, and keeps the deluded "prostrate upon the sickbed of the eighty-four thousand evils."[50] Shōsan himself was convinced of the matter and vitally interested in it. Perhaps "vitally" is not the word. For on his own final sickbed he laughed as he told a worried visitor: "Shōsan has been dead these thirty years."[51]

How to effect the cure? Total dedication to service and to status is Shōsan's answer. The elaboration is to be found in his major work, *Banmin tokuyō* (Functional virtue in all walks of life). Buddhahood must be achieved in the daily experience of this world: the samurai attacks all obstacles to gain it; the peasant digs for it as he tills his field; the artisan fashions it with his hands; the merchant earns it even as he makes general profit increase. Profit to Shōsan means public benefit, not private gain. The concept totally excludes the notion of the self. And the search for profit is not confined to the merchant. All classes must contribute to the common weal. Each individual participates and serves according to the station in life ordained for him. In short, what Shōsan was preaching was nothing but the ideology of the Tokugawa social order.

To be sure, his preachments bear a Buddhist guise. This fact makes them appear unconventional: one does not expect this sort of secularism from a monk. But it may be said that layman's Buddhism is the very basis of the Mahayana; and Shōsan was only too faithful to that tradition. The critical spirit was not the essence of his life. Professor Nakamura Hajime performs a Procrustean exercise when he finds in Shōsan's thought "an aspect of Buddhism which would naturally have developed into the spirit of capitalism, if only it had developed."[52] He further tells us that Shōsan's notion of freedom approached "rather closely to the modern meaning" and that he therefore "expressed his opposition to the various kinds of feudalistic ethics that existed in his time and he made an attempt at reformation—though it was of little avail."[53] And finally we are confronted with this: "If in place of Shōsan's Heaven and 'the way of Heaven' you substitute 'God,' and if in place of 'freedom' you put 'the salvation of God,' can you not find, word for word, the ethics of capitalism of the early period of modern Europe, tracing its foundation to Calvinism?"[54] Perhaps, if you substitute, you can find.

Professor Nakamura's elevation of the *Banmin tokuyō* into a gospel of capitalism, and of Shōsan into a Weberian prototype, is based upon sentences which read as follows:[55]

Those who would engage in trade should first engage in the mental discipline which will increase profit. And that mental concern is nothing else but this: Give yourself up to Heaven's Way and learn to tread the straight and narrow. The heavens bless the straightforward man, the Buddhas and the gods protect him. He will escape disasters and his wealth will naturally increase. Men will love and respect him; he will be able to handle everything as his heart pleases . . . Abandon the notion of private profit. Be always aware in your enterprise that you have been designated by Heaven's Way to an official position: your task is to bring about self-sufficiency[56] in the entire country.

Professor Nakamura would have us think that in the first few phrases "the ethics of the pursuit of gain are openly stated," and that the notions of the accumulation of capital and of its advantageous circulation inhere in Shōsan's teaching.[57] I find great difficulty with his entire argument.

Shōsan does not speak of business as a "calling" or a "vocation" from God. His Heaven's Way is simply the natural order. The proper Buddhist complexion may be put on it with the simple identification of worldly elements with Buddhist dharmas; and Shōsan does precisely that.[58] But, on the other hand, he also finds little difference between the Buddha and the Confucian Sage who stresses worldly ethics.[59] His acceptance of the social standards of his age would seem complete. How else are we to interpret the following statement?

The One Tathagata of Original Illumination assumes ten billion separate shapes in order to profit the world. Without smiths, carpenters, and the other workmen the needs of the world could not be filled. Without samurai the world could not be governed. Without peasants there would be no food for the world. Without merchants there would be no self-sufficiency in the world.[60]

The *Banmin tokuyō* is merely a Buddhist adaptation of the *taigi meibun* formula.

Shōsan's disciple Echū tells us that his master wrote the *Banmin tokuyō* because he wanted "to profit the public" (*seken o ri-sen*). Another phrase clearly defines the context and the quality of that profit: Buddhism is preached to the people in order to facilitate the land's governance (*kokudo o osamen*). The True Law ensures true order, religion is an instrument of rule, the priest a functionary of the régime. *Busse funi*, the Buddha and the profane are undifferentiated—even in the political realm. "Monks are officials who set the land in order by transmitting to the world the virtue of their own religious discipline and repairing thereby the minds of the populace."[61] This is the conventional propagandist's rationale. Shōsan had found his niche in the Tokugawa system, and he strove conscientiously to play his role. He has been called a lone wolf and an aberrant within Zen.[62] But he was not an individualist nor a free lance when active service for the Bakufu was needed. The shogunate used Buddhism to tranquilize and police the people. Shōsan, true to himself, pitched right in.

His activities in Amakusa are best understood within that organizational context. His brother Shigenari, the *daikan*, re-structured the islands' administration into ten subdivisions and attempted to restore the devastated economy. Shōsan, the monk, founded thirty-two temples and tried to refashion the islanders' pattern of spiritual allegiance. To symbolize his purpose, he installed the statues of Ieyasu and Hidetada in the Jōdo Sect affiliate among his foundations (the others were all Sōtō Zen); as, indeed, in his own temple, the Onshinji in Mikawa, images of these two Tokugawa shoguns flanked Kannon on the altar.[63]

When the populace was herded back to register in the Buddhist temples Amakusa could be considered pacified. But the disastrous effects of the peasant war remained. The area had suffered a huge population loss: the number of inhabitants had shrunk to no more than ten thousand, and much arable land lay fallow.[64] The islands' putative yield, however, remained fixed at the 42,000 *koku* of Terazawa days, when there had been thrice as many people to work the land. The tax assessment was practically impossible to meet. Shigenari seems to have petitioned repeatedly for the estimate's reduction, but the Bakufu did not grant it. In 1653 the *daikan* proved that he too was one who was ready to die: suicide was his final remonstrance. The Bakufu recognized the merit of his deed by permitting his adopted son, Shōsan's child Shigetatsu, to succeed him as the administrator of Amakusa. Under the intendancy of this second *daikan*, in 1659, the estimate of the islands' product was finally halved.[65] On account of all these memories the two brothers and the son are hallowed as deities. The Suzuki Jinja stands to this day in the hills inland from Hondo and remains the principal Shinto shrine on the islands.

Shōsan spent three years in Amakusa. Before he departed he vowed to make certain that the pernicious faith be extirpated forever, and to that end left behind a copy of *Christians Countered* in each of the temples.[66] His propaganda work was to be continued on the proper doctrinal basis, and the tract laid down the guidelines. These lines are very compact. At the start Shōsan asserts that Deus is a fraud: anyone who casts away his life for him is not only foolish but a national disgrace. The way to salvation is direct: enlightenment does not depend on words or letters but rather on the realization that there is no such thing as independent existence. The gods and the Buddhas appear in a multitude of shapes to make the individual's task easier: the man who esteems them is paying obeisance to the cosmic order, just as the man who obeys his immediate superior is demonstrating his allegiance to the political order. For similar reasons the sun and moon are to be worshipped also: they represent the forces of Yin and Yang, which form the basis of all existence. But there is no such thing as miracles: the mind which transcends elemental limitations by its own discipline is by that very fact possessed of super-powers. Nor is there such a thing as a real soul: in teaching actual existence the Kirishitans do not even reach the level of pre-Buddhist infidels' views. All sentient beings without exception contain the Buddha-Nature: but they must train themselves to use their capabilities. It follows that the eradication of the self and the extinction of the idea of permanence constitute the cure of all spiritual ills. If these precepts are followed, all hindrance ceases.

The tract concludes with threats of dire punishment upon anyone who does not conform to the national standard; for Japan can tolerate neither external aggression nor the internal subversion which is part of the barbarians' plot.

We may assume that *Christians Countered* represents the content of the sermons which Shōsan preached in Amakusa between 1642 and 1645. The booklet was not published until 1662, seven years after Shōsan himself had finally expired. The fact that it saw print makes it unique. Japanese Buddhist monks may have assiduously tried to live up to their charge by watching out for Kirishitans, but until the Bakumatsu period hardly any were stirred to try their pens in anti-Christian intellectual exercise. That may imply a lack of need more than a lack of wit. At any rate, we only find one other Buddhist tract to note. Its title is *Taiji jashūron* (On quelling the pernicious faith), and it was composed in 1648 but not printed until 1861.[67] It may be significant to add that the author, Sessō, had at one time been associated with Suzuki Shōsan.

Little is known of this monk beyond the few terse notes of Shōsan's disciple and biographer Echū, who states that Shōsan spent some time at the Hōryūji together with "the priest Sessō of Bu[ngo]" and that Sessō was a "subordinate of Kanzan," *i.e.* the Myōshinji faction of Zen.[68] Shinmura Izuru provides some further details: Sessō was the resident of the Tafukuji in Usuki; in 1647 he went to preach at the Kōfukuji, one of the famous "Chinese temples" of Nagasaki, at the instance of the *bugyō* Baba Saburōzaemon.[69] The preparation of these sermons (a series lasting twenty-one days) may have led naturally to the composition of *Taiji jashūron*, but the tract's contents (unlike those of *Ha Kirishitan*) are not homiletic as much as expository. Sessō's argumentation is much more effusive than Shōsan's and leans heavily upon formidable buttresses of quotation from the sutras. He makes at least one interesting point: the Christians also attacked Confucianism and Shinto, but were most intent on countering Buddhism because of its great similarity to their own religion.

The Christians "change the name of Brahma and call him Deus; of the Brahma-Heaven devas and call them *anjo*; of Heaven's Palace to *Paraiso*; of the human realm to *Purgatorio*; of hell to *Inferno*; of anointment to *baptismo*; of contrition to *confissan*; of the Ten Good Laws to the ten *mandamento*; of nuns to *virgem* . . . They change the name of prayer beads and call them *contas*."[70] Christianity, in short, is just a Buddhist heresy. Of course, "Jesus secretly studied Buddhism; but he could not penetrate its wondrous hidden depths."[71]

It would seem that we have come full circle and are right back where we started, with Xavier and the Shingon monks of Yamaguchi. The identification, however, was an extremely dangerous one for Sessō to make. As we shall shortly see, a Confucian mind expanded it and turned it against Buddhism.

Sessō's tract contains little else that is new, and his arguments often reflect the language of his predecessors, whose writings he claims to have studied minutely.[72] He was certainly very well informed, and his outline of Christian procedures is remarkably accurate. He borrowed much from Fabian and from Ferreira, and could have consulted the latter directly. He arrived, of course, at the foregone conclusion:[73]

Those who adhere to a religion which wants to usurp sovereignty betray their ruler and their obligations to their land. Those who do not venerate their ancestors disregard their parents' virtue and their debt for their upbringing. Those who do not pray at the gods' mausolea undercut the customs of the country to which they owe their very lives. Those who love deeply the members of their own religion only to hate strongly those of another faith do not know what the communion of friend and friend means. Those who destroy temples and shrines and burn sacred scriptures and images commit actions which damn them to the three realms of suffering. Do not fall for this demonic trickery, you people! Mark this well, by all means mark this well!

We note that a manuscript copy of this work was deemed worthy of inclusion in the collection of the Hayashi family, the hereditary heads of the official Bakufu college.

Sessō, however, was just one Buddhist monk, and his influence was limited by that very fact. Suzuki Shōsan was an outsider even from his own sect; the direct effects of his activity were felt in Amakusa but hardly extended beyond the islands. And the *Kirishitan monogatari* genre is vulgar by definition. For the full brunt of the anti-Christian propaganda we must look elsewhere. A thorough appreciation of the mental climate which governed the Tokugawa period's attitude toward Christianity cannot be attained unless more influential and official makers of opinion are taken into account. Therefore we revert to Hayashi Razan.

When Razan held his disputation with Fabian in 1606, he was debating the representative of a tradition which was outlandish but not yet condemned by the Tokugawa. Accordingly, the *Anti-Jesuit* stops short of the no-holds-barred assault and is still essentially a scholastic critique. Nevertheless, one sentence from Razan's appraisal of the *Myōtei mondō* sticks in the mind. "Nothing like burning the book!" According to Heine's famous epigram, where they burn books they burn people. Hayashi Razan was one honest scholar and public servant who poured oil upon the billowing flames.

Razan is the archetypal *goyō gakusha*, that is to say, purveyor of intellectual wares to the government. He first met Ieyasu in 1605, and lectured before the Second Shogun, Hidetada, in

1607; he began drafting diplomatic documents for the Bakufu in 1610, and thereafter was increasingly employed in that task. For some years he shuttled between Kyoto and Sunpu, Ieyasu's residence after his "retirement" in 1605; but from 1613 he was never far from Ieyasu's side, accompanying him to scholarly discussions, falconry expeditions, and the Osaka Winter Campaign. Indeed, Razan helped to compose for Ieyasu his specious *casus belli* against Hideyori.[74]

The number of the writings Razan produced to shape the shogunate's policy and ideology is legion. More than anyone else, he contributed to the establishment of the Chu Hsi brand of Neo-Confucianism as the official orthodoxy of Tokugawa Japan. And he directed the attitude of ruthless orthodoxy against Christianity and its real or imagined effects.

In the official documents concerned with Christianity Razan's tone changed from that of the *Hai Yaso*. The treatise had refuted the barbarian teachings as irrational on Confucian grounds. Those same standards underlay Razan's perennial critiques of the otherworldly religion of Buddha, a word he habitually wrote with characters reading "Futo" and meaning "floating death." But his denunciations of Buddhism were mainly carried on in private correspondence; they were venomous, but they did not possess a public sting. Buddhism, after all, performed a useful police function.[75] No restraints governed his declarations on Christianity. Scholarly refutation is not a feature of the series of pronouncements which he composed on behalf of one Bakufu functionary or another; all is strident condemnation. Bakufu policy had changed to rigorous persecution in accordance with the thesis Razan himself helped to establish: Christianity perverts society. And he served up prolix elaborations on this point to worthies such as Suetsugu Heizō, Inoue Chikugo, Kagazume Minbu, and Soga Hisasuke. All of these were front-line fighters against Christianity. Razan's involvement was more distant. He merely sent them paper ammunition.

The language of this propaganda contains much that is of interest. In 1625, for instance, Razan wrote in a message destined for the Ming governor of Fukien:[76]

The shrike-tongued monsters from South Barbary, the ones called Jesuits, came riding on trade vessels and, insinuating their pernicious trickery [into our land], stirred up and deluded the foolish and the common. Thus it came about that the populace, craving the profit of the trade ship, mixed with these shrike-tongued barbarians and bearers of discord, entered into concourse with them, and traded with them . . . But in these present days our whole land has been unified, the polity upraised. Society has been reformed and evils remedied. A new start has been made, a thorough renewal. Governmental ordinances are strict and clear. But observed with particular stringency is the measure to exclude the barbarian doctrine and bar the way sinister, to deny the Jesuits entry; so that there be no violators.

The expletives are the first to strike the eye. But there is also a grave new argument in Razan's words, one that would be repeated by all of his epigones. Internal reform requires stringent measures. When the country is in disarray, the Christians intrude. When the land is unified, the exotics are excluded. Those who work to refashion society must first undo the barbarians' wiles.

Thorough renewal is in Razan's consciousness a notion firmly tied to the extinction of the barbarian doctrine: the upraised polity presupposes that the way sinister be cut. Therefore all Christians who smuggle themselves into Japan will be killed; all those who bring Christian books to Japan will be killed; and all those who do not report Christian attempts to infiltrate will be killed.[77]

Needless to say, the news of the Shimabara Uprising did nothing to calm Razan. Nor was he moved to moderate his strident tones by the events which followed, the issuance of the final Sakoku Edict in 1639 and the execution of the Macao ambassadors in 1640. The message sent to Macao to give notice of the envoys' fate is the product of a Razan at high pitch and in true form.[78] Its passages crawl with "wriggling barbarians" (*shunban*) and Bateren wielding their perverse arts: these execrable creatures have wormed their way into society and eat away at its fabric. They have generated a noxious swarm of wasps and flies: when their sectarians clustered together and rose up in Shimabara, that was akin to history's worst of peasant rebellions— or did the Yellow Turbans of Chang Lu and the notorious Sun En's Five Pecks of Rice wreak greater damage? In such a case the mass execution of the rebels, the thorough hate of the barbarians, and the total exclusion of the foreigners' evil influence constitute the only solution.

And yet the poison remained in the land, kept circulating in channels that were no longer purely Jesuit. As Razan's age advanced, the specters haunting him increased. The Christian monsters blended with the Buddhist floating death and merged with yet more dangerous active spirits.

Razan confided his private fears in letters to his old friend Ishikawa Jōzan. The Jesuit doctrine (he said in 1654) has changed its form and assumed the shape of heterodoxy just like the fox monster that ate the maiden and assumed her shape. The perspicacious, however, will always detect the truth. Of course, to transform Buddha into Jesus is as easy as turning the palm of one's hand. But that an entire school of Confucianism should have been possessed by the Jesuits is as uncanny as it is insidious. That heterodox branch, the outgrowth of the teachings of Wang Yang-ming, can no longer be termed Confucian: its followers have merely stolen the true Confucians' doctrine of the Way of Heaven and now spew forth the dregs of it. Their hearts and hopes are founded in the Lord of Heaven, Tenshu, Deus; him they worship, in him they trust, and his religion they secretly plan to spread. From the Buddhists they have usurped the theory of the void nature; their basic thesis is the identity of mind and principle, and the result is a thorough confusion of essentials. This misshapen thing is un-Confucian, un-Taoist, un-Buddhist—"call it the three-legged cat-demon."[79]

This long letter is one series of staggering paralogisms. Razan could not have been conscious of his fallacies. He was overwhelmed by the suggestiveness of his own construction, the all-pervading image of perniciousness. All consideration of heterodoxy is colored by reference to this image; every utterance on a rival persuasion alludes to it. In this sort of sensibility cognition melds with emotion and perceived forms with prior concepts, until all adversaries—and most of all the spiritual kind—become identical, deriving from one seedbed of perdition.

Or, if we get down to cases: The followers of the Wang Yang-ming school and of its principal Japanese representative, Kumazawa Banzan, are the enemy within. The rōnin cabal of Yui Shōsetsu proves it.

The background of this putsch is to be sought in the air of disquiet surrounding the accession of a ten-year-old as the Fourth Shogun, Ietsuna, in 1651.[80] The shogunate's bannermen (hatamoto) were already facing a crisis of sustenance. A daimyo from the ancestral lands of the Tokugawa, Matsudaira Sadamasa, demonstratively announced that he was returning his fief and all his properties to the Bakufu for distribution among the hatamoto, and himself walked the streets of Edo in the garb of a beggar monk. The authorities treated him as a madman, but took no positive steps to meet the grievances he had brought into the open. Yui Shōsetsu was inspired by this atmosphere to attempt the overthrow of the Bakufu. And he availed himself of the name of one of Ieyasu's sons to mobilize a band of discontents.[81]

The plan seems to have called for Shōsetsu's lieutenant, Marubashi Chūya, on a windy night to explode the shogunate's arsenal and burn down the city of Edo. The Bakufu Elders (*rōjū*) who would come rushing to the shogun's castle would be waylaid and killed; the castle would be taken. Shōsetsu himself would in the meantime take over Sunpu, raid Ieyasu's tomb on Kunōzan and plunder its treasure, and then disburse the wherewithal to his fellow conspirators for use as campaign funds. The entire land would soon be theirs to rule and govern.

Of course the plan leaked. Its details soon reached the ears of Clever Izu, Matsudaira Nobutsuna. Chūya was captured in Edo, and Shōsetsu committed suicide in the middle of a ring of minions of the law (September 1651). He left behind a note to the effect that he did not mean to overthrow the Bakufu but only to correct its wrongs and relieve the sufferings of the people.

The involvement of Kumazawa Banzan in this plot is, needless to say, a slander.[82] The followers of Chu Hsi's rationalism were traditionally averse to the intuitionism of Wang Yang-ming. But the two schools possessed equally impeccable Confucian credentials. Their history of intellectual rivalry can scarcely justify Razan's incontinent statements.

"Almost all of this gang"—wrote Razan to Ishikawa Jōzan in November 1651—"were followers of that heterodox school and accepted its false teachings . . . These are proxies for the Jesuits and represent their transformation."[83] And in the pamphlet *Sōzoku zenki* he named names: When Matsudaira Izu no Kami questioned Marubashi Chūya and his fellow plotter, Kawara Jūrōbei, whether they were Jesuits, these two stated that indeed they were not, but that they were followers of the school of a certain Kumazawa. "This Kumazawa is a minor retainer of [the lord of Bizen]. He uses witchcraft to delude the deaf and blind, and those who hear him go astray and cannot be enlightened . . . At bottom this is but Jesuitry transformed . . . These bandits all listened to Kumazawa's monstrous words."[84] And Razan caps his point with a citation of the *Wang chih*: "Who takes the way sinister and thereby deranges government, who preaches falsehood and defends it, studies the untrue and follows it, who constructs strange devices and composes discordant sounds and thereby deludes the populace, who misappropriates the spiritual beings and falsifies the times of the calendar—all of these shall be killed without mercy."[85]

We recall that the *Anti-Jesuit* contains a similar quotation. The metastasis was now complete. The orthodox must look out for the Jesuit/Wang Yang-ming witches. Had Razan had his way, all doctrines other than his own would have been eradicated.

Hayashi Razan died on 7 March 1657 (Meireki 3/1/23), in his seventy-fifth year. Arai Hakuseki was born a little more than two weeks later, on 24 March (Meireki 3/2/10). An entire cycle of life-and-death separated these two scholars, and their temperaments were vastly different. Yet there is a curious point of affinity in the roles they played in the historical drama of interest to us. Razan's attitude toward Christianity was first formed by the bruising encounter with the Jesuit Fabian Fucan. Hakuseki's views were more dispassionate, his partner having been perforce more docile. Yet the condemnation of Christianity which issued out of Hakuseki's meeting with Giovanni Battista Sidotti was scarcely less devastating than Razan's or, for that matter, the anti-Jesuit Fabian's.

In 1708, when the missionary Sidotti was dropped by a ship from the Philippines on an island off Kyushu, Hakuseki was on the threshold of a new rise to prominence. For some fifteen years he had served and tutored the lord of Kōfu, Tokugawa Tsunatoyo; and that lord had been designated successor to the Fifth Shogun, Tsunayoshi, and was destined the very next year to become under the name Ienobu the Sixth Shogun. Hakuseki in turn became the shogunate's principal policy planner. His statements on Christianity clearly had more than academic significance.

Hakuseki interrogated Sidotti four times in the last days of 1709 and the first few of 1710, and submitted his recommendations on 8 January 1710 (Hōei 6/12/9). His report, the very model of a concise memorandum, contains one sentence which is often cited: "When the people of those [Christian] countries spread their doctrine to other lands, that is not a plot of aggression; this fact is clear." Less famous is the next sentence: "However, once that doctrine begins to flourish, rebellious subjects *ipso facto* arise in the land; that also is the inevitable natural consequence."[86] And he goes on to note that the fall of the Ming Empire has been attributed to Christianity's activity in China. The Japanese should be proud, and the shogun Iemitsu praised, for eradicating the Christian peril.

In short, Hakuseki divorced the notion of internal subversion from that of external aggression, which he deemed a false fear; but that is all he did to revise the prevalent image of the pernicious faith. It is his sympathy for Sidotti that has gained him the undeserved reputation of having been tolerant—or even sympathetic—toward Christianity. He suggested to the Bakufu that the best policy would be to send Sidotti back home: this step would be a demonstration of the humanity which prevailed in Japan under the enlightened Tokugawa rule, but would also serve as a warning, for Sidotti would transmit the message of the Japanese determination to cut down on the spot any missionary who might follow. The Bakufu took neither this alternative nor that of execution. Instead, it took the middle course and kept Sidotti a prisoner in the Kirishitan Yashiki at Kobinata, the site of Inoue Chikugo's triumphs. There Sidotti committed an indiscretion. He proselytized his caretakers, an elderly couple who had previously come under the influence of one of the members of the Second Rubino Group. After these two confessed their Christianity, Sidotti was confined in a hole in the ground on a starvation diet; and there he perished, on 28 November 1714 (Shōtoku 4/10/21).

Sidotti's act of faith must have shocked Hakuseki. After all, he had counseled that the priest be kept alive without even the customary requirement of formal apostasy. His counsel was now discredited. This embarrassment made Hakuseki want to clear the record; and the further shock of Sidotti's sad end moved him to set down his observations in expanded form. The famous treatise *Seiyō kibun* (Tidings of the West), which he drafted in 1715, was the result.[87]

Hakuseki seems to have visited Sidotti several times after the initial interrogations were concluded. Years later he was to write to the Mito scholar and historian Asaka Tanpaku that his encounters with the Roman constituted the wonderful chance of a lifetime (*isshō no kikai*). He learned an abundance of marvellous things from the Roman, he states; and he wishes that he could tell the full tale of these meetings, but he dare not, on account of the laws prohibiting the spread of Christian information.[88] During the Tokugawa period the *Seiyō kibun* could on that account circulate only in manuscript, and in private. The text was not published until 1882, and its appearance in print was anteceded by several translations.[89]

Yet the *Seiyō kibun* is far from being a mere summary of Christian teachings. Nor is it just a transcript of conversations with the Catholic priest. Hakuseki had been given the title Chikugo no Kami in 1711, but unlike that other Chikugo of Kirishitan Yashiki fame he possessed a genuine and far-ranging intellectual curiosity. His treatise accordingly incorporates information gleaned from the Dutch as well as from Sidotti, Chinese material as well as Japanese; it deals with history and geography at least as much as with theology. Hakuseki knew his sources well. Quite naturally he referred to the testimony of the fallen Jesuit Padre Giuseppe Chiara—Okamoto San'emon—and to the other materials contained in the *Kirishito-ki*. It also seems certain that he had read Razan's *Hai Yaso*; he applies terminology used by Sessō; and his discussion of Christian cosmology is obviously a condensed copy of Fabian's First Step, complete with its skilled craftsmen and house laws.[90] The treatise which resulted is short but nevertheless comprehensive. What is its total effect?

Hakuseki is clearly more interested in the problems of Christian lands than in Christianity. For instance, he finds it noteworthy that the king of England should have cast away his proper wife and put a concubine in her stead; the head of the Christian religion thereupon cut relations with that land, and all who owed allegiance to him followed suit.[91] He treats in some detail the Portuguese dynastic problem and concludes that the royal house of Portugal became extinct because too many of its heirs despised the world and imitated Jesus Christ.[92] And he spends a goodly portion of Part Two of his book in fighting the War of the Spanish Succession.[93]

The picture which emerges here is one of chaos, a European Sengoku. The lord of Germany proposes that his son become Carolus Tertius of Spain; the lord of France counters with his own grandson, Philippus Quintus. Holland and England help the Germans, and all the princes move their troops, on land and on the sea. The king of Poland also dies. Then Lithuania leaps into the fray, and seven thousand Poles are slain. The Swedes, the Danes, the Turks, the Muscovites—all butcher one another. And one after the other, strongholds collapse, fortresses fall: Tournai, Douai, Béthune and Saint Amand, and Mons.

In short, only the strains of *Malbruck s'en va-t'en guerre* are missing from this account. It is little wonder that Hakuseki should have concluded, after hearing some of this sort of thing from Sidotti, that Europeans could not "even in their wildest dreams plot aggression" against Japan.[94] They all too obviously had other preoccupations. For that matter, the factors of geography would make a fantasy of any such plans.

But there is yet another point behind Hakuseki's list of minutiae. He has heard, he states, that the cause of all the wars that have plagued Europe since ancient times has been the failure of the line of succession.[95] For the Confucian the reasons are not hard to find: they lie in the foreigners' ignorance of the essentials of ethics. The natural duty of preserving the family line is sacred; *kō*, filial piety, requires it; the veneration of the ancestors cannot be carried out if there are no heirs. The Europeans, on the other hand, attribute primacy to the beck and call of their Deus. And that to Hakuseki seems impious indeed.

Hakuseki viewed Christianity through spectacles made by Chu Hsi. The first image they registered was that of "wild absurdity and utter shallowness (*kōtan senrō*), unworthy of consideration." Hakuseki makes short shrift of it. The Christians' anthropomorphic and capricious Deus has at best an affinity with the sham deities of vulgar Taoism; not for him to be compared with the Shang Ti of the Confucian classics, for that term is identical with *li*, the organizing pattern which rules over the process of natural creation. "If Deus is autogenous," Hakuseki asks, "then why cannot nature be autogenous?"[96] Nor is the origin of the Christian heresy hard to find, for Judeola, the locale of Deus' birth, is not far from Western India: Christianity is an offshoot of Buddhism, itself a heresy. "Now what do we hear of Jesus' law? It has images and ordinations, it has anointments, and litanies, and beads, it has paradise and hell, rebirth and retribution—there is nothing here unlike the Buddhist talk." Of course no rational Confucianist can countenance this nonsense; no wonder the Ming fell if they permitted it to spread. "Our country's strict prohibition of this doctrine is by no means an excessive countermeasure."[97] The entrails of society are torn apart by Christian perversity. In Arai Hakuseki's view, the vicious Christian disregard of the most basic rules of life was brought precisely into focus.

The strict constructionist of *taigi meibun* gave the *coup de grâce* to the enemy in one brisk paragraph:[98]

As I see it, when [Sidotti] says that discussions of a country must not be based upon that land's small or great size, near or far distance, he has a good argument. And when he says that what corrupts a country is not its religion but its people, his words also have the ring of truth. But [the Christians] teach that Deus[99] produced heaven and produced earth, and make him out to be the Great Lord and Great Father who generated the myriad things. In other words: I have a father, but I do not love him; I have a lord, but I do not revere him. Now this is what we call impious and disloyal. Nor is that all! This Great Lord and Great Father cannot be served without exhausting all one's love and all one's reverence—is what they say. But the *Li chi* reserves the rites of serving Shang Ti, the Lord On High, to the Emperor, the Son of Heaven; no such prerogative of worshipping Heaven is given the various princes or those ranking below. And that is in order to prevent the disturbance of the distinction between the exalted and the base. However: The sovereign is Heaven to the subject; the father is Heaven to the child; the husband is Heaven to the wife. And therefore, he who serves his sovereign with loyalty thereby serves Heaven. He who serves his father with filial piety thereby serves Heaven. She who serves her husband with propriety thereby serves Heaven. Outside of the constancy of these Three Bonds there is no way of serving Heaven. If I have a Great Lord to serve beyond my lord and a Great Father to serve beyond my father, and if this [Great Lord and Father] is sacred beyond my lord and my father, then not only are there two sacred personages in the house and two lords in the land but the highest duty must be to set at naught the lord and set at naught the father. Even if they do not go as far as teaching to set the father and the lord at naught, still the atrocious nature ingrained in their doctrine is of such enormity that even at the point of regicide or parricide they must not look back, and in the end think nothing of it.

The conclusive analysis of the Christian poison had been made.

There matters rested. As the eighteenth century progressed, the Christian threat seemed to fade into nonexistence. The Kirishitan Yashiki fell into disuse after Sidotti died, was for a time reduced to housing common criminals, and was abandoned in 1792. Along with it, the office of the *shūmon-aratame yaku* was abolished.[100] But as the century turned, the image of perniciousness re-emerged and reared its head. The sense of an impending foreign crisis made it necessary once again.

One of the causative factors of Sakoku had been the fear of the Christian menace. Paradoxically, one of the major streams of thought which led to the sea change of the Meiji Restoration and thus (although indirectly) to renewed intercourse with foreign nations also contained the dark stain of anti-Christian effluvia. The advocates of *sonnō jōi*, that ideology of blustering patriotism and antiforeign truculence, revivified and put to their own uses the image of the Christian peril. The most strident of all were the three leading lights of the Late Mito School, Aizawa Seishisai, Fujita Tōko, and Mito's model lord, Tokugawa Nariaki.

The barbarians were at the gates. How to repel them? The slogans which flowed from Mito were those of national unity and a reconstitution of the Bakufu. The Late Mito thinkers insisted on the abandonment of one part of the shogunate's ancestral law—the Bakufu-First principle designed to keep the other political units weak—while cleaving with all their might to the other, Sakoku. Nothing illustrates better the abortive nature of their reformist thesis. The vilification of Christianity is so much part and parcel of their doctrine that it seems at times to obscure the positive aspects of their construction. They fully believed their predecessors' propaganda. Their view of the West was conditioned by it: they were seduced by the mass of accumulated disinformation.

The *sonnō jōi* slogan is first applied as a formula in the Late Mito School's canonical scripture, the *Kōdōkanki* of 1838.[101] The context is an appreciation of Ieyasu as the founder of the Sakoku policy:

> Our Lord of the Eastern Radiance
> Made order out of chaos and
> Restored the rightful course:
> *Revered the Emperor, repelled barbarians,*
> Perfected Arms, perfected Arts;
> Establishing thereby the fundament of
> Universal peace.

Lest there be any doubt concerning the identity of the barbarians whom Tōshōgū repelled, Fujita Tōko provides an exegesis of the phrase:[102]

At the time of the Sengoku disturbances the foreign barbarians spied out our difficulties, took advantage of our dilapidated government and slack mores, and dared to spread their monstrous doctrine. Toyotomi at one time prohibited this. And at the time of Our Lord of the Eastern Radiance, new and expansive legal measures were undertaken. An investigation was conducted throughout the land, all their temples were torn down, and the sectarians executed. Nor were the successors remiss in enunciating their Ancestor's principles. Accordingly, preparedness against the foreign barbarians and prohibition of their monstrous doctrine are the everlasting first essentials of the Law.

It is difficult to say what outraged Tōko more, the knowledge that the barbarians and their monstrous doctrine had once been permitted to pollute the Land of the Gods or the thought that they might come again. It is, however, certain that the Christian peril and the foreign threat were indistinguishable entities in his mind. Looking back upon history, he congratulated Iemitsu for crucifying the Macao ambassadors of 1640 and burning their ship: this deed made Japan's fame resound abroad, so that "for over a hundred years not even the shadow of a foreign ship was seen."[103] He cannot forget the Shimabara Rebellion or Iemitsu's glory in putting it down. In all, he states, 280,000 sectarians were executed. "This single point makes it apparent how hateful is the pernicious doctrine." The barbarians must not be permitted to approach. "If they do, then smash them, crush them!"[104]

All barbarians—all those who use "crab writing," letters running sideways—are the same to Tōko. He laments the fact that the Dutch have been permitted to continue trading with Japan: how dangerous that is he knows by experience, for he has encountered three of the enemy in Edo. These three Hollanders' hats and clothes were similar to what he had seen in the portrait of a Russian. From this similarity he concludes that Holland has been taken over by Russia and forced to submit to that aggressor country's religion, Roman Catholicism. "Aah! The Holland of today is not the Holland of yesteryear!"[105] A little kakubutsu kyūri, it would seem, could take the sober "investigator into things" quite a long way.

Tōko must be taken seriously, if only because he was the brain behind one of the most prominent personages in the transformation scene of Bakumatsu politics, his daimyo Tokugawa Nariaki. Nariaki began beating the drums of internal reform and outward preparedness soon after succeeding to the Mito *han* in 1829, and his policy proposals are neatly comprehended in the celebrated "eyes only" remonstrance, the *Bojutsu no hōji* of 1838. This appeal to the shogun begins with a thurification of Ieyasu and then proceeds to the obligatory tattoo on corruption and luxury in high places. The Dutch trade, of course, is one of the major reasons for these extravagances; therefore it ought to be stopped. The Dutch at one time were not contaminated with the pernicious faith; but they write in letters running sideways, which amounts to the same thing. "Lands with letters running sideways all belong to the *jashūmon*; and the intent of the *jashūmon* is to drag members of other religions into that same faith and step by step to convert the entire world . . . For that reason they always and forever have designs on other lands."[106]

The rapacious and subversive nature of those whose main deity is a criminal crucified on a stake is evident: they caused the Shimabara Rebellion, and they are this very moment machinating through a heretical group of scholars—*Rangakusha*, addicts of the "Dutch Learning"—to infuse their evil poison into the Land of the Gods. Buddhism also is an imported doctrine; therefore it also is a pernicious doctrine. Its temples have been entrusted with the control of Kirishitans, but even these police functions can better be handled by others. "Once the Dutch Learning is prohibited and the sprouts of the pernicious faith thus kept from growing, the religious scrutiny may also be abandoned and instead . . . all Japanese without exception made into parishioners of Shinto shrines."[107]

Nariaki's was not, however, a pristine nativism: his disdain for the Buddhists was purely Confucian; and on occasion he used one barbarous faith to control the other. In 1855 he dignified the Mito reissue of a late Ming thesaurus of anti-Christian writings with his own preface, a simple vituperation against the barbarians; and much of this Collection Countering Perniciousness (*P'o-hsieh chi*) is Buddhist.[108] And the Mito *han*, true to its tradition of historical research, compiled its own collection of Japanese anti-Christian sources, the *Sokkyohen* (Writings to put an end to deviation).[109] The table of contents is very informative. It includes, among many similar texts, all the works translated in my study. The materials which fed the minds of Mito thinkers being what they are—a hotchpotch with ingredients by

Fabian, Razan, Chūan, Shōsan, Sessō, and much novelese pulp thrown in—it is no wonder that their cognition was laid lame.

The most instructive case of intellectual paralysis in confronting deviltry occurred when Aizawa Seishisai took time off from his new proposals to engage in antique fulminations against Christianity. His tract, *Sangan yokō* (The third eye: some added views), takes the form of a series of glosses on Hakuseki's *Seiyō kibun*; and, indeed, its sole measure of rationality is that already provided by Hakuseki.[110] We see here the dead end of the traditional propagandistic line which had started with the seventeenth century's vehement condemnation of Christianity, seemed to be rationalized by Hakuseki in the eighteenth, and sputtered out in the nineteenth.

Fabian ranted at times, but he did so with style. Hakuseki condemned Christianity, but he did so with detachment. Aizawa's jottings have neither rhyme nor reason, and the fact that they appear side by side with Hakuseki's observations makes them seem particularly inept. Where Hakuseki merely refers to "child's talk," Aizawa cannot resist an expostulation.

Aizawa's argument founders completely as he reaches midstream, in the chase after Moses in the shallows of the Red Sea. Pharaoh is apostrophized as a *meikun*, a model lord, because he did not believe in the pernicious doctrine. It was true principle (*dōri*) that led him to chastise those who had banded together in rebellion. Deus, on the other hand, is denounced for his lack of humane qualities (*jinshin*) because he drowned the poor Egyptian soldiers who, presumably, were only following the dictates of loyalty to their illustrious sovereign.[111]

It is clear to Aizawa that Deus is the root of all rebellion. This theme he pursues with the rigidity of a monomaniac. His order of battle is composed of a veritable phalanx of Confucian rubrics. But the village atheist will out. Who will prove, he asks, that Joseph and Mary did not have their child in the usual way? How could Deus' blood remain in existence generations after he had been crucified for breaking the law of the land? The vulgarity of one of the major luminaries of late Tokugawa intellectual history is truly appalling: the chapbook is the proper vehicle for such talents.

How badly acuity had deteriorated over the centuries may be demonstrated by a simple comparison of Aizawa and Fabian Fucan. Fabian was far better informed; but that is not the heart of the matter. Unlike Aizawa, Fabian worked within a precise intellectual frame. Whether he was writing as a Jesuit or as an anti-Jesuit, he kept his sights on the supreme importance of the conceptual scheme. He too had much to say concerning the juxtaposition of the human sphere with the divine: one plane was higher than the other, and Fabian, a true enantiomorph of himself, showed why with perfect consistency of method. In *Myōtei mondō* Deus had been omnipotent and all-active, vastly superior to the human Buddhas and gods. In *Ha Daiusu* the reverse was true: the Buddhas were removed into the realm of total abstraction, one far beyond a Deus possessed of human frailities. In each instance, the inferior deity is treated on the level to which its adherents have reduced it. Aizawa lays no such basis. Instead, he merely visualizes a single banal standard and is indignant when Deus does not meet it. Imagine! Deus is not *humane*! No wonder that his followers, such as Noah, did not know righteousness either. Of course, Aizawa cannot fairly be termed unfaithful to himself. He had a penchant for proving reality by myth, and the *idée fixe* was his hallmark.

Deus was a sham. But Japan was the Land of the Gods. Irrationality can be a positive element of propaganda, and Aizawa indulged in it freely. The construction of the myth of Japan's unique sacred character is his most significant contribution to history. The Emperor of Japan and the Divine Progenitrix, Amaterasu Ōmikami, were consubstantiated. Out of this theory arose the doctrine of the *kokutai*, the mystical body of Japan. Others amended Aizawa's doctrine to signify that the Japanese Emperor was the supreme and absolute value. This was indeed the unsurpassable symbol: it was divine, nativistic, and familial all at once.

In this sign was won the battle to overthrow the Tokugawa shogunate. For better or for worse, Japan's entry into the modern era proceeded under the aegis of the imperial myth. This myth was purely exoteric, but it became the basis of the Meiji ideological structure. The emperor system in the course of the nineteenth century's last decades evolved into a strong governmental form. Its measure of success in repelling barbarians is a well-known story.

Christianity was no challenge to the nativist buttresses, the political makeup, or the social integrity of modern Japan. The Meiji government for a few years maintained the prohibition of the pernicious faith, and indeed punished by exile from their homes some *Kakure* who had come out into the open. But the proscription was abandoned in 1873. In the modern era there were clearly more dangerous enemies to confront and far more dangerous ideologies to quell or persecute.

Conclusion

THE GESÙ is sublime. Indeed, this greatest of Jesuit churches is one of Rome's most magnificent monuments. The transports and ecstasies of its imagery draw the mind to the empyrean. But the exalted view of the heavens is an illusion made possible by trickery with light. False shadows are cast over parts of the structure. The depictions of glory overcrowd the architectural frame and seem to distend it. The dramatic effect is achieved by a spectacular *trompe l'oeil.*

This religious edifice may be the proper symbol of the Christian activity in Early Modern Japan. The missionaries' enterprise was of heroic proportions, and the news they sent of it to Europe as embellished with images of triumph and apotheosis as the church. But the perspective of history confines the view of their accomplishment within narrower limits. Seen in strict terms, the sum of their cultural contribution to Japan was nil.

Some amplification is necessary. The effect of the Christian presence on the political disposition of Early Modern Japan was unquestionably great. But it was a negative and annihilating effect for the Christians. The importance of the mission's literary production is considerable: the Japanese works of the Jesuit press represent the best of Azuchi-Momoyama literature, and they fascinate the modern student. But they did not reach any significant portion of the contemporary Japanese audience to start with; and when the doors shut on Sakoku all the European writers (with the exception of that most innocuous of authors, Aesop) passed into total oblivion. The Jesuits contributed to Japanese intellectual history one very important figure. But that figure, Fabian Fucan, disavowed them, and they in turn disavowed him. In short, the missionaries left no lasting influence.

Historians of the "Christian Century" have in many instances labored under an obvious bias. The Christian encounter with Japan was also the first meeting of the European and Japanese cultures, and the tendency has been to attribute a positive value and a superior rationality to the European input of this interchange.[1] The failure of the encounter accordingly must have had tragic consequences for Japan. But the routine assumptions are highly questionable. Were the Christian missionaries indeed representatives of modernity? In what sense did they negate traditionalism? Did they in fact bear with them the scientific spirit?

In the sixteenth century the Christians taught the Japanese that the earth was round. But in the seventeenth century the man who taught that it also moved around the sun was condemned in Europe by the highest authorities of the Christian Church. The scholars who do not fail to point out the first fact usually neglect to mention the second. The year when the Inquisition moved against Galileo was 1633, the missionaries and their converts were being hounded throughout Japan, and Inoue Chikugo had just been made *sōmetsuke*.

For that matter, the Europeans did not yet possess a vastly superior stock of scientific information to dispense in Japan. It is hardly necessary to point out that sixteenth-century Europe's view of the universe was still dominated by Ptolemy. To be sure, Copernicus had launched modern astronomy into orbit in 1543, the year when the first Portuguese reached Japan. But the heliocentric conception was not generally accepted in Europe until after the "Christian Century" of Japan had ended. The full impact of the scientific revolution was not felt until the end of the seventeenth century. The missionaries' view was pre-Copernican. They were anything but Cartesians. It is an anachronism to assume that they drew the picture of a universe substantially more rational than Chu Hsi's.

What makes plausible the notion of a tragedy for Japan is not only the great spectacle of the "Christian Century's" initial acts but also the stark brutality of the drama's dénouement. The Europeans were barbarized, the Christians exterminated by the despotic Tokugawa régime. None will defend these deeds of the shogunate, and they neither can nor need be vindicated. The apologetic technique is not a proper part of the historian's method. Historical understanding, however, requires a long, comprehensive, and unprejudiced view.

The "feudal" Bakufu has not had a good press. The idea of Sakoku does not now enjoy popularity; by and large, its associations are bad. But if we take a new look at Tokugawa history we are forced to recognize that the Edo period was no

dark age, nor the Sakoku policy a bane on cultural development.[2] An equilibrium was achieved within Japan, and internal
stability maintained remarkably well for a period exceeding two
centuries. Japan was isolated from the rest of the world, but in
the country's major cities the arts flourished and a uniquely
Japanese mode of expression was created: the townsmen's genre
scene of the Tokugawa era is the golden age of Japanese culture.
On another level there occurred a brilliant synthesis of East
Asian thought: there was great vitality in the Tokugawa intellectual world, which the Confucian tradition dominated but did
not oppress. Nor was the flow of information from Europe
terminated. Scholars of the "Dutch Learning" maintained the
contact, although some irreconcilables found their presence irk-
some. The Christian missionaries were excluded, but for all that
Japan did not stagnate.

What sources of information were cut off when the missionaries
were eliminated? They had brought to Japan some splendid
representations of the rich Christian heritage, most notably the
matchless spiritual bouquets of Thomas à Kempis and Luis de
Granada. But they had also brought with them the spirit of
the Counter Reformation. We must remember that this spirit,
for all its pure composition, still shied away from the vernacular
Gospel. Its bearers adhered tightly to the official teaching of the
Church. An image of perfect consistency was required in the
mission country. No distortion and no adulteration should disturb
it. That is why the Jesuits worked so insistently to keep other
religious orders out of Japan. Within Japan their reaching was
trimmed rigorously, and they cut hard to the bone of orthodoxy.

The intellectual Jesuit is a cliché. But we have seen how
much even that most sapient of the Jesuits of Japan, the *Visitator*
Valignano, distrusted the philosophers. What occurred under such
auspices was the separation of philosophy from religion. Materials
which were not merely objects of scholarly concern but
constituted the basic food of cultivation in Europe were by
design kept from Japan. This may indeed be termed an element
of tragedy; for the design cost the missionaries the last slim
chance of perpetuating their traces in Sakoku.

They recognized, for instance, that Cicero was pre-eminent in
rhetoric. But was his philosophical advice of value? That question
of value was the crux, and the bearers of the Western message
to Japan were highly censorial. They rejected the aid of pagan

philosophers out of hand. Yet these philosophers could have afforded them a wider avenue of entry. Aristotle's advice on the superiority of the contemplative life could have been made attractive to those immured in the Five Mountains of Zen, for it was certainly amenable to them. But the invocation of Aristotle, upon whom was built the dialectic which the missionaries used, occurs nowhere in the innumerable accounts of the "Christian Century's" dogmatic debates.[3] The Japanese observer was not given as much as a glimpse of a Platonic shadow—nor, for that matter, were the many Japanese investigators into noumena and phenomena, the accidents of existence and their underlying substance, introduced to Thomas Aquinas. Or, to return to Cicero, could not the moral categories of De Officiis have been discussed on friendly terms with the Confucian? Such discussions, however, were considered dangerous from the doctrinal standpoint.

Today that doctrinal spirit is dead. Jesuits and other Catholic religious not only study Buddhist methods but apply them. Christian theologians speak of the close affinities between Thomas Aquinas and Zen. A vast literature has arisen to mark out the identities of the Christian quest for perfection and the Buddhist approach to enlightenment.[4] The insight into the Nature is set equal to the Aquinian *simplex intuitus veritatis*. It has been discovered that Meister Eckehart shared the experience of *mu* with the masters of Zen. We find remarkable passages, such as this:

Mahayanist, Taoist, and Zen thought are very much [in] accord with the thought of St. Thomas on the transcendence of God. The Ultimate Reality is incomprehensible, innominable, and ineffable because of its transcendence; and it is called Nonbeing because of its supra-substantiality. The doctrine of the eminence of the Deity in the Buddhist, Taoist and Zen thought reveals a striking similarity to the doctrine of the eminence of the Christian Deity in the supernatural order.

At least some of the twentieth-century Catholic writers agree with the anonymous fourteenth-century English mystic who cautions that God must not be sought by the activity of the mind but rather within the dark cloud of unknowing:[5]

So much so, that unless God in his great goodness intervenes with a miracle of mercy and makes [the seeker] stop and submit to the advice of those who really know, he will go mad, or suffer some other dreadful form of spiritual mischief and devilish deceit. Indeed, almost casually as it were, he may be lost eternally, body and soul. So for the love of God be careful, and do not attempt to achieve this experience intellectually. I tell you truly it cannot come this way. So leave it alone.

The accomplished Zen monk would say Amen.

Valignano, Organtino, and Francisco Pasio, Orfanel, Juan Pobre, and Francisco de Morales could not agree to any such comparison because they were the children of their times. The missionaries left the field of spiritual affinities unexplored. They served a different ideal. They were convinced that they were in possession of the absolute truth, and they knew how to circumscribe it with catechetical formulas. Most of them were selfless and self-sacrificing men. But when they were finally expelled or executed, they left behind no foot of ground on which a positive image could rest or a small positive atavism remain. Their seed was ruthlessly extirpated. All their traces were wiped out. Or, in the golden words of their own *Qincuxŭ*:[6] "Rŏxite cô naxi," much effort to no effect.

The missionaries of the "Christian Century" could not indulge in a free discourse with the heathen. That was not their mission. They came to convert Japan, not to enlighten it. It is therefore all the more ironical to note that they shared an ecumenical fate with some of their spiritual adversaries. The Christian order of allegiances clashed with the secular claims of the emerging Early Modern state in the same manner as did that of several Buddhist sects. When Oda Nobunaga ravaged the Tendai monasteries and burnt, boiled, or crucified Ikkō sectarians, there were put on the Japanese stage those "terrible and piteous actions" which the Tokugawa would imitate, to complete Aristotle's definition of tragedy. Not only Kirishitans were scrutinized in Early Modern Japan. Nevertheless, Christianity was a special case.

The Satsuma *han* maintained a strict prohibition of the True Pure Land faith throughout the Tokugawa period. The adjoining Hitoyoshi *han* retained the services of an *Ikkōshū metsuke* to spy out all single-directed religionists. As a natural consequence, *Kakure monto* communities developed in these areas of Kyushu, which lie directly across from Amakusa. During the seventeenth and eighteenth centuries there occurred here several martyrdoms of Ikkō believers.[7] The traditional aversion which underlay the measures against tightly knit religious groupings dated back to Sengoku days and was founded in the fear of peasant *ikki*. To be sure, there also existed an ideological pool which could be drawn upon to ratify the antipathy.

Edo period Confucians from Hayashi Razan on down to Fujita Tōko maligned Buddhism in practically the same language they used for Christianity.[8] They and their employers knew, however, that history can at best be bent, not done away with. Buddhism had set deep roots in Japan and adapted to Japanese conditions. Christianity could do neither, and was an alien religion. That was the crucial difference. Buddhism could not be erased and was used; Christianity could not be used and was erased.

The universal persecution which the missionaries and their converts suffered was not the karma of their actions but rather what Fabian called it: their inescapable fate.[9] The agony of torture and death was not within the compass of their own determination. Their free will could be exercised only in the choice between martyrdom and apostasy. These are the true elements of this Christian tragedy. The spirit which engendered Tokugawa Japan also bore the fruit which poisoned it; but in the clash of principles with Christianity it was victorious. The Christians' heroism could not avert this fate: they could do nothing to arrest this force, and were ground up before it.

If all that is the case, then what remained after the "Christian Century" had run its course? A few peasants, the *Kakure*, continued guarding in deepest secrecy a faith which gradually deteriorated and merged with the grassroots of native popular religion. A few museum pieces, the *Nanban byōbu*, bore witness of a rapidly receding age in which exotics daily mingled with the populace on the streets of Japanese cities. There also remained the seeds of xenophobia. A hundred and fifty years free of unwanted foreign intrusions nourished them quietly; and they emerged full-blown in the early nineteenth century, when the foreigners' Black Ships again appeared on the horizon.

But rationality did not entirely collapse before xenophobia. *Shishi* zealots who engaged in frenzied antiforeign activities during the Bakumatsu period metamorphosed into responsible bureaucrats of the Meiji government. The *jōi* slogan helped to bring down the Bakufu, but was hidden deep in the cupboard of the modern state's priorities. The foreigners could not be denied entry, and they again brought Christianity with them. Again, a small group of intellectuals was attracted by the religion's ethos, and the weight of their influence exceeded that of their number. Again, the converts amount to somewhat more than one percent of the population. But it has been neither a Catholic nor a Protestant spirit that moved Japan into the first rank of powers.

The historian's task is to interpret a complex of events, not to call an impression into being. The poet's conceits allow him to evoke richer associations. For that reason the final word belongs to Akutagawa Ryūnosuke. He also considered Deus Destroyed, and he gave his peculiar twist to the image. His story "When the Gods Smile" concludes as follows:[10]

Padre Organtino of the Temple of Southern Barbarians—no, not just Organtino. From amidst the fairy-tale laurels and roses washed with the glimmer of dusk, the high-nosed Redhairs, calmly trailing the skirts of their habits behind them, retreated into a folding screen. Into a folding screen three centuries old, with the picture of a Southern Barbarian ship entering harbor.

Farewell, Padre Organtino! You and your comrades are now walking along a Japanese beach, gazing at the colossal Southern Barbarian ship with its banners all flying in the golden-brown mist. Will Deus win? Will Amaterasu win? I suppose that can't easily be determined even today. But this is a problem which our efforts should presently clear up. Go on, look at us in peace from that seashore of the past. You and your fellow figures on the screen—the *capitão* leading his dog by a leash, the little blackamoor with the parasol upraised—you all have sunk into oblivion. But our black ships have made their first appearance on the horizon. There's no denying it: The time will come when the sound of fire from these ships will blast your musty old dream to pieces. Till then—goodbye, Padre Organtino! Goodbye, Urugan Bateren of the Temple of Southern Barbarians.

TRANSLATIONS

DEUS DESTROYED
by Fabian Fucan

PREFACE

What is the cult of Deus? What are the scriptures on which this cult's adherents rely, and the terminology they use? Who is the main deity they worship, and what do they say about his Causal State?[1] What are the principles they teach? Because the followers of the Buddhas do not inquire into these matters, they are not able to strike down and defeat this sect. Because the priestly attendants of the gods are not familiar with these matters, they are not able to vanquish this cult's adherents and chase them from the land. And therefore the cursed doctrine has grown day by day; wickedness has flourished many months—how many years have passed thus!

I joined this creed at an early age; diligently, I studied its teachings and pursued its practices. Due to my stupidity, however, I was long unable to realize that this was a perverse and cursed faith. Thus fruitlessly I spent twenty years and more! Then one day I clearly perceived that the words of the adherents of Deus were very clever and appeared very near reason—but in their teaching there was little truth. So I left their company. Some fifteen years have passed since: every morning I have lamented my desertion of the Great Holy True Law; every evening I have grieved over my adherence to the crooked path of the barbarians. All that effort to no effect! But I had a friend who remonstrated with me, saying: "'If you have made a mistake, do not be afraid of admitting the fact and amending your ways.'[2] Here, this is the Confucians' golden rule of life—act on it! Before, you learned all about the cursed faith of Deus; take pen in hand now, commit your knowledge to writing, and counter their teachings. Not only will you thereby gain the merit of destroying wickedness and demonstrating truth; you will also supply a guide toward new knowledge."

All right. Though I am not a clever man, I shall by all means try to act on this advice. I shall gather the important points about

the teachings of the Deus sect and shall skip what is not essential;
my aim is to write concisely. Thus shall I mount my attack; and
I shall call my volume DEUS DESTROYED.

In the sixth year of Genna, *kanoe saru*,
on the sixteenth day of the first month,
a Zen recluse in my hermitage,[3]
at random I write this Preface.

For those initially entering the Deus sect
there is a seven-step gate to the doctrine.
And the sum of the FIRST STEP is as follows——

    In the myriad phenomena of heaven and earth, we recognize
an all-powerful creator; in the unaltering change of the seasons,
we recognize his regulating hand. To use an analogy: When we
see a splendid palace, we realize that there existed a skilled
craftsman who built it; when we see that house laws exist within
a family and the family is governed according to their intention,
we realize that the family must certainly have a household head.
Such realization is the universal rule. Therefore, since there was
a time when heaven did not exist and earth did not exist and
nothing existed and all was a lonely void, then the fact that
heaven and earth emerged, that the sun, the moon, and the stars
with boundless brilliance shed their light in the heavens, rising in
the east and setting in the west in unaltered sequence, that the
thousand grasses and the myriad trees grow on earth, sprouting
fresh buds and shedding old leaves exactly in the appointed season
—this fact would be inconceivable without the existence of an
all-powerful creator. This all-powerful creator we call 𝕯.[4]

To counter, I reply:

    What is so amazing about all this? What schools fail to discuss
this? It is stated:[5]

> There was something before heaven and earth:
> The shapeless original emptiness;
> It acts as the lord of the myriad phenomena,
> It does not wane in accord with the four seasons.

And also:[6]

> Heaven does not speak;
> Yet the four seasons run their course thereby,
> The hundred creatures, each after its kind,
> Are born thereby.

Moreover, Buddhists discuss this in terms of the process of origination, continuation, destruction, and void;[7] and in Shinto the Age of the Gods is divided between the Seven Gods of Heaven and the Five Gods of Earth. And the first of the Seven Gods of Heaven are the Three: Kuni-tokotachi no Mikoto, Kuni-sazuchi no Mikoto, and Toyokunnu no Mikoto; they are the ones who opened up heaven and earth.[8] The lord who always rises to the land's government: this is the meaning of the worshipful name Kuni-tokotachi no Mikoto. Why then do the adherents of Deus press their tedious claims with the pretence that they alone know the lord who opened up heaven and earth? Idle verbosity without substance, and most annoying!

The adherents of Deus claim:

𝕯 is *infinitus*—without beginning or end. He is *spiritualis substantia*—true substance without material shape. He is *omnipotens* —all is in his power. He is *sapientissimus*—the wellspring of wisdom without superior. He is *justissimus*—the wellspring of universal law. He is *misericordissimus*—the wellspring of universal mercy and universal compassion.[9] Aside from all this, he is the wellspring of all good and all quality. Since the Buddhas and the gods all are merely human beings, they do not possess the above-mentioned qualities. Since they are subject to the process of birth and death, how can they be said to be the creators of heaven and earth?

To counter, I reply:

To regard the Buddhas and the gods as merely human is but the wicked view of ignorant men, a supposition truly befitting the adherents of Deus. The Buddhas all possess the Three Bodies: the Law Body, the Recompensed Body, and the Accommodated Body.[10] The Tathagata in the Accommodated-Transformed Body did undergo the Eight Stages of Earthly Life, for the sake of salvation of all sentient beings and as a means of bestowing grace.[11] However, the Tathagata in the Law Body is the Buddha of Eternal Existence and Eternal Constancy in kalpas boundless and without beginning: he is the True Buddha of the Law Body of Thusness.[12] He therefore transcends all attempts to define him; one does not speak of "good" or "evil" in him. And so the scriptures also say:[13]

> Constant dwells the Tathagata;
> There is in him no change.

Only the deluded and unenlightened consider him merely human. And those who say that the gods also are merely human likewise are ignorant.

The August Gods in their origins are manifestations of the Buddhas under the figures of Japanese deities.[14] For instance, Tenman Daijizai Tenjin in his original state is the all-merciful all-compassionate Kanzeon; but when in subdued brilliance he became part of this world of dust, he appeared in the person of the Grand Minister Kan Shōjō and left his evidence for posterity at Kitano; he is celebrated as the God Protector of the Hundred Kings.[15] Where the god of shrine or mausoleum to whom this principle does not apply?! But let us go further, let us take up the example of Kuni-tokotachi no Mikoto. How could you ever say he is a mere human, he who was a god before even one human existed, before heaven and earth were opened up! Don't dare say it, don't dare say it! Accept as understood the things you can understand, admit you do not fathom the things you can not fathom.[16] Even the Sage Confucius spoke about the gods as follows:[17]

> They cause the men of the world
> To fast and be purified and wear
> Their finest clothing:
> Thereby to carry out religious ritual.
> In mighty overflow, they are above
> And on the right
> And on the left as well.

The proverb says: The blind man does not fear the snake. And so the ignorant adherents of Deus babble on, unmindful of the fate they shall incur. O horror of horrors!—their tongues shall indeed be ripped out!

Japan is the Land of the Gods. Owing to the eastward advance of Buddha's Law it may also be called the Land of the Buddhas. That being so, then the adherents of Deus who pile abuse on the Buddhas and the gods must still in this world suffer the punishment of the Buddhas and the gods, without even the chance to await the other world; that is their inescapable fate, so swift a punishment that they cannot turn their heels on it. And soon men have forgotten their very names. It is impossible to count the examples: an unbroken procession passes before the eye.

Look! Look at Ōtomo Sōrin of Bungo.[18] In the days when Sōrin was still devoted to the Buddhas and gods he brandished his power over all of Kyushu and the glory of his name spread throughout the Four Seas. But after he entered the ranks of Deus the fortunes of war suddenly turned against him. With his eldest son Yoshimune he fell over Hyūga to fight the Shimazu, suffered a crushing defeat at Mimigawa, and had to flee home deserted by all and in desperate straits. After that his house gradually fell to ruin; so prosperous, so flourishing for many generations, the family is practically extinct today. Are any offspring left, or not? —such is the sad state of the house at present.

The like fate befell Konishi Lord Settsu.[19] Because he was the ringleader of the Deus sect he lost the protection of the Buddhas and gods. He joined the atrocious rebellion of Mitsunari; but he wound up dragged down the avenue to the execution ground and was beheaded. One and all, his relatives were eradicated; he left no survivors.

Takayama Ukon also was a pillar of the Deus sect; but where are his descendants now?[20] Akashi Kamon, too, became an adherent of Deus, brought ruin over his house, and lost his life.[21] To give yet other examples: the family of Juan Kikyōya[22] in the Capital and the house of Higoroya in Sennan no Tsu,[23] though merchants, became prominent benefactors of the Deus sect; most members of these families were not blessed with a peaceful death but finished miserably. Where are their descendants now?

All these stories are clearly known to all. But the adherents of Deus, though they have heard these facts, still say that the Buddhas and gods are merely human. It seems that they consider but surface appearance. Lord Shaka had the Great King Jōbon for his father and the Lady Maya for his mother, assuming the State of Incarnation; and in Crane Forest he entered Nirvana.[24] Hachiman Daibosatsu was born with Emperor Chūai for his father and Empress Jingū for his mother.[25] Therefore, the adherents of Deus conclude, they are but human. If that be so, then what about the main deity of the Deus sect, Jesus Christus? Joseph was his father, Santa Maria his mother. His birth was issue from simple humans, that's all. And they tell us that a human being cannot be the Lord of Heaven and Earth!

The adherents of Deus claim: Jesus Christus represents the Causal State, human in its nature and in this no different from the Buddhas' Causal State or the gods' manifestations; I shall set aside this step for treatment later. Since the gods have their original state as Buddhas, it shall not enter into discussion. Let us now compare the Law Body of Thusness with 𝕯.

As stated above, 𝕯 is the wellspring of all good and all quality. But the Law Body of Thusness is defined as *muchi yaku mutoku*— no knowledge and no quality.[26] If that be so, then how is it possible from a position of no knowledge and no quality to create heaven and earth and the myriad phenomena? Further, if the original wellspring does not possess knowledge and quality, how could it be that forethought, knowledge, and discrimination exist in us today?

To counter, I reply:

The adherents of Deus do not understand the obvious truth. Hearing that the Law Body of Thusness possesses no knowledge and no quality, they consider this impossible and reject it. Hearing that 𝕯 possesses knowledge and quality, they consider this possible and accept it. Just wait! I will teach the obvious to you!

To start with, the word *mu* is inscrutable—

The word *mu* is an iron barrier
Ten-million-fold!
Who can pass over this word
And break through to the other side?[27]

Mu therefore is one word which the likes of the adherents of Deus can never understand. All right, then! Let us proceed to *muchi yaku mutoku*. Take the expression literally: no knowledge and no quality. Now *muchi mutoku* indeed is absolute truth. But that 𝕯 possesses knowledge and quality cannot be affirmed with ease. Generally, where knowledge is present it is impossible to avoid the discrimination between hate and love. But hate and love are human feelings. If this 𝕯 were possessed of hate and love, he would be unworthy of mention together [with the Law Body of Thusness]. But I shall explain this at a later spot.

> Thusness is like unto the ocean,
> Transcending attributes of
> "Good" or
> "Evil."[28]

How absolutely true this is!

The adherents of Deus also boast that their 𝕯 possesses quality. But there is not a shred of evidence for this; this is but the talk of fools incapable of enlightenment.

> Superior quality is not to claim quality;
> This is wherein quality lies.[29]

But this is said even of humans; so to say that 𝕯 possesses this or that quality makes him full of deficiencies. Let me cite the three words of Lao Tzu: *i* (no form), *hsi* (no sound), *wei* (no shape). "These three cannot be further inquired into."[30] It is indeed proper to term these three concepts—invisible, inaudible, intangible—inexpressible in words and intransmissible in writing.

𝕯 possesses wisdom and discrimination, and therefore surpasses Thusness, you claim. The very idea! I can't help laughing out loud! The Pure Undisturbed Absolute[31] is something you fools can never understand.

The adherents of Deus also claim:

If the original wellspring does not possess knowledge and quality, then how can be explained the forethought and knowledge possessed by humans, and whence stems the quality of order inherent in the myriad phenomena? One can not escape the view that such a nature of things would be quite impossible if the original wellspring were not endowed with knowledge and quality.

To counter, I reply:

Willows are green, flowers are red; this is but the order of nature. Crush the willow roots and see: there is no green. Smash to pieces the flowering tree—now see: there is no red. And yet this is the essence of nature manifest.[32]

> The mountain cherry of Yoshino
> Bears blossoms every year.
> Split up the tree and see:
> Do you find flowers?

For something not at the base of the root to be found at the end of the branch is but the usual state of things.

> Tao produced the One.
> The One produced the two.
> The two produced the three.
> And the three produced the
> ten thousand things.[33]

All the following stem from the original wellspring of the Pure Undisturbed Absolute: Yin and Yang were born; the pure and turbid, dynamic and quiescent material force came to exist;[34] heaven, earth, and man together produced the myriad things; we possess forethought, knowledge, and discrimination; the birds fly about and sing, and the beasts run about and roar; the grasses and the trees blossom forth in flower, wither away, and die. All these comply with the double variance, the pure and turbid, dynamic and quiescent principle. From antiquity immemorable down to the present day, not one of the Thousand Sages and Ten Thousand Worthies has failed to affirm the truth of this process! The adherents of Deus are not the ones to surpass Confucius or excel Lao Tzu. Their creeping tendrils of sophistry, their twisted vines of discord I shall sever at the root!

SECOND STEP

The adherents of Deus claim:

𝔇 is the Lord both of this world and of the world to come, and he is the wellspring of all reward and all punishment. Though there be such a Lord, he would be inconceivable without the knowledge of the factor involved in the allotment of reward or punishment in the next world according to the effect of good or evil done in this world.

All things with a material shape—men, animals, grasses and trees—have an end. Burnt, they turn to ashes; buried, they turn to dust. But how are we to conceive of the entity remaining to live on after death, to receive agony or bliss in the life to come? There are diverse kinds of animating principles in things.

First, let us take up the spirit of grasses and trees: it is called *anima vegetativa*. *Anima vegetativa* has the meaning of vital principle endowed solely with the capabilities of birth, growth, luxuriance, and withering, of sprouting fresh buds and shedding old leaves. Next, we take up the vital principle of birds and beasts: it is called *anima sensitiva*. *Anima sensitiva* is vital principle which possesses not only the capabilities of birth and growth but also of perception, motion, and the like. For instance, the sparrow in seeing a hawk recognizes it for an enemy; and his kind of vital principle feels hunger and thirst, irritation and pain. The above-mentioned two kinds of *anima* constitute a type of vital principle which proceeds from matter and thus gives forth capabilities applicable only to a material state; such an animating spirit accompanies the material state into destruction as it reverts to the Four Great Elements of matter.[35] Finally, we take up the mind of man: it is called *anima rationalis*. This *anima* which is termed *rationalis* not only possesses the capabilities of the above-mentioned two but is capable also of discrimination between right and wrong; this is why it is called *rationalis anima*. This *rationalis anima* does not proceed from matter; rather, it determines matter. It is *spiritualis substantia*, true substance without material shape.

That it does not proceed from matter is evident from the following. Because human beings also have a material state, they feel hunger and thirst, cold and heat; in this they are no different from the birds and beasts. However, in the face of starvation and desire to eat, a human being will rather die than eat if he feels that in the particular situation he will incur disgrace by eating. On the battlefield, though every sinew dictates retreat, a man will think of his duty rather than flee and make people point their fingers at his back; against his own instincts he will seek a hero's death. And demonstrated in this way is *anima rationalis* which proceeds not from matter! It is clear that 𝔇 created it to be master over the body. This being so, since it is *anima rationalis* quite separate from the material body, it does not accompany the material body into destruction but remains to live on in the other world; and in accord with the effect of its actions in this world, it is assigned agony or bliss, eternal and without decrease. The good place is called *Paraiso* and is in heaven. But the bad place is called *Inferno* and is in the bowels of the earth.

To counter, I reply:

I shall give each of the above three kinds of *anima* its proper designation; let me explain them one by one. Best of all the three is supposed to be the *anima* of humans: it is *rationalis* and does not proceed from a material body, they claim, but has been created as a separate entity by 𝕯; according to the effects of its actions in this world it is assigned agony or bliss in the life to come.

O how awful it is!—the adherents of Deus do not understand the obvious truth. And how wretched, alas!—unenlightened fools of our own realm, taken in by this heresy. I shall teach the truth to you. You just listen!

All things have two aspects: object and principle.[36] If a particular object exists it is impossible for its principle not to exist. This principle we call the thing's natural endowment. Though there may exist an infinite variety of things, there exist not two principles, not three principles, but only one principle. The difference in functioning accords with the kind of object. To use an analogy: Rain is one—it is the principle. The receptacles are of thousandfold variety—they are the objects. When the heavens send down streams of rain, one puts out receptacles to gather the rainwater in. Rainwater is not endowed with the attributes of long or short, square or round; it does not possess odor, fragrant or foul; clearness and turbidity are not inherent in it; and it does not have flavor, sweet or bitter or whatever. Rather, for rainwater a square or round shape, the Five Flavors,[37] fragrant or foul odor, clearness or turbidity, and so forth—all is determined by the receptacles' square or round shape, good or bad quality, pure or defiled state.

And so it is with a thing's natural endowment. According to differences in material force and its manifestant tangible matter[38] —clear or turbid, thick or thin—its functioning will also differ. So how is it possible to divide up this principle into individual parcels?—*vegetativa, sensitiva, rationalis,* et cetera! Especially does this hold true of the human mind: they term it *anima rationalis,* claim that it is a separate entity and therefore controls bodily desires, make this the fundamental principle, and think that the various schools know nothing of this. Really, for narrow-mindedness this tops it all!

The wilful mind (*jen hsin*) is what Confucianism calls the desires that stem from material force and its manifestant; and mindfulness of duty is called the righteous mind (*tao hsin*).[39] This Confucian striving for the perfection of good and beauty is something which the crooked barbarian teachings of the adherents of Deus shall never be able to match. To illustrate this concept:[40]

> The wilful mind is unstable;
> Subtle is the righteous mind.

And in Buddhism there is no lack of detailed discussions concerning the three concepts of mind, volition, and consciousness.[41] The unrisen concentrated mind is the mystical body of Fudō the Mind-Ruler.[42] The rise of concentrated egoistic desire is called volition. And to devise minute distinctions such as "green" or "red" is termed consciousness. But let me illustrate: Though fire is one, it is like unto three—combustion, flame, and embers.

Not knowing a jot about the true facts so exhaustively defined by the various schools, the adherents of Deus with smug countenance prate about *anima sensitiva, anima vegetativa* or *rationalis* or what have you. So much Chinaman's gibberish it is, crooked twaddle to dupe idle fools! And they say that to the *anima rationalis* 鬼 in the world after death will assign agony or bliss in accord with the effect of its actions in this world. So him who perpetrates such injustice we are to call 鬼! Such action is to be condemned even in a human ruler.

After succeeding to the throne, Yü of Hsia once—

> In sighting a criminal
>> descended from his chariot
>> and uttered, shedding tears:
> Men of Yao and Shun
>> patterned their hearts
>> on the hearts of Yao and Shun.
> I am king;
> And all the hundred families
>> pattern their hearts
>> each to his own intention.
> This
> I lament.

Thus he took the blame upon himself.[43]

The subjects of King T'ang of Shang were suffering under a terrible seven-year drought. The Court Astrologer performed his divinations and reported to the throne, saying: "The right course to take is offer people as sacrifice." But King T'ang thought: "This all is disaster sent down by Heaven due to my fault; the people are not to blame." So in order to sacrifice himself, he took an unadorned plain wood chariot drawn by white horses, and—

> His body girt with white reeds,
> and thus himself the sacrificial object,
> he prayed in the wilderness
> of Mulberry Wood.

> Six things
> he took upon himself in blame,
> saying: "Yes—
> government is intemperate;
> the people are negligent of duty;
> the palace is luxurious;
> feminine intrigue flourishes;
> bribery is rampant;
> and slander thrives.
> Yes, it is so."

> Before he finished speaking,
> abundant rain came down
> for thousands of miles around.[44]

> And he took the gold of Chuang Shan
> and minted it into coin
> and saved the lives of his subjects.[45]

Thus the histories attest.

Such were the Sage Sovereigns and Enlightened Rulers, albeit they were humans! But 𝕯—who asked him? who hired him?—created human beings countless as the sands of the Ganges, and now he thrusts them into hell. And is it hell for only a day, or for a month? Oh, no! It is hell for all eternity, agony without surcease. And him who keeps raking torment upon agony we are to call the all-merciful, all-compassionate 𝕯! Him only shall you call all-merciful and all-compassionate who sweeps away suffering and grants joy!

THIRD STEP

The adherents of Deus claim:

𝔇 is *spiritualis substantia*—true substance without material shape. Not a hair can be inserted into space where he is not; he fills up all heaven and all earth. But in a special way he has demonstrated his power and his glory: above all the heavens he created a world of boundless bliss, in order to bestow joy upon the good; this place we call *Paraiso*.

At its beginning, before he brought man into being, he created a countless, immeasurable number of heavenly beings called *anjo*: but he did not yet show his holy self to them. He set down the sacred law that none was to aspire to the rank of chief over the rest: if they kept this sacred law, for their virtue they would in adoration of the presence of 𝔇 partake to fullest measure of inexhaustible bliss; but if they broke this law, they would be thrust into that pool of perfect agony called *Inferno* and would suffer the torments of noxious cold and noxious heat in hell.

But no sooner had they been created than from among the countless number of *anjo* there arose the one called Lucifer and, taking pride in his own excellence, urged upon the others: "It is I who am 𝔇. Adore me!" Among this boundless number of *anjo*, one part in three followed Lucifer's behest; but the greater part did not ally themselves with him. So 𝔇 then took Lucifer and all of his confederates, one part in three among the *anjo*, and, casting them down to the underworld, he thrust them into *Inferno*. And so the *anjo* due to their sin of pride became the devils known as *diabo*.

To counter, I reply:

O you adherents of Deus! What you have exposed here is entirely 𝔇's own fault and altogether serves him right. First of all: What you have said about 𝔇's overflowing omnipresence makes one wonder whether he has not misheard a discussion of the process in which the Active Law Nature of Thusness fills up all heaven and earth and pervades the Six Directions.[46] Two lookalikes don't both have to be right—here's your perfect example of that fact. But did you not say that 𝕯 is *sapientissimus*, Wisdom pervading the Three Worlds?[47] If that be so, and if he created these *anjo*, then it indeed is inconceivable for him not to have known that the *anjo* on the instant would fall into sin. If he did not realize this, then it is utter nonsense to call him Wisdom encompassing the Three Worlds. And if he did know that they would fall into sin and nevertheless created them, then he committed the most nefarious of cruelties. If he is the all-powerful 𝕯, why ever did he not make sure the *anjo* would not fall into sin—why did he not create them sinless? Contentedly to let them fall into sin was, in effect, to create a band of dreadful demons. What manner of action is this, this creation of useless devils, this spawning of a wicked hindrance? But perhaps 𝕯 bungled the job of creation? Or do the *anjo* represent chips that fell during the work of constructing heaven and earth and the myriad phenomena, to be used for kindling the flames of *Inferno*? Haha! What a joke!

FOURTH STEP

The adherents of Deus claim:

After 𝕯 had created heaven and earth and the myriad phenomena which crowd the universe, he created man to be master over all the myriad things. Not that from the beginning he created the countless, immeasurable number of humans that exists today. Rather, he created a pair of humans: Adam as the husband, and Eve as the wife. He gave them all the categories of wisdom and discrimination in abundance, and he left them in a region called *Paraiso Terreal*, a world of boundless bliss upon the face of this earth. This *Paraiso Terreal* was a place without cold and without heat, separated from any sorrow. While in this place, Adam and Eve would suffer no want and no illness; they would live in ease and satisfaction, and the thousand cares and ten thousand troubles would never even approach their precincts. But here also

𝔅 set down a law, for Adam and Eve to follow: of every herb and tree of the garden he let them freely eat, but not of the fruit called *maçan*.[48] If they kept this law, Adam and Eve themselves (needless to say), and also their children and descendants down to the furthest generation would not age and would not die, but rather would live on in peace and satisfaction, and in due course would ascend to the Supreme Heaven which is called *Paraiso*. But if they proved transgressors of the law, they would be chased from *Paraiso Terreal* and would fall prey to death, disease, and the other multitude of sorrows. Never would they be raised up to the Supreme Heaven, *Paraiso*; but instead they would in the end have to dwell sunk in the hell of *Inferno*. Such was the commandment.

But the aforesaid devil Lucifer grew jealous in the expectation that humans, if only they stayed true to 𝔅's behest, would usurp the honors of Supreme Heaven, which he himself had lost. Craftily he crept in to *Paraiso Terreal* and prevailed upon the woman Eve, saying: "Why should you not eat of this fruit called *maçan*? This is the fruit of knowledge, of insight into the Three Worlds; and if you eat thereof you shall be like unto 𝔅. For 𝔅 only set down this law so that humans would not become like unto him."

And Eve ate of this fruit. And her husband Adam also did eat. By this they broke the sacred law, and for this they were chased from *Paraiso Terreal*. This curse has descended down even to us, the progeny of Adam and Eve today: death, disease, and all the other sorrows have multiplied hereby. But, worst of all, our lot now is to be subject to descent into *Inferno*.

To counter, I reply:

Although they were contrary to reason, the first two Steps did at least possess a minute measure of logic. But as one progresses from the Third Step into this Fourth, one expects in vain to go from shallowness on to greater profundity, and finds instead that even the shallows gradually lose in depth. And just to imagine what lies in store ahead!

But first let us consider: Though the term "sacred law" itself implies something holy, still such a precept must contain the stuff of which laws are made. But this business of "Don't you dare eat the *maçan*!'' (a fruit somewhat like the persimmon) truly is the height of absurdity! It's just like tricking an old woman or cajoling a crying child. A persimmon does not suffice to serve as direct or indirect cause for such all-important matters as the possession of Supreme Heaven or the fall to hell. Among the Five Commandments or the Ten Laws or all the codes of the School of Discipline, I have not heard of one precept which cautions against persimmons.[49] When the late Hachiya Nyūdō heard this disquisition on *maçan*, he aptly termed it the persermon of the adherents of Deus.[50]

To demonstrate their determination to destroy demons, the gods and Buddhas shed their dress of detachment and appear girt in the appurtenances of anger: sword and spear, bow and arrow. Thus they extend their protecting hand. To hear of such protection is to wonder all the more about 𝕯. For not only did 𝕯 create the devil Lucifer and leave him to his own devices, but he stood by nonchalantly as this devil was about to ensnare Adam and Eve, and he offered them no protection as they fell into sin. 𝕯 looked on and laughed as Adam and Eve ate the persimmon; and thereupon he immediately chased them out of *Paraiso Terreal*. And now, not only Adam and Eve but every human being he wants to cram into hell! Just like 𝕯, isn't it? But how like is it to reason?

Did not 𝕯 know that Adam would break his law? If he did not know, then he is not Wisdom encompassing the Three Worlds. And if he did know, then from his position of mercy and compassion he certainly should have taught to Adam and Eve the determination not to fall into sin. Either way, the explications of the adherents of Deus are gross invention and completely outrageous.

FIFTH STEP

The adherents of Deus claim:

After the aforesaid Adam and Eve had broken the law, they saw that they were subject to the pain of death and disease, of discomfort and of discontent. And especially when they reflected upon the fact that after death the fall to *Inferno* would be their sorry lot, they raised in their hearts the repentance we call *contriçan*. "Come what may in this life—but save us in the life to come, and all those who shall repent of their sins!" Thus they prayed in walking and in resting, in sitting and in lying down, facing the heavens and prostrate upon the ground. And 𝕯, from the standpoint of universal mercy and universal compassion, wished to save them. But from the standpoint of universal law, human beings with their limited faculties cannot possibly render appropriate atonement, no matter how fervent their desire to atone sufficiently for their sins. That is because the sin of Adam and Eve was a boundless sin.

Let me use a paraphrase. When we strike a person's face with the hand, the offence is shallow or deep according to the other's slight or weighty position. If the other is of lower standing, then we shall not suffer for slapping him. If he is of the same rank, then he will hit back. But if we were to strike someone of superior rank (the ruler of a country, for example), then naturally the offence is a grievous crime and condemns even our children, grandchildren, and their descendants to the most severe of punishments. A crime perpetrated against the boundless 𝕯 cannot be recompensed except by boundless atonement. But human beings with their limited faculties cannot render such atonement, not ever; and 𝕯 might well have abandoned them to this state.

But in that case the omnipotence of 𝕯 would have been obscured. And therefore, the twin qualities of merciful compassion and universal law being requisite to his omnipotence, 𝕯 gave to Adam and Eve his divine promise that he would without fail assume human form, enter this world, and accomplish atonement for man. And Adam and Eve received this promise, passing it down to their descendants, lived to the age of nine hundred and thirty years and finally died.

To counter, I reply:

This is just what people mean by the common saying, "A cut-and-patch carpenter!" At times nothing is better than something. A patched-up thing may be all right; yet it is better not to have the problem of patching arise in the first place. But let me use an example. A carpenter might want to fit a piece of good wood into a certain space—say to cut it into a cross-beam spanning thirty feet. If the piece turns out overly short he won't just throw it away but rather he will add an extension onto it; and this, to be sure, speaks well for his ability. Nevertheless, it is not right to make a wasteful mistake by cutting a long piece of wood too short; in fact, it is inexcusable. No different is the story of 𝕯's attempt to repair the damage after his wasteful mistake in creating Adam and Eve without directing them to the rightful path. In a halfhearted way 𝕯 set about creating human beings—who hired him?—and he botched the job. And now we, too, are put to pain in overabundance! Really, it's nothing to be thankful for! And the adherents of Deus take this story in and feel grateful and nothing will change them. The worst of fools! The worst of fools![51] But words fail me.

Well, then: let us continue. You adherents of Deus have claimed above that since the offence is determined by the slight or weighty position of the other party, an offence perpetrated against the boundless 𝕯 is a boundlessly grievous crime, and so human beings with their limited capabilities cannot possibly render atonement for it. But all this is quite dubious. If the offence of eating one persimmon becomes a boundless offence when perpetrated against 𝕯, then what about the good of the feelings of shame, self-abasement, contrition, and penitence raised up to 𝕯?[52] When repentance flares up eight thousand times to scorch the heart, to sink it in a flood of crimson tears—is this not a boundless source of good?

But perhaps your 𝕯 is a Lord who nourishes the evil in man and for the good in man offers but neglect. Or does evil puff up in presumption when connected with 𝕯, and good collapse to nothingness upon confronting him? Come, you adherents of Deus! Your stand must certainly be on one of this pair of propositions! But your theses are of such base value: to criticize them one by one, I could take heaven and earth for paper and all the grasses and trees for pens, and still I would not exhaust my refutations. I have now held up one corner for a moment. The wise man will certainly come back with the other three.[53] And thus let it be.

SIXTH STEP

The adherents of Deus claim:

The above-mentioned entry of 𝕯 into this world occurred after some five thousand years had passed from the time when heaven and earth were opened up. His birth took place during the reign of an emperor named Caesar, in a village called Belem, in the country of Judea. His mother's name was Santa Maria, and Joseph was the name of his father. But both Santa Maria and Joseph were *virgem*, by which is meant to say that throughout their lives they did not have marital relations; and in these circumstances he was conceived and born.

But how did all this come about? How are we to understand this entry of 𝕯 into the world? Well, first of all, this Santa Maria not only possessed the virtue of lifelong chastity but also, because she was endowed with the various good qualities and all the virtuous accomplishments, she paid zealous attention to devotional pursuits and to the recitation of prayers. One day at dusk, as she had composed her mind toward the open window of spiritual contemplation, an *anjo* suddenly appeared before her. And he knelt down, his hands upraised and joined, and uttered: *Ave, gratia plena. Dominus tecum.* The meaning of these words is: "Hail Maria, full of 𝕯's grace. The Lord is with you." And from that moment she conceived and after the ten months were fulfilled she gave birth in the aforesaid Belem, at deepest midnight, in a stable. And angels descended from the heavens, playing music, and a wonderful fragrance pervaded the four directions. And marvellous signs were seen at this time, to testify that 𝕯 had entered this world.

Now the name of the Lord who was thus born is Jesus Christus. For thirty-three years he remained on this earth, to teach the way of goodness to all sentient beings. But because he claimed that he was 𝕯 a group of people called Jews on hearing this said it was deviltry. And, swaying their judges, they heaped blows and tortures upon him, and then they suspended him upon a stake known as the *cruz*. And thus he crushed sin and gave effect to good for mankind, and by this merit he accomplished atonement for the sin of Adam and Eve. And thus in his thirty-third year he summoned forth death. But on the third day he rose again from the dead, and after forty days he ascended into Heaven. Some one thousand and six hundred years have passed since.

To counter, I reply:

So it took all of five thousand years after heaven and earth were opened up for 𝕯 to enter this world! Was the atonement so late in coming because heaven and earth are so far apart? Were so many years expended along the way on this distant route? Or were all those years spent on fuss and preparation for the journey? Since atonement was not accomplished for five thousand years all the human beings in the world had to fall into hell— a measureless, countless number! All those people falling down to hell! Really, it must have been like a torrent of rain. And him who watched this and did not even feel sad, who for five thousand years was not disposed to find a way to redeem sentient beings—are we to call him the all-merciful, all-compassionate Lord? One simple look at this will make it clear that all the teachings of the adherents of Deus are fraud.

And what they say about the total number of years is also extremely dubious. Five thousand years from the opening up of heaven and earth until the coming of Jesus Christus added to the one thousand and six hundred years since his coming make a sum of six thousand and six hundred years. In balancing this number of years against that recorded in the Japanese and Chinese histories one finds the number exceedingly short. But perhaps the heaven and earth of the adherents of Deus are somewhere outside this heaven and this earth, and came into existence at a later date. Perhaps there is yet another, a separate heaven and earth. Dubious, dubious!

So Jesus Christus was born with lifelong virgins, the virtuous Joseph and Santa Maria, as father and mother. What sort of ideal virtue is this? "Man and wife have separate functions."[54] The universal norm of moral law is that one and all shall enter into marital relations. Actually, to counter the universal norm is evil; and evil may be defined as the departure from the Way. If marital relations were not completely the standard of moral law in the world, then what else could we expect but the extinction of the human seed in every province and district, down into the last village! So it is obvious now that the standard Way is virtuous and all outside it not virtuous.

So Jesus Christus assumed the name of Lord of Heaven and Earth and because of this the group of Jews, saying that this was deviltry, sued him before their judges, suspended him upon a stake, and took his life. Now this, to be sure, is both plausible and proper! *The Odes* say:[55]

> To hack an axe-haft
> an axe
> hacks;
> the pattern's near.

And now, before our very eyes here in Japan, you adherents of Deus are preaching a doctrine wicked and contrary to the Way of the Sages; and therefore the wise ruler has decided to stamp out your doctrine, and the people also hate it and inform on it and denounce its followers, so that they are beheaded or crucified or burnt at the stake. The methods of government of the wise men of former and of latter days agree perfectly, like the halves of a tally joined.[56] But the doctrine you adherents of Deus preach is a perverse faith; I shall unmask it later, point by point.

Well, then: What you say about the resurrection and ascent to Heaven sounds quite splendid; but in a faith perverse from its very roots everything must be devilish illusion, magical trickery.

The right and wrong of enlightenment, right or wrong, is all resolved as right. The right and wrong of delusion, right or wrong, is all resolved as wrong.[57] The right and wrong of true doctrine, right or wrong, is all resolved as truth. The right and wrong of deviltry, right or wrong, is all resolved as devilish. There is no ground for indecision about this!

SEVENTH STEP

The adherents of Deus claim:

The above six Steps contain the outstanding and necessary teachings of our faith. Those who can find assent to these Steps will accept our doctrine; but after embracing our doctrine they must by all means observe ten statutes known as the Ten *Mandamentos*. The first of these is: "You shall hold the one 𝔇 dear above all things and him shall you worship." The second:

"You shall not invoke the holy name of 𝔇 in baseless oaths."
The third: "You shall endeavor to keep every seventh day as
your *domingo*." The fourth: "You shall observe filial piety to
your father and your mother." The fifth: "You shall not kill
human beings." The sixth: "You shall not commit adultery." The
seventh: "You shall not steal." The eighth: "You shall not make
false charges against others." The ninth: "You shall not lust for
the spouse of another." The tenth: "You shall not have wicked
desires for the property of another." These are the commandments.

And of these the First *Mandamento*—"You shall hold 𝔇 dear
above all things and him shall you worship"—means that one
should esteem this 𝔇 even above one's ruler, more even than
one's father and mother. Refuse to follow the orders of ruler or
parent if compliance would mean the denial of 𝔇's will! Do not
grudge your life in such a situation! And not to mention all
else that this *Mandamento* implies!

One is given a name at the time of entry into our faith.
The names of virtuous men and virtuous women, those who in
times past fulfilled 𝔇's will, are now used for everybody, so
that everybody may turn to these virtuous personages for
mediation in the Holy Presence. One is also given a taste of
salt. As salt is a thing which adds taste to something without
taste, so does this signify: "I now give you a taste of the life
to come." And one has a taper placed in the hand, to signify:
"You have found the True Light." *Ego te baptizo in nomine
Patris, et Filii, et Spiritus Sancti*—these required words are intoned
and water is sprinkled upon the forehead. The meaning of these
words is: "I cleanse you in the name of 𝔇 the Father, and
𝔇 the Son, and their Reciprocal Love."[58] At this time the merit
of the blood which Jesus Christus shed on the cross com-
mingles with the water, to wash away all stain of sin. And after
this, if a man die without committing sins of his own, there is no
doubt that the gain of Heaven is his. But if a man receive not
this blessing of *baptismo*, though he be righteous there is for him
no salvation.

To counter, I reply:

So you propound a ten-point statute called *mandamentos*. But
aside from the first of the ten points nothing here exceeds the

scope of the Five Commandments which prohibit killing, theft, adultery, falsehood, and drunkenness.[59] The ninth and tenth *mandamentos* contain restraints against wicked desires of the mind; but the injunction against drunkenness also is aimed at restraining all licentiousness of the mind. In drinking wine and in drinking water the act of drinking may be all the same; but wine leads to licentiousness, so that lust, cupidity, and other such wicked desires arise when one is drunk. And therefore drunkenness is prohibited, and the commandment which proscribes drunkenness is meant for to prevent the mind's corruption.[60]

So you talk about filial piety. O you adherents of Deus! Filial behavior is in the Empire accepted as the way to righteousness, and therefore you mouth adherence to it for mere form's sake. That is the way it seems to me; but we shall hear more about this point later.

The first *mandamento* urges disobedience to the orders of sovereign or father if compliance would mean denial of 𝔇's will; it entreats one to hold life itself cheap in such a situation. In this precept lurks the intention to subvert and usurp the country, to extinguish Buddha's Law and Royal Sway. Quick, quick! Put this gang in stocks and shackles!

"One does not usually expect to find precepts for attaining to ultimate good outside the realm of morals constantly preserved in the people's daily life."[61] There are a great many divisions within moral law, but they all come within the scope of the Five Social Relationships and the duties they involve. Sovereign and subject, father and child, husband and wife, elder brother and younger brother, friend and friend—what else can a man do if he has performed his duties within these relationships! And if a man derange these, then what is the iniquity, what the atrocity to which he will not stoop?

The duties of sovereign and subject toward each other are loyalty and reward. The duties of father and child toward each other are filial piety and parental affection. The duties of husband and wife are in the propriety of separate functions. The duties of elder brother and younger brother are in fraternal service and love. The duties of friend and friend are contained in good faith. To bestow upon man a nature consistent with these Five Relationships is the part of Heaven's Will. And here is how you regard all this, you adherents of Deus! If adherence means denial of 𝔇's will, then cast aside the loyalty of subject to sovereign,

repudiate the bonds of filial piety and of fraternal service!—
such is your counsel. What greater iniquity than this?

The expression "denial of 𝔇's will" means, first and foremost, to abandon 𝔇 and adhere to the Buddhas and the gods.
And therefore, no matter how grave be the ruler's command to
convert from the cult of Deus and adhere to the Buddhas and
the gods, the adherents of Deus do not grudge their lives and
would rather court chastisement under the Five Penalties, and
would delight in it.[62] Look, look! They value above the ruler's
command the orders of the Bateren. For Bateren preachments
they feel more debt of gratitude than for their own parents'
beneficence.

Japan is the Land of the Gods. The generations of our rulers
have received the Imperial Dignity from Amaterasu Ōmikami,
through U-gaya-fuki-awasezu no Mikoto and his August Child
Jimmu Tennō, who became the progenitor of our Hundred
Kings. The Three Divine Regalia became the protectors of the
Empire, so that among all the customs of our land there is not
one which depends not on the Way of the Gods.[63]

And the divine Prince Shōtoku, being a Buddha manifest in
human form,[64] took on the will of Amaterasu Ōmikami to
expand the Way of our land, and to that end he made Buddha's
Law flourish. From that time on our land also became the Land
of the Buddhas.

And this, this the adherents of Deus plan to subvert! They
bide their time with the intent to make all of Japan into their
own sectarians, to destroy the Law of Buddha and the Way of
the Gods. Because the Law of Buddha and the Way of the Gods
are planted here, the Royal Sway also flourishes; and since the
Royal Sway is established here the glory of the Buddhas and
the gods does grow. And therefore the adherents of Deus have
no recourse but to subvert the Royal Sway, overthrow the
Buddhas and the gods, eliminate the customs of Japan, and then
to import the customs of their own countries; thus only will
advance the plot they have concocted to usurp the country
themselves.

They have dispatched troops and usurped such countries as
Luzon and Nova Hispania, lands of barbarians with nature close
to animal. But our land by far surpasses others in fierce bravery;
and therefore the ambition to diffuse their faith in every quarter
and thus to usurp the country, even if it take a thousand

years, has penetrated down to the very marrow of their bones. Ah!—but what a gloomy prospect awaits them! For the sake of their faith they value their lives less than trash, than garbage. *Martyr*, they call this. When a wise sovereign rules the Empire good is promoted and evil is chastised. Rewards promote good and punishments chastise evil. There is no greater punishment than to take away life; but the adherents of Deus, without even fearing that their lives be cut, will not change their religion. How horrible, how awful it is! And whence did this flagrant wickedness arise? One look will show that its origin is in the first *mandamento*: "You shall hold 𝕯 dear above all things and him shall you worship." The spread of such a cursed doctrine is completely the working of the devil.

But I need not dissect these cursed teachings into little pieces to proffer to my august audience. Our ruler truly possesses perspicacity and sagacity; so he need hear but one part in ten to understand the whole ten.[65] From the top on down this entire gang will be subjugated and stamped out. And the benefit of this action will a hundred times surpass the merit of the Sage Rulers of another land in ancient times who, as tradition has it, subdued the wild beasts, tamed the flooding waters, and put at peace the dwellings of the people. Wild beasts and flooding waters are enemies harmful to the body. This gang, however, would subvert the truth; these are enemies of the Buddhas and of all Law. And, worst of all, this is a perfidious band which plots to usurp the country. Who is there that would not hate them?

Well, to continue: It is scarcely worthwhile to discuss the right or wrong of the part about the bestowal of a name, the taste of salt, and the taper in the hand. So 𝕯 will not save men who have not received the blessing of this *baptismo*, though they be righteous men! This is completely unheard-of. A man may not have received the blessing, but if he is righteous what reason could there be to condemn him?

The Great Brilliance keeps no light to itself; the Great Benevolence keeps no love to itself. In contrast, listen to 𝕯 talk! "This is mine, all mine!" "This does come up to my expectations!" This is a 𝕯 with an ego, fraught with human caprice. The presumption that human caprice can measure up to Heaven's Will is the abyss of ignorance.

I have presented above a summary of the Deus sect's seven-step sequence of sermons; and now I conclude my discussion. I have always been rather short of wit, so that my argumentation has by no means been anything but shallow. Nevertheless: "a question for every answer, an answer for every question"[66]—that is the time-proven method. Do not scoff at it, if you are wise! I intend below to take on whatever other questions may arise, and to record everyday matters connected with the Deus sect.

Let this be
AN EVENING'S CONVERSATION.

You say: I have heard the statement of Confucius: "Look closely into his aims, observe the means by which he pursues them, discover what brings him content—and can the man's real worth remain hidden from you, can it remain hidden from you?"[67] If that be so, then what is the daily behavior of the Deus sect's Bateren like?

And I answer: All temples must have a temple regimen. To speak of temple regimen: In the temples of the adherents of Deus also they have morning and evening services (nothing especially wrong in that). The morning service is called the *missa*; here they read the scriptures. And they claim that when the required words are uttered over the *ostia* (something like a Southern Barbarian cracker made of wheat flour), it turns into the true flesh of Jesus Christus. And they also claim that when some grape wine is poured into a goblet and certain words, in like fashion, are uttered over it, the wine turns into the true blood of Jesus Christus. Then they eat the cracker and they drink the wine; and that is their service. That a wheat cracker should become the flesh of Jesus Christus and that grape wine should change into blood most people will not find credible. And yet the adherents of Deus consider these proceedings quite splendid!

"Pride is the root of all evil, and humility the foundation of all good; so make humility your actions' base"—is what they urge upon people. And yet the devil himself could not measure up to them in arrogance! Could it be their inborn national character? And because of this arrogance they sink to brawls and quarrels with the Bateren of other factions in contentions for influence, outdoing even laymen in their wrangles. It's quite a sad thing to see, worse even than you could imagine—you can be sure of that!

I have heard of one event which was gross indeed. They say that it came to a real fight some seven or eight years ago in Macao.[68] With their superior Valentim Carvalho in the van, a broken stick at the ready, the Bateren surged upon another faction's temple, the Iruman and acolytes all brandishing blunt instruments and yelling, "Me first!" They burst inside the temple and even fired off their guns from the tower! Now I ask you: Isn't this sort of buffoonery rather unbefitting brother monks?

You ask: I suppose there do exist some courtesies between the Southern Barbarians and the Japanese within the temple.
And I answer: This also you can guess from the story I have related above. Because of their arrogance they do not even consider the Japanese to be human. And the Japanese, considering this outrageous, in their turn do not tender courtesy with sincerity.

And moreover, so that the Bateren and Iruman residing in Japan might continue to receive their financial support from the Emperor of South Barbary, we Japanese could not possibly see our true desire satisfied. "Henceforth, do not let Japanese become Bateren!"—we all felt terribly nonplussed by this principle of operation. But you can guess what kind of a feeling it is to know that one's real purpose can never be attained. And the reason is that the Southern Barbarians feel that in their designs against Japan they will find the natives partial, after all, to the interests of their native land. You can be sure of that!

You ask: I have heard that for the most part the adherents of Deus are unselfish and that they make charity their basic practice. Is this true?

And I answer: For them the border between unselfishness and pure cupidity just does not exist. They greedily seek parishioners; and dazzlement at the sight of gold or silver is their very own invention. A parishioner may keep all their precepts and may be praised as a righteous man: but if he is poor they will just compliment him out the door. And another may be an impious transgressor of their laws: but if he is rich they will feast him and fawn upon him and treat him as their prime parishioner. And when he goes bankrupt they won't even deign him another look.

And also: If their basic practice is to give alms for charity, then it all is done only for the sake of prestige and profit. It's only done to make people think, "My, how praiseworthy!," and thereby to attract more converts; you can be sure of that!

You ask: Whatever else may be said about the Deus sect's Bateren, one has to admit that they have severed all inclination to adultery. What about that?

And I answer: That may well be true, according to the individual. It depends upon the person—you know what I mean. In Japan they have still been afraid of disgrace, and so only the tenth part of their goings-on has become known here. But in Luzon, South Barbary, and Nova Hispania, as I have heard people tell, their shameful conduct is a public scandal.[69] And especially they say that the Bateren known as *clerigo* keep women for wives, and have children by them. But I suppose that to have children is their true purpose, as their very name implies. The word Bateren means "father." And without children it is hard indeed to do justice to the meaning of a father!

You ask: What is the origin of this *confissan* of the adherents of Deus?

And I answer: Here is what it is. When Jesus Christus was on this earth, he made the following promise to Pedro, the first among his disciples: "The offences that you forgive on earth I will also forgive in Heaven." And this, they claim, was the beginning of *confissan*. And so, at the time of *confissan* the individual and the Bateren meet privately, just the two of them without allowing anyone else to draw near, and the individual penitently declares his offences, leaving nothing out. Even if a man has perpetrated banditry or piracy, or if he has killed his father and his mother and has committed the Five Unpardonable Sins;[70] even if he has been guilty of treason and rebellion in plotting to subvert the state, and of other capital crimes—if the Bateren upon hearing him forgives his offences, they are nullified. So they claim. A devilish doctrine, indeed! "Though the crime be capital and its extent the country's overthrow, if the Bateren hears and forgives, the offence is nullified"—is what they teach. It is really the same as spreading around the notion: "Even if you commit a crime you won't suffer for it!" To look upon this is but to conclude that the Bateren should be branded pillars of banditry, masterminds of rebellion and murder. In any case, this is a disgusting religion; you can be sure of that!

You ask: I have heard that there have been many miraculous happenings connected with the Deus sect, and especially that there have been many marvellous signs about those people called *martyrs*, the ones who throw away their lives for the sake of their doctrine. Is is true or not? What about it?
And I answer: Here is how it is. You can take this as a general principle: To hear of it, it's heavier than a ton; to see it, it's lighter than an ounce. Whatever the adherents of Deus may claim to be mysterious just is not so! I left my home at the age of nineteen and after that spent some twenty-two or twenty-three years at spiritual exercises in their temple, and was held to be of some account among them; but I did not see even one thing that could be described as a miraculous happening. And I didn't see any marvellous signs appear about a *martyr*.

It is a general fact that at the start of a new religion's establishment pressures are put upon its first founder, to test whether his doctrine be pernicious or true. So it was with the Great Founder Nichiren Shōnin. Four times he encountered critical difficulties, and countless times he conquered lesser per-

plexities; and for the sake of his doctrine he experienced outright
sink-or-swim situations. Once in Kamakura Lord Sagami gave
the order to cut off the Great Founder's head.[71] Already the
Saint had been made to kneel on the mat of execution, and already
the swordsman had brandished the naked blade, had stepped
around to Nichiren's back. But as he was raising high the great
sword, Divine Light flooded about the Great Founder, the sword-
blade began to quiver, the swordsman's eyes were blinded, blood
spurted from his nose, and he dropped to the ground. And
further, it was made abundantly clear that the Saint was a Buddha
Manifest by a mystical dream in which a radiance like that of
lightning seemed to flash through the entire palace, and by other
marvellous signs; and so even Lord Sagami was astounded, and
he abandoned his intent to execute the Saint. And more details
can be found in the histories.

When such signs appear, they make it penetratingly clear that
Buddha's Law is being spread, that True Doctrine is being
preached. Yes, even in this our depraved age, in these our days
of the Decline of the Law, look upon this, all you people! With
parched throats, with looks of longing, with necks outstretched,
witness these signs and believe! But when the Bateren who spread
a cursed doctrine are condemned and killed, no marvels and no
signs are seen.

But I have heard people tell the story—wasn't it some seven
or eight years ago?—of the execution of some Bateren in
Nagasaki. All shrunk into themselves, the cowering Bateren and
their sectarians thought, "Aah! There must surely be a miracle!,"
their inmost hearts devoid of anything but this vain expectation.
The chief magistrate of Nagasaki at the time was Hasegawa
Sahyōe no Jō Fujihiro.[72] Knowing full well that this was just a
bunch of babbling babes, he decided to play a trick on them.
He had a children's toy made, a kite, with a lit taper affixed to
its top. The kite was sent aloft after dusk, and on its string it
rode the wind from a place called Inasa over to Nagasaki. The
Bateren and their sectarians all burst into a tumult: "Aah! Look,
look over there! Didn't we predict it? A white cloud is suspended
above us, and brilliant light descends from Heaven!" Sahyōe
only smiled and put on an innocent expression; but the truth of
the matter did not remain hidden in the end, and the adherents
of Deus were mortified to find out they had been tricked.
And there was nothing they could do but grin and bear it.

Such was the story I heard; and I wonder whether such goings-on could be called miracles for *martyrs*. Nothing especially astonishing was either seen or heard.

You say: Well, you've really stripped the religion of Deus naked! And now I'm sure its followers must all hate you deeply indeed!

And I answer: Just as you say. It's easily guessed! When I first quit their temple I felt quite uncomfortable at the thought of coming across one of them in the street and having to say something; so I thought I'd go to a place where this sect would not be likely to exist, and I repaired to Nara. Just then my luck went bad. Wasn't Ōkubo Iwami the chief magistrate of the area at the time?[73] The Bateren had me denounced to one of his submagistrates, who was an adherent of Deus. They even urged him to have me killed on the sly; but somebody warned me of what might happen. "Do not stay in a danger-fraught state," goes the saying.[74] How much the more should I have quit this place where danger threatened me directly! I took the Kizu River boat and went to a spot called Nakamiya, above Hirakata.[75] And for a while I remained in seclusion at this place. I heard that even afterwards they had designs upon me, but in this our well-ordered reign they could not easily bring their stored-up malice to fruition; so nothing further came about.

I am reminded of the *Chant of Tōru*:

> How useless this long tale
> Of an autumn night!
> Let me now go
> Dip sea water, dip salt.

—thus the Old Man's intonation.[76] But I have told this useless long tale, and the night went up in smoke. The thousand nights of autumn could be condensed into one, and still I could talk on—the night would grow light, and some words would still be left unsaid. But you can guess it all.

> In the sixth year of Genna,
> *kanoe saru,*
> first month,
> Fabian set his hand to this.

DECEIT DISCLOSED
by
Christovão Ferreira
sive
Sawano Chūan

All things encompassed by heaven and earth have their specific propensities. Birds and beasts, insects and fishes, grasses and trees, earth and rock, wind and water—not one of them which possesses not its own quality! Beasts only desire to run about; birds desire to rise in flight; fishes desire to swim in the water; and insects desire to chirp their songs. Trees want to grow big and tall, and grasses want to spread their blades to the sides. Earth gives birth to things and rock gives birth to fire. Water creates moisture and wind produces coolness. Not one among them which possesses not its own quality! All this is the working of the shaping forces. Man is the potent lord over the myriad things; and therefor Heaven has endowed him with a nature of Goodness, Propriety, Ritual, and Knowledge. For that reason man is inclined to strive toward good and abhor evil; and he esteems quietude.

I was born in the distant region of South Barbary. I wandered in delusion along a perverse path; for I knew not the True Way. I was quite like the man who walks bearing a plank on one shoulder,[1] like one who does not know his right from his left. I resembled one watching a tree stump thinking to catch a rabbit.[2] From my earliest years I devoted myself exclusively to the teachings of the Kirishitan religion, and finally I left my home to become a monk. And as I grew older I formed in my heart the deep desire to spread this faith in Japan, and I did not deem the thousands and tens of thousands of miles too far a distance. When I reached this Realm of the Sun, for years on end I endured hunger and cold, labor and privation, and that without complaint: it was all for the sake of preaching this doctrine to every creature. I hid myself in the wilderness of the mountains and of the plains; I did not grudge my very life. I feared not law or regulation; I floated between east and west. And I spread this doctrine.

Yet when I saw the customs of Japan, when I heard the truths of Confucianism and Buddhism, though I understood but the thousandth part of their meaning, I repented of my delusion and I reformed. And therefore I cast off the Kirishitan religion and settled my heart on the teachings of Lord Shaka. And now I do not hold the Kirishitan obscurities to be true. But I will present here a summary exposition of their doctrines, to preach their condemnation and to make known the truth. Let my words be an admonishment to those who have become addicted to a pernicious faith in following the Kirishitan religion.

I

The basic mystery of this religion concerns the being called
Deus (that is to say, substance without beginning and without
end). To be specific: He is the Creator of Heaven and Earth;
among the myriad phenomena of the universe, those with a
consciousness and those without,[3] there is not one which is not
of Deus' creation. He is the wellspring of moral force, of
compassion, of law, and of wisdom. He is the self-determining,
self-sufficing Lord Deus. And therefore, outside our faith there is
no salvation for man in the life to come. But why is that?

Six thousand years ago, Deus with the one word "Fiat" (that
is to say, "Let the myriad things be born!"), with the single act
of his will—"Let it thus be!"—created the myriad phenomena
of the universe. And after that he created *Adam* and *Eve* as man
and wife. All this Deus himself revealed, some two thousand
years or more after heaven and earth were opened up; and it
can all be seen in the histories and in the Kirishitan scriptures.
And the very words of Deus' revelation likewise are in the
scriptures. And so, it is inconceivable for a thing to exist without
the existence of its maker. For example: if there is a sword, it is
inconceivable that there was no smith to make it. A poem
cannot be transmitted to the world if there is no poet. There is
no such thing as a child without a father and a mother. And
therefore the Creator of Heaven and Earth is the one and
omnipotent Deus. This is the teaching on which they concentrate
and which they propagate to the public.

As I now carefully ponder the origin of heaven and earth,
I find the Kirishitan teachings about a heaven and earth created

by Deus hard to fathom indeed. Not one thing about their reasoning is clear. If Deus were the creator of heaven and earth and the myriad things, then the news of this should be a matter of tradition passed down in every country. But in the chronicles of the Three Countries there is no record of this.[4] It is not true that heaven and earth were produced six thousand years ago. Considering the chronology of China, one sees that from the first of the Three Emperors, Fu Hsi, down to the end of the Shang there passed 19,994 years.[5] This can be seen in the reference books. And therefore the chronology of an event which pertains to their foremost mystery is greatly mistaken.

Moreover, before the birth of *Jesus Christus* (his father was Joseph and his mother Santa Maria), there lived in South Barbary a great scholar named *Aristoteles*, who in discussing the beginning of heaven and earth correctly noted that heaven and earth have no beginning. The category known as *mixta* (by which is meant to say, compounded things) are things resulting from the conjunction of the Four Basic Elements.[6] Such are termed *artificial* (by which is meant to say, made by man). Since they are things produced by the artifice of human beings, created by a superior borrowing the skill of another in applying his own contrived plan, and because their existence is inconceivable without a creator, they have a beginning and an end. The category known as *simplex* (uncompounded things)—earth, water, fire, air, and heaven—are not created things and therefore have neither beginning nor end: they are the mysterious effects of the conjunction of Yin and Yang. But that is plain before everyone's eyes. To explain all this by teaching that there is a creator of heaven and earth, the one Lord of all, is merely a device to establish the Kirishitan religion.

First of all, heaven and earth are not created things. The sequence of the four seasons; the sun, moon, planets, and constellations; East, West, South, North—these follow an ordered cycle without change, and this is the pattern of nature. If Deus were the beginning of heaven and earth, the myriad phenomena, and all the sentient beings, then one and all, down to the savages of the East and the hordes of the West, the barbarians of the South and the wild men of the North, should honor and adore him; but outside of the Kirishitan religion no one at all knows of him. Measuring the number of Kirishitans against the world's entire population is even more absurd than likening one strand of hair to nine head of cattle. If Deus is the Creator of Heaven and Earth, Lord over the myriad phenomena, and the wellspring of wisdom, why then did he not create the men of this world in such a way that they would know all this? If he is Lord over the myriad phenomena, omnipotent and self-determining, why then did he not from ancient times prohibit all but the Kirishitan religion? If he is the wellspring of compassion, why did he create the Eight Sorrows for human beings, the Five Signs of Decline for devas, and the Three Realms of discontent in this world of suffering?[7] If he is the wellspring of universal law, why then does he not proclaim a law based on truth and befitting the times?

When one considers all this, one sees that the point they place uppermost in their teachings is but a contrivance they utilize in their design to delude people. Country upon country despise this and hate this, not Japan alone! Unenlightened fools in foreign lands without understanding the truth revere Deus and honor the *Padres* (by that is meant to say, priests); and that is the extremity of shallow judgment and lack of direction. It is no different from the proverb: "One dog barks a lie, ten thousand take it up as truth." How pitiful! How wretched!

II

The Kirishitans teach that there is an afterlife. Differing with the established doctrines of the various sects, they attach to it the nameless name of Deus. And they expound it as follows.

The Five Parts of the human body do not differ from those of birds and beasts, being compounded of the Four Basic Elements; their processes of origination and dissolution are the same.[8] But within the human body is contained a soul called *anima*. This *anima* is *spiritus* and indestructible. Though the Five Parts be destroyed, the *anima* remains and is not destroyed. And therefore, according to its good or evil actions upon this world it will sink or swim in the next. Accordingly, only humans are capable of an afterlife; and universally they desire it. The soul of birds and beasts, being contingent upon the Five Parts, originates together with them and is destroyed together, and therefore cannot be saved in the afterlife.

That outside the Kirishitan religion there is for humans no salvation in the afterlife is Holy Doctrine. The place of salvation is called *Paraiso* (that is to say, paradise) and is above the heavens. In *Paraiso* shines brilliant light, and manifold delight abounds to fulfillment. But they who are not saved fall down into *Inferno* (that is to say, hell) and suffer the pains of water and of fire, and for endless kalpas into the future can never rest in peace. Thus they teach.

In all countries men devote themselves to the pursuit of the afterlife. But the above doctrines would construct man in their own image, onesidedly and at variance with the several sects. These teachings are garnished in metaphors and embellished with fancy words and indeed do appear to possess the semblance of truth. But since their basic mystery is Deus, substance of *spiritus*, they totally lack anything of any particular accord with reason. This thing called *anima* by definition is substance of *spiritus*, cannot be taken in the hand nor seen by the eye, and is without material shape. Then what is there to be grasped and named indestructible substance? The soul of birds and beasts also is without material shape and cannot be taken in the hand or seen by the eye, and therefore should also in the same manner be *spiritus*. But according to the doctrines of the Kirishitan religion it is not *spiritus*, and is destroyed together with the body. And therefore the Kirishitan doctrines abound only in things unheard-of.

First of all, it is colossal deceit to claim that this thing called *anima* has been bestowed by Deus. Not even six thousand years have passed since Deus' creation of humans in the world. Then who was it that bestowed the *anima* upon the people of all the lands which came into existence before that? On top of that they claim that those who are not Kirishitan cannot be saved in the afterlife. But that again is quite outrageous. Among the humans of the world those of the Kirishitan religion do not even come up to one part of ten thousand! And even among the Kirishitans the *predestinados* (by that is meant to say, the elect for the afterlife) are elected and chosen by Deus from all eternity without beginning or end, and they are saved; but the remainder from among the same religion, called *reprobos* (by that is meant to say, the abominated for the afterlife) fall down into *Inferno*.

Thus they teach. Is this to be called the wellspring of mercy and compassion? And moreover, the *predestinados* are saved no matter what evil they commit; and the *reprobos* fall down into hell no matter how they strive toward good. Thus they teach. But there is no distinction between good and evil in this; this is not the wellspring of universal law but merely the doctrine of wilfulness. Yet to express doubt at this and to question the doctors of this religion is but to obtain the answer: "In Deus' scriptures is the intent to save all." This is a duplicious rejoinder, spoken with a forked tongue. In everything they but deceive the people; using religion they plot to usurp the country.

And all those people in country upon country who never heard of the Kirishitan doctrine even in their dreams—why, for what offence should they all be thrust into hell? And they also teach that young children, though they be of the Kirishitan religion, who have not received the blessing of *baptismo* (that is to say, the blessing of water sprinkled onto the top of the head) shall all be thrust into hell. Unheard-of! Babes who cannot yet distinguish east from west—of what possible offence could they be capable? There is not one rational thing about this, and nothing that could be called the wellspring of compassion or the wellspring of universal law.

But why should all this be? The Kirishitan teachings state that all human beings are subject to the Eight Sufferings and to the fall into hell because of the sin of *Adam*. What was this sin? After Deus had opened up heaven and earth, he created the man named *Adam*, and at first settled him in the place called *Paraiso Terreal* (by that is meant to say, a place of boundless bliss upon the face of this earth). And Deus set down the law that he was not to eat of the fruit of the tree called *maçan*. But *Adam* ate of the fruit of this tree, and because of his sin in breaking the law Deus thrusts all human beings into hell. This is not the wellspring of reason, of universal law, or of compassion.

The Kirishitan scriptures state that it is better not to be born on this earth than to be subject to *Inferno*. But if this be so, then why did Deus—the wellspring of wisdom— create *Adam* liable to commit sin? If he is self-sufficing and omnipotent, why did he not create *Adam* sinless, direct all sentient beings to the Kirishitan faith, and make all be born in *Paraiso*? That he was unable to do this merely goes to prove that this is a religion of pure fabrication. Yet to confront the doctors with this accusation is but to obtain the answer that Deus bestowed upon man the faculty of a free will and that therefore it is up to every individual to strive for good or to commit evil. To do good is to be saved in the afterlife and to abound in bliss. To do evil is to fall into hell and to undergo suffering. Such is the reward for good and the punishment for evil, they answer.

According to the Kirishitan teachings, human beings are not capable of doing good and avoiding evil merely through their own faculty of a free will. They are not capable unless they receive Deus' assistance, *graça* (that is, assistance). Thus they teach. But if this be so, then why does Deus not provide his assistance to draw man away from evil and direct him toward good? Their religion expounds at length Deus' special assistance to *Santa Maria* (who is the mother of *Jesus Christus*), who was thereby rendered immaculate of even one sin. If he is the self-sufficing Deus, then why did he not bestow upon all sentient beings the same special assistance he granted to *Santa Maria*? Why did he not plan them all to be sinless? Not one of these teachings satisfies the dictates of reason! They make fabrication their teachings' base; their plot is to spread disturbance throughout the land and to pervert society. Not the scantiest trifle of substance in their account of the afterlife! At its most profound this religion has no bearing on reason.

III

In the Kirishitan teaching, precepts leading to the road of salvation in the afterlife culminate especially in the following ten articles:

1. You shall worship no other Buddhas beside the one Deus.
2. You shall not invoke the holy name of Deus in baseless oaths.

3. You shall endeavor to keep every seventh day as your holy day *domingo*.
4. You shall observe filial piety to your parents.
5. You shall not kill human beings.
6. You shall not commit adultery.
7. You shall not steal.
8. You shall not make false charges against another.
9. You shall not have wicked desires for the property of another.
10. You shall not lust for the wife of another.

In ancient times Deus set down these ten articles, on the mountain called *Sinai* in the country of *Arabia*. Using the man named *Moses* as intermediary, Deus transmitted this law to the subjects of *Judea* (this is the name of a country), and therefore the Kirishitans teach that this is the True Path. But these laws, difficult to keep, are not meant for the sake of the country nor for the sake of the people, and are altogether dissimilar to legislation consistent with propriety and reason.

In all the lands where the Five Constant Virtues are preserved and the Five Commandments kept,[9] where the people pray for peace and tranquillity in the present world and beseech repose in the good place for the afterlife, therefore does the subject look up to the ruler and the child is filial to his father and mother, the aged are esteemed and the young are loved, and the ruler treats his subjects with sympathy and bestows compassion upon the people. There indeed the families prosper, the country flourishes, and all under heaven is regulated. All this can readily be seen. To treat the Buddhas with ceremony and the gods with esteem, and to offer prayers to the ancestors, is to practice humanity and propriety in this world and to accumulate merit for the afterlife. But the Kirishitan teachings have no use for humanity or propriety; they do not keep the Five Commandments and moreover they inveigh against the worship of the Buddhas and the gods. Not one thing consistent with reason!

The First Article is: "You shall worship no one beside the one Deus." It teaches that one must invoke and worship the one Deus, Lord over this life and the afterlife, the omnipotent and self-sufficing wellspring, and that therefore one must admit no other considerations. For countries which are not Kirishitan such a doctrine constitutes the root of rebellion and the inception of reign's overthrow. In every land those who become Kirishitans refuse to reverence the Buddhas and the gods; they tear down the temples and pagodas, demonstrate no respect for the sovereign's will, show no awe of the military, and do not even observe the parent's command. And therefore examples where they have cast the land into disorder and overthrown the reign are great in number, in every country. And in Japan also we have witnessed many such examples before our very eyes. When we refer to the commentaries of the Kirishitan doctors concerning this law, we find only statements that are completely unheard-of. Let us take one example.

One meets a Kirishitan and asks him: "Are you a Christian?" He will not clearly say, "I am not a Christian," but rather he will answer by twisting his words to leave the impression that he is not a Kirishitan. Thus the commentary on this article teaches him. All this simply means that they make lies their actions' base. Concerning everything they but produce a multitude of suchlike fabrications.

The Second Article is: "You shall not invoke the holy name of Deus in oaths." However, when they find themselves in a personal perplexity they twist their words in all sort of ways in order to escape the difficulty. These lies and distortions—are they not also oaths in the name of Deus?

The Third Article teaches: "You shall endeavor to keep your holy day *domingo*." This certainly is of no benefit to the people. To be specific, in one year the number of *domingos* amounts to some eighty of these "holy days." If on these days the governor does not attend to the management of public affairs and in the Four Classes[10] men and women alike do not severally perform their allotted duties, then neither the interests of the sovereign nor of the individual will be served.

The Fourth Article sets down as law: "You shall observe filial piety to your parents." Nevertheless, in matters of religion this article would have the Kirishitan deny the will of his parents and pay no heed to the orders of his ruler, and throw his very life away; nay, more!—set his father's and his mother's life at naught! But this is completely contrary to law. When an only child wishes to become a monk, no matter how the parents grieve over the extinction of the family line, they are not to be heard; so this article would have it. To extinguish progeny forever, as has happened many times—is this to be called filial piety?

The Fifth Article sets down as law: "You shall not kill human beings." In matters of religion, however, they kill altogether too many people. One might ask them, for example: "When many people are killed due to the desperate resolution of one Bateren to remain hidden—is this not the taking of life?" And they will answer: "While the law of religion is being proclaimed to save all sentient beings, not to accept these teachings but rather to kill those who are of the religion—that sort of murder is not what we have committed but what has been committed by the others!" In the Kirishitan scriptures one may see the statement: "Look at the customs of the country. Leave behind you a country which finds not agreement in our law; but proclaim the gospel in a country which believes." Then is it not the taking of one's own life to defy the law in setting forward the religion?

The Sixth Article sets down as law: "You shall not commit adultery." But in *Judea* (this is the name of a country) they also received this law from Deus, and nevertheless they kept a great many wives and committed adultery, as indeed can be seen in the scriptures. And the Bateren also, according to the individual, had wives and children, in South Barbary as well as in Japan. Or they had love affairs with courtesans and dancing girls, or seduced widows and made them pregnant. That this is a lewd piece of legislation is plain before everyone's eyes.

The Seventh Article sets down as law: "You shall not steal." Nevertheless, in spreading the gospel of the Kirishitan religion it is a matter of course to tear away and usurp country after country. *Nova Hispania* (this is the name of a country), *Luzon* (ditto), *India* (ditto), and others have been torn away and taken over by *Europe* (South Barbary). Their present course of action speaks as evidence. And spreading the gospel always proceeds this way.

Fifty years ago[11] the emperors of two countries called *Portugal* and *Castela* designed to construct Black Ships, dispatch men, search out yet unknown countries, open routes thereto, and do commerce. When the *pappa* (that is to say, the head of the Kirishitan religion, the representative of *Jesus Christus*) heard of this plan, he divided the routes of navigation into two. And here is the message he dispatched to the aforementioned two emperors: "Your plans, of course, are of great benefit to the wealth and reputation of your countries, and to the spread of the faith.

However, it appertains to my position to determine the directions to which those who spread the faith are dispatched. The emperor of *Portugal* to the east, the emperor of *Castela* to the west: thus dispatch your men and spread the faith! And if at any time you should tear away and take over some lands, any place, treat them as you please." Thus the *pappa* determined; and accordingly men of those two countries crossed the seas to the several directions, tore away and took over many places with no trouble, and thus they continue to act this way. Is this not theft by religion?

The Eighth Article is: "You shall not make false charges against another." This prohibits falsehood in bringing to light a man's unknown offence by spreading false tales to people. But if one looks at the commentaries on this law he sees the amplification that if a man has lost his reputation, has come to grief, or is in trouble, one will not suffer for making his offences known. And also the commentaries teach that if one tells people things of pure invention, but with an ulterior intention—this is called *amphibologia* (that is, empty words)—he will not suffer for it. And therefore this is not a law which restrains falsehood but rather one which deceives people.

The Ninth Article is: "You shall not have desires for the property of another." And yet, once they have dragged one into their religion they dispose of all his goods as they please. When one of their religionists dies, they confiscate his goods for their temple or extort them for the *misericordia* (meaning, the dispensation of mercy) under the pretext of using the property for works of compassion. Is not all this the usurpation of the property of another? And the regulation that daimyo of their religion must take one tenth of their lands' proceeds and cede this produce to the temples: is this not desiring the property of another?

The Tenth Article is: "You shall not lust for the wife of another." Since I have already written of this under the Sixth Article, "You shall not commit adultery," I shall cut my words short and not discuss this here.

Added to the aforesaid ten articles are laws set down by the *pappa*. This person called *pappa*, being the representative of *Jesus Christus*, is the chief regulator of all the religious beliefs held by the Kirishitans concerning the afterlife; he is a man of exalted rank. Succession to this rank is not determined in the same manner as that to the rank of the ruler of a country. The senior councilors of the *pappa*, called *cardinales* (that is to say, senior councilors of the *pappa* who themselves can later attain to the rank of *pappa*), simply select a suitable person from the body of their religionists, whatever nationality he may be of. All the people reverence him, for he is the representative of *Jesus Christus*. Men of the highest families prostrate themselves in front of him; even emperors kiss his feet; he is without peer in the amount of veneration shown him. He has substantial estates, yet is not lord over a country but rather a priest. His place of residence is in *Italia* (this is the name of a country), in a city called *Roma* (the capital of *Italia*). Resting upon his authority as the representative of *Jesus Christus*, he sets down all sort of laws. But close inspection of these laws will expose them as unheard-of. Regulations born of rapacity, they are of no benefit to the people.

First of all, there is the regulation that they who become Bateren of the type called *clerigo* must necessarily possess appropriate estates known as *patrimonio* (that is meant to say, estates passed on from the ancestors). The rationale behind this regulation is that the *clerigo*, were they bereft of property, would become subject to many ignoble habits and, concentrating on making their way through this world, would leave aside their lamentation for the afterlife and would rather occupy themselves with commerce, which is quite unbefitting the priestly calling. And yet, there additionally exists the regulation that one tenth of the people's property and grain fields must be turned over to the temples of the aforementioned priests. This is an immense imposition, and certainly is of no benefit to the people. It is but natural that people's aspirations are aroused by mention of the afterlife, and that is the way it should be; but in this case it is a pretext for crude agglomeration of domains throughout the land, and is not merely rank greed but an obstruction of the national interest.

And moreover, sometimes they perform the *missa* (that is to say, perform the morning service), sometimes they preach sermons, or at other times officiate at memorial ceremonies for the dead; and for suchlike they take silver and gold. This would certainly still be all right if the believers were to donate the money each according to his heart's desire. But there is a regulation which allows them to size up the person willy-nilly

The factions known as *São Domingos, São Francisco, Companhia,* and so on, each keeps its own regulations and pursues its own set of ascetic practices. These are called *religião* and are constituted houses. But the *clerigo* are priests outside the aforementioned groups and do not pursue ascetic exercises; these men may also become priests with official functions.[12]

and determine, on the part of the temple, how much he is to give. The idea is to sell the afterlife.

And there are still other unheard-of things! To mention one: in order to gather in money, the *pappa* sometimes issues a writ of *cruzada*. And, moreover, those who do not possess a *bulla* (this is a license from the *pappa*) cannot gain any merit from the *contas* (rosary) or attain remission of sins through the *jubileo* (that is to say, grand remission) or be absolved of the *caso reservado* (this is the withholding of remission at certain times). Once one possesses the *bulla*, however, one need but request the aforementioned merit; or, upon saying *confissan* (that is to say, repentance and contrition) to any Bateren, one can obtain remission of any *caso reservado* (deep offence), not to speak of the usual sins! But for those who apply for a *bulla* there is a list of prices. Is this not avaricious trafficking with the afterlife? The *pappa*, as lord over the afterlife, selling licenses—how about that? Deluding the people, selling the afterlife for gold and silver, is not what he was meant to do!

Likewise there exists a regulation in regard to the Bateren which provides that no layman—be he the emperor himself— can chastise a priest for a crime, no matter how foul, or restrain him from a lifelong career of villainy. This indeed is a law contrary to reason. To be more precise: though the *bispo* (the head of the *Padres*) may admonish an offending priest, nevertheless the offender cannot be brought to justice. For this reason the behavior of priests is depraved indeed, for they do not reform in their wickedness. And accordingly the laity also, witnessing the priests' behavior with their eyes and ears, from top to bottom are beset with foul behavior.

And also there is this thing called *excomunhão* (that is to say, expulsion). This regulation can be put into effect by the *pappa* first and foremost, and also by the *bispo*. The word *excomunhão* means "to expel." Those who incur *excomunhão* may not receive the blessings of the faith, nor associate with members of the faith in the exchange of words, greetings, or items of commerce. And therefore—to say nothing of the afterlife—they are deprived of the society of men; and for this reason people consider this regulation to be exceedingly afflicting, more even than the others. And therefore the *pappa* in administering the regulations very often puts this *excomunhão* into effect. For the most part, of their myriad regulations all are of this nature.

Whereas religious regulations should serve to secure the way to salvation in the afterlife, and peace and happiness in the present life, theirs are not like that. Rather, they bandy about with the aforesaid *excomunhão* to take in gold and silver aplenty, and their so-called remissions of sins serve no other purpose but to rake in money. Unheard-of manner of action! But words fail me.

In the first place, none of this is of benefit to the country's ruler or to society. To be specific, when this *excomunhão* is invoked against the population of a country, it necessarily follows that the country will be thrown into turmoil. Examples of that are many, in country upon country.

The regulations that remain are of various sorts, but all of similar ilk, and all unheard-of. For example, on the holy days which recur during the year, twice every seven days, it is prohibited to eat the flesh of bird or beast. It comes down to that sort of level.

ABOUT JESUS CHRISTUS   (*Joseph* was his father,
                          Santa Maria his mother)

Above I have described the moral precepts which lead to salvation, and the laws of the *pappa*. Since there exists an after-life, there must also exist a savior for the afterlife—so the Kirishitans claim, and therefore the foremost of their teachings concerns this savior for the afterlife. According to these teachings, in order to save human beings Deus himself was born as a human, one thousand six hundred and thirty-six years ago.

Let us investigate the evidence. The woman named *Maria*, a descendant of Emperor *David* of the country of *Judea*, was betrothed to the man called *Joseph*. In the womb of this woman Deus took upon himself the human condition and became man; and after the nine months were fulfilled she gave birth and Deus entered this world. And he is the one called *Jesus Christus*. He is the savior of mankind; or so the Kirishitans teach. It is the customary claim of all Kirishitans that *Maria*, the mother of *Jesus Christus*, conceived without any marital converse; and they esteem this very highly and worship her for it. But let us inquire into the truth and examine precedents. Never since heaven and earth were opened up has there been an example of a child born without two parents. *Santa Maria* herself pointed out *Joseph* to *Jesus Christus*, saying: "This is your father." One can see this in the Kirishitan scriptures, and so the teachings I have described above must be mere falsehood.

Inquiring into the birthplace of *Jesus Christus*, we see that the two parents went to a locality called *Belem*, but could not find admission at an inn; so they went to a place nearby where there was a cave, and here *Jesus Christus* was born. The Kirishitans call his birthday *Natal*, and it is an especially celebrated holy day among them. On the eighth day after that, he received the blessing known as *circuncisão* (that is to say, the skin of his hidden part was cut off), and he was given the name of *Jesus*. This day has been set down as New Year's Day for the Southern Barbarians, and the Kirishitans everywhere celebrate it as a holy day. Some dubious things are connected with this. The blessing of *circuncisão* corresponds in meaning with *baptismo* (that is to say, the blessing of water poured), which is practiced by the Kirishitans today. This blessing is received in order that the *original* sin (that is to say, the offence passed on to the descendants) be forgiven. But since *Jesus Christus* was actually Deus and therefore free of sin and offence—as they teach—then why did he receive this blessing?

On the thirteenth day after *Natal* (the birthday of *Jesus Christus*) three *Magos* (that is to say, learned men or doctors) came to *Jerusalem*, the capital of *Judea*. It is not known from what country they came; but it was from the East. "Where is the newborn Emperor of *Judea*? We saw his star in the Eastland and came to worship him"—thus they spoke. When *Herodes*, the emperor of that country, heard this story he said: "If that is why you came, go to *Belem* (the birthplace of *Jesus Christus*) and seek out that child. When you find him, let me know. And I will go myself and reverence him." When the three heard him say this they left *Jerusalem*. The star they had seen in the East was visible here also, and they made it their guide. They went to *Belem* and they found *Jesus Christus* in that cave, and they gave him presents of *mirra* (that is to say, a medicine), of incense, and of gold. But they did not thence return to *Jerusalem*; rather, they changed their route and returned to their own country. And therefore *Herodes* was greatly angered at being deceived by the three, and he dispatched his men and had them cut down and kill all the little children born within the previous two years in *Belem* itself, needless to say, as well as in the nearby villages and countryside. And they left not a one alive.

But this also does not appear to be true. First of all, though the home country of the three is not known with certainty, it is generally thought to have been the country of *Arabia*. But this country is several hundred leagues distant from *Judea*, and therefore it is most unlikely that within thirteen days the three could have traveled as far as *Jerusalem*. The learned men of the Kirishitans teach that these three all were emperors; but this also is a lie quite distant from the truth. The meaning of the word *Magos* does not correspond to the word "emperor." The meaning simply signifies "learned man" or "doctor." And, moreover, if the three were emperors, then they must have ruled separate countries. If that be so, then they must first have seen the star which appeared on the day of *Natal*, then met each other, and within the short time of thirteen days traveled from their several countries as far as *Jerusalem*. But this is not reasonable. Furthermore: when they inquired in *Jerusalem*, "Where is the newborn emperor of *Judea?*," why did not Emperor *Herodes* go to *Belem* himself, without using the three as intermediaries, since the road from *Jerusalem* to *Belem* is a bare three leagues? And if the three were emperors, how could they have kept hidden the fact of their return to their native lands?

Realizing that he had been deceived by the three *Magos*, *Herodes* resolved to kill all the little children in the city and the vicinity of *Belem*. When *Joseph* and *Maria* heard this, they grew affrighted and agitated and, taking *Christus* with them, they fled to the land of *Egypt* and spent some six or seven years in that country. But if *Jesus Christus* were truly Deus, the omnipotent being, then why did he fear *Herodes*? Why did all this come about? It was a design to teach the Kirishitans that in a time of legal measures it is all right to flee and hide some place—thus the Kirishitans respond. And all such tales are products of rank fabrication.

Afterward *Jesus Christus* returned from *Egypt* to his native land; and when he reached the age of thirty years, he withdrew himself into mountains away from all civilization, and there he fasted for a period of forty days. The Kirishitans strive to imitate him in this, and in the regulations of the *pappa* there is prescribed a forty-day period called *jejum* (that is to say, one meal per day) or *quaresma*, which is to say the same thing as *jejum*.[13] There is a regulation that everyone must say his *jejum confissan* during the aforesaid forty-day period. And outside of that, they perform various violent practices in disciplining their bodies. This is the season when their minds are particularly intent on the performance of all their religious duties, and therefore at this time those who are Kirishitans at heart are most easily recognized and found out.

And afterward *Jesus Christus*, grown up a man of wide talent and profound wisdom, decided to preach the law. He selected twelve disciples and taught them the innermost tenets of his religion. For the period of three or four years, drawing many parables and embellishing his language, he spread about his teachings, appealing to the people with pathos, and exerting all effort to sway the lower classes. When he held forth at his sermons, he defamed persons of authority; and the people were swayed, and those who turned to his doctrines were as plentiful as raindrops in a shower that drenches the land. As soon as they noticed this, the potentates of the country and the Lord Constable grew apprehensive.

While a countless number of people—several thousands or tens of thousands—were once listening to his sermon, it so happened that all shouted as with one voice: "*Jesus Christus* we want for emperor!" When the elders heard of this agitation they realized that they were faced by no mere superficial crisis, and that unless they killed this *Jesus Christus* before the plot came to fruition he would certainly take over the country and usurp the royal title. In the end they decided to have *Jesus Christus* arrested and killed.

And now from among the twelve disciples there appeared one who said: "As the matter stands, I am willing to renounce my loyalty to *Jesus Christus*, to spy out his movements, and hand him over to you." The elders' joy was not in minor key. And they had a number of men go along with the disciple, arresting *Jesus Christus*. Handing him over to *Pilatos*, the Lord Constable of the country, they had him questioned under various tortures as a criminal. They denounced him for constantly gathering disciples and for claiming during his sermons, "It is I who am emperor of this country," for deluding the populace and causing rebellion in the realm. And therefore the Constable, hearing of this design, in the end after examining him minutely had him suspended upon a cross. But the Kirishitan religionists claim that *Jesus Christus* was suspended upon the *cruz* (that is to say, cross) and died in order to save humanity, and they revere and esteem this above all.

The reason why he was suspended upon the *cruz* is as I have described above. And therefore, from that time on until the present, country upon country has hated this religion: those executed for it number in the countless thousands and tens of thousands. The Kirishitans' customary claim is that on the third day he came back to life and on the fortieth day after that ascended into Heaven. But these are matters of sixteen hundred years' antiquity, without trustworthy evidence. These are but tales composed by the disciples of *Jesus Christus*, that is all.

About the BLESSINGS of the KIRISHITANS

Among the many blessings established by *Jesus Christus* during his span of life the first is called *baptismo*, the blessing of water. One must receive this blessing when first becoming a Kirishitan. The manner of administering it is as follows. Some water is sprinkled upon the brow of the person becoming a Kirishitan, accompanied by the intonation of the formula: "I cleanse you in the holy name of *Deus Pater* (the meaning is, Deus the father) and *Filius* (meaning son) and *Spiritus Sanctus* (meaning to say, holy substance without material shape, without beginning or end)." When the ritual forms can be fulfilled, a Bateren administers the blessing. In actual practice, however, anyone— man or woman—may serve: if only the aforementioned formula is intoned, then the blessing takes effect. Those who receive this blessing become Kirishitans and are infused with *graça* (that is to say, assistance which renders man capable of satisfying Deus' will), and all the sins which they have committed up to that time are washed away without a trace. Thus they teach.

But much of dubious nature is connected with this. All things possess limitations within their very natures and are ineffective outside these limitations. For instance, the limitation of the eyes is shape: a shapeless thing cannot be perceived by the eyes. The limitation of the ears is sound: a soundless thing cannot be heard. The limitation of the nose is odor: an odorless thing cannot be smelled. The limitation of the tongue is flavor: a flavorless thing cannot be tasted. The limitation of the body is *corpo* (substance with a material shape), and therefore things which are not *corpo* cannot be touched, and things which are not *corpo* cannot be produced. Things which are not *corpo* are *spiritus* (that is to say, without material shape). *Spiritus* is not within the limitations of the Five Parts of the body. And therefore, its proper locus is not in the Five Parts but in *anima* (the soul). *Anima*, according to the Kirishitan teachings, is substance of *spiritus*. *Graça* also is the same substance. And therefore: how can *graça*, substance of *spiritus*, be produced by the use of water, which appertains to the Five Parts? How can substance of *spiritus* be produced by the use of words audible to the ear? How can water wash away the stain of sin on the *anima*, which is substance of *spiritus*? Not one thing in all this teaching is reasonable. And such sort of reason is repeated in all their blessings. All is empty fabrication.

The second blessing is called *confissan*, meaning the repentance and acknowledgment of sins. Only a Bateren can hear it. The sinner—man or woman, noble or mean—recalls to mind all the sins he has committed by thought, word, or deed, and repentantly resolves never to commit another sin again. If he enumerates all his sins to the Bateren without leaving one out, then all his sins, even the weightiest, are forgiven by the Bateren's mere words: "I absolve you." Thus they teach.

Looking at their scriptures one is hard put to find a clear explanation of this blessing. Of course, among the sayings of *Jesus Christus* there is the statement: "The sins of any man you forgive shall also be forgiven before Deus." But the part about enumerating all one's sins without leaving one out has been made up by the Kirishitans with the *pappa* at their head. To ponder this blessing carefully is to find it inadmissible. But why do I say that?

The learned men of the Kirishitans teach that when one repents of his prior sins and resolves not to sin again, then even if he does not say *confissan* his offence does vanish. But what profit does he gain who, even after saying his *confissan*, commits sins again? To cast this doubt and raise this question is but to obtain the answer: "There are two types of repentance. One is called *contrição* (deep repentance), a feeling of regret for having offended Deus with one's sins. This is perfect repentance, difficult to accomplish, and is rare. The other type is called *atrição* (shallow repentance), consisting of a loss of pleasure because of a feeling of guilt. Since it is merely regret at incurring distress it is not perfect repentance." So we see that both this *contrição* and also the above *confissan* are completely unheard-of. And the learned men of the Kirishitans all teach that one must still say *confissan* even after he has accomplished *contrição*. And, there are also some learned men who teach that one cannot merit remission of sins by *atrição* only, even if he says *confissan*. When there are different schools of thought among even the Kirishitans themselves, it is obvious that to be saved is a difficult matter indeed, one way or the other. In short, it is all quite unacceptable.

The third blessing is called *eucharistia* (that is to say, the blessing of bread and wine). On the evening before he was suspended upon the *cruz*, *Jesus Christus* had supper with his twelve disciples, and during it he took bread in his hands, and he said: "This is my body; eat of it." And in the same manner he took grape wine and said: "This is my blood; drink of it. And henceforth when you do this, do it in remembrance of me." And therefore—not to speak of that original occasion—even now when the Bateren as the representative of *Jesus Christus* performs the *missa* and says over the bread, "This is my body," and in the same manner over the wine, "This is my blood," then *Jesus Christus* is truly present in this blessing. Thus they teach.

The Kirishitans hold this to be the foremost of their blessings; but it is not at all in conformity with reason. That by the use of words bread should turn into flesh and wine into blood is outside the range of comprehension. Among the sayings of *Jesus Christus* there is the statement: "My word is the life of man." If his word were the life of man, then there should be no death. But statements of this sort are all *metaphora* (that is to say, parables) and have the intent of being taken as such. If that be so, then the statements, "This bread is my body," and, "This wine is my blood," must also be *metaphora*.

The blessings that remain beyond these do not deserve discussion. Moreover, they are not administered to all Kirishitans. And therefore I have omitted them.

ABOUT JUIZO GERAL   (*Juizo* means to inquire into things, *Geral* means universal)

According to the Kirishitan teachings, directly upon any man's death his good or evil is inquired into, and according to his good or evil he receives reward or punishment in the world to come. Those who perform good are saved in the later world; their glory is supreme and their bliss exhaustive. Those who work evil fall down into *Inferno* (hell); they incur punishment and suffer pain. This scrutiny is an inquiry into individuals one by one, and is therefore called *juizo particular* (that is to say, separate investigation of each). The verdict of this investigation will remain unchanged; but there will also occur the *Juizo Geral*. It will proceed under the following circumstances.

Sometime in the future—it is not clear just when—according to Deus' plan this world will burn up and vanish. Needless to say, humans will not vanish together with the other creatures, those with consciousness and those without; rather, humans will be resurrected, each in his original bodily form. Those saved in the afterlife will appear in majestic, radiant brilliance, and those fallen into *Inferno* will gather in wretched, miserable countenance; together they will assemble in the country of *Judea*, in the vale of *Josaphat*. And at that time *Jesus Christus* will descend from Heaven and will place the saved on his right and those bound to *Inferno* on his left; one by one, he will inquire into the good or evil of each. Now the evil he will thrust down into *Inferno* forever. But the good he will summon up with him to *Paraiso* (meaning, paradise). Thus they teach.

And after that—not to speak of human beings—not one living creature will remain in this world. The sun, the moon, the constellations—the Three Brilliances will cease their revolutions. The grasses and trees will no longer exist. Thus they teach.

To consider this teaching is to recognize it as unheard-of. At a time when everything in the entire world has burnt up and vanished, can the evil be thrust any place?—and be it hell! To burn up and kill the good demonstrates a lack of discrimination between good and evil; certainly this action stems not from any wellspring of reason, justice, or compassion! And also, it is ridiculous to claim that all the human beings to exist from the day heaven and earth were opened up until that future time could possibly assemble in the vale of *Josaphat*. If at the time of the *juizo particular* good or evil will be looked into, and if the verdict will remain unchanged—is not then the *Juizo Geral* superfluous? The investigation of the utterly boundless number of humans is to be performed within the space of a mere day!—this is outside the realm of reason. Shallow indeed must be the wisdom of a religion which esteems such teachings and considers them something to be thankful for!

To teach that all human beings will be resurrected in their original bodies at the prime of life is even farther removed from reason. How can bodies turned to ash, turned to dust, withered into decay assume their original form? Moreover, there will be those who died young, and those who died in old age. And they are all to be resurrected in their original bodies at the prime of life, aged thirty years? Isn't the very notion laughable, disgraceful? That the Five Parts of a one-year-old, a two-year-old, or a three-year-old resurrected as the Five Parts of a thirty-year-old—in the prime of life— still constitute an "original body" is very difficult to maintain. And if it is not the original body, then the man in question is a different person. And the teaching is pure deceit. Furthermore: in some countries there are also men who eat other humans. How are they to be reborn in their "original bodies" whose bodies have been eaten up by others?

And thus they devote themselves to deceiving the people with such extravagant talk, thereby to establish their religion. And there are a great many teachings of similar ilk beside these; but their nature is such that when one part is raised the other hundred are easily perceived. And therefore I do not see it fit to record them all.

Juizo Geral is the end of man, and so I have written of it at the end of this volume. And here I stop, inviting judgment of my readers.

The above volume presents a summary of the secrets of the Kirishitan religion; it discloses truth and deceit and discusses right and wrong. For that reason I have called it DECEIT DIS-CLOSED.

I desired to record everything minutely; but I am ignorant of letters. I wished to speak of everything fully; but I am mystified by differences in the Five Sounds.[14] So I have made little sense. Nevertheless, their abstrusities of doctrine are all contained in this volume. People, do not make the mistake of casting doubt on what is written here!

In the thirteenth year of Kan'ei,
with the Dragon Constellations of heaven
at the sign of *hinoe ne*,
in the ninth month, the first day,[15]

the resident of the country of Portugal,
Chief Bateren of Japan and Macao,
Christovão Ferreira,
reformed in religion and turned
an adherent of Zen,

Chūan
set his hand to this.

KIRISHITAN MONOGATARI
Anonymous Chapbook

How the Kirishitans First Crossed Over to Japan

In the reign of Mikado Go-Nara no In, the hundred and eighth Emperor since the days of Jimmu, some time about the Kōji Period, a Southern Barbarian trading vessel came to our shores.[1] From this ship for the first time emerged an unnamable creature, somewhat similar in shape to a human being, but looking rather more like a long-nosed goblin or the giant demon Mikoshi Nyūdō.[2] Upon close interrogation it was discovered that this was a being called Bateren.

The length of his nose was the first thing which attracted attention: it was like a conch shell (though without its surface warts) attached by suction to his face. His eyes were as large as spectacles, and their insides were yellow. His head was small. On his hands and feet he had long claws. His height exceeded seven feet, and he was black all over; only his nose was red. His teeth were longer than the teeth of a horse. His hair was mouse-grey in color, and over his brow was a shaved spot in the outline of a winebowl turned over. What he said could not be understood at all: his voice was like the screech of an owl. One and all rushed to see him, crowding all the roads in total lack of restraint. And all were agreed that this apparition was even more dreadful than the fiercest of goblins could ever be. His name was Urugan Bateren.[3] Though at heart he planned to spread the Kirishitan religion, he seemed intent first to survey the wisdom of the Japanese people. He brought with him all sort and manner of curious things from South Barbary.

Onlookers are startled by the apparition of the first Bateren;
a merchant hails him ashore.

In the Province of Tsu there lived at that time Takayama Lord Hida and his son Ukon Daibu. They extended reverence to this Bateren and became followers of his religion. Introducing him to the likes of Miyoshi Shūri no Daibu and Matsunaga Sōtai, they enabled him to remain in Japan.[4]

How the Bateren Was Summoned to Azuchi in the Province of Ōmi

At that time Prince Oda Nobunaga, Taira no Ason, Lord Kazusa, was master over the Empire. Like the wind that makes all the grasses and trees bend before its gusts, he vanquished and subjugated the savages of the East, the barbarians of the South, the wild men of the North, and the hordes of the West, thus setting at peace the Empire. At Azuchi in the Province of Ōmi he built his castle, furnishing it with a splendor the likes of which even Hsien Yang Palace had never seen.[5]

Once in the course of an evening's conversation he heard tell of that Urugan Bateren, and he uttered the desire to see this creature as soon as possible. Suganoya Kuemon no Jō was given orders to convey the Bateren to Nobunaga's residence;[6] and thus he arrived at Azuchi.

After two or three days the Bateren appeared before Nobunaga to pay obeisance. He was dressed in a garment called *habito*, which looked somewhat like a piece of felt carpet; it was mouse-grey in color, with long sleeves and the skirts slit. Wearing this garment he looked for all the world like a bat spreading its wings. Word had spread that he was coming to pay obeisance to Nobunaga, so that great lords and lesser lords of all Japan, minor officials, townsmen, all rushed to see the sight. Really, it was like the Gion Procession or the Sannō Festival: you could hardly push your way through the crowds!

The Bateren bearing gifts is conveyed into Nobunaga's presence.

For presents he brought ten muskets, far-seeing and near-seeing spectacles, a mosquito net big enough to cover an eight-mat room yet fine enough to fit into a tiny perfume container when folded, some thirty yards of cloth of orangoutang,[7] picture scrolls, medicines, goats and sheep, Cathay dogs, and many other artifacts in overwhelming number. Prince Nobunaga was not at all displeased. He gave to the Bateren a plot of land for a residence and had a colossal temple built for him.[8]

And after that the two Bateren called Gerigori and Yariisu were brought over.[9] Rorensu, a native of the Province of Hizen, acted as their Japanese interpreter.[10] Also there were Gōzumo and Shimon, men of Sakai in Izumi; these two took turns in preaching sermons.[11] They were given the appellation of Iruman. And also they sought out renegade Japanese bonzes who had become disillusioned with the world and, bribing them with colossal sums of money, they made them into Iruman. These thereupon made up a seven-step sequence of sermons incorporating Confucian and Buddhist materials; and this they preached to the people. What they said seemed to have no hidden intent. First of all they made a simple statement of the teachings of the Way of the Gods and of the Buddhist scriptures, then down to the fifth step they reviled these teachings, rending into them layer by layer; and finally in the sixth and seventh steps they taught their own doctrine.

On the Kirishitan Version of Buddhist Doctrine

Well, then: The Kirishitan version of Buddhist doctrine tells us that at the time heaven and earth were opened up the One Buddha—called Deus, as well as the Great Lord—made his appearance, creating the sun and moon and illuminating the world.[12] He created man and beasts, grasses and trees, the universe and all the myriad phenomena therein. Once he had constructed the terrestrial domain he let man live there in opulence; but he did not give man specific instruction on doing good or doing evil. The age of the Decline of the Law came about: man's wisdom being but scant, he offended against Deus' law and for that, as befits a sentient being of evil mind and lack of righteous course, he is expediently thrust into *Inferno*, a place of darkness in the bowels of the earth. And there, invested with the form of a beast or fowl, he undergoes suffering.

But they who do not diverge from Deus' teachings fly from here to *Paraiso*, a place of ease and pleasure in the heavens above. They are reborn there to enjoy full freedom and every abundance; and that is *Paraiso*.

From the facilities inherent in all sentient beings have arisen the Eight Sorrows and Eight Impediments.[13] But in the grace of Deus there has been no inconsistency from the beginning. To use an analogy: no parent in bringing up a child wishes him to grow up bad; but on gaining adult age many do turn out sick, or undutiful to their parents, or even become thieves. There is no fault in Deus. But the facilities of men take many different paths; and so it stands to reason that he holds bad men in deep abomination.

Not to diverge from Deus' teachings—by what means can this ambition be attained? There is *confissan*: to come into the presence of the Buddha, do penance and contrition, and pray for happiness in the future world. There is *quaresma*,[14] similar to the Japanese devotion of reading the sutras: while reciting his scripture, the Kirishitan strikes his chest with resounding blows; this appears to be a practice meant to demonstrate that there is in the heart no thought but earnest adoration of Deus and Santa Maria. Next, he raises a pointing finger while directing his gaze up at heaven; this signifies worship reciprocating the protection which Deus from heaven above bestows upon this world. Thereupon the believer horizontally passes his hand over both eyes; this practice expresses the wish that the mind not be attached to any object which the eyes may see. Next he appears to press his mouth and gnash his teeth; this seems to be a practice expressing the determination not to allow falsehoods or lies to pass the mouth. And for the evening there is the *penitencia*: in his mouth the believer mutters contrition for all his accumulated misdeeds, and flogs his back with an object somewhat like a fly-swatter spiked with copper thorns, besmirching himself with blood—and all the while intoning, "Zensumaru, Zensumaru." For an amulet the Kirishitan strings around his neck the *contas*, images of Deus linked together by thin metal knots. To these beads is tied a cruciform: and he fingers them in the order away from his body, continuously intoning, "Zensumaru, Zensumaru."[15] And the thing called *cruz* he values as all-important. All the profundity of a saucer's depths! Or so it would seem.

But what is the appearance of the Kirishitan temple? It contains a Room of Mystery, in which is on display an image of Deus, fashioned in the most gruesome manner, hanging upon a cross. This appears to be a device to extract tears of emotion from their sectarians, by showing off this figure of agony and mortification. And in back of this room is the Meeting Room. On display here is an image of the matron Santa Maria after she gave birth to Deus, holding in her arms an infant in his second year. Now the particular background of this image is as follows. The Buddha

The Kirishitan version of Buddhism: the portrait of Santa Maria presides over the flagellation scene.

called Deus, deeming it unlikely that sentient beings would themselves learn of Buddha's Law and even of wordly law, and certain that they would doubt the mere statement that he is the Lord of Heaven and Earth, decided to be born himself into this world. And he caused the womb of Santa Maria to conceive and to give birth. Such is the Meeting Room.

And the chamber in back is called the Room of Repentance. Here the Bateren and Iruman and their adherents all sit in a circle, while the penitent in its center publicly proclaims contrition of his sins and misdeeds, begging forgiveness and subjecting himself to severe humiliation. Thereupon the Bateren, taking into his hands the aforementioned *penitencia*, flogs the sinner, causing the flow of blood. Then he wipes the blood off with a piece of cloth and, without washing his hands, offers up prayers to the Buddha. And they call this a great deed!

But here is what the Kirishitans believe. Those who perform such acts of mortification obtain the protection of Deus: to them he is like a shadow, at their side constantly, by day and by night; and therefore the body should be valued less even than dew or dust. Those who hear the doctrines of Deus have come upon uncommon good fortune, more extraordinary than gleaning gold from the bottom of the sea, more unexpected than the one-eyed tortoise's coming upon the one floating tree in the middle of the ocean.[16] And so they praise this religion and find satisfaction in it; indeed, they think determinedly that this way they can attain Buddhahood. Though they be roasted alive, be torn in two by oxen or carriages, or be crucified head down— though they meet with such tortures, there appear to be none among them that would grudge their lives, so confident are they of attaining their desire of Buddhahood. How pitiful it is!

Once a fool has turned a ready ear to something and set his heart on it, nothing will change his mind. To use an analogy: a child of two or three in seeing a reflection in a mirror thinks it an actual figure; a monkey in seeing the moon on the surface of the water tries to grab it with his paws—for such is the simplicity of their minds. All fools are like that. But heretical doctrine must be of deviltry.

How the Kirishitans Were Dragged through the Land in Carts during the Reign of the Taikō Hideyoshi

Some time about the Bunroku Period, during the reign of the Taikō Hideyoshi, a great many Bateren called Furaten were sent over to Japan.[17] It appears that in their own country they had been priests much given to devotions. But here in Japan they went out on the streets and gathered beggars and the outcasts of society about them. They gave remarkable medical treatment to the harelipped, to lepers, to wretches afflicted with boils and carbuncles, with the Chinese pox and with mange, thus enticing them to join their religion. And hale beggars were given a meal if they expressed the desire to become members of their religion. To those of the middle level of society who had been disillusioned with this world they taught their heretical doctrines and made their way through life seem easier; in return they were pulled into the Kirishitan religion. The young, the extravagant, the indiscreet, and the affected were tricked with newfangled bric-a-brac. Those whom they deemed great lords they flattered with gifts of baubles and beads, long-seeing spectacles, and similar fare, thus involving them in an ever-deepening relationship and finally deluding them into joining the Kirishitan faith. They built temples every place and everywhere: in Osaka, in Sakai, in Nagasaki, in Yamaguchi of Suō Province, in Hiroshima, in Okayama of Bizen, in Himeji. And in the Capital they built great temples at Gojō Horikawa and Ichijō Abura no Kōji.[18]

The Bateren are sent off with their noses slit.

Morons, menials, and misfits—they took in everybody and rejected nobody. And thus (a matter of notoriety) they gathered about themselves a bunch of good-for-nothings.

One day a group of Iruman concocted a plot together with some of their most trusted parishioners. News of their criminal activity leaked out. And now the wrath of the Taikō Hideyoshi exceeded all bounds. Hearing of their secret plans to spread their pernicious doctrines and to delude the populace, he decided that it was high time to slash at their very roots. How fortunate for Japan!—for he determined to purge the land of them.

But now all sorts of apologies were sent from Nagasaki, so that he relented on the point of expelling them all from Japan. Only the actual criminals were put in carts at the Ichijō crossroads and were sent off,[19] their ears and noses slit. There were twenty-five in all. Six of them were Bateren, eight Iruman; the rest were oblates and lay believers. They were dragged through the Capital, and then by relays straight along the roads of Harima and all the way to Tsukushi on the Western Sea. Thus they were dragged to Nagasaki of Hizen. Along the way they were constantly looking for a miracle from Deus, gazing up at the sky, peering across the mountains—but there wasn't even a dewdrop of a miracle, and their faces became drawn with fright and disappointment.

They were crucified in Nagasaki. For a while a guard was posted at the site; but then the bodies rotted on the crosses. Their bones and skulls were stolen by other believers, and afterwards the crosses, too, were whittled down to toothpicks. These relics were used as amulets, and what is more (so report has it), were later bartered at high prices.

How the Kirishitans Made Light of the Japanese Monks

How different are the habits of Japanese monks from the custom of South Barbary! Japanese monks fawn upon their parishioners. They crave after fame and fortune and are sunk in lust. Bereft of merciful compassion, they are given to unfeeling covetousness. From their high thrones they preach, "Cast off all desire!"—but what others cast off they contrive to pick up again. In every sermon we hear them talk of the Pure Land of the West, and how the blessed who attain this paradise will be dressed in garments embellished with the Seven Precious Things, will wear jewel necklaces of delicate workmanship, will be endowed with the Thirty-Two Bodily Signs of Buddhahood,[20] and will enjoy a life without want in food, drink, or clothing— for in the Pure Land there is not one thing to be dissatisfied with. And yet our doubts refuse to clear. For when these priestly gentlemen of wisdom are taken ill, they do drink medicines, submit themselves to acupuncture, and have moxa burned—so terribly precious is life to them. So the Pure Land they preach must be pure fiction. Thus the Kirishitans ridiculed the Japanese religious.

So let the sawdust out of them![21] To be sure, the Kirishitans' arguments seem quite to the point. Lamentable behavior is rife among the Eight Schools and Nine Sects.[22] To start with, Japanese monks engage in public activities and amusements most unbefitting the religious. They dabble in the tea ceremony and in other such artistic fancies, in the composition of linked verse,

Alms: bestowing a piece of cloth.

dance performances, football, archery, in flower-viewing parties and drinking bouts—things without profit all! They are unfamiliar with learning, and when questioned about Buddhist doctrine prove quite inferior to the layman in knowledge.

The word for "giving alms" is written with the characters *fuse*—"bestowing a piece of cloth." The commentaries to the scriptures make the derivation of this word quite clear. When women (who are beings much encumbered by karma and the attachment to earthly things), all their energies entwined and entangled in the task, after much pain and effort in weaving the strands of linen down to the last fine mesh finally produce a piece of homespun, then the Buddha, appreciating the nobility of their devotion, takes great pleasure in this and deems it an act worthy of salvation, a thread connecting the human to Buddhahood. But in these our days gold and silver are the currency, and prices are reckoned high. And yet, priests without even a fixed income (and without savings) must do constant repairs on their temples and halls of prayer, must make the offerings of food, incense, and flowers before the Buddha, must purchase sutras, scriptures, and saints' commentaries, must bring up their disciples and arrange for their own food—or else Buddha's seed would be choked by the cares of this world and would vanish. That much must be said in defense of our own priests. Bear in mind here the words of the saint: though the sins of the wise man be many, he shall not fall down into hell; but the fool shall fall down into hell, though his sins be few!

It is not by a miracle that the Kirishitans are not covetous and refrain from fawning on their parishioners. For the King of South Barbary each year dispatches a Black Ship or a *galliot*, to eliminate any want in all their temples; and everyone gets his share—including simple parishioners, if their faith be deep. So it is no wonder that they appear to be uncovetous and prudent. And, moreover, day and night they eat the flesh of cows, horses, swine, chickens, and meaner yet! Anxious thus to adopt the manner of wild beasts, many became members of their religion mainly for the taste of such foods. Or so report has it.

How a Japanese Lay Monk and a Kirishitan Iruman
Held a Debate on Religion

About the first year of the Genna Period the Kirishitan faith
was enjoying great prosperity in Osaka.[23] Samurai, townsmen,
and masterless desperadoes, all gathered before the gates of the
Kirishitans' temple and made of it a marketplace. And the widow
of a daimyo, though she was past her sixth decade, having the
Kirishitan faith pressed quite urgently upon her, was heard to
say, constrained by the entreaties: "I am about to reach the age
of seventy and have no desire for glory, pomp, or luxury.
There is nothing in which I feel want; but I have set my heart
on the life in the next world, and day and night I stray not
from this one desire. In fine, my only object is to attain Buddhahood. But down to this day I have not understood the logic in
Buddhism. By saying 'Namu Amida Butsu' one is supposed to
go to the Pure Land of the West; by saying 'Myōhō Rengekyō'
one is supposed to go to the Land of Liberation and Brilliance—
this is all I know, and I have earnestly applied myself to these
devotions.[24] But if there were a way in which Buddhist doctrine
were made clear to me near enough to grasp in hand, then
I certainly would not retain allegiance to any sect. I would
certainly change my religion."

An Iruman, hearing of this and considering that women are very easily cheated, now said to the widow: "True, true is what you say. In the Buddhist doctrine of Deus the place of repose is called *Paraiso*, a place of comfort and delight where the persons of the blessed will be radiant with a golden brilliance. It is a place which knows neither heat nor cold, a place where musical instruments called *organs* play delightful tunes (indeed, much like those of Japan) for the amusement and enjoyment of the blessed. Shaka! Amida!—how could they be Buddhas! Shaka, if you'd really like to know, was the son of King Jōbon of India. He was disinherited by his father and lived withdrawn on Dandoku Mountain, and there, giving his mouth free rein, he worked deception upon all sentient beings.[25] And the person now known as Amida was actually called Hōzō Biku and was a mere human being.[26] But he who is called Deus is the Buddha who opened up heaven and earth. To be deluded by the teachings of Shaka (who was just an everyday person) is just like falling under the spell of a fox. But it does seem that by his clever tongue Shaka managed to trick the fools of the Three Countries."[27]

To this the widow replied: "I am a mere woman and therefore cannot follow all these distinctions. But it does seem to me that what you say here is but very clever talk and cannot be right. In the final analysis, here is the best thing to do. Select from among the Kirishitans one well-versed Iruman, and have him come here before me. And I will seek out a person learned in the Buddhist doctrine of Shaka and have him come forward. We can have them debate religion, and I shall join the side of the one who wins."

Hearing this, the Iruman answered: "Just what we want! We shall be pleased to act entirely in accord with your arrangements." Making this solid promise, the Iruman returned to his quarters.

Then the widow said: "I hear that even when the greatest abbots of the Zen and Pure Land Schools were called on, the Kirishitans have countered and defeated arguments from the Way of the Gods, the Interior Scriptures, and the Exterior Scriptures,[28] and have put forward their own perversities. But I have heard of a lay monk named Hakuō Koji who is supposedly superior to all the religious.[29] Let us send someone to invite him, and

The widow decides to send for Hakuō.

see if he will take part in a disputation." And she dispatched a swift courier to Kyoto.

Now this Devotee of the Way named Hakuō Koji had made for himself a humble hut on the northern outskirts of the Capital. To cover his body he wore only hempen cloth or paper garb, and in the winter merely a coverlet of paper. For his two meals a day he had only some groats with a side dish of parched coarse salt. Altogether, he presented quite an ascetic figure.

Day and night he remained at his book stand, never relaxing once to blink an eye in his study of the Interior and Exterior Scriptures. From his earliest years he was bent to Buddhist studies. In the Southern Capital he listened to sermons on the doctrine of Mere-Ideation.[30] At the Miidera he heard the Story of the Higher Special Dharma, and especially the Chapter on Worlds; and he held the Three Thousand Realms in the palm of his hand.[31] He scaled the peak of the Enryakuji and for twelve years remained in residence there, mastering the Preliminary Mysteries, the Exegeses, Meditation by the Abrupt Method of Calmness and Insight, Unbudging Concentration, the Sutra of Prohibitions, and other such materials and practices.[32] Peering across the Purple Plain he listened to the sound of Green Cliff.[33] Becoming a follower of the Myōshinji School, he looked into the Mirror of the Faith, founding himself upon the Platform Sutra of the Sixth Patriarch.[34] In the Five Great Monasteries he studied the writings of Tōba, the works of Sankoku, and the Literary Selections.[35] And he also delved into the Miwa Branch of Shinto.[36] Entering the gates of the Pure Land School as well, he chose to apply himself to the Tracts on Selection,[37] and penetrated the Meaning of the Two Treasures.[38]

Thus he realized the identity of all elements. Rapt in Zen Meditation and Concentration, his body clouded by drifts of incense smoke, he looked quite like a mystic sage. And the eloquence of this disciple of Buddha would have baffled even the matchless Furuna![39]

So this was the man to whom the courier from Osaka came on his religious errand. For a while Hakuō considered within himself whether it was a good idea to take part in a debate without the presence of a trustworthy judge; but since it was the noble lady's wish, and since the Kirishitan gang had for all

Hakuō on his way to Osaka, passing Yodo.

too long been given excessive leeway in spewing forth their devilish doctrine to the lower classes and to various other fools, he finally agreed, thinking to put the Kirishitans to shame. And he took a fast boat from Fushimi, and thus arrived at the lady's residence in Osaka.

The widow's joy at this was not in minor key. Forthwith she sent a messenger to the Kirishitans' temple. "Have an Iruman with a wide grasp of learning and a ready tongue come to my residence. Let's have the promised disputation, and see whose Buddhist doctrine is victorious and whose falls short!"—this was her message.

Now it so happened that resident in the Kirishitans' temple at this time was one Fabian. It appears that he had been a Zen monk originally and then turned renegade. The insides of his eyes kept turning round and round, and his mouth also kept revolving, with a flood of words like swift-running water, and never a hitch. He was about fifty years old, while Hakuō was sixty-four or perhaps a year older. During dinner he treated Hakuō to sundry compliments and flattery on a great range of trifling topics.

Night came and candles were lit. It was time to start the religious bout. Screens and room partitions were removed and a great hall thus created. In it an audience of some two hundred sat all eager to take in the proceedings. Not even a cough disturbed the silence.

After a while Fabian had some scripture cases brought out and took from them the Lotus Sutra, the Diamond Sutra, the Three Sutras, and other volumes, neatly ranging them side by side.[40] Seeing this, Hakuō quickly turned the debate in another direction, exclaiming: "No! No!—there's nothing strange to us in the arguments of Shaka's doctrine. We're deeply acquainted with Japanese knowledge, hearing it as we do day and night. Just stick to the explanation of the elements of Deus' law." And he put the volumes back in their cases. For it had obviously been Fabian's intent to read selected sentences from the sutras and then, maliciously twisting the meaning, to disrupt, deform, and destroy their arguments.

Now there was in the room a set of boxes nestled in each other, such as are used for the serving of sweets. Using these boxes as an example, the Iruman asked: "Were these boxes made by somebody's skill? Or did they merely appear by accident?" And Hakuō replied: "The carpenter's skill. These are not things that could have dropped out of nothing all of a sudden."

The Iruman now said: "I'm glad you understand this point— this will make it easy for you to follow my further meaning. The Buddha called Deus is the Buddha who opened up heaven and earth and gave them a beginning. Before that there was but a misty void, with not a thing existing in it. And in this emptiness Deus created the myriad phenomena of the universe, man and beasts, grasses and trees, sun and moon, everything. Thus, the construction of the world—et cetera, et cetera. Not to worship this creator, and instead to invoke Shaka and Mida (who have at best a two- or three-thousand-year history)—what kind of reliance can be placed in that! And, moreover, Shaka's scriptures all represent the point of view of Non-Being. But all the elements of Deus' doctrine represent the point of view of Recompensed Being.[41] And accordingly, all those who perform good and do not diverge from Deus' regulations shall reside in a place called *Paraiso*, in ease and fulfillment of delight. But the wicked are thrust down into *Inferno*, the place of the extremity of all suffering. Originally there was no good or evil, delight or suffering; but as the Age of Decline came about, the nature and the wisdom of sentient beings became warped and they ceased to be submissive.[42] Disturbed at this, Deus created *Paraiso* and *Inferno*.

"What is the history of the gods and Buddhas of Japan? They may be called that, but originally all were humans. The one in the Grand Shrines of Ise is the child of Izanagi and Izanami, and in Izumo Province the child of a fisher girl. And the 'Great Bodhisattva' Hachiman is actually the emperor Ōjin, who was a human.[43]

"The reason for the state of delusion of sentient beings was that they placed their hopes astray, their prayers in the wrong direction, knowing nothing at all of the True Law. And therefore Deus decided to show his figure to human beings, thus bestowing his grace upon them; and he was conceived in the womb of a beautiful lady called Santa Maria, and finally manifested to the world his diamond-countenance of unyielding might, thus fulfilling all of mankind's desires.

"South Barbary is a great country, and compared to it five hundred (or even a thousand) Japans would be like the one strand of hair set against the nine head of cattle. In his edict the King of South Barbary expressed the thought: 'The people of Japan are to be pitied for their ignorance of the True Law.' And so he caused his emissaries to cross over to Japan, braving the perils of ten thousand miles of the deep blue sea." Thus spoke Fabian.

Hakuō listened carefully to all the details of this speech. "And is there no deeper meaning, beyond this, in all the elements of Deus' doctrine?," he asked now. The Iruman answered: "The expanse of all the elements of Deus' doctrine is wide and great, knowing no borders, hardly comprehensible to human wisdom. Mountain upon mountain of scriptures are ranged to support our view."

To this Hakuō replied: "Let's strike at the flaws! And you just listen, without interruptions. You tell me that someone called Deus is the Buddha who opened up heaven and earth. No doubt they insist on believing that in South Barbary—let them! But in China, in India, and in Our Empire, we know of the Seven Gods of Heaven and the Five Gods of Earth; day and night we look upon their record in the *Nihongi* as well as in Chinese books. This thing about Deus—it's the first time I've heard of it! He cannot possibly be the Buddha who opened up heaven and earth. At best, he may be a demon who arose after the opening up of heaven and earth.

"First of all—leaving aside the nonsense about Deus creating the myriad phenomena of the universe, man and beasts, grasses and trees, sun and moon, and everything—first of all, let's find out just why he might have created humans. What could his purpose have been, I ask you? For it couldn't possibly have been no purpose at all. So was it to have a plaything, like a pet bird, say? Or perhaps Milord felt lonely by himself and created man in order to have a confidant, a partner in conversation? Or a jester?[44] No, my doubts refuse to clear. The set of boxes in this room is meant to be a container for sweets and appetizers. And among all the other implements there is not one which lacks its purpose: so this pot is meant for preparing tea to drink; these fire tongs are for grasping hot coals. Each has

Hakuō disputes with Fabian; the widow takes it all in.

its appointed purpose. And for humans, too, Deus must have had some set purpose in mind. Or didn't he? Well, answer!" But Fabian, thrown into confusion, only talked into the four winds and could not come up with a quick response.

Then Hakuō continued: "My second objection is this. If it were true that Deus created human beings, why then did he not at the same time establish one religion for all the people encompassed by heaven and the Four Seas? So now he has to face the dangers of a journey of thousands—nay! tens of thousands —of miles, all for the sake of spreading his doctrine to this little land. What a stupid Buddha he must be! And, of course, bereft of super-powers.

"And here is my third objection. Deus was crucified, another time driven amongst thorns and brambles, and otherwise subjected to deranging pains, pressures, and persecutions. Or so you say in your seven-step sequence of sermons, as I am told. To make such a criminal, rebellious individual into an object of worship is most ill-considered, shameful, and base.

"Fourth. Without anybody asking him, Deus created human beings, and then he also created *Paraiso* and *Inferno*, paradise and hell. And now he lifts humans up, or drops them down, ruled only by his own caprice and fancy. Human beings, be they noble or mean, are all without exception subject to the Four Pains and Eight Sorrows.[45] Perhaps they nailed him to the cross because of the grudge they bore him for causing this suffering. At any rate, this Deus looks like a devil to me."

For a while the Iruman kept his mouth shut, but then he said: "As proof that Deus is the Great Lord of the universe you can take this exploit. If he were to climb onto the roof of the Holy of Holies of Amaterasu Ōmikami, or Kasuga, or Hachiman, and defecate and urinate thereon, no punishment would strike him. From this you can tell that he is the Basal Buddha."[46]

What a detestable bastard! And what a big mouth, too! I'd like to bust up the skin around that trap of his! No mercy!— so thought Hakuō. He sat up straight and began: "Fabian, now listen carefully! You call it a grand exploit to climb onto the roofs of the Holy of Holies of the Three Shrines, to defecate and urinate thereon, and to escape unpunished for the effort. Of course, there is no prior example of punishment striking oxen, horses, or other beasts for suchlike misdeeds. But this Buddha whom you worship is so insignificant that he does not even rank among the beasts, the birds, or even the infinitesimal creatures. Let's have Santa Maria out here! The one that gave birth to this capricious, this deceitful Deus, this child without a father! I'll soil and sully her from head to toe, I'll kick and trample her with my feet, I'll show you! And if punishment does strike me on the spot, then I and all my family and followers will take up your religion.

"And what is more: It may be true that you don't resort to walking the streets blaring the empty lie, 'This is the true Deus!' But it is fact that you hold all other faiths in great contempt, defaming all the laudable and commendable things about them. Your own heresy you make out to be a wondrous faith; the idiots, the ignorant, the animal-like dolts among your followers you indoctrinate with your seven-step sequence of sermons, a caricature of the truth. Unheard-of things from distant lands you embellish with flowered words, thereby thrusting so many people straight down the devil's path. And that is most lamentable."

Hakuō finished thus, pressing Fabian for a response. But Fabian merely gulped with his mouth, as though choking on a peach, and finally he let out a wail like a dog's when he turns tail and runs. "No use talking to a bigot!," he yelped in exasperation, stood up, and left. And afterward those who had pressed the Kirishitan faith upon the widow were seen no more.

Some Learned Comments of Hakuō Koji, Inserted Here
at This Opportunity

A general inspection of the Story of the Higher Special
Dharma will reveal that the problem, "When did this world,
its lands and territories, and its people have their beginning?,"
does not exist. There is no report of gods or Buddhas creating
these. And in the future yet to come, eternity following upon
eternity, there will be no such creation.

Every hundred years man's average span of life decreases by
one year until an age of ten years becomes longevity. Then it
increases again, by one year in each century, until an age of
830,000 years becomes average. Thereafter it decreases again, until
an average life span of one hundred years is reached.[47] After
this process is completed, then will Miroku come into this
world,[48] succeeding Shaka, who was the ninth Buddha thus to
appear.[49] And after twenty-one Buddhas appear in this world in
this fashion, then will this world vanish; thus it may be stated.
But then the world will come into existence anew, like a
pagoda of multilevel construction, and after this process sentient
beings will have neither increased nor decreased: no exhaustion
will have resulted.

The appearance of one Buddha in this world takes place in
four thousand years of Tōriten Heaven,[50] which are 5,670,000,000
years of this world. But human beings for kalpas without
beginning have been subject to Constant Flow: the Law of
Cause and Effect is like unto a wheel.[51] Just as a stone possesses

Hakuō expounds the Story of the Higher Special Dharma to the widow.

within itself the potential nature of fire, so are human beings endowed with a nature capable of attaining Buddhahood; but this they fail to apprehend, thus falling into darkness and delusion. And therefore they in whom covetousness is deep fall into the Realm of Hungry Spirits; they in whom ignorance thrives fall into the Realm of Beasts; and they in whom anger is rampant fall into the Realm of Fighting Spirits or the Realm of Hellish Beings.[52] And after this term of anguish and agony expires, then again the World of Created Elements affects the fruit of the womb of human beings or of beasts.[53] According to the specific character of each,[54] there are then those who successfully pursue the Path of Buddha, and there are those who are dragged down the path of evil. Et cetera, et cetera.

There is only one Law, not two. But for those desirous of accomplishing the Way of Buddha and attaining the afterlife there are three styles of instruction: the straight, the cursive, and the accomplished.[55] The ignorant and those of low quality are taught never—walking or standing, sitting or lying down—to neglect the invocation "Namu Amida Butsu," and additionally to weigh carefully in their hearts the meaning of good and evil, to make the straight and righteous path their actions' base and thus avoid incurring the hate of others, to devote themselves to works of charity and to mercy and compassion, and to pray with single-mindedness and constancy to be saved and taken to the Pure Land of the West of Mida Nyorai. This is the process urged upon the various people of low quality, those wholly ignorant of letters; they are taught to have unbudging trust in its efficacy. Then there are those who chant the five-syllable invocation "Myōhō Rengekyō."[56] Of course, the contents of the eight volumes of the Lotus Sutra are unsurpassed, for such concepts as enlightenment in Original Illumination and Initial Illumination,[57] and for the blessed Abrupt Round Doctrine of the Great Vehicle.[58] But people not at all conversant with letters are taught merely to keep intoning this sutra's name, "Myōhō Rengekyō," morning and evening, thus to aim at rebirth in the Pure Land of Liberation and Brilliance, trusting in the uninterrupted accumulation of merit.[59]

And here is the process of instruction for those of a middling intelligence. Since Japan is the Land of the Gods, they must first of all believe in the gods and Buddhas and worship them, and especially take to heart the Revelation of the Three Shrines of Ise, Kasuga, and Hachiman;[60] and mornings they must pray for peace in the Empire, security in the land, and respect for the ruler. "In subdued brilliance sharing this world of dust is the beginning of the tie [between Buddha and man]; the Eight Stages [of the Buddha's earthly life] and the Establishment of the Way are the end of all beneficial things."[61] Thus it is said, and these words are a safe guide to the extreme moment of death; this is because between the Buddhas and the gods there is but the difference between water and waves. Give attention, evenings, to the impermanence of all things. Consider that a human life has but the span of fifty years; know not the morrow. From the human mind arise varicolored lascivious thoughts and evil ideas; and therefore a close rein on your mind must never be relaxed, so you avoid being drawn into excesses. And, in order to pass safely through this world, maintain humanity, righteousness, decorum, wisdom, and good faith, and preserve within yourself the aspiration to Buddhahood. No matter how great a hoard you keep of gold or silver, it is like gathering riches in a dream. And yet this is not to say that each and every desire must be cast away. This instruction is meant to proscribe wickedness, excess, and immoderation.

For those of superior wisdom who desire to attain disengagement from this world the procedure is as follows. All the sutras of Shaka make a distinction between delusion and enlightenment. From the human mind arises enlightenment; but delusion also arises from the human mind. The way to Buddhahood is not by reliance on any man, nor by reliance upon any Buddha. The one simple fact is: if you do not give a polish to your own character and thereby produce from within yourself the Buddha with whom your own self is endowed, then it is difficult indeed to attain Buddhahood, though you pass through eternity upon future eternity. To use an analogy: rock crystal possesses within itself a brilliance; yet if it is not shined and polished with diamond dust it will never become a jewel. And, for another example: a mirror, being a thing without cognition, does not retain the shade which floats upon it. The true mind of man is not inferior to a mirror in brightness; but it retains and attaches to itself all of life's experience which floats upon it, and thus it wanders in delusion on the road of covetousness and conceit. In the Zen School they use the expression, "To follow along the course of the myriad phenomena without becoming involved," to mean a refusal to become attached to the myriad experiences of life. And in Tendai they say, "One conscious moment raises the three thousand forms of life," meaning that three thousand delusions arise from the human mind; and this they hold to be their inmost teaching.[62] Of course, this can never be communicated to the unenlightened fools of this world. And yet, though great is the number of men who have sufficient wisdom to perceive the truth of this, few are those who become enlightened. Those who won't hear are useless, like a cart with one wheel and without remedy.

A monk denounces the Kirishitans before the Council of Elders.

How a Man Appeared to Accuse the Kirishitans of Desiring to Subject Japan to South Barbary

Some time about the Genna Period a monk came up from Higo Province and presented himself at Suruga.[63] Received before the Council of Elders, he reported as follows: "In the Province of Higo there is a Kirishitan temple called *Natal*, being a temple much reverenced by Konishi Lord Tsu.[64] Here they bade me do much that is unreasonable and unjust, and finally they chased me out. For I, too, was an Iruman and preached sermons; but now I would have my revenge on them.

"The King of South Barbary plans to subjugate Japan. His means is the diffusion of his brand of Buddhism. To that end he has sent a great many Bateren over here, and has diverted the income of five or ten provinces of his country toward the needs of his Japanese undertaking. Under the pretext of annual trading vessels he ships over all sort and manner of articles to entangle Japan in his web.[65] Each of the Kirishitans' temples in the Capital and in the countryside gets its share, so that they do not lack the wherewithal. Moreover, annually they compile a great list of the people (so many hundreds, so many thousands) whom they have that year persuaded to join their religion, and they send this list from Japan to South Barbary. This is a plot to take over the country without even a battle fought with bow and arrow. Right before our eyes, in Luzon and Nova Hispania, the King of South Barbary has installed his own governors, and has new officials sent over every three years. In sum, the plot consists of the design to spread religion.

"Quickly, dispatch someone to Higo to summon forth my adversaries, so we can have a confrontation before the August Presence. Naturally, if it proves that I have spoken but idle lies, then please dispose of me as you wish, though I be ripped apart by oxen or carriages. Until my adversaries appear I must, of course, be kept in prison." Thus spoke the former Iruman, with never a hesitation.

All this was brought to the attention of His Highness, who favored the report with much apparent satisfaction, being heard to comment, "A loyal individual!" Orders were transmitted to Katō Lord Higo, who thereupon had the suitor's adversaries brought up to court.[66] A confrontation between the two sides now took place. The Kirishitans made a confession in all particulars, and it was determined that they had, in fact, been steeped in the plot to take over the country. From that point on His Highness grew to hate them deeply and had their temples destroyed. And he gave strict notice as follows: "Those among the followers of this religion who choose to fall away upon this occasion shall remain further unmolested; but should there be any who persist, they shall meet with immediate chastisement."

How the Followers of the Kirishitan Religion
Were Inserted in Straw Sacks

Now a careful inquisition was conducted among the towns-
people of the Capital—in back-alley tenements, in shacks for rent,
and in a nunnery—even as far as the outlying districts; but
many were those who merely pretended to fall away and kept
an attachment to the Kirishitan faith lurking in their hearts.[67] At
that time the Resident Commissioner in Kyoto was Itakura
Katsushige, Lord Iga.[68] He tried many kinds of stratagems on
them; but this rabble, possessed of an animal kind of square-
mindedness, refused to go back on something once inserted in
the brain. Since they held their lives to be less dear than dew,
being completely set on the one objective of salvation in the life
to come, Itakura could not very well punish them as he would
pickpockets or burglars, and he worried himself sick in trying to
decide how to act. At this point the authorities in Edo sent
Ōkubo Lord Sagami to act as special magistrate.[69] Wherever he
caught wind of a possible Kirishitan—in the Capital, in Osaka,
Sakai, or Nara—he made arrests. And he had the Kirishitans
inserted into straw sacks.

Wrapped in two sacks each, bound in five places, with only
the neck sticking out, they looked for all the world like tree-
bugs encased in their self-spun houses. First, all the ones from
the Capital were piled on top of each other on the riverbank at

The Kirishitans are bundled in straw sacks; the constabulary holds dry twigs ready.

Shijō and Gojō, like so many hundredweights of rice; but the old men and the grannies were laid out in a tightly-packed row. The whole city of Kyoto seemed roused together, so many were the spectators on hand.

From morning until noon their tongues were capable enough to keep blabbing, "Zensumaru, Zensumaru." And they kept telling one to the other: "Well, now, how fortunate! Just us, and us alone—meeting with the final extremity, we'll obtain salvation from Deus and be born in *Paraiso*, where no want will disturb our life of ease, where we'll have jewels dangled from our necks. Every *domingo* we hear this in the sermon. Quick, let them go ahead and kill us!" Thus they kept whispering to each other.

The hour of noon passed, two o'clock was approaching. And now one of them spoke up: "Hey, how about all of us falling away together! You can't just go have a quick look at the afterlife—no one I know's ever come back. So let's leave that for later! At any rate, I'm so hungry my eyes are dizzy. Remember what we've been hearing in all those sermons? When we meet with the final extremity, we're supposed to get a hundred different sorts of food and drink, and be taken up to heaven above. But today we didn't even get a cracker, not even one pasty bun! Not a thing to eat since last night!—the worm's gnawing at my insides."

And someone packed in at the bottom of the pile said: "Pressed down from above, layer upon layer—can't hardly breathe, weight's too much to bear! Duty—forget it! Reputation—who cares? Come on, let's fall away!" Different words, same tune. On all sides, the rest of them took up the melody. And the entire riverside rocked with howls of laughter.

Now the constabulary were sent scurrying around town for guarantors and affidavits; and all were released to go back to their homes. But some fifty or sixty remained, reviling the others: "For shame! For shame!" But these merely answered: "This bit of shame we whistle at.[70] Now everything's turned out all right, and we don't care if we're reborn as rats or weasels." Kirishitan unity disrupted, they returned home.

The constabulary of course were furious at the abominable creatures that remained. They now brought over some four or five horseloads of kindlewood, and showed them off with the promise: "Throughout the night, some two or three hundred more bunches of fine dry twigs will be arriving from Yase, Ōhara, Iwakura, Nagatani, Shizu no Hara, and Hanazono.[71] Tomorrow at dawn we'll stack them mountain-high, and give you a good roasting!" Hearing this, they were terrified and set to shivers and trepidations. Calling the heads of the constabulary— Matsuo, Matsumura, Ogino, and Igarashi—they said: "One day's endurance for honor's sake is enough. Please let us fall away now!" Accompanying this plea with divers additional explanations, they were let out of the straw sacks, to the sound of much laughter. Or so I've heard.

How the Kirishitan Religion Was Subjugated

This first time the ruler thought it quite pitiable that poor illiterates upon hearing the teachings of this devilish heresy should take them for the truth, and bestowing his grace upon them he granted pardon to those who would fall away. This news did not remain unheard in South Barbary. Forthwith the doctrinal standpoint was changed, to state that one was free to renounce the faith any number of times, as long as his internal devotion remained unchanged. This was transmitted to Japan, along with a bit of gold for each Kirishitan, which was secretly distributed. In this case also there appeared an informer. More and more, their plans to subvert the country came out into the open.

The ruler's hate for them now grew deep indeed. Orders were sent to the Lords Protector, Lords Steward, Magistrates, and other officials throughout Japan[72] to scour every last place in the country for Kirishitans: village by village, mountain hut upon mountain hut, island by island, fishers' cove upon fishers' cove—no place was to be omitted. Down to the last baby born yesterday or today, all were to be registered in the rolls of Buddhist parish temples. Pledges written in the most uncompromising terms had to be presented to the authorities: "I and my whole family, children and grandchildren, definitely declare ourselves to be parishioners of this temple. If even one among us should prove to be of the Kirishitan persuasion, then the temple shall be confiscated and the priest subjected to any applicable punishment." To make sure that none who reneged escaped undetected, these pledges had to be repeated once a year: by townsmen to the ward elders and their assistants on monthly rotation, by villagers to the village headman and chief peasant, by samurai to their group leader. Moreover, notice boards offering rewards for information about Kirishitans were erected in settlements throughout every province. All too often, some ten or twenty were discovered here and there and were put to the fire, or crucified upside down, or subjected to the ordeal by water. And despite these various punishments more are being discovered even these days. How strange it is! Et cetera, et cetera.

How the Kirishitans Raised a Revolt in Amakusa and Shimabara of Hizen in Tsukushi

About the middle of the eleventh month of the fourteenth year of Kan'ei a rebellion flared up in Shimabara and Amakusa.[73] The comings and goings of express couriers and post-horse messengers now covered all of Japan like a fine-toothed comb, without regard for the borders of day and night. Upon investigation it was discovered that the fount of the rebellion was in the fief granted to Matsukura Lord Nagato. In a domain designed to yield 60,000 *koku* of rice he made his own land survey, arbitrarily setting the yield at 120,000 *koku* and taking from the peasants fifty or sixty percent of this estimate, being inordinately greedy. Year by year the peasants grew more exhausted, and were not able to have either the children or the cattle and horses due normally. How could they sustain life itself under those circumstances! Rather than starve to death, they preferred at least to be remembered in the records of future generations, and thus they rose in rebellion, making Amano Shirō their general.

They had Kirishitan sermons preached, and these incited the religionists into a state of blind fanaticism, so that they cut down any dissenter on the spot. For an emblem around the waist, a badge upon the cap, and an amulet about the neck they used a thing called the *cruz*.

Detecting their chance when Lord Nagato was away in Edo, the peasants burned down not only his castle town but also everything within two or three leagues of it. Readying plentiful provisions of rice, bean paste, salt, and gunpowder, they spent day and night in devising fortifications for the Old Castle of Shimabara.

A general description of this castle might be given as follows. On the east there was the raging sea, on the west a marsh swilled by the tides so that there was no ground for even one horsehoof to stand on; on the south and north towered craggy cliffs. The castle was some 2150 yards in length, and some 1200 across.[74] Three empty moats were dug traversing the inside, and excavations made along the waist of the hill. Musket loopholes were opened up and a small donjon constructed in the inner castle; pennants flew over the turrets. Earth walls, abatises, and barricades of shields were erected; thus they laid out a second and even a third ring of fortifications to a well-considered plan. The number of those who shut themselves up in this castle amounted to some thirty-four or thirty-five thousand soldiery. Among them were four or five hundred bowsmen able to hit even the eye of a needle, and some eight hundred musketeers that would not miss a boar or a hare on the run, nor even a bird in flight. On earthen parapets they set up catapults to hurl stones at the approaching enemy. Even the women had their tasks apportioned to them: they were to prepare glowing-hot sand and with great ladles cast it upon the attackers, and also to boil water seething hot and pour it upon them. There were also those assigned to fling football-sized rocks at the invaders. Thus they designated someone for each defensive duty.

Itakura Naizen no Kami and Ishigae Jūzō no Suke were appointed government envoys to subjugate the revolt.[75] In addition, Matsudaira Lord Izu was sent as special magistrate. The Tsukushi daimyo present at the fighting were Hosokawa Lord Etchū, Kuroda Uemon no Suke, Nabeshima Lord Shinano, Arima Genba no Jō, Tachibana Lord Hida, Terazawa Hyōgo no Kami, and Ogasawara Ukon no Daibu.[76] Mizuno Lord Hyūga and Toda Saemon no Kami were among the generals present;[77] the mention of others is here omitted.

Making their preparations carefully, they built an earth wall, set up an abatis, put a palisade of strong wood stakes around their encampment, raised lookout towers, constructed a hedge of cross-hatched twigs and bamboo, prepared testudos, surrounded themselves with several dozen water-filled moats, set up a barricade of shields toward the seaside, built great ships with superstructures covered all over, raised turrets above their fort, and kept up a nonstop bombardment with fire-arrows and artillery. Indeed, none of the besieged could now escape, unless he were a bird. During the daytime, musketeers were sent out, and they kept up a fire patterned as close as raindrops falling; but the Kirishitans did not turn a hair. From inside the castle they started a violent counterfire, having dug trenches along the waist of the mountain and having opened up three layers of loopholes.

There were two roads leading up to the castle, one to the front and one to the rear; but they were both merely narrow paths running from cliff to cliff. Single encounters might take place there, but their continuation down to the flat ground below was quite unthinkable. At night those in the castle lit many torches and bonfires, so that they could even discover an ant creeping low on the ground. And therefore those who tried to approach the castle merely invited injury upon themselves, by day or by night.

The castle was on a craggy cliff, on a steep precipice. Looking up at it was like peering at the nine apex rings of a pagoda. Weary of attacking such a place, the generals spent their days conferring, without being able to reach agreement upon one set plan. At this point the following instructions arrived from Edo: "The troops are not to be exposed to injury due to attacks made in haste. The rebellious rabble and their steep cliff are to be kept invested. No matter how many they may be, none of them are of account as adversaries. Surround, do not attack." One after the other, fast couriers kept arriving with messages of this purport.

The various daimyo now gathered at the government envoy's headquarters to make an estimate of the situation. "To be sure, this castle—though composed of rocky caverns and cliff walls, and harnessed in a triple fold of iron—is no more than an assembly of gadflies and mosquitoes trying to raise thunder. One attack would trample and scatter them all: that is obvious. But it would be lamentable to expend the lives of samurai in fighting peasants, outcasts, and beggars. So what is to be done?

After all, they do not have with them supplies to last several years, having entrenched themselves in this castle with makeshift preparation. Food or gunpowder, the one or the other will give out, and there is no worry at all of the contrary. Moreover, the orders we have received strictly enjoin us, in consideration of the above, first to leave them unmolested for a month." And they all agreed on this course of action.

At this point those in the castle made a night attack on scouts sent out by Nabeshima Lord Shinano. But these had suspected that such would take place and were well prepared. Played just right!—and they surrounded the attackers and took some hundred and forty or fifty heads, capturing some twenty or thirty alive. The rest, over two hundred men, beat a hasty retreat back up to the castle. And when the stomachs of the dead enemy were cut open, it was discovered that they had been eating seaweed, treeleaves, unripe barley, and suchlike. Not one was there whose stomach had rice in it.

Now that it was clear that there was no food left in the castle, the order for the general attack was transmitted to all headquarters, the action to start at midnight, the twenty-seventh of the first month, the fifteenth year of Kan'ei.[78] At the first blast of the conch trumpet all were fed, at the second they fitted themselves out for battle; upon the signal of the third trumpet they girt themselves with their swords and put on identifying marks, most going to the attack without armor, and only the lower ranks wearing cuirasses of straw. Swift as a flock of finches or sparrows, they made nothing of obstacles: earth walls, abatises, cliffs, rocks, iron spikes—they climbed and leapt over them, thus penetrating to the second ring of fortifications, each eager to be second to none.

"We can't stand for that!"—must have been the defenders' foremost thought. Opening the gate, they rushed out in a phalanx of spears, thrusting their weapons out and drawing them in again, making sparks fly in two or three such passes. But they were slashed down by the attackers, who followed them back into the castle as they retreated, making a forced entry close upon their heels; and one after the other of them had his head taken. Finally they were all pressed back into the innermost castle.

Fire-arrows now flew in on them from eight directions, like a deluge of rain; and as they sallied forth again, desperate for lack of cover, they were slashed and skewered, cut through the body, pursued and beaten down. Thus the castle fell in two hours, with corpses piled as high as mountains.

The heads taken by the attacking troops were fifteen or sixteen thousand in number; the total count of those who died by fire or by sword, including women and children, was in excess of forty thousand. The attackers also suffered terrible damage, which was a very sad thing. It is difficult to divide up the praise among all the great lords, and also those of lesser rank, who contributed their own hand in this campaign, or who marshaled their troops in so wonderful a fashion. Even in the romances of old there is heard no other example of so many killed in battle.

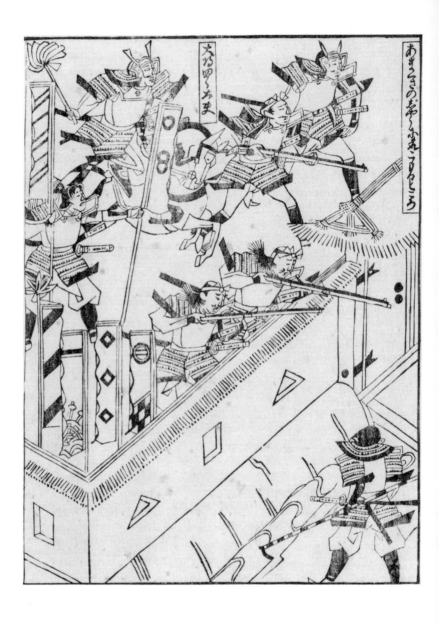

*Shirō rushes to lead the resistance as the shogunate's hosts storm
the castle of the Amakusa rebels.*

How Matsukura Lord Nagato Brought Ruin upon Himself

In times past Matsukura Lord Bungo was one of the principal councilors of Tsutsui Junkei of Yamato.[79] A man of much merit, he gained pre-eminence by several distinguished exploits and, his loyalty not remaining concealed from the world, was granted the fief of Shimabara. There he lived in all abundance of comfort until he passed on to the other world due to old age. His son and heir Matsukura Lord Nagato was granted succession in the fief without prejudice, and received countless other favors. He was quite steadfast in his attendance at Edo, and was never remiss in his service.

But one day his eye lit upon a fellow who appeared to have some cleverness in him, one of his musketeers; and he entrusted all his affairs to this man, and to him alone. The management of his fief (that goes without saying), but also the disposition of retainers whose families had served the house for generations—all was subjected to the orders of this one man. Now this fellow's particular talents lay solely in trucking for profits and in niggardliness; day and night he spent in conniving.

Quarrels soon arose, as could be expected. Some forty-five old cavaliers were displaced, and as a result the administration of the fief fell entirely into the hands of parvenus. From that time on he gained still more of the favor of his lord, until he could well imagine that his strength was as the strength of a thousand. There were some who lamented this state of affairs in the shadows, or signaled their discontent in secret—by a furtive tug at the friend's sleeve, a meaningful glance of the eye—but none were there that would intercede with him in all things. Or so I've heard. Such a state of affairs amounted to the devil's own plan: it was a sure omen for the downfall of the house.

Matsukura's calculating official lords it over the local peasantry.

How to Treat Subordinates,
Whether They Be of High or Low Degree

There are several ways of employing subordinates, whether they be of high or low degree. But the way that a ruler of deep wisdom chooses is to treat them whose families have served the house for generations as pedigreed swords of Masamune or Sadamune, those newly taken into his service as newly forged blades, and the retainers of lower degree as workmanlike short swords of Magoroku or Masatsune. Treated thus with much consideration, none will hold a grudge against the master. All will bear for him the deepest gratitude and never will depart from this feeling.

The wise ruler does not show any discrimination among his retainers, nor does he play favorites. But rather he treats all as his own children, with special regard to employ them according to the special qualifications of each. He does not pass down instructions after listening to one side only. But rather he acts with deep compassion and cordial feeling for all, thus conducting his affairs always with an easy mind. If this be the case, then his retainers will show complaisance in all things and prudence in their manner, will obey his regulations, and will not be addicted to excesses, thus fitting the statement, "Like lord like servant." In the siege of a castle or in a pitched battle they will never take a step backward but rather, obeying the whisk of their lord's command, they will strive to crush the enemy in the instant. And this is because they will remember in their hearts the lord's constant and repeated demonstrations of sympathy, which is at such times the insurance that none there be who become useless.

And here is how the ruler who is clever but only of median wisdom treats his subordinates. He holds their personalities up to the light and those whom he does not like, though they be individuals of long and distinguished service to the house, he puts aside as he would an old sword with dulled blade, so that they humble themselves before him and assent with him in all things. But the one (though he may only have come into service yesterday or today) who carries out all his orders promptly and without objection, who has an apt tongue, whom he deems more clever than the ordinary run—to him alone does he grant his favor, singling him out head and shoulders above the other retainers, so that no others dare even whisper an accusation into the lord's ear against him, no matter what occasion may arise. And therefore everyone, old retainer as well as parvenu, pays homage to this powerful figure, gathering at his gatefront as if it were a marketplace. To those who are on close terms with him he opens up his heart, treating them in friendly fashion. But those with whom he is on distant terms he tries to provoke, as the opportunity arises, to counter the opinion of the lord, of which he has made himself a prior estimate. Though flames of anger scorch the hearts of those grieved in this fashion, there is nothing they can do now but greet the foul situation with an even countenance. The higher the rank the more ingenuous the judgment—and therefore, if he puts on a good front and presents his intentions in a true-seeming light, his superior does not realize how much trouble he is causing on the side.

Among the many retainers, there are those who follow a rightful path and behave with profound discretion. But there are also many of those in the world who think that as long as they maintain the lord's favor nothing else matters. Making employ of retainers is quite like joining stones to build a wall. The big stones are piled on each other, and the small stones form the filling for the gaps. And so, according to the way the lord employs his retainers, each has his function, and none appears to lack the talent or the judgment necessary to his task. Matsukura Lord Nagato was of only average intelligence, and very slow in his reactions. Thus it was that he handed over the administration of his domains to a treacherous villain. Not one was there that would praise his conduct of affairs. Lord Nagato fell, deprived of his fief. And thus he fulfilled a foregone conclusion.

*   *   *   *   *

During this reign the Kirishitan religion has been cut down at its root and cast out of our land. Such must indeed have been the judgment of the Buddhas, Gods, and Bodhisattvas—and it is a blessing deserving universal gratitude, of proportion to render Mount Sumeru low and the blue ocean shallow in comparison. How can mere words and similes do justice to this favor!

But why was the outcome so fortunate? Japan is called the Land of the Gods. But it is also terrain where Buddha's Law is widely spread. It is traditional in the Three Countries that the Royal Sway, the Way of the Gods, and the Path of Buddha are like unto a tripod's legs: if one of them be broken off, then the sun and moon are fallen from the sky and the lantern is lost which lights up the gloomy night.

Barbarians from foreign lands came here, to spread their cursed doctrine and, despising the Buddhas and the Gods, to destroy them and do away with them, determined thereby to make of Japan a domain of devils. How wretched it was, how lamentable! Men of wisdom spent their days and nights in grief and sorrow over this. But then the Kirishitans were exterminated, without being allowed to grasp an inch of our soil, to stand on a foot of our land. And all the major and minor deities of our sixty and more provinces, all the Buddhas of the Three Worlds rejoiced thereat, extending their protection for ten thousand eternities and a myriad years.

The Empire is at peace, the land in tranquillity, the reign of longevity. The people partake of the virtue of the ruler and his subject princes. Verily, our age can be called another sainted reign of Engi, a golden age indeed.[80]

> In the sixteenth year of Kan'ei,
> *tsuchinoto u,*
> the eighth month,
> on a propitious day.

CHRISTIANS COUNTERED
by Suzuki Shōsan

I

According to the Kirishitan teachings, the Great Buddha named Deus is the Lord of Heaven and Earth and is the One Buddha, self-sufficient in all things. He is the Creator of Heaven and Earth and of the myriad phenomena. This Buddha made his entry into the world one thousand six hundred years ago in South Barbary, saving all sentient beings. His name is Jesus Christus. That other lands do not know him, worshipping instead the worthless Amida and Shaka, is the depth of stupidity. Thus they claim, as I have heard.

To counter, I reply: If Deus is the Lord of Heaven and Earth, and if he created the terrestrial domain and the myriad phenomena, then why has this Deus until now left abandoned a boundless number of countries without making an appearance? Ever since heaven and earth were opened up, the Buddhas of the Three Worlds in alternating appearance have endeavored to save all sentient beings, for how many thousands and tens of thousands of years![1] But meanwhile, in the end Deus has not appeared in countries other than South Barbary; and what proof is there that he did make an appearance of late, in South Barbary alone? If Deus were truly the Lord of Heaven and Earth, then it has been great inattention on his part to permit mere attendant Buddhas to take over country upon country which he personally created, and allow them to spread their Law and endeavor to save all sentient beings, from the opening up of heaven and earth down to the present day. In truth, this Deus is a foolscap Buddha!

And then there is the story that Jesus Christus upon making his appearance was suspended upon a cross by unenlightened fools of this lower world. Is one to call this the Lord of Heaven and Earth? Is anything more bereft of reason? This Kirishitan sect will not recognize the existence of the One Buddha of Original Illumination and Thusness.[2] They have falsely misappropriated one Buddha to venerate, and have come to this country to spread perniciousness and deviltry. They shall not escape Heaven's punishment for this offence! But many are the unenlightened who fail to see through their clumsy claims, who revere their teachings and even cast away their lives for them. Is this not a disgrace upon our country? Notorious even in foreign lands, lamentable indeed!

II

The direct way to Buddhahood for all sentient beings is the true import of the appearance of the Buddhas of the Three Worlds upon this impure earth.[3] For that reason it is said:[4]

> Direct pointing at the heart of man,
> Seeing into one's nature:
> the attainment of Buddhahood.

The World-Honored One[5] entered this world and accumulated merit through twelve years of austerities and mortifications, and on the eighth day of the Month of Wax,[6] looking up at the bright stars, he was enlightened to the True State of all elements. And then he descended out of the mountains and, after preaching the various scriptures—

> Touching the flower, he showed it
> to the disciples' assembly.
> And then the disciples all were silent:
> There was only the Venerable Kāśyapa
> whose face broke out in a subtle smile.

> And the World-Honored One said:
> "I have
> the exquisite, the wondrous gate
> to the Doctrine

of the Treasure of the Eye of the True Law,
the Wondrous Nirvana-Mind,
the True State or No State:

"Without dependence on words or letters,
a special transmission outside the scriptures.
I entrust it to you, Mahākāśyapa!"[7]

And from Kāśyapa it has been passed on to a direct line of disciples, and has been transmitted to Japan. Down to this day is preserved the meaning of transmission from mind to mind.

But the Kirishitan teachings concentrate on the view of actual existence, multiply remembrance, will, consciousness, and attachment, postulate a Creator of Heaven and Earth, pile karma onto the Wheel of Life, and take this to be the way to Buddhahood![8] And with such ill-contrived opinions they have come to this country and have ventured to oppose the True Law! It is no different from the swallow's matching his wings against the roc, from the firefly's debating his brightness with the moon.

III

That gods are esteemed and worshipped in Japan is a perversity. And the reason for it is because the Japanese know not Deus. Thus the Kirishitans claim, as I have heard.

To counter, I reply: Japan is the Land of the Gods. To be born in the Land of the Gods and refuse to adore and worship the gods is the ultimate of irreverence. "In subdued brilliance sharing this world of dust is the beginning of the tie [between Buddha and man]; the Eight Stages [of the Buddha's earthly life] and the Establishment of the Way are the end of all beneficial things."[9] Accordingly, the Buddhas have first appeared as gods and manifested their traces in this country; this is an expedient to pacify the mind of man and turn him to the True Way. The word "Buddhas" and the word "gods"—these have but the difference between water and waves. The One Buddha of Original Illumination and Thusness appears in transformation and pursues his work of salvation in accommodation with the mind of man. And thus, the mind which esteems and worships the gods is but acknowledging and worshipping this One Buddha.

A similar instance is the established rule which holds that to honor and serve the sovereign one must esteem his ministers and councilors and then, each according to his gradation, the military headmen and civil administrators also; and the people honor them down to the local magistrate and his assistant. All this is the process of honoring and serving the one superior. But the likes of the Kirishitan teachings would have one honor and serve the one superior without paying attention to his representatives! Do not the Kirishitans term this proper? Can such irreverence be tolerated?

IV

That the sun and moon are revered and worshipped in Japan is a perversity. They are but the lamps of the world; but the reason for this perverse worship is because the Japanese know not Deus. Thus the Kirishitans claim, as I have heard.

To counter, I reply: the human form has Yin and Yang for its base; the body is formed by the combination of the Four Great Elements.[10] The wheel of the sun is Yang incorporate; the wheel of the moon is Yin incorporate. How can this body of ours ever be maintained apart from Yin and Yang? Since Yin and Yang constitute the basis of us all, we can never worship them enough! Do not use water or fire, you who term Yin and Yang worthless!

The sun and moon are in the heavens and thus illuminate the world. This debt of gratitude is difficult to repay. Man has two eyes and thus illuminates his self. Is this not by virtue of the sun and moon? May the Kirishitans have their eyes crushed for calling worthless the worship of the sun and moon! Such is ignorance of truth, depth of stupidity indeed.

V

The Kirishitan sect, as I have heard, in general places high value on miraculous occurrences, claiming that they are testimonies to the glory of Deus. Contriving various sorts of trickery, they delude the people.

To counter, I reply: If miraculous occurrences are to be esteemed, then one should worship the King of Evil. Even the foxes and badgers of our own country work miraculous happenings. It is said that when Indra fought the asuras and these lost the battle, they hid inside the hollow of a lotus filament, and taking 84,000 of their cohorts along at that![11] Is one to honor suchlike miracles also?

But let us take up the subject of the Six Super-Powers. They are the Power of the Deva-Eye, the Power of the Deva-Ear, the Other-Mind Power, the Accumulated-Life Power, the Power of Flight, and the Evil-Extirpating Power.[12] The Power of the Deva-Eye is the power to see at a glance everything in the Greater Chiliocosm.[13] The Power of the Deva-Ear is the power to hear on the spot everything in the Greater Chiliocosm. The Other-Mind Power is the power to perceive clearly the innermost mind of another. The Accumulated-Life Power is the power to know the events of life in previous existences. The Power of Flight is the power to transport oneself freely to the heavens and beyond. These five powers are granted to the King of Evil and to infidels; but the Evil-Extirpating Power is not within the reach of the King of Evil or of infidels—it is Buddha-Wisdom which severs evil at the root. And yet there is nothing miraculous about the Six Super-Powers of the Buddhas. And one may say that there is nothing miraculous about the True Law. Those who do not understand this truth must have been deluded by the King of Evil or by infidels.

The Six Super-Powers of the Buddhas mean but the following. With the eyes to see shape, and be unhindered; with the ears to hear sound, and be unhindered; with the nose to smell odor, and be unhindered; with the tongue to taste flavor, and be unhindered; with the body to touch, and be unhindered; to reside in the elemental realm and be unhindered by the myriad elements, to be like the shade reflected in a mirror—such a mind, void and unhindered, one and undifferentiated, appertains to the six-super-powered, unimpeded Devotee of the Way. And he is also called bereft of specific character and bereft of remembrance. And therefore the scriptures teach: it is better to make offerings to a single no-minded Devotee of the Way than to make offerings to all the Buddhas of the Three Worlds.[14] Men who endeavor to practise the Buddha's Way devote themselves to the study of this path. They have no use at all for miracles.

VI

According to the Kirishitan teachings, animals do not possess a real soul. And accordingly, when their body dies, the soul dies as well. Human beings, however, have been endowed by Deus with a true soul. And therefore, though their body dies, the soul does not die: according to men's good or evil actions in this life, their souls are assigned pleasure or pain in the next. For those who have worked good, Deus has created *Paraiso*, a world of happiness inexhaustible; and to this world he summons them. But for those who have worked evil, he has created *Inferno*, a world of pain; into this place he thrusts them, to burden them with suffering. Thus they claim, as I have heard.

To counter, I reply: If Deus made such a careful distinction in creating the souls of animals and humans, then why did he fix evil-mindedness upon the human soul? Why thrust men's souls down into hell? For in that case it is entirely Deus' own doing to cast humans down into hell.

When the Tathagata Sakyamuni was dwelling on this earth, infidel sects were enjoying great prosperity in India. Their intelligence was wide, their wisdom great; they put forward various views and discoursed upon truth. And yet their doctrines —similar though they were to the Buddha's Law—were unclear to their own eyes and only amounted to sophistries.

The infidel Sāṁkhya school put forward the Twenty-Five Principles in analyzing the elements of the universe.[15] And the first is called the Profound Principle [of Prakṛti].[16] Before heaven and earth were yet separated, it was: unaffected by changes of fortune, not to be apprehended by perception or by intellectual insight. It is difficult to affix a name to this principle. Pressed for a label, one calls it the Profound Principle. It is permanent and not subject to transformation in the states of birth, continuation, change, and extinction.

The twenty-fifth principle is called the Principle of Puruṣa.[17] The unenlightened label it mind and call it soul. This principle also may be termed permanent. And the twenty-three principles in between are the states of the various transformations (changes of fortune, et cetera) of the finite world. These are called created elements.

When Puruṣa occasions differentiations between the states of long or short, square or round, the Profound Principle in motion manifests shapes. Accordingly, the process of transformation in the world of created elements depends upon the generation of mental activity by Puruṣa. When Puruṣa does not generate the various mental activities and is resolved into the Profound Principle in this fashion, then the process of transformation of created elements long ceases and the bliss of the noncreated state is of itself attained.[18] Though the material body is destroyed and vanishes, Puruṣa does not vanish; this may be compared to the house burning up while the owner exits.

By the use of such propositions they tried many ways of explicating the truth. But finally they extended reverence to the Tathagata and were directly enlightened to the Specific Nature.[19] And all without exception became disciples of Buddha. But the Kirishitans of our present day, failing entirely to reach even the level of the infidels' views, think that theirs is the True Law— frogs inside the well which delimits their universe.[20]

VII

Forty-nine years long the World-Honored One preached the most profound Law, and yet in the end he stated: "I have not taught a single word."[21] And that itself is the teaching designed to make known the Buddha-Nature directly. "I have not taught a single word"—the meaning does not come within the grasp of mental estimate. And therefore he described the teaching of the sutras as a finger pointing at the moon. The men of old said, indicating the Absolute Mind: with conscious mind it cannot be sought out, nor with no-mind attained; with words it cannot be reached, nor with quietude penetrated. Such is the teaching which has been passed on. Indeed, it does not come within the realm of verbal explanation!

The like is true of the appearance in this world of the Seven Buddhas: Vipaśyin, Śikhin, Viśvabhu, Krakucchanda, Kanakamuni, Kāśyapa, Sakyamuni. Even the Dharma of one of these Buddhas lasted many tens of millions of years; how much more boundless is the Dharma of all seven![22]

The appearance of the Tathagata Amida in this world was ten kalpas ago, and he was called Hōzō Biku. Amida is Sanskrit; in Chinese letters, we write it Muryōju, and translate as Infinite Life. *The Sutra of the Meditation on Amitayus* says:[23] "The body of the Buddha of Infinite Life is like unto a billion Yama-Heavens; its color is of the gold washed in the Jambu-Grove River. Between his brows he has a white hair; coiled beautifully in righthand revolution, it is like unto five Sumeru Mountains. The Buddha's eyes are like unto the waters of the Four Oceans, blue-white, bright and clear. His body emits variegated brilliance, like unto Mount Sumeru. The aureole of light surrounding this Buddha is like unto the ten milliard Triple-Thousand Greater Chiliocosms." How vivid and brilliant these words are! "His height is sixty billion nayutas, as many yojanas as there are sandgrains in the Ganges; the white hair between his brows is like unto five Sumeru Mountains, and his eyes are like unto the waters of the Four Oceans"—so it says. Can there be a greater Buddha than this? Even the Greater Chiliocosm measured against Amida's body must amount to less than the one strand of hair compared with the nine head of cattle!

Purity ascendant became heaven and turbidity descendant became earth; thus they separated into Yin and Yang. Heaven rules over Yang. Earth takes Yin for its substance. And thus, ever since the beginning of the world, all things which arose have had heaven for their father and earth for their mother: from the combination of Yin and Yang was born the universe and emanated the myriad phenomena. And all this by virtue of the One Buddha's power! In Zen, this One Buddha is called the Great One, or the One of Great Power. The poem of Wu-men says about the One of Great Power:[24]

> He raises his legs and
> Flying
> Treads over the Sea of Perfume.
>
> He lowers his head and
> Bowing
> Peers over the Four Dhyana Heavens.

And the various scriptures and commentaries all make similar report. The Buddha-Nature pervades the elemental realm and acts as lord over all sentient beings. And accordingly we are taught: "All sentient beings without exception contain the Buddha-Nature."[25] To use a parable: It is like the one moon in the heavens above reflecting in the myriad waters—in the ocean is one moon, and in every drop of dew is one moon also.

Mind is formless, but it brings to manifestation marvellous capabilities. It is in the eyes, and sees things. It is in the ears, and hears sounds. It is in the nose, and smells odors. It is in the mouth, and says things. It is in the hands, and grasps things. And it is in the feet, and walks.[26] When this mind becomes enlightened to the Buddha, it is Buddha. When this mind is deluded about the Buddha, it is an unenlightened fool. Accordingly, as an expedient to make known the Buddha-Nature in each individual self, many appellations are used: Original Aspect, Basal Locus, All-Encompassing Illumination, Buddha of the Victory of All-Penetrating Wisdom.[27] Dainichi, Yakushi, Kannon, Jizō Bosatsu, and so on—many are the different names, and yet the Buddha is not-two, the Law is not-two. When one considers the True State of all elements, the wind in the pines and the flow of the waters turn into Wonderful Melody. When one becomes enlightened to the identity of all elements, the grasses and the trees and all the terrestrial domains become Buddha.[28] And yet, these Bateren have never dreamed of the actuality of the direct attainment of Buddhahood; instead, they venerate the teachings of Jesus Christus. It is no different from hoarding fish eyes, taking them to be bright pearls.

VIII

The Buddha is the Great Physician. It is his vow to cure all sentient beings of the ill of delusion. When sentient beings believe and take advantage of this vow, the ills which stem from the Obstacles of Evil and of Karma cannot but be cured. But unenlightened fools, being unaware of the ill of delusion, are unable to make use of the medicine.[29]

What is the origin of this ill? To cleave to the notion that the self, this dream and phantasm, is real—that is the cause of the ill which day and night torments the mind. Covetousness, hatred, ignorance—the mental functions of the Three Poisons arise to torment the individual. And the root of all this is simply the concentration of thought upon the self. Even while prostrate upon the sickbed of the eighty-four thousand evils that have these Three Poisons for their seed, the unenlightened fools would nevertheless not recognize the truth and rather would love their ill.[30] But that is without question their own determined karma, the suffering of their entire span of life. And when they die, their delusions of permanence and attachment to this life turn into demons that vie with each other in the infliction of torments. Indeed, it is beyond description! At this time the Mountain of Death and the River of Three Crossings also make their appearance.[31] And the unenlightened fools who have suffered in life are afflicted like this even unto death. And all this stems from the mind's fall into delusion.

The fall into delusion means, first of all, the mind enjoying its own suffering and taking it for pleasure, ignorant of true pleasure. Second, it means the mind ignorant of the truth of impermanence, attached to this world, steeped in the idea of permanence. Third, it means the mind taken with a body stained with the Ten Evils and the Eight Sorrows,[32] bound with the fetters of evil, and nevertheless deeming this body free. Fourth, it is the mind ignorant of the fact that this body is unclean, and deeming it pure. In such fashion do errors arise.

Again and again I say: you must be totally unaware how impure is the body! The Five Organs and the Six Intestines,[33] the sweat exuded from hairy pores, feces and urine, wax from the ears, snot from the nose—not one of these is clean. Reflect upon this body which we love, look upon it once again!

To make known this truth, the View of Impurity was estab-lished.[34] Let those who wish to practice the View of Impurity take up their dwelling alongside the graves that hold the multitude of corpses! This is the teaching which warns: sever perverse attachment to this foul flesh! Cut all connection with such a mind!

As long as mind lives there is suffering and pleasure. When mind vanishes all hindrance ceases. With mind, know Mind! The difference between Buddha and all sentient beings is like unto the difference of water and ice. When the remembrance of evil congeals into scum, that is like water turning into ice. When all remembrance is extinguished and vanishes, and when hindrance ceases, that is like ice melting and turning into water. And therefore the scriptures say:[35]

> The Three Realms are but One Mind:
> Outside of Mind there is no other Dharma.

> Mind, Buddha, and all sentient beings:
> These three are without difference.

But the Kirishitans are utterly ignorant of what this One Mind is.

IX

The Bateren who have come in recent years have had no fear at all of Heaven's Way. They have wilfully made up a Creator of Heaven and Earth, and have destroyed shrines of the gods and temples of the Buddhas. They nurture the plot to annex our land to South Barbary, and to that end they have deluded the people with all sorts of empty lies. Some thieving bonzes of our own country have thrown their lot in with these foreigners and, taking the name of Bateren or Iruman, have dragged a great many people down into perdition. The Buddhas of our country are not Buddhas, the sun and the moon are to be despised, the gods are nonexistent; so they claim. Their offence is grave in the extreme. The punishment of Heaven, the punishment of the Buddhas, the punishment of the gods, the punishment of man—not one of these shall they escape! All, all shall be suspended by the rope and killed! Their followers' hearts also brim with this offence. And accordingly a countless number have perished—how many thousands upon tens of thousands! This all is the fruit of deviltry; it is not only official determination that has stamped them out.

In fraud they have misappropriated the worship of the Way of Heaven, have flaunted falsehoods, and have dragged an untold number of people down into hell. By their treacherous villainies, their foul atrocities, by their own works they have perfected their own destruction. This is plain before everyone's eyes.

To a true disciple of the Buddha it is clear that it is through the Curse of Heaven that even one of these Bateren should perish. But a great many Bateren and a countless number of our land's Kirishitan religionists have met with the punishment of death. What manner of curse could this be?

No matter how often they come here, as long as the Way of Heaven prevails they will all, all come to their own destruction. No doubt of it! Keep this fact in mind, keep it in mind.

END

I pray that the merit of this
Spread out to reach everyone;

That we and all sentient beings
All together accomplish Buddha's Way.[36]

In the second year of Kanbun,
the second month,
on a propitious day.

Tsutsumi Rokuzaemon

ABBREVIATIONS
NOTES TO THE TEXT
NOTES TO THE TRANSLATIONS

Abbreviations

Cartas.   *Cartas qve os Padres e Irmãos da Companhia de Iesus escreuerão dos Reynos de Iapão & China aos da mesma Companhia da India, & Europa, des do anno de 1549. atè o de 1580.* Nellas se conta o principio, socesso, & bondade da Christandade daquellas partes, & varios costumes, & falses ritos da gentilidade. Impressas por mandado do Reuerendissimo em Christo Padre dom Theotonio de Bragança Arcepispo d'Euora. Impressas com licença & approuação dos SS. Inquisidores & do Ordinario. Em Euora por Manoel de Lyra. Anno de M.D.XCVIII. 2 vols. in one.

GJ.   Frois, Luis, SJ, *Die Geschichte Japans (1549–1578),* tr. G. Schurhammer and E. A. Voretzsch (Leipzig: Asia Major, 1926).

KK.   *Kirishitan kenkyū* (Kirishitan studies), published since 1942 by the Kirishitan Bunka Kenkyūkai (Tokyo: Yoshikawa Kōbunkan since 1959).

MN.   *Monumenta Nipponica* (Tokyo: Sophia University, 1938–).

NST 25. *Kirishitan sho, Hai-Ya sho* (Kirishitan and Anti-Christian texts), ed. Ebisawa Arimichi, H. Cieslik, Doi Tadao, and Ōtsuka Mitsunobu, Nihon Shisō Taikei 25 (Tokyo: Iwanami, 1970).

SP.   Frois, Luis, SJ, *Segunda Parte da Historia de Japam que trata das couzas, que socedarão nesta V. Provincia da Hera de 1578 por diante, começado pela Conversão del Rey de Bungo, (1578–1582),* ed. João do Amaral Abranches Pinto and Okamoto Yoshitomo (Tokyo: Edição da Sociedade Luso-Japonesa [Nippo Kyōkai], 1938).

SPPY.   Ssu-pu pei-yao.

SPTK.   Ssu-pu ts'ung-k'an.

Taishō.   *Taishō shinshū daizōkyō // The Tripitaka in Chinese,* ed. Takakusu Junjirō, 85 vols. (Tokyo: Taishō Issaikyō Kankōkai, 1924–1932).

VMJ.   Schütte, Josef Franz, SJ, *Valignanos Missionsgrundsätze für Japan* (Rome: Edizioni di Storia e Letteratura). I. Band I. Teil: *Das Problem (1573–1580),* 1951. I. Band II. Teil: *Die Lösung (1580–1582),* 1958.

YNT.   *Yasokaishi Nihon tsūshin* (Jesuit relations from Japan), ed. and trans. Murakami Naojirō and Watanabe Yosuke, 2 vols., Ikoku Sōsho (Tokyo: Yūshōdō, 1966 revised reprint).

Notes to the Text

Introduction

1. The text of the final Sakoku Edict is most conveniently found in *Shiryō ni yoru Nihon no ayumi: Kinsei-hen*, ed. Ōkubo Toshiaki, Kodama Kōta, Yanai Kenji, and Inoue Mitsusada (Tokyo: Yoshikawa Kōbunkan, 1963, 9th printing), pp. 129–130. The date, Kan'ei 16/7/5, corresponds to 4 August 1639. I have found the conversion of lunar calendar dates necessary for the sake of coordination between the Japanese and the Western sources upon which large parts of my study equally depend; and I have relied on Paul Yachita Tsuchihashi SJ, *Japanese Chronological Tables* (Tokyo: Sophia University Press, 1952). The Julian calendar is followed until 4 October 1582; the next day is 15 October according to the Gregorian system. For a brief consideration of the Shimabara rebellion's Christian flag, see Fernando Gutiérrez SJ, "A Survey of Nanban Art," *The Southern Barbarians: The First Europeans in Japan*, ed. Michael Cooper SJ (Tokyo and Palo Alto: Kodansha International, 1971), pp. 170–171. There is a large illustration on p. 161.

2. Padre João Rodriguez Girão SJ, Nagasaki, 15 March 1616; quoted in C. R. Boxer, *The Christian Century in Japan* (Berkeley: University of California Press, 1951), p. 331.

3. A good introductory discussion of the role of Buddhism is Kashiwabara Yūsen, Yamamoto Takeo, and Yanai Kenji, "Bakuhan taisei no seiritsu to shūkyō no tachiba," *Taikei Nihonshi sōsho*, XVIII, *Shūkyōshi*, ed. Kawasaki Yasuyuki and Kasahara Kazuo (Tokyo: Yamakawa Shuppansha, 1964), 281–326.

The *goningumi* were not created specifically for the anti-Christian purpose, but were intimately associated with it. See Hubert Cieslik SJ, "Die Goningumi im Dienste der Christenüberwachung," *MN*, 7.1/2:102–155 (January 1951).

Copious examples of the wide range of contracts requiring assurances that the party entering service was not a Christian are given in Ishii Ryōsuke, *Zoku Edo jidai manpitsu: Edo no yūjo sono ta* (Tokyo: Inoue Shobō, 1961); see particularly chs. xii–xvi, pp. 89–171.

4. On the applicability of Neo-Confucianism to the Tokugawa order, see the classic analysis by Maruyama Masao, *Nihon seiji shisōshi kenkyū* (Tokyo: Tōkyō Daigaku Shuppankai, 1962, 9th printing), pp. 7–44 and 195–207.

5. Kitajima Masamoto, *Edo jidai*, Iwanami Shinsho 332 (Tokyo: Iwanami, 1958), pp. 63–64. For illustrations of the changing attitudes, see Ishige Tadashi, "Sengoku/Azuchi-Momoyama jidai no rinri shisō: Tentō shisō no tenkai," *Nihon ni okeru rinri shisō no tenkai*, ed. Nihon Shisōshi Kenkyūkai (Tokyo: Yoshikawa Kōbunkan, 1965), pp. 141–168.

6. The Christian definition of *Tentō* is given in the *VOCABVLARIO DA LINGOA DE IAPAM com adeclaração em Portugues* published in Nagasaki in 1603–4; facsimile edition prepared by Doi Tadao, *Nippo jisho* (Tokyo: Iwanami, 1960), p. 509: "*Tentŏ. Tenno michi.* Caminho, ou ordẽ, & prouidencia do ceo. Commummente chamamos ja a Deos por este nome.

Postoque os gẽtios não parece que atinauão mais que com o primeiro sentido.— —The way, or order, & providence of heaven. Now we commonly call God by this name. Although it does not seem that the pagans have hit upon more than the first meaning." Ishige Tadashi, p. 163, cites the interesting example of a compact involving the Christian daimyo Ōmura Sumitada, who in the anathema clause vows to observe the terms or lose the grace of Divine providence, *Tentō no garasa*.

7. See below, *Deus Destroyed*, pp. 282–283.

8. See below, *Deceit Disclosed*, pp. 303–304.

9. For one example, see *Nanbanji kōhaiki*, ed. Hiyane Antei, Kirishitan Bunko, II (Tokyo: Keiseisha, 1926), 2–3.

10. Some references give 1640 as the year of Shigenari's appointment, but it dates to Kan'ei 18/9/20 (24 October 1641); *Tokugawa jikki*, III, ed. Kuroita Katsumi, Kokushi Taikei, XL (Tokyo: Yoshikawa Kōbunkan, 1964), 238.

11. Ienaga Saburō, "Waga kuni ni okeru Bukki ryōkyō ronsō no tetsugakushiteki kōsatsu," *Chūsei Bukkyō shisōshi kenkyū*, 4th ed. (Kyoto: Hōzōkan, 1963), pp. 112–116.

12. The letter to the Viceroy of the Indies is dated Tenshō 19/7/25 (12 September 1591); text in *Shiryō ni yoru*, pp. 56–57; translation in *Sources of Japanese Tradition*, ed. Ryusaku Tsunoda, Wm. Theodore DeBary, and Donald Keene (New York: Columbia University Press, 1959, 2nd printing), pp. 325–327. The date of Sūden's labors is Keichō 18/12/22–23 (31 January–1 February 1614); text in *Shiryō ni yoru*, p. 124.

13. Cited by Kitajima, *Edo jidai*, p. 64. The first statement is attributed to Seika by his disciple Hayashi Razan: *Seika sensei no gyōjō* (Seika's way of life), *Razan sensei bunshū*, ed. Kyōto Shisekikai, II (Kyoto: Heian Kōkogakkai, 1918), 20. The second is from Seika's *Kana shōri* (The Principle in the Nature; a *kana* treatise), *Fujiwara Seika shū*, II (Tokyo: Kokumin Seishin Bunka Kenkyūjo, 1939), 408. Seika caps this dictum with a sentence on the corruption of the Buddhist clergy written in terms of disapproval scarcely less harsh than those the Christians used.

14. *CONTEMPTVS mundi jenbu. CORE YO VO ITOI, IESV CHRIStono gocŏxeqiuo manabi tatematçuru michiuo voxiyuru qiŏ.* (Contempt of the world; complete. Being a scripture that teaches the way to despise the world and imitate the merits of Jesus Christ.) NIPPON IESVSNO COMPANHIA no Collegio nite Superiores no goguegiuo motte coreuo fanni firaqu mono nari. Toqini goxuxxeno nenqi. 1596.

For the bibliographical details, see Johannes Laures SJ, *Kirishitan Bunko: A Manual of Books and Documents on the Early Christian Mission in Japan*, MN Monographs 5, 3rd ed. (Tokyo: Sophia University Press, 1957), no. 16, pp. 51–54. This text is in Roman letters. Two copies are extant, at the Bodleian Library and at the Biblioteca Ambrosiana in Milan. Photographic copies are available at Sophia University and at the Tenri Library. An abridged version in Japanese characters is: *CONTEMPTVS MVNDI. MIACI EX OFFICINA FARADA ANTONII.* Cum facultate ordinarij, et Superiorum. Anno 1610. The latter is the text published with a critical introduction by Shinmura Izuru and Hiragi Gen'ichi in *Kirishitan bungakushū*, I, Nihon Koten Zensho (Tokyo: Asahi Shinbun-sha, 1957), 171–390. Described in Laures, *Kirishitan Bunko*, no. 32, pp. 77–79.

15. Inoue Mitsusada, *Introduction to Japanese History—Before the Meiji Restoration*, Series on Japanese Life and Culture, III (Tokyo: Kokusai Bunka Shinkokai, 1962), 81.

16. The number of Christian martyrs in Early Modern Japan is impossible to determine with any precision. There were certainly more than three thousand; and Johannes Laures, counting those who were executed as well as those who lost their lives for other reasons directly connected with the persecution, arrives at the number 4,045 of those who "in the true sense of the word became martyrs for the sake of Christ." Laures' scrupulous calculations, presented in "Die Zahl der Christen und Martyrer im alten Japan," *MN*, 7.1/2:84–101 (January 1951), do not yet exhaust the sources. Also see J. F. Schütte SJ, *Introductio ad Historiam Societatis Jesu in Japonia, 1549–1650* (Rome: Institutum Historicum Soc. Jesu, 1968), pp. 435–446. For the number of Christians in Japan at a given time during the "Christian Century," see the tables in *Introductio*, pp. 428–433. For instance, a relation sent to the King of Spain and Portugal, and by him to the Pope, claims that 500,000 baptized Christians were living in Japan in November 1614, when most of the missionaries were forced to leave the country. That figure may be an exaggeration, for a carefully itemized list composed in 1609 gives the number of 222,000 souls under the care of the Jesuits in Japan that year. When those under the charge of other pastors are included, 300,000 appears as a reasonable rough estimate for the peak, the first decade of the seventeenth century. The country's total population was between twenty and twenty-five million, so that the Christians may have constituted somewhat more than one percent.

Chapter 1 : Attitudes of Entry

1. *Epistolae S. Francisci Xaverii aliaque eius scripta*, ed. Georg Schurhammer SJ and Josef Wicki SJ, II, Monumenta Historica Societatis Iesu 68 (Rome: Monumenta Historica Soc. Iesu, 1945), no. 90, 186; Kagoshima, 5 November 1549, to the Jesuits of Goa.

2. This estimate of Cabral's knightliness was made by the Bishop of Macao, Melchior Carneiro SJ, the contrast being with the *villein* P. Organtino Gnecchi-Soldo; *VMJ*, I-1, 250. Schütte gives an extensive critique of Cabral in *VMJ*, I-1, ch. iii, 237–313. Matsuda Kiichi deals with Cabral's approach to Japan in *Kinsei shoki Nihon kankei Nanban shiryō no kenkyū* (Tokyo: Kazama Shobō, 1967), pp. 609–644. My criticism echoes Valignano's; see *VMJ*, I-1, 322. *VMJ* is cited by permission of Edizioni di Storia e Letteratura, Rome.

3. Cabral to P. João Alvarez SJ, Portuguese Assistant in Rome; Goa, 10 December 1596, cited extensively in *VMJ*, I-1, 308–311.

4. See below, *Deus Destroyed*, "An Evening's Conversation."

5. Valignano to General SJ, Usuki, 27 October 1580; original Spanish text in *VMJ*, I-2, 487–494; extensive German citation in *VMJ*, I-1, 322–325 and 333–335. Cabral is said to operate without consultation but with much force (*con mucho imperio*); *VMJ*, I-2, 488.

6. Valignano to General SJ, Goa, 23 November 1595; cited in *VMJ*, I-1, 321. There may be some overstatement in Valignano's retrospective account. If Cabral had truly prevented the Japanese from learning Portuguese or Latin, and if the Portuguese had been rendered unable to learn Japanese, then no communication would have been possible between shepherds and flock, or only that of the most primitive sort. The very fact of the mission's quantitative success belies the blunt allegation. The problem is resolved by the recognition of Valignano's extreme eagerness to develop formal structures, and of his dismay at Cabral's subjectivism.

7. *Tratado Em q̃ se contem M^(to) susinta e abreuiadamente algũas contradisões & diferencas de custumes Antre agente de Europa e esta prouincia de Japão* . . . f^(to) Em canzusa aos 14 de Junho de 1585 Annos—. Published with a critical introduction and German translation by Josef Franz Schütte SJ: *Kulturgegensätze Europa-Japan (1585), MN* Monographs 15 (Tokyo: Sophia University, 1955). An annotated Japanese translation by Okada Akio is included in Volume XI of the Dai Kōkai Jidai Sōsho series: *Nichiō bunka hikaku* (Tokyo: Iwanami, 1965), pp. 495–636. "Topsyturvydom" is Okada's apt word.

8. Cited in *VMJ*, I-1, 364, from Valignano's *Summario de las cosas que pertenecen a la Provincia de la India Oriental y al govierno della,* second version, original draft; October 1579, Shimo. This draft registers the full force of the *Visitator*'s initial impression of Japan; in the final text, completed by August 1580, many of the most vivid passages had been struck. (The first version of the "Indian *Summario*" was composed in Goa in November–December 1577.)

9. *VMJ*, I-2, 65; *Introductio,* pp. 564 and 693–708.

10. Text in Ebisawa Arimichi and Matsuda Kiichi, *Porutogaru Evora shinshutsu byōbu monjo no kenkyū* (Tokyo: Natsume-sha, 1963), pp. 156–169. At the time he edited the *byōbu* text, Ebisawa held that Organtino (who was a representative of Valignano's school of thought) was the source of the Instructions and Azuchi their locale; *Evora byōbu,* pp. 55–56. Three years later, following Matsuda, he had switched to the conjecture that Valignano was the instructor, and the place Usuki; Ebisawa, *Nihon Kirishitan shi* (Tokyo: Hanawa Shobō, 1966), pp. 241 and 257, n. 8.

11. *Evora byōbu,* p. 164. My citations are commonly identical with the form of the original; no attempt is made to correct the erratic spelling of the source or to *sic* the purist onto spots which might offend him; he will at any rate know what the proper orthography is. In some phrases there would be more (!) corrections than words.

12. *Evora byōbu,* pp. 166–167.

13. See below, *Deus Destroyed,* "An Evening's Conversation."

14. *ARTE DA LINGOA DE IAPAM* COMPOSTA PELLO Padre Ioão Rodriguez Portugues da Cõpanhia de IESV diuidida em tres LIVROS. COM LICENÇA DO ORDINARIO, E SVPERIORES EM Nangasaqui no Collegio de Iapão da Companhia de IESV Anno. 1604. (The colophon is dated 1608.) A facsimile edition has been published by Shima Shōzō: *Rodorigesu Nihon daibunten* (Tokyo: Bunka Shobō Hakubunsha, 1969). There is a meticulously prepared Japanese translation by Doi Tadao: *Nihon daibunten* (Tokyo: Sanseidō, 1955).

15. Valignano to General SJ, Goa, 23 November 1595; cited in *VMJ*, I-1, 327.

16. Cabral to General SJ, Kuchinotsu, 30 August 1580; *VMJ*, I-2, 497–498. Compare Frois, *SP*, ch. x, "How the army of Bungo was destroyed by the King of Sacuma," pp. 64–72.

17. In discussing the daimyo institution I draw upon the schemata of John Whitney Hall, *e.g.* the outline presented in "Foundations of the Modern Japanese Daimyo," *The Journal of Asian Studies,* 20.3: 317–329 (May 1961), reprinted in *Studies in the Institutional History of Early Modern Japan,* ed. Hall and Marius B. Jansen (Princeton: Princeton University Press, 1968), pp. 65–77. For a specific consideration of the Ōtomo case, see the two articles by Toyama Mikio: "Kyūshū ni okeru daimyō ryōkoku no keisei: Ōtomo-uji o chūshin to shite," *Nihon rekishi,* 101: 27–34 (November 1956); "Shugo daimyō to shite no Ōtomo-uji no seikaku ni tsuite: kashindan hensei katei o shu to shite mitaru," *Hisutoria,* 18: 40–55 (June 1957). There is a biography of

Ōtomo Sōrin, but it is the work of an amateur: Hakusui Kōji (pseud. for Endō Tsunehisa), *Kirishitan daimyō Ōtomo Sōrin* (Tokyo: Shunjūsha, 1970).

The fortunes of the House of Ōtomo deserve much further study. Not only will the scholar find the topic of this provincial power structure fascinating; he will be blessed with a singular abundance of sources which have been published but not yet evaluated. There is a wealth of materials on the Ōtomo in the various multivolume compilations issued by Kyushu prefectures in the past decade and a half (*Ōita-ken shiryō* and *Kumamoto-ken shiryō* are but the most obvious examples). Military chronicles also provide a plethora of information (or, as the case may be, romantic misinformation). The most notable of them are assembled in *Ōita-ken kyōdo shiryō shūsei*, ed. Kakimoto Kotoo, 2 vols. (Ōita: Ōita-ken Kyōdo Shiryō Kankōkai, 1936–1938). Above all, there is the splendid labor of love of Takita Manabu, himself a descendant of a collateral family of the Ōtomo, who over a period of three decades compiled and issued a massive series of documents dealing with the house, most of it privately published:

(1) *Ōtomo shiryō*, 2 vols. (Ōita: Kin'yōdō Shoten, 1937–1938);
(2) *Hennen Ōtomo shiryō*, 2 vols. (Tokyo: Fuzanbō, 1942–1946);
(3) *Zoku Ōtomo shiryō*, 6 vols. (Vol. I, Beppu Daigaku-kai; the rest privately published, Ōita, 1955–1956);
(4) *Zoku hennen Ōtomo shiryō*, 10 vols. (Ōita, privately published, 1956–1959);
(5) *Zōho teisei hennen Ōtomo shiryō*, 30 vols. (Ōita, privately published, 1962–1969).

18. Note the remarkable example of Documents 349 and 350, *Ōtomo shiryō*, I, 259–260. Sōrin exempts his vassals, the Tamura, from their corvée obligations and specifically grants them the right of no-entry and freedom from interference in internal affairs (*kendan funyūken*). The year of issue is unclear; but Takita Manabu in commenting upon the documents' extraordinary character notes that they date to a time when Sōrin's power was at its zenith. For a *sengoku daimyō* such concessions surely meant a crying anachronism.

19. On the provenance of the Hekki Tachibana and their connection with the Ōtomo, see Fujino Tamotsu, *Bakuhan taiseishi no kenkyū* (Tokyo: Yoshikawa Kōbunkan, 1961), pp. 613–618.

20. *GJ*, p. 199.

21. Concerning the baptism of Sebastião, see *GJ*, pp. 468–469, and cf *VMJ*, I-1, 289.

Frois tells the story "How the King repudiated Izabel, and took another for his wife, whom he made hear the sermons, and be baptized, and the name Julia was given her" in *SP*, ch. ii, pp. 7–14. The appellation "perversa Jzabel" will be found in *SP*, p. 155. The Jesuit sources depict Sōrin's first wife as an unregenerate harpy, with only the occasional and perfunctory sigh: "May God give her the light so that she know Him." Typical is Frois' statement (to Cabral, October 1578; *Cartas*, I, 432): "Of Iesabel we have the news that she threw a fit of choler, and was incensed in the extreme, when she found out that the prince ordered a chapel to be made so close to where she resided." Frois' spelling is erratic, yet it is clear from the characterization that the intended cognomen is Jezebel, not Isabel, and might as well have been Xanthippe. On Sōrin's marital problems, see Kataoka Chizuko, "Ōtomo Sōrin no kon'in mondai," *Kirishitan Bunka Kenkyūkai kaihō*, 11.1: 19–35 (December 1968). On his baptism, see *SP*, ch. iii, pp. 15–24.

22. See for instance *Ōtomo-ki* (Ōtomo chronicle), *Ōita-ken kyōdo shiryō shūsei*, II, 268–282.

23. Dated [Tenshō 8]/2/16 (1 March 1580), in *Ōtomo shiryō*, II, no. 89, 56–66. Also included in *Ōtomo kōhaiki* (The rise and fall of the Ōtomo), *Ōita-ken kyōdo shiryō shūsei*, I, *Senki-hen* (Military chronicles), 335–343.

24. Yamaga Sokō, *Shinpen Buke jiki* (Tokyo: Shin Jinbutsu Ōrai-sha, 1969), pp. 909–911.

25. See below, *Deus Destroyed*, First Step.

26. *SP*, ch. xiv, "How the Prince of Bungo began to falter in his intentions, and to distance himself from the Church, and to be one with the enemies," pp. 89–95; and ch. xvi, "How there arose the persecution against the Church after the Prince was all spent in vices, and Idolatries, and zeal against conversion," pp. 101–112.

27. Yoshimune's last hurrah is treated in several chronicles included in *Ōita-ken kyōdo shiryō shūsei*, II, 770–842.

28. *GJ*, pp. 367–375. The patents were Nobunaga's *shuinjō* dated Eiroku 12/4/8 (24 April 1569), and the *seisatsu* of Shogun Yoshiaki, Nobunaga's protégé.

29. *GJ*, p. 398. Frois takes the text from his own letter to Figueiredo, Miyako, 12 July 1569; *Cartas*, I, 274v; *YNT*, II, 58.

30. *GJ*, pp. 372–373.

31. *GJ*, p. 425.

32. See Laures, *Nobunaga und das Christentum*, *MN* Monographs 10 (Tokyo: Sophia University Press, 1950), pp. 33–42.

33. *GJ*, pp. 152–153. See also Almeida to the Irmãos of India, 17 November 1563; *Cartas*, I, 118–131.

34. *VMJ*, I-1, 291–292. Frois treats "the conversion of Yoshisada Dom André, the Yakata of Takaku in the realm of Hizen, and his personal qualities" in *GJ*, ch. cviii, pp. 473–477.

35. *SP*, ch. xix, "Of the conversion of Arimandono: and else that occurred in Tacacu," pp. 120–132.

36. Frois treats the "further things that happened in this area: and of the assistance given him by the P͞e Vizitador" in *SP*, ch. xx, pp. 132–139. Cf. p. 133: Valignano "ordered as well that succor be given the fortresses that were under fire, provisioning them with victuals, and some silver, as much as he could, and also provisioning them with lead, and saltpetre whereof he had laid in a good stock from the *nao* toward this effect, and expending in these matters close to six hundred cruzados." The *nao* was the Great Ship of Dom Leonel de Brito, on which Valignano had first arrived in Japan. We note that the ship had departed on its return journey to Macao by the end of December 1579. Valignano's influence had caused it to call at Arima's harbor Kuchinotsu in the first place. Compare *VMJ*, I-1, 404–407.

37. Valignano to General SJ, Goa, 23 November 1595; cited in *VMJ*, I-1, 328.

38. *GJ*, p. 232.

Chapter 2:
The Christian Attempt at an Ethical Synthesis

1. "Bateren" is the period's Japanese approximation of the word "Padre," as is "Kirishitan" of *Christam* or *Christão*, the Portuguese for "Christian." The original exotic value of such usages is apparent, and I usually retain

them in my translations. "Kirishitan" is standard in modern Japanese historiography treating the period, the specific character of the topic being apparent in the practice: a Kirishitan is a Christian of Sengoku-Edo Japan. The Kirishitan terminology absorbed a whole series of Portuguese and Latin words. The most convenient list is in João Rodriguez Tçuzzu, *ARTE DA LINGOA DE IAPAM*, f. 179–179v; *Nihon daibunten*, pp. 642–645.

2. I cite approximately 20 percent of the speech, which is contained in *GJ*, pp. 337–340. Sanga Hōki no Kami Yoriteru was baptized in 1564 by Padre Gaspar Vilela, after being instructed by Irmão Lourenço. On the Sanga family, see Matsuda Kiichi, *Nanban shiryō no kenkyū*, pp. 645–682.

3. "Día de nuestra Señora de Agosto año de 1549": Xavier to the Jesuits of Goa, Kagoshima, 5 November 1549; *Epistolae*, II, no. 90, 185. Xavier's European companions were Padre Cosme de Torres SJ and Irmão João Fernandes SJ.

The most recent comprehensive study of Xavier's activity in Japan is by Paul Aoyama Gen SVD, *Die Missionstätigkeit des hl. Franz Xaver in Japan aus japanischer Sicht*, Studia Instituti Missiologici Societatis Verbi Divini Nr. 10 (St. Augustin/Siegburg: Steyler Verlag, 1967). On the Saint's stay in Kagoshima, see Aoyama, "Zabieru taizaiki no Kagoshima," *KK*, 13:51–89 (1970).

4. On Yajirō and his meeting with Xavier, see particularly the *Historia da Igreja do Japão* of João Rodriguez Tçuzzu, trans. and ed. Doi Tadao et al., *Nihon kyōkai shi*, II, Dai Kōkai Jidai Sōsho X (Tokyo: Iwanami, 1970), pt. 3, chs. vi–vii, 295–314. The Portuguese edition by João do Amaral Abranches Pinto (Macao: Noticias de Macau, 1954–1955) unfortunately covers only the first two parts of the work.

The name of Xavier's companion is sometimes given as Anjirō; but Rodriguez specifically states that "Angero" is mistaken and "Yajirŏ" correct (*Nihon kyōkai shi*, II, 296). Diego Pacheco SJ gives 1544 as the date of his departure from Japan on a Portuguese ship; "The Europeans in Japan, 1543–1640," *The Southern Barbarians: The First Europeans in Japan*, ed. Michael Cooper SJ, p. 36.

5. *GJ*, p. 3, quoting Cosme de Torres to the Jesuits of Portugal, Goa, 25 January 1549; *Cartas*, I, 5.

6. See Xavier's letter to Dom João III, King of Portugal, Malacca, 20 June 1549; *Epistolae*, II, no. 83, 116–119.

7. To Padre Simon Rodrigues in Portugal; *Epistolae*, II, no. 79, 71.

8. Schurhammer in *Das Kirchliche Sprachproblem in der Japanischen Jesuiten-mission des 16. und 17. Jahrhunderts* (Tokyo: Deutsche Gesellschaft für Natur- und Völkerkunde Ostasiens, 1928; "Mitteilungen," Vol XXIII) has published sources dealing explicitly with Xavier's use of the term "Dainichi" and with the subsequent problems of a Kirishitan terminology. The confusion caused by a whole series of "dangerous words" seems, at least initially, to have been substantial; see pp. 66–75.

9. Schurhammer, *Sprachproblem*, pp. 27–29, cites Almeida's original text. The published version of Almeida's letter to his Jesuit confrères, 25 October 1562, *Cartas*, I, 105–105v, omits the passage dealing with Dainichi.

10. *GJ*, p. 15.

11. Schurhammer, *Sprachproblem*, p. 30, cites a letter of P. Camillo Constantio SJ to General SJ (Macao, 25 December 1618) to the effect that "Dainichi" was a common contemporary circumlocution for the phallus. Presumably the derivation is mudric: *kongōken*, the "wisdom-fist." Schurhammer's gloss on Xavier's own account of his Yamaguchi experience best

describes what must have been the Saint's mental state when he was enlightened to the meaning: "Xaverius stupefactus." Cochin, 29 January 1552, to the Jesuits of Europe; *Epistolae*, II, no. 96, 266, n. 57.

12. *GJ*, p. 10; Yamaguchi, 1550. For Xavier's own words on the language difficulty, see *Epistolae*, II, no. 90, 201; Kagoshima, 5 November 1549, to the Jesuits of Goa: "May it please our Lord God to give us the tongue so that we be able to speak of the things of God, for then we shall reap much fruit with his aid and grace and favor. Now we are like statues among them."

13. *GJ*, p. 6; *Epistolae*, II, no. 96, 260; *Epistolae*, II, no. 96, 266.

14. Valignano, *Historia del Principio y Progresso de la Compañía de Jesús en las Indias Orientales,* ed. Josef Wicki SJ, Bibliotheca Instituti Historici S.I. 2 (Rome: Institutum Historicum S.I., 1944), pp. 167–168. This book is commonly known as *Historia Indica*. Part One, written in Spanish, concentrates upon the role of Saint Francis Xavier, and was composed in Japan, 1580–1581. Part Two, written in Portuguese, was composed in Cochin, 1583.

The question of Xavier's relations with the Shimazu has been the subject of some debate. Aoyama Gen attempts to shed a more favorable light on Takahisa's intentions: *Missionstätigkeit*, pp. 82–91; "Zabieru taizaiki," pp. 75–83; "Zabieru no Kagoshima jikyo ni tsuite," *Kirishitan Bunka Kenkyūkai kaihō*, 11.2/3: 52–60 (February 1969). Also see Tanaka Tomoe, "Shimazu Takahisa no Kirishitan kinsei ni tsuite," *Kirishitan Bunka Kenkyūkai kaihō*, 10.1: 1–22 (September 1967).

15. The emperor was Go-Nara. Xavier's own account is in *Epistolae*, II, no. 96, 261–262. See also *GJ*, p. 13, and *Historia Indica*, pp. 171–175; cf. Matsuda, *Nanban shiryō no kenkyū*, pp. 541–565.

16. *GJ*, p. 14. See *Epistolae*, II, no. 96, 262–263, for the measure of Ōuchi's return largesse: "He gave us a monastery after the fashion of a college, for us to stay therein." The visit took place at the end of April 1551. Xavier appeared as the ambassador of the Portuguese Governor of the Indies, Dom Garcia de Sá, and also presented a parchment from the Bishop of Goa, Dom João de Albuquerque. On the episode and its ramifications, see Aoyama, *Missionstätigkeit*, pp. 135–154.

17. *GJ*, pp. 9–11.

18. *GJ*, p. 232.

19. *Epistolae*, II, no. 96, 270: "quando pregavão imterpretavão o nome de Deus como eles querião, dizemdo que Deus e 'daiuzo' são de huma mesma cousa. Daiuzo em limgoa de Japão quer dizer 'gramde mentira,' por iso que se guardasem de nosso Deus. E outras muitas blasffemias dizião comtra Deus . . ."

20. *Epistolae*, II, no. 96, 275. The location of the college was the Ashikaga no Shō in Shimotsuke, one of the Bandō (Kantō) provinces. Its date of foundation is unclear, but its prominence was established under the patronage of Uesugi Norizane, who took over the administration of the *shōen* in 1432. The school has been termed mediaeval Japan's only secularly oriented institution of higher learning, and it did play an important role in maintaining an academic interest in the continental cultural tradition. But it has also been criticized for its simple functionality during Sengoku, when its graduates seem to have peddled their expertise in the *I-ching* to the superstitious *bushi*, who sought in divination the answers to their uncertainties. See Wajima Yoshio, *Chūsei no jugaku*, Nihon Rekishi Sōsho 11 (Tokyo: Yoshikawa Kōbunkan, 1965), pp. 226–261.

21. *GJ*, p. 43.

22. *GJ*, p. 463.

23. *CATECHISMVS CHRISTIANAE FIDEI, IN QVO VERITAS nostrae religionis ostenditur, & sectae Iaponenses confutantur,* editus à Patre Alexandro Valignano societatis IESV . . . Olyssipone, excudebat Antonius Riberius. 1586. *CATECHISMI CHRISTIANAE FIDEI, in quo veritas nostrę religionis ostenditur, & sectę Iaponenses confutantur, LIBER SECVNDVS.* Authore Alexandro Valignano societatis IESV. Olyssipone excudebat Emmanuel de Lyra, Typog. 1586. There is a Japanese translation, done by Ieiri Toshimitsu: *Nihon no katekizumo,* Tenri Toshokan Sankō Shiryō 7 (Tenri: Tenri Toshokan, 1969).

The text is described by Laures, *Kirishitan Bunko,* no. 2, pp. 27–29. Laures knew of two extant copies; Ieiri mentions a third (p. ii), and Arai Toshi appends a brief description of all three to Ieiri's translation (pp. 191–192). They are all in Portugal; but there are photographic copies in the Kirishitan Bunko of Sophia University, Tokyo, and in the Tenri Library. Schütte takes exhaustive reference to the *CATECHISMVS* in *VMJ,* I-2, 88–118; see p. 89 on the question of the time of composition.

The Japanese text found in the *byōbu* was published by Ebisawa and Matsuda in *Evora byōbu,* pp. 127–156, and is reprinted in Ieiri, pp. 193–221. Ebisawa rejects the possibilities that the *byōbu* text is either a preliminary Japanese manuscript used in the catechism's compilation or a Japanese translation of Valignano's Western-language manuscript, and asserts instead that it represents notes of lectures based on Valignano's catechism given at the Jesuits' Azuchi *seminario; Evora byōbu,* p. 51. The reasoning is somewhat tenuous; nor was Ebisawa consistent in his subsequent discussions of the *byōbu* text's specific character. Compare the contradictory statements in *Nihon Kirishitan shi,* pp. 104 and 159.

24. *VMJ,* I-2, 90. The opportunity to make revisions never came: in 1583 Valignano was appointed Provincial of India, and the post consumed all his time. For the relevant dates, see *VMJ,* I-2, 579.

25. *GJ,* pp. 95–96. Schurhammer's gloss concerning the books in which Yōhōken collaborated is incorrect: the catechism mentioned by Frois is Valignano's, and not the *FIDES NO DŌXI to xite P. F. Luis de Granada amaretaru xo no riacu* (Epitome of a book composed by P. F. Luis de Granada as a Guide to the Faith; Amakusa, 1592); Laures, *Kirishitan Bunko,* no. 11, pp. 43–44. On the various activities of Yōhōken, see Doi Tadao, *Kirishitan bunken kō* (Tokyo: Sanseidō, 1963), ch. v, pp. 123–157.

26. *VMJ,* I-2, 117.

27. Published with an extensive commentary by Doi Tadao in *KK,* 5:59–113 (1959), and in *Kirishitan bunken kō,* ch. viii, pp. 259–322.

28. See the "Prooemium" to Book One for the statement of the work's purpose. *CATECHISMVS,* I, 3; Ieiri, p. 4.

29. *CATECHISMVS,* I, 3v–4; Ieiri, pp. 5–6. Compare the *byōbu* text: *Evora byōbu,* pp. 128–129; Ieiri, pp. 195–196.

30. ". . . omnes tamen in vno verbo communi opinione consentiunt, nimirum *Gonijt,* quod duo significat, veritatem, & veritatis speciem, idest verum, & apparens." *CATECHISMVS,* I, 4v; Ieiri, p. 6. *Evora byōbu,* p. 129; Ieiri, p. 196.

31. *CATECHISMVS,* I, 4v–5; Ieiri, pp. 6–7. *Evora byōbu,* p. 129; Ieiri, pp. 196–197.

32. *CATECHISMVS,* I, 5–5v; Ieiri, pp. 7–8. *Evora byōbu,* pp. 130–131; Ieiri, pp. 197–198.

33. *CATECHISMVS*, I, chs. ii–iii, 12v–34; Ieiri, pp. 19–54. *Evora byōbu*, pp. 135–145; Ieiri, pp. 202–211 (ch. ii only). Cf. *VMJ*, I-2, 99–104.

34. Torres to Xavier, Yamaguchi, 20 October 1551; *Cartas*, I, 18v. Cited by Schurhammer, *Sprachproblem*, p. 55.

35. *CATECHISMVS*, I, 35 *et seq.*; Ieiri, p. 56 *et seq.* Unfortunately there is a lacuna in the *byōbu* text.

36. *CATECHISMVS*, I, 49v–50; Ieiri, pp. 82–83. Cf. n. 40 below on "Forengequio" = *Hōrengekyō*.

37. *CATECHISMVS*, II, 2v–8; Ieiri, pp. 134–150. The original Japanese text of Book Two is not extant.

Those unfamiliar with the Ten Commandments will find versions of them listed below (*Deus Destroyed*, Seventh Step, and *Deceit Disclosed*, III). Valignano's treatment of their particular application to Japan is discussed in *VMJ*, I-2, 113–114.

38. *CATECHISMVS*, II, 5; Ieiri, p. 142.

39. *GJ*, p. 86. To take only this first part of Frois' *Historia* for an example: other disputations on pp. 6, 16, 18, 21–26, 32–33, 54, 62, 79, 84, 86, 89–91, 94, 97–100, 108–109, 139, 145, 150, 265, 272, 319, 379–385, and 412.

40. The quotation is from *Historia Indica*, pp. 160–161; but the point is made in the same fashion in *CATECHISMVS*, I, 48–48v (Ieiri, pp. 79–80). Valignano restated it in somewhat more restrained language in his most celebrated work: *Sumario de las Cosas de Japon (1583)*, ed. José Luis Alvarez-Taladriz, *MN* Monographs 9 (Tokyo: Sophia University Press, 1954), pp. 66–67; Japanese translation by Matsuda Kiichi and Sakuma Tadashi, *Nihon junsatsuki*, Tōzai Kōshō Ryokōki Zenshū 5 (Tokyo: Tōgensha, 1965), pp. 200–201. *Sumario* is cited by permission of Monumenta Nipponica, Tokyo.

But (*butsu*) and *fotoque* (*hotoke*): Buddha. *Meo* (*Myō*): *Myōhō rengekyō*, the Lotus Sutra, the invocation of which is stressed by the Nichiren Sect of Buddhism. The invocation of the name of Amida—*Namu Amida Butsu*—is the way to salvation preached by the Pure Land sects in their emphasis upon the *sola fide* approach.

41. *Historia Indica*, pp. 139–140. The text of *Sumario*, p. 29, is identical; Matsuda and Sakuma, p. 190. The *Dayri* (*Dairi*) is, of course, the Emperor.

42. John Whitney Hall, "Foundations of the Modern Japanese Daimyo," *The Journal of Asian Studies*, 20.3:317–329 (May 1961), reprinted in *Studies in the Institutional History of Early Modern Japan*, ed. Hall and Marius B. Jansen (Princeton: Princeton University Press, 1968), pp. 65–77. Hall offers a more elaborate treatment in *Government and Local Power in Japan: 500 to 1700* (Princeton: Princeton University Press, 1966), chs. ix–xiii, pp. 238–423. Cf. Nakamura Kichiji, "Sengoku daimyō ron," *Iwanami kōza: Nihon rekishi*, VIII (*Chūsei* 4; Tokyo: Iwanami, 1963), 189–237; see especially p. 218, n. 6.

43. *GJ*, p. 255, based on a letter from Almeida to his Jesuit confrères, 25 October 1565; *Cartas*, I, 168.

44. *From Max Weber: Essays in Sociology*, ed. H. H. Gerth and C. Wright Mills (New York Oxford University Press, 1958; Galaxy Book 13), p. 253.

45. *Giya do pekadoru jōkan*, Nihon Koten Zenshū, 2nd ser. (Tokyo: Nihon Koten Zenshū Kankōkai, 1927), pp. 20–21. The book is described by Laures, *Kirishitan Bunko*, no. 21, pp. 60–62.

46. Text in Anesaki Masaharu, *Kirishitan shūkyō bungaku* (Tokyo: Dōbunkan, 1932), pp. 326–327.

47. Text in Anesaki, *Kirishitan shūkyō bungaku*, p. 673. Cf. Ebisawa, *Kirishitanshi no kenkyū* (Tokyo: Unebi Shobō, 1942), pp. 23–24. The *SANCTOS NO GOSAGVEO* is described by Laures, *Kirishitan Bunko*,

no. 9, pp. 39–41. The sole extant copy of the Jesuit *Taiheiki nukigaki* (Laures, no. 34, pp. 80–81) is in the Tenri Library. The date and place of publication are unknown.

48. Ebisawa, *Kirishitanshi no kenkyū*, p. 30.

49. *SP*, pp. 194–196. Laures, in *Takayama Ukon und die Anfänge der Kirche in Japan*, Mission Studies and Documents 18 (Münster i. Westf.: Aschendorffsche Verlagsbuchhandlung, 1954), p. 93, strives mightily to exonerate Ukon: "According to the conceptions of Japanese *bushidō*, the vassal had to preserve loyalty to his immediate lord, although he could present eventual misgivings in due humility. But if the lord persisted in his initial decision, then the vassal had to submit. Accordingly, by his representations against the war with Nobunaga, Ukon had proved the genuineness of his chivalrous disposition even by the standard of old Japan; but, by the same standard, he had to sacrifice his scruples to his fealty after Araki had declared war. *It is of great credit to Ukon's [Christian] faith that he had second thoughts about this traditional standard.* Organtino, above all, feared as fatal to the Christian cause the general scandal which a mutiny of Ukon against Nobunaga would stir. This fact seems to indicate at least that even non-Christian contemporaries, contrary to the traditional conceptions of *bushidō*, followed their healthy instincts of right and justice, and assigned precedence to the responsibility toward the higher sovereign. After all, even the much-heralded loyalty of *bushidō only made sense and had purpose when it served the common weal,* when it was, in other words, in the final event directed toward the Emperor or Tennō. *And the Tennō was certainly better represented by the Naidaijin Nobunaga than by the false and treacherous Araki.*" The italics are mine. *Takayama Ukon* is cited by permission of Verlag Aschendorff, Münster in Westfalen.

50. P. João Francisco Stephanoni SJ stated that Nobunaga threatened him with the crucifixion of the Padres and their Christians if the Takayama remained unpersuaded. Stephanoni to P. Manoel Teixeira SJ in Bassein, Miyako, 22 October 1579; *Cartas*, I, 452v; *YNT*, II, 457–458.

Organtino, in the meantime, had proceeded to Takatsuki, to be received with a cautious welcome. Dom Dario invited him to climb the donjon and from that vantage point observe the manoeuvres of Nobunaga's soldiery. The Padre at first declined to budge from the church, suspecting a ruse to imprison him and then turn him over to Kōsa, the Monk of Osaka; but he finally agreed to inspect the fortifications, in order to scout a feasible spot for a nighttime escape from the castle. His intentions were found out, and he was put under guard. In mortal fear that Nobunaga would interpret his detention in Takatsuki as collaboration with the Takayama, and would make good his threats against the Christians, Organtino surrendered to his sorrow and fell supine in prayer. Frois in *SP*, pp. 200–203, displays a great story-teller's talent which Laures emulates and almost matches in *Takayama Ukon*, pp. 101–102.

51. *Nobunaga [Shinchō] kōki*, comp. Ōta Gyūichi, ed. Okuno Takahiro and Iwasawa Yoshihiko, Kadokawa Bunko 2541 (Tokyo: Kadokawa, 1969), 11:256; entry for the events of Tenshō 6/11/9 (7 December 1578) *et seq.*

Nippo jisho, p. 584, defines *shami* as follows: "Xami. Bôzos da Tera que são como pateiros, & seruem nos officios da casa.——Temple bonzes who are like lay pantrymen and attend to the house services." The assumption of priestly orders—or at least the gesture of taking the tonsure--was in Japan a common device of escaping the onus of worldly responsibility.

52. Frois, *SP*, pp. 203–204, purports to transcribe Ukon's speech of justification. The reporter's language is too turgid to be an accurate representation

of the samurai's statements; nevertheless, the appalling nature of the dilemma emerges quite clearly.

53. *SP*, pp. 207–208.

54. The persistence of the story has been fostered by television. The immensely popular serial *Taikōki* devoted an evening to the affair in the summer of 1965. The NHK series *Nihonshi tanpō* (History Excursions) in April 1971 presented a half hour on Ukon and the locales of his famous deeds; the program was billed as the story of a *sengoku daimyō* who, while a Christian, stabbed three of his liege lords in the back, including his own father.

55. Ming Ti of the Later Han ruled A.D. 58–76; it was during the first century that Buddhism made its initial entry into China. Wu Ti of Liang ruled 502–549.

56. Fabian utilizes this same quotation in the Second Step of *Deus Destroyed* to support an anti-Christian position. In the latter instance, the Sage Sovereigns and Enlightened Rulers of China are contrasted with a Deus whose lack of a sense of responsibility, justice, and mercy appears especially reprehensible because this moral sense was abundantly present in those human rulers.

The Drum of Plaints: a large drum placed in the palace courtyard to enable anyone making a petition to the sovereign to declare his intent; a practice supposedly initiated by Yü.

57. Shōhei-Tengyō no Ran: Fujiwara no Sumitomo in 934 (Shōhei 4) refused to relinquish his post in the government of the province of Iyo and revolted, terrorizing the area of the Inland Sea until he was suppressed in 941 (Tengyō 4); Taira no Masakado at the same time extended his power over a substantial area of the Kantō, proclaiming himself emperor, and meeting his end at the hands of local aristocrats in 940 (Tengyō 3).

Hogen no Ran (1156) and Heiji no Ran (1159): conclusive demonstrations of the rise of the military aristocracy; events preparatory to the Taira Dominance.

58. Shōkyū no Hen (1221): the confrontation between the Retired Emperor Go-Toba and the Hōjō Regent Yoshitoki, meant to bring about the reassertion of imperial control over *shugo* and *jitō* but ending rather in the triumph of the Kamakura Shogunate and the exile of Go-Toba.

59. It is difficult to say whether Fabian is innocent of knowledge or merely being deceitful. The text will be found in NST 25, pp. 174–176.

Chapter 3 : The Accommodative Method

1. "More than twenty thousand" according to Vilela's letter to General SJ, Goa, 3 November 1571; but "some thirty thousand" according to his report of 23 January 1572. *VMJ*, I-1, 256.

2. Laures, "Zahl der Christen," p. 85. Schütte's chart, *Introductio*, p. 429, gives the number 100,000.

3. *VMJ*, I-1, 281–282 and 293–301.

4. In evaluating a 1576 report from Cabral to the *Visitator*, Schütte notes that it was at that point *Valignano* who resisted *Cabral's* urgent pleas for permission to admit Japanese into the Society! *VMJ*, I-1, 299.

5. *VMJ*, I-1, 307. Cabral himself speaks of the latter point with great pathos. See his letter to General SJ, Cochin, 15 December 1593; *VMJ*, I-2, 471: "... fundados em humildade, pobresa e grande confiança em Deus e desconfiança da propria industria," etc. with biblical allusions.

6. The first comment is cited by Valignano as a particularly frequent expression of Cabral's; *VMJ*, I-1, 325. The source is the *Visitator*'s long retrospective letter to General SJ, Goa, 23 November 1595; cited extensively in *VMJ*, I-1, 325–330. This letter is consistent in concept, if not entirely in tone, with the message Valignano wrote on the spot in Usuki on 27 October 1580 (original Spanish in *VMJ*, I-2, 487–494; German translation of extensive portions in *VMJ*, I-1, 322–325 & 333–334). These two reports to the General SJ add up to a stinging indictment of Cabral's direction of the Japanese mission.

7. Letter of 23 November 1595; *VMJ*, I-1, 328–330 passim.

8. *Sumario*, p. 230; Matsuda and Sakuma translation, pp. 271–272.

9. *Sumario*, p. 235; Matsuda and Sakuma, p. 272.

10. *Sumario*, p. 241; Matsuda and Sakuma, pp. 274–275.

11. Alvarez-Taladriz supplies the full text of Question XVIII in *Sumario*, ch. xxiii, n. 23, pp. 245–247.

12. Published with an Italian translation by Josef Franz Schütte SJ, *Il Cerimoniale per i Missionari del Giappone* (Rome: Edizioni di Storia e Letteratura, 1946). For a brief account of the factors which inspired the treatise, see Schütte's "Introduzione," pp. 78–79, and cf. *VMJ*, I-2, 221–222. The work was composed in a day and a night in October 1581.

13. *Il Cerimoniale*, pp. 274–278. *Yakata*: major daimyo; a term of the late Muromachi period. Cf. *Nippo jisho*, p. 631: "*Yacata*. Certa dignidade de senhores principaes que não são Cûgues.——A particular rank of principal lords who are not of the imperial aristocracy." *Zashiki*: formal reception room. Cf. *Nippo jisho*, p. 656: "*Zaxeqi. i, Zaxiqi*. Camara, ou sala onde se aßenta, ou ajunta gente.——A chamber or hall where people take their seats or gather in assembly."

14. Alvarez-Taladriz supplies the full text of Question XVII in *Sumario*, ch. xxiii, n. 23, pp. 241–245; the quoted portion is from pp. 244–245. The biblical allusion is to Romans 14:3, "Let not him that eateth set at nought him that eateth not: and let not him that eateth not judge him that eateth."

15. *Evora byōbu*, p. 162.

16. Ibid., p. 161.

17. *VMJ*, I-2, 221–222.

18. *VMJ*, I-2, 185.

19. *Il Cerimoniale*, pp. 124–126.

20. For an example, see *Il Cerimoniale*, pp. 144–146: "Because it is the universal custom of the *chōrō* of the sects of Japan to go about by palanquin rather than horse, the Japan Superior in crossing pagan territory or in calling on a pagan lord may also go by palanquin, and the three overall superiors of Shimo, Bungo, and Miyako may also do the same; but when traveling among Christians they should usually go on horseback."

21. On the preliminary Shimo Consultation, see *VMJ*, I-1, 459–464. The *Visitator*'s preliminary estimate of the situation is given in the important letter to the General SJ, Kuchinotsu, 10 December 1579; quoted extensively in *VMJ*, I-1, 372–384.

22. See Hubert Cieslik SJ, "The Training of a Japanese Clergy in the Seventeenth Century," *Studies in Japanese Culture*, ed. Joseph Roggendorf SJ (Tokyo: Sophia University Press, 1963), p. 44. A somewhat expanded

Japanese version of this important article is: "Nihon ni okeru saisho no shingakkō (1601nen–1614nen)," *KK*, 10:1–55 (1965); cf. p. 4.

23. *VMJ*, I-1, 408–409.

24. *VMJ*, I-2, 150–153. Schütte points out (p. 151) that it was only Organtino's "extraordinary manner of action" that reduced the initial problem of finding an enrollment. Organtino was already engaged in recruiting students in the year 1580, although the school's mechanism would not be regulated until Valignano did it in person the following year. "This type of seminary—its academic program patterned after the European model (although extensively adjusted to Japanese character and customs), and its instruction in great part of a European content—was a completely unknown entity in Japan. Therefore [Organtino] at first found no understanding for it among Japanese Christians, the parents or the children. The manner in which he finally invited the first eight noble youths (from Takatsuki) to come to a feast in Azuchi and then talked them into staying . . . does not exactly leave one with a favorable impression. The mediation of Takayama Ukon . . . succeeded in mollifying the parents."

25. Cieslik, "Training," pp. 44–45; *KK*, 10:4.

26. Ebisawa Arimichi, "Kirishitan no denrai to sono bunka," *Nihon bunkashi gairon*, ed. Ishida Ichirō (Tokyo: Yoshikawa Kōbunkan, 1968), p. 353. Where the Jesuits could have got the personnel to teach such an extensive curriculum is a question which does not seem to have concerned Mr. Ebisawa. Their number in Japan during the Tenshō period (to 10 January 1593) never exceeded 142, Padres and Irmãos, Europeans and Japanese (see *Introductio*, charts on p. 317 and pp. 321–322), and it is not likely that their various native servitors knew enough of the listed Western subject matter to teach it. Ebisawa has somewhat moderated his statements (but not his overly enthusiastic general orientation) in his article on "The Meeting of Cultures," *The Southern Barbarians: The First Europeans in Japan*, ed. Michael Cooper SJ, pp. 123–144; see particularly p. 139, where the number of schools still stands at two hundred (by 1580), but "much of the curriculum" is occupied by catechism lessons. In October 1580 there were 59 Jesuits in Japan; in November six more arrived.

27. *Sumario*, p. 171; Matsuda and Sakuma, p. 238.

28. *Introductio*, p. 742.

29. *Regimento pera os Semynarios de Japan 1580, Para nuestro P. General*; original text in *VMJ*, I-2, 479–485; see especially p. 484. *Sumario*, ch. xii, "De la importancia de los seminarios de los naturales y del modo que se ha de tener en ellos," pp. 170–175; Matsuda and Sakuma, pp. 238–240.

30. *VMJ*, I-2, 481. Attached to the *Regimen* is a daily schedule for the younger pupils, *Distribuição das horas pera os minimos do seminaryo*: *VMJ*, I-2, 485–486; German translation, *VMJ*, I-1, 438–440. This *Distribution of hours*, circumscribing as it does a major part of the early Western contribution, is a very important document of the history of education in Japan, and reads as follows:

1. In summer they shall arise at half past four, and finish their oration at five together with that of the Padres; and in winter they shall accord with the same order while doing everything one hour later, this change beginning in the middle of October and lasting until the middle of February.

2. At the conclusion of the oration the mass shall be said immediately, with its paternosters; and in the time remaining until six o'clock they shall sweep the *zashiki*.

3. The time between six and half past seven they shall spend on their studies, memorizing their lesson; the smaller ones learning their Latin vocabulary, as their master may see it fit.

4. From half past seven until nine they shall be with the master who teaches Latin, giving their account of the lesson and of what they have learned by heart, and listening to what the master reads to them; the small ones during this time doing their school problems and the rest that the master may assign to them. And the master shall take care to instruct in such a manner that the big ones and the small ones do not get in each other's way and lose time. He may utilize for this the assistance of some of the more advanced students to hear the lesson and correct the assignment of the smaller ones.

5. From nine until eleven they shall have their meal and ordinary recreation.

6. The time between eleven and two they all shall spend in reading and writing Japanese, and those who are already proficient shall compose some epistles in Japanese, according to what their Japanese master will assign them. He shall hear their lesson and correct their assignments, arranging everything in such a manner that they make progress and lose no time.

7. The time between two and three they shall spend in singing and playing musical instruments, and the time left over shall be for their recreation. Selected for [training in music] shall be those more gifted for it. The master may utilize for this the assistance of some of the more advanced, so that he gain the extra time to teach something or other.

8. From three until half past four they shall again be with the master who teaches Latin, who will during this time have them write a composition and read to them some other lesson which he deems most appropriate for their profit. The smaller ones he shall occupy in Latin reading or writing exercises, as appears better to him. And the half hour that remains until five, before supper, he will let them rest.

9. From five until six they shall have supper and their recreation.

10. From six until eight those who are studying Latin shall go over their lessons again, and the smaller ones shall spend this time either in writing Japanese or in writing Latin or in some other thing, as appears better at the time.

11. At eight they shall make their examination [of conscience], do the Litany of Our Lady, and immediately go to sleep.

12. When no holy days fall in a particular week, they shall on Wednesday be given the day off, from one o'clock and after, so that they only have two hours of reading and writing Japanese, and recreation the rest of the time. But they shall spend some time in singing chants to organ accompaniment, and in playing the clavichord and viola and other such instruments.

13. On Saturdays they shall spend the entire morning in repetition of the Latin which they have learned in the preceding week, and after dinner they shall have two hours of reading and writing Japanese. And from one o'clock and after they shall have the time off. Some time shall be given them to bathe and attend to their hair and to make their confessions, and the hour which remains after supper and recreation they shall spend half in hearing the lecture that shall at this time be given them on spiritual matters, and the other half in rehearsing and discussing what they have just heard and Christian doctrine.

14. On Sundays and holy days they shall after dinner go for play at the country house or out in the open air. If it rains or if it is very cold, so that it is impossible to go, then they shall have the entire day for recreation

in the residence; but those who are proficient should spend some time in singing and in playing musical instruments.

15. At the time of great heat in summer they shall be given more rest on some days; one may give them a vacation or remit some portion of their studies, according to what appears more convenient to the Superior of the seminary.

ALEXANDRO.

31. *CHRISTIANI PVERI INSTITVTIO, ADOLESCENTIAEQVE perfugium*: autore Ioanne Bonifacio SOCIETATIS IESV. cum libri unius, & rerū accessione plurimarū. Cum facultate Superiorum apud Sinas, in Portu Macaensi in Domo Societatis IESV. Anno 1588. The book is described by Laures, *Kirishitan Bunko*, no. 4, pp. 30–32. The only extant copy is in the Ajuda Library in Lisbon; I have utilized the photocopy in the Tenri Library.

32. Cicero: Laures, *Kirishitan Bunko*, no. 36, p. 87. Virgil: ibid., pp. 90–91.

33. See Arcadio Schwade SJ, "Funai no korejiyo ni tsuite," *KK*, 10:56–66 (1965).

34. *VMJ*, I-2, 467.

35. *VMJ*, I-1, 293–297.

36. Frois to the Jesuits of Portugal, Usuki, 16 October 1578; *Cartas*, I, 424. *Yasokaishi Nihon tsūshin: Bungo-hen*, trans. and ed. Murakami Naojirō, II, Zoku Ikoku Sōsho (Tokyo: Teikoku Kyōikukai Shuppanbu, 1936), 299.

37. P. Lourenço Mexia to General SJ, Bungo, 20 October 1580; *Cartas*, I, 472; *Bungo-hen*, II, 422–423. Cf. *SP*, ch. xxiii, "Of the *Collegio* which the P.ᵉ Vizitador ordained for the city of Funay, and of other events," pp. 158–165; and *VMJ*, I-2, 66–67.

38. Schwade, pp. 60–61.

39. Cieslik, "Training," p. 45; *KK*, 10:4–5.

40. Cieslik, "Training," p. 45. Interestingly enough, in the *KK* version of the article, p. 5, he escalates the number on the potential graduation list to three hundred.

41. On the end of the institution, see Schwade, pp. 62–64.

42. Cieslik, "Training," p. 46; *KK*, 10:5.

43. On the "Christian Century's" bishops of Japan, see João Rodriguez Tçuzzu's contemporary historical sketch, included in *Nihon kyōkai shi*, II, 605–667. Also see Cieslik, "Kirishitan jidai ni okeru shikyō mondai," *KK*, 9:366–468 (1964); pp. 404–436 contain the biographical details.

The first bishop-designate of Japan, Sebastião de Morais SJ, died in 1588 on board ship off Moçambique before reaching his see. The second bishop, Pedro Martins SJ, arrived in Japan in 1596, accredited to Hideyoshi as the envoy of the Portuguese Viceroy of India; but he could only remain a half-year, being forced to depart in the aftermath of the *San Felipe* Affair. Bishop Cerqueira arrived in Nagasaki on 5 August 1598 and exercised his office for sixteen years, dying of an ulcer on 16 February 1614, just as the general persecution was breaking out. The fourth bishop-designate, Diogo Correa Valente SJ, was in 1619 prevented from taking ship for Japan by the Macao authorities, who were fearful of provoking the Bakufu into repressions against their trade.

44. The letter is dated Nagasaki, 10 October 1601; quoted by Cieslik in "Training," p. 49, and *KK*, 10:10. For biographies of some Japanese priests of the period, including Sebastião Kimura, see Cieslik, *Kirishitan jinbutsu no kenkyū: hōjin shisai no maki* (Tokyo: Yoshikawa Kōbunkan, 1963).

45. *Epistolae*, II, no. 97, 291; Cochin, 29 January 1552.

46. Cieslik, "Training," p. 75.

47. *Sumario*, ch. xiv, pp. 181–187 passim; Matsuda and Sakuma, pp. 244–247. The resolution of Question X of the Japan Consultation— "Whether Japanese should be received into the Society"—is stated in similar language; the full text is provided by Alvarez-Taladriz in *Sumario*, ch. xiv, n. 2, pp. 181–183. It is noteworthy that Valignano devoted five whole chapters (xiv–xviii) of the *Sumario* to the development of the thesis: Japanese are fully fit to be Jesuits.

48. *Sumario*, p. 198; Matsuda and Sakuma, p. 250.

49. *Sumario*, ch. xvi, pp. 198–202 passim; Matsuda and Sakuma, pp. 250–253.

50. *Sumario*, ch. xvii, pp. 203–206 passim; Matsuda and Sakuma, pp. 254–256.

51. *Sumario*, ch. xviii, pp. 207–211 passim; Matsuda and Sakuma, pp. 256–260.

52. *Historia Indica*, ch. xviii, "De algunas otras estrañas costumbres de los japones," pp. 140–142. Text identical in *Sumario*, ch. ii, pp. 30–31: Matsuda and Sakuma, p. 191.

53. Okada Akio, "Kirishitan shinkō to hōken shakai dōtoku," *Nihon bunka kenkyū*, no. 5 (Tokyo: Shinchōsha, 1959).

54. *Asakura Sōteki waki*, in *Zokuzoku gunsho ruijū*, X (Tokyo: Kokusho Kankōkai, 1907), 2. Cited by Ishige Tadashi, "Sengoku/Azuchi-Momoyama jidai no rinri shisō: Tentō shisō no tenkai," p. 154.

55. *Takeda Shingen kahō*, in *Nihon kyōiku bunko, Kakun-hen* (Tokyo: Dōbunkan, 1910), pp. 220–236; quotations from pp. 228 and 230; cited by Ishige, p. 154. Both precepts are taken from the second portion of Shingen's "house laws," dated 1558, which itemizes in "99 articles" (in actuality there are only 98) the moral standards expected of retainers of the Takeda, buttressing the instructions with copious citations from the classics. (The first portion, in 55 articles, deals with practical matters of administration and is dated 1547; there is an appendix dated 1554.)

The second example is, of course, an old saw. It is included in the Jesuit edition of East Asian homiletic maxims published together with the *Heike* and Aesop at Amakusa in 1593: *XIXO, XIXXO nadono vchiyori nuqi idaxi, qincuxŭ to nasu mono nari* (Compilation of Golden Words, selected from among the Four Books, Seven [Military] Texts, and others). A photocopy and detailed analyses are provided by Yoshida Sumio, *Amakusa-ban Kinkushū no kenkyū//On the Qincuxŭ (Kinku-syu) Published in 1593 by the Amakusa Collegio of the Jesuit Mission in Japan*, The Tôyô Bunko Ronsô Series A, Vol. XXIV (Tokyo: The Tôyô Bunko, 1938). See photocopy, p. 532: "Qimi qimi tarazu, xin motte xin tarazumba arubecarazu." Cf. Yoshida, p. 41 and p. 220. João Rodriguez Tçuzzu also cites the precept, giving the *Heike* as the provenance: *ARTE*, f. 39v; *Nihon daibunten*, pp. 161–162.

56. The focus of *chū* in *Hagakure* is remarkably narrow. One of the very first statements of the prologue is: "Neither Shaka nor Confucius nor Kusunoki nor Shingen served the Ryūzōji and Nabeshima, and therefore they could not possibly attain to observance of the values of the House." *Hagakure*, account of Yamamoto Tsunetomo recorded by Tashiro Tsuramoto, ed. Watsuji Tetsurō and Furukawa Tesshi, I (Tokyo: Iwanami, 1970 eleventh imprint; Iwanami Bunko 2305–2306), 17; cited along with several other extravagant dictums by Kitajima Masamoto, *Edo jidai*, p. 78. Perhaps even more extreme is the following rule of conduct (*Hagakure*, I, 20): "On no account do I aspire to attain Buddhahood; nothing of the sort! I am

determined to be reborn and reappear in seven lives as a Nabeshima samurai."

57. For an example, see *GJ*, p. 56, the source being Vilela's letter to the Jesuits of India and Portugal, Hirado, 29 October 1557, *Cartas*, I, 54v; *Bungo-hen*, I, 188–189. The italics are mine:

> The means and manner which the King of Bungo applied (according to the custom of Japan) in the punishment of rebels were the following. On the very same day which he had set for their death, and while each of the traitors (and they lords of some standing) was still unbound and free, he was sent word from the King that he must die that day. And he answered that if it be the will of His Lordship, then he shall kill himself. And if the King granted this to him, then he deemed it a great honor, and dressed in his best clothing he took a dagger and slit open his bowels crosswise, and so he died. *And such men are not considered dishonored and their children are not disinherited.* But if the King answered the rebel that he should not kill himself but that someone would be sent to punish him, then he and all his servitors, friends, relations, and sons threw themselves to their weapons. And the King sent a *tono* . . . with the necessary men to punish the culprit, while all the townspeople watched the struggle. The traitor defended himself as best he could, first with arrows, then with spears, and finally with the sword. And so the traitor died with all his sons, servitors, and friends; *and his house was immediately burnt, and his memory extinguished and with him also that of his entire family.* And thus they go to hell.

58. See below, *Deus Destroyed*, First Step.

59. The source of the melodramatic traditional accounts of Dom Agostinho Konishi's end is the letter from P. Valentim Carvalho to General SJ, dated 25 February 1601; *Lettera dei P. Alessandro Valignano, Visitatore della Compagnia di Giesù nel Giappone, e nella Cina, del 1599. Con un supplimento del P. Valentino Caruaglio della medesima Compagnia dell'Anno 1601* (In Venetia, M.DCIII., Appresso Gio. Battista Ciotti, All'insegna della Aurora), pp. 92–102. Another excellent representation may be found in *The History of the Church of Japan*, Written Originally in French By Monsieur L'Abbe de T. [pseudonym for Jean Crasset SJ], II (London, 1707), 92–97. At the execution site, we are told, a Christian sent by the Jesuits "march'd up boldly thro' the Guards" and urged Konishi to make a perfect act of contrition; he replied that he had already done so. He brusquely rejected the "superstitious Ceremonies" and "apish Tricks" of the bonzes who busied themselves about Ishida, and instead "said his Beads, holding in his Hand a curious Picture of our Lady, with our Saviour in her Arms." He was beheaded "at the third Stroak."

Yukinaga's death, no matter how much in the spirit of Christian chivalry, was a major blow for the Church in Japan. His lands came into the possession of Katō Kiyomasa, a notorious anti-Christian adherent of the Nichiren Sect. By 1603 the number of Christians in the province of Higo had dwindled from 80,000 to 20,000.

Japanese accounts bear out the story of Dom Agostinho's Christian motivations. See for one instance *Tsukushi shoke kōhaiki* (The rise and fall of Kyushu noble houses), *Ōita-ken kyōdo shiryō shūsei*, II, 885: "Defeated in the Battle of Sekigahara, he came to the precincts of a temple to the east of Ibukiyama, and he said: 'I am a Jesuit and revere the law of the Emperor of Heaven. Therefore I reject suicide. Bind me and turn me in.' Now there was a priest called Hayashi Zōsu there who denounced him, and he was made prisoner. Thus he died." The story of Mitsunari's persimmon is cited by Imai Rintarō, *Ishida Mitsunari*, Jinbutsu Sōsho 74 (Tokyo: Yoshikawa Kōbunkan, 1961), pp. 218–219.

60. *Historia Indica*, p. 127. Text identical in *Sumario*, p. 6; Matsuda and Sakuma, p. 181.

61. For an example, see *GJ*, p. 114.

62. ". . . which play was fit to confound the pagan women who in this land kill their children, demonstrating to them the force of the natural love that a mother has for her child." Irmão João Fernandes to his Jesuit confrères, Bungo, 8 October 1561; *Cartas*, I, 79; *Bungo-hen*, I, 349.

63. See Baltezar Gago to Dom João III, King of Portugal, Hirado, 20 September 1555; *Cartas*, I, 42; *Bungo-hen*, I, 116–117. Cf. Ebisawa Arimichi, *Kirishitan no shakai katsudō oyobi Nanban igaku* (Tokyo: Fuzanbō, 1944), p. 66. Ebisawa gives a survey of Christian institutions for the care of infants on pp. 139–145.

64. *Sumario*, pp. 170–171; Matsuda and Sakuma, p. 238. Cf. the Japan Consultation's Question V—"Whether seminaries for Japanese natives are to be founded"—in *Sumario*, ch. xii, n. 5, pp. 172–174.

65. *Sumario*, pp. 343–344; Matsuda and Sakuma, pp. 299–300.

66. Chapter xi of the *Sumario*, pp. 162–169, is devoted to this problem; Matsuda and Sakuma, pp. 233–237.

67. *VMJ*, I-2, 190–191.

68. *SP*, ch. xxxii, pp. 251–258.

69. *SP*, ch. xxxiii, pp. 258–263.

70. *SP*, p. 257.

71. *Regimento pera os Padres que estão nas Residencias do Japão*, composed in the middle of November 1581 with an appendix written in January or February 1582; cited extensively in *VMJ*, I-2, 278–293.

72. *Summario d'algumas cousas que se hão de guardar polos Padres nas casas e residensias de Japão para que sejão todos conformes*, appended to the *Regimen*; cited extensively in *VMJ*, I-2, 294–300.

73. *Sumario*, p. 342; Matsuda and Sakuma, p. 299.

74. "Como no conviene ir a Japon otras religiones," *Sumario*, pp. 143–149; Matsuda and Sakuma, pp. 223–228.

75. *Sumario*, p. 148; Matsuda and Sakuma, p. 227.

76. Alvarez-Taladriz, in *Sumario*, ch. ix, n. 17, pp. 148–149. Cf. Boxer, *Christian Century*, p. 160.

77. See Schütte, "Wichtige Japandokumente in einem Band der Propaganda-Kongregation im Staatsarchiv von Florenz," *Archivum Historicum Societatis Iesu*, 35.69:232–241 (January–June 1966). This catalogue of documents from the archives of the Congregatio de Propaganda Fide offers interesting glimpses into the controversy between the several orders and their Japanese confraternities. It will be noted that Clement VIII on 12 December 1600 explicitly permitted mendicants to proceed to Japan, but only by way of Portugal and Goa. On 11 June 1608 Paul V lifted even that restriction.

For a contemporary friar's account of the decision to send Franciscans from the Philippines to Japan, see Marcelo de Ribadeneira OFM, *Historia de las islas del Archipiélago filipino y reinos de la Gran China, Tartaria, Cochinchina, Malaca, Siam, Cambodge y Japón*, ed. Juan R. de Legísima OFM (Madrid: La Editorial Católica, 1947), pp. 326–334. Ribadeneira himself went to Japan in 1594, and his book was originally published in Barcelona in 1601.

78. The date after much debate has been determined as 1584 by Bernward Willeke OFM, "Saisho no Furanshisuko-kaishi no raichō," *KK*, 8:249–265 (1963).

79. See Arcadio Schwade SJ, "Saisho no Furanshisuko-kaishi no raichō ni kansuru hōkoku hosoku," *KK*, 8:266–271 (1963).

80. Joanbaptista de Baeça SJ to Pedro Morejón SJ, [Nagasaki], 16 March 1621. Text in Diego Pacheco SJ, "Hoan Baputisuta de Baeza Shinpu no nishokan ni tsuite," *KK*, 10:97 (1965); translated into Japanese, ibid., pp. 79–80. Baeça was near the point of utter distraction: it is hard to tell whether this letter is written in Spanish or Portuguese.

81. Laures, "Zahl der Christen," p. 85.

82. For the precise tabulation, see *VMJ*, I-2, 385–386, and cf. *Introductio*, p. 321 and pp. 329–330.

83. *Sumario*, p. 147; Matsuda and Sakuma, p. 227.

84. For samples of the traditional Japanese accounts of the Honnōji Affair, see: *Nobunaga kōki*, Kadokawa Bunko 2541, 15:414–423; *Tenshōki* (Tenshō chronicle), comp. Ōmura Yūko, pt. 2, *Koretō muhonki* (Account of the rebellion of [Akechi]), *Taikō shiryōshū*, ed. Kuwata Tadachika, Sengoku Shiryō Sōsho 1 (Tokyo: Jinbutsu Ōrai-sha, 1965), pp. 23–43; *Kawazumi Taikōki*, comp. Kawazumi Saburōemon (?), *Taikō shiryōshū*, pp. 229–237. For a portrait of the hegemon Nobunaga as teaman, see Kuwata Tadachika, *Oda Nobunaga*, Kadokawa Shinsho 192 (Tokyo: Kadokawa, 1964), pp. 173–198; an account of the final tea party will be found on pp. 194–198.

85. The Western accounts tally perfectly with the Japanese. See particularly *SP*, ch. xli, pp. 325–332; the quotation is from p. 330. There is a very convenient chronological table of the relations between Nobunaga and the Southern Barbarians in Matsuda, *Nanban shiryō no kenkyū*, pp. 470–484.

86. *SP*, p. 352.

87. *SP*, p. 242.

88. See Chapter 5, pp. 137–139.

Chapter 4: The Donation of Bartolomeu

1. Padre Gaspar Vilela to the Jesuits of India and Portugal, dated Hirado, 29 October 1557, attributes the conversation with Sōrin which led to the Funai hospital's foundation to the very last days of 1556 or the very first of 1557; *Cartas*, I, 55v–56; *Bungo-hen*, I, 195–196. The hospital is discussed by Ebisawa in *Kirishitan no shakai katsudō*, pp. 85–120. The physician was Irmão Luis de Almeida, who himself describes the onrush of patients which necessitated the expansion of hospital facilities: to P. Belchior Nuñes in Cochin, late 1559; *Cartas*, I, 62–62v; *Bungo-hen*, I, 293–294.

2. *GJ*, p. 167.

3. *Regimento pera o Superior das partes do Ximo*, dated 12 February 1582. Synopsis in *VMJ*, I-2, 354–357.

4. Valignano, *Historia Indica*, p. 444.

5. *GJ*, pp. 152–153.

6. Boxer, *The Great Ship from Amacon: Annals of Macao and the Old Japan Trade, 1555–1640* (Lisbon: Centro de Estudos Históricos Ultramarinos, 1959), p. 45 and n. 67, pp. 45–46. To Cabral, Almeida's silver capital was the root of all evil. See the letter to Francisco de Borja, General SJ, Nagasaki, 5 September 1571; *VMJ*, I-2, 465. After discussing the apostolic poverty in which Xavier, Torres, and Fernandes founded the Japanese mission, and how they endured "many injuries and persecutions at the hands of the pagans,

and poverty, not having anything but the alms they received from the ships [of the Portuguese] . . . of which there were only two or three in that time," Cabral waxes indignant. "And in this poverty Our Lord granted them mercy, and by His resources many souls were converted. And they lived in this manner until the Irmão Luis d'Almeida entered [the Society], who brought 4 or five thousand cruzados, with which began the mercantile trade, in Japan as in China; and as it increased so also did luxury in the residences increase. So much that 7 or 8 years ago silks began to be introduced in these parts, in beds as in clothing . . . abundance in foods, multitude of servants, little labor and prayer, etc.; little by little the matter grew to the point where in Japan a Padre resembled a lord more than a Padre of the Society. Whence began the murmurings of the Portuguese that came here, about this as about the increased loose behavior in crooked trading and profiteering (*demasiada soltura na chatinaria e mercancia*)."

7. *Historia Indica*, pp. 445–446.

8. Christianity in Hirado existed at the lowest level of life, on account of the attitude of the Matsuura daimyo. Harassment of Christians noticeably ceased when the China Ship came into port, to resume again when the *nao* departed (*GJ*, p. 60). Despite Jesuit appeals for sanctions, Portuguese ships from 1555 to 1561 (with 1560 the likely exception) annually called here. For details, see Boxer, *The Great Ship from Amacon*, pp. 21–27.

A severe provocation occurred in 1561, when more than a dozen Portuguese (including the Captain-Major, Dom Fernão de Souza) were killed in a quarrel over a piece of cloth worth only a few *monme*, while Matsuura Takanobu, according to Frois, "shrugged off the matter without punishing or chastising the evildoers." *GJ*, p. 155; date corrected to 1561, following Boxer.

In 1564 the Great Ship of Dom Pedro de Almeida, battered by forty-two days of storms, was forced to put in at the roadstead of Hirado. Disregarding Frois' urgent pleas that the *nao* proceed elsewhere, the seasick and weary merchants did not budge from their decision to enter the port (*GJ*, p. 212). A *quid pro quo* was arranged: in exchange for the trade of the *nao*, Matsuura would permit the mission's re-establishment and the construction of a church. But by 1565 the situation was again intolerable for the Christians of Hirado. Accordingly, Dom João Pereira, taking the Jesuits' recommendation, anchored at Fukuda in the Ōmura domain. Infuriated, the Matsuura in conspiracy with some Sakai merchants who owned large vessels sent out a fleet to take the *nao*. Artillery from a Portuguese galliot, which also happened to be in the harbor, managed to drive off the fierce attack, inflicting severe casualties upon the Japanese. It had, of course, been a Padre that warned the *nao*. *GJ*, p. 262; Boxer, *The Great Ship from Amacon*, pp. 30–31. For an outline of Christian missionary activity in the Hirado area, see Schütte, *Introductio*, pp. 464–470. Fujino Tamotsu gives a comprehensive survey of the transformation of the Matsuura from petty leaders of mediaeval military groupings into *kinsei daimyō* in *Bakuhan taiseishi no kenkyū*, pp. 499–531.

9. *GJ*, p. 190; Boxer, *The Great Ship from Amacon*, p. 29.

10. *GJ*, p. 160.

11. The progenitor of the house, Naozumi (a grandson of Fujiwara no Sumitomo) is said to have settled in the area in 994; Fujino Tamotsu, *Bakuhan taiseishi no kenkyū*, p. 559. Fujino treats the transformation of the Ōmura from *sengoku daimyō* into *kinsei daimyō* on pp. 559–567 of his study of the Ōmura *han* (pp. 559–612); my outline follows his discussion.

12. Fujino, p. 561. On the events of Sumitada's rule, see Ōmura-ki, Shiseki zassan, I (Tokyo: Kokusho Kankōkai, 1911), 147–154; the account is one long list of troubles.

13. Fujino, pp. 562–564.

14. GJ, p. 188. On the events of 1563 and the rebellion of Gotō Takaaki, which seems to have been motivated at least in part by the anti-Christian reaction of a Buddhist party in Ōmura, see pp. 205–230 of the very elaborate biographical sketch by Matsuda Kiichi, "Ōmura Sumitada den," Nippo kōshōshi, Shinwa Bunko 6 (Tokyo: Kyōbunkan, 1963). The rebellion may well have been triggered by an action of the new Christian zealot Dom Bartolomeu on the occasion of the Bon observances: instead of burning incense before the votive statue of his (adoptive) and Takaaki's (real) father, Sumisaki, he burnt the statue—"which the bonzes took for an extremely disgusting crime, on account of the profits which had flowed to them" from such ceremonials. So states Frois (GJ, p. 186); but the modern historian cannot fail to remark upon the highly provocative nature of this transgression against the most sacred traditional dictates of filial piety.

15. GJ, p. 307. Valignano treats the ups and downs of Sumitada's career as one of the examples of the great and mysterious judgments of God in conducting the work of the Japan mission through a series of voltes of fortune. Sumario, pp. 272–274; Matsuda and Sakuma, pp. 277–278.

16. VMJ, I-1, 285–286.

17. GJ, p. 463.

18. VMJ, I-1, 287.

19. GJ, p. 465.

20. Shimazu Takahisa (1514–1571) was the true founder of the Shimazu power in the sixteenth century. His son Yoshihisa (1533–1611) was its consolidator: he was the victor of Mimigawa over the Ōtomo; and in 1584 his forces routed the Ryūzōji at Okitanawate on the Shimabara Peninsula. Ryūzōji Takanobu lost his life in this battle. See Kawasoe Hiroshi, Ryūzōji Takanobu, Nihon no Bushō 45 (Tokyo: Jinbutsu Ōrai-sha, 1967), pp. 336–345.

21. Boxer, The Great Ship from Amacon, pp. 30–35. The nao of 1570, with Manuel Travassos as Captain-Major, is cited by Matsuda, "Ōmura Sumitada den," pp. 267–268, as an exception to the Ōmura rule, visitor instead of Shiki on Amakusa; but Boxer states that this ship also called at Nagasaki.

Okamoto Yoshitomo, Jūroku-seiki Nichiō kōtsūshi no kenkyū (Tokyo: Rokkō Shobō, 1942 revised edition), is another invaluable study. A major portion, pp. 293–503, is devoted to a year-by-year consideration of the traffic of European vessels from its beginnings to 1590; there is a convenient table on pp. 504–514. The critical decade 1561–1570 is treated in great detail, pp. 369–414.

22. For accounts of the campaign, see: Ōtomo kōhaiki (The rise and fall of the Ōtomo), Ōita-ken kyōdo shiryō shūsei, I, Senki-hen, 182–197; also Ryōhōki (The chronicle of Buzen and Bungo), ibid., II, 462–464. For the developments as they bore on Ōmura, see Matsuda, "Ōmura Sumitada den," pp. 257–259.

23. GJ, p. 404.

24. GJ, p. 433. The date cannot be determined from Frois' text. Schütte gives 1571 (VMJ, I-1, 413), which Boxer follows in The Great Ship from Amacon, p. 36. Matsuda, after a careful examination of relevant Japanese sources, settles on 1570; "Ōmura Sumitada den," pp. 264–267.

25. *GJ*, p. 441. The date under which Frois gives his account is 1573; the best efforts of Matsuda, "Ōmura Sumitada den," pp. 269–295, cannot determine its accuracy.

26. See *Ōmura-ki*, pp. 152–153, for a brief description of this uncomfortable visit.

27. P. Gaspar Coelho to General SJ, *annua* for 1581, dated Nagasaki, 15 February 1582; *Cartas*, II, 18v–19v. Matsuda, "Ōmura Sumitada den," pp. 310–315. On the fate of Kamachi Shigenami, see also Kawasoe, *Ryūzōji Takanobu*, pp. 325–330. Shigenami had planned overtures to the Shimazu. Takanobu evidently lured him out of his impregnable fortress of Yanagawa under the pretext of a *sarugaku* party. Frois treats the incident in *SP*, pp. 160–170.

28. Alvarez-Taladriz, "Introduccion" to *Sumario*, n. 179, pp. 70–71, offers the very interesting speculation that Ōmura's donation of 1580 was merely a renovation of a contract made previously, the basis of the assertion being the mention by Frois in *GJ*, p. 433, that "the necessary agreements were concluded with Dom Bartholomeo" at the time of initial settlement in Nagasaki. Alvarez further speculates that Ōmura, acting under pressure from Ryūzōji, had revoked the first donation, that the Padres for that reason kept the *nao* of 1579 from going to Nagasaki, and that the repentant Ōmura thereupon undertook reparations. The pressions of Ryūzōji, according to Alvarez, were motivated by reasons of state and ultimately directed at the Padres as principal purveyors of munitions to Ōtomo Sōrin, "on whose behalf—even before his baptism—they annually used to negotiate the investment of 3,000 ducats in the China trade." The extrapolation seems a trifle extreme.

29. Spanish text in *VMJ*, I-2, 477–478; photocopy of the nearly identical document sent by 2nd route in *VMJ*, I-1, facing p. 416. The latter text is used by Alvarez-Taladriz and published in his "Introduccion" to *Sumario*, p. 70. Schütte gives a German translation in *VMJ*, I-1, 411–412. For Japanese translations, see: Cieslik, "Kirishitan chigyōchi Nagasaki," *Kirishitan Bunka Kenkyūkai kaihō*, 6.3:7 (September 1962); Matsuda's biographical sketch of Valignano, Matsuda and Sakuma, pp. 73–74; Iwao Seiichi, *Sakoku*, Vol. XIV of *Nihon no rekishi* (Tokyo: Chūō Kōron-sha, 1966), 46–47.

Schütte's is the pre-eminent research into Western sources: *VMJ*, I-1, 411–418, and *Introductio*, pp. 722–726. Okamoto's investigation of Japanese sources, *Jūroku-seiki Nichiō kōtsūshi no kenkyū*, pp. 569–571, has been the basis of all subsequent commentary from that standpoint. The best integrated discussion of the "Donation of Bartolomeu" is by Alvarez-Taladriz, "Introduccion" to *Sumario*, pp. 68–81. Also see Matsuda, "Ōmura Sumitada den," pp. 315–319. Boxer's discussion, *Christian Century*, pp. 100–102, is inadequate.

30. *VMJ*, I-1, 412.

31. Alvarez cites a major portion of this letter's text in his "Introduccion" to *Sumario*, pp. 71–72. Ōmura's income from the merchants' dues was some three thousand ducats: Schütte, *Introductio*, p. 723; *VMJ*, I-1, 369 and 412.

32. Valignano states explicitly that all the Padres of Shimo, of Bungo, and of Miyako were consulted. Much of the discussion was, of course, conducted by correspondence. The formal seal was put on the matter in the Japan Consultation's Question XIV, "Whether it is good to keep the localities of Nagasaki and Mogi." Valignano's resolution was: "It appears good to continue holding these localities of Nagasaki and Mogi, with the reservation that the Japan Superior have the liberty to give them up if, in consultation, such should appear better; making certain that Don Bartolomé of Omura

act with the *yakunin* in such a manner that justice be done." The text is provided by Alvarez, "Introduccion" to *Sumario*, pp. 73–74.

33. The preceding account is based on Schütte, *VMJ*, I-1, 414–416. Valignano, the prolific writer of statutes, apparently also wrote a *Regimen* for the *yakunin* of Nagasaki and Mogi. This is indicated in his *Regimen for the Japan Superior* of 24 June 1580; see *VMJ*, I-1, 430: "The Superiors are not to intrude into the exercise of justice by the *yakunin*, be it to let mercy prevail over the letter of the law; that would be the cause of unrest among the Japanese, who know no other justice but the sword, and the ruin of obedience among subordinates, nay! even of the Church. The *yakunin* have their *regimentos*. As long as they proceed accordingly, they should not be hindered by the Superiors, though they judge with severity (but also with justice)." In addition, Valignano's statement on the *Faculties of the Vice-Provincial of Japan* (2 February 1582) authorizes the Vice-Provincial to make the necessary dispositions in Nagasaki and Mogi, "the two harbors of the Church," and to promulgate new *regimentos* and laws to secure good government and better fortifications; *VMJ*, I-2, 352.

34. *VMJ*, I-1, 417–418.

35. *VMJ*, I-1, 429–430.

36. *VMJ*, I-2, 276.

37. *Apologia en la qual se responde a diversas calumnias que se escrivieron contra los Padres de la Comp.ª de Jesús de Jappón y de la China*; composed in Macao in January 1598 and revised and expanded in Japan in October 1598. The text of the portions relevant to the question of Nagasaki is provided by Alvarez, "Introduccion" to *Sumario*, n. 204, pp. 80–81.

38. *Ōmura-ke hiroku*, in *Shiseki zassan*, I, 163; the text gives the date as Tenmon (1532–1555), but this is an apparent slip of the pen for Tenshō (1573–1593) and is accordingly emended. The obviously tendentious Japanese sources deserve very little credence. Certainly the *Ōmura-ke hiroku* contains sheer fantasies of the sort that even the authors of the *Kirishitan monogatari* genre did not excel. The extravagant nature of this text is evident from its very first sentences, which detail the inception of the Southern Barbarians' monstrous plot to subvert Japan by religious means. The impression of extravagance increases as the narrative proceeds to attribute the untimely deaths of Sumitada's successors to Christian poisoners. Into the caldron with the Iewes!

39. The text proper of this chronicle was compiled in 1764 by Tanabe Mokei. For the relevant accounts, see *Nagasaki shi seihen*, ed. Koga Jūjirō (Nagasaki: Nagasaki Bunko Kankōkai, 1928), pp. 246–248. In one interpretation given here, Nagasaki Jinzaemon Sumikage figures as a loyal helpmate of Ōmura in the wars against Ryūzōji: "In the first year of Genki [1570], in order to equip himself with weaponry, he borrowed silver from the barbarians, turning over the area of Nagasaki in pawn." He thereby becomes an unwitting tool of the Kirishitans; for his successors the Ōmura and Arima "conferred and decided instead of repaying the loan to turn over the area of Nagasaki and make it into Southern Barbarian temple domain."

40. In Alvarez, "Introduccion" to *Sumario*, n. 204, p. 80.

41. One might only add that Jesuit financial assistance to Ōmura (if not Ōmura's explicit financial indebtedness under explicit conditions) is a fact acknowledged by Valignano: "At times it is necessary [to assist] some Christian lords with much expenditure, whom it is necessary to aid with money during the time of their wars, for one would otherwise run the peril of losing them together with their lands; and this has been done many

times with Don Bartolomé, lord of Omura, and with the lord of Arima." *Sumario*, ch. xxvii, "Of the great expenses that are made in Japan and our mode of support and of the income necessary to enable forward progress in this enterprise," p. 310; Matsuda and Sakuma, p. 288.

42. *Sumario*, pp. 309–311 passim: Matsuda and Sakuma, pp. 287–289. I do not treat the question of Jesuit involvement in the China trade with all the detail it deserves because there is little improving over Boxer's general treatment of the theme of God and Mammon in *Christian Century*, ch. iii ("Christianity and the Kurofune"), pp. 91–136.

43. Valignano has left behind a fascinating analysis of this problem in ch. xxviii ("Of the cause and reason why the Christian lords are not able to support the Padres and their churches in Japan") of the *Sumario*. We have here an instance of the Western perspective providing the clearer view. Bungo is obviously the model: the *Visitator*'s theoretical structure draws on the terminology of the Ōtomo vassal organization. *Sumario*, pp. 312–317; Matsuda and Sakuma, pp. 290–293.

44. For an integration of sources concerning Ichijō Kanesada (1543–1585), see Matsuda Kiichi, *Kirishitan kenkyū daiichibu: Shikoku-hen* (Osaka: Sōgensha, 1953), pp. 49–62.

Kanesada was the son of a sister of Ōtomo Sōrin. The traditional Japanese accounts paint him as a thoroughly despicable character; but Matsuda asserts that a large portion of the stories constitutes propaganda spread abroad by party-takers of Chōsogabe Motochika to justify his usurpation, which occurred in 1574. Kanesada fled to Sōrin, and during this inauspicious visit expressed the desire to become Christian; but the unsavory stories had evidently preceded him to reach the ear of Cabral, who at first refused to baptize him. He finally received the sacrament in 1575. Sōrin gave Kanesada one of his daughters in marriage and sent him back to Tosa "with a great fleet and in grand style"—each of the ships displayed a cross on its banners, for Dom Paulo intended not only to recover his domains but also to Christianize them; but Chōsogabe was soon able to chase him from Tosa again.

Coelho's *annua* for 1581 (*Cartas*, II, 46–46v) states that Valignano on his return from the inspection tour of the Kansai in 1581 met "the good king of Tòsa" near his hiding place of Kojima in Iyo. The *Visitator* praised the Christian zeal of Dom Paulo, who preserved his hope of salvation although he lived alone among pagans, made his faith known to all by fingering his rosary continuously, and asked that his thirteen-year-old son be accepted into a *seminario*. Cf. *SP*, pp. 264–265. Kanesada died in 1585, at a time when his enemy Chōsogabe was hard-pressed by Hideyoshi's invasion. Valignano adduces his fate as one of the examples of the mysterious workings of God in the spread of His doctrine: *Sumario*, p. 280; Matsuda and Sakuma, p. 280.

45. See the relevant text from ch. xvi of Valignano's *Apologia*, in *VMJ*, I-2, 455–460. Schütte has translated a portion into German; *VMJ*, I-1, 234–235.

46. Summary in *VMJ*, I-1, 394–398.

47. *Sumario*, ch. xxix, pp. 331–339; Matsuda and Sakuma, pp. 294–298.

48. A convenient summary of the varying dispositions by European authorities concerning the Jesuit involvement in the China-Japan trade is given by Alvarez-Taladriz in *Sumario*, ch. xxix, n. 4, pp. 334–335. The period covered is 1567–1633.

49. Question XIII of the Japan Consultation: "Of the remedy which has to be procured for the temporal sustenance of Japan." Text provided by Alvarez in *Sumario*, ch. xxix, n. 2, pp. 331–334.

50. *GJ*, pp. 430–431; Boxer, *The Great Ship from Amacon*, pp. 37–38.
51. *Sumario*, p. 336; Matsuda and Sakuma, p. 295.
52. *Sumario*, pp. 336–337; Matsuda and Sakuma, pp. 295–296. For details of the shipwreck, see Okamoto, *Jūroku-seiki Nichiō kōtsūshi no kenkyū*, pp. 431–441.
53. *Sumario*, ch. xxix, p. 338; Matsuda and Sakuma, p. 297: "In the name of the entire Society in Japan and of this province, I ask our Father [General] . . . that he truly see after the search of remedy for Japan, with His Holiness and with His Majesty and with the other Cardinals, because I discharge my conscience upon you, Father General, for I cannot do aught more. And that which must be procured for Japan is at the very least ten thousand ducats [of yearly support] and the capital of thirty or forty thousand ducats."

Chapter 5: Hideyoshi and the Sectarians

1. *Kanpaku*: Tenshō 13/7/11 (6 August 1585). *Daijō daijin*: Tenshō 14/12/19 (27 January 1587). On Tenshō 19/12/27 (9 February 1592) Hideyoshi passed on the rank of *kanpaku* to his nephew and adopted son, Hidetsugu, and thereby assumed the title of *taikō*, which applies to the Regent's father. Strictly speaking, it is an anachronism to call him by that title in contexts prior to 1592; but his popular identification with it has become so complete that the word "Taikō" is for all practical purposes synonymous with the name Hideyoshi.

2. Laures, *Takayama Ukon*, pp. 183–184. Gamō Ujisato was baptized just before the Negoro campaign (*c.* January–March 1585). Kuroda Josui Yoshitaka (Kodera Kanbei) followed shortly thereafter. Ibid., p. 174.

3. Prenestino, Hirado, 1 October 1587; quoted by Laures, *Takayama Ukon*, pp. 193–194.

4. Cf. Suzuki Ryōichi, *Toyotomi Hideyoshi*, Iwanami Shinsho 171 (Tokyo: Iwanami, 1954), pp. 92–95; also Kuwata Tadachika, *Toyotomi Hideyoshi*, Kadokawa Shinsho 198 (Tokyo: Kadokawa, 1965), pp. 76–78.

5. To Kita no Mandokoro, Tenshō 15/5/9; text in *Nihon shiryō shūsei* (Tokyo: Heibonsha, 1956), p. 255.

6. Frois to Valignano, Shimonoseki, [4] October 1586; *Cartas*, II, 178v. Matsuda Kiichi, *Taikō to gaikō* (Tokyo: Tōgensha, 1966), p. 50, corrects the letter's date from the accepted 17 October.

7. Coelho had left Nagasaki on 6 March 1586 with the express purpose of interceding with Hideyoshi on behalf of Sōrin and the other Christian daimyo of Kyushu. He arrived in Sakai at the end of April. Takayama Ukon, Konishi Ryūsa, and Ai Gozaemon arranged the audience for him. Hideyoshi was at the time occupied with the completion of Osaka Castle, and received the Vice-Provincial at the site. Frois tells the story of Coelho's journey to Osaka and interview with the Taikō in *Cartas*, II, 173–179v.

A discussion of the Osaka audience, with very extensive quotations of Frois' accounts, is given by Okamoto Yoshitomo in *Tenshō 14nen Ōsaka-jō ekkenki* (Tokyo: Kasahara Shoten, 1942); *n.b.* p. 31. See also the same author's *Toyotomi Hideyoshi: Nanbanjin no kiroku ni yoru*, Chūkō Shinsho 28 (Tokyo: Chūō Kōron-sha, 1963), pp. 50–76. Organtino's report is in the Roman Archives of the Society of Jesus (JapSin 11 I, 70) and has not yet been published. Laures paraphrases portions of it in his account of the audience, *Takayama Ukon*, pp. 187–192, and it is also utilized by Matsuda Kiichi in *Taikō to gaikō*, pp. 47–57.

8. Laures, *Takayama Ukon*, p. 190; cf. Matsuda, *Taikō to gaikō*, pp. 51–52.

9. Matsuda, *Taikō to gaikō*, pp. 40–42.

10. Boxer, *Christian Century*, pp. 257–259, discusses the project and cites excerpts, as does Matsuda, *Taikō to gaikō*, pp. 42–44.

11. Okamoto, *Ōsaka-jō ekkenki*, pp. 119–120.

12. Cf. Laures, *Takayama Ukon*, p. 198: "Valignano states that [Coelho] had the ship made so that he could more easily undertake his diplomatic journeys; and one might conceivably understand the armament's being meant against pirates. And he evidently thought he would thereby cut a more imposing figure; as he loved a pompous and brilliant stage presence in any case, thinking it necessary for suitable representation of the Church. At the audience in Osaka Coelho's train consisted of thirty persons, and Pasio complains about this as also about his senseless profligacy with presents, unheard-of in Japan." This is a clear instance of the perversion of Valignano's dicta on ceremonial bearing.

13. The sole extant copy of the Japanese original is in the Matsuura Shiryō Hakubutsukan in Hirado. Published in: *Shiryō ni yoru Nihon no ayumi*, p. 51; *Nihon shiryō shūsei*, p. 271; Matsuda, *Taikō to gaikō*, pp. 64–65; Ebisawa, *Kirishitanshi no kenkyū*, pp. 146–147; Ebisawa, "Nihon Nijūroku Seijin kankei Nihon bunken," *KK*, 8:138 (1963); Ebisawa, *Nihon Kirishitan shi*, pp. 266–267.

The contemporary Portuguese translation (which is preserved in the Jesuit Archives in Rome) is reproduced by photocopy in Matsuda, *Taikō to gaikō*, p. 65, and printed in that author's *Nanban shiryō no kenkyū*, pp. 497–498. *Cartas*, II, 209v, has somewhat edited the original. There is a German translation of the Portuguese text in Laures, *Takayama Ukon*, pp. 207–208, and an English translation from the Portuguese in Boxer, *Christian Century*, p. 148.

14. Frois' effusive account of this lurid matter is found in *Cartas*, II, 202–213 (to General SJ, Arima, 20 February 1588).

Matsuda devotes a substantial portion of *Nanban shiryō no kenkyū* (pp. 127–538) to the examination of Frois' historiography. Case 32, pp. 490–503, is a scholarly review of Frois' treatment of the expulsion edict; *Taikō to gaikō*, pp. 61–75, covers fundamentally the same ground in more popular fashion. Also see Boxer, *Christian Century*, pp. 144–152, and cf. Laures, *Takayama Ukon*, pp. 198–212. Laures notes (p. 202, n. 73) that Valignano severely edited Frois' report, leaving out all "superfluous" matter, so that it may be the *Visitator* who is to blame for the published account's apparent omissions.

15. Document in the Ise Jingū Bunko, published in: *Shiryō ni yoru Nihon no ayumi*, pp. 50–51; *Nihon shiryō shūsei*, p. 270; Ebisawa, *Nihon Kirishitan shi*, p. 268; Ebisawa, *Kirishitanshi no kenkyū*, pp. 159–160; Ebisawa, "Nihon Nijūroku Seijin kankei Nihon bunken," pp. 139–140.

16. My discussion follows Inoue Toshio, "Shūkyō ikki," *Iwanami kōza: Nihon rekishi*, VIII (*Chūsei* 4), 157–188. On the social structure of the Honganji "religious monarchy" and its political and economic base, also see Inoue, *Ikkō ikki no kenkyū* (Tokyo: Yoshikawa Kōbunkan, 1968), ch. vi, pp. 479–555. The True Pure Land Sect (Jōdo Shinshū) is also known as the Single-Directed Sect (Ikkōshū); the terms are used interchangeably.

17. Inoue, "Shūkyō ikki," p. 167.

18. The greatest activity in the founding of such confraternities did not,

however, occur until after Hideyoshi's expulsion edict, constituting the preparation of infrastructures designed to continue the activity of the Church under persecution. Cf. Sukeno Kentarō, *Kirishitan no shinkō seikatsu* (Tokyo: Chūō Shuppansha, 1957), p. 15 and ch. i passim. Matsuda has published and discussed a series of recently discovered documents dealing with Christian *kumi* under persecution: *Nanban shiryō no kenkyū*, pp. 1022–1221; the dates span 1617–1622. On Ikkōshū *kumi*, see Inoue, *Ikkō ikki no kenkyū*, pp. 499–534.

19. See the schematic representation of the Ikkō role structure in Inoue, "Shūkyō ikki," p. 180, and also the schema presented by the same author in collaboration with Kasahara Kazuo in "Jōdo Shinshū," *Taikei Nihonshi sōsho*, XVIII, 175.

20. Hall's 1961 article, "Foundations of the Modern Japanese Daimyo," developed these distinctions. But Hall seems to have been himself dissatisfied with the modality of his approach, dropping the *shokuhō daimyō* category altogether in his subsequent *Government and Local Power in Japan* (1966).

21. Inoue, "Shūkyō ikki," p. 183.

22. A Zen monk who was eyewitness to the Kaga *ikki* thus describes the activities of the *monto*: "They attack and calumniate the various sects and make [their adherents] into followers of their own faction; they kill *shugo* officials and usurp [their functions]. They intimidate tax collectors and they plunder, and there is no stopping their impetus." Quoted by Inoue, "Shūkyō ikki," p. 171.

23. *Nobunaga kōki*, Kadokawa Bunko 2541, 7:175; entry for Tenshō 2/9/29 (13 October 1574). My outline of events largely follows Inoue and Kasahara, "Jōdo Shinshū," pp. 178–182, and Suzuki Ryōichi, *Oda Nobunaga*, Iwanami Shinsho 649 (Tokyo: Iwanami, 1967), pp. 107–122.

24. Matsuda, *Taikō to gaikō*, p. 67.

25. Matsuda, *Nanban shiryō no kenkyū*, p. 500.

26. See Laures, *Takayama Ukon*, pp. 202–205. The details are taken from a letter from Prenestino to General SJ, dated 1 October 1587, in the Jesuit Archives in Rome.

27. *Kyūshū godōza-ki* (Account of the Kyushu Expedition), quoted by Matsuda in *Nanban shiryō no kenkyū*, p. 502, and *Taikō to gaikō*, pp. 67–68. The anonymous author was probably Ōmura Yūko, one of Hideyoshi's *otogi-shū* sycophants and author of several other narratives of his deeds. The professional story-teller's touch is evident.

28. Prenestino, quoted by Laures, *Takayama Ukon*, pp. 202–203.

29. The name Ukon is in actuality an honorific court title, and refers to a rank in the Palace Guards of the Right (*u-konoe*). The precise gradation in this case is as indeterminable as the actual duties were nonexistent, and Takayama is variously called Ukon no Daibu, Ukon no Jō, Ukon no Shōgen, and Ukon no Suke. His childhood name was Hikogorō, and subsequently he seems to have been called Nagafusa and Shigetomo. As a teaman he used the name Minami no Bō. His further sobriquets are Tōhaku and Yūshō. See Matsuda, *Nanban shiryō no kenkyū*, pp. 726–727, and Kataoka Yakichi, *Takayama Ukon Daibu Nagafusa den* (Tokyo: Katorikku Chūō Shoin, 1936), pp. 8–14.

30. For more information on Matsunaga, see below, n. 4 to *Kirishitan monogatari*. Matsunaga (if one may further indulge in the popular genre) lives on as the grandiose villain of the *jōruri* and *kabuki* stage in the play *Kinkakuji* (The Golden Pavilion; 1757).

31. Frois, Usuki, 20 August 1576; *Cartas*, I, 364: "Daijodono grãde inimigo, & impugnador do nome Christão." Cf. Laures, *Takayama Ukon*, pp. 10–11.

32. *GJ*, pp. 131 and 220.

33. See the biographical letter of 20 August 1576, *Cartas*, I, 364; *YNT*, II, 302.

34. Yūki Yamashiro no Kami Shinsai Tadamasa was from a family of Ashikaga Bakufu functionaries and had connections also at the Imperial Court. Matsuda, *Nanban shiryō no kenkyū*, pp. 682–684, summarizes the information available on him. Frois praises him as a great scholar, astrologer, and master of the epistolary style; *GJ*, pp. 138 and 220. Irmão João Fernandes in a letter to a Padre in China (9 October 1564; *Cartas*, I, 144) attributes great necromantic expertise to both Yūki and Kiyohara, and asserts that while the one tutored the Ashikaga shogun in idolatry the other counseled Miyoshi Chōkei on military strategy, first consulting the devil; the two were frequently called upon to act as arbiters of sectarian matters. Kiyohara Ekata (Dōhaku) was a court noble and at the time of his conversion, apart from his secretarial title of *dai geki*, bore also the titles *shōnagon* (lesser councilor), *jijū* (chamberlain), and *hakase* (doctor): He was advanced to the Third Rank in 1581, and died in 1590, apparently having abandoned the Christian faith; see Matsuda, *Nanban shiryō no kenkyū*, pp. 720–721. Presumably his doctorate was obtained from the *Onmyōryō* (Yin-Yang Department) established in the classical codes. Although it would be rash to assume that the unsympathetic Jesuits made an accurate estimate of the academic standards of Kyoto, one might note that the *Nippo jisho*, p. 149, defines the degree as follows: "*Facaxe*. Feiticeiro, ou adeuinho.——Witch doctor, or soothsayer."

Frois treats the entire affair in *GJ*, pp. 138–147. See also the commentaries of Laures in *Takayama Ukon*, pp. 9–17, and in *Die Anfänge der Mission von Miyako* (Münster i. Westf.: Aschendorffsche Verlagsbuchhandlung, 1951; Mission Studies and Documents 16), pp. 72–83.

35. On this intrigue, see *GJ*, pp. 279–286. Vilela, who had been forewarned, left Miyako on 27 July 1565. The edict was promulgated on 31 July; the shogun Yoshiteru, who had shown himself well-disposed toward the missionaries, had been murdered on 17 June, On the interconnection between the two events, see Matsuda, *Nanban shiryō no kenkyū*, pp. 407–411; and cf. Laures, *Die Anfänge der Mission von Miyako*, pp. 107–119.

36. 1563 has been the accepted date; I follow Matsuda's correction, *Nanban shiryō no kenkyū*, pp. 721–726.

37. Wada Koremasa is eulogized in Frois' letter to Padre Antonio de Quadros SJ, Provincial of India, dated Miyako, 28 September 1571; *Cartas*, I, 311–315v. See also *GJ*, pp. 414–422; and cf. Laures, *Takayama Ukon*, pp. 44–45.

38. Aida Yūji, *Haisha no jōken: Sengoku jidai o kangaeru*, Chūkō Shinsho 62 (Tokyo: Chūō Kōron-sha, 1965), p. 166. For Frois' melodrama, see his letter to Cabral, Miyako, 20 April 1573, *Cartas*, I, 341v–342v; *YNT*, II, 249–254 (where a citation of the *Intoku Taiheiki* account is included). Cf. *Intoku Taiheiki* (also known as *Intoku-ki*), *Tsūzoku Nihon zenshi*, XIV (Tokyo: Waseda Daigaku Shuppanbu, 1913), 153. The book is a military chronicle rather than an assembly of sources. The preface is dated Genroku 8 (1695), and the proofreader's postscript to correspond to 1712. The unusually rich sweep of the work covers practically the entire Sengoku period, from 1490 to the eve of the Grand Pacification of 1600 (hence *Taiheiki*), and encompasses the Kansai and most of the rest of Western Japan.

Kataoka, *Takayama Ukon Daibu*, p. 30, cites another Japanese source which places Korenaga's death in the year 1600; but that source must be mistaken or refer to a different person, for Frois, while shivering at the pagan rites, describes our young unfortunate's funeral in detail. Also see *GJ*, pp. 422–423; and cf. Laures' attempt at exoneration, *Takayama Ukon*, pp. 49–53.

39. "'How welcome indeed is your progress to the Capital!' And both shed tears." *Kawazumi Taikōki, Taikō shiryōshū*, p. 257. On Ukon's role in the battle, see pp. 263–264. He shared the honor of leading the cavalry van (*onma no sakite*) with Nakagawa Sebyōe no Jō Kiyohide.

40. Laures, *Takayama Ukon*, p. 138: "Ukon besiegt Akechi." The subsequent section bristles with such formulations. Laures never hesitates at total acceptance of the contemporary Jesuit propaganda. It suits his point: Ukon's strength was that of a thousand men because his heart was pure. Hideyoshi's army, according to those sources, was nowhere in sight when Ukon with his valiant thousand cast himself upon the sinister myriad of Akechi. Losing one man only, he smote two hundred. The Christians were overjoyed at "Ukon's victory." And Oda Nobutaka, we are supposed to believe, was heard to remark that Ukon had achieved this brilliant victory only because he was Christian.

41. Ukon had the joint command of the eleventh company of the advance guard on the march and was backing up Nakagawa Sebyōe when that rash warrior was killed in Sakuma Morimasa's famous attack; *Tenshōki*, pt. 3, *Shibata kassenki* (Account of the Shibata wars), *Taikō shiryōshū*, pp. 48–53. Kataoka, *Takayama Ukon Daibu*, pp. 76–90, cites a series of other sources. Cf. Laures, *Takayama Ukon*, pp. 145–150.

42. To the historian the sole (but very substantial) value of Laures' *Takayama Ukon* is the extensive quotation of contemporary Jesuit sources which are not available elsewhere. Laures' intention to serve the process of canonization is clear from the language of his summary. Consider p. 377:

> Ukon desired that truth and amity alone should act and recruit. It will be difficult to discover in all of world history a hero in whom truth shone in more purity or sought adherents with greater amity . . .
>
> Ukon is indeed great as a human being, as a general, as an artist, and above all as a Christian. His life was a living sermon to his contemporaries. His missionary zeal occasioned the richest of fruit, and his Christian heroism under three great tests of fire has secured for him a place of honor among the glorious martyrs of the Church.
>
> And so it is understandable that the Catholics of Japan should like to see their great compatriot elevated upon the altars and placed before the eyes of all Christianity as a shining example. During his living days he was accounted by his astonished non-Christian friends the incarnation of the highest ideal of humanity. His moral purity was an object of universal admiration. The heroism with which he sacrificed all for the sake of his Christian conviction stirred the admiration of such men as Maeda Toshiie and Hosokawa Tadaoki. Even today's non-Christian Japan with pride sees in Takayama Ukon one of the noblest of the sons of Nippon, and would welcome most eagerly his canonization as an honor upon the entire nation. Takatsuki and Kanazawa view him as the greatest man of their long history and hallow his memory.

For more of this sort of thing, see also Ulderico Romani SDB, *Un Samurai Senza Macchia e Senza Paura* (Rome: Officium Libri Catholici, 1959).

43. Johan Huizinga, *The Waning of the Middle Ages* (Garden City, N.Y.: Doubleday, 1954; Anchor Book A42), p. 183. Huizinga states that the conception of the Counter Reformation saint did not differ from that of the Middle Ages; the assertion is certainly proved in this case.

44. Laures, *Takayama Ukon*, pp. 164–165.

45. See Suzuki Ryōichi, *Toyotomi Hideyoshi*, pp. 71–75.

46. Laures, *Takayama Ukon*, pp. 180–182. The bonzes' intermediary, the Jesuits state, was the former bonze Yakuin Zensō (Tokuun), the foiling of his devices being part of the reason for the rancor he subsequently vented.

47. Quoted by Laures, *Takayama Ukon*, p. 177, n. 84.

48. As a teaman Ukon was numbered among the "Seven Accomplished Disciples" of Sen no Rikyū (*Rikyū Shittetsu*); and one of the Japanese anecdotes concerning his fall from Hideyoshi's grace has the Taikō send Rikyū himself to plead with Ukon to recant. Ukon replied, in effect, that the steadfast samurai must hold to the higher duty. Kataoka, *Takayama Ukon Daibu*, pp. 104–105.

49. Cf. Matsuda, *Taikō to gaikō*, p. 68.

50. Matsuda, *Taikō to gaikō*, p. 71.

51. Alfons Kleiser SJ, "P. Alexander Valignanis Gesandschaftsreise nach Japan zum Quambacudono Toyotomi Hideyoshi," *MN*, 1.1:78 (January 1938), quotes Valignano's reference to Hebrews 11:38—"wandering in deserts and mountains and caves, and the holes of the earth."

52. See Boxer, *Christian Century*, p. 149: Coelho "endeavored to get Arima to induce the other Christian daimyo to unite in armed resistance against the expulsion edict. In this he failed, so he fell back on a more temporizing policy. But he still had not learned his lesson entirely, since he wrote to Manila, Macao, and Goa begging for two or three hundred soldiers and firearms wherewith to stiffen the Christian daimyo. The Spanish authorities contented themselves with referring his request to Madrid, and the Jesuit Superior at Manila sent him a severe reprimand for his imprudence. The Portuguese sent him some weapons but no troops."

The precise nature of Coelho's plans is unclear; and Matsuda Kiichi laments (*Taikō to gaikō*, p. 86) that although the existence and place of repose of voluminous Jesuit correspondence on the topic are known the material's confidential nature has kept it from publication.

53. Quoted by Matsuda, *Taikō to gaikō*, pp. 88–89.

54. See below, *Deceit Disclosed*, III.

55. Philip Habsburg was of Castile the Second and of Portugal the First. The Portuguese dynastic crisis was caused by the death of Sebastião I at the Battle of Alcazar Quivir in 1578, on an ill-advised Moroccan crusade. His successor Dom Henrique was a cardinal and perforce heirless. When he died in 1580, seven claimants vied for the throne, and the Spanish Philip (son, nephew, and husband of members of the Portuguese royal house) conquered. But the party of Dom Antonio of Crato remained active: backed now by the French and then by the English, he continued armed interventions until 1589, and was to stay a focus of Portuguese recalcitrants' hopes until his death in 1595. Interestingly enough, the Jesuits in Portugal itself "generally supported" Philip's accession; John H. Elliott, *Imperial Spain: 1469–1716* (Harmondsworth, Middlesex: Penguin Books, 1970), p. 273.

To whose *conquista* did Japan properly belong? In discussing the decision to send Spanish Franciscans to Japan, a Spanish friar gives the answer: "conforme a la división que hizo Alejandro VI del mundo . . . Japón, como parte occidental (según dicen los cosmógrafos), es de la corona de Castilla." Ribadeneira, *Historia de las islas del Archipiélago*, p. 332.

56. Boxer, *Christian Century*, p. 162.

57. The table is adapted from Matsuda, *Nanban shiryō no kenkyū*, p. 891. Matsuda treats the *San Felipe* incident on pp. 853–898, and deals extensively

with the incident's prior historiography. A more concise statement of his views is given in *Taikō to gaikō*, ch. xi, pp. 200–223.

58. Cieslik, "Nihon Nijūroku Seijin junkyō kankei shiryō," *KK*, 8:114 (1963). Cieslik's article presents in Japanese translation four Jesuit documents (in the British Museum) concerned with the *San Felipe* incident and the subsequent martyrdom.

The single most interesting contemporary Jesuit account is by Frois: *Relatione della gloriosa morte di xxvi. posti in croce . . .*, fatta in Italiano dal P. Gasparo Spitilli di Campli (In Roma, Appresso Luigi Zannetti 1599). An English version "Translated oute of the Jtaliã Copie" with a preface dated "the last of this month of december 1600" is included in a heretofore unconsidered collection of manuscripts in the possession of the Houghton Library (MS. Jap 3): "The Report of the glorious death of xxvj persons executed upon the Crosse by the commandement of the King of Japonia"; cited by permission of the Harvard College Library.

The Franciscan case has been amply stated and documented by Lorenzo Pérez OFM in "Cartas y relaciones del Japón," a long series published in *Archivo Ibero-Americano* between the years 1915 and 1923; of particular importance are the portions included in vols. 13–19 (1920–1923) and dealing with the Franciscan missionaries' persecution and martyrdom. The friar Ribadeneira, who was himself in Nagasaki at the time of his confrères' martyrdom, devotes major portions of his *Historia* to the affair's antecedents (Book Four, pp. 319–426), events (Book Five, pp. 427–533), and personages (Book Six, pp. 535–638).

59. *Testimonio del Obispo del Japón sobre las causas del embargo del navío San Felipe, prisión y martirio de los frailes franciscanos* (text in Portuguese), dated Macao, 17 November 1597, in Pérez, "Cartas y relaciones del Japón," *Archivo Ibero-Americano*, 15:344–349 (1921); quotation from pp. 347–348. Along with the *Testimonio* is included on pp. 337–344 a report sent by Martins to King Philip in 1597. The King of Spain was ill-served by this Bishop of Japan: the relation is a model of colored reportage if not outright distortion of the facts.

60. Martins, *Testimonio*, p. 345. Mashita Uemon no Jō Nagamori (?–1615) was one of the Five *Bugyō*, special commissioners and right-hand men of Hideyoshi. He was employed in various administrative tasks, such as the land surveys of Ōmi (1591) and Awa (1593). During the conflict of 1600 he was the Western Army's Lord Lieutenant (*rusui*) of Osaka; after Ieyasu's victory, his extensive domains (Yamato Kōriyama with *c.* 200,000 *koku* of income) were confiscated and he was subjected to a heavy monetary fine. After the fall of Osaka Castle in 1615 he was ordered to commit suicide, ostensibly because his son Moritsugu had been one of Hideyori's stalwarts in the siege. *Sengoku jinmei jiten*, ed. Takayanagi Mitsutoshi and Matsudaira Toshikazu (Tokyo: Yoshikawa Kōbunkan, 1963), pp. 228–229.

61. Pérez, "Fray Juan Pobre de Zamora: su relación sobre la pérdida del Galeón 'San Felipe', y martirio de San Pedro Bautista y compañeros," *Erudición Ibero-Vltramarina*, 2:221–223 passim (1931). For a complete translation of "Fray Juan Pobre's testimony on the Pilot-Major of the San Felipe," see Boxer, *Christian Century*, App. III, pp. 420–424. The story of the Jesuits' disavowal of the "tyrant and usurper" Philip and their protestations of allegiance to "King D. Antonio" is repeated also in the testimony of the Spaniard Don Pedro de Figueroa Maldonado, who was on board the galleon; *Archivo Ibero-Americano*, 15:355. Figueroa Maldonado denounces the Jesuits for not mentioning Philip's name in the intentions of their mass and instead

praying only for the Supreme Pontiff and "our Emperor Maximilian" (p. 358). He complains further that the Jesuits have gone native, speak the vernacular, dress and eat *à la Japonaise*, and have even composed a book called *Das costumes y ceremonias del Japon* which they use in their seminaries.

Excerpts of several varying contemporary and near-contemporary accounts of the causes of the disaster and the role of Francisco de Olandía may be found also in supplementary note 4 to *Nippon Ōkoku ki*, the richly annotated translation by Sakuma Tadashi, Aida Yū, and Iwao Seiichi of the *Relaçion Del Reyno del Nippon Aque LLaman Coruptamente Jappon* by Bernardino de Avila Girón; in Dai Kōkai Jidai Sōsho, XI (Tokyo: Iwanami, 1965), 643–644. Cited are the Franciscans Pedro Bautista and Juan Pobre, as well as Pedro Morejón SJ, the annotator of the Jesuit copy of Avila Girón's work.

Avila Girón was a Spanish merchant who first arrived in Japan in 1594, on the same ship which bore the third Philippine embassy to Hideyoshi. He traveled widely and observantly in Japan, and also voyaged to much of the rest of the maritime periphery of Asia, as far as India and Ceylon. He was unquestionably well-informed; what lends his work a particularly high value, however, is that it is written from a neutral position— he demonstrates no particular prejudice for or against Jesuits or friars, Portuguese or Spaniards, and is not interested either in scandalmongering or in dogmatic expostulations. He was the eyewitness of a series of critical events in the history of Christianity in Japan, and he recorded them with a faithful eye to detail, particularly in regard to Nagasaki, which was his residence and base of operations. His work is one of the most interesting Western sources on Japan in a dramatic period. Unfortunately, the publication of the original was interrupted by the outbreak of the Spanish Civil War and not continued after its conclusion. Only the initial fifteen chapters were issued, edited with an introduction by Doroteo Schilling OFM and Fidel de Lejarza: "Relación del Reino de Nippon," in *Archivo Ibero-Americano*, Vols. 36–38 (1933–1935). The *San Felipe* incident and the subsequent martyrdom are treated in chs. vi–viii: *Archivo Ibero-Americano*, 37:516–554, and *Nippon Ōkoku ki*, pp. 228–270.

62. "I furthermore certify that it is the greatest of falsehoods to maintain that the Portuguese were the cause of the ship's seizure, and that they said in Meaco that the King of Spain was not the king of the Portuguese, and that the Spaniards came in order to conquer [Japan], and other lies that [Uemon no Jō] told the Spaniards in Urando, claiming that the Portuguese had stated so; for when the ship came to Urando, Antonio [Garçes] and his companions already were in Nangasaqui, and were not at that time in Meaco. And when I arrived in Meaco with the Portuguese who were with me, that was already after [Uemon no Jō] had gone to Urando to seize the cargo. And so not one of those statements could have been uttered by the Portuguese at the time of the ship's arrival, because not a single one was at that time in Meaco." Indeed (adds the Bishop), the Portuguese are exceedingly grieved at the Spanish ship's confiscation: the plunder caused a glut on the market, the price of the goods from Macao fell, and "to this day" (November 1597) much remains unsold. Martins, *Testimonio, Archivo Ibero-Americano*, 15:346–347.

That Martins could not have had a direct influence upon the decision for confiscation is indeed clear from the dates of Mashita's departure and the Bishop's arrival in Kyoto. And there is the bare possibility that the stories of Jesuit and Portuguese derogations at the court of the Taikō do constitute "the greatest of falsehoods." There is, of course, no implication that Martins actively agitated for *bloody* persecution of the Jesuits' rivals. Cf. Boxer, *Christian Century*, App. III, n. 7, p. 421.

63. Matsuda, *Nanban shiryō no kenkyū*, p. 893. Figueroa Maldonado (*Archivo Ibero-Americano*, 15:356) specifies that Organtino was a key informer against the Spaniards, along with Bishop Martins and Rodriguez; his phrase for the actions of the Bishop and his consorts is "treason and wickedness," *traycion y maldad*. This witness, however, cannot be trusted: he is much too intent on painting the Jesuits in the blackest possible color.

64. I am indebted for this information to Michael Cooper SJ, the author of a forthcoming biography of Rodriguez Tçuzzu. Father Cooper convincingly notes in a personal communication: "The Nagasaki process was obviously convened to provide pro-Jesuit evidence. Nevertheless, it is hard to believe that all the witnesses erred, deliberately or otherwise, on this point. In any case, Rodrigues was a well known figure and the matter could be easily verified. The Jesuits would hardly have made this a key issue in their judicial investigation if there was any possibility of the matter redounding to their discredit."

65. For an analytical list of the martyrs' names, see Matsuda, "Nihon Nijūroku Seijin no jinmei ni tsuite," *KK*, 8:3–39, and an expanded version of the same article in *Nanban shiryō no kenkyū*, pp. 899–939. A detailed description, with sketch map, of their progress to the site of martyrdom is given by Diego Pacheco SJ, "Nihon Nijūroku Sei Junkyōsha no tabiji ni kansuru oboegaki," *KK*, 8:40–86. Also see Kataoka Yakichi, "Saigo no michi," *KK*, 8:87–105, and cf. Kataoka, *Nagasaki no junkyōsha*, Kadokawa Shinsho 113 (Tokyo: Kadokawa, 1957), pp. 89–99.

Chapter 6: Pilgrim's Progress

1. Akutagawa Ryūnosuke, "Rushiheru," *Hōkyōnin no shi, hoka jūsanpen*, Iwanami Bunko 3742–3743 (Tokyo: Iwanami, 1970 eighteenth printing), pp. 59–67.

2. See below, *Deus Destroyed*, Preface.

3. Fujita Kankai, "Habian to Hakuō: Kirishitan zokusho shikō," *Kokugo to kokubungaku*, 30.8:32–41 (August 1953).

4. See below, *Kirishitan monogatari*, "How a Japanese Lay Monk and a Kirishitan Iruman Held a Debate on Religion."

5. *Nanbanji kōhaiki*, ed. Hiyane Antei, Kirishitan Bunko, II, 13–15.

6. Cf. *Kirishitan shūmon raichō jikki* (A true account of the Kirishitan religion's advent to Our Empire), in *Kirishitan monogatari hoka sanshu*, ed. Hiyane Antei, Kirishitan Bunko, I (Tokyo: Keiseisha, 1926), 104–106. M. Paske-Smith in *Japanese Traditions of Christianity* (Kobe: J. L. Thompson & Co., 1930), pp. 6–48, gives a reprint of the anonymous translation first published in the *Japan Herald* in 1864; the title used is "A History of the Introduction of Christianity into Japan," and the relevant pages are 26–27.

7. Anesaki Masaharu, *Kirishitan hakugaishichū no jinbutsu jiseki* (Tokyo: Dōbunkan, 1930), p. 466, speculates that "Unquio" might represent the romanization of the characters for "cloud dweller." Those characters indeed compose the name of a contemporary Zen priest—Unko Keyō, one of Suzuki Shōsan's mentors. No identity with Fabian is implied.

8. Ajuda codex 49–IV–56, *Jesuitas na Asia*; cited by Pierre Humbertclaude SM in prefatory notes to his translation, "Myôtei Mondô; une apologétique chrétienne japonaise de 1605," *MN*, 1.2:224 (July 1938).

9. Louis Delplace SJ, *Le Catholicisme au Japon*, I (Brussels: Librairie Albert

Dewit, 1909), 278; original in the Roman Archives of the Society of Jesus, JapSin 25, ff. 48–52v.

10. *Rol das casas e residencias que tem a comp^a na Vice prouincia de Japão neste mez de nouembro do anno de 92. cõ os nomes dos p^es e Jrmãos q̃ nellas residem*; British Museum, Add.MSS. 9860; published by Doi Tadao in *Kirishitan bunken kō*, pp. 323–341. Fabian's name is No. 94 in the list, p. 330.

11. *NIFON NO COTOBA TO Historia uo narai xiran to FOSSVRV FITO NO TAMENI XEVA NI YAVA RAGVETARV FEIQE NO MONOGATARI.* IESVS NO COMPANHIA NO Collegio Amacusa ni voite Superiores no go menqio to xite core uo fan ni qizamu mono nari. Go xuxxe yori M.D.L.XXXXII.

The bibliographical details will be found in Laures, *Kirishitan Bunko*, no. 13, pp. 46–49. The only extant copy is in the British Museum. There are two photocopy editions: (1) *"Amakusa-bon Heike monogatari" ken'an*, ed. Shima Shōzō (Tokyo: Ōfūsha, 1967), provides a reproduction of the Roman-letter original and a *katakana* collation; (2) *Kirishitan-ban Amakusa-bon Heike monogatari*, ed. Kamei Takanori (Tokyo: Yoshikawa Kōbunkan, 1969), gives the clearer reproduction but at a far higher list price. There is a readily available edition put into Sino-Japanese characters: *Habiyan-shō Kirishitan-ban Heike monogatari*, ed. Kamei Takanori and Sakada Yukiko (Tokyo: Yoshikawa Kōbunkan, 1966 revised ed.).

12. *FEIQE*, p. 3; cf. Kamei & Sakada, p. 5, for the transliteration.

13. Doi Tadao, *Kirishitan gogaku no kenkyū* (Osaka: Seibunsha, 1942), p. 301.

14. Yoshida, *Amakusa-ban Kinkushū no kenkyū*, English introduction, p. 4; cf. Japanese text, p. 85.

15. *ESOPONO FABVLAS. Latinuo vaxite Nippon no cuchito nasu mono nari.* IEVS NO COMPANHIA NO Collegio Amacusani voite Superiores no gomenqiotoxite coreuo fanni qizamu mono nari. Goxuxxe yori M.D.L.XXXXIII.

The best and most convenient of several modern editions are the two following: Inoue Akira, ed., *Amakusa-ban Isopo monogatari* (Tokyo: Kazama Shobō, 1964); Ōtsuka Mitsunobu, ed., *Kirishitan-ban Esopo monogatari*, Kadokawa Bunko 2632 (Tokyo: Kadokawa, 1971). Inoue Akira presents the results of his extensive research into this work in *Amakusa-ban Isopo monogatari no kenkyū* (Tokyo: Kazama Shobō, 1968).

Aesop was the only one of the authors imported by the Jesuits to survive under Sakoku. Some eleven variants published during the Tokugawa period are extant. Ōtsuka includes one (n.d.; in the possession of the Imperial Household) in Kadokawa Bunko 2632. Another (n.d.; National Diet Library) is included in *Kana zōshi shū*, ed. Maeda Kingorō and Morita Takeshi, Nihon Koten Bungaku Taikei 90 (Tokyo: Iwanami, 1965). The version printed by Itō San'emon in Manji 2 (1659) is particularly interesting because of its illustrations. I have consulted the original in the Kyoto University Library (3 *kan* in 1 volume). This book has also been published in facsimile: *Isopo monogatari*, 3 *kan*, Kisho Fukuseikai, fourth series, nos. 6–8 (Tokyo: Yoneyama-dō, 1925).

16. Doi, *Kirishitan bunken kō*, p. 14. Yoshida Sumio proposes a compromise solution in regard to the *Qincuxŭ*: "It is known that [Fabian] had been a Zen Buddhist before he entered the Jesuit Mission. A number of maxims from Zen Buddhism was embodied in the [*Qincuxŭ*] of the Amakusa Edition. From this, one can see that Fabian had something to do with the compilation of this book. It also seems that Tacay Cosme took some part in it. The

writer surmises that Cosme made the commentaries. It may be a safe guess to say that both Fabian and Cosme collaborated in compiling this book." *Amakusa-ban Kinkushū no kenkyū*, English introduction, p. 5; the argument of the corresponding Japanese text, pp. 106–108, is more facile and persuasive.

17. Hideyoshi ordered the Nanbanji destroyed in March 1588, and it had not been replaced by anything of a similar scale when the Taikō's second persecution began in late 1596. Soon after Ieyasu's victory at Sekigahara (by February 1601), João Rodriguez Tçuzzu obtained from him "provisions" officially permitting the Jesuits to resume their activities in Kyoto, Osaka, and Nagasaki; the church of Shimogyō, in which the first mass was said on Christmas Day 1605, became their headquarters in the Capital. This second Temple of Southern Barbarians remained in existence until February 1614. See Schütte, *Introductio*, pp. 614–615; and pp. 615–616 on the Kamigyō establishment. Schütte quotes a letter by João Rodriguez Girão, Nagasaki, 15 February 1607, on the motives for the latter's foundation. The Jesuits were displaced hence in 1612 by order of the shogunal authorities.

18. *Catalogo das Casas que a Comp.ª tem em Japão *** de 1606 e dos pessoas que nellas morão*; British Museum, Add.MSS. 9860; published by Doi in *Kirishitan bunken kō*, pp. 359–365. Jr. fabiaõ of Ximoguio (Miacö de baixo) figures on p. 365. Also Doi, *KK*, 3:196–204 (1948); see p. 203.

Several hints of Fabian's presence in the Kyoto area before 1606 may be found in published Jesuit relations: his name is not specifically mentioned, but the mode of operation appears distressingly familiar. For instance, Mattheus de Couros (writing from Nagasaki on 6 October 1603) describes a disputation between "an extraordinary bonze" and an "extremely well versed Japanese Irmão." It is a typical Fabian act. Although the bonze is "heathenry's most eminent master (*der allerfürnembst Maister der Heidenschafft*)," he more than meets his match in our Irmão, who launches into "such a lengthy *discursum*, or speech, on the doctrine of *Xaca* that everyone was stupefied and amazed that he knew so much about it." The performance concludes with a *reductio ad absurdum* of the Buddhist's position, and even the pagan audience roars with laughter. *Historische Relation Was sich inn etlichen Jaren hero im Königreich Iapon, so wol im geist- als auch weltlichem Wesen namhafftes begeben vnd zugetragen* (Getruckt zu München Durch Nicolaum Henricum im Jahr M.DC.IX.), pp. 48–51.

And who could have been the Irmão who demonstrated Western astronomical instruments to Toyotomi Hideyori in 1604? Characteristically, the lesson in cosmography involved the humiliation of a bonze: the Irmão's *ken* impressed the eleven-year-old prince so much that he gave the Buddhist a fillip on the nose, exclaiming, "You know nothing!" João Rodriguez Girão, 23 November 1604; *Historische Relation*, p. 104.

19. The letter (original in the British Museum, Add.MSS.9860) is cited by Pierre Humbertclaude SM, "Notes complémentaires sur la biographie de l'ex-Frère Jésuite Fabien Fucan," *MN*, 4.2:293, n. 15 (July 1941). An account of the funeral episode may also be found in Fernão Guerreiro SJ, *Relaçam annal das covsas que fizeram os Padres da Companhia de IESVS, nas partes da India Oriental, & em algũas outras da conquista deste Reyno nos annos de 607. & 608. & do processo da conuersaõ & Christandade daquellas partes, com mais hũa addiçam á relaçam de Ethiopia* (Em Lisboa: Impresso por Pedro Crasbeeck, Anno M.DCXI.), ff. 108v–111v.

20. The best available text is in NST 25, pp. 490–491; there is also a very convenient transcription of the original *kanbun* into Japanese on pp. 413–417. The text in the standard collection of Razan's essays, *Razan sensei*

bunshū, ed. Kyōto Shisekikai, II (Kyoto: Heian Kōkogakkai, 1918), 56:228–230, is marred by several errors. The most notable of these mistakes is in the name of one of the principals: "Fukan" is written "Fu-u" throughout. There is a German translation by Hans Müller SJ: "Hai-Yaso—Anti-Jesus," *MN*, 2.1:268–275 (January 1939).

The date of the confrontation converts to 19 July 1606. Shōyū is the important *haikai* poet Matsunaga Teitoku (1571–1653). Nobuzumi is Razan's younger brother (also known as Eiki; 1585–1638), himself destined to develop into a talented Neo-Confucian scholar and Razan's valued collaborator. A detailed discussion of this episode and treatise will be found in Hori Isao, *Hayashi Razan*, Jinbutsu Sōsho 118 (Tokyo: Yoshikawa Kōbunkan, 1964), pp. 101–121. Hori notes (p. 104) that it was the essay collection's original compiler, Razan's son Shunsai (1618–1680), who added the last sentence of the *Razan sensei bunshū* text: "The above was composed in the Keichō period, at an early age."

21. I-hsing (672–717) was a Tantrist monk whom Joseph Needham calls "the greatest Chinese astronomer and mathematician of his time": *Science and Civilisation in China*, II (Cambridge, At the University Press, 1956), 427. Shen Kua (1030–1093) was an astronomer and high official of the Sung.

Razan's cosmology is a relic of the Kai-t'ien theory; cf. Needham, III, 210–216, and Chu Hsi, *Lun-yü huo-wen*, in *Chu Tzu i-shu* (Taiwan), III, 2:1. The *Wang chih* is ch. v of the classic *Li chi*: see SPTK, II, 4:12b.

22. Ebisawa, *Evora byōbu*, p. 79. The identical criticism may be seen in Ebisawa's volume of modern Japanese renditions of Kirishitan-related literature, *Nanbanji kōhaiki, Jakyō taii, Myōtei mondō, Ha Daiusu*, Tōyō Bunko 14 (Tokyo: Heibonsha, 1964), pp. 117–118 (hereafter cited as Tōyō Bunko 14).

23. *Litterae Iaponicae anni M.DC.VI. Chinenses anni M.DC.VI. & M.DC.VII.*, Illae à R. P. Ioanne Rodrigvez [Girão], hae à R. P. Matthaeo Ricci (Antverpiae, Ex Officina Plantiniana, Apud Viduam & Filios Io. Moreti, M.DC.XI.), pp. 117–124. The issue is in the pathetic story of a youth who goes down from Kyoto to Nagasaki on business but through the special grace of God "gains far greater profit than he had hoped": for he sees the true light and becomes converted to Christianity. He returns to Kyoto. His parents refuse to countenance his novel turn of faith. He refuses to relapse into darkness. A swarm of bonzes exert themselves in pressuring him. He will not be moved. Finally, in exasperation, he makes an agreement: he will become Buddhist again if the most eminent bonze of the Hokke Sect will vanquish in disputation our aforesaid Irmão. And the melodrama unfolds.

The bonze and a mob of adherents debouch upon the Temple of Southern Barbarians. But the Buddhist is only given the opportunity to relish a few initial taunts before Fabian puts him on the defense and presses him "into such a tight corner that he is ensnared in his own traps." His disciple rushes to his assistance, but he too is defeated, and begins spouting words that contradict his master. A verbal embroglio now results among the heathen, and the master is abandoned to his own devices. Thus, in the Buddhist's shock and Fabian's triumph, is the Christian youth justified.

24. *Catalogo das Casas da Companhia desta V'prouincia de Japam & dos P^es E Jrmaõs que nellas moraõ feito em Feur^o de 1607*; British Museum, Add.MSS. 9860; Doi, *Kirishitan bunken kō*, pp. 365–372, Jr. fabiam at Miaco on p. 371; *KK*, 3:204–213, *n.b.* p. 212.

Catalogo dos P^es E Irmaõs de Japaõ, repartidos pollas casas, E residencias em q̃ cada hũ delles reside, f^o em Octubro de 1607; British Museum, Add.MSS. 9860; Doi,

Kirishitan bunken kō, pp. 372–380, Jř. Fabiaõ at Miaco on p. 379; *KK*, 3:213–224, *n.b.* p. 223.

25. Doi, *Kirishitan bunken kō*, p. 397.

26. Schütte, *Introductio*, p. 211.

27. "O apostata Fabian esta aqui y ehego (*sic*; chego?) a morte. Escribio hun libro cheo de herexias y blasfemias." The letter is dated 16 March 1621 and addressed to P. Pedro Morejón SJ, "wherever he may be"; published in the original and in Japanese translation by Diego Pacheco SJ, "Hoan Baputisuta de Baeza Shinpu no nishokan ni tsuite," *KK*, 10:92–98 and 72–80; see p. 96.

28. Fabian's year of birth is difficult to determine. Jesuit catalogues are not reliable guides to years of birth, sometimes listing age inaccurately. Several such errors occur in the catalogue given by Delplace. For instance, the entry for Valignano (p. 276) overestimates his age by five years while giving his years in the Society accurately: *aetatis anno* 59, *societatis anno* 27 in 1593 (cf. *VMJ*, I-1, 37–39: Valignano was born in February 1539 and entered the Jesuit Order in May 1566). Delplace's catalogue, however, provides the only external indication of Fabian's birthdate: *aetatis anno* 27, *societatis anno* 6 in 1592. Hence, tentatively: born 1565, Irmão 1586. The year of entry is confirmed by the Ajuda codex cited by Humbertclaude.

In 1620 Fabian wrote in the Preface to *Ha Daiusu*: "So I left their company. Some fifteen years have passed since." 1605 is not the correct date of his departure from the Company of Jesus, but it is of some value in collating his own obscure chronological statements with known dates. In the same Preface he also states that he spent "twenty years and more (*nijū-yo nen*)" as a Christian: *ergo*, conversion 1585–. In the concluding "Evening's Conversation" he amplifies: "I left my home [*shukke*, became affiliated with a religious order] at the age of nineteen and after that spent some twenty-two or twenty-three years at spiritual exercises at their temple, and was held to be of some account among them." Counting from 1605, we arrive at 1583 or 1582 for entry into religion (which raises the possibility that Fabian became at that time a probationary associate or *dōjuku* of the Society). If we then subtract "the age of nineteen" (certainly in the Japanese mode of counting, *kazoetoshi*, and therefore eighteen in the Western manner), we have 1565 or 1564 as the year of birth.

If one takes the "twenty-two or twenty-three years" at face value and counts from 1586, the known date of his entry into the Society, then 1608 or 1609 is the year of his departure. This extrapolation is proved correct, and 1608 indicated, by Couros' reference to "thirteen years ago" in the 1621 letter quoted immediately below.

29. See below, *Deus Destroyed*, "An Evening's Conversation."

30. The original of this very important letter is in the Jesuit Archives in Rome, JapSin 37, ff. 180–181, and has not yet been published. I am very grateful to P. Michael Cooper SJ for providing me with a copy of the relevant portion of the Portuguese text. Ide Katsumi has included a Japanese translation of the paragraphs dealing with Fabian in the valuable article "Haikyōsha Fukansai Fuabian bannen no ichi shiryō," *Kirishitan Bunka Kenkyūkai kaihō*, 9.3: 27–28 (October 1966).

"Gonrocu Presidente de Nagasaqui": the Nagasaki *Bugyō* Hasegawa Gonroku. "Tóan": Antonio Murayama Tōan. "Feizo": João Suetsugu Heizō.

31. "Sattaixu" perhaps was originally written "fattaixu," and the f mistaken for a cursive f. Ide, p. 27, romanizes "Hattaixu," which from the standpoint of the contemporary orthography is not very likely: the Hepburn

system's "ha" was written "fa" in the Kirishitan usage. "fattaixu" is a near approximation of *Ha Daiusu*; but one must not exclude the possibility that Fabian circulated another version of his anti-Christian tract, perhaps under a somewhat different title. The question would be resolved if the translation of which Couros speaks were extant; and it may indeed rest in the dust of the Roman Archives of the Society of Jesus, awaiting discovery. Those archives, unfortunately, are far from being in the public domain.

32. The work in question is the *Compendium Catholicae Veritatis*, completed *c.* 1593; Schütte, "Drei Unterrichtsbücher für Japanische Jesuitenprediger aus dem XVI. Jahrhundert," *Archivum Historicum Societatis Iesu*, 8.2:232 (1939).

33. Tōyō Bunko 14, pp. 276–277; identical language in *Nihon Kirishitan shi*, pp. 203–204.

34. Shinmura Izuru, *Nanban kōki* (Tokyo: Iwanami, 1925), pp. 95–96.

35. See below, *Deus Destroyed*, Preface.

36. The proverbial statement's provenance is *Analects*, I:8 and IX:25.

37. Guerreiro, *Relaçam annal*, f. 129–129v: Vice-Provincial Pasio turned to Honda Kōzuke to beg intercession with Ieyasu, in order to obtain "perfect liberty for the promulgation of our holy law in all Japan, so that anyone, high or low, whoever so desired, could accept it without falling therefore into disgrace with the Cubo. To that purpose Conzuquedono was handed in writing a disquisition on the doctrine & truth of our holy law, & how there was a creator of Heaven & of the earth, & of the soul, & its immortality, & how there was another life, & that being eternal, & consequently a reward for the good & punishment for the evil which one committed in this life. Of the ten commandments of the law of God, which we teach, & in particular of the forcefulness of the oaths of the Christians, & how they keep & preserve them more inviolable than do the pagans. (A stumbling block for many, for it seems to them, because they are ignorant of the actual truth, either that we do not have oaths or that if we do have them, then we make little of them; which opinion once introduced by the devil, enemy of all good, has caused great harm to us, & to all of this Christianity.) Finally of the falsety & frauds of the sects of Japan, & how there is in them no salvation, adducing therefor multiple authorities & texts from the books of those very sects, which they could not contradict; & all of it in elegant style, & in suave & unassuming language, which irmão Fabiam (well versed in the sects of Japan) composed in order to give to the aforesaid Conzuquedono." The disquisition described here certainly fits the nature of the *Myōtei mondō*, Razan's contrary comments on its style notwithstanding.

38. P. Fr. Jacinto Orfanel OP, *Historia de la Iglesia del Japón*, Archivo de la Provincia del Santisimo Rosario (Manila), Division de MSS., Seccion: Japon, Tomo 1 (former cat. no. 288), insert between pp. 426 and 427. The context is ch. liv, which describes several martyrdoms. The preceding paragraph is also dedicated to Tōan. The date of the manuscript is 24 May 1621. I am greatly indebted to P. J. F. Schütte SJ for drawing Orfanel's statement to my attention, and I am particularly grateful to P. Fr. Pablo Fernandez OP of the Archivo for permitting me to consult the manuscript.

"Tocuã": André Murayama Tokuan, Tōan's eldest son. By "emperor" is meant the shogun, as is often the case in Western sources of the Tokugawa period.

39. Mattheus de Couros to P. Luís Pinheiro, Portuguese Jesuit *Procurator* in Madrid, dated Nagasaki, 23 February 1619; in Alvarez-Taladriz, "Fuentes

Europeas sobre Murayama Toan (1562–1619)," *Tenri Daigaku gakuhō*, 51:259 (March 1966), the Portuguese original translated into Castilian.

The Dominicans maligned Tōan's adversary, Suetsugu Heizō, in similar terms. For an example, see Diego Aduarte OP, *Historia de la Provincia del Sancto Rosario de la Orden de Predicadores en Philippinas, Iapon, y China* (En Manila En el Colegio de Sãcto Thomas, por Luis Beltran impressor de libros, Año de 1640), II, 193, where Heizō figures as "este ministro de Satanas." Aduarte's account of the entire incident, "Competencias entre los governadores de Nangasaqui, grande occasion de la destruicion de aquella Christiãdad," begins (II, 88) with the cut-and-dried characterization of the two contestants: "Antonio Toan Christano catholico, y Feizo Christiano renegado."

40. Another variant of the Dominican side is Francisco Carrero, *Triunfo del Santo Rosario y Orden de Santo Domingo en los Reinos del Japon, desde el año del Señor 1617 hasta el de 1624* (Manila: Imprenta del Colegio de Santo Tomás, 1868), a book originally published in Manila in 1626. Ch. xix, pp. 176–187, is designed to promote the cause of Tōan's martyrdom; see pp. 176–177 on the attempts of Suetsugu Heizō—"segundo Judas, ó Juliano Apóstata"—to destroy "los mayores pilares y estribos" of Christianity, "como era el Toan." This chapter is also included in the comprehensive assembly of sources on Tōan published in *Dai Nippon shiryō*, comp. Shiryō Hensanjo, pt. 12, Vol. XXXII (Tokyo: Tōkyō Teikoku Daigaku, 1935). Carrero was Orfanel's epigone. In particular, he followed Orfanel's account of Fabian's "testimony in favor of Toan" almost word for word (pp. 185–187).

41. *Diary of Richard Cocks, Cape-Merchant in the English Factory in Japan, 1615–1622*, ed. Murakami Naojirō, I (Tokyo: Sankōsha, 1899), 251; entry for 20 April 1617 (note that Cocks customarily follows the Julian calendar).

42. See Avila Girón, ch. xix, "What sort of a man Tōan was, and what sort he is now," *Nippon Ōkoku ki*, pp. 422–426. The account is dated 11 June 1614.

43. For one instance, see the letter of the *Visitator* Francisco Vieira to Pinheiro, Nagasaki, 21 February 1619; in Alvarez, *Tenri Daigaku gakuhō*, p. 252.

44. Avila Girón, *Nippon Ōkoku ki*, p. 424, gives the year as 1594. Several Japanese sources also deal with the interview, but the nature of those accounts is legendary and confusion reigns in them concerning terms, date, and occasion. Cf. *Dai Nippon shiryō*, 12/XXXII, 290–294 and 314–318.

45. Couros to Pinheiro, 23 February 1619; Alvarez, *Tenri Daigaku gakuhō*, p. 260. See Schütte, *Introductio*, p. 741: After Terazawa Hirotaka (Shima no Kami Masanari, who had governed Nagasaki since 1592) fell out of favor with Ieyasu and was removed from his charge, the administration of the city in the first months of 1603 passed to five elders with Murayama at their head. When Rodriguez at about the time of the Japanese New Year (11 February 1603) met Ieyasu in audience, he had the powers of superintendence—"superiorem quandam in Nagasakiense gubernium auctoritatem ('superintendência')"—placed into his and the Society's hands. It would be interesting to find out how Ieyasu conceived of these "powers of superintendence." At any rate, the Jesuits relinquished whatever the authority was no later than 1606.

According to Alvarez (n. 8, pp. 247–246), Rodriguez Tçuzzu's disagreement with Terazawa over the disposition of the Portuguese China trade resulted in the latter's removal and Tōan's elevation. When the time came later, the Dominican friars, looking back upon the antecedent case of

Terazawa, might well think that the Jesuits, unable to change their spots, were machinating with Suetsugu Heizō against Murayama. Avila Girón found out abroad (in Macao) in 1604 that Tōan had become head of the *otona* of Nagasaki, and he further states that Ieyasu handed over the authority over Nagasaki to Tōan in 1605; *Nippon Ōkoku ki*, p. 425.

46. The ship is also known as the *Madre de Deus*. The causes and the spectacle of this rich vessel's disastrous end have been described in great detail by Boxer in *Christian Century*, pp. 269–283, *The Great Ship from Amacon*, pp. 71–77, and elsewhere. Also see Schütte, *Introductio*, pp. 181–182 and 193. Avila Girón's eyewitness report, ch. xi (*Archivo Ibero-Americano*, 38:120–127; *Nippon Ōkoku ki*, pp. 292–301), is very picturesque; the Jesuit Morejón adds to it a note naming the *bugyō* Hasegawa Sahyōe and Tōan as the culprits who persuaded Arima Harunobu to attempt the vessel's seizure (*Archivo*, 38:122, n. 3; *Nippon Ōkoku ki*, p. 295, n. 5).

Hayashi Razan has also contributed a vivid account, based on his brother Nobuzumi's report of what he saw and heard in Nagasaki: *Nagasaki itsuji* (A curious tale from Nagasaki; 1610), *Razan sensei bunshū*, I, 22:246–248. The preamble is as curious as the tale itself: After stating that the Christians teach the effectual retribution after death for actions performed in this life, Razan wonders "whether they might not be a tribal group from the ancestral lands of the Mohammedans." Then he abominates "the foolish and lovers of the exotic and those who put their trust in marketplace profits," who have been taken in by the Christians and have taken up their doctrine. Hori Isao, *Hayashi Razan*, pp. 384–385, comments that these utterances signal a new stage in the formation of Razan's anti-Christian attitude.

47. A good example of the Jesuits' attitude is to be found in the letter from Couros to Pinheiro, 23 February 1619; *Tenri Daigaku gakuhō*, pp. 260–259: Tōan "developed such a ferocious hate against the Society that he not only presented false testimony of the gravest order against one or the other, or almost all of [the Society's] Padres that were in Japan, but sought with all his powers to make sure that none of ours could remain here. And in order to accomplish his damnable design he closely allied himself with the Castilian friars that come from the Philippines, especially with the Dominicans, whose [Vicar Provincial], Fray Francisco de Morales by name, confesses that he bears no fondness for the Society, and has always put that [animosity] on view and continues to put it on view, in such a manner that even the secular remark upon it, and even the most virtuous among his Religious share it." Couros adds that some eight years previously the lord of Arima had told him that Tōan aimed at nothing less than the total extirpation of the Jesuits in Japan, so that Japanese diocesan clergy and Castilian friars would be the only ones remaining; to which end he engaged in the forgery of documents with the friars' connivance. "And since these Castilian friars seek to put this Christianity and commerce under the crown of Castile, with intentions which Your Reverence will judge for yourself and which they themselves openly proclaim in their own words, they show themselves insouciant [about their means] on suchlike occasions in order to obtain their ends." Exactly three weeks after the date of this letter, Francisco de Morales was captured at Nagasaki in the house of Tōan's son André Tokuan. Aduarte, II, 134–135.

48. Avila Girón, *Nippon Ōkoku ki*, p. 426.

49. Avila Girón, *Nippon Ōkoku ki*, ch. xviii, pp. 412–421.

50. Avila Girón, *Nippon Ōkoku ki*, p. 426.

51. Iwao Seiichi, "Nagasaki Daikan Murayama Tōan no Taiwan ensei to

kenminshi," *Taihoku Teikoku Daigaku shigakka kenkyū nenpō*, 1:283–359 (1934); *n.b.* pp. 330–340.

52. *Diary of Richard Cocks*, I, 131. That Hideyori had somehow survived the fall of Osaka Castle and escaped abroad was, of course, the current rumor.

In an "eyes only" memorandum dated 23 February 1619, Vieira stated to Pinheiro that "all Japan knows that Toan and his sons favored the party of Hideyori" (*Tenri Daigaku gakuhō*, p. 249). The knowledge was not soon forgotten. Hayashi Razan was still ruminating on it in a letter he wrote to Ishikawa Jōzan in 1654 (*Razan sensei bunshū*, I, 7:95): "In a bygone year, during the Naniwa Campaign, the Jesuit Akashi [Kamon] had been enlisted [into the camp of Hideyori] and was in the castle. There was a rich Nagasaki merchant named Murayama Tōan. He offered to render assistance by a secret dispatch of soldiers and supplies into the castle, asking in return that after the war's victorious conclusion the Jesuit doctrine be widely spread throughout the entire land. This was agreed upon. Accordingly, Murayama had his son bring succor into the castle. Fortunately the Great Divine Lord [Ieyasu] applied his glorious majesty, so that the armies came and were beholden to him and Naniwa Castle was made to fall. In the next year the fire died our by itself and was extinguished together with the Jesuits. Murayama's head was put on exhibition. Retribution follows swiftly after crime. How awesome! But you are acquainted with all this."

53. Alvarez-Taladriz, *Tenri Daigaku gakuhō*, n. 13, pp. 246–245.

54. Vieira to Pinheiro, "eyes only," 23 February 1619; *Tenri Daigaku gakuhō*, p. 249.

55. Cocks, II, 10–11, 29 January; II, 39, 4 June; II, 69, 19 August 1618.

56. Couros to Pinheiro, 21 March 1620; *Tenri Daigaku gakuhō*, p. 253: "Among the effects left behind by Toan that were confiscated, there were found various papers and among them a letter from that same Toan to our Father General, in Japanese letters and comprising some fifteen leaves of paper, in which he speaks ill of the Padres of Japan and that we were the cause of this persecution with our manner of operation, etc. The governor of this place, named Gonroku, read this letter and said that it was not possible for Toan to have composed this letter by himself without the aid of others . . . From this manner of speaking of the pagan governor may be understood that he thinks that the friars were in charge of this business. I am stunned by the sight of the efficiency with which these Castilian religious, especially the Dominicans, endeavor to throw us out of Japan . . . Pray God that they do not cause such a stir with this pretension and hubbub about their conquests that the king of Japan, to rid himself of his fears, decides to send an army of twenty or thirty thousand Japanese to descend upon the Philippines, a thing he could do with the greatest of ease, and that the Dutch aid them; and I know that there already has been talk of just that for a few years."

57. Alvarez-Taladriz, *Tenri Daigaku gakuhō*, p. 244, n. 21, citing P. Fr. José de San Jacinto OP, 25 March 1620.

58. Vieira to Pinheiro, "eyes only," 23 February 1619; *Tenri Daigaku gakuhō*, p. 250. An affidavit signed by two city elders of Nagasaki (Christians and party-takers of Heizō) is given on pp. 257–255: "Certificação de alguns christãos de Japam, como nam tiveram os da Companhia parte alguma no caso de Toan Antonio com Feizo, nem na guerra de Vosaca de Findioyri com o Xogun." The two swear on the Gospel and deny that: (1) the Jesuits counseled Heizō and assisted him with money; (2) the Jesuits

sent men to aid Hideyori in Osaka; (3) the Jesuits' counsel and direction were involved in the sale and parceling out of the Nagasaki properties of the Dominicans, Franciscans, and Augustinians.

59. See Daniello Bartoli SJ, *Dell'Historia della Compagnia di Giesv: Il Giappone; Seconda Parte Dell'Asia* (In Roma, M.DC.LX, Nella Stamperia d'Ignatio de'Lazzeri), Book Four, pp. 25–29, on "Mala vita, e mala fine di Toan Antonio rinnegato," and especially note p. 27: "Comperatasi dunque a buoni denari, la fede, e l'anima d'vn nostro catechista Simone (che poi i Christiani, per lo simile tradimento, chiamauano Simone Giuda) e d'vn altro Fabiano, doppiamente apostata, dalla Religione, e dalla Fede, n'hebbe in iscritto i nomi di quanti Padri nostri (che solo de'nostri ne volle) erano in Giappone, e chi gli albergaua . . ."

There is a parallel passage in Pedro Morejón SJ, *Historia y relacion de lo svcedido en los reinos de Iapon y China, en la qual se continua la gran persecucion que ha auido en aq̄lla Iglesia, desde el año de 615. hasta el de 19.* (Año 1621, Con licẽcia en Lisboa por Iuan Rodriguez), f. 129: "no faltô vn Iudas, que fue primero Bonço Gentil, y despues estuuo algunos años en nuestra casa, el qual . . . presentô delante de los Iuezes vna lista, acusando al dicho Feizo, y a los Regidores Christianos, que tenian los Padres escondidos."

It is a pity that Morejón does not reveal the actual name of this "Judas, who first was a Pagan Bonze, and then was for some years in our house." If this were a clear reference to Fabian, it would constitute proof of his often assumed but never established prior career as a Buddhist priest. But the statement might also fit the catechist Simon, whom Bartoli names as the list's other author.

60. See Couros to Pinheiro, 21 March 1620; *Tenri Daigaku gakuhō*, pp. 255–254. Cf. Carrero, *Triunfo*, p. 180: While Tōan was in exile on the island, there occurred the martyrdom of his eldest son Tokuan. "Infuriated, the Emperor said, 'Since Toan has a son so insolent that he keeps Religious in his house, go and cut off his head.' Forthwith the sentence was carried out, and in the city of Yendo they cut off good Toan's head, the King of the world repaying his services with such a cruel death, and the King of Heaven bestowing upon him the palm of martyrdom for the holy zeal that he bore for the Faith and the shelter he gave the Religious." See also Léon Pagès, *Histoire de la Religion Chrétienne au Japon depuis 1598 jusqu'a 1651,* I (Paris: Charles Douniol, 1869), 415–416; Japanese translation by Yoshida Kogorō, *Nihon Kirishitan shūmon shi,* II, Iwanami Bunko 1640–1642a (Tokyo: Iwanami, 1968 eighth printing), 104.

61. Pierre F. X. de Charlevoix SJ, *Histoire et Description Generale du Japon,* V (A Paris, Chez Julien-Michel Gandouin et al., M.DCC.XXXVI), Livre XIV, ch. vii, 522. Charlevoix extensively copies Bartoli.

62. Ōkubo Iwami no Kami Nagayasu/Chōan (1545–1613) was a parvenu who rose to a position of great power under Ieyasu through the administration of gold and silver mines (*Iwami Ginzan Bugyō*, 1605; *Sado Kinzan Bugyō*, 1605; *Izu Kinzan Bugyō*, 1608) and of land surveys (Echigo, Shinano, Mino, 1609). The sphere of his activities was so widespread that it gained him the popular sobriquet *Tenka no Sōdaikan* (General Administrator of the Empire). For a short sketch of his career, see Murakami Tadashi, "Ieyasu to Ōkubo Chōan," *Nihon jinbutsushi taikei,* III (Tokyo: Asakura Shoten, 1963 third edition), 126–157. Fabian claims (*Deus Destroyed*, "An Evening's Conversation") to have had a near-fatal encounter with one of Ōkubo Iwami's subordinates in Nara, and Chōan's long arm did reach the area: he seems to have been appointed *daikan* of Yamato in 1600. See *Sōgō chihōshi dainenpyō,*

ed. Kodama Kōta, Okayama Yasushi, and Kanai Madoka (Tokyo: Jinbutsu Ōrai-sha, 1967), p. 960. Data concerning his activities and influence in Yamato are, however, as unreliable as they are scanty.

63. Cf. the listing of the qualities of Deus in the *Myōtei Dialogue*, NST 25, p. 153, with that of the First Step of *Deus Destroyed*.

64. NST 25, pp. 146–147.

65. NST 25, pp. 150–151.

66. NST 25, p. 147. In the First Step of *Deus Destroyed*, Fabian revoked this statement in ultra-zealous fashion, threatening the Christian blasphemers with a "horror of horrors!—their tongues shall indeed be ripped out!"

67. NST 25, pp. 171–173.

68. NST 25, p. 154.

69. NST 25, p. 147.

70. In Anesaki Masaharu, *Kirishitan hakugaishichū no jinbutsu jiseki*, pp. 487–495. Also in NST 25, pp. 103–112. For a detailed outline, see below, n. 108.

71. NST 25, p. 180. The complete text is as follows:

> The intent of this *Myōtei Dialogue* stems from the fact that ladies of quality and widows have no proper way of giving easy interview to men, though they be monks, and of inquiring about doctrine, though it be eminently true. And accordingly, though they have the desire it must remain fruitless. I have therefore compiled this dialogue, so that they may read it by themselves and come to the light, appreciating in full measure the salutary value of the Kirishitan evangel.
>
> I have divided the number of volumes into three. In the first volume I have damned and dismissed Buddhism for a totally pernicious doctrine, since its base is of the void non-ens. In the second volume, I have discussed the purport of Confucianism and of Shinto, demonstrating the fact that they differ vastly from the true, Kirishitan teachings. In the third volume, I have further elevated the teachings of our Kirishitan religion for manifestation of their truth. Despite my general lack of skill with words, and regardless of my short measure of talent, I have only cherished the one desire that the True Lord 𝇇 be hallowed in the world. Thus I am entirely oblivious of any derision that may be directed at me. And that is because I look forward to the Divine bond of future life in Heaven.
>
> Fukansai Habian
with due humility

72. Fabian did outdo himself somewhat in the *Myōtei Dialogue*'s illustration of the Padres' lack of aggressive intentions: gratuitous is the citation of the famous anecdote, from the *Chuang Tzu*, about the phoenix, the owl, and the rotten rat. The Padres of lofty intent may indeed have only desired to save souls, with no use for temporal power. But was the Japanese polity in 1605 such an insignificant carcass? Or its protectors as owlish as the woe-begone Hui Tzu of Liang in the story? NST 25, p. 177. Cf. *Chuang Tzu*, *Ch'iu-shui* xvii; SPPY, 6:15. See the English translation by Burton Watson, *The Complete Works of Chuang Tzu* (New York: Columbia University Press, 1968), "Autumn Floods," p. 188.

73. See especially NST 25, pp. 162–163.

74. NST 25, p. 157.

75. The Second Step of *Deus Destroyed* is a good example of Fabian's eclectic use of terminology. Fabian uses Buddhist terms to initiate his

argument ("object" or state of conditioned elements, generated by causation; "principle" or state of unconditioned elements, noumenal Thusness). But the conclusion is in the specific Neo-Confucian distinction between the "human mind" and the "mind of the Way," and the illustration of rainwater receptacles also has a Neo-Confucian source. See the great anthology of Chu Hsi, *Chin-ssu lu*, SPPY, 2:18, on the Nature and the accumulation of water in various sorts of receptacles.

76. NST 25, p. 169. Note the delayed parallel in the Fifth Step of *Deus Destroyed*. For another example, see the *Myōtei Dialogue*'s account of the fall of Adam and Eve (NST 25, pp. 168–169) and its elaboration in the Fourth Step of *Deus Destroyed*, where "the aforesaid devil Lucifer" tempts the ancestral pair with a persimmon. (The fruit had not been mentioned by the Christian Fabian, and Deus' sacred law left undefined, perhaps in a conscious omission, to avoid producing the type of criticism which Fabian the apostate would later utilize himself.)

77. *Myōtei mondō*, NST 25, p. 170. *Ha Daiusu* (Genna period original), p. 38b; NST 25, p. 439.

78. (1) *NIPPON NO IESVS no Companhia no Superior yori Christan ni sŏtŏ no cotouari uo tagaino mondŏ no gotoqu xidai uo vacachi tamŏ DOCTRINA.* IESVS NO COMPANHIA NO COLLEgio Amacusa ni voite Superiores no von yuruxi uo cŏmuri, core uo fan to nasu mono nari. Toqini go xuxxe no NENQI. 1592. A reproduction of this Roman-letter *DOCTRINA* is appended to Hashimoto Shinkichi, *Bunroku gannen Amacusa-ban Kirishitan kyōgi no kenkyū*, Tōyō Bunko Ronsō 9 (Tokyo: Tōyō Bunko, 1928). Quotations from *DOCTRINA*, pp. 50–51.

(2) A parallel Japanese-character version was published by the mission press in 1591 (or early 1592), and is included in NST 25, pp. 13–81: *Dochiriina Kirishitan*. See p. 48: "Goittai no Deusu o uyamai tattobi tatematsurubeshi."

(3) *DOCTRINA CHRISTAN.* IN COLLEGIO IAPONICO SOCIETATIS IESV Cum facultate Ordinarij, & Superiorum ANNO 1600. This is the Roman-letter version of another parallel set. A reproduction is included, under the title *Seikyō yōri*, in the Chinsho Taikan Kirishitan Sōsho series (Osaka: Ōsaka Mainichi Shinbun-sha, 1928). See f. 29: "Goittaino Deusuo vyamai tattomi tatematçurubexi."

(4) *DOCTRINA CHRISTAM.* NAGASAQVI EX OFFICINA Gotŏ Thome Sŏin Typographi Societatis IESV. Cum facultate Ordinarij, & Superiorum. Anno. 1600. This Japanese-character version is included in *Kirishitan bungakushū*, ed. Shinmura Izuru and Hiragi Gen'ichi, II, 45–174. See p. 106: "Goittai no 🈁 o uyamai tatto[bi] tatematsurubeshi."

79. See below, *Deus Destroyed*, Seventh Step.

80. There is no recurrence of the preoccupation with Sung Neo-Confucianism in *Ha Daiusu* because that book was not as much meant to demonstrate erudition applied to apologetics as to prove reconversion to an unobjectionable religious persuasion. Hence the Buddhist tone dominates. It is also possible, however, that Fabian for one reason or another was forced to hurry his work and therefore had to curb his pedantry. The First Step is highly elaborate, the rest rather slim in comparison.

81. NST 25, pp. 126–127. Material force: *ch'i* (*ki*). Manifestant tangible matter: *chih* (*shitsu*).

82. NST 25, p. 114. The phrase is quasi-proverbial. *Funi* and *ichinyo*— "not two," "one and undifferentiated," "thus"—are descriptions of the absolute noumenal Law Nature of Thusness, which ultimately is identical

with phenomenal manifestations. It is a cardinal Mahayanist doctrine that all elements are interpenetrant; this doctrine was developed especially by the Kegon School. The Nirvana School and Tendai extended the notion to arrive at the pansophistic statement that all elements share the Buddha-nature. The Pure Land schools placed the idea into a universal soteriological context, and its ultimate development was Shinran's stress that it is especially the evil man who will, undistracted by trust in self, be saved by Amida. The complex of ideas was consistently attacked by the Christian missionaries. In the fragments of the putative Volume I of *Myōtei mondō* there is much sniping at this target.

83. NST 25, pp. 114–115. The famous couplet of the *Lao Tzu*, 42, is utilized in the First Step of *Deus Destroyed* to the contrary effect.

The *Myōtei Dialogue's* argument utilizes the famous *Diagram of the Great Ultimate* (*T'ai-chi t'u*) of Chou Lien-hsi, and Chou's exposition of it. Diagram and text in *Tseng-pu Sung-Yüan hsüeh-an*, SPPY, II, 12:1–1b. See the following translations and commentaries: Wing-tsit Chan, *A Source Book in Chinese Philosophy* (Princeton, N.J.: Princeton University Press, 1963), pp. 463–464; Shimada Kenji, *Shushigaku to Yōmeigaku*, Iwanami Shinsho 637 (Tokyo: Iwanami, 1967), pp. 31–32; Joseph Needham, *Science and Civilisation in China*, II, 460–462, which last is the most enlightening. Fabian may also have been familiar with Chu Hsi's commentary on Chou's diagram, *T'ai-chi t'u chieh-i*, or at least the portions of it cited in *Chin-ssu lu*, which begins with the words, "Master Lien-hsi said: 'The Ultimateless, and the Great Ultimate!'"

84. NST 25, pp. 116–117.

85. NST 25, p. 124.

86. Needham, II, 472–485. Chu Hsi states that the Great Ultimate "is at the centre of all things, but not their centre." Needham, II, 465–466, explains Chu Hsi's paradox by an allusion to Pascal's: "Une sphère dont le centre est partout, la circonférence nulle part."

87. Chan, *Source Book*, p. 638, from *Chu Tzu chüan-shu*, 49:8b and 49:10b–11; cited by permission of Princeton University Press, Princeton, N.J., and Oxford University Press, London and New York.

88. Needham, II, 475.

89. This discussion forms the second of seven interchanges "On Confucianism"; NST 25, pp. 117–119. Ebisawa, Tōyō Bunko 14, pp. 152–153, mistakenly annotates it with a reproduction of Chou's diagram; but it is quite clear that Fabian had Shao Yung in mind. Shao's basic diagram (*Hsien-t'ien kua-wei t'u*) is more familiar in linear form; see *Tseng-pu Sung-Yüan hsüeh-an*, SPPY, I, 10:1–5b. But it is perfectly adaptable to a circular representation, and is used thus by Fabian, who combines Shao's series into one graph.

90. NST 25, p. 118. Emending "coordinate pivot" (*sōsū*) for the original text's "coordinate vessel" (*sōki*) accords with the text's subsequent usage (p. 119) as well as with the current analogy, if not with the previous (p. 117) analogy of the medicine box (*yakushu no iritaru hitotsu no hitsu*).

91. NST 25, p. 119.

92. Chan, *Source Book*, p. 641, from *Chu Tzu chüan-shu*, 49:14.

93. A good instance of the amalgamation of terms is Fabian's usage of the phrase *kyorei fumai* (*hsü-ling pu-mei*). In the First Step of *Deus Destroyed*, Fabian uses the expression to denote Thusness, the Buddhists' noumenal True State of total lack of discrimination. The sense here is that of the unobscured, all-permeating, but essentially undifferentiated and void body of the Buddha

(*komushin*). But intruding into the text is also the citation of the Taoist ineffable trigram from *Lao Tzu*, 14. In the *Myōtei Dialogue* (NST 25, p. 126) Fabian had used the phrase correctly, citing the initial passage of the *Great Learning*—"Ta-hsüeh chih tao tsai ming ming-te . . ."—and Chu Hsi's exegesis of it. Fabian's definition of *meitoku* (*ming-te*) appears there as follows: "Illustrious virtue is what man obtains from Heaven, and is called the Vacuous Spirit Unobscured (*kyorei fumai*). The Vacuous Spirit Unobscured may be compared to the mirror's brightness—barbarian coming, barbarian reflected; Chinese coming, Chinese reflected—beyond discussion of good or evil. But the ego of human desire arising upon the circuit of the eyes', ears', nose's, tongue's, and body's craving, because of the distinction between 'self' and 'other', the vacuous, spiritual, unobscured original mind is beclouded. To dispel that ego of human desire is what is meant by the phrase, 'The Way of the Great Learning is in the exemplification of illustrious virtue.'" Compare Chu Hsi's *Sententiae* on the Great Learning, *Ta-hsüeh chang chü*; *Gaku Yō shōku*, ed. Kanno Dōmei (Tokyo: Meiji Shoin, 1927), pp. 9–10.

What the Neo-Confucian means by "vacuous" (*kyo/hsü*) is quite different from the Buddhist's meaning. See Chan, *Source Book*, p. 788, on the Neo-Confucian conception: "As a description of a state of mind, it means absolute peacefulness and purity of mind and freedom from worry and selfish desires and not to be disturbed by incoming impressions or to allow what is already in the mind to disturb what is coming into the mind . . . profound and deep continuum in which there is no obstruction." The mirror image is used in exemplary clarity by Ch'eng I-ch'uan in discussing the "human mind." See *Chin-ssu lu*, SPPY, 4:8; Chan's translation, *Reflections on Things at Hand* (New York: Columbia University Press, 1967), pp. 143–144: "Suppose here is a clear mirror. It is its normal nature to reflect all things. It is difficult not to have it reflect them. Similarly, the human mind cannot but interact with the myriad things, and it is difficult not to have it engaged in thinking. If one wants to avoid confusion and disturbance, his mind must have a master. What can be its master? Seriousness, and seriousness only. With a master, the mind will be vacuous and if it is vacuous depravity cannot enter into it."

The translation "Transconceptual Eminently Active" might better fit *kyorei fumai* into the Buddhist context; and I am very grateful to Professor Masatoshi Nagatomi for suggesting this alternative. Such a phrasing would, however, eliminate the ambiguity of Fabian's usage. I therefore translate "Pure Undisturbed Absolute," to suit both *Myōtei mondō* and *Ha Daiusu*.

94. In *Chu Tzu ta-ch'üan*, SPPY, IX, 72:16–23b.

95. Ibid., p. 23b. For the provenance of Fabian's quotations, also see Chu Hsi's response to Lü Tzu-yüeh, *Chu Tzu ta-ch'üan*, SPPY, VI, 47:4. NST 25, p. 124.

96. NST 25, pp. 127–128.

97. NST 25, pp. 129–130.

98. *Chin-ssu lu*, SPPY, 1:17; Chan, *Reflections*, p. 32. This portion of the statements "On Shinto" is to be read in connection with "On Confucianism," NST 25, p. 123, where Chang Tsai, Ch'eng I-ch'uan, and Chu Hsi are cited on *kuei-shen* as the functioning of nature.

99. NST 25, p. 130.

100. NST 25, p. 133.

101. NST 25, pp. 133–136 passim.

102. NST 25, p. 138.

103. *Evora byōbu*, p. 79; Tōyō Bunko 14, pp. 117–118; *Nihon Kirishitan shi*, p. 202.

104. See below, *Kirishitan monogatari*, "How a Japanese Lay Monk and a Kirishitan Iruman Held a Debate on Religion."

105. Although the first part of Humbertclaude's translation (*MN*, 1.2:223–256, July 1938) leaves off with the seeming promise that Shinto will be discussed, "Mais quelle est votre pensée sur cet âge des kami?," the second part (*MN*, 2.1:237–267, January 1939) begins with Fabian's summary of Christian doctrine. No indication is provided that anything has been omitted.

106. *Giya do pekadoru gekan, Myōtei mondō, Ha Daiusu, Kengiroku*, Nihon Koten Zenshū, second series (Tokyo: Nihon Koten Zenshū Kankōkai, 1927), pp. 31–32. Unexpurgated text in NST 25, p. 140.

107. The discussion of the Age of Men is the sixth interchange "On Shinto," NST 25, pp. 140–141. Cf. *Deus Destroyed*, First Step.

108. An outline of the twelve points of *Buppō no shidai ryaku nukigaki* is as follows:

(1) "General discussion of Buddhism."

(2) "On the causal state and birth of Shaka; abbreviated." The culmination of this fragment on the Buddha's life is the assertion that Sakyamuni was a mere human.

(3) "On the causal state of Amida; abbreviated." The assertion is: "Now this again is not in the slightest way different from Shaka. [Amida] had a father, and he had a mother, and he had a wife, and he had children, and he was a human no different from you and me."

(4) "On Dainichi; abbreviated." Dainichi possesses neither shape nor form, and is in the two realms (Diamond and Womb) a mere symbolic representation of the male and female elements. The Buddha is not to be found apart from the human body.

(5) The Middle Way. The mind and its desire for a good rebirth.

(6) *Gonkyō* and *jikkyō*, the expedient doctrine and the true. Sakyamuni's transmission of the unspoken Zen doctrine to Mahākāśyapa. "If one smashes to pieces the tree and looks, there is neither green nor red." There is in Buddhism no concept of morality: *zen'aku funi, jashō ichinyo*.

(7) The Buddhists lack a concept of morality because they recognize no Lord Supervisor, stressing instead the irresponsibility of the Ultimate Void. The names of their sects may differ. "But the reeds of Naniwa Bay are simply the bulrushes of Ise" and smell, presumably, as sweet.

(8) The name of Buddhist sects is legion; but they do not differ in teaching the doctrine of non-ens.

(9) The Buddhist teachings are a palliative for illiterates. That the sun "rotates to rise from the east is clear proof that the shape of the world is not square. Further, it is evident from the science called *philosophia*. And moreover, from measurements made by circumnavigation in the Black Ships, it has been recorded that [the earth] is approximately 7,772 leagues [around]. In that case, where is this Western Land the other side of ten billion other lands?—what country is meant thereby? Don't laugh so hard, you'll make yourself sick! The Western Paradise nonexistent, it's clear that neither does Amida exist."

(10) "The *Sutra of Meditation* says: 'The length of the body of Amida is sixty billion nayutas, as many yojanas as there are sandgrains in the Ganges. Between his brows he has a white hair; coiled beautifully in righthand revolution, it is like unto five Sumeru Mountains. The Buddha's eyes are like unto the waters of the Four Oceans, blue-white, bright and clear.' What a frightfully tall body and huge eyes!" (Compare Suzuki Shōsan, *Christians Countered*, VII.)

(11) Unedifying anecdotes about Shinran; scorn of the notion of salvation for the depraved.

(12) Pseudo-etymology of the invocation of Amida (*namu = minami nashi*) compounded by solecist coordinance with the *Changes*. "To turn to Namu" is a mere restatement of "Born out of void, to void shalt return." There is in Buddhism no promise of an afterlife. Shaka himself stated, "In forty-nine years I have not taught a single word."

109. Ebisawa, Tōyō Bunko 14, p. 118, commits it. After commending Fabian's intellectual superiority over his Japanese contemporaries, Ebisawa condemns his farfetched sophistries: "The flighty verdicts we see in the *Buppō no shidai ryaku nukigaki*, especially in the likes of the first passage, show us the figure of an overexcited, a belligerent Fabian indeed . . . Fabian is supposed to have been knowledgeable about Buddhism: how, then, could he have indulged in so many ignorant statements? They even make it seem unbelievable that he wrote the book! These flaws may well be reflections of his character and his emotions, as well as results of the frank and unguarded nature of a preliminary draft. In the final analysis, what he has done is make use of Buddhist preachings and parables current among the plebs, in reckless fashion ignore the internal religious ideals, refute the arguments in a manner which begs the question, and argue therefrom that Buddhism is absurd nonsense. But the same sort of thing can be said about the Kirishitan faith if one uses the same methods of argument."

110. See below, *Kirishitan monogatari*, "How a Japanese Lay Monk and a Kirishitan Iruman Held a Debate on Religion."

111. Hayashi Nobuzumi, in *Hai Yaso*, this chapter. Fabian, *Deus Destroyed*, First Step.

112. Kiyū Dōnin Ugai Tetsujō (1814–1891) was the seventy-fifth *monshu* of the Chion'in of Kyoto, the headquarters of the Jōdo (Pure Land) Sect. He was a truly indefatigable compiler, editor, and publisher of anti-Christian tracts. His efforts, aside from the reissue of Fabian's *Ha Daiusu* and of *Nanbanji kōhaiki*, include also the publication of Japanized versions of seventeenth-century Chinese polemics against Christianity. Among his own works is one titled *Jesus Ridiculed* (*Shō-Ya ron*; 1869). For a biographical sketch, see *Chion'in shi*, ed. Yabuuchi Genzui (Kyoto: Chion'in, 1937), p. 429.

The citations are from Kiyū Dōnin's 1869 edition of *Ha Daiusu*; the sole extant copy is in the Tenri Library. The postscript is signed Manjidō Itsunin.

113. Tōyō Bunko 14, p. 117.

Chapter 7: The Final Solution

1. See below, *Deceit Disclosed*, II.

2. Endō Shūsaku and Miura Shumon, *Kirishitan jidai no chishikijin*, Nikkei Shinsho 59 (Tokyo: Nihon Keizai Shinbun-sha, 1967), pp. 155–156.

3. The diary of the Dutch factory of Nagasaki records under the date of 6 November 1650 that Ferreira died the previous day; *Nagasaki Oranda shōkan no nikki*, ed. and trans. Murakami Naojirō, III (Tokyo: Iwanami, 1958), 33. For further data, see Matsuda Kiichi, *Nanban junrei* (Tokyo: Asahi Shinbun-sha, 1967), pp. 195–196.

4. Robert Jay Lifton, *Thought Reform and the Psychology of Totalism* (New York: Norton, 1963; The Norton Library N 221), pp. 68–69.

5. Pagés, *Histoire de la Religion Chrétienne au Japon*, I, 794–796; Japanese translation by Yoshida Kogorō, *Nihon Kirishitan shūmon shi*, III, 254–255.

6. Hubert Cieslik SJ and Gustav Voss SJ, "Einleitung" to *Kirishito-ki und Sayo-yoroku: Japanische Dokumente zur Missionsgeschichte des 17. Jahrhunderts*, *MN* Monographs 1 (Tokyo: Sophia University Press, 1940), p. 15.

7. Pagés, I, 436–437, n. 5; Yoshida, II, 159, n. 19.

8. Chronology in Obara Satoru Augustinus SJ, "Kirishitan jidai no kagaku shisō: Pedoro Gomesu-cho 'Tenkyūron' no kenkyū," *KK*, 10:174–175 (1965).

9. Pagés, I, 374; Yoshida, II, 41.

10. Matsuda, *Nanban junrei*, p. 193.

11. Pagés, I, 436–437; Yoshida, II, 132.

12. Matsuda, *Nanban junrei*, pp. 193–194.

13. Cieslik, "The Great Martyrdom in Edo 1623," *MN*, 10.1/2: 1–44 (April 1954); see p. 27, n. 41. Also see Schütte, *El "Archivo del Japon": Vicisitudes del Archivo Jesuitico del Extremo Oriente y Descripción del Fondo Existente en la Real Academia de la Historia de Madrid*, Archivo Documental Español, XX (Madrid: Real Academia de la Historia, 1964), 414–416.

14. Matsuda, *Nanban junrei*, pp. 193–194.

15. "Copia de hūa carta que o Pᵉ Christovão Frrᵃ escreveo de Japão ao Pᵉ Andre Palmrᵒ, visitador da provincia de Japão," Pagés, II, Annexe 110, 369–374. Cited extensively by Cieslik, *Kirishitan jinbutsu no kenkyū*, pp. 98–107.

16. Takenaka Uneme no Kami Shigeyoshi was the daimyo of Funai in Bungo, Ōtomo Sōrin's old domain. He was appointed *Nagasaki Bugyō* in the eighth month of Kan'ei 3 and relieved of his duties on Kan'ei 10/2/11 (20 March 1633); see the relevant entries in *Tokugawa jikki*, II, Kokushi Taikei, XXXIX, 377 and 585. On Kan'ei 11/2/22 (21 March 1634) his fief was confiscated, and he himself and his son committed suicide as ordered; ibid., p. 624. Cf. Cieslik, *Kirishitan jinbutsu*, p. 93.

17. Pagés, II, Annexe 105, 356–359.

18. Pagés, II, Annexe 110, 370.

19. *Japan: The Official Guide*, ed. Tourist Industry Bureau, Ministry of Transportation, rev. enl. ed. (Tokyo: Japan Travel Bureau, 1959), pp. 853–854.

20. Ferreira quotes Ishida's letter; Pagés, II, Annexe 110, 372: "brotavão e fervião os tanques con tanta furia, qᵉ so a vista poderá fazer desmayar a qué a graça dna não confortara mᵗᵒ." Cf. Cieslik, *Kirishitan jinbutsu*, p. 104, and further compare Arnoldus Montanus, *Atlas Japannensis: Being Remarkable Addresses by way of Embassy from the East-India Company of the United Provinces to the Emperor of Japan*, English'd, and Adorn'd with above a hundred several Sculptures, By John Ogilby Esq; Master of His Majesties Revels in the Kingdom of Ireland (London, Printed by Tho. Johnson, M.DC.LXX.), f. 263: "But besides their burning them by degrees, the *Japanners* us'd also the waters of *Singok*, that is to say, *Hell*. These waters being Sulphureous and hot, flow from the Foot of an exceeding steep mountain, with such force and noise, that it strikes terror and amazement to the Beholder. It rushes forth between the Rocks, and sends its noysom and choaking Vapors up to the Sky."

21. From a poem by Jean Le Fèvre, *c.* 1376; Huizinga, *The Waning of the Middle Ages*, p. 144. Only the imagination of a Bosch could ever do justice to the description of the scene as it must have appeared to its

victims. But which triptych should one choose as illustrative? Perhaps "Juizo Geral" is even more horrid than "Paraiso Terreal."

22. Pagés, II, Annexe 110, 373: "Este foi o victoriozo fim desta batalha em q^e nossa s^{ta} ley ficou sobre ma^{ra} accreditada, os xpãos animados, e o tyraño vincido, e confuso todo contra o que elle pretendia e se prometia."

23. Pagés, I, 771; *sc.*: "Viva la fè de Christo! Ea! soldados valorosos y cavalleros de Christo, viva su fè santa!" Cf. Cieslik, *Kirishitan jinbutsu*, pp. 109–110.

24. The *Visitator* Antonio Rubino's apostrophe to the fallen Ferreira gives the details: "Are you then that same Christopher whom our Society on the 23rd day of December of the year 1632 entrusted with the government of the Province and the Bishopric of all Japan?" Schütte, *Introductio*, p. 259, n. 29. For further chronological details, compare Matsuda, *Nanban junrei*, pp. 189–195; Pagés, I, 790–795 (Yoshida, III, 251–254); Delplace, *Le Catholicisme au Japon*, II, 217.

25. See Schütte, *El "Archivo del Japon"*, pp. 393–394. The Jesuits of the wider world had at least been spared the immediate knowledge of the scandal: the Portuguese ships had left Nagasaki for Macao just before the torture was completed. When the *Visitator* André Palmeiro on 20 March 1634 wrote from Macao to his General, he could still take it for granted that Ferreira by then was in glory, *já agora está martyr glorioso*. There is but the slightest trace of uncertainty in the afterthought—"although," he adds, "at the ships' departure, having put him to the torture of the pit for several hours, they had taken him out again; but some Portuguese say that as the sails were unfurled he once again was being martyred." The portion of the letter dealing with Japan is given by Schütte in *Introductio*, pp. 256–258; see p. 257.

26. Aduarte, *Historia de la Provincia del Sancto Rosario*, II, 415.

27. *Tokugawa jikki*, IV, Kokushi Taikei, XLI, 356.

28. Cf. Cieslik and Voss, pp. 4–5. For obvious reasons, it is difficult to find contemporary evidence of Inoue's Christianity, and the assumption is based upon two brief references in the 1650 compilation by P. Antonio Francisco Cardim SJ, *Batalhas da Companhia de Jesus na sua Gloriosa Provincia do Japão*, ed. Luciano Cordeiro (Lisbon: Imprensa Nacional/Sociedade de Geographia de Lisboa, 1894), pp. 63 and 65: "chicaudono, que fôra christão" and "Checandono renegado," in a context where Inoue Chikugo is unmistakably meant. Cited by Cieslik and Voss, p. 25, nn. 43 and 44.

29. *Tokugawa jikki*, III, Kokushi Taikei, XL, 84.

30. For a brief summary of details, see *Kumamoto-ken shi*, compiled and published by the Kumamoto Prefectural Government (Kumamoto, 1965), *Sōsetsu-hen*, pp. 536–542.

31. *Tokugawa jikki*, III, Kokushi Taikei, XL, 192.

32. Text in *Shiryō ni yoru Nihon no ayumi*, pp. 129–130.

33. See Boxer, *The Great Ship from Amacon*, pp. 163–166, and *Christian Century*, pp. 384–385.

34. The entry is for Kan'ei 17/6/27 (14 August 1640); *Tokugawa jikki*, III, Kokushi Taikei, XL, 194–195.

35. Compare the *Tokugawa jikki* entry with the text of Razan's message to the Ming merchants on the prohibition of Christianity, *Razan sensei bunshū*, II, 58:147–148 (where the date is given as Kan'ei 17 *chūshū*, the eighth month). Also see *Razan sensei bunshū*, I, 8:103–107, for several instructional epistles (on the *Changes*) addressed to Inoue; and likewise the two brief cosmological essays, ibid., 30:332–335.

36. Anesaki Masaharu, *Kirishitan shūmon no hakugai to senpuku* (Tokyo: Dōbunkan, 1925), pp. 1–9. The office was not abolished until 1792; Cieslik and Voss, p. 4.

37. Cieslik, *Kirishitan jinbutsu*, pp. 160–164.

38. *Kirisuto-ki* is the better reading for the characters of the title; but I retain the variant made familiar by Cieslik and Voss. The original Japanese documents may be found in: *Zokuzoku gunsho ruijū*, XII, 626–668; Hiyane Antei, ed., *Nanbanji kōhaiki hoka nihen*, Kirishitan Bunko, II, 45–143; Anesaki, *Kirishitan shūmon no hakugai to senpuku*, chs. ii–iv, incomplete in form but interspersed with extensive commentaries. For this citation, see: *Zokuzoku*, p. 647; Hiyane, pp. 91–92; Anesaki, pp. 75–76; Cieslik and Voss, pp. 78–79 (with incorrect annotation of date). Sanuki no Kami is the *tairō* Sakai Tadakatsu.

The *Visitator* Rubino in reporting to Rome the apostasy of two Padres apparently could not bear to continue in Portuguese but couched the key phrase in Latin: "apregoárão que defecerunt a confessione Fidei, e . . . preguntados quem os sustentava, respondérão que os Portuguezes de Macao; donde se vierão a resolver a quebrar o comércio com esta Cidade." This latter allegation—that when the apostate Jesuits were "questioned who supported them, they had answered that it was the Portuguese of Macao; whence they came to the decision to break off the trade with this City"— is particularly interesting in view of the presence of Iemitsu at the interrogation. This very important letter also contains a Portuguese translation of the final Sakoku edict. Rubino to Mutio Vitelleschi, General SJ, Macao, 2 November 1639; text in Schütte, *Introductio*, pp. 263–265; citation from p. 264.

39. Pagés, I, 850; Yoshida, III, 331.

40. The letter is addressed to Padre Nuño Mascarenhas SJ, Portuguese Assistant to the General of the Society. Cited by Cieslik, *Kirishitan jinbutsu*, pp. 125–126.

41. Those who would like more details will find that Cieslik's biographical sketches of Kibe read better than the proverbial novel. See "P. Pedro Kasui (1587–1639): Der letzte japanische Jesuit der Tokugawa-Zeit," *MN*, 15.1/2:35–86 (1959/1960); also *Kirishitan jinbutsu*, pp. 111–168.

42. My account is a synopsis of Pagés, I, 827–839; Yoshida, III, 302–314. Pagés asserts that Mastrilli's voyage to Japan, and the ardor of the 33 Jesuits who set sail with him from Lisbon in 1635, were caused directly by the desire to atone by martyrdom for Ferreira's defection. The statement does not deserve credence: there was not enough time for news of the apostasy (which occurred in October 1633 and was not immediately reported outside Japan) to have spread so far; and it is to be kept in mind that Ferreira was not expelled from the Society until November 1636. Pagés' direct association of motive is of the unconscious and unquestioning sort, and testifies above all to the ingrained nature of the traditional juxtaposition, which in its origin certainly was conscious.

One example of the typical Baroque construction is Crasset (London, 1707), II, 505–526. See p. 525: "Now the same Year that [Ferreira] apostatis'd, St. *Francis Xaverius* appear'd to Father *Mastrilli*, and oblig'd him by Vow to go for *Japan, to repair this Scandal*, which he did by hanging four Days in the Pit, and shedding his Blood in the *same Place*, the *same Month*, and *same Day*, that the other renounc'd his Faith, and this to attone for his Fault, and settle the poor Christians, who began upon the others Apostacy, to Stagger in the Faith . . . as one falls, another rises, and as one deserts, another bears away the Crown." Another edifying work is Bartoli's: the major portion of the concluding Book Five of his *Dell'Historia della Compagnia di Giesv: Il Giappone,* pp. 434–491, is devoted to a hagiography of Mastrilli.

In the possession of the Houghton Library is what appears to be one of the earliest pamphlets on Mastrilli's martyrdom: *Relacion del insigne martyrio, qve padecio por la Fe de Christo el Milagroso P. Marcelo Francisco Mastrilli de la Compañia de IESVS en la Ciudad de Nangasaqui de los Reynos del Iapõ a 17. dias del mes de Octubre deste año pasado de 1637* [Manila, Colegio de la Compañia de Jesus, por Tomás Pinpín, 1638?]. The association with Ferreira does not yet appear in this tract.

43. On the Magindanau Expedition (February–March 1637) and Mastrilli's role in it, see Horacio de la Costa SJ, *The Jesuits in the Philippines: 1581–1768* (Cambridge, Mass.: Harvard University Press, 1961), pp. 383–385. Cf. Bartoli, Book Five, pp. 467–475.

44. This item of information is from the confession signed by the apostates of the Second Rubino Group. *Zokuzoku gunsho ruijū,* XII, 655; Hiyane, *Nanbanji kōhaiki hoka nihen,* p. 109; Anesaki, *Kirishitan shūmon no hakugai to senpuku,* p. 101; Cieslik and Voss, p. 92.

45. *Zokuzoku,* p. 653; Hiyane, pp. 105–106; Anesaki, pp. 98–99; Cieslik and Voss, pp. 90–91. *Yoriki* and *dōshin:* constables, *yoriki* being the higher rank. Baba Saburōzaemon was in his capacity as *Nagasaki Bugyō* present at the inquisition of Mastrilli.

46. Pagés, I, 868–876; Yoshida, III, 356–361. Cf. Pagés, I, 869: "le motif principal était toujours le désir de ramener le P. Ferreyra."

47. *Deshima Rankan nisshi,* ed. and trans. Murakami Naojirō, I (Tokyo: Bunmei Kyōkai, 1938), 268–269, entry for 21/22 August 1642, states very simply that the apostate Joan was told by his victims to go to hell; and posthaste he departed the spot. The alternate version, *Nagasaki Oranda shōkan no nikki,* I, 174, gives the story without this elaboration.

The entry for 17 March 1643, the day the members of the First Rubino Group were suspended in the pit, states about Chūan: "Christopho Ferreda, born in Lisbon, abandoned his faith in the Roman religion after four days (!) of suspension in the pit." Was that what Ferreira himself claimed? *Deshima Rankan nisshi,* I, 348–349; *Nagasaki Oranda shōkan no nikki,* I, 213.

48. *Deshima Rankan nisshi,* I, 368–369; *Nagasaki Oranda shōkan no nikki,* I, 222.

49. Montanus, *Atlas Japannensis,* f. 319. I quote throughout from this account, which (with numerous digressions) takes up the following forty folios.

50. *Atlas Japannensis,* ff. 356–358. The Dutch eyewitness accounts drifted back to the Jesuits somewhat mangled. On 2 May 1649, for instance, P. Philippo Marino wrote to the General SJ that it was certain that Chiara "finì martire glorioso." The rest of his miscellanea includes the information that the mathematician Cassola frequents the ruler's palace to give instruction in astronomy (*la sphera*). Text in Schütte, *Introductio,* pp. 373–374.

51. *Atlas Japannensis,* f. 367.

52. *Zokuzoku,* pp. 650–652; Hiyane, pp. 98–103; Anesaki, pp. 92–96; Cieslik and Voss, pp. 84–88.

53. Cited from Gordon Rupp, *Luther's Progress to the Diet of Worms* (New York: Harper & Row, 1964; Harper Torchbooks TB 120), pp. 29–30. The image of the sphere and the tangential line is Luther's; I have redrawn it slightly.

54. See Introduction, above, p. 6.

55. See below, n. 69.

56. *Zokuzoku*, pp. 656–668; Hiyane, pp. 114–143; Anesaki, pp. 106–130; Cieslik and Voss, pp. 95–109.

57. Cieslik and Voss, pp. 5–6.

58. *Zokuzoku*, pp. 635–637; Hiyane, pp. 69–76; Anesaki, pp. 86–91; Cieslik and Voss, pp. 58–63.

59. Kobinata in Edo was the site of the Kirishitan Yashiki, the place of detention of the apostates of the Second Rubino Group. The last of these (Nikan Donatus of Cochin) did not die until 1700. Thereafter only one Christian missionary was destined to be incarcerated here: Giovanni Battista Sidotti (captured off Kyushu in October 1708; brought to Kobinata in December 1708; died in November 1714), the partner of celebrated conversations with Arai Hakuseki; see Chapter 8. Cieslik and Voss treat the Kirishitan Yashiki in App. VIII, pp. 191–202. Also see Max von Küenburg SJ, "Kirishitan Yashiki, das ehemalige Christengefängnis in Koishikawa," *MN*, 1.2:300–304 (July 1938). *Sayō yoroku*, the diary of one of the *yoriki* guards of the Kirishitan Yashiki, gives a fascinating summary of the routine of the place between 1672 and 1691. Text in *Zokuzoku gunsho ruijū*, XII, 598–625; translation in Cieslik and Voss, pp. 110–157.

60. A traction torture. The victim was made to mount a wooden horse, and stone weights were attached to his ankles. There is an illustration in Anesaki, *Kirishitan shūmon no hakugai to senpuku*, p. 85.

61. Cieslik and Voss, p. 60, translate *meiyo* as *Wunder*. But the inquisitor is questioning the very notion of the "glory of martyrdom" rather than the existence of miracles.

62. The suspect renounced Christianity and called upon the Christian God to damn him for a Judas if he ever revoked his apostasy! By way of reinsurance, he was also required to swear by the Japanese gods that he was now and would forevermore be orthodox. See Cieslik and Voss, App. III, "'Christlicher' und 'Japanischer' Eid," pp. 164–166, for such a document from the year 1645, and the attestation of its originality and efficacy by Ferreira. Boxer, *Christian Century*, pp. 441–442, gives an English translation.

63. *Kirishito-ki*, Document V, "The Method of Religious Scrutiny." *Zokuzoku*, p. 632; Hiyane, p. 62; Anesaki, p. 83; Cieslik and Voss, pp.53–54.

64. Ebisawa, *Nanban gakutō no kenkyū* (Tokyo: Sōbunsha, 1958), pp. 90 and 501.

65. Ebisawa, *Nanban gakutō*, pp. 498–501.

66. *Deshima Rankan nisshi*, III, 333, 334, 367; *Nagasaki Oranda shōkan no nikki*, II, 199–200, 200, 215. Also see the entries for: 25 September, *Nisshi*, III, 360–361/*Nikki*, II, 212; 7 October, *Nisshi*, III, 363/*Nikki*, II, 214; 18 October, *Nisshi*, III, 366/*Nikki*, II, 214. These latter detail further medical and astronomical errands Ferreira ran on Inoue Chikugo's behalf.

67. *Nanbanryū geka hidensho*; interior title *Nanbanryū gekasho*; MS. in·the Fujikawa Collection, Kyoto University, Faculty of Medicine. The final words of the volume are: "The above, Chūan the Southern Barbarian's secret treatment of wounds and use of herbs, is to be kept secret, secret, etc. etc."

68. *Oranda-ryū geka shinan*, Kyoto University copy, 5 *kan* in 4 vols. (Kyoto: Izumoji Izumi no Jō, Hōei 2 [1705]), I, 1:1. On Ferreira's medical activities and the variants of this book, see Ebisawa, *Nanban gakutō*, pp. 497–512. Ebisawa's major proof that this is properly termed a "Southern Barbarian" rather than a "Dutch" tract consists of a list of technical terms which seem more Latin than Dutch.

69. *Kenkon bensetsu*, in *Bunmei genryū sōsho*, II (Tokyo: Kokusho Kankōkai, 1914), 1–100. On Ferreira's use of "barbarian characters," see Mukai Genshō's Preface, p. 2, and explanatory note, p. 3. Nishi Kichibei read off the draft and Genshō did the transcription. The MS. which became the basis of the published text is in the possession of the Kyoto University Library. It contains 7 *kan* in 3 vols., but lacks the Section on Stars included on pp. 92–100 of the *Bunmei genryū sōsho* text and representing *kan* 8. Mukai Genshō's Preface bears the date Meireki *tsuchinoto* i/9/15; but we note that there was no such year in the Meireki period (1655–1658) and that the cyclical combination corresponds rather to Manji 2 (1659). A copyist's error?

For a synopsis and brief discussion of the *Kenkon bensetsu*, see Shigeru Nakayama, *A History of Japanese Astronomy: Chinese Background and Western Impact* (Cambridge, Mass.: Harvard University Press, 1969), pp. 88–98; Nakayama appends a table of contents of the treatise on pp. 235–237.

70. On the question of original authorship, see Obara Satoru, "Kirishitan jidai no kagaku shisō," *KK*, 10:168–178.

71. *Bunmei genryū sōsho*, II, 6–8.

72. Genshō's rejoinders are replete with phrases à la "This is the same as the Confucian theory." The strained attempt to find classical authorities is perhaps best exemplified by one of the final sallies: "But Chuang Tzu says that heaven is 90,000 leagues high." *Bunmei genryū sōsho*, II, 100; Genshō's appreciation of the master of parables would seem to be at least several leagues off the mark.

73. See *Bunmei genryū sōsho*, II, 25–29, for the discussion of the roundness of the earth. For a general critique of Mukai Genshō's effort, see Satō Shōsuke, *Yōgakushi kenkyū josetsu* (Tokyo: Iwanami, 1964), pp. 24–29, and cf. Ebisawa, *Nanban gakutō*, pp. 90–113.

74. *Bunmei genryū sōsho*, II, 8 (Ferreira), and pp. 1 and 2 (Mukai).

75. See Bartoli, Book Five, pp. 416–421. An excellent synopsis is also given by Schütte, "Ist P. Christovao Ferreira als Martyrer gestorben?," Appendix IX to Cieslik and Voss, pp. 202–208. Schütte answers his own question in the affirmative.

Also see Schütte, *El "Archivo del Japon"*, pp. 394–396 and p. 412.

76. Delplace, *Le Catholicisme au Japon*, II, 243.

77. Bartoli, Book Five, p. 421. Also see Crasset (London, 1707), II, 542–545. Crasset's text closes with an apology for Ferreira, and the final words are St. John Chrysostom's: "It's the Property of Man to sin, of a Christian to do Penance, and of the Devil to persevere in his Crime."

Chapter 8: The Effects of Propaganda

1. I draw on Bruce L. Smith, "Propaganda," in *International Encyclopedia of the Social Sciences*, ed. David L. Sills, XII (New York: The Macmillan Company and The Free Press, 1968), 579–589. The quotation is from p. 579.

2. *Christianity in Japan: A Bibliography of Japanese and Chinese Sources*, pt. 1 (1543–1858), comp. Arimichi Ebisawa (Tokyo: Committee on Asian Cultural Studies, International Christian University, 1960), pp. 38–41. The best overall review of the popular genre remains Hubert Cieslik's: "Nanbanji-Romane der Tokugawa-Zeit," *MN*, 6.1/2:13–51 (1943).

3. In the one manuscript volume of *Ibuki no yomogi: Kirishitan shūmon no yurai* (The mugwort of Ibuki: the origins of the Kirishitan faith), Kyoto University Library copy (*terminus a quo* 1689), there may be found any number of examples. For instance, *hakyaku* (to demolish) has not merely the *kana* provided but also the translation *yaburu* (to wreck).

4. The edict was issued on Kan'ei 16/7/5; the *Kirishitan monogatari* is dated Kan'ei 16/8. The *Baterenki* (Tale of the Bateren) seems to antedate the *Kirishitan monogatari* (Ebisawa, *Nihon Kirishitan shi*, p. 206, speculates that it was composed some time after 1607 in the area of Hakata), but cannot properly be placed in the genre. This book introduces much Christian legendary material and develops the theme of aggression, but its plot lines differ completely from those of the later chapbooks—if, indeed, a plot can be attributed to it, for it is merely a series of vignettes.

Contrary to Ebisawa's notation (*Christianity in Japan*, p. 22), the *Baterenki* MS. is not to be found in the Tenri Library. The text has been published in: *Zokuzoku gunsho ruijū*, XII; *Kirishitan monogatari hoka sanshu*, ed. Hiyane Antei, Kirishitan Bunko, I; *Kaihyō sōsho*, ed. Shinmura Izuru, I (Kyoto: Kōseikaku Shoten, 1927).

5. *Kirishitan raichōki* (Account of the Kirishitans' advent to Our Empire), MS. copy dated Hōreki 11, Kyoto University Library. The *terminus a quo* of the composition of the *Nanbanji kōhaiki* would seem to be Genroku 8 (1695), the date of appearance of Nishikawa Joken's *Ka-i tsūshō kō*. The chapbook's first printed text is Kiyū Dōnin's edition of 1868; a second edition followed immediately that same year. See Ebisawa's commentary, Tōyō Bunko 14, pp. 3–8; the modern Japanese version which follows on pp. 9–78 is valuable for its annotations. It may be added, however, that the copyist of *Banshū seikinroku* (Record of the barbarian sect's proscription), 20 *kan* in 5 MS. vols. (Library of the Department of History, Kyoto University), a work dressed up as history, reproduced the absurdities unhesitatingly in 1846!

6. *Kirishitan shūmonki* (Account of the Kirishitan religion), interior title *Yaso shūmon raichō kongenki* (Account of the origins of the Jesuit religion's advent to Our Empire), 3 MS. vols. in the Kyoto University Library (*terminus a quo* 1689). The other chapbooks usually call Urugan's homeland the Kirishitan Country.

7. The *Nanbanji kōhaiki* describes Furukomu as a scholar who, after arriving in Nagasaki, read all the sutras thrice in one year and was therefore well conversant with Buddhism. He rode standing up on the saddle of his horse and lit tobacco by striking fire from his own claws. When he saw a bird perched on a tree, he fixed it with his stare, rode over and broke off the branch; the bird remained sitting on it. And he amazed all with other such feats of magic. Kiyū Dōnin, 1st ed., pp. 17b–18; Hiyane Antei, Kirishitan Bunko, II, 20–21.

8. *Nanbanji kōhaiki*: Kiyū Dōnin, 1st ed., pp. 7–11b; Hiyane, pp. 8–13. There are some slight variations in the other chapbooks, but they generally contain the mantra *Shigo Shōten Haraizō Zensu Maro*: "After-death Rebirth Paradise Jesus Mary." The mantra found its way into the kabuki, and that surely is yet another indication of the chapbooks' popularity. Tsuruya Nanboku IV, the late Edo period's greatest playwright, used it in *Tenjiku Tokubei ikoku banashi* (Tenjiku Tokubei's outlandish tale; 1804)—the arch-villain and would-be usurper Tokubei repeats "Shigo Shōden Haraiso" or "Dei, Dei, Haraiso" in order to vanish into thin air or summon forth his familiar, a huge toad; *Tsuruya Nanboku zenshū*, I, ed. Gunji Masakatsu

(Tokyo: San'ichi Shobō, 1971), 35–36 and 48. The play proved a wild success, not least because Nanboku spread about the rumor that its dazzling quick changes and stage tricks were indeed only made possible by the application of Kirishitan magic. It did not hurt attendance any when the city magistrate's office decided that the rumor was worth investigating and actually conducted a search of the theater. Ihara Toshirō, *Kinsei Nihon engeki shi* (Tokyo: Waseda Daigaku Shuppanbu, 1913), pp. 210–211 and 675.

9. Kiyū Dōnin, 1st ed., pp. 13–13b; Hiyane, pp. 15–16.

10. See below, *Kirishitan monogatari*, pp. 357–360.

11. Avila Girón, *Nippon Ōkoku ki*, p. 401. Also see Crasset (London, 1707), II, 226–227: "In *Meaco*, there was one Street call'd the Street of the Christians, because no Heathen was permitted to dwell amongst them, and here it was, where the Tyrant made his first Onset. Having turn'd out all the Men, he bound up the Women in Rice Sacks, and so very streight, that they had no Manner of Use of their Limbs; but for Fear any should be stiffl'd, he took Care to lay them Side to Side, and in this Manner, they were expos'd Day and Night to the Cold, and Snow, which at that Time fell in great Abundance. What's remarkable, the very Children were so importune with the Officers, to share with their Parents, in the Torments, that they were forc'd to bind them also, in the same Manner."

12. *Kinka keiranshō* (Golden flowers and violent storms), 30 *kan* in 15 MS. vols., Kyoto University Library; the first six *kan* contain the usual chapbook material.

13. I do not mean to imply that all the specifications are present; but enough analogues may be detected to make the comparison feasible. For a general discussion of the problem in Europe, see the brilliant study by Norman Cohn, *The Pursuit of the Millennium* (New York: Harper, 1961; Harper Torchbook TB 1037). My argument also draws on the provocative article by Fukaya Katsumi, "Junkyō no ronri to hōki no ronri," *Shisō*, 565:40–55 (July 1971). See also two other articles by Fukaya: "Shūkyō to teikō," *Rekishi hyōron*, 185:40–49 (January 1966); "'Shimabara no ran' no rekishiteki igi," *Rekishi hyōron*, 201:20–42 (May 1967). Both of these are dogmatic, but the latter incorporates a wealth of previously unevaluated primary materials.

14. See below, *Kirishitan monogatari*, "How the Kirishitans Raised a Revolt in Amakusa and Shimabara of Hizen in Tsukushi."

15. *Shimabara Hantō shi*, ed. Hayashi Tetsuyoshi, I (Shimabara: Nagasaki-ken Minami Takaki Gunshi Kyōikukai, 1954), 983–984.

16. Kitajima, *Edo jidai*, p. 32. Kitajima notes that the Matsukura were pressed for funds in part because they had attempted to get into the shogunate's good graces by volunteering to contribute to the construction of Edo Castle an amount appropriate to a domain of 100,000 *koku* whereas theirs produced only 40,000. The shogunate increased their holdings to a yield of 60,000 *koku*.

17. Diego Pacheco SJ, "The Europeans in Japan, 1543–1640," *The Southern Barbarians: The First Europeans in Japan*, ed. Michael Cooper SJ, p. 93.

18. Schütte, *Introductio*, p. 431.

19. Avila Girón: *Archivo Ibero-Americano*, 38:410; *Nippon Ōkoku ki*, p. 377. Banzuii Chiyo was the 33rd abbot of the Hyakumanben Chionji in Kyoto. On his exploits in the Arima area, see *Dai Nippon shiryō*, 12/IX (1906), 568–570.

20. From the *Arima kiroku* (The Arima record), an account of the Nabeshima *han*'s role in suppressing the rebellion; *Shimabara Hantō shi*, II,

273. The text goes on to blame the *ikki* on the evil ways of government and the extortionism which prevailed in the Matsukura domain, and mentions the prophecies which circulated about the personage of Amakusa Shirō, "who was to be revered as the emissary of Deus and possessed of divine super-powers." There would surely be a portent which "would move heaven and earth, and none should be surprised, etc. etc." For further examples of texts referring to mass apostasy and subsequent return to Christianity (*tachikaeri*), see Fukaya, "Junkyō no ronri to hōki no ronri," pp. 47–49. Volume II of the *Shimabara Hantō shi* is the single most important compilation of sources on the rebellion, containing almost a thousand pages of materials devoted to the topic.

21. Jesús López Gay SJ, *El Catecumenado en la Mision del Japon del S. XVI* (Rome: Libreria dell'Universitá Gregoriana, 1966), p. 116, states flatly: "The missionaries molded the Christians to be able—regardless of the ideology of their surroundings—to resist their superiors." It is true that the Christian propaganda was directed against the ideology of the surroundings; but it never called for the active deed against superiors nor even implied that it was desirable or possible. The Christian definition of resistance was that of a spiritual act of commitment to Deus and fortitude in the face of all pressures to abandon Him. The superiors, of course, interpreted this stress on an ulterior loyalty as another instance of social subversion. For examples of the exhortation to martyrdom in seventeenth-century Japan, see Anesaki Masaharu, *Kirishitan shūmon no hakugai to senpuku*, ch. v, "Maruchiriyo no shiori" (The guide to martyrdom), pp. 131–240. Anesaki reproduces here the text of a manuscript which circulated after 1614; a portion is included under the title *Maruchiru no michi* (The way of the martyr) in NST 25, pp. 323–360, and Cieslik provides a commentary on pp. 623–626. The depictions of the glory of martyrdom are combined with gruesome threats of punishment against those who apostatize; for the guilt of those who reject what they know to be the truth is more grievous than that of the ignorant heathen, and so shall their punishment be. Cf. Anesaki, p. 190, and NST 25, p. 335: "Those who fall away from being *Xpāos* shall be the slaves of the devil, kindling for the flames of Inferno; nor shall there be an end to their suffering, for they shall be burnt more mercilessly even than the others. Their punishment not only shall be torment and agony in the life to come; already in this life they shall begin to suffer many spiritual and bodily losses." Everyone shall despise them; they shall be cast away from humanity and execrated by men, saints, and angels.

22. The perfect example of this dissolution may be found in a compact the rebels swore to attest their readiness to do anything and to die for the Kirishitan faith "to which we have returned." The formulas of the oath are terribly corrupt, and the vow is addressed to the "Heavenly Master Shirō Tokisada the Good Lord." This last appellation is written in the characters often used for the name of Jesus: Zensu or Zesu. The possibility cannot be excluded that part or all of the text is a latter-day falsification, for it occurs in the *Yaso Tenchūki* (How Heaven's punishment struck the Jesuits), which is not an immediately contemporary account. But this chronicle's compilation of reports of the rebellion's progress is generally reliable. And millenarian enthusiasm is notoriously bereft of discrimination and susceptible to such identifications. The form of address rings true, as does another name applied to Shirō, "Heavenly Child" (*Tendō*). The oath is dated [Kan'ei 14]/11/8 (Christmas Eve 1637). *Shimabara Hantō shi*, II, 878; also see the preliminary account on p. 877.

23. The circular is dated [Kan'ei 14]/10/15 (1 December 1637); *Yaso Tenchūki, Shimabara Hantō shi*, II, 846. For another view of Shirō's provenance, see Tsuruta Yasunari, "Shijitsu Amakusa Shirō no kenkyū: sono keireki to kazoku-ensha soshite rekishiteki igi," *Kirishitan Bunka Kenkyūkai kaihō*, 10.3/4:1–60 (October 1968).

24. Dated 10/25; *Yaso Tenchūki, Shimabara Hantō shi*, II, 851–852.

25. Ibid., p. 919; message attached to an arrow and shot into the enemy camp, dated [Kan'ei 14]/12/12 (26 January 1638).

26. On Beheim and Wirsberg, see Cohn, *The Pursuit of the Millennium*, pp. 237–251. There is a splendid characterization of Amakusa Shirō as Magus in *Yaso Tenchūki, Shimabara Hantō shi*, II, 842–843.

27. Document dated [Kan'ei 15]/7/19 (28 August 1638); *Shimabara Hantō shi*, II, 980–981.

28. For an account of Chie Izu's activities in connection with the *ikki*, see the diary compiled in 1663 by his son Matsudaira Kai no Kami Terutsuna; *Shimabara Amakusa nikki*, ed. Hiyane Antei, Kirishitan Bunko, III, 1–49. For a list of the two dozèn lookout stations which resulted, see Document III of *Kirishito-ki*: Cieslik and Voss, pp. 44–46, include a map; Hiyane, Kirishitan Bunko, II, 49–52. Cf. *Tokugawa jikki*, III, entry for Kan'ei 18/5/10 (18 June 1641), Kokushi Taikei, XL, 225–226.

29. A wealth of materials on the crypto-Kirishitans will be found in the definitive study by Tagita Kōya, *Shōwa jidai no senpuku Kirishitan* (Tokyo: Nihon Gakujutsu Shinkōkai, 1954). This is a truly fascinating book, in which the scriptures, prayers, and practices of Nagasaki Prefecture's present-day *Kakure* are analyzed with great perceptiveness and in great detail. A multitude of illustrations accompanies the text. Of particular interest is ch. x, pp. 355–456, which reconstructs a series of orational formulas.

One example of the rote degeneration over the centuries might be given, from a *Kakure* oration tape-recorded by Tagita on Ikitsuki in 1953. The transcription (p. 377) reads as follows: "Atobiya oremus, biya tettoro gruriyosa. Sempero pepero, jimis mariya. Kiyons miyons domino, entera serusha gruriyoza, mosporoteruka, yotsu atsu bideka, terutowa kaina, tenna terukiris todeno noshitsurushi ammeizusu. Bedekawamos domino, biya garassa ammeizus." Originally these were the concluding sentences of the Litany of the Blessed Virgin Mary (the *Sancta Virgo virginum* transformed by the *Kakure* into "Santa brôga brôshima"), and the Latin reads as follows: "Oremus. Beatae et gloriosae semper Virginis Mariae quaesumus, Domine, intercessione gloriosa nos protegat et ad vitam perducat aeternam. Per Christum Dominum Nostrum, Amen. Benedicamus Domino. Deo gratias, Amen."

Also deserving special notice is the *Kakure* scripture *Tenchi hajimari no koto* (On the beginnings of heaven and earth), which Tagita treats in ch. iv, pp. 76–163. Over the years Tagita was able to obtain nine manuscript variants of this text in several locales of Nagasaki Prefecture, in transcriptions dating from the early nineteenth century into the middle of the twentieth. One is included in NST 25, pp. 381–409; Tagita gives a commentary on pp. 631–634. There is a German translation by Alfred Bohner, "Tenchi Hajimari no Koto: Wie Himmel und Erde entstanden," *MN*, 1.2:173–207 (July 1938); original text on pp. 208–222.

30. The catalogue of the Amakusa Kirishitan-kan (which exhibits some forty ritual implements and images of the *Kakure*) states that the practices continued into the beginning of the Shōwa period, *sc.* the 1930s (September 1969 ed., p. 18). The author of the handbook *Amakusa* (Kumamoto:

Kinryūdō, 1968 revised edition), Yamaguchi Osamu, is more circumspect and gives the Meiji period as the terminal date (p. 126).

31. It will be noted that it took Tagita Kōya more than twenty years to obtain the confidence of the *Kakure* and gather the information included in his work (see its preface).

32. This incident is described exhaustively by Furuno Kiyoto, *Kakure Kirishitan*, Nihon Rekishi Shinsho (Tokyo: Shibundō, 1959), pp. 45–87. Furuno cites the ample day-by-day records of the inquiry; and he goes on to discuss the nature of the *Kakure* religion in Amakusa on pp. 87–100. On this mass roundup, see also Shimoda Kyokusui, *Zantei Amakusa Kirishitan shi* (Kumamoto: Kumamoto Toshokan Kan'yūkai, 1941), pp. 331–357.

33. The total number of *Kakure* in Nagasaki Prefecture was in 1959 estimated at 30,000 (Furuno, p. 43), meaning a 2:5 ratio of crypto-Kirishitans to Roman Catholics. On Ikitsuki there were in that same year some 380 Catholics (Furuno, p. 106); and Tagita stated in 1954 that well over ten thousand of the island's population continued to some extent the subterranean religion's practice (p. 2).

34. *Kirishito-ki*, Document VII, Item 18; see above, Chapter 7; Cieslik and Voss, p. 62.

35. Yamazaki Kai no Kami Ieharu was ordered transferred to Marugame in Sanuki on Kan'ei 18/9/10, and Suzuki Shigenari appointed *daikan* on 9/20 (24 October 1641); see the relevant entries in *Tokugawa jikki*, III, Kokushi Taikei, XL, 238. Shigenari arrived in Amakusa in December 1641; Shimoda Kyokusui, p. 223.

36. The biographical details may be found in three sketches compiled by Shōsan's disciple Echū: *Sekihei Dōnin gyōgōki* (An account of [Shōsan's] actions); a detailed defense of the account, *Sekihei Dōnin gyōgōki bengi*; *Sekihei Dōnin shisō* (The four stages of [Shōsan's] life). The three are included in *Suzuki Shōsan Dōnin zenshū*, ed. Suzuki Tesshin (Tokyo: Sankibō Busshorin, 1962).

The best general treatment of Shōsan's approach to Zen is by Akizuki Ryōmin, in *Zenmon no iryū*, Nihon no Bukkyō 12 (Tokyo: Chikuma Shobō, 1969 third printing), pp. 99–160. The discussion by Furuta Shōkin, in *Kinsei no Zenshatachi* (Kyoto: Heirakuji Shoten, 1956), pp. 147–161, may also be recommended.

37. His earliest tract, *Mōanjō* (The blind man's staff) was composed in 1619, while Shōsan was a member of the Osaka garrison; included in *Suzuki Shōsan Dōnin zenshū*, pp. 49–60, and in *Kana hōgo shū*, ed. Miyasaka Yūshō, Nihon Koten Bungaku Taikei 83 (Tokyo: Iwanami, 1964), pp. 241–261. The motive for composition is described by Echū as explicitly controversialist: among Shōsan's fellow samurai there was a Confucianist who held that Buddhism was contrary to the wordly norm, and Shōsan wanted to demonstrate the opposite; see *Roankyō* (The donkey's saddlebone), *kan* 3, no. 132, *Zenshū*, p. 277. The *Roankyō* consists of Shōsan's analects and anecdotes about him. Suzuki Daisetsu appends a valuable commentary to his edition of this work: *Roankyō*, Iwanami Bunko 3767–3769 (Tokyo: Iwanami, 1948).

38. *Sekihei Dōnin gyōgōki bengi*, *Zenshū*, p. 31.

39. *Roankyō*, *kan* 3, no. 70, *Zenshū*, p. 258.

40. Note the remorseless attack on the grasping and corrupt type of bonze in *Fumoto no kusawake* (Parting the grass at the foot of the mountain): Shōsan revels in examples of such monks' ghastly end; *Zenshū*, pp. 91–92. On the ancient masters' lack of perfection in practice, see *Roankyō*, *kan* 1,

no. 34, *Zenshū*, p. 148. It will also be noted that Shōsan did not consider even Dōgen, the patriarch of Sōtō Zen in Japan, to have been enlightened; *Roankyō, kan* 3, no. 121, p. 274. Shōsan's major objection seems to be that Zen-men have become too gentle and lack the ferocity needed to achieve satori: *Roankyō, kan* 1, nos. 1–4, pp. 138–139. Also see *Sekihei Dōnin gyōgōki bengi, Zenshū*, p. 20.

41. Cf. Kitajima Masamoto, *Edo jidai*, pp. 72–74.

42. Nakamura Hajime is the advocate of this view. For a lengthy exposition, see his *Kinsei Nihon ni okeru hihanteki seishin no ichi kōsatsu* (Tokyo: Sanseidō, 1949); pp. 1–243 deal with Shōsan. A more concise statement is ch. iii of *Nihon shūkyō no kindaisei*, in *Nakamura Hajime senshū*, VIII (Tokyo: Shunjūsha, 1964), 145–164; there is a translation by William Johnston, "Suzuki Shōsan, 1579–1655, and the spirit of capitalism in Japanese Buddhism," *MN*, 22.1/2:1–14 (1967).

43. *Roankyō, kan* 1, no. 170, *Zenshū*, p. 187.

44. *Roankyō, kan* 1, no. 2, pp. 138–139.

45. *Banmin tokuyō* (Functional virtue in all walks of life): *Zenshū*, p. 68; *Kana hōgo shū*, p. 272.

46. *Hogoshū*: *Zenshū*, pp. 315–316; *Kana hōgo shū*, pp. 328–330. These "scraps and jottings" represent another set of analects and anecdotes, and were probably also compiled by Echū.

47. *Roankyō, kan* 1, no. 107, *Zenshū*, p. 171.

48. *Hogoshū*: *Zenshū*, p. 316; *Kana hōgo shū*, pp. 330–331.

49. *Roankyō, kan* 3, no. 13, *Zenshū*, p. 239. Cf. Chapter 2, pp. 46–48 above.

50. See below, *Christians Countered*, VIII.

51. *Roankyō, kan* 3, no. 128, *Zenshū*, p. 276.

52. "Suzuki Shōsan, 1579–1655, and the spirit of capitalism in Japanese Buddhism," trans. William Johnston, *MN*, 22.1/2:3.

53. *MN*, 22.1/2:4–5.

54. *MN*, 22.1/2:9.

55. *Banmin tokuyō*: *Zenshū*, p. 71; *Kana hōgo shū*, pp. 277–278.

56. The word is *jiyū* but clearly does not mean "freedom" in any modern sense and at best denotes a premodern conception of economic autarky. In many contexts of the Tokugawa period the expression merely means "prosperity." For instance, chapbooks of the *Raichō jikki* type invariably include as the first element in Kōshinpi's plot the intelligence that Japan, albeit small, had plenty of gold and silver, rice and grain, so that it was *jiyū jizai*—self-reliant and self-sufficient, in other words rich.

57. *MN*, 22.1/2: 9 and 11.

58. For a bit of dialectical spiritualism, see in *Hogoshū* the "four questions and four answers" which are meant to contain the essence of Shōsan's thought: *Zenshū*, pp. 293–294; *Kana hōgo shū*, pp. 292–294. The first set defines the identity of worldly elements and Buddhist dharmas. In *Banmin tokuyō* Shōsan cites the Kegon Sutra to that effect: see *Zenshū*, p. 61, or *Kana hōgo shū*, p. 263; cf. *Kegon-kyō*, ch. xix, *Taishō*, X, no. 278, 105.

59. *Roankyō, kan* 2, no. 46, *Zenshū*, p. 203. Note also the simple eclecticism of the *Hogoshū* discussion of moral obligations: *Zenshū*, pp. 290–292; *Kana hōgo shū*, pp. 288–291.

60. *Banmin tokuyō*: *Zenshū*, p. 70; *Kana hōgo shū*, p. 276.

61. Quotation from *Sekihei Dōnin shisō, Zenshū*, p. 37; for the wider context, see pp. 37–39.

62. "The lone wolf of Zen" (*Zenmon no ippiki ōkami*) is the title of Akizuki's introduction to Shōsan; *Zenmon no iryū*, pp. 101–109.

63. *Sekihei Dōnin gyōgōki, Zenshū*, pp. 7–8.

64. For estimates of the islands' population after the rebellion, see Yamaguchi Osamu, *Amakusa*, p. 136.

65. Yamaguchi, pp. 137–139.

66. *Sekihei Dōnin gyōgōki, Zenshū*, p. 8.

67. The best manuscript copy is in the Library of Congress. The first printed text is an abbreviated transcription of the original *kanbun*, included in Kiyū Dōnin's compilation *Byakuja kankenroku* ([Edo]: Enzan, Bunkyū 1 [1861]), 1:24b–31b. Kiyū Dōnin also included the transcribed epitome, under the title *Jakyō taii* (The gist of the pernicious doctrine), in both of his 1868 editions of the *Nanbanji kōhaiki*. Volume X of *Nihon shisō tōsō shiryō* (Tokyo: Tōhō Shoin, 1930) contains the *Taiji jashūron* (pp. 391–402) as well as the *Jakyō taii* (pp. 309–317). The most convenient edition of the *kanbun* text is in NST 25, pp. 492–502; Ebisawa provides a slightly abbreviated but nicely annotated transcription on pp. 460–476, and a brief discussion on p. 640.

68. *Sekihei Dōnin gyōgōki* and *Bengi*; *Zenshū*, pp. 4 and 17.

69. Shinmura Izuru, *Nanban kōki*, pp. 105–106.

70. NST 25, pp. 494 and 462.

71. NST 25, pp. 496 and 465.

72. NST 25, pp. 497 and 467. Sessō's outline of Christian teachings and practices (pp. 497–499 and 467–471) seems entirely derived from Fabian and Ferreira; there are also echoes of the *Kirishitan monogatari*.

73. NST 25, pp. 502 and 476.

74. The *casus belli* was the inscription on the bell Hideyori ordered to be cast for the rebuilt Hōkōji in Kyoto, his father's foundation (the bell bears a date corresponding to 24 May 1614). It contained the phrase *kokka ankō*, "the realm is at peace," but the malevolent noted that the two characters of Ieyasu's name were split in this phrase by a third; and this was interpreted as lese-majesty or worse. Leading priests of the *Gosan* were consulted, and were unanimous in their condemnation. Razan contributed his piece, and stated that the offence against the August Name outraged all the classical laws, regulations, and ritual codices of Japan and of China: it was "the height of irreverence and lawlessness." See Hori Isao, *Hayashi Razan*, pp. 187–199; the text of Razan's exegesis is given on pp. 195–196. Ieyasu had for several years prior to 1614 demonstrated an uncommon interest in Chinese precedents for righteous tyrannicide; and Razan obliged him with scholarly responses to his queries on this possible form of justification for the move against Hideyori. See Hori, pp. 156–172, for a discussion and ample citations.

75. On Razan's attitude to Buddhism, see Hori, pp. 400–410.

76. Written on behalf of the *Nagasaki Daikan* Suetsugu Heizō; *Razan sensei bunshū*, I, 12:136. Cited by Hori, pp. 385 and 260–261. I owe much of my argument to Hori, pp. 384–400. Razan does not use the word *Yaso*, which I translate "Jesuit," in the precise sense (a member of the Society of Jesus), but rather to denote a follower of the religion of Jesus, or the religion itself. The usage is analogous to Fabian's term *Daiusu*: adherent of Deus.

77. Warning to the Ming traders, 1641; *Razan sensei bunshū*, II, 58:248–249.

78. Written in 1640 on behalf of Inoue Chikugo's fellow *ōmetsuke* Kagazume Minbu no Shōshō Tadazumi, who was sent from Edo to settle the matter of the Macao embassy (the sixty-one executions took place on the 4th of August); *Razan sensei bunshū*, II, 58:246–247. Compare *Tokugawa jikki*, III, Kokushi Taikei, XL, 193–194 (entry for Kan'ei 17/6/27).

79. *Razan sensei bunshū*, I, 7:93. The letter is dated to correspond to the second or third week of May 1654.

80. I follow the outline of Kitajima Masamoto, *Edo jidai*, pp. 54–55. Matsudaira Sadamasa was the daimyo of Kariya in Mikawa. Shōsetsu was the son of a draper who made a success of himself as a tutor in military science: daimyo and *hatamoto* were among his students. Those privy to his conspiracy were mostly rōnin; but samurai in daimyo employ were also among the participants, as were *hatamoto*, rich peasants, and even Buddhist priests. Their number is sometimes given as three thousand, but Kitajima believes that to be an exaggeration.

81. Shōsetsu is said to have forged the seals of Yorinobu, Ieyasu's tenth son and founder of the Kii branch of the Tokugawa, one of the family's Three Houses (*gosanke*).

82. Banzan himself scorned Buddhism and Christianity as much as any other Japanese Confucian, including Razan. What is more, he too had a propensity for altogether facile identifications. Buddhism and Christianity were to him undifferentiated: the Kirishitan barbarians were the Southern Buddhists, barely distinguished from the accepted Western kind. See the colloquy *Miwa monogatari* (1685?), *kan* 6, *Banzan zenshū*, ed. Masamune Atsuo, V (Tokyo: Banzan Zenshū Kankōkai, 1942), 63–64: "South Barbary is a land of beasts who merely look human." All they do is plot how to take over other lands. The Southern Barbarians' brand of Buddhism (*i.e.*, Christianity) is a device toward this end. The populace of Japan had already been stultified and impoverished by the Western Barbarians' Buddhism (*i.e.*, Buddhism), so that the Kirishitans thought it would be an easy thing to take over the country, in fifty or at most a hundred years. The *Miwa monogatari* then continues (8:75) to spell out the details: "When the Kirishitans say, 'We employ two Bateren to convert Japan,' they mean Dengyō and Kōbō . . . But do not the Kirishitans also loathe Buddhism? I say that is just like the Nenbutsu Sect and the Nichiren Sect, who are enemies and allies at the same time. Shaka told the Bateren about the afterlife; the end result is the same, the people are deluded. Call it the Buddha Tathagata, call it Zensu Maru; in actuality they are one. Shaka studied the pernicious crafts of the Bateren and made them out to be divine super-powers; the Kirishitans take the Buddha Tathagata and label him Zensu Maru." Dengyō and Kōbō, the founders of Tendai and Shingon in Japan, are revealed as Kirishitan Bateren in disguise, and that is interesting in itself. But it is even more interesting to note that the allusion is unmistakably to Urugan and Furaten, and testifies to the spread of the popular anti-Christian literature beyond the circles of the vulgar.

If there is any doubt whether the opinions of the colloquy's personages properly represent Banzan's own, it is dispelled by the explicit dictums of *Shūgi gaisho* (The complex of morals and its application: an additional treatise; 1679?), *Banzan senshū*, II (1941): "If the Buddhists are permitted to carry on as before, there will be disturbance. And upon disturbance will immediately follow the Kirishitan turnover" (14:233). "As long as Buddhism remains, the Kirishitans cannot be eliminated" (2:26). In fact, what differentiates the two religions is that the Kirishitans are more rational and more clever than the Buddhists (10:175). Japan need not fear foreign aggression: external perfidy can easily be fended off. "But the Kirishitans are an internal disease, one difficult to cure" (8:148–149).

Another colloquy (which may, however, be spurious) defines the nature of the dual peril best of all. See *Banzan zenshū*, V, *Usa mondō*, 1:6——It is said that Shaka was born in the West, but his homeland actually was in southern India and bordered on South Barbary. The Buddhist magic was an import from South Barbary, and the Kirishitans knew full well where it would lead: Buddhism became the fifth column of Christianity and paved the way for Southern Barbarian aggression. "So that Japan be taken over by South Barbary, it was first taken over by the Western Buddha."

83. *Razan sensei bunshū*, I, 7:87.

84. *Sōzoku zenki*, in *Jijitsu bunpen*, IV, ed. Gokyū Toyotarō and Gokyū Tomotarō (Tokyo: Kokusho Kankōkai, 1911), 502–503. This edition does not give the author's name; but there is no doubt that Razan wrote the tract, for he himself refers to a *Sōzoku ki* in the May 1654 letter to Jōzan, and gives him permission to show it to others (*Razan sensei bunshū*, I, 7:96).

85. Cf. *Li chi, Wang chih* v; SPTK, II, 4:12–12b.

86. Miyazaki Michio has compiled an invaluable assembly of sources dealing with the Sidotti episode in his definitive edition of Hakuseki's *Seiyō kibun*, Tōyō Bunko 113 (Tokyo: Heibonsha, 1968). This volume contains not only the final version of the *Seiyō kibun* and a profuse apparatus, but also Hakuseki's notes preparatory to the treatise, several antecedent variants, and a whole series of related texts. Hakuseki's recommendations on how best to dispose of Sidotti (*Rōmajin shochi kengi*) and his brief analysis of the implications of Catholicism (*Tenshukyō taii*) will be found on pp. 193–200; the quotations are from pp. 199–200.

87. I follow Miyazaki's commentary, Tōyō Bunko 113, pp. 420–424. The final version of the treatise was completed in 1724 or in the year of Hakuseki's death, 1725; see Tōyō Bunko 113, pp. 424–431, on the stages of composition. There is a detailed consideration of the *Seiyō kibun* on pp. 203–263 of Miyazaki's *Arai Hakuseki no kenkyū* (Tokyo: Yoshikawa Kōbunkan, 1969 revised edition), and of Hakuseki's attitude toward Christianity on pp. 559–608. On the latter topic, see also Miyazaki, "Arai Hakuseki no Kirishitan-kan," *Nihon rekishi*, 92:14–28 (February 1956), and 93:28–32 (March 1956); and cf. Hirai Naoko, "Arai Hakuseki no Kirisuto-kyō kan," *Kirishitan Bunka Kenkyūkai kaihō*, 8.3/4:32–50 (March 1966).

88. Tōyō Bunko 113, p. 388. The letter's date is tentatively set as Kyōhō 7 (1722)/10.

89. These translations are: "Sei yo ki-bun, or Annals of the Western Ocean," trans. S. R. Brown, *Journal of the North-China Branch of the Royal Asiatic Society*, New Series, 2:51–78 (December 1865) and 3:40–62 (December 1866), complete but for the appendix to Part One; "The Capture and Captivity of Pere Giovanni Batista Sidotti in Japan from 1709 to 1715, Translated from the [*Seiyō kibun*] of Arai Haku-seki, by the Rev. W. B. Wright," *Transactions of the Asiatic Society of Japan*, 9:156–172 (1881; Yūshōdō reprint edition, 1964), Part One only. In September 1882 the Yokohama journal *The Chrysanthemum* also published a synopsis: "Père Sidotti in Japan (A Condensed Translation from the Seiyo-kibun)," 2.9:390–399. Cf. Tōyō Bunko 113, pp. 417–418.

90. Compare *Seiyō kibun*, Tōyō Bunko 113, pp. 83–84, with the First Step of *Deus Destroyed*.

91. *Seiyō kibun*, p. 41.

92. Ibid., pp. 34–35.

93. Ibid., pp. 59–63.

94. *Tenshukyō taii*, Tōyō Bunko 113, p. 199.

95. *Seiyō kibun*, Tōyō Bunko 113, pp. 96–97.

96. Ibid., pp. 93–94.

97. Ibid., pp. 97–98.

98. Ibid., p. 79.

99. The text has *Tenshu*, the Lord of Heaven. Hakuseki uses this term interchangeably with Deus, but criticizes Matteo Ricci for having applied it to his deity in the first place, such a usage being inconsistent with that of the Confucian classics.

100. Cieslik and Voss, App. VIII, "Das Kirishitan-Yashiki," p. 198.

101. Motoyama Yukihiko, "Meiji Ishin to sonnō jōi shisō," *Meiji shisō no keisei* (Tokyo: Fukumura Shuppan, 1969), p. 20. I owe my interest in Mito thought to Professor Motoyama, and my general formulations concerning its character developed out of the translation work I undertook on his article, "The Political Thought of the Late Mito School," to be published under the auspices of the Japanese National UNESCO Committee in *Philosophical Studies of Japan*, no. 11.

102. *Kōdōkanki jutsugi* (Exegesis of the *Kōdōkanki*; 1852), in *Shintei Tōko zenshū*, ed. Kikuchi Kenjirō (Tokyo: Hakubunkan, 1940), p. 168.

103. Memorial of Tenpō 2/7/29 (5 September 1831), *Tōko zenshū*, p. 808.

104. *Hitachi obi* (A Hitachi sash; 1844), *Tōko zenshū*, pp. 113–114. Also see *Kaiten shishi* (Turn Heaven round: a poetical history of the reversal of affairs; 1844), *Tōko zenshū*, pp. 38–39.

105. *Oranjin o miru no ki* (On seeing some Hollanders), *Tōko zenshū*, p. 446. Also see the memorial of Bunsei 11/12/14 (19 January 1828), *Tōko zenshū*, p. 1059. The episode occurred in 1826; one of the three Westerners was the famous Dr. Siebold (who, incidentally, was not a Hollander but a German from Würzburg). Cf. Richard Chang, *From Prejudice to Tolerance: A Study of the Japanese Image of the West, 1826–1864*, MN Monographs (Tokyo: Sophia University, 1970), pp. 45–47.

106. *Mitogaku taikei*, ed. Takasu Yoshijirō, V (Tokyo: Mitogaku Taikei Kankōkai, 1942 second printing), 216–217. The draft is dated Tenpō 9/8/1 (19 September 1838).

107. *Mitogaku taikei*, V, 227–228. The preceding argument is contracted from pp. 215–228.

108. The *P'o-hsieh chi* (*Hajashū*) was originally compiled in 1640 by Hsü Ch'ang-chih. The 1855 Mito reissue is in eight volumes. Nariaki's preface is also included in *Mitogaku taikei*, V, 309–310.

109. A table of contents of this manuscript collection will be found in Ebisawa, *Christianity in Japan: A Bibliography of Japanese and Chinese Sources*, pt. 1, p. 119.

110. *Sangan yokō*, in *Nihon shisō tōsō shiryō*, X, 405–431. The date is commonly given as 1849 but cannot be determined accurately. The pamphlet's preface states that Aizawa had consulted the official history of the Ming on the advent of the pernicious faith to China, and had gleaned also from the *P'o-hsieh chi*; the insights he derived were summarized in his *Ryōgankō* (Views from two eyes). Hakuseki provided him with the third eye; and, indeed, the Japanese are triply perceptive, for they do not permit the barbarians' entry; p. 412.

111. *Sangan yokō*, p. 418.

Conclusion

1. Ebisawa Arimichi is the principal exponent of this view, and has in the course of a prolific career developed it into a widely accepted thesis. The best brief illustration is his article "Kirishitan no denrai to sono bunka,"

Nihon bunkashi gairon, ed. Ishida Ichirō, ch. xxi, pp. 351–366. Another good instance is his approach to "The Meeting of Cultures," *The Southern Barbarians*, ed. Michael Cooper SJ, pp. 125–144. This essay begins with the assertion that the humanist spirit characterized the Society of Jesus of the sixteenth century, and the author draws the required corollaries; for all that, this is one of his more persuasive pieces.

The debate over the meaning of Sakoku finds some of the greatest names of modern Japanese historiography ranged on opposite sides of the argument. At the end of a comprehensive and still valuable book, Nakamura Kōya arrived at a positive evaluation: *Edo Bakufu Sakoku shiron* (Tokyo: Hōkōkai, 1914), pp. 395–396. The economic historian Uchida Ginzō also drew attention to the positive aspects of Sakoku: *Kinsei no Nihon* (Tokyo: Fuzanbō, 1919), pp. 77–81. Uchida referred to Shinmura Izuru's critique of Tsuji Zennosuke's *Kaigai kōtsū shiwa* (Tokyo: Tōadō Shobō, 1917), and himself took issue with the essentially negative judgment on Sakoku's effects which Tsuji expressed in ch. xxiv, pp. 433–449. Tsuji maintained his stand in the revised and expanded version of his book: *Zōtei Kaigai kōtsū shiwa* (Tokyo: Naigai Shoseki Kabushiki Kaisha, 1930), ch. xxxiv, pp. 619–639. The most famous study of all is by Watsuji Tetsurō, and its basic orientation is indicated in the title, *Sakoku: Nihon no higeki* (Sakoku: a tragedy for Japan; Tokyo: Chikuma Shobō, 1950). Iwao Seiichi gives a brief survey of the changing attitudes toward Sakoku in the conclusion of his own very interesting study, Volume XIV of the Chūō Kōron-sha *Nihon no rekishi* series: *Sakoku*, pp. 456–464.

2. Cf. John Whitney Hall, "The New Look of Tokugawa History," *Studies in the Institutional History of Early Modern Japan*, pp. 55–64.

3. Needless to say, Aristotle neither could be nor was totally excluded: he was indispensable at the higher levels of training in theology and philosophy. One of the three Latin manuscripts attributed to Pedro Gomez and used by him in the Jesuits' Japanese *collegio c.* 1593 is in effect an epitome of Aristotle's *De anima*; another, "De sphaera," repeatedly invokes Aristotle's authority. But this utilization occurred within the closed confines of the *collegio* and was accordingly not of a public nature. It is remarkable that the public treatise *Myōtei mondō*—apologetics at a high intellectual level—does not apply Western philosophers. Fabian could have digested them as he did Confucius and Chu Hsi.

Gomez' manuscripts are described in Schütte, "Drei Unterrichtsbücher für Japanische Jesuitenprediger aus dem XVI. Jahrhundert," *Archivum Historicum Societatis Iesu*, 8.2:223–256 (1939). "De sphaera" is discussed in Obara Satoru, "Kirishitan jidai no kagaku shisō: Pedoro Gomesu-cho 'Tenkyūron' no kenkyū," *KK*, 10:101–178 (1965); Obara provides the original text and a Japanese translation as well. A sketch of Kirishitan science and its Japanese setting is given by Itō Shuntarō in supp. n. 1 to Rodriguez, *Nihon kyōkai shi*, II, 671–676.

4. For a brief introduction into this literature, see the review article by Horst Rzepkowski SVD, "Thomas von Aquin und der Zen-Buddhismus," *Neue Zeitschrift für Missionswissenschaft*, 24.2:146–150 (1968). The quotation is from Augustin Hideshi Kishi, *Spiritual Consciousness in Zen from a Thomistic Theological Point of View*; cited by Rzepkowski, p. 146. Also very informative is Rzepkowski's own essay, *Thomas von Aquin und Japan*, Studia Instituti Missiologici Societatis Verbi Divini Nr. 9 (St. Augustin/Siegburg: Steyler Verlag, 1967).

5. *The Cloud of Unknowing*, translated into Modern English with an Intro-

duction by Clifton Wolters (Harmondsworth, Middlesex: Penguin Books, 1961), p. 58.

6. *Qincuxú*, p. 535; Yoshida Sumio edition, p. 46.

7. On the Hitoyoshi *han* and its policy, see Harada Toshiaki, ed., *Kumamoto-ken no rekishi* (Tokyo: Bungadō, 1957), pp. 216–223.

8. For instance, we find in a colloquy attributed to Kumazawa Banzan that it was a fortunate flaw in Nobunaga's character that caused him to ravage Hieizan: "He did a good thing for Japan." The Ikkō Sect and the Nichiren Sect should be prohibited along with Christianity, for they are as harmful and as abhorrent. *Banzan zenshū*, V, *Usa mondō*, 1:8–9.

Tōko called Buddhism "hateful" and found the Ikkō Sect especially pernicious, because its adherents esteemed their Buddha "more than the lord or the father." He praised Satsuma for its refusal to permit even one Ikkō priest in its domain. Christianity, however, was infinitely more harmful than even the Ikkōshū. *Hitachi obi, Tōko zenshū*, p. 113.

9. See below, *Deus Destroyed*, p. 264.

10. Akutagawa Ryūnosuke, "Kamigami no bishō," *Hōkyōnin no shi, hoka jūsanpen*, p. 126.

Notes to the Translations

Bibliographical Note

The extant original of Fabian Fucan's *Ha Daiusu* is a woodblock volume which indicates neither the place nor the year of publication. The preface and the postscript are dated Genna 6 (1620), and the assumption is that this imprint does not postdate the Genna period (*sc.*, 1624). The possibility of another contemporary edition cannot be excluded, but is only suggested by secondary evidence.

The bibliography compiled by Ebisawa Arimichi, *Christianity in Japan*, pt. 1 (1960), p. 20, lists three extant copies of the original: in the Kyoto University Library, the Tenri Library, and the Shōkōkan in Mito. I have consulted the two former.

The more recent *Kokusho sōmokuroku*, VI (Tokyo: Iwanami, 1969), 640, lists six exemplars but is undependable: it omits mention of the Kyoto University book and errs in at least one other instance, attributing a copy of the original to the Nagasaki Prefectural Library.

The basis of my translation was the reproduction of the Kyoto University book: *Ha Daiusu*, Chinsho Taikan Kirishitan Sōsho (Osaka: Ōsaka Mainichi Shinbun-sha, 1928).

The most convenient edition is the text included in the recently published Volume XXV of the Nihon Shisō Taikei series: *Kirishitan sho, Hai-Ya sho*, ed. Ebisawa Arimichi, H. Cieslik, Doi Tadao, and Ōtsuka Mitsunobu (Tokyo: Iwanami, 1970).

Other editions which I utilized were:

(1) copies in the Kyoto University Library and the Tenri Library of the 1868 (*tsuchinoe tatsu chūshun*) edition by Kiyū Dōnin Ugai Tetsujō;

(2) the Tenri Library copy of the 1869 (*tsuchinoto mi banka*) edition by Kiyū Dōnin;

(3) in *Zokuzoku gunsho ruijū*, XII (Tokyo: Kokusho Kankōkai, 1907);

(4) in *Kirishitan monogatari hoka sanshu*, ed. Hiyane Antei, Kirishitan Bunko, I (Tokyo: Keiseisha, 1926);

(5) in *Giya do pekadoru gekan, Myōtei mondō, Ha Daiusu, Kengiroku*, Nihon Koten Zenshū, second series (Tokyo: Nihon Koten Zenshū Kankōkai, 1927);

(6) in *Nihon shisō tōsō shiryō*, X (Tokyo: Tōhō Shoin, 1930);

(7) in *Nihon tetsugaku shisō zensho*, X (Tokyo: Heibonsha, 1956).

These seven are all of the same genus: their common source is the editor's pen of Kiyū Dōnin, one of the leading anti-Christian publicists of the period of the Meiji Restoration. Texts (3) through (7) are for all practical purposes merely subsequent versions of (1) and (2), with little emendation of the errors accountable to Kiyū Dōnin.

Ebisawa Arimichi has done a modern Japanese rendering of *Ha Daiusu* and of several other texts of the Kirishitan genre: *Nanbanji kōhaiki, Jakyō taii, Myōtei mondō, Ha Daiusu*, Tōyō Bunko 14 (Tokyo: Heibonsha, 1964). This work was published after my translation was completed; but I found it of use in revising my first draft. Ebisawa's modern Japanese is uninspired, and is not free of errors of interpretation. His annotation is somewhat erratic.

An attempt was made by Esther Lowell Hibbard ("Assisted by Professor Yoshimori Hiraishi") to translate *Ha Daiusu* into English: "Refutation of Deus by Fabian," *Contemporary Religions in Japan*, Vol. III (1962). Miss Hibbard's translation was published after mine was completed; and I found her attempt of little utility. Her translation is neither facile nor accurate; nor is the Preface satisfactory. She has had no recourse to the original text and has used (7) as her source.

Textual Notes

1. Causal State (*in–i*): the state of a Buddha actively engaged in the salvation of all sentient beings; his Bodhisattva career. The Christian parallel, so Fabian feels, is the career of Jesus Christ on this earth. Cf. *Nippo jisho*, p. 262: "*In–i*. Fotoque no tempo que era homem ordinario como os outros.— —Buddha during the time when he was an ordinary human being like the others."

2. *Analects*, I:8 and IX:25. Translation by Arthur Waley, *The Analects of Confucius* (New York: Random House; Modern Library Paperbacks P66), p. 143; IX:24 in Waley's classification. The precept is cited in the *Qincuxŭ*, p. 507: "Ayamatteua aratamuruni, fabacarucoto nacare" (Yoshida Sumio transcription, p. 1). "All that effort to no effect" is, of course, that same *Rŏxite cŏ naxi* of the *Qincuxŭ*, p. 535, in a different guise.

3. The date corresponds to 19 February 1620. The "recluse" (*Gōko no yasu*) possesses very strong Zen associations: *Gōko* in the sense of an abbreviation for the names of the two Chinese provinces Kiangsi and Hunan refers to places where the Zen Sect particularly flourished, and the word by transference is used for devotees of Zen in general. See Oda Tokunō, *Bukkyō daijiten*, 2nd rev. ed. (Tokyo: Daizō Shuppan, 1962), p. 510.

4. The original uses a Gothic D as a hieroglyph for Deus, the Christian God. A transcription into three Chinese characters is used when *Daiusu* is meant to denote the (Christian) adherents of Deus. I translate accordingly, except in the title *Ha Daiusu* which, rendered literally, would read "The Adherents of Deus Destroyed."

5. A standard Zen phrase used to describe the unchanging basal nature or Buddha-nature of all things; cf. *Zengo ji–i*, comp. Nakagawa Jūan and Imai Fukuzan (Tokyo: Morie Shoten, 1956 second printing), p. 711. Originally perhaps a paraphrase of *Tao Te Ching*, 25:

> There was something undifferentiated
>   and yet complete,
> Which existed before heaven and earth.
> Soundless and formless, it depends
>   on nothing and does not change.
> It operates everywhere and is free from danger.
> It may be considered the mother of the universe.
> I do not know its name; I call it Tao.

Translation by Wing-tsit Chan, *The Way of Lao Tzu* (Indianapolis and Copyright (c) 1963, by The Bobbs-Merrill Company, Inc., reprinted by permission of The Liberal Arts Press Division of The Bobbs-Merrill Company, Inc.

6. *Analects*, XVII:19. Waley, p. 214.

7. *Jōjū-ekū no shidai*: the cycle of existence of the world of sentient beings; the Four Kalpas (*shikō*).

8. Cf. Chapter 6, p. 178 above.

9. In this case, Fabian gives *katakana* approximations of Portuguese terminology. I have chosen to use the related Latin for the sake of easier comprehension.

10. The Three Bodies (*sanjin*; trikāya): the Law Body (*hosshin*; dharmakāya), the Recompensed Body (*hōjin*; sambhogakāya), the Accommodated Body (*ōjin*; nirmāṇakāya). For a brief description of the "immense influence" which the concept of the Law Body has had on Mahayana Buddhism, see Takakusu Junjirō, *The Essentials of Buddhist Philosophy*, 3rd edn., ed. Wing-tsit Chan and Charles A. Moore (Honolulu: Office Appliance Co., 1956), pp. 127–128. The Accommodated Body (*ōjin*) and the Transformed Body (*keshin*) are largely synonymous; the combined usage—as here in *ōge no Nyorai*—is frequent. In this instance, the Tathagata in the Accommodated-Transformed Body is identifiable with Sakyamuni Buddha; but the expression may be applied to any Buddha or Bodhisattva who appears in a visible shape to preach the Law for the benefit of all sentient beings, thus accommodating their inherent desire to learn the truth.

11. The eight stages (*hassō*) of Sakyamuni Buddha's career were: descent from heaven, entrance into the womb, departure from home, defeat of Mara, establishment of the Way, turning the Wheel, entrance into Nirvana.

12. *Hosshō hosshin no honbutsu*: *Hosshō*—literally Dharma-nature—is for all practical purposes synonymous with Thusness (*shinnyo*; tathatā), from the standpoint of the elements' being devoid of special characteristics (*mujishō*), as well as from the standpoint of Mahayanistic universalism (the Dharma-nature or the Buddha-nature is possessed in common by all). The term *hosshō hosshin* is used in technical contradistinction to *hōben hosshin* (also *ōge hosshin*), the Law Body of Expediency, or the Law Body in its Transformed aspect.

13. *Daihatsu nehankyō*, ch. xxvii; *Taishō*, XII, no. 374, 522.

14. *Honji suijaku no iware*: The absolute "original substance" (*honji*) of the Buddha "manifests traces" (*suijaku*) in various areas and under various forms, as an expedient in the endeavor to save all sentient beings. The transformation may well assume the person of a deity. The identification of a particular Buddha or Bodhisattva with a specific Japanese deity developed into a syncretistic doctrine which worked toward the amalgamation of Shinto into Buddhism. The doctrine was especially popular during the Kamakura period; but its articulation dates back at least to Ōe no Masafusa (1041–1111). The Muromachi period saw the development of a school of thought which reversed the positions in the association: the Japanese deity was described as the original substance, the Buddha was the trace manifestation.

In Fabian's example, the Bodhisattva Kanzeon is the *honji*, and Tenman Daijizai Tenjin represents the *suijaku* transformation.

15. *Hikari o yawarage chiri ni majiwaritamau*: For the origin of the phrase, cf. *Tao Te Ching*, 4; Chan, p. 105:

> It softens its light.
> It becomes one with the dusty world.

Fabian's allusion is to the *wakō dōjin* doctrine, the euhemerist complement of *honji suijaku*: the Buddhas and Bodhisattvas—and thus also the Japanese gods—as an expedient in the endeavor to lead all sentient beings to salvation appear in this world with the original radiance of their supreme wisdom obscured, in the guise of humans. See *Maka shikan*, ch. vi-2; *Taishō*, XLVI, no. 1911, 80:

> In subdued brilliance sharing
> this world of dust
> is the beginning of the tie
> [between Buddha and man];
> the Eight Stages
> [of the Buddha's earthly life]
> and the establishment of the Way
> are termed its completion.

In Fabian's example, Tenman Daijizai Tenjin is held to have appeared in this world as Kan Shōjō, which is the sobriquet of Sugawara Michizane (845–903; Minister of the Right from 899 to 901). The Kitano Tenmangū of Kyoto was in 987 officially established as the center of the cult of Michizane.

16. Cf. *Analects*, II:17; Waley, p. 91:

> The Master said, Yu, shall I teach you
> what knowledge is? When you know a thing,
> to recognize that you know it, and when
> you do not know a thing, to recognize that
> you do not know it. That is knowledge.

The precept is cited in the *Qincuxǐ*, p. 546: "Xireranuoba xirerito xeyo: xirezaranuoba xirazuto xeyo: core xireru nari." Yoshida, p. 66.

17. *Chung Yung*, 16. The intended meaning may be understood better if the strophe is cited in context from *The Mean*; see James Legge, *The Chinese Classics* (Hong Kong: Hong Kong University Press, 1960 reissue), I, 397–398:

> The Master said,
> "How abundantly do spiritual beings display
> the powers that belong to them! We look
> for them, but do not see them; we listen to,
> but do not hear them; yet they enter into
> all things, and there is nothing without them.
> They cause all the people in the kingdom . . ."

18. Look at Chapter 1, pp. 21–25 above.

19. Material on the Konishi family will be found in Matsuda, *Nanban shiryō no kenkyū*, pp. 756–788.

20. In answer to Fabian's question: In 1620 five of Ukon's grandsons probably were in Manila, where Ukon had died in exile in 1615. There exists a tradition that they eventually returned to Japan; and there have been individuals in recent decades who have claimed descent from Ukon. See Laures, *Takayama Ukon*, pp. 369–371; and cf. Kataoka Yakichi, "Takayama Ukon," *MN*, 1.2:168–172 (July 1938). A genealogical summary of the Takayama family is further provided by Matsuda, *Nanban shiryō no kenkyū*, pp. 718–752.

21. Akashi Kamon (Dom João), a ranking Bizen samurai, was baptized at the end of 1596 or the beginning of 1597. He was related to Ukita Hideie, the daimyo of Bizen, and was in his service at the time of the Battle of Sekigahara. When the Ukita were dispossessed by Ieyasu after the Western Army's defeat, Dom João became a rōnin. He was related also to the Kuroda family, and in 1602 was able to secure employ with Kuroda Naoyuki, the daimyo of Akizuki. Some time later, after his wife's death,

he went to Nagasaki, where he seems to have planned to enter the Jesuit Order.

Kamon's notoriety derives from the part he took in Toyotomi Hideyori's last stand against the Tokugawa: he fought at the head of the two thousand Kirishitan samurai who buttressed Hideyori during the siege of Osaka Castle. He survived the fall of the castle in 1615 and escaped to a mountain village in Shikoku. The date of his death is unknown. For a brief sketch of his career and family, see Morejón, *Historia y relacion*, Book Two, ch. x, ff. 77v–80; and cf. Cieslik, *Geibi Kirishitan shiryō || Sources and documents concerning the history of Kirishitan in the provinces of Aki and Bingo* (Tokyo: Yoshikawa Kōbunkan, 1968), pp. 133–136. (Cieslik bases his account on Morejón, and reprints the relevant chapter among his Western sources, pp. 136–139; there is a Japanese translation on pp. 434–438.) Matsuda Kiichi found in Kōchi Prefecture in Shikoku two families bearing the name of Akashi who possess genealogies to support their claims of descent from Kamon; *Kirishitan kenkyū daiichibu: Shikoku-hen*, pp. 63–71.

22. Ebisawa (Tōyō Bunko 14, p. 289, n. 27; and NST 25, pp. 428–429) identifies Kikyōya with Hashimoto Tahyōe, martyred in Kyoto in 1619. Another possibility is one of the Twenty-Six Saints of Japan, whom Matsuda identifies as Kinuya Juan: contemporary variants of his name include Quiquia Juan and Quinquia Joan; *Nanban shiryō no kenkyū*, p. 914, and *KK*, 8:19. Alvarex-Taladriz, *Sumario*, p. 282, n. 47, shares this conjecture.

23. The Higoroya (or Hibiya) of Sennan no Tsu (Sakai) were some of the very first adherents of Christianity in the Kansai. On the family, see Matsuda, *Nanban shiryō no kenkyū*, pp. 752–756, and cf. Alvarez-Taladriz, *Sumario*, p. 129, n. 73, where a family tree is given.

24. The parents of the Buddha Sakyamuni were King Śuddhodana (Jōbon Daiō) and his queen, the Lady Maya. The Crane Forest is the grove of Śāla trees (Sharajurin) which "turned white as white cranes" at Sakyamuni's entry into Nirvana; *Daihatsu nehankyō*, ch. i; *Taishō*, XII, no. 374, 369.

25. Hachiman is the Japanese deity most intimately associated with Buddhism, first coming into prominence at the building of the Tōdaiji in 749, when his protection was officially invoked and he was festively transported from his shrine at Usa in Kyushu to Nara. The *honji suijaku* theory holds that Hachiman represents the divine manifestation of Amida, the original substance. See Ōe no Masafusa's account of Shin'en Shōnin's vision of the "Great Bodhisattva Hachiman": "in his state of original enlightenment, he is the Tathagata Muryōju (Amida) of the West"; *Zoku honchō ōjō den*, in *Gunsho ruijū*, IV (Tokyo: Keizai Zasshi-sha, 1898 second printing), 427.

Hachiman "shared the world of dust" as Ōjin Tennō, the first Japanese emperor whose historicity may be accepted. Chūai Tennō and Jingū Kōgō are quasi-mythical. See Inoue Mitsusada, *Nihon kokka no kigen*, Iwanami Shinsho 380 (Tokyo: Iwanami, 1960), pp. 119–128.

26. The provenance of Fabian's *muchi yaku mutoku* (no knowledge and no quality) is unclear, and may well be a mistaken rendering of the homonym *muchi yaku mutoku* (no knowledge and no attainment), a phrase which occurs in the highly popular brief text *Hannya shingyō* (Prajñāpāramita hṛdaya); *Taishō*, VIII, no. 251, 848. Cf. the translation by Daisetz Suzuki, in *Manual of Zen Buddhism* (New York: Grove Press, 1960; Evergreen Original E-231), pp. 26–30. See p. 27: "no knowledge, no attainment, [and] no realization, because there is no attainment. In the mind of the Bodhisattva who dwells depending on the Prajnaparamita there are no obstacles; and, going beyond the perverted views, he reaches final Nirvana."

27.   Provenance unclear. Perhaps inspired by the introductory verse written by Mumon Ekai (Wu-men Hui-k'ai) for the popular late Sung Zen text *Mumonkan* (*Wu-men kuan*; The Gateless Barrier):

> The Great Way has no gate,
> For all its thousand varied paths;
> But if you penetrate this barrier,
> You walk the universe in solitary
> splendor.

Mumonkan, ed. Furuta Shōkin, Kadokawa Bunko 1383 (Tokyo: Kadokawa, 1965 eighth printing), p. 104; Japanese translation, p. 13.

See also the text's famous First Case, "Jōshū's Dog." Jōshū (Chao-chou) upon being asked whether a dog possessed the Buddha-nature answered: *Mu*! Mumon's comment is that in the study of Zen one must first pass through the barrier erected by the ancient masters. And—

> What is the barrier of the masters?
> Just one word: *Mu*!

Furuta, pp. 107 and 15.

28.   *Bosatsu shotaikyō*, ch. xiii; *Taishō*, XII, no. 348, 1035.

29.   I have tried to convey Fabian's meaning; but see *Tao Te Ching*, 38, for the fuller context. Chan, p. 167:

> The man of superior virtue is not (conscious of) his virtue,
>   And in this way he really possesses virtue.
> The man of inferior virtue never loses (sight of) his virtue,
>   And in this way he loses his virtue.
> The man of superior virtue takes no action, but has no ulterior
>   motive to do so.

30.   *I, hsi, wei*: Fabian has paraphrased *Tao Te Ching*, 14. Chan, p. 124:

> We look at it and do not see it;
>   Its name is The Invisible.
> We listen to it and do not hear it;
>   Its name is The Inaudible.
> We touch it and do not find it;
>   Its name is The Subtle (formless).
>
> These three cannot be further inquired into,
>   And hence merge into one.

Although "these three cannot be further inquired into," they have been objects of much speculation, fancied and ingenuous at the same time, on the part of an antique group of Western savants who professed to see concealed in the ineffable trigram nothing other than the Tetragrammaton itself. If this quaint exegesis were correct, then Fabian would be in the anomalous position of attempting to drive out 田 by using Jehovah!

31.   See above, n. 93 to Chapter 6.

32.   "Willows are green, flowers are red" is a standard Zen phrase of unestablished original authorship. Although it is commonly attributed to Su Shih, it is not to be found in his works; but it recurs in various Zen copybooks of the *Kuzōshi* genre. For an example, see the 1656 version included in Yoshida, *Amakusa-ban Kinkushū no kenkyū*, p. 300. Suzuki Shōsan uses the expression in *Mōanjō* (*Kana hōgo shū*, p. 254; *Suzuki Shōsan Dōnin zenshū*, p. 56). The poem on "The mountain cherry of Yoshino" also is a standard Zen saying of uncertain provenance; cf. *Zenrin sego shū*, ed. Tsuchiya Etsudō (Kyoto: Kichūdō, 1957), p. 126. Ebisawa, NST 25, p. 430, tentatively identifies it as a homiletic verse (*dōka*) by Ikkyū (1394–1481). The

lines occur nowhere in the Complete Works of the Priest Ikkyū (*Ikkyū oshō zenshū*, comp. Mori Taikyō; Tokyo: Kōyūkan, 1898), although Ikkyū's tract *Gaikotsu* (The skeleton; Mori, p. 6) does contain a similar stanza:

> Smash to pieces the cherry tree—
> See: there are no flowers!
> The flowers are borne
> On the skies of spring.

A variation on this poem is found in Ikkyū's *Ninin bikuni* (Two nuns; Mori, p. 4).

Ikkyū utilizes the flower and willow pattern in his Nō chant *Yamanba* (The witch; Mori, *Yōkyoku*, p. 8):

> Each time you look, all things
> Are as they are
> In their appearance:
> Willows are green, flowers are red.

33. *Tao Te Ching*, 42; Chan, p. 176. The initiation of the argument "On Confucianism" in the *Myōtei mondō* proceeds from this quotation.

34. *Seidaku dōjō no ki*: Fabian's eclecticism reflects that of the Sung Neo-Confucians, some of whose most important formulae stemmed from Taoism. Cf. *Ch'ing-ching ching* (Scripture of the Pure Quiescent), *Tao shu ch'üan chi* (1682 edition in the Harvard-Yenching Library), 22:76b—

> The Tao contains the pure, the turbid,
>   dynamic and quiescent:
> Heaven is pure, Earth turbid,
>   Heaven dynamic, Earth quiescent.
> Male is pure, female turbid,
>   male dynamic, female quiescent.

35. *Shidai*: earth, water, fire, and air.
36. See above, n. 75 to Chapter 6.
37. *Gomi*: spicy, sour, salty, bitter, sweet.
38. See above, n. 81 to Chapter 6.
39. Fabian here makes the basic Neo-Confucian distinction between *jen hsin* ("human mind," "mind of the body") and *tao hsin* ("mind of the Way," "mind of the spirit"), and I have attempted to be faithful to his meaning. The distinction is quite unequivocal; for an example, see Chu Hsi's Introduction to *Chung-yung chang chü*; Kanno Dōmei, *Gaku Yō shōku*, p. 52. Impeded by the limitations of material force, which generates man's physical makeup and egoistic desires, the "human mind" shows a dangerous proclivity to fall into an immoral path. The "mind of the Way"—the inherent capacity of the mind for virtue and righteousness—is all too often obscured by those selfish desires. Rectification of the mind and concordance with the original nature are to be attained by the extension of knowledge.

40. *Shang Shu, Ta Yü mo*; cf. Legge, III, 61: "The mind of man is restless,—prone to *err*; its affinity for the *right* way is small." Legge cautions against the very distinction which Fabian has made, and rejects the Sung dualistic tendency: "we seem to want in [*tao*] some entity or being corresponding to [*jen*]. But that cannot be. The [*tao hsin*] is still the [*jen hsin*], the mind of man in its relation to the path of duty."

41. *Shin-i-shiki*: For the distinction, see *Jō-yuishiki ron*, ch. v; *Taishō*, XXXI, no. 1585, 24.

42. Shinnō Fudō: *Shinnō* denotes the Absolute Mind, in contradistinction

to *shinjo*, the concomitant mental functions. Esoteric Buddhism identifies the Absolute Mind with the Tathagata Vairocana of the Diamond Element (Kongōkai Dainichi Nyorai), the universal Buddha-body of wisdom (*chihōshin*); and the concomitant mental functions are depicted as Vairocana's retinue. Fudō Myōō is the manifestation of Vairocana in the Dogmatic Body (*kyōryō rinshin*), representing his wrathful aspect (*funnu*), so that the two names may even be combined into one: Dainichi Daishō Fudō Myōō.

43. The quotation appears at first sight to stem lightly paraphrased from *Shuo yüan, Chün tao*; SPTK, I, 1:5b. But one ought not attribute such an extensive grasp of the sources to Fabian: he did take recourse to shortcuts. The actual provenance is the very popular Yüan dynasty epitome compiled by Tseng Hsien-chih, *Shih-pa shih lüeh*: cf. Fabian's text with *Jūhachi-shi ryaku shinshaku*, ed. Nakayama Kyūshirō and Shiono Shinjirō, I, Shōwa Kanbun Sōsho (Tokyo: Kōdōkan, 1930), 37.

44. Nakayama and Shiono, p. 52.

45. The final strophe is not in the standard *Shih-pa shih lüeh*, but may be found in the *Kuan-tzu, Shan ch'üan shu* lxxv; SPTK, IV, 22:9b.

46. *Rikugō*: east, west, south, north, up, down.

47. *Sanze*: the world of the past, the present world, and the world of the future.

48. *Maçan* or *mação*, the Portuguese for "apple."

49. The Buddhist Five Commandments (*gokai*) prohibit: (1) killing; (2) theft; (3) adultery; (4) false words; (5) drunkenness.

The most common listing of the Ten Laws (*jūkai*) includes the Five Commandments and the additional prohibitions of: (6) eating flesh foods; (7) false views; (8) slander; (9) backbiting; (10) fraud.

The codes of the Ritsu School, according to Takakusu, *Essentials*, pp. 185–186, contain "250 articles for priests and 348 for nuns."

50. The text has Kohachiya Nyūdō, complete with *furigana*, but that seems to be a mistake. The surname Hachiya figures several times among the retainers of Hideyoshi, and the most likely candidate for this reference would seem to be Hachiya Daizen Daibu (?–1593), whose name in religion (*sc.* as a lay monk, *nyūdō*) was Kennyū. See *Sengoku jinmei jiten*, pp. 195–196. Persermon: *amaboshi dangi*, persimmon sermon.

51. Cf. *Analects*, XVII:3; Waley, p. 209:

> The Master said,
> It is only the very wisest
> and the very stupidest who
> cannot change.

52. *Zangi sange*: For the distinction between these four mental functions, see *Daijō gishō*, ch. ii; *Taishō*, XLIV, no. 1851, 492. Also *Maka shikan*, ch. vii-2; *Taishō*, XLVI, no. 1911, 98.

53. The allusion is to *Analects*, VII:8; Waley, p. 124:

> The Master said,
> Only one who bursts with eagerness do I instruct;
> only one who bubbles with excitement, do I enlighten.
> If I hold up one corner and a man cannot come back to
> me with the other three, I do not continue the lesson.

54. See the Seventh Step for the wider context of Fabian's discussion of this basic Confucian precept and the others of the Five Social Relationships. The precise meaning of *kakon*—marital relations in the sense of sexual union—

is clear from *Nippo jisho*, p. 60: "*Cacon. Totçugui, u.* Aiuntamento de femea, & macho."

55. *Shih Ching*, Mao 158. I use the translation by Ezra Pound, *The Classic Anthology Defined by Confucius* (Cambridge, Mass.: Harvard University Press, 1954), p. 79. Pound's passage is not notable for its lucidity, although it is good onomatopoeia; but Fabian's citation of a few isolated lines is not very lucid either. The full context is:

> How cut haft for an axe?
> Who hacks
> holds a haft.
> To take a wife
> properly
> one gets a notary.
>
> To hack an axe-haft
> an axe
> hacks;
> the pattern's near.
>
> Let who weds never pass
> too far
> from his own class.

Copyright 1954 by the President and Fellows of Harvard College; cited by permission of Harvard University Press and Faber & Faber, Ltd.

56. An allusion to *Mencius*, 4B:1. The original comparison is of Shun and Wen Wang, born over a thousand years and over a thousand leagues apart, yet complementing each other.

57. Suzuki Shōsan uses the identical phrase in *Mōanjō* (*Kana hōgo shū*, p. 247; *Suzuki Shōsan Dōnin zenshū*, p. 52). The provenance is uncertain: the paradigm was used by the Shingon monk Kakuban (1095–1143), but it also occurs in works such as the popular mediaeval collection of Buddhist fables *Shasekishū*, and that would seem to be our authors' most likely source; cf. the Watanabe Tsunaya edition, Nihon Koten Bungaku Taikei 85 (Tokyo: Iwanami, 1966), p. 474. Even that may be looking too far afield. The expression evidently was a contemporary cliché. Ōkubo Hikozaemon—who was anything but erudite—used this dictum to begin the text of the *Mikawa monogatari*, his 1622 contribution to the annals of *bushidō*. *Genpon Mikawa monogatari*, ed. Nakada Norio (Tokyo: Benseisha, 1970), II, 5; vol. I is a facsimile of Hikozaemon's original MS.

58. *Taisetsu* in Fabian's translation of the Latin baptismal formula means "love." Cf. *Nippo jisho*, p. 475: "*Taixet.* Amor." The circumlocutory "Reciprocal Love" was standard Kirishitan usage for "Holy Ghost."

59. The comparison is with the Buddhist *gokai* (above, n. 49).

60. *Kokoro oba urasaji ga tame nari*. See *Nippo jisho*, p. 576, for the verb: "*Vraxi, su, aita*. Fazer amadurecer como fruita, &c," with the added notation that the word is peculiar to Kyushu. Perhaps "ripen" in the sense of the proverb "Soon ripe soon rotten"?

61. From Chu Hsi's Introduction to *Ta-hsüeh chang chü*; Kanno Dōmei, *Gaku Yō shōku*, p. 5.

62. *Gokei*: There are several catalogues of the Five Penalties; but a glance at the entry "*Goqei*" in *Nippo jisho*, p. 706, convinces that Fabian is referring to the rather picturesque list of Chou times: (1) tattooing the forehead; (2) cutting off the nose; (3) cutting off the legs; (4) castration; (5) capital punishment. João Rodriguez Tçuzzu (*ARTE*, f. 224v; *Nihon*

daibunten, p. 802) gives the same list. Cf. *Shang Shu, Lü hsing*, Legge, III, 604–606; and *Shang Shu, Shun tien*, Legge, III, 38.

63. More properly: Hiko-nagisa-take-u-gaya-fuki-aezu no Mikoto. Jimmu was his fourth son. The Three Divine Regalia are: the Curved Jewel of Yasaka; the Eight-Hand Mirror; the Heavenly Cloud Sword.

64. *Gonke no shinsei*: *Gonke* (expedient transformation) denotes the Buddhas' and Bodhisattvas' use of super-powers to appear in a variety of shapes or produce a multitude of manifestations. The two characters may also be read *gonge*, in which case the expression becomes synonymous with *gongen*, a term intimately associated with the doctrine of *honji suijaku*. The *gongen* is the Transformed Body (*keshin*) of the original substance of a Buddha or Bodhisattva, active in the realm of trace-manifestation in order to lead all sentient beings to enlightenment. Oda, *Bukkyō daijiten*, p. 580.

65. Fabian seems to be addressing this paragraph directly at Tokugawa Hidetada, the Second Shogun. Perspicacity and sagacity: *sōmei eichi*; *Lü-shih ch'un ch'iu, Shen shih*, SPTK, V, 26:12b—

> . . . perspicacious of ear and eye,
> sagacious in mind and will . . .

He also alludes to *Analects*, V:9; Waley (V:8), p. 109—

> . . . Hui has but to hear one part in ten,
> in order to understand the whole ten.
> Whereas if I hear one part, I understand
> no more than two parts. The Master said,
> Not equal to him—you and I are not
> equal to him!

66. A standard Zen phrase found in the *Kuzōshi*; Yoshida, *Amakusa-ban Kinkushū no kenkyū*, p. 312.

67. *Analects*, II:10; Waley, p. 90.

68. Fabian's extravagant anecdote refers to the climax of the dispute between the Jesuits and the friars of Japan; see Boxer, *Christian Century*, p. 326. The fraternal rivalry attained the proportions of a minor schism when the Bishop of Japan, Luis de Cerqueira SJ, died in February 1614, and the mendicants refused to acknowledge the Jesuit Carvalho as his successor in the administration of the diocese. The spectacle was especially demeaning because the events took place on the eve of expulsion from Japan. "Both parties circulated public manifestos denouncing each other, right up to the day that they were forcibly interned in a few fishermen's huts before being placed on board ship." The scandal did not end there: the displaced Padres carried the quarrel to Macao.

69. *Sanmyō o sagaitaru koto*: the unwary, misled by the fact that the sonant mark (*dakuten*) is missing in the original, will read the verb *sakaitaru* and as a result lose track of the meaning. *Nippo jisho*, p. 435, makes it clear: "*Sanmiǒuo sagasu. i, Fagiuo sarasu.* Ficar enuergonhado, & afrontado diante de gente.——To be publicly embarrassed, & shamed." Also see p. 152 under "*Fagi*," p. 430 under "*Sagaxi, su, aita*," and p. 438 under "*Saraxi, su, aita*." A *clerigo* is a diocesan (secular) priest, as opposed to a monk (religious).

70. The Five Unpardonable Sins (*go gyakuzai*; also known as *go fukyūzai*) include, apart from the two mentioned by Fabian: (3) killing an arhat; (4) causing discord in the assembly of priests; (5) shedding a Buddha's blood.

71. The celebrated *Tatsu no Kuchi no hōnan* took place in 1271; Tatsu no Kuchi was the execution ground of Kamakura. Lord Sagami is Hōjō

Sagami Tarō Tokimune (1251–1284), Regent from 1268. The story with various embellishments may be found in any number of popular biographies of Nichiren. For one example, see *Nichiren Daishōnin chū gasan*, compiled by Nitchō with glosses by Nisshū (Eishō period, 1504–1521), in *Nichiren Shōnin denkishū*, ed. Nichirenshū Zensho Shuppankai (Tokyo: Suwaraya Shoten, 1910), p. 69.

72. Hasegawa was *Nagasaki Bugyō* from 1605 to January 1615 (Keichō 19/12/22).

73. See above, Chapter 6, p. 164.

74. *Kihō ni wa orazu*: a slightly inaccurate allusion to *Analects*, VIII:13. Cf. Waley, p. 135:

> Do not enter a state that pursues dangerous courses,
> nor stay in one where the people have rebelled.
> When the Way prevails under Heaven, then show yourself;
> when it does not prevail, then hide.

The maxim is included in the *Qincuxŭ*, p. 529: "Qifŏniua irazu, rampŏniua vorazu: tenca michi aru toqimba mamiye: michi naqi toqimba cacuru"; Yoshida, p. 38.

75. Nakamiya is now a part of the city of Hirakata, some twenty miles east of Osaka.

76. *Tōru*, in *Yōkyokushū*, I, ed. Yokomichi Mario and Omote Akira, Nihon Koten Bungaku Taikei 40 (Tokyo: Iwanami, 1960), 300.

DECEIT DISCLOSED by Christovão Ferreira *sive* Sawano Chūan

Bibliographical Note

The basis of this translation of *Kengiroku* is the sole printed text, in *Giya do pekadoru gekan, Myōtei mondō, Ha Daiusu, Kengiroku*, Nihon Koten Zenshū, second series (Tokyo: Nihon Koten Zenshū Kankōkai, 1927). That text was in turn based on a manuscript in the possession of the Ōkōchi family, the former daimyo of Ōtaki, and dating back to 1670. The Nagasaki Prefectural Library MS. listed by Ebisawa, *Christianity in Japan*, p. 28, is a copy made in 1913. The Kyoto University entry of *Kokusho sōmokuroku*, III, 103, also represents two recent MS. copies.

Textual Notes

1. The *Kuzōshi* of 1656 explains this standard Zen phrase by noting that a man who carries a plank on one shoulder has only the other side unobstructed, and hence is capable only of a one-sided view—a man who shoulders the heavy burden of prejudice. Yoshida, *Amakusa-ban Kinkushū no kenkyū*, p. 293.

2. The reference is to the celebrated anecdote in the *Han Fei Tzu, Wu tu* (SPTK, 19:1): A farmer in Sung while tilling his field saw a rabbit dash himself headlong into a tree stump and fall over dead. He then stopped working his field and spent his days in watching for another rabbit to fling himself against the stump and fall into his hands—fruitless expectation

born out of stupidity and stubbornness. Translated by Burton Watson in *Basic Writings of Mo Tzu, Hsün Tzu, and Han Fei Tzu* (New York: Columbia University Press, 1967), *Han Fei Tzu*, "The Five Vermin," p. 97.

3. *Ujō hijō*: *Ujō* is synonymous with *shujō*, sentient beings. *Hijō* refers to grasses, trees, and (as the *Nippo jisho*, p. 180, puts it) "the rest of the things that lack a sensitive soul."

4. The Three Countries: China, India, Japan.

5. The semi-divine (demi-human/demi-snake) culture hero Fu Hsi is said to have drawn the Eight Trigrams for the first time, invented the writing system, and designed nets for hunting and fishing. The end of the Shang dynasty is traditionally given as 1122 B.C. or 1027 B.C.

6. The Four Basic Elements: earth, water, fire, air.

7. The Eight Sorrows for human beings (*ningen no hakku*) are those of: (1) birth; (2) aging; (3) disease; (4) death; (5) separation from a beloved object; (6) confrontation with a hateful object; (7) seeking without obtaining; (8) the five *skandhas*, aggregates of personality (form, perception, conception, volition, consciousness). *Daihatsu nehankyō*, ch. xii; *Taishō*, XII, no. 374, 435.

The Five Signs of Decline for devas (*tennin no gosui*), which appear when their term of life is about to end, are: (1) their robes become soiled; (2) the flowers in the crown wilt; (3) the body gives off an unpleasant odor; (4) perspiration flows from the armpits; (5) they no longer enjoy their position. *Daihatsu nehankyō*, ch. xix, p. 478.

The Three Realms (*sangai*) are divisions of the world of delusion traversed by those tied to the cycle of life and death: the realm of desire (*yokkai*), the realm of form (*shikkai*), the realm of no-form (*mushikkai*). For a detailed categorization, see Oda, *Bukkyō daijiten*, pp. 607–608.

8. Several listings are available of the Five Parts of the human body (*gotai*). The most common is: head, neck, breast, arms, legs. João Rodriguez Tçuzzu gives: the two arms, the two legs, the head; *ARTE*, f. 225; *Nihon daibunten*, p. 803.

9. The Five Constant Virtues (*gojō*) are: humanity, righteousness, decorum, wisdom, and faith. See Rodriguez, *ARTE*, f. 224: "*Gojŏ. Iin, Gui, Rei, Chi, Xin*. i. as cinco virtudes morais. s. piedade, Iustiça, Reuerencia, Prudencia, Fee." For the Buddhist Five Commandments, see above, n. 49 to *Deus Destroyed*.

10. The text is specific in enumerating *shi, nō, kō, shō*: samurai, peasants, artisans, and merchants.

11. A mistake for "one hundred and fifty years ago" if the reference is to be to the Treaty of Tordesillas (7 June 1494). Perhaps the mistake is conscious and the date advanced by a century to lend the threat greater actuality.

12. *Kansō* are high-ranking priests involved in official secular functions by secular sanction, as opposed to priests of the strict observance; Oda, *Bukkyō daijiten*, p. 346. One is set before the image of a highly secular Prince-Bishop à la Albrecht von Brandenburg or the contemporary Richelieu.

13. *Jejum* means fasting in Portuguese, as defined by Ferreira. But the specific meaning of *quaresma* is Lent.

14. *Nippo jisho*, p. 241, gives two definitions of the "five sounds": musical tones and Japanese vowels. Ferreira means the latter, in a self-deprecatory reference to a lack of ability in the Japanese language. "*Goin. Itçutçuno coye*. Cinco vozes, tons, ou toadas conforme ao vso da musica de Iapão.//Item, As cinco vogais de Iapão. A. I. V. YE. VO."

15. The date translates to 29 September 1636.

KIRISHITAN MONOGATARI, Anonymous Chapbook

Bibliographical Note

Ebisawa Arimichi, *Christianity in Japan*, p. 33, lists three extant copies of the early Edo period woodblock imprint of the *Kirishitan monogatari*: in the Tenri Library, the National Diet Library, and in his own collection (*kan* 1 missing). I have used the Tenri copy, which contains the two *kan* in a single volume. Neither the place nor the date of publication is indicated; but the text is dated Kan'ei 16 (1639), and it is assumed that the publication was nearly contemporaneous with the compilation. *Kokusho sōmokuroku*, II (1964), 574, lists seven copies.

The *Kirishitan taiji monogatari* (Tale of the quelling of Kirishitans) is for all practical purposes identical with the *Kirishitan monogatari*, but omits the brief terminal section. The unique virtue of this chapbook is the splendid set of illustrations which accompanies the text. Three extant copies of the seventeenth-century original are listed in *Kokusho sōmokuroku*, II, 574. *Christianity in Japan*, p. 33, lists only the Kyoto University book, which I have consulted. This is a single woodblock volume which indicates neither the date nor the place of publication; but the library notes that the work was printed by Nakano Tarōzaemon in Kyoto in Kanbun 5 (1665). The Kisho Fukuseikai published a facsimile in 3 *kan*: sixth series, nos. 1 & 2 (1928) and no. 9 (1929).

The *Kirishitan monogatari* is included in Volume XII of *Zokuzoku gunsho ruijū* (1907), and has also been published by Hiyane Antei in *Kirishitan monogatari hoka sanshu*, Kirishitan Bunko, I (Tokyo: Keiseisha, 1926). Hiyane has provisioned the original's cursive *hiragana* text with Chinese characters; his edition, however, is not without errors and must be used with caution.

My translation proceeded on the basis of a collation of the aforementioned editions.

Textual Notes

1. Xavier, the first Bateren to land in Japan, arrived in 1549, during the reign of Go-Nara (1536–1557) but not during the Kōji period (1555–1558). Go-Nara is listed as the 105th Emperor according to the current standard.

2. Long-nosed goblin: *tengu*, a denizen of dark mountains, somewhat similar in shape to a human being, but with an exceedingly long nose, long claws on hands and feet, and wings which enable it to fly about freely; affects the appearance of an ascetic of the Mountain Brotherhood (*yamabushi*). Mikoshi Nyūdō is a genie looking like a monk of extraordinary size: the more one looks the bigger he gets.

3. Urugan Bateren: a reference to Padre Organtino Gnecchi-Soldo SJ, who was somewhat of a confidant of Nobunaga's. The account of his arrival represents an overlap of images. Organtino landed in Japan on 18 June 1570 and that same year was sent to Kyoto to assist Frois, himself becoming mission superior of the area of the Capital in 1577 (see *VMJ*, I-2, 137). The details of the *Kirishitan monogatari* story of the Bateren's introduction evidently apply more to the establishment of the mission of the Capital by Padre Gaspar Vilela, 1559–1563 (see *GJ*, pp. 128–145). The mention of the Padre's extraordinary height is perhaps a distorted memory

of the unusually tall Valignano, as Hubert Cieslik points out in "Nanbanji-Romane der Tokugawa-Zeit," *MN*, 6.1/2:19 (1943).

4. Miyoshi Shūri no Daibu: Miyoshi Chōkei (Nagayoshi), prominent *sengoku daimyō* (1522–1564). He rose at the expense primarily of the Hosokawa house of Awa and reached a position of near supremacy in the Home Provinces, becoming the true power behind the shogun Ashikaga Yoshiteru. There is a convenient biography: Nagae Shōichi, *Miyoshi Nagayoshi*, Jinbutsu Sōsho 149 (Tokyo: Yoshikawa Kōbunkan, 1968).

Direct contacts between Chōkei and the Jesuit missionaries date from 1560, when Vilela called on him to ask for his protection (Irmão Lourenço to the missionaries in Bungo, 2 June 1560; *Cartas*, I, 71; *YNT*, I, 15). Frois, *GJ*, p. 128, asserts that Vilela was able to obtain from Chōkei a patent of privileges, but the specifics are unclear. That Vilela in 1560 did, however, obtain such a patent from the shogun Yoshiteru is clear: for the original text, see Nagae, pp. 235–236, Matsuda, *Nanban shiryō no kenkyū*, p. 401, or *Nihon shiryō shūsei*, p. 269; *GJ*, pp. 88–89, gives it in translation.

Matsunaga Sōtai: Matsunaga Danjō Hisahide (?–1577), one of Japanese history's more notorious figures. He was associated with Miyoshi from Chōkei's childhood and in 1549 became his representative in the Capital. After 1560 Sōtai extended his talents to the conquest of Yamato, acting at first on Chōkei's behalf but later (especially after his patron's death) in furtherance of his own ambitions. Sōtai's most notorious exploit was the treacherous attack (1565) upon Ashikaga Yoshiteru, in which the shogun lost his life. Sōtai's partner in the conspiracy had been Chōkei's adopted son, Miyoshi Yoshitsugu; but soon there occurred a falling out between Sōtai and the Miyoshi party, and during the fighting our hero committed the second of his famous deeds, burning the Great Buddha Hall of the Tōdaiji in Nara (1567). He initially adopted a pro-Nobunaga posture when that hegemon appeared upon the scene of the Capital (1568), and participated in several campaigns on Nobunaga's side; but by 1573 he was engaged in an anti-Nobunaga adventure with Miyoshi Yoshitsugu. Coming back to Nobunaga's fold, Sōtai destroyed Yoshitsugu. But at the end of his days he had turned against Nobunaga again and died in the flames of his fortress at Shigi under assault by Oda forces.

5. Nobunaga's castle is here compared to the nonesuch palace of Ch'in Shih Huang-ti. The Padres themselves were among the greatest admirers of Nobunaga's pleasure domes, and engaged in similar superlatives. For an example, see the verbal transports of Frois on the subject of Nobunaga's earthly paradise at Gifu (*Cartas*, I, 272–272v; *YNT*, II, 44–49; to P. Belchior de Figueiredo SJ, 12 July 1569).

It is fruitless to attempt a correlation between the account of the *Kirishitan monogatari* and a particular Jesuit visit to Nobunaga's castle. One might point out that the Mission Superior of Japan, Francisco Cabral, in the company of Frois and Irmão Lourenço, called on Nobunaga at Gifu during the first few months of 1572 (*GJ*, pp. 424–427). Organtino first visited Nobunaga in Azuchi in 1577 (*Cartas*, I, 413v; *YNT*, II, 410–411; letter of P. Giovanni Francesco Stephanoni, 14 January 1578). Perhaps the image cast is that of Valignano, whose 1581 journey to Nobunaga's presence had caused a popular sensation, "with the amazement being directed particularly at the giant stature of the *Visitator* and the black color of the Negro who came along in the train" (*VMJ*, I-2, 126). The Negro (*kurobōzu*) figures pointedly in the *Nobunaga kōki* account of Valignano's first audience with Oda (Kyoto, late March 1581), and the color of the servant, whose "entire body was black like that of an ox," might well have been transferred in the popular imagination to the master (*Nobunaga kōki*, Kadokawa Bunko 2541, 14:339–340). In 1581 Valignano made two visits to Azuchi, each of a month's duration, and was entertained by Nobunaga in the most friendly fashion; for the chronology, see *VMJ*, I-2, 163–167.

6. Suganoya Kuemon Nagayori, Oda retainer, one of the three in charge of preparing the plot of ground which Nobunaga gave to the missionaries in Azuchi; see *Nobunaga kōki*, 13:320, entry for Tenshō 8/interc. 3/16.

7. The text strives for the exotic effect, and I therefore retain the literal "cloth of orangoutang" for the highly suggestive *shōjōhi*; the meaning is scarlet wool cloth. The list of gifts includes the item *tōken*, which completes the menagerie with leonine Chinese dogs. *Zokuzoku gunsho ruijū*, however, edits with a homonym to read "swords," and Hiyane follows.

8. Not the residence itself but rather the plot of ground for one is meant by *on'yashiki*. Cf. *Nippo jisho*, p. 636: "*Yaxiqi*. Chão da casa." The story of Nobunaga's meticulous choice of a favorable location for a Jesuit establishment in the immediate propinquity of Azuchi Castle is told in Stephanoni's letter of 1 September 1580; *Cartas*, I, 479v–480; *YNT*, II, 484–485.

9. Gerigori is most likely Padre Gregorio de Cespedes SJ, who arrived in Japan in 1577 and after an initial stay in Ōmura was active in the Home Provinces for some twenty years. Cespedes was probably the leading Jesuit optimist in the speculation concerning Nobunaga's possible conversion, basing his hopes on Nobunaga's evident hate of the Buddhist establishment but also upon signs which he claimed to detect in him of an inherent readiness to be persuaded by (Christian) reason; see Laures, *Nobunaga und das Christentum*, *MN* Monographs 10 (Tokyo: Sophia University Press, 1950), p. 34. Cespedes was also associated with Nobunaga's son Nobutada, to whose residence in Gifu he made four visits in 1581–82, and who treated him with much favor (*VMJ*, I-2, 196–199).

Yariisu would seem to be either Luis de Almeida, who was famous for his medical skills, or the prolific letter-writer and historian Luis Frois, who arrived in Japan in 1563 and after an initial stay in Yokoseura and Hirado spent the years 1565–1576 in the area of the Capital; thereafter he was active in various locations in Kyushu, and died in Nagasaki in 1597.

10. Rorensu is indubitably the celebrated Irmão Lourenço. (Hiyane incorrectly edits his birthplace as Bizen.) Lourenço was converted by Saint Francis Xavier in Yamaguchi in 1551. A near-blind mountebank, and ugly, he proved to be possessed of unusually sharp wit and was an indefatigable worker for the cause of Christianity in Japan, which moved Frois (*GJ*, p. 16) to cite the Apostle Paul: "And the base things of the world, and the things that are despised, did God choose" (I Corinthians 1:28). Lourenço accompanied Vilela through the vicissitudes of the attempt to establish a mission in Kyoto in 1559 and after. In 1563 he was permitted to become an Irmão, being the first Japanese accepted into membership in the Society of Jesus. He was present at several Jesuit audiences with Nobunaga and Hideyoshi and engaged in picturesque exchanges with them. For a detailed consideration of his career, see Ebisawa, *Kirishitanshi no kenkyū*, pp. 356–372.

11. Shimon is not readily identifiable, but Gōzumo is most likely Cosme Takai, one of the relatively few natives of the city of Kyoto to become a Christian in the mission's early decades. Cosme was the first to break the pattern of neighborhood ostracism of the missionaries in Shijō no Bōmon Ubayanagi, since 1560 the site of a Jesuit residence. Gaspar Vilela's arrival

and the delivery of shogun Yoshiteru's patent safeguarding the Padre caused a riot in Ubayanagi, and Cosme's decision to be baptized and become a *dōjuku* (1565 or 1566) was a scandal. His father disinherited Cosme and continued his violent opposition to the Christians into 1581 (*GJ*, pp. 111 and 452–455). In 1574 Cabral received Cosme into the Society as an Irmão; two years later, he was sent to Azuchi on the important mission of obtaining Nobunaga's sanction for the building of the Kyoto Nanbanji. In 1592 we find him, along with Fabian Fucan, in the Jesuit college of Amakusa as an instructor in Japanese and collaborator in the publications of the mission press. For further data, see Schütte, *Introductio*, pp. 608–609, and Alvarez-Taladriz, *Sumario*, p. 120, n. 46.

12. The original title of the chapter is *Kirishitan Buppō no koto*: literally, "On Kirishitan Buddhism." Deus is quite specifically called a Buddha. Such a usage may have been natural, and the intention innocuous, in 1549 when Xavier was confounded by his own and his opponents' syncretist propensities. But by 1639 the distinction should have been clear. The studied identification points toward the portrayal of the Kirishitan faith as a heresy. The subsequent depiction of foul Kirishitan practices fixes in the plebeian mind the image not merely of an exotic intrusion but of an execrable aberration.

13. The Eight Sorrows are listed above, n. 7 to Ferreira, *Deceit Disclosed*.

The Eight Impediments (*hachinan*) which obstruct sentient beings in their quest of Buddhahood, blocking the opportunity of the accomplishment of religious practice, are:

(1) *jigoku*, the realm of hellish beings;

(2) *gaki*, the realm of hungry spirits;

(3) *chikushō*, the realm of beasts;

(4) *mōryō onna*, bodily impediments—the blind, the deaf, the dumb, the mute are incapable of being taught the Law;

(5) *sechi bensō*, wordly wisdom, which makes the pseudo-sophisticate persist in his heresy;

(6) *Butsuzen Butsugo*, the misfortune of living at a time when one Buddha's career has finished and the career of the next not yet begun, and there is no one to lead the Way;

(7) Uttan'otsu, the realm of Uttarakuru, the northern of the four continents to the west of Mount Sumeru;

(8) *chōjuten*, the heavens of longevity, the longest of which lasts eighty thousand kalpas.

It may be noted that Impediments (1) through (3) mean residence in the Three Evil Realms, where no saintly being is seen, suffering prevails, and religious practice is impossible; whereas (7) and (8) mean residence in realms where pleasure abounds unabated, no pain exists, and desire to seek Buddhahood is not present. The list is from *Daijō gishō*, ch. viii; *Taishō*, XLIV, no. 1851, 628.

14. The raconteur is misinformed about the word's meaning: *quaresma* is Lent, a time of recollection, penitence, and abstention.

15. "Zensumaru, Zensumaru" = "Jesus Maria, Jesus Maria."

16. The coincidence is all the more striking when one considers that the tortoise (blind or near-blind) only sticks its head out of the water once every hundred years and that it is to find the one hole in the tree floating free in the ocean, blown by the winds. Moral: Easier it is for the tortoise to fit through the hole in the tree than for the unenlightened man . . . etc. *Zō agongyō*, ch. xv; *Taishō*, II, no. 99, 108.

17. Furaten are Franciscans, members of the *Ordo Fratrum Minorum*. The

plot of this chapter of *Kirishitan monogatari* is that of the events treated in Chapter 5 above; see also Chapter 3, pp. 79–81, and cf. Boxer, *Christian Century*, chs. iv and v. Boxer's treatment of the relations between Jesuits and friars puts much emphasis upon differences in mission method: where the Jesuits concentrated their efforts upon the upper classes, the mendicants did their work among the poor. The thesis is correct in general outline, although the Jesuits did not entirely neglect social work and medical missionary activity. But the Franciscans' work among "beggars and the outcasts of society" and their "remarkable medical treatment" remained more alive in the popular imagination, as the *Kirishitan monogatari* testifies. The Franciscans followed the policy of establishing a leprosarium with each mission from the very beginning of their activity in Japan. Ribadeneira, *Historia de las islas del Archipiélago*, p. 380, states that in Kyoto alone more than three thousand lepers sought treatment; and when the persecution struck in late 1596, the Franciscans were operating two hospitals in the capital city (Ribadeneira, Book Four, ch. xii, pp. 355–357). A leprosarium was founded in Osaka as early as 1594; the Franciscans' work there was interrupted by the persecution, but it is significant to note that when their mission was reopened in Osaka and Sakai, the number of converts gained from among the patients treated exceeded one thousand in 1603 alone (Ebisawa, *Kirishitan no shakai katsudō*, p. 182). In 1603 the Franciscans had six hospitals in Japan, with physicians adept in internal medicine and surgery (Ebisawa, pp. 230–231). Their activity extended to Edo, where Ieyasu, who had been approached by Geronimo de Jesús OFM immediately after Hideyoshi's death, had permitted them to settle in 1599, and where they operated the famous leprosarium of Asakusa (Ebisawa, pp. 203–207).

18. The text diverges here from a description of the Franciscans' activities to a mention of the locations of Kirishitan temples. There is no conflict concerning the location of the celebrated Kyoto Nanbanji, the three-story Church of the Assumption of the Blessed Virgin Mary. Its elaborate construction began in late 1575 and was completed in the spring of 1578 on the site of the old and rotted residence in Shijō no Bōmon Ubayanagi which Vilela had first occupied in 1560 (the present-day Takoyakushi Muromachi nishi-iru). But there is some confusion concerning the nature of the church here described as the "great temple" of Gojō Horikawa. It is to be noted that there was in this area of the city a concentration of Christians sizable enough to warrant the popular place name Daiusu-chō. See Ebisawa, *Kirishitanshi no kenkyū*, p. 284, and the sketch map on p. 287. Ribadeneira, p. 342, in speaking of the location of the Franciscans' Church of Santa Maria de los Angeles merely notes that "although it was within the city, it was free of neighbors, on the bank of a river."

Ichijō Abura no Kōji may have been the location of the Jesuit house established in 1600 in Kamigyō, the northern quarter of the Capital, to take advantage of the proximity of aristocrats' residences; cf. n. 17 to Chapter 6. For an extensive treatment of the several Jesuit establishments in Kyoto, see Schütte, *Introductio*, pp. 603–616.

19. The above portion of this paragraph is present in both the *Kirishitan monogatari* and the *Kirishitan taiji monogatari*, but was dropped from the *Zokuzoku gunsho ruijū* text. Hiyane repeated the lapse. A parallel account is given by Frois, Houghton Library MS. Jap 3, "The Report of the glorious death of xxvj persons," ch. vii, "How euery one of them had one eare cutt of, and how they weare, shamefullie caried in cartes," pp. 62–63: On 3 January 1597 the martyrs "had their handes bound behinde them,

and weare lead on foote, throughe a cheefe streete of the higher towne of *Meaco*, where euery one of them had a peece of his lefte eare cropped of: which *Gibonoscio* caused to be donne (otherwise than the king gaue commandment, which was that they should haue both their eares cutte of and their noses slitte) . . . Now when their eares weare cutte, they weare all caused (according to the ancient vse of *Iaponia*) to gette vp into cartes, 3 and 3 into a carte . . . The people weare infinite both in the streetes and windowes and on the toppes of howses, who came to beholde this rare spectacle of so many persons, whose innocency was manifest vnto them all" (Gibonoscio: Ishida Jibu no Shōyū Mitsunari). Also see Ribadeneira, Book Five, ch. vi, "Cómo los gloriosos mártires fueron sacados en carretas y traídos por las calles de Miaco," pp. 446–449.

20. The Seven Precious Things (*shippō*) are : gold, silver, emerald, mother of pearl, agate, pearl, ruby. The Thirty-Two Bodily Signs of Buddhahood (*sanjū-ni sō*) are prominent and easily apperceptible features of the physical body of a Buddha or of a Cakravartin King. These anatomical prodigies range from (1) flat feet and (5) webbed hands and feet, through (15) radiant body and (22) forty teeth, to (29) dark blue eyes and (32) topknot-shaped mound of flesh on the head. For the full catalogue, see Oda, *Bukkyō daijiten*, pp. 635–636.

21. I render with the proverbial expression, where the literal translation would be: "There appears some substance even in sawdust, when presented with a persuasive argument."

22. This is a general appellation from the standpoint of the Pure Land Sect for the other Japanese sects of Buddhism. The Eight Schools are: (1) Abhidharma-kośa (Kusha); (2) Completion of the Truth (Jōjitsu); (3) Mere-Ideation (Hossō); (4) Three-Treatise (Sanron); (5) Wreath (Kegon); (6) Disciplinary (Ritsu); (7) Tendai; (8) Shingon. The Eight Schools with the addition of Zen constitute the Nine Sects.

23. Genna (Genwa): 1615–1624.

24. Pure Land of the West: *Saihō Jōdo*, the region appertaining to Amida, whose vow it is to bestow rebirth in the Buddha-land of the West on all sentient beings who invoke his name; the paradise of the Amida-pietist sects.

Land of Liberation and Brilliance: *Jakkōdo*; more properly *Jōjakkōdo*, the Land of Permanence, Liberation, and Brilliance. Permanence refers to the Law Body of the Tathagata; liberation means the cessation of all human desire; and brilliance is the all-illuminating Buddha-wisdom. This is the ultimate of the Four Buddha-lands (*shido*) of the Lotus Sect, which is so labeled after the text of its ultimate reliance: Sutra of the Lotus of the Good Law, *Myōhō Rengekyō*.

25. King Jōbon is Sakyamuni's father Śuddhodana. Dandoku Mountain or Dantaloka is where Sakyamuni embarked upon his Bodhisattva career.

26. Hōzō Biku: Amida's name during his Bodhisattva career (Dharmakara).

27. The Three Countries: India, China, and Japan.

28. The Interior Scriptures (*naiten*) are, from the Buddhist standpoint, orthodox Buddhist scriptures, as opposed to the Exterior Scriptures (*geten*), scriptures of other religions or secular tracts (such as Confucian treatises).

29. A *koji* devotes himself to Buddhism in his own home, without entering a religious order.

30. The Doctrine of Mere-Ideation: *Yuishiki-ron*; more properly *Jō-yuishiki-ron*, Doctrine of the Completion of Mere-Ideation (*Vijñānamā-trasiddhi-śāstra*; *Taishō*, XXXI, no. 1585), the basic text of the Hossō School, whose headquarters is at the Kōfukuji in Nara, the Southern Capital.

31. The Miidera, or Onjōji, is the headquarters of the Jimon branch of the Tendai Sect, and is located in Ōtsu across the range of hills which flank Kyoto to the east. It produced a series of famous commentators on the Story of the Higher Special Dharma, the *Kusha-ron* or *Abidatsuma kusha-ron* (*Abhidharma-kośa-śāstra*; *Taishō*, XXIX, no. 1558), the text by Vasubandhu containing an exposition of all elements of reality enumerated in seventy-five dharmas. See Takakusu, pp. 57–73, for a concise explanation and chart.

The Kusha School proposes a universal Great Chiliocosm of 1000 small, 1000 middle, and 1000 large worlds as the elaboration of an extensive world-system. But cf. Takakusu, p. 137, for the basic Tendai doctrine of the Three Thousand Worlds: "The whole universe is said to have the constituency of 'three thousands,' but the theory is quite different from other pluralistic systems. It is not an enumeration of all *dharmas*; nor is it the world system of three Chiliocosms . . . The expression 'three thousands' does not indicate a numerical or substantial immensity, but is intended to show the inter-permeation of all *dharmas* and the ultimate unity of the whole universe." The Tendai doctrine stresses the ultimate identity of phenomenon and noumenon: the True State is Thusness. Phenomena are further held to be identical with conscious action; and therefore, since all the elements are interpermeating, the whole three-thousand-fold universe is immanent in one moment of thought. If not in the palm of his hand, Hakuō Koji does apprehend the Three Thousand Worlds in one conscious instant (*ichinen sanzen*). Cf. Takakusu, p. 140.

32. The Enryakuji, located on Mount Hiei to the northeast of Kyoto, is the headquarters of the Sanmon branch of the Tendai Sect.

Preliminary Mysteries (*Gengi*): In Tendai practice, the elucidation of the deeper meaning of a sutra is given preliminary to a reading of the text itself (Oda, *Bukkyō daijiten*, p. 441). The most prominent compendium of such elucidations is, of course, that for the Lotus Sutra itself, the *Hokekyō gengi*; *Taishō*, XXXIII, no. 1716. Exegeses (*Mongu*): The generic term applies particularly to the *Hokekyō mongu*; *Taishō*, XXXIV, no. 1718. Calmness and Insight: *shikan*, the Tendai method of meditation; see Oda, pp. 696–697. The *Maka shikan* of Chih-k'ai (538–597), *Taishō*, XLVI, no. 1911, is one of the most prominent texts of the Tendai School, and together with the aforementioned two scriptures is included in the *Tendai sandaibu*, which Hakuō as an expert in Tendai doctrine is certain to have studied. Unbudging Concentration (*shuryōgon*): *Shuryōgon sanmai* is the perfection of meditative concentration attained by the Buddha, that of a firmness impenetrable to Maras or other evil influences. The *Shuryōgon-kyō* (*Śūraṁgama Sutra*; *Taishō*, XIX, no. 945) is a popular text of Zen and of the esoteric schools, although it has been attacked as spurious. See Oda, p. 841, and cf. Suzuki, *Manual of Zen Buddhism*, pp. 64–72. Sutra of Prohibitions: *Kaikyō*, more properly *Bosatsuji jikyō* (*Taishō*, XXX, no. 1581), the basis of the regulations of the Tendai Sect, was applied by Dengyō Daishi in contradistinction to the rules of the Ritsu School at the time he introduced Tendai into Japan and established the Enryakuji.

33. The "Purple Plain," Murasakino, is the location in the north of Kyoto of the great monastery of the Rinzai branch of Zen, the Daitokuji.

Green Cliff: Hekigan, an obvious allusion to the *Hekiganroku*, the famous Zen classic compiled by the Sung period monk Yüan-wu (1063–1135) and first published in 1128.

34. The Myōshinji is another major Rinzai temple in Kyoto. The Mirror

of the Faith: *Shūkyōroku*, a highly popular tract by the Sung monk Yen-shou (904–975). Daisetz Suzuki, *Essays in Zen Buddhism*, third series (London: Rider, 1958 third ed.), p. 23, describes this work as the culmination of a syncretist movement within Zen, an attempt to "melt all the differences of Buddhist thought in the doctrine of Mind-only—understanding by 'Mind' an ultimate reality which is aware of itself, and is not the seat of our empirical consciousness." The Platform Sutra of the Sixth Patriarch: *Enō dankyō*, more properly *Rokuso dankyō*. The Sixth Patriarch of the Zen School in China, in the traditional line of transmission from Bodhidharma, was Hui-neng, called Enō in Japanese (638–713); the Platform Sutra purports to be a collection of his statements, includes a fictionalized autobiography, and is an eighth-century work compiled by his disciples.

35. The Five Great Monasteries or "Five Mountains" (*Gosan*) of the Zen Sect in Kyoto were ranked by the shogun Ashikaga Yoshimitsu as follows: Nanzenji in a special position at the head; (1) Tenryūji; (2) Shōkokuji; (3) Kenninji; (4) Tōfukuji; (5) Manjuji. The Manjuji suffered a disastrous fire in 1434 and lost its independent status, eventually being absorbed into the Tōfukuji.

Tōba (Tung-p'o) is the sobriquet of Su Shih, as Sankoku (Shan-ku) is of Huang T'ing-chien (1045–1105), a disciple of Su Shih and himself a literary figure of major importance.

Literary Selections: *Monzen* (*Wen hsüan*), the great anthology of Chinese poetry from the Ch'in to the Six Dynasties period, compiled by the Liang prince Chao-ming (501–531). The mention of these works in connection with the Five Great Monasteries is designed to allude to *Gosan Bungaku*, the representative school of letters of the Muromachi period: poetry, diaries, and anecdotes written in Chinese and particularly influenced by Sung literature. The patronage of Chinese letters by Zen monks of the *Gosan* is also noteworthy as the source for the introduction of Neo-Confucianism into Japan.

36. The Miwa Branch of Shinto is representative of the syncretist trend in mediaeval Japanese religion, which resulted in the amalgamation of traditional Shinto cults and Buddhist superstructures. Miwa Shinto is a faction which emerged in the eleventh and twelfth centuries from the Shingon-based rationalization known as Ryōbu Shinto, an attempt to represent Japanese native deities as manifestations of the Buddhas graphically arrayed in the Two Mandalas (*kontai ryōbu no mandara*) of the Diamond Element and of the Womb. The emphasis of Miwa and of the other factions of Ryōbu Shinto is on ascetic practice and the esotericism of mystic incantations. The cult lacks a systematized body of doctrine but is generally based on the Shingon proposition that the universe itself is the manifestation of Dainichi Nyorai and that Dainichi is the original substance (*honji*) of all deities, who are his trace manifestations (*suijaku*).

37. Tracts on Selection: *Senchakushū*, more properly *Senchaku hongan nenbutsushū*, Tracts on Invocation of the Select Original Vow (of Amida); perhaps the greatest commentary on Pure Land doctrine, the principal work of Hōnen Shōnin (1133–1212). The Original Vow is select because for those who invoke him Amida has chosen rebirth in the best of all possible worlds, the Pure Land of the West.

38. The Meaning of the Two Treasures: *Nizōgi*, more properly *Shaku jōdo nizōgi*, The Meaning of the Two Treasures of the Buddha's Pure Land, an Amidist tract by Ryōyo Shōkei (1341–1420). The reference is clear not

only from the context but also from the *Kirishitan taiji monogatari*, 1:20, where the Chinese characters are supplied; *Zokuzoku gunsho ruijū*, however, constructs as *nisōgi*, and Hiyane follows.

39. Furuna: Pūrna, one of the Ten Great Disciples of Sakyamuni, and the one most clever in preaching the Law.

40. Lotus Sutra: *Hokekyō* (*Saddharma-pundarīka*; *Taishō*, IX, no. 262), the principal text of Tendai and the Nichiren Sect. Diamond Sutra: *Kongōkyō* (*Vajra-cchedikā*; *Taishō*, VIII, no. 235), a basic Mahayana text, concentrating upon the Prajñāpāramita teaching with emphasis upon the doctrine of Śūnyata. The text is particularly popular in the Zen School. The Three Sutras: *sanbukyō*; the three principal sutras of any particular sect. The reference here probably is to the three principal texts of the Pure Land Sect: (1) *Dai Muryōju-kyō* (*Sukhāvatī-vyūha*), *Taishō*, XII, no. 360; its résumé, (2) *Amida-kyō*, *Taishō*, XII, no. 362; (3) *Kan Muryōju-kyō* (*Amitāyur-dhyāna*), *Taishō*, XII, no. 365.

41. Non-Being: *mu*. Recompensed Being: *u*, a term which may be re-phrased as *kahō*, the results of karma.

42. Age of Decline: *masse*, also termed *mappō*, the Age of Decline of the Law, which is to last 10,000 years, following upon the Age of the True Law (*shōbō*, 500 years after Sakyamuni's entry into Nirvana) and the Age of the Simulated Law (*zōhō*, the subsequent 1000 years). For the details, see Oda, *Bukkyō daijiten*, p. 773. This chiliastic doctrine was extremely wide-spread in the Japanese Middle Ages.

43. Amaterasu Ōmikami, who is enshrined at the Ise Daijingū, was the offspring of the primal pair. The deity of the Izumo Taisha is Ō-mononushi no Mikoto, progeny of the "fisher girl" Kushi-inada Hime and Susanoo. On Hachiman, see above, n. 25 to *Deus Destroyed*.

44. The *kusurimono* (medicinal article) of the text makes no sense, and is probably a mistake for *kusugurimono* (jester).

45. See above, n. 7 to Ferreira, *Deceit Disclosed*. The Four Pains are the first four of the Eight Sorrows.

46. The original does not make it clear just who it is that is supposed to climb onto the shrine roofs and perform the "exploit"—an explicit subject of the sentence is lacking. But the next paragraph in its contrast between Deus and the transgressor birds and beasts implies overwhelmingly that Hakuō, at least, assumed that Fabian was volunteering Deus' services and not his own.

Scatology in reference to the deity is, of course, a common cultural phenomenon and lies but thinly submerged in the shallows of the primitive mind. The identical story is, for instance, contained in the collection of jottings and anecdotes involving Suzuki Shōsan, the *Hogoshū* (*Kana hōgo shū*, pp. 338–339; *Suzuki Shōsan Dōnin zenshū*, pp. 321–322): A samurai maintains to Shōsan that the Buddhas and gods are nonexistent; for proof, he has already committed that most primitive of sacrileges, and no punish-ment has struck him. Shōsan replies: "Is there a punishment greater than that! The true samurai is one who with true sincerity reveres the Buddhas and gods, honors his superiors and treats his inferiors with compassion, who exhausts himself in loyalty and exerts himself in filial piety, who is humane, righteous, courteous, and wise—in short, one who acts with propriety. The beasts, of course, do not know the Buddhas and the gods; they shit and piss at random on the altars. Your deed makes you identical with the beasts." The point strikes home, the samurai is converted.

47. The *Kusha-ron* contains cosmological speculation in which cycles of

degeneration and regeneration succeed each other, and the convenient index of an age's quality is the extent of human longevity. The text's postulate of 830,000 years as ultimate longevity is, strictly speaking, not accurate: 84,000 is standard usage. But 84,000 is a conventionalized Buddhist numerological representation of great numerical extent or multiplicity; there is no necessity to attribute real value to this stenograph. The discussion is commonly made in terms of a definition of kalpas: great, middle, and small.

One small kalpa (shōkō) is:

either	*or*
one cycle of degeneration—human longevity decreasing from infinity/ 84,000 by one year every century until a standard age of 10 years is reached	one cycle of regeneration—human longevity increasing from 10 by one year every century until a standard age of 84,000 years is reached

One middle kalpa (chūkō) is the combination of one cycle of degeneration and one cycle of regeneration; one middle kalpa equals two small kalpas.

One great kalpa (daikō) is the complete cycle of existence of the world of sentient beings—origination, continuation, destruction, and void. For each of the four periods of the cycle twenty middle kalpas are postulated; one great kalpa equals eighty middle kalpas.

Cf. Kusha-ron, ch. xii; Taishō, XXIX, no. 1558, 63.

48. Miroku (Maitreya): the most prominent figure of Buddhist eschatology, whose legend became popular c. 200 B.C. in India under the influence of speculation concerning the Age of the Decline of the Law. See Edward Conze, Buddhism: Its Essence and Development (New York: Harper, 1959; Harper Torchbooks TB 58), pp. 115–117. Miroku resides in Tuṣita Heaven (Tosotsuten), whence he will return unto earth after 4,000 celestial years, which are 5,670,000,000 years by human reckoning. He will preach the Law under the Dragon Tree in the Flower Garden to innumerable masses of humans and devas, and will lead them to enlightenment. See Oda, Bukkyō daijiten, p. 1689.

49. The text makes the association of one Buddha with one increase/ decrease cycle. The present period of twenty middle kalpas has Miroku regnant over its tenth segment, succeeding Sakyamuni, who is associated with the ninth.

A more standard listing than the text's (Oda, p. 411) attributes 1000 Buddhas to the present period of twenty middle kalpas. No Buddhas appeared during the first eight. The ninth segment saw the appearance of four Buddhas, Sakyamuni being the last of this series. The first Buddha to appear in the tenth middle kalpa is to be Miroku.

50. Tōriten (Trāyastriṁśa): the residence of Indra on Mount Sumeru. An apparent mistake for the Tuṣita Heaven of n. 48.

51. Constant Flow: ruten (saṁsāra), dynamic life-flux, the key element in the basic Buddhist doctrine of causation by action-influence, which postulates that life is created by the accumulated energy of the actions of a previous life. Schematically: Life A is in the action-influence sphere of its antecedent $Z(Y+X+...)$, and is inextricably tied to it in the process of generation; but the effectual A is also causative to A_1. The water and wave analogy is used as a favorite device to explain this never-ending cycle of causations and becomings; e.g. Takakusu, p. 35: "Life is like the waves on water; the vibration of one particle causes the vibration of the next particle and thus the waves are transmitted a long distance. One wave is one life, and

the series of lives is *sansara*. In Buddhism the series of lives do not go on infinitely as in a straight line. They turn in a circle and repeat the circle over and over again. The Wheel of Life is a small circle of one life, while the great circle (the series of the Wheel of Life) is *sansara*." The Law of Cause and Effect is like unto a wheel because there is no fixed beginning in it, just as there is none in a circle; a cause is a cause when viewed from its effect, but it is an effect when viewed from its antecedent cause. A cause is an effect is a cause. Takakusu gives a clear explanation on pp. 30–36, complete with diagram.

52. Enumerated here are the Three Poisons (*sandoku*) which are products of the deluded mind and form the root of all evil. Each leads to descent into one of the Three Evil Realms: covetousness (*ton'yoku*), the Realm of Hungry Spirits; stupidity (*guchi*), the Realm of Beasts; anger (*shin'i*), the Realm of Fighting Spirits or of Hellish Beings.

53. The text has "World of Specific Character" (*u-sō sekai*), used in the sense of "Created-Conditioned Elements" (*u-i hō*), a key phenomenological phrase. All elements exist merely as combinations of causes and therefore possess characteristics which are merely temporary or illusory. The sole exception—bereft of specific character (*musō*), noncreated element (*mu-i hō*)— is in the several categories of Thusness, which transcends all specific character and is as is, the void. See *Dai chidoron*, ch. xxxi; *Taishō*, XXV, no. 1509, 288.

54. Specific character (*sō*) is created by ideation. All things are products of universal causation and are therefore interdependent and free to exist in harmony with all other things. It follows that cleaving to determinate character is one of the principal evils produced by the mind: delusion. Conversely, illumination is the realization of non-individuality and recognition of the interpenetrated totality of the elemental world; Mahayanist universalism postulates that the True Character is No Specific Character (*jissō musō*). Ideation, however, has a cumulative effect: mind-action through perception causes reactions which are stored as seeds of future action. The Ideation Store (*araiya-shiki*; ālaya-vijñāna) carries over across the border of life and death. When the causes emanating from it are good, the specific character of becoming will be good, and ultimately will mean the attainment of Buddhahood, for potentially none are excluded. Bad causes, on the other hand, lead down the path of evil.

55. This is originally a calligraphic distinction describing the three styles of writing: *shin, sō, gyō*.

56. The invocation of the Lotus Sutra is particularly associated with the Nichiren Sect and labeled *daimoku*.

57. *Shikaku hongaku no satori*: In Mahayanistic parlance, the basal nature (*honshō*) of Mind is originally undefiled and is itself the substance of enlightenment. The Ideation Store, which subsists in all created elements, is the seedbed of enlightenment of two categories:

(1) Original Illumination (*hongaku*) is a description of the original nature of the Ideation Store, which is clear and unperturbed by delusion, and is ultimately identifiable with the basis of enlightenment, the True State of Thusness.

(2) The manifestation of Thusness, when effected by an impure cause, may take an impure form. Takakusu states, p. 39: "The ideation-store of a human being is determined by his nature as a human being and this nature is a particular dynamic form of Thusness." The ālaya-vijñāna may have been polluted by an influx of delusionary ideations, being in actuality unenlightened. But it is possible by religious practice to progress in wisdom

and to clear away the seeds of unenlightenment, for the first time making manifest the original nature and illuminating the mind; this result is termed Initial Illumination (*shikaku*).

From the standpoint of enlightenment, since Initial Illumination is merely the activation of the immanent Original Illumination, the two categories are in fact identical.

58. The Abrupt Round Doctrine of the Great Vehicle (*Daijō endon*): The Round Doctrine (*enkyō*) of the Mahayana stands at the apex of the Tendai School's critical classification of the nature of Buddhist teaching: it is the True Doctrine (*jikkyō*), perfect in the sense of all-permeating (*ennyū*) and all-fulfilling (*enman*). The Round Doctrine is the ultimate expression of Mahayanistic universalism: it teaches the perfect interpenetration and mutual identification of all elements, and asserts the completion of a perfect synthesis. Undifferentiation (*muji mubetsu*) ultimately means that, just as water is identical with wave, so is Evil with Bodhi, the process of life and death with Nirvana, sentient beings with Original Illumination; all the myriad elements of the universe are identical with Thusness and Thusness with the myriad elements (*manbō ze shinnyo shinnyo ze manbō*). For a Christian view of this dialectic, see *Evora byōbu*, p. 130.

Since all elements are interpermeating, all elements are immanent in any one; one conscious instant apprehends the Three Thousand Worlds (*ichinen sanzen*) and Buddhahood therefore can be attained abruptly. This subitist aspect of enlightenment based on perfect immanence is termed *endon*, and for its concentration upon the doctrine the Tendai Sect is sometimes called *Endon-shū*. See Oda, *Bukkyō daijiten*, pp. 1868–1871, and Takakusu, pp. 131–141.

59. Uninterrupted accumulation: *futaiten*, the progress to Buddhahood along the straight, unbending, and unretrogressing road of religious practice.

60. The Revelation of the Three Shrines (*Sanja takusen*) is a figment of Ryōbu Shinto, particularly current in the Muromachi period. The text—supposedly of divine origin—is not distinguished by any coherence; this fact is illustrative of its nature as a pseudo-profound formula for popular consumption. The revelation may be sampled in the encyclopaedic dictionary *Daigenkai*, comp. Ōtsuki Fumihiko (Tokyo: Fuzanbō, 1961 thirteenth revised edition), p. 840.

61. See above, n. 15 to *Deus Destroyed*.

62. *Ichinen sanzen*. See nn. 31 and 58.

63. Higo is the present-day Kumamoto Prefecture on the island of Kyushu; in this area there was a major concentration of Christians. Suruga is the present-day Shizuoka Prefecture; in this province was the castle of Sunpu, Ieyasu's residence after he passed on the shogunal office to Hidetada in 1605.

64. Konishi's fief was Uto in Higo Province. The reference to a "Kirishitan temple called *Natal*" is unclear.

65. *Itomakimono* is a rather difficult image to translate. *Itomaki* means a spool used to wind thread, and the reference may merely be to the import of silk thread, the trade of the *nao*. But the phrase bears within it a secondary allusion: *itomaki no tachi* is a type of sword with hilt wrapped with cords or thin leather thongs, and that would suggest the more sinister import of weapons. I consciously choose the Western cliché, which may be farfetched but is comprehensive.

66. Katō Higo no Kami: Katō Kiyomasa (1562–1611), prominent favorite of Hideyoshi and great competitor of Konishi Yukinaga, with whom he vied for the laurels of the most successful general in Hideyoshi's Korean

adventure. After the death of Hideyoshi he emerged as one of the principals of the "military" faction among Hideyoshi's former retainers, juxtaposed with the "civil" faction headed by Konishi and Ishida Mitsunari. In the factional disputes among members of the Toyotomi league lay the opportunity which Ieyasu utilized masterfully at the Battle of Sekigahara in 1600. In this struggle Katō adhered to Ieyasu's party, and was rewarded by the extension of his fief to cover all of Higo; thus Dom Agostinho Konishi's lands passed into the hands of his arch-rival, who made short shrift of Konishi's Christian converts.

It is difficult to say whether the incident recounted in this chapter has some sort of historical basis or is random fiction meant to serve as a transition to the story which follows. The image of the Iruman may well be yet another reflection of Fabian Fucan, whose denunciatory *Ha Daiusu* was composed in the sixth year of Genna. The mention of a "confrontation before the August Presence" may possibly have for its distant source the quarrel between Murayama Tōan and Suetsugu Heizō, which was also an occurrence of the Genna period, the stated time of the action.

67. The straw sack incident took place in 1614; see Chapter 8 above. The inquisition in a nunnery also is historical: among the Christian victims was a group of Japanese women who lived a monastic life. The Jesuit relation dated 25 October 1614 gives a detailed account: *Lettera annva del Giappone del M.DCXIV.* (In Roma, Appresso Bartolomeo Zannetti, M.DCXVII.), pp. 23–32. Another contemporary source is Avila Girón, *Nippon Ōkoku ki,* pp. 400–402. It is interesting to note that Avila Girón transforms the Japanese verb *korobu* (which I translate literally, "to fall away") into the Spanish *corondear,* and gives it Spanish inflections: thus a *corondeado,* one who has fallen away, is an apostate.

See also Bartoli, *Dell'Historia della Compagnia di Giesv: Il Giappone,* Book Three, pp. 743–754, where the date of the straw sack torture is given as 3 March (p. 745). Compare Crasset (London, 1707), II, 225–229; included is an account of the indignities suffered by the residents of "a House of young Women, and old Virgins, that vow'd Chastity, and liv'd together in Community"—they scorned the threats to "lead them Naked thro' the streets," and were finally bound up in sacks and "flung upon the Ground . . . to be insulted by the Dregs of the People." Apparently even such methods of intimidation did not suffice. "Ten considerable Ladies also were carried to the Stews, in Order to be deflowr'd, but by the Mercy of God, they converted this abominable Place, into a House of Prayer and Devotion, and sanctifi'd it with their Presence."

68. Itakura Iga no Kami Katsushige was appointed by Ieyasu to the position of *Kyōto Shoshidai* in 1601, and served in that post until 1619. Charitable feelings toward Christians are attributed to him by Laures, *Takayama Ukon,* pp. 349–350. Apparently his "careful inquisition" was rather lax: Laures claims that he consciously diminished the number of Christians in the census he conducted in Kyoto from an actual 7,000 to 1,600.

69. Ōkubo Sagami no Kami Tadachika appeared in Kyoto in late February 1614 (Crasset, II, 226, gives the date 26 February); the straw sack affair was the immediate result. Sagami no Kami had been the patron of the notorious Ōkubo Chōan, and that association was utilized in attempts to discredit him by Honda Kōzuke Masazumi and his father Masanobu, two of the most eminent *éminences grises* of the Bakufu. The intrigues and counter-intrigues of the Honda and Ōkubo Sagami form an altogether notorious chapter of early Tokugawa history, and seem to have barely

avoided the inconceivable climax of a swordfight within the precincts of the shogunal castle. It is tempting to surmise that Sagami no Kami was shunted away from the center of power on a wild Christian chase as the result of a palace intrigue of the Honda clique, who then used his absence to work measures against him. That at least is what Tadachika's uncle Ōkubo Hikozaemon suggests in the concluding passages of the *Mikawa monogatari*; Nakada Norio edition, II, 295–297.

Tadachika was deprived of his fief on Keichō 19/1/19 (27 February 1614), while he was away on his straw sack mission. For a brief account of his contretemps, see Kitajima Masamoto, *Edo Bakufu no kenryoku kōzō* (Tokyo: Iwanami, 1966 second printing), pp. 449–451. A sympathetic biography by Murakami Tadashi is included among the "tragic cases" of *Daimyō retsuden*, III, ed. Kodama Kōta and Kimura Motoi (Tokyo: Jinbutsu Ōrai-sha, 1967), 17–73.

70. "To whistle" is the meaning evident from *Nippo jisho*, p. 218: "*Vso uo fuqu. Asuuiar.*"

71. Villages on the northern outskirts of Kyoto. The readings of place names accord with *Kirishitan taiji monogatari*, 2:10.

72. A conventional narrative enumeration of no relevance to the historical actuality of the Edo period.

73. Kan'ei 14 is equivalent to 1637, but the middle of the eleventh month (11/1 = 17 December) is approximately New Year's 1638. Cf. the chronological volume of *Kumamoto-ken shi*, p. 162, where the major dates are given as follows: Kan'ei 14/10/25, *ikki* begins in Shimabara; 10/29, *ikki* spreads to Amakusa; 11/14, resounding victory of the joint *ikki* forces over the troops of the Terazawa; 12/10, Itakura Shigemasa lays siege to Hara Castle.

74. The original has 18 *chō* by 10 *chō*. One *chō* = 119 yards.

75. Itakura Naizen no Kami Shigemasa, the son of Itakura Katsushige, died in a futile assault upon Hara Castle on the lunar New Year's Day of Kan'ei 15. Ishigae Jūzō no Suke Sadakiyo lived up to his fierce warrior's reputation in that same attack, penetrating to the second ring of fortifications. On the role of Matsudaira Izu no Kami, see above, Chapter 8, p. 222.

76. Hosokawa Etchū no Kami Tadatoshi: daimyo of Kumamoto. Kuroda Uemon no Suke Tadayuki: daimyo of Fukuoka. Nabeshima Shinano no Kami Katsushige: daimyo of Saga. Arima Genba no Jō Toyouji: daimyo of Kurume. Tachibana Hida no Kami Muneshige: daimyo of Yanagawa. Terazawa Hyōgo no Kami Katataka: daimyo of Karatsu and Amakusa; deprived of the latter part of his fief after the campaign's conclusion. Ogasawara Ukon no Daibu Tadazane: daimyo of Kokura.

77. Mizuno Hyūga no Kami Katsunari: daimyo of Fukuyama in Bingo; formerly a Konishi vassal and familiar with the terrain. Toda Samon Ujikane: daimyo of Ōgaki in Mino; frequent collocutor of Hayashi Razan; after the rebels were all slaughtered he was charged with the task of conveying the grisly trophies to Edo.

78. The actual date was Kan'ei 15/2/27 (11 April 1638).

79. Matsukura Bungo no Kami Shigemasa, who died in 1630, had been the retainer of Tsutsui Sadatsugu, whose father Tsutsui Junkei (1549–1584) had successively served Oda Nobunaga, Akechi Mitsuhide, and Toyotomi Hideyoshi, and was at the end of his life master of Yamato Province and much of Kawachi.

80. The fabled era of Engi was 901–923. The eighth month of Kan'ei 16: 29 August–26 September 1639.

CHRISTIANS COUNTERED by Suzuki Shōsan

Bibliographical Note

The basis of this translation of *Ha Kirishitan* is the text contained in *Suzuki Shōsan Dōnin zenshū*, ed. Suzuki Tesshin (Tokyo: Sankibō Busshorin, 1962). A more convenient annotated edition has recently been published in Volume XXV of the Nihon Shisō Taikei series: *Kirishitan sho, Hai-Ya sho*, ed. Ebisawa Arimichi, H. Cieslik, Doi Tadao, and Ōtsuka Mitsunobu (Tokyo: Iwanami, 1970).

I have also utilized the Kyōto Furitsu Sōgō Shiryōkan copy of the wood-block volume printed by Ogawa Tazaemon (Kyoto: Zenke Shorin Ryūshiken, Kanbun 2 [1662]). Ebisawa, *Christianity in Japan*, p. 45, lists three other editions published in Kyoto that year; these four are the first known imprints of Shōsan's tract.

The seventeenth-century work *Kirishitan hakyaku ronden* (Christians crushed; tracts and glosses) comprises in the final of its three volumes the text of *Christians Countered* and commentaries on it. The compiler was the prolific poet, essayist, and writer of *kana* chapbooks Asai Ryōi (?–1691), who signed the work with his sobriquet Hyōsuishi. This variant is of interest chiefly on account of the ingenuity which Hyōsuishi applied to construct solecisms in his Chinese-character transcriptions of the word "Kirishitan." A complete copy of the original is in the possession of the Kyoto University Library; Yamada Ichirōbei was the printer, but the date of publication is not indicated. A facsimile was published by the Kisho Fukuseikai: sixth series, nos. 10, 12, and 14 (1929). The text is included in *Kaihyō sōsho*, ed. Shinmura Izuru, Vol. I (Kyoto: Kōseikaku Shoten, 1927).

Textual Notes

1. The Three Worlds (*sanze*)—of the past, the present, and the future—are the periods of change undergone by all elements subject to karma, and relative to the term of existence of each. The Buddhas of the Ten Directions—an unlimited, countless number of Buddhas—appear in the Three Worlds to save all sentient beings.

2. See above, n. 57 to *Kirishitan monogatari*.

3. The Buddhist implications of *shusse* comprise the appearance of a Buddha in the impure world of the unenlightened, his own enlightenment, and his ensuing efforts to preach the Law to all sentient beings.

4. One half of the famous quatrain, of uncertain authorship, which serves as a summation of the method of Zen:

> A special transmission outside the scriptures,
> No dependence upon words and letters,
> Direct pointing at the heart of man,
> Seeing into one's nature:
> the attainment of Buddhahood.

Cf. Daisetz Suzuki, *Zen Buddhism: Selected Writings of D. T. Suzuki*, ed. William Barrett (Garden City, N.Y.: Doubleday, 1956; Anchor Books A 90), pp. 9 and 61.

5. *Seson* (Lokanātha; Bhagavat), an honorific for the Buddha, the most sacred and most venerated personage of this world.

6. *Rōgatsu yōka*, the eighth day of the twelfth month; a traditional date for Sakyamuni's attainment of satori, and celebrated as such in the Zen Sect.

7. From the Sixth Case of *Mumonkan*; Furuta Shōkin edition, pp. 110 and 20. Kāśyapa is regarded as the first patriarch of the Zen Sect.

8. The view that beings are endowed with real and individual existence (*jitsu-u*) is held by Buddhists to be erroneous: what appears to be real is temporary and illusory, since all things in the universe derive their existence from an indeterminate series of causes. A conscious attachment to this delusion affixes the unenlightened to the Wheel of Life. Cf. nn. 51 and 54 to *Kirishitan monogatari*.

9. See above, n. 15 to *Deus Destroyed*.

10. Earth, water, fire, and air.

11. The asuras (ashura) are fighting spirits engaged in perpetual war among themselves and against Indra (Tentaishaku), who dwells on the summit of Mount Sumeru as lord over Trāyastriṁśa Heaven and, vanquishing the asuras, acts as one of the prime protectors of Buddha's Law.

12. There are various catalogues of Super-Powers (*tsū*): the Five, the Six, the Ten; see Oda, *Bukkyō daijiten*, pp. 1231–1232.

13. The Greater Chiliocosm (*dai sen-sekai*), more properly the Triple-Thousand Greater Chiliocosm (*sanzen dai sen-sekai*), is a Buddhist cosmological elaboration postulating:

a. a minor cosmos with Mount Sumeru at its center, encompassing the Seven Mountains and Eight Oceans, and with the Iron Circuit Mountain Tetchisen (Cakravāḍa) as its limit;

b. the minor cosmos × 1000 = the minor chiliocosm;

c. the minor chiliocosm × 1000 = the middle chiliocosm;

d. the middle chiliocosm × 1000 = the Greater Chiliocosm. The Greater Chiliocosm is the precinct of one Buddha's productive enterprise of transformation (*kekyō*). See Oda, p. 643.

14. The citation (as Ebisawa notes in NST 25, p. 453) is not from a sutra but from the T'ang period tract *Denshin hōyō* (Essential rules for the Transmission of the Mind) attributed to Ōbaku Kiun (Huang-po Hsi-yun). The work was compiled in the middle of the ninth century by that Zen Master's lay disciple Fei-hsiu. See *Taishō*, XLVIII, no. 2012 A, 380.

15. As Nakamura Hajime points out (*Kinsei Nihon ni okeru hihanteki seishin*, p. 222), Shōsan's expository text (from "The infidel Sāṁkhya" to "this may be compared to the house burning up while the owner exits") is borrowed from a fourteenth-century work by the great Zen Master Musō Soseki. See Musō Kokushi, *Muchū mondō*, ed. Satō Yasukiyo, Iwanami Bunko 1046–1047 (Tokyo: Iwanami, 1934), ch. lxvi, pp. 152–153. For a particularly lucid exposition of the "infidel Sāṁkhya" (*Shuron gedō*) system, see S. Radhakrishnan, *Indian Philosophy*, rev. 2nd ed., II (London: George Allen & Unwin, 1931), 248–335. A brief diagram of the Twenty-Five Principles (*nijū-go tai*) of the Sāṁkhya is given on p. 273, n. 4.

16. The *myōtai* of Shōsan's text is synonymous with *jishō*, to denote prakṛti, the Sāṁkhya explanation of the ultimate basis of the empirical universe: "before creation," uncaused cause; independent, all-pervading, eternal, imperceptible, unconscious, material force; the not-self.

17. Puruṣa (*shingatai*) in the Sāṁkhya system is the unalterably constant principle of consciousness, the qualityless pure spirit which coordinates all experience; the self.

18. The Buddhist parallel is the noncreated state of Thusness.

19. *Jishō* is used here in the sense of a dialectically established idea of

Void, a characterless state of No State (*musō*), bereft of specific identity. The ultimate specificity is that of lack of independent reality. See Takakusu, p. 106.

20. The expression is proverbial, but its provenance is the *Chuang Tzu, Ch'iu-shui* xvii; see Burton Watson, trans., *The Complete Works of Chuang Tzu*, "Autumn Floods," p. 175: "You can't discuss the ocean with a well frog—he's limited by the space he lives in."

21. *Shichi-kan Ryōga-kyō*, Ch. iv; *Taishō*, XVI, no. 672, 608.

22. Although the Buddhas of the Past are immeasurable in number, a conventionalized representation is sometimes made of a series of seven regnant over a succession of kalpas. See Oda, *Bukkyō daijiten*, pp. 739–740.

23. *Kan Muryōju-kyō*; *Taishō*, XII, no. 365, 343. The same citation is included in Point 10 of *Buppō no shidai ryaku nukigaki*, the putative anti-Buddhist fragment of *Myōtei mondō*. Cf. n. 108 to Chapter 6 above.

24. From the Twentieth Case of *Mumonkan*; Furuta Shōkin edition, pp. 116–117 and 31.

25. *Issai shujō shitsu u busshō*. *Daihatsu nehankyō*, ch. xxi; *Taishō*, XII, no. 374, 488. Also in ch. xxvii, p. 522.

26. Cf. *Rinzairoku*, ed. Asahina Sōgen, Iwanami Bunko 1202 (Tokyo: Iwanami, 1938 fourth printing), pp. 36–37.

27. Buddha of the Victory of All-Penetrating Wisdom: Daitsūchishō Butsu, a Tathagata who appeared 3000 kalpas ago. At the time of his appearance there were sixteen princes who became monks and, following him, heard the Lotus Sutra, endeavoring later to proclaim it to all sentient beings. The ninth of these prince-disciples was Amida and the sixteenth was Shaka. His legend is told in *Hokekyō*, ch. iii; *Taishō*, IX, no. 262, 22–27.

28. Wonderful Melody (Myōon): a reference to Myōon Bosatsu (also known as Daibenzaiten), a deification of the mellifluous sound of the Sarasvatī River. The legend of this Bodhisattva is told in *Hokekyō*, ch. vii; *Taishō*, IX, no. 262, 55–56. "The grasses and the trees" is a parable for all sentient beings, upon whom falls the gentle rain of Buddha's salutary work. The phrase cited by Shōsan, *sōmoku kokudo shikkai jōbutsu*, is falsely attributed to various sutras and is instead a standard Buddhist expression, part of an exhortatory poem which sums up the Mahayana teaching on universal salvation: "When one Buddha establishes his Way, Inspects and sees the elemental world, The grasses . . ." etc. See Oda, *Bukkyō daijiten*, pp. 597 and 82–83.

29. The Great Physician: Dai Iō (Great King of Cures); cf. *Zō agongyō*, ch. xv; *Taishō*, II, no. 99, 105. Compare *Banmin tokuyō* (*Kana hōgo shū*, p. 267; *Suzuki Shōsan Dōnin zenshū*, p. 64).

The Obstacles of Evil and of Karma: *bonnō gosshō*, two of the Three Obstacles (*sanshō*) which bar entry into the True Way. The karma is more specifically that of the Five Unpardonable Sins (*q.v.* in n. 70 to *Deus Destroyed*).

30. Compare the use of the Three Poisons ascribed to the Christians in *Buppō sōron*, the putative fragment of Fabian's anti-Buddhist volume; Chapter 6, p. 182, above. "The eighty-four thousand evils" is another standard Buddhist phrase; 84,000 is a conventional stenograph for great numerical extent or multiplicity.

31. The Mountain of Death: Shide no Yama, originally used in the metaphorical sense but later conceptualized as the residence of the Plutonic Enma-ō. The River of Three Crossings: Sanzu no Kawa, popularized into a Stygian stream in similar fashion. These obstacles are encountered on the

seventh day after death. Shōsan is more elaborate in *Banmin tokuyō*: see *Kana hōgo shū*, p. 269 and add. nn. 290–291, pp. 466–467; *Suzuki Shōsan Dōnin zenshū*, p. 65.

32. The Ten Evils (*jūaku*) are transgressions against the Ten Laws (see n. 49 to *Deus Destroyed*). The Eight Sorrows are listed in n. 7 to *Deceit Disclosed*.

33. The Five Organs (*gozō*) are: the heart, kidneys, lungs, liver, spleen. The Six Intestines (*roppu*) are: the great intestine, small intestine, stomach, gall, bladder, urinary tract.

34. The View of Impurity (*fujōkan*) is one to which Shōsan returned again and again. To give but three examples: *Ninin bikuni* (Two nuns), *Suzuki Shōsan Dōnin zenshū*, p. 104; *Roankyō, kan* 1, no. 51, *Zenshū*, p. 153; *Hogoshū, Zenshū*, pp. 296–297 (*Kana hōgo shū*, pp. 298–299). The *Ninin bikuni* in particular is essentially a dirge elaborating upon the theme of impermanence with detailed attention to the decomposition of the human body.

The theme was standard in Japanese Buddhism (as, indeed, it was in European Christianity) and was picked up by the missionaries. One of the Jesuits' Japanese-letter publications includes a series of poems on the Nine Stages (of decomposition; *kusō*) and on impermanence (*mujō*): *ROYEI. ZAFIT. IN COLLEGIO IAPONICO SOCIETATIS IESV.* Cum facultate Ordinarij, & Superiorum. ANNO 1600. This work has been reproduced in facsimile: *Keichō 5nen Yasokai-ban Wakan rōeishū*, ed. Kyōto Daigaku Bungakubu Kokugogaku Kokubungaku Kenkyūshitsu (Kyoto: Kyōto Daigaku Kokubungakkai, 1964). A transcription is included, with the poems occupying pp. 42–46. A detailed commentary by Doi Tadao accompanies the text. Doi also discusses the book in *Kirishitan bunken kō*, pp. 19–60.

35. Nakamura Hajime (*Kinsei Nihon ni okeru hihanteki seishin*, p. 234, n. 2) points out that Shōsan uses a phrase joined together from two sources. The first two lines are found in the 80-chapter *Kegon-kyō*, ch. xxxvii; *Taishō*, X, no. 279, 194. The second couplet is in the 60-chapter *Kegon-kyō*, ch. x; *Taishō*, IX, no. 278, 465. There is more than a faint echo of *Denshin hōyō*, which has for its very first statement: "The Buddhas and all sentient beings are all one Mind; there is beyond it no other dharma." *Taishō*, XLVIII, no. 2012 A, 379–380. Ōbaku Kiun's entire tract may be said to be an exposition of this formula.

36. The concluding poem is a standard formula used at the end of expositions of the Law. The second month of Kanbun 2: 20 March–18 April 1662. Tsutsumi Rokuzaemon was the publisher of the variant Suzuki Tesshin utilized in his compilation of The Complete Works of Shōsan.

BIBLIOGRAPHY
GLOSSARY
INDEX

Bibliography

Aduarte, Diego, OP. *Historia de la Provincia del Sancto Rosario de la Orden de Predicadores en Philippinas, Iapon, y China*. Por el Reverendissimo Don Fray Diego Aduarte Obispo de la Nuevasegovia. Añadida por el muy Reverendo Padre Fray Domingo Gonçalez . . . Con Licencia, En Manila En el Colegio de Sãcto Thomas, por Luis Beltran impressor de libros. Año de 1640. 2 vols. in one.

Aida Yūji 会田雄次. *Haisha no jōken: Sengoku jidai o kangaeru* 敗者の条件—戦国時代を考える (The loser's condition: thoughts on the Sengoku period). Chūkō Shinsho 中公新書 62. Tokyo, Chūō Kōron-sha 中央公論社, 1965.

Akizuki Ryōmin 秋月龍珉. *Zenmon no iryū* 禅門の異流 (Zen aberrations). Nihon no Bukkyō 日本の仏教 12. 3rd printing. Tokyo, Chikuma Shobō 筑摩書房, 1969.

Akutagawa Ryūnosuke 芥川竜之介. *Hōkyōnin no shi, hoka jūsanpen* 奉教人の死他十三篇 (The death of a believer; and thirteen other stories). Iwanami Bunko 岩波文庫 3742–43. 18th printing. Tokyo, Iwanami 岩波, 1970.

Alvarez-Taladriz, José Luis. "Fuentes Europeas sobre Murayama Toan (1562–1619): I.—El pleito de Suetsugu Heizo Juan contra Murayama Toan Antonio (1617–1619), según el Padre Mattheus de Couros, Provincial de la Compañía de Jesús en Japón," *Tenri Daigaku gakuhō* 天理大学学報 (Bulletin of Tenri University) 51:262–241 [(93)–(114)], March 1966.

Anesaki Masaharu 姉崎正治. *Kirishitan shūmon no hakugai to senpuku* 切支丹宗門の迫害と潜伏 (The persecution and subterranean activity of the Kirishitan faith). Tokyo, Dōbunkan 同文館, 1925.

——— *Kirishitan kinsei no shūmatsu* 切支丹禁制の終末 (The end of the official proscription of Kirishitans). Tokyo, Dōbunkan, 1926.

——— *Kirishitan dendō no kōhai* 切支丹傳道の興廢 (The rise and fall of the Kirishitan mission). Tokyo, Dōbunkan, 1930.

——— *Kirishitan hakugaishichū no jinbutsu jiseki* 切支丹迫害史中の人物事蹟 (Historical traces of personages during the persecution of Kirishitans). Tokyo, Dōbunkan, 1930.

——— *Kirishitan shūkyō bungaku* 切支丹宗教文學 (Kirishitan religious literature). Tokyo, Dōbunkan, 1932.

Aoyama Gen 青山玄. "Zabieru no Kagoshima jikyo ni tsuite" ザビエルの鹿児島辞去について (On Xavier's departure from Kagoshima), *Kirishitan Bunka Kenkyūkai kaihō* キリシタン文化研究会会報 (Bulletin of the Association for the Study of Kirishitan Culture) 11.2/3:52–60 (February 1969).

——— "Zabieru taizaiki no Kagoshima" ザビエル滞在期の鹿児島 (Kagoshima at the time of Xavier's stay), *Kirishitan kenkyū* キリシタン研究 (Kirishitan studies) 13:51–89 (1970).

———, Paul, SVD. *Die Missionstätigkeit des hl. Franz Xaver in Japan aus japanischer Sicht*. Studia Instituti Missiologici Societatis Verbi Divini Nr. 10. St. Augustin/Siegburg, Steyler Verlag, 1967.

Arai Hakuseki 新井白石. *Seiyō kibun* 西洋紀聞 (Tidings of the West), ed. Miyazaki Michio 宮崎道生. Tōyō Bunko 東洋文庫 113. Tokyo, Heibonsha 平凡社, 1968.

——— *Seiyō kibun*, tr. S.R. Brown, "西洋紀聞 Sei yo ki-bun, or Annals of the Western Ocean," *Journal of the North-China Branch of the Royal Asiatic Society*, new series, 2:51–78 (December 1865) and 3:40–62 (December 1866).

Arai Hakuseki. *Seiyō kibun*, Part One, "The Capture and Captivity of Pere Giovanni Batista Sidotti in Japan from 1709 to 1715. Translated from the 西洋紀聞 of Arai Haku-seki, by the Rev. W.B. Wright," *Transactions of the Asiatic Society of Japan* 9:156–172 (1881; Yūshōdō 雄松堂 reprint, 1964).

———*Seiyō kibun*, anonymous synopsis, "Père Sidotti in Japan (A Condensed Translation from the Seiyo-kibun)," *The Chrysanthemum* 2.9:390–399 (Yokohama, September 1882).

Asakura Sōteki waki 朝倉宗滴話記 (Conversations with Asakura Sōteki), in *Zokuzoku gunsho ruijū* 續々群書類從 (Classified textual corpus; second continuation), X, 1–12. Tokyo, Kokusho Kankōkai 國書刊行會, 1907.

Asao Naohiro 朝尾直弘. "Toyotomi seiken ron" 豊臣政権論 (On the Toyotomi régime), *Iwanami kōza: Nihon rekishi* 岩波講座日本歴史 (Iwanami symposium: Japanese history), IX, 159–210. *Kinsei* 近世 1; Tokyo, Iwanami, 1963.

———"Sakokusei no seiritsu" 鎖国制の成立 (The formation of the Sakoku order), *Kōza Nihonshi* 講座日本史 (Japanese history symposium), ed. Rekishigaku Kenkyūkai 歴史学研究会/Nihonshi Kenkyūkai 日本史研究会, IV, 59–94. 3rd printing. Tokyo, Tōkyō Daigaku Shuppankai 東京大学出版会, 1971.

Avila Girón, Bernardino de. "Relación del Reino de Nippon," chap. 1–15, ed. Doroteo Schilling OFM and Fidel de Lejarza, *Archivo Ibero-Americano* 36:481–531 (1933); 37:5–48, 259–275, 392–434, 493–554 (1934); 38:103–130, 216–239, 384–417 (1935).

———*Relaçion Del Reyno del Nippon Aque LLaman Coruptamente Jappon*, annotated Japanese translation by Sakuma Tadashi 佐久間正, Aida Yū 会田由, and Iwao Seiichi 岩生成一, *Nippon Ōkoku ki* 日本王国記, in Dai Kōkai Jidai Sōsho 大航海時代叢書, XI, 15–494. Tokyo, Iwanami, 1965.

Banshū seikinroku 蠻宗制禁錄 (Record of the barbarian sect's proscription). 20 *kan* in 5 vols. MS. dated Kōka 弘化 3 (1846), Library of the Department of History, Kyoto University.

Bartoli, Daniello, SJ. *Dell'Historia della Compagnia di Giesv: Il Giappone; Seconda Parte Dell'Asia*. In Roma, M.DC.LX. Nella Stamperia d'Ignatio de'Lazzeri.

Bohner, Alfred, tr. "Tenchi Hajimari no Koto: Wie Himmel und Erde entstanden," *Monumenta Nipponica* 1.2:173–207 (July 1938); original text, 天地始りの事, pp. 208–222.

Boxer, C.R. *The Christian Century in Japan: 1549–1650*. Berkeley, University of California Press, 1951.

———*The Great Ship from Amacon: Annals of Macao and the Old Japan Trade, 1555–1640*. Lisbon, Centro de Estudos Históricos Ultramarinos, 1959.

Cardim, Antonio Francisco, SJ. *Batalhas da Companhia de Jesus na sua Gloriosa Provincia do Japão*, ed. Luciano Cordeiro. Lisbon, Imprensa Nacional/Sociedade de Geographia de Lisboa, 1894.

Carrero, Francisco, OP. *Triunfo del Santo Rosario y Orden de Santo Domingo en los reinos del Japon, desde el año del Señor 1617 hasta el de 1624*. 2nd ed. Manila, Imprenta del Colegio de Santo Tomás, 1868.

Cartas qve os Padres e Irmãos da Companhia de Iesus escreuerão dos Reynos de Iapão & China aos da mesma Companhia da India, & Europa, des do anno de 1549. atè o de 1580. Nellas se conta o principio, socesso, & bondade da Christandade daquellas partes, & varios costumes, & falses ritos da gentilidade. Impressas por mandado do Reuerendissimo em Christo Padre dom Theotonio de Bragança Arcepispo d'Euora. Impressas com licença & approuação dos SS. Inquisidores & do Ordinario. Em Euora por Manoel de Lyra. Anno de M.D.XCVIII. 2 vols. in one.

Chan, Wing-tsit, comp. and tr. *A Source Book in Chinese Philosophy*. Princeton, Princeton University Press, 1963.

Chan, Wing-tsit, tr. *The Way of Lao Tzu*. Indianapolis and New York, Bobbs-Merrill, 1963; The Library of Liberal Arts 139.

Chang, Richard T. *From Prejudice to Tolerance: A Study of the Japanese Image of the West, 1826–1864. Monumenta Nipponica* Monographs. Tokyo, Sophia University Press, 1970.

Charlevoix, Pierre F.X. de, SJ. *Histoire et Description Generale du Japon*, vol. 5. A Paris, Chez Julien-Michel Gandouin et al., M.DCC.XXXVI.

CHRISTIANI PVERI INSTITVTIO, ADOLESCENTIAEQVE perfugium: autore Ioanne Bonifacio SOCIETATIS IESV. cum libri unius, & rerũ accessione plurimarũ. Cum facultate Superiorum apud Sinas, in Portu Macaensi in Domo Societatis IESV. Anno 1588. Photocopy in the Tenri Library of the original in the Ajuda Library.

Christianity in Japan: A Bibliography of Japanese and Chinese Sources, pt. 1 (1543–1858), comp. Ebisawa Arimichi 海老沢有道. Tokyo, The Committee on Asian Cultural Studies, International Christian University, 1960. Pt. 2 (1859–1912), *A Bibliography of Christianity in Japan: Meiji Era // Nihon Kirisutokyō bunken mokuroku: Meiji-ki* 日本キリスト教文献目録―明治期, ed. The Committee on Asian Cultural Studies. Tokyo, International Christian University, 1965.

Chu Hsi 朱熹. *Chin-ssu lu* 近思録, Ssu-pu pei-yao 四部備要.

———*Chin-ssu lu*, tr. Wing-tsit Chan, *Reflections on Things at Hand*. New York, Columbia University Press, 1967.

———*Chu Tzu ta-ch'üan* 朱子大全 (Complete works of Chu Hsi), Ssu-pu pei-yao.

———*Chung-yung chang chü* 中庸章句 (Sententiae on the *Mean*) and *Ta-hsüeh chang chü* 大學章句 (Sententiae on the *Great Learning*), in Kanno Dōmei, ed., *Gaku Yō shōku.*

———*Lun-yü huo-wen* 論語或問 (Questions on the *Analects*), *Chu Tzu i-shu* 朱子遺書 (Posthumous works of Chu Hsi), vols. 3–4. Taiwan, I-wen Yin-shu-kuan 藝文印書館, n.d.

Chuang Tzu 莊子. Ssu-pu pei-yao.

Cieslik, Hubert, SJ. "Nanbanji-Romane der Tokugawa-Zeit," *Monumenta Nipponica* 6.1/2:13–51 (1943).

———"Die Goningumi im Dienste der Christenüberwachung," *Monumenta Nipponica* 7.1/2:102–155 (January 1951).

———"The Great Martyrdom in Edo 1623," *Monumenta Nipponica* 10.1/2:1–44 (April 1954); Japanese version, "Edo no dai-junkyō" 江戸の大殉教, *Kirishitan kenkyū* 4:55–112 (1957).

———"P. Pedro Kasui (1587–1639): Der letzte japanische Jesuit der Tokugawa-Zeit," *Monumenta Nipponica* 15.1/2:35–86 (1959/1960).

———"Kirishitan chigyōchi Nagasaki" キリシタン知行地長崎 (The Kirishitan fief Nagasaki), *Kirishitan Bunka Kenkyūkai kaihō* 6.3:1–11 (September 1962).

———*Kirishitan jinbutsu no kenkyū: hōjin shisai no maki* キリシタン人物の研究―邦人司祭の巻 (Studies of Kirishitan personages: native Japanese priests' book). Tokyo, Yoshikawa Kōbunkan 吉川弘文館, 1963.

———"Nihon Nijūroku Seijin junkyō kankei shiryō" 日本二十六聖人殉教関係史料 (Historical sources related to the martyrdom of the Twenty-Six Saints of Japan), *Kirishitan kenkyū* 8:111–135 (1963).

———"The Training of a Japanese Clergy in the Seventeenth Century," in *Studies in Japanese Culture*, ed. Joseph Roggendorf SJ, pp. 41–78. Tokyo, Sophia University Press, 1963. Japanese version, "Nihon ni okeru saisho no shingakkō (1601nen–1614nen)" 日本における最初の神学校（一六〇一年―一六一四年）(The first theological seminary in Japan: 1601–1614), *Kirishitan kenkyū* 10:1–55 (1965).

———"Seminariyo no kyōiku seishin ni tsuite" セミナリヨの教育精神について (On the educational spirit of the *seminarios*), *Kirishitan Bunka Kenkyūkai kaihō* 8.1:1–27 (June 1964).

———"Kirishitan jidai ni okeru shikyō mondai" キリシタン時代における司教問題

(The problem of an episcopacy in the Kirishitan period), *Kirishitan kenkyū* 9:366–468 (1964).

Cieslik, Hubert, SJ. *Geibi Kirishitan shiryō* 芸備キリシタン史料 // *Sources and documents concerning the history of Kirishitan in the provinces of Aki and Bingo.* Tokyo, Yoshikawa Kōbunkan, 1968.

——and Gustav Voss SJ, trs. *Kirishito-ki und Sayo-yoroku: Japanische Dokumente zur Missionsgeschichte des 17. Jahrhunderts. Monumenta Nipponica* Monographs 1. Tokyo, Sophia University Press, 1940.

Cocks, Richard. *Diary of Richard Cocks, Cape-Merchant in the English Factory in Japan, 1615–1622,* ed. Murakami Naojirō 村上直次郎. 2 vols. Tokyo, Sankōsha 三光社, 1899.

Cohn, Norman. *The Pursuit of the Millennium.* New York, Harper, 1961; Harper Torchbook TB 1037.

CONTEMPTVS mundi jenbu. CORE YO VO ITOI, IESV CHRIStono gocŏxeqiuo manabi tatematçuru michiuo voxiyuru qiŏ. (Contempt of the world; complete. Being a scripture that teaches the way to despise the world and imitate the merits of Jesus Christ.) NIPPON IESVSNO COMPANHIA no Collegio nite Superiores no goguegiuo motte coreuo fanni firaqu mono nari. Toqini goxuxxeno nenqi. 1596. Photocopy in the Tenri Library of the original in the Bodleian Library.

Conze, Edward. *Buddhism: Its Essence and Development.* New York, Harper, 1959; Harper Torchbook TB 58.

Cooper, Michael, SJ, ed. *The Southern Barbarians: The First Europeans in Japan.* Tokyo and Palo Alto, Kodansha International, 1971; in cooperation with Sophia University, Tokyo.

[Crasset, Jean, SJ.] *The History of the Church of Japan.* Written Originally in French by Monsieur L'Abbe de T. And Now Translated into English. By N.N. [Webb]. Volume II. London, Printed in the Year MDCCVII.

Dai Nippon shiryō 大日本史料 (Japanese historical materials), pt. 12, vol. 9, comp. Tōkyō Teikoku Daigaku Bunka Daigaku Shiryō Hensangakari 東京帝國大學文科大學史料編纂掛. Tokyo, Tōkyō Teikoku Daigaku 東京帝國大學, 1906. Pt. 12, vol. 32, comp. Tōkyō Teikoku Daigaku Bungakubu Shiryō Hensanjo 東京帝國大學文學部史料編纂所. 1935.

Daigenkai 大言海, Japanese encyclopaedic dictionary, comp. Ōtsuki Fumihiko 大槻文彦. 13th rev. ed. Tokyo, Fuzanbō 冨山房, 1961.

de la Costa, Horacio, SJ. *The Jesuits in the Philippines: 1581–1768.* Cambridge, Mass., Harvard University Press, 1961.

Delplace, Louis, SJ. *Le Catholicisme au Japon.* 2 vols. Brussels, Librairie Albert Dewit, 1909–1910.

DOCTRINA CHRISTAN. IN COLLEGIO IAPONICO SOCIETATIS IESV Cum facultate Ordinarij, & Superiorum ANNO 1600. Facsimile titled *Seikyō yōri* 聖教要理 (Essentials of Holy Doctrine). Chinsho Taikan Kirishitan Sōsho 珍書大観吉利支丹叢書. Osaka, Ōsaka Mainichi Shinbun-sha 大阪毎日新聞社, 1928.

Doi Tadao 土井忠生. *Kirishitan gogaku no kenkyū* 吉利支丹語學の研究 (On Kirishitan language studies). Osaka, Seibunsha 靖文社, 1942.

——*Kirishitan bunken kō* 吉利支丹文獻考 (Considerations of Kirishitan documents). Tokyo, Sanseidō 三省堂, 1963.

Ebisawa Arimichi 海老澤有道. *Kirishitanshi no kenkyū* 切支丹史の研究 (Studies in Kirishitan history). Tokyo, Unebi Shobō 畝傍書房, 1942.

——*Kirishitan no shakai katsudō oyobi Nanban igaku* 切支丹の社會活動及南蠻醫學 (Kirishitan social activity and Southern Barbarian medicine). Tokyo, Fuzanbō, 1944.

Ebisawa Arimichi. *Nanban gakutō no kenkyū* 南蛮学統の研究 (Studies in the lineage of the Southern Barbarian Learning). Tokyo, Sōbunsha 創文社, 1958.

――"Nihon Nijūroku Seijin kankei Nihon bunken" 日本二十六聖人関係日本文献 (Japanese documents related to the Twenty-Six Saints of Japan), *Kirishitan kenkyū* 8:137–175 (1963).

――*Nihon Kirishitan shi* 日本キリシタン史 (History of the Kirishitans of Japan). Tokyo, Hanawa Shobō 塙書房, 1966.

――"Kirishitan no denrai to sono bunka" キリシタンの伝来とその文化 (The advent of the Kirishitans and their culture), in *Nihon bunkashi gairon* 日本文化史概論 (An outline of Japanese cultural history), ed. Ishida Ichirō 石田一良, chap. 21, pp. 351–366. Tokyo, Yoshikawa Kōbunkan, 1968.

――and Matsuda Kiichi 松田毅一. *Porutogaru Evora shinshutsu byōbu monjo no kenkyū* ポルトガル・エヴォラ新出屏風文書の研究 (A study of the documents recently discovered in a folding screen at Evora in Portugal). Tokyo, Natsume-sha ナツメ社, 1963.

Elliott, John H. *Imperial Spain: 1469–1716.* Harmondsworth, Middlesex, Penguin Books, 1970.

Endō Shūsaku 遠藤周作 and Miura Shumon 三浦朱門. *Kirishitan jidai no chishikijin* キリシタン時代の知識人 (Intellectuals of the Kirishitan period). Nikkei Shinsho 日経新書 59. Tokyo, Nihon Keizai Shinbun-sha 日本経済新聞社. 1967.

FIDES NO DŌXI to xite P.F. Luis de Granada amaretaru xo no riacu. (Epitome of a book composed by P.F. Luis de Granada as a Guide to the Faith.) Core uo Companhia no Superiores no go saicacu vomotte Nippon no cotoba ni vasu. IESVS NO COMPANHIA NO Collegio Amacusa ni voite Superiores no go menqio toxite core uo fan ni qizamu mono nari. Go xuxxe yori M.D.L. XXXXII. Photocopy in the Tenri Library of the original in the Library of the University of Leiden.

Frois, Luis, SJ. *Relatione della gloriosa morte di xxvi. posti in croce Per comandamento del Re di Giappone, alli 5. di Febraio 1597. de quali sei furno Religiosi di S. Francesco, tre della Compagnia di Giesù, & dicesette Christiani Giapponesi.* Mandata dal P. Luigi Frois alli 15. di Marzo al R.P. Clavdio Acqvaviva Generale di detta Compagnia. Et fatta in Italiano dal P. Gasparo Spitilli di Campli della medesima Compagnia. In Roma, Appresso Luigi Zannetti 1599.

――*Die Geschichte Japans (1549–1578)*, tr. G. Schurhammer and E.A. Voretzsch. Leipzig, Asia Major, 1926.

――*Segunda Parte da Historia de Japam que trata das couzas, que socedarão nesta V. Provincia da Hera de 1578 por diante, começãdo pela Conversão del Rey de Bungo, (1578–1582)*, ed. João do Amaral Abranches Pinto and Okamoto Yoshitomo 岡本良知. Tokyo, Edição da Sociedade Luso-Japonesa (Nippo Kyōkai 日葡協會), 1938.

――*Tratado Em q̃ se contem M^{to} susinta e abreuiadamente algũas contradisões & diferencas de custumes Antre agente de Europa e esta prouincia de Japão . . . f^{to} Em canzusa aos* 14 de Junho de 1585 Annos――. Critical edition and German translation by Josef Franz Schütte SJ, *Kulturgengensätze Europa–Japan (1585). Monumenta Nipponica* Monographs 15. Tokyo, Sophia University Press, 1955.

――*Tratado Em q̃ se contem*, annotated Japanese translation by Okada Akio 岡田章雄, *Nichiō bunka hikaku* 日欧文化比較, in Dai Kōkai Jidai Sōsho, XI, 495–636. Tokyo, Iwanami, 1965.

Fucan Fabian (Fukansai Habian 不干齋巴鼻庵). *NIFON NO COTOBA TO Historia uo narai xiran to FOSSVRV FITO NO TAMENI XEVA NI YAVA RAGVE-TARV FEIQE NO MONOGATARI.* (Heike no monogatari, simplified into the popular tongue for the sake of those desirous of learning the language and history of Japan.) IESVS NO COMPANHIA NO Collegio Amacusa ni voite Superiores no go menqio to xite core uo fan ni qizamu mono nari. Go xuxxe yori

M.D.L.XXXXII. Facsimile published by Kamei Takanori 亀井高孝, *Kirishitan-ban Amakusa-bon Heike monogatari* キリシタン版天草本平家物語 (Heike monogatari, the Amakusa Kirishitan press variant). Tokyo, Yoshikawa Kōbunkan, 1969.

Fucan Fabian. *FEIQE NO MONOGATARI*, facsimile and *katakana* collation by Shima Shōzō 島正三, *"Amakusa-bon Heike monogatari" ken'an* 「天草本ヘイケモノガタリ」検案 (An examination of the "Heike monogatari, Amakusa variant"). 2 vols. Tokyo, Ōfūsha 桜楓社, 1967.

———*FEIQE NO MONOGATARI*, Japanese transcription by Kamei Takanori and Sakada Yukiko 阪田雪子, *Habiyan-shō Kirishitan-ban Heike monogatari* ハビヤン抄キリシタン版平家物語 (Heike monogatari, the Kirishitan press variant compiled by Fabian). Rev. ed. Tokyo, Yoshikawa Kōbunkan, 1966.

———*Myōtei mondō* 妙貞問答 (Myōtei Dialogue), tr. Pierre Humbertclaude SM, "Myôtei Mondô: Une apologétique chrétienne japonaise de 1605," *Monumenta Nipponica* 1.2:223–256 (July 1938), and 2.1:237–267 (January 1939).

———*Ha Daiusu* 破提宇子 (Deus Destroyed). Tenri Library and Kyoto University Library copies of the early Edo period woodblock imprint; n.d.

———*Ha Daiusu*, facsimile of the Kyoto University exemplar, Chinsho Taikan Kirishitan Sōsho. Osaka, Ōsaka Mainichi Shinbun-sha, 1928.

———*Ha Daiusu*, ed. Kiyū Dōnin 杞憂道人, 1868 ([Keiō 慶應 4] *tsuchinoe tatsu chūshun* 戊辰仲春) version, Tenri Library and Kyoto University Library copies.

———*Ha Daiusu*, ed. Kiyū Dōnin, 1869 ([Meiji 2] *tsuchinoto mi banka* 己巳晩夏) version in the Tenri Library; contains a postscript signed Manjidō Itsunin 卍堂逸人.

———*Ha Daiusu*, tr. Esther Lowell Hibbard, "Refutation of Deus by Fabian," *Contemporary Religions in Japan*, vol. 3 (1962).

Fujino Tamotsu 藤野保. *Bakuhan taiseishi no kenkyū* 幕藩体制史の研究 (Studies in the history of the *bakuhan* system). Tokyo, Yoshikawa Kōbunkan, 1961.

Fujita Kankai 藤田寛海. "Habian to Hakuō: Kirishitan zokusho shikō" ハビアンと伯翁—キリシタン俗書私攷 (Fabian and Hakuō: some personal reflections on the Kirishitan chapbook), *Kokugo to kokubungaku* 国語と国文学 (Japanese language and literature) 30.8:32–41 (August 1953).

Fujita Tōko 藤田東湖. *Shintei Tōko zenshū* 新定東湖全集 (Complete works of Tōko, newly determined), ed. Kikuchi Kenjirō 菊池謙二郎. Tokyo, Hakubunkan 博文館, 1940.

Fujiwara Seika shū 藤原惺窩集 (Collected works of Fujiwara Seika). 2 vols. Tokyo, Kokumin Seishin Bunka Kenkyūjo 國民精神文化研究所, 1938–1939.

Fukaya Katsumi 深谷克己. "Shūkyō to teikō" 宗教と抵抗 (Religion and resistance), *Rekishi hyōron* 歴史評論 (Historical review) 185:40–49 (January 1966).

———"'Shimabara no ran' no rekishiteki igi" 「島原の乱」の歴史的意義 (The historical significance of the "Shimabara Rebellion"), *Rekishi hyōron* 201:20–42 (May 1967).

———"Junkyō no ronri to hōki no ronri" 殉教の論理と蜂起の論理 (The logic of martyrdom and the logic of rebellion), *Shisō* 思想 (Thought) 565:40–55 (July 1971).

Furuno Kiyoto 古野清人. *Kakure Kirishitan* 隠れキリシタン (The crypto-Kirishitans). Nihon Rekishi Shinsho 日本歴史新書. Tokyo, Shibundō 至文堂, 1959.

Furuta Shōkin 古田紹欽. *Kinsei no Zenshatachi* 近世の禅者たち (Zen-men of the Early Modern period). Kyoto, Heirakuji Shoten 平楽寺書店, 1956.

Giya do pekadoru jōkan ぎや・ど・ぺかどる上巻 (GVIA DO PECADOR, I). Nihon Koten Zenshū 日本古典全集, 2nd ser. Tokyo, Nihon Koten Zenshū Kankōkai 刊行會, 1927.

Giya do pekadoru gekan, Myōtei mondō, Ha Daiusu, Kengiroku ぎや・ど・ぺかどる下巻, 妙貞問答, 破提宇子, 顯偽録 (GVIA DO PECADOR, II; Myōtei Dialogue; Deus Destroyed; Deceit Disclosed). Nihon Koten Zenshū, 2nd ser. 1927.

Guerreiro, Fernão, SJ. *Relaçam annal das covsas qve fizeram os Padres da Companhia de IESVS, nas partes da India Oriental, & em algũas outras da conquista deste Reyno nos annos de 607. & 608. & do processo da conuersaõ & Christandade daquellas partes, com mais hũa addiçam á relaçam de Ethiopia.* Em Lisboa: Impresso por Pedro Crasbeeck. Anno M.DCXI.

Hagakure 葉隠 (In the shadow of a leaf). Account of Yamamoto Tsunetomo 山本常朝 recorded by Tashiro Tsuramoto 田代陣基, ed. Watsuji Tetsurō 和辻哲郎 and Furukawa Tesshi 古川哲史. 3 vols. Iwanami Bunko 2305–10. 11th printing. Tokyo, Iwanami, 1970.

Hakusui Kōji 白水甲二 (pseud. for Endō Tsunehisa 遠藤常久). *Kirishitan daimyō Ōtomo Sōrin* きりしたん大名大友宗麟. Tokyo, Shunjūsha 春秋社, 1970.

Hall, John Whitney. "Foundations of the Modern Japanese Daimyo," *The Journal of Asian Studies* 20.3: 317–329 (May 1961).

—— *Government and Local Power in Japan: 500 to 1700.* Princeton, Princeton University Press, 1966.

——and Marius B. Jansen, eds. *Studies in the Institutional History of Early Modern Japan.* Princeton, Princeton University Press, 1968.

Han Fei Tzu 韓非子. *Ssu-pu ts'ung-k'an* 四部叢刊.

Harada Toshiaki 原田敏明, ed. *Kumamoto-ken no rekishi* 熊本県の歴史 (History of Kumamoto Prefecture). Tokyo, Bungadō 文画堂, 1957.

Hashimoto Shinkichi 橋本進吉. *Bunroku gannen Amakusa-ban Kirishitan kyōgi no kenkyū* 文祿元年天草版吉利支丹教義の研究 (Studies in the Amakusa press Kirishitan Doctrine of 1592). Tōyō Bunko Ronsō 東洋文庫論叢 9. Tokyo, Tōyō Bunko 東洋文庫, 1928.

Hayashi Razan 林羅山. *Razan sensei bunshū* 羅山先生文集 (Collected essays of Hayashi Razan), ed. Kyōto Shisekikai 京都史蹟會. 2 vols. Kyoto, Heian Kōkogakkai 平安考古學會, 1918.

—— *Sōzoku zenki* 草賊前記 (The grass-roots bandits, first account), in *Jijitsu bunpen* 事實文編 (Compilation of factual accounts), ed. Gokyū Toyotarō 五弓豊太郎 and Gokyū Tomotarō 五弓友太郎, IV, 501–504. Tokyo, Kokusho Kankōkai, 1911.

—— "Hai-Yaso 排耶蘇—Anti-Jesus," German translation by Hans Müller SJ, *Monumenta Nipponica* 2.1: 268–275 (January 1939).

Hayashi Tetsuyoshi 林鉄吉, comp. *Shimabara Hantō shi* 島原半嶋史 (History of the Shimabara Peninsula), vols. 1–2. Shimabara, Nagasaki-ken Minami Takaki Gunshi Kyōikukai 長崎県南高来郡市教育会, 1954.

Hirai Naoko 平井直子. "Arai Hakuseki no Kirisuto-kyō kan" 新井白石のキリスト教観 (Arai Hakuseki's view of Christianity), *Kirishitan Bunka Kenkyūkai kaihō* 8.3/4: 32–50 (March 1966).

Historische Relation Was sich inn etlichen Jaren hero im Königreich Iapon, so wol im geistals auch weltlichem Wesen namhafftes begeben vnd zugetragen. . . . Durch Aegidivm Albertinvm . . . auß vnderschidlichen der Societet Iesu Jtalianischen vñ Frantzösischen Jahrschreiben vnd anderer Herrn Missiuen menigklich zu gutem in vnser hochteutsche Sprach vbersetzt. Getruckt zu München Durch Nicolaum Henricum im Jahr M.DC.IX.

Hiyane Antei 比屋根安定, ed. *Kirishitan monogatari hoka sanshu* 吉利支丹物語他三種 (Kirishitan monogatari; and three others). Kirishitan Bunko 吉利支丹文庫, vol. 1. Tokyo, Keiseisha 警醒社, 1926.

——, ed. *Nanbanji kōhaiki hoka nihen* 南蠻寺興廢記他二篇 (The rise and fall of the Temple of Southern Barbarians; and two others). Kirishitan Bunko, vol. 2. 1926.

——, ed. *Shimabara-Amakusa nikki hoka shihen* 嶋原・天草日記他四篇 (Shimabara-Amakusa diary; and four others). Kirishitan Bunko, vol. 3. 1927.

——, ed. *Hara-jō kiji* 原城紀事 (The record of Hara Castle). Kirishitan Bunko, vols. 4–5. 1927–1928.

Hondo Shiritsu Amakusa Kirishitan-kan shiryō mokuroku 本渡市立天草切支丹館資料目録 (Catalogue of materials in the Hondo Municipal Amakusa Kirishitan-kan). Hondo, Amakusa Kirishitan-kan Shinkōkai 天草切支丹館振興会, September 1969.

Hori Isao 堀勇雄. *Hayashi Razan* 林羅山. Jinbutsu Sōsho 人物叢書 118. Tokyo, Yoshikawa Kōbunkan, 1964.

Houghton Library MS. Jap 3. Seven unrecorded contemporary English translations of Jesuit letters from Japan; from the Japanese Collection of E.G. Stillman; with a transcript (MS. Jap 3.1) made by Frederica Oldach, 1948–1949.

Huizinga, Johan. *The Waning of the Middle Ages.* Garden City, N.Y., Doubleday, 1954; Anchor Book A 42.

Humbertclaude, Pierre, SM. "Notes complémentaires sur la biographie de l'ex-Frère Jésuite Fabien Fucan," *Monumenta Nipponica* 4.2:291–295 (July 1941).

Ibuki no yomogi: Kirishitan shūmon no yurai 伊吹蓬切支丹宗門之由来 (The mugwort of Ibuki: the origins of the Kirishitan faith). MS. in the Kyoto University Library; n.d.

Ide Katsumi 井手勝美. "Haikyōsha Fukansai Fuabian bannen no ichi shiryō" 背教者不干斎フアビアン晩年の一史料 (A historical source on the last years of the apostate Fukansai Fabian), *Kirishitan Bunka Kenkyūkai kaihō* 9.3:26–31 (October 1966).

Ienaga Saburō 家永三郎. "Waga kuni ni okeru Bukki ryōkyō ronsō no tetsugakushiteki kōsatsu" 我が國に於ける佛基兩教論爭の哲學史的考察 (The debate in our country between the two religions Buddhism and Christianity, and its import in the history of philosophy: an inquiry), *Chūsei Bukkyō shisōshi kenkyū* 中世佛教思想史研究 (Studies in the history of mediaeval Buddhist thought), pp. 111–180. 4th ed. Kyoto, Hōzōkan 法藏館, 1963.

Ihara Toshirō 伊原敏郎. *Kinsei Nihon engeki shi* 近世日本演劇史 (History of the Japanese theatre [in the late Edo period]). Tokyo, Waseda Daigaku Shuppanbu 早稲田大學出版部, 1913.

Ikkyū Sōjun 一休宗純. *Ikkyū oshō zenshū* 一休和尚全集 (Complete works of Ikkyū), comp. Mori Taikyō 森大狂. Tokyo, Kōyūkan 光融館, 1898.

Imai Rintarō 今井林太郎. *Ishida Mitsunari* 石田三成. Jinbutsu Sōsho 74. Tokyo, Yoshikawa Kōbunkan, 1961.

Inoue Akira 井上章, ed. *Amakusa-ban Isopo monogatari* 天草版伊曽保物語 (The Amakusa press Tales of Aesop). Tokyo, Kazama Shobō 風間書房, 1964.

——— *Amakusa-ban Isopo monogatari no kenkyū* 天草版伊曽保物語の研究 (Studies of the Amakusa press Tales of Aesop). Tokyo, Kazama Shobō, 1968.

Inoue Mitsusada 井上光貞. *Nihon kokka no kigen* 日本国家の起源 (The origins of the Japanese nation). Iwanami Shinsho 岩波新書 380. Tokyo, Iwanami, 1960.

——— *Introduction to Japanese History—Before the Meiji Restoration.* Series on Japanese Life and Culture, vol. 3. Tokyo, Kokusai Bunka Shinkokai, 1962.

Inoue Toshio 井上鋭夫. "Shūkyō ikki" 宗教一揆 (Religious *ikki*), *Iwanami kōza: Nihon rekishi*, VIII, 157–188. *Chūsei* 中世 4; Tokyo, Iwanami, 1963.

——— *Ikkō ikki no kenkyū* 一向一揆の研究 (Studies of *Ikkō ikki*). Tokyo, Yoshikawa Kōbunkan, 1968.

——— and Kasahara Kazuo 笠原一男. "Jōdo Shinshū" 浄土真宗 (The True Pure Land Sect), in *Taikei Nihonshi sōsho* 体係日本史叢書 (A topical library of Japanese history), vol. 18: *Shūkyōshi* 宗教史 (History of religion), ed. Kawasaki Yasuyuki 川崎庸之 and Kasahara Kazuo, pp. 158–182. Tokyo, Yamakawa Shuppansha 山川出版社, 1964.

Intoku Taiheiki 陰德太平記, also known as *Intoku-ki* 陰德記 (Tales of hidden virtue), comp. Kagawa Masanori 香川正矩 and Kagawa Kagetsugu 香川景繼 (Gyōshin Senna 堯眞宣阿), *Tsūzoku Nihon zenshi* 通俗日本全史 (Popular histories of Japan), vols. 13–14. Tokyo, Waseda Daigaku Shuppanbu, 1913.

Ishige Tadashi 石毛忠. "Sengoku/Azuchi-Momoyama jidai no rinri shisō: Tentō shisō no tenkai" 戦国・安土桃山時代の倫理思想—天道思想の展開 (Ethics in the Sengoku/Azuchi-Momoyama periods: the development of the notion of *Tentō*), in *Nihon ni okeru rinri shisō no tenkai* 日本における倫理思想の展開 (The development of ethics in Japan), ed. Nihon Shisōshi Kenkyūkai 日本思想史研究会, pp. 141–168. Tokyo, Yoshikawa Kōbunkan, 1965.

Ishii Ryōsuke 石井良助. *Zoku Edo jidai manpitsu: Edo no yūjo sono ta* 続江戸時代漫筆—江戸の遊女その他 (Further jottings on the Edo period: Edo whores and other such). Tokyo, Inoue Shobō 井上書房, 1961.

Isopo monogatari 伊曾保物語 (Tales of Aesop). 3 *kan* in 1 vol. Printed by Itō San'emon 伊藤三右衛門, Manji 萬治 2 (1659); Kyoto University Library.

Isopo monogatari. 3 *kan*. Facsimile published for the Kisho Fukuseikai 稀書複製會, 4th ser., nos. 6–8. Tokyo, Yoneyama-dō 米山堂, 1925.

Itō Shuntarō 伊東俊太郎. "Kirishitan jidai ni okeru Nihon no kagaku chishiki no haikei" キリシタン時代における日本の科学知識の背景 (The background of Japanese scientific knowledge in the Kirishitan period), supp. n. 1 to Rodriguez, *Nihon kyōkai shi*, II, 671–676.

Iwao Seiichi 岩生成一. "Nagasaki Daikan Murayama Tōan no Taiwan ensei to kenminshi" 長崎代官村山等安の臺灣遠征と遣明使 (The Taiwan expedition and Ming embassy of the *Nagasaki Daikan* Murayama Tōan), *Taihoku Teikoku Daigaku shigakka kenkyū nenpō* 臺北帝國大學史學科研究年報 (Annual Bulletin of the Department of History, Taihoku Imperial University) 1:283–359 (1934).

———"Sakoku" 鎖国 (The Closed Country), *Iwanami kōza: Nihon rekishi*, X, 57–100. *Kinsei* 2; Tokyo, Iwanami, 1963.

———*Sakoku*, vol. 14 of *Nihon no rekishi* 日本の歴史 (A history of Japan). Tokyo, Chūō Kōron-sha, 1966.

Japan: The Official Guide, ed. Tourist Industry Bureau, Ministry of Transportation. Rev. enlarged ed. Tokyo, Japan Travel Bureau, 1959.

Kaihyō sōsho 海表叢書 (An overseas library), ed. Shinmura Izuru 新村出, vol. 1. Kyoto, Kōseikaku Shoten 更生閣書店, 1927.

Kanno Dōmei 簡野道明, ed. *Gaku Yō shōku* 學庸章句 (Sententiae on the *Learning* and the *Mean*). Tokyo, Meiji Shoin 明治書院, 1927.

Kanzaki Issaku 神崎一作, comp. *Haja sōsho* 破邪叢書 (Library of works countering perniciousness). 2 vols. Tokyo, Tetsugaku Shoin 哲學書院, 1893.

Kashiwabara Yūsen 柏原祐泉, Yamamoto Takeo 山本武夫, and Yanai Kenji 箭內健次. "Bakuhan taisei no seiritsu to shūkyō no tachiba" 幕藩体制の成立と宗教の立場 (The formation of the *bakuhan* system and the position of religion), in *Taikei Nihonshi sōsho*, vol. 18: *Shūkyōshi*, pp. 281–326. Tokyo, Yamakawa Shuppansha, 1964.

Kataoka Chizuko 片岡千鶴子. "Ōtomo Sōrin no kon'in mondai" 大友宗麟の婚姻問題 (Ōtomo Sōrin's marital problems), *Kirishitan Bunka Kenkyūkai kaihō* 11.1:19–35 (December 1968).

Kataoka Yakichi 片岡彌吉. *Takayama Ukon Daibu Nagafusa den* 高山右近大夫長房傳 (Biography of Takayama Ukon). Tokyo, Katorikku Chūō Shoin カトリック中央書院, 1936.

———"Takayama Ukon," *Monumenta Nipponica* 1.2:159–172 (July 1938).

———*Nagasaki no junkyōsha* 長崎の殉教者 (The martyrs of Nagasaki). Kadokawa Shinsho 角川新書 113. Tokyo: Kadokawa 角川, 1957.

———"Saigo no michi" 最後の道 (The final journey), *Kirishitan kenkyū* 8:87–105 (1963).

Kawasoe Hiroshi 川副博. *Ryūzōji Takanobu* 龍造寺隆信. Nihon no Bushō 日本の武将 45. Tokyo, Jinbutsu Ōrai-sha 人物往来社, 1967.

Kenkon bensetsu 乾坤辨説 (Debate on astronomy), commentary by Mukai Genshō 向井玄松 upon information compiled by Sawano Chūan 澤野忠菴 (Christovão Ferreira). 7 *kan* in 3 vols. MS. in the Kyoto University Library.

Kenkon bensetsu, in *Bunmei genryū sōsho* 文明源流叢書 (Wellsprings of civilization library), II, 1–100. Tokyo, Kokusho Kankōkai, 1914.

Kinka keiranshō 金花傾嵐抄 (Golden flowers and violent storms). 30 *kan* in 15 vols. MS. in the Kyoto University Library; n.d.

Kirishitan bungakushū 吉利支丹文學集 (Collection of Kirishitan literature), ed. Shinmura Izuru and Hiragi Gen'ichi 柊源一. 2 vols. Nihon Koten Zensho 日本古典全書. Tokyo, Asahi Shinbun-sha 朝日新聞社, 1957–1960.

Kirishitan denrai hiroku 切支丹傳来秘録 (A confidential record of the Kirishitans' introduction [into Japan]). Chapbook MS. in the Dōshisha University Library; n.d.

Kirishitan denraiki 切支丹傳来記 (Account of the Kirishitans' introduction [into Japan]). Chapbook MS. in the Tenri Library; n.d.

Kirishitan hakyaku ronden 鬼利至端破却論傳 (Christians crushed; tracts and glosses), comp. Hyōsuishi 瓢水子 (Asai Ryōi 淺井了意), at the shop of Yamada Ichirōbei 山田市郎兵衞. Seventeenth-century work in 3 *kan*, Kyoto University Library.

Kirishitan hakyaku ronden, facsimile published for the Kisho Fukuseikai, 6th ser., nos. 10, 12, and 14. Tokyo, Yoneyama-dō, 1929.

Kirishitan jitsuroku 吉利支丹実録 (The facts about the Kirishitans). Chapbook MS. dated Bunka 文化 9 (1812), Tenri Library.

Kirishitan kenkyū キリシタン研究 (Kirishitan studies). Published since 1942 by the Kirishitan Bunka Kenkyūkai キリシタン文化研究會. Tokyo, Yoshikawa Kōbunkan since 1959.

Kirishitan monogatari 吉利支丹物語. Tenri Library copy of the early Edo period woodblock imprint; text dated Kan'ei 寛永 16 (1639).

Kirishitan raichōki 切支丹来朝記 (Account of the Kirishitans' advent to Our Empire). MS. dated Hōreki 寶暦 11 (1761), Kyoto University Library.

Kirishitan sho, Hai-Ya sho キリシタン書排耶書 (Kirishitan and Anti-Christian texts), ed. Ebisawa Arimichi, H. Cieslik, Doi Tadao, and Ōtsuka Mitsunobu 大塚光信. Nihon Shisō Taikei 日本思想大系 25. Tokyo, Iwanami, 1970.

Kirishitan shūmon no koto 切支丹宗門之事 (On the Kirishitan religion). Chapbook MS. in the Tenri Library; n.d.

Kirishitan shūmon raichō jikki 切支丹宗門来朝実記 (A true account of the Kirishitan religion's advent to Our Empire). Chapbook MS. dated Tenpō 天保 4 (1833), Kyōto Furitsu Sōgō Shiryōkan 京都府立総合資料館.

Kirishitan shūmon raichōki 切支丹宗門来朝記 (An account of the Kirishitan religion's advent to Our Empire), interior title *Kirishitan shūmon raichō jikki*. Chapbook included in *Kaigai ibun* 海外異聞 (Strange tales from overseas), MS. collection in the Kyoto University Library; n.d.

Kirishitan shūmon raichōki. MS. in the Tenri Library; n.d.

Kirishitan shūmonki 切支丹宗門記 (Account of the Kirishitan religion), interior title *Yaso shūmon raichō kongenki* 耶蘇宗門来朝根元記 (Account of the origins of the Jesuit religion's advent to Our Empire). 3 vols. MS. in the Kyoto University Library; n.d.

Kirishitan taiji monogatari 切支丹退治物語 (Tale of the quelling of Kirishitans), Kyoto University Library. The volume bears no colophon which would indicate the date of publication; but the library notes that the work was published in the eighth month of Kanbun 寛文 5 (September 1665) at the shop of Nakano Tarōzaemon 中野太郎左衞門 in Kyoto.

Kirishitan taiji monogatari, facsimile of the 1665 original, published in 3 *kan* for the Kisho Fukuseikai, 6th ser., nos. 1–2 and no. 9. Tokyo, Yoneyama-dō, 1928 and 1929.

Kirishitan yurai jikki 切支丹由来実記 (A true account of the origins of the Kirishitans). Chapbook MS. dated Kaei 嘉永 7 (1854), Dōshisha University Library.

Kitajima Masamoto 北島正元. *Edo jidai* 江戸時代 (The Edo period). Iwanami Shinsho 332. Tokyo, Iwanami, 1958.

——*Edo Bakufu no kenryoku kōzō* 江戸幕府の権力構造 (The power structure of the Edo Bakufu). 2nd printing. Tokyo, Iwanami, 1966.

Kiyū Dōnin 杞憂道人 (Ugai Tetsujō 鵜飼徹定), comp. *Byakuja kankenroku* 闢邪管見録 (Perniciousness laid open: a record of my humble researches). 2 *kan*. [Edo], Enzan 縁山, Bunkyū 文久 1 (1861), Kyōto Furitsu Sōgō Shiryōkan copy.

——*Shō-Ya ron* 笑耶論 (Jesus ridiculed). Preface and text dated Meiji 2 (1869), Tenri Library copy.

Kleiser, Alfons, SJ. "P. Alexander Valignanis Gesandschaftsreise nach Japan zum Quambacudono Toyotomi Hideyoshi 1588–1591," *Monumenta Nipponica* 1.1:70–98 (January 1938).

Kokusho sōmokuroku 國書總目録 (General catalogue of Japanese texts). 8 vols. Tokyo, Iwanami, 1963–1972.

Kuan Tzu 管子. Ssu-pu ts'ung-k'an.

Küenburg, Max v., SJ. "Kirishitan Yashiki, das ehemalige Christengefängnis in Koishikawa," *Monumenta Nipponica* 1.2:300–304 (July 1938).

Kumamoto-ken shi 熊本県史 (History of Kumamoto Prefecture), compiled and published by the Kumamoto Prefectural Government (Kumamoto, 1965), *Sōsetsu-hen* 総説編 (General outline) and supp. vol. 1, chronology.

Kumazawa Banzan 熊澤蕃山. *Banzan zenshū* 蕃山全集 (Complete works of Kumazawa Banzan), ed. Masamune Atsuo 正宗敦夫. 6 vols. Tokyo, Banzan Zenshū Kankōkai, 1941–1943.

Kuwata Tadachika 桑田忠親. *Oda Nobunaga* 織田信長. Kadokawa Shinsho 192. Tokyo, Kadokawa, 1964.

——*Toyotomi Hideyoshi* 豊臣秀吉. Kadokawa Shinsho 198. Tokyo, Kadokawa, 1965.

Laures, Johannes, SJ. *Nobunaga und das Christentum. Monumenta Nipponica* Monographs 10. Tokyo, Sophia University Press, 1950.

——*Die Anfänge der Mission von Miyako.* Mission Studies and Documents 16. Münster i. Westf., Aschendorffsche Verlagsbuchhandlung, 1951.

——"Die Zahl der Christen und Martyrer im alten Japan," *Monumenta Nipponica* 7.1/2:84–101 (January 1951).

——*Takayama Ukon und die Anfänge der Kirche in Japan.* Mission Studies and Documents 18. Münster i. Westf., Aschendorffsche Verlagsbuchhandlung, 1954.

——, comp. *Kirishitan Bunko: A Manual of Books and Documents on the Early Christian Mission in Japan. Monumenta Nipponica* Monographs 5. 3rd ed. Tokyo, Sophia University Press, 1957.

Legge, James, tr. *The Chinese Classics.* 5 vols. Hong Kong, Hong Kong University Press, 1960 reissue.

Lettera annva del Giappone del M.DCXIV. Al molto Reuer. Padre Generale Della Compagnia di GIESV. Scritta dal Padre Gabriel de Mattos della medesima Compagnia di GIESV. In Roma, Appresso Bartolomeo Zannetti. M.DCXVII.

Lettera dei P. Alessandro Valignano, Visitatore della Compagnia di Giesù nel Giappone, e nella Cina, del 1599. Con un supplimento del P. Valentino Caruaglio della medesima Compagnia dell'Anno 1601. In Venetia, M.DCIII. Appresso Gio. Battista Ciotti, All'insegna della Aurora.

Li chi 禮記, Ssu-pu ts'ung-k'an.

Lifton, Robert Jay. *Thought Reform and the Psychology of Totalism.* New York, Norton, 1963; Norton Library N 221.

Litterae Iaponicae anni M.DC.VI. Chinenses anni M.DC.VI. & M.DC.VII. Illae à R.P.

Ioanne Rodrigvez [Girão], hae à R.P. Matthaeo Ricci . . . Latinè redditae à Rhetoribus Collegij Soc. IESV Antuerpię. Antverpiae, Ex Officina Plantiniana, Apud Viduam & Filios Io. Moreti, M.DC.XI.

López Gay, Jesús, SJ. *El Catecumenado en la Mision del Japon del S. XVI.* Studia Missionalia, Documenta et Opera 2. Rome, Libreria Dell'Università Gregoriana, 1966.

Lü-shih ch'un-ch'iu 呂氏春秋, Ssu-pu ts'ung-k'an.

Maeda Kingorō 前田金五郎 and Morita Takeshi 森田武, eds. *Kana zōshi shū* 假名草子集 (Collection of *kana* chapbooks). Nihon Koten Bungaku Taikei 日本古典文學大系 90. Tokyo, Iwanami, 1965.

Maruyama Masao 丸山眞男. *Nihon seiji shisōshi kenkyū* 日本政治思想史研究 (Studies in the history of Japanese political thought). 9th printing. Tokyo, Tōkyō Daigaku Shuppankai, 1962.

Matsuda Kiichi 松田毅一. *Kirishitan kenkyū daiichibu: Shikoku-hen* キリシタン研究第一部四国篇 (Kirishitan studies, Part one: Shikoku collection). Osaka, Sōgensha 創元社, 1953.

―――*Nippo kōshōshi* 日葡交渉史 (History of Luso-Japanese intercourse). Shinwa Bunko 親和文庫 6. Tokyo, Kyōbunkan 教文館, 1963.

―――"Nihon Nijūroku Seijin no jinmei ni tsuite" 日本二十六聖人の人名について (On the names of the Twenty-Six Saints of Japan), *Kirishitan kenkyū* 8: 3–39 (1963).

―――*Taikō to gaikō* 太閤と外交 (Hideyoshi's foreign affairs). Tokyo, Tōgensha 桃源社, 1966.

―――*Kinsei shoki Nihon kankei Nanban shiryō no kenkyū* 近世初期日本関係南蛮史料の研究 (Studies in Southern Barbarian historical sources relating to Japan at the beginning of the Early Modern period). Tokyo, Kazama Shobō, 1967.

―――*Nanban junrei* 南蛮巡礼 (A Southern Barbarian pilgrimage). Tokyo, Asahi Shinbun-sha, 1967.

Mitogaku taikei 水戸學大系 (A compendium of the Mito Learning), ed. Takasu Yoshijirō 高須芳次郎, vol. 5. 2nd printing. Tokyo, Mitogaku Taikei Kankōkai, 1942.

Miyasaka Yūshō 宮坂宥勝, ed. *Kana hōgo shū* 假名法語集 (Collection of Buddhist *kana* homilies). Nihon Koten Bungaku Taikei 83. Tokyo, Iwanami, 1964.

Miyazaki Michio 宮崎道生. "Arai Hakuseki no Kirishitan-kan" 新井白石のキリシタン観 (Arai Hakuseki's view of Christianity), *Nihon rekishi* 日本歴史 (Japanese history) 92:14–28 (February 1956) and 93:28–32 (March 1956).

―――*Arai Hakuseki no kenkyū* 新井白石の研究 (Studies of Arai Hakuseki). Rev. ed. Tokyo, Yoshikawa Kōbunkan, 1969.

Montanus, Arnoldus. *Atlas Japannensis: Being Remarkable Addresses by way of Embassy from the East-India Company of the United Provinces to the Emperor of Japan,* English'd, and Adorn'd with above a hundred several Sculptures, By John Ogilby Esq; Master of His Majesties Revels in the Kingdom of Ireland. London, Printed by Tho. Johnson, M.DC.LXX.

Monumenta Nipponica. Tokyo, Sophia University, 1938–.

Morejón, Pedro, SJ. *Historia y relacion de lo svcedido en los reinos de Iapon y China, en la qual se continua la gran persecucion que ha auido en aꝗlla Iglesia, desde el año de 615. hasta el de 19.* Año 1621. Con licēcia en Lisboa por Iuan Rodriguez.

Motoyama Yukihiko 本山幸彦. "Meiji Ishin to sonnō jōi shisō" 明治維新と尊王攘夷思想 (The Meiji Restoration and *sonnō jōi* thought), *Meiji shisō no keisei* 明治思想の形成 (The forms of Meiji thought), pp. 1–67. Tokyo, Fukumura Shuppan 福村出版, 1969.

Mumon Ekai (Wu-men Hui-k'ai) 無門慧開. *Mumonkan (Wu-men kuan)* 無門關 (The gateless frontier pass), ed. Furuta Shōkin. Kadokawa Bunko 角川文庫 1383. 8th printing. Tokyo, Kadokawa, 1965.

Murakami Naojirō 村上直次郎, tr. *Deshima Rankan nisshi* 出島蘭館日誌 (Daghregister des Comptoirs Nangasacque). 3 vols. Tokyo, Bunmei Kyōkai 文明協會, 1938–1939.

———, tr. *Nagasaki Oranda shōkan no nikki* 長崎オランダ商館の日記 (Dagregister des Comptoirs Nangasaqui). 3 vols. Tokyo, Iwanami, 1956–1958.

Murakami Tadashi 村上直. "Ieyasu to Ōkubo Chōan" 家康と大久保長安 (Ieyasu and Ōkubo Chōan), in *Nihon jinbutsushi taikei* 日本人物史大系 (Compendium of personages in Japanese history), III, 126–157. 3rd printing. Tokyo, Asakura Shoten 朝倉書店, 1963.

——— "Ōkubo Tadachika" 大久保忠隣, in *Daimyō retsuden* 大名列伝 (Daimyo biographies), III, 17–73, *Higeki-hen* 悲劇篇 (Tragic cases), ed. Kodama Kōta 児玉幸多 and Kimura Motoi 木村礎. Tokyo, Jinbutsu Ōrai-sha, 1967.

Musō Kokushi 夢窓國師. *Muchū mondō* 夢中問答 (Dialogue in a dream), ed. Satō Yasukiyo 佐藤泰舜. Iwanami Bunko 1046–47. Tokyo, Iwanami, 1934.

Nagae Shōichi 長江正一. *Miyoshi Nagayoshi* 三好長慶. Jinbutsu Sōsho 149. Tokyo, Yoshikawa Kōbunkan, 1968.

Nagasaki shi seihen 長崎志正編 (Nagasaki chronicle: the text proper), comp. Tanabe Mokei 田邊茂啓, ed. Koga Jūjirō 古賀十二郎. Nagasaki, Nagasaki Bunko Kankōkai 長崎文庫刊行會, 1928.

Nakamura Hajime 中村元. *Kinsei Nihon ni okeru hihanteki seishin no ichi kōsatsu* 近世日本における批判的精神の一考察 (An inquiry into the critical spirit in Early Modern Japan). Tokyo, Sanseidō, 1949.

———*Nihon shūkyō no kindaisei* 日本宗教の近代性 (The modern characteristics of Japanese religion), *Nakamura Hajime senshū* 中村元選集 (Selected works of Nakamura Hajime), vol. 8. Tokyo, Shunjūsha, 1964.

——— "Suzuki Shōsan, 1579–1655, and the Spirit of Capitalism in Japanese Buddhism," tr. William Johnston, *Monumenta Nipponica* 22.1/2: 1–14 (1967).

Nakamura Kichiji 中村吉治. "Sengoku daimyō ron" 戦国大名論 (On *sengoku daimyō*), *Iwanami kōza: Nihon rekishi*, VIII, 189–237. *Chūsei* 4; Tokyo, Iwanami, 1963.

Nakamura Kōya 中村孝也. *Edo Bakufu Sakoku shiron* 江戸幕府鎖國史論 (On the history of the Closed Country under the Edo Bakufu). Tokyo, Hōkōkai 奉公會, 1914.

Nakayama, Shigeru. *A History of Japanese Astronomy: Chinese Background and Western Impact*. Harvard-Yenching Institute Monograph Series, vol. 18. Cambridge, Mass., Harvard University Press, 1969.

Nanbanji kōhaiki 南蠻寺興廢記 (The rise and fall of the Temple of Southern Barbarians), ed. Kiyū Dōnin, Keiō 4 (1868), Kyoto University Library copy; includes *Jakyō taii* 邪教大意 (The gist of the pernicious doctrine), abbreviated transcription into Japanese of the *kanbun* text by Sessō 雪窓, *Taiji jashūron* 對治邪宗â (On quelling the pernicious faith).

Nanbanji kōhaiki, ed. Kiyū Dōnin, Keiō 4 (1868). 2nd ed., Kyōto Furitsu Sōgō Shiryō-kan copy; includes *Jakyō taii* and a postscript signed Gensuishi 原水子.

Nanbanji kōhaiki, Jakyō taii, Myōtei mondō, Ha Daiusu 南蛮寺興廃記・邪教大意・妙貞問答・破提宇子 (The rise and fall of the Temple of Southern Barbarians; The gist of the pernicious doctrine; Myōtei Dialogue; Deus Destroyed), Modern Japanese versions by Ebisawa Arimichi. Tōyō Bunko 14. Tokyo, Heibonsha, 1964.

Nanbanryū geka hidensho 南蠻流外科秘傳書 (Secret transmission of the Southern Barbarian style of surgery), interior title *Nanbanryū gekasho* 南蠻流外科書 (Text on the Southern Barbarian style of surgery). MS. in the Fujikawa 富士川 collection, Library of the Faculty of Medicine, Kyoto University.

Needham, Joseph. *Science and Civilisation in China*, vols. 2–3. Cambridge, At the University Press, 1956–1959.

Nichiren Daishōnin chū gasan 日蓮大聖人註畫讃 (Lauds on the portrait of the Great Saint

Nichiren), comp. Nitchō 日澄 with glosses by Nisshū 日收, in *Nichiren Shōnin denkishū* 日蓮上人傳記集 (Collected biographies of Nichiren Shōnin), ed. Nichirenshū Zensho Shuppankai 日蓮宗全書出版會. Tokyo, Suwaraya Shoten 須原屋書店, 1910.

Nihon shiryō shūsei 日本史料集成 (Collection of Japanese historical sources). Tokyo, Heibonsha, 1956.

Nihon shisō tōsō shiryō 日本思想鬪諍史料 (Historical sources on controversies in Japanese thought), vol. 10. Tokyo, Tōhō Shoin 東方書院, 1930.

Nihon tetsugaku shisō zensho 日本哲學思想全書 (Collected works of Japanese philosophy), vol. 10. Tokyo, Heibonsha, 1956.

NIPPON NO IESVS no Companhia no Superior yori Christan ni sŏtŏ no cotouari uo tagaino mondŏ no gotoqu xidai uo vacachi tamŏ DOCTRINA. IESVS NO COMPANHIA NO COLLEgio Amacusa ni voite Superiores no von yuruxi uo cŏmuri, core uo fan to nasu mono nari. Toqini go xuxxe no NENQI. 1592. Facsimile appended to Hashimoto Shinkichi, *Bunroku gannen Amakusa-ban Kirishitan kyōgi no kenkyū.*

Nishikawa Joken 西川如見. *Ka-i tsūshō kō* 華夷通商考 (Considerations on commerce with the civilized and the uncivilized world). 2 vols. Kyoto, Rakuyō Shorin Kansetsudō Gakuryōken 洛陽書林甘節堂學梁軒, Genroku 元祿 8 (1695).

Nobunaga [Shinchō] kōki 信長公記 (The chronicle of Nobunaga), comp. Ōta Gyūichi 太田牛一, ed. Okuno Takahiro 奥野高広 and Iwasawa Yoshihiko 岩沢愿彦. Kadokawa Bunko 2541. Tokyo, Kadokawa, 1969.

Obara Satoru 尾原悟, Augustinus, SJ. "Kirishitan jidai no kagaku shisō: Pedoro Gomesu-cho 'Tenkyūron' no kenkyū" キリシタン時代の科学思想ーペドロ・ゴメス著「天球論」の研究 (Scientific thought in the Kirishitan period: a study of Pedro Gomez, "De sphaera"), *Kirishitan kenkyū* 10: 101–178 (1965).

Oda Tokunō 織田得能. *Bukkyō daijiten* 佛敎大辭典 (Encyclopaedic dictionary of Buddhism). 2nd rev. ed. Tokyo, Daizō Shuppan 大藏出版, 1962.

Ōe no Masafusa 大江匡房. *Zoku honchō ōjō den* 續本朝徃生傳 (Continued accounts of those of Our Empire who were reborn [in the Pure Land]), in *Gunsho ruijū* 群書類從 (Classified textual corpus), IV, 416–434. 2nd printing. Tokyo, Keizai Zasshisha 經濟雜誌社, 1898.

Ōita-ken kyōdo shiryō shūsei 大分縣郷土史料集成 (Collection of sources on the provincial history of Ōita), ed. Kakimoto Kotoo 垣本言雄. 2 vols. Ōita, Ōita-ken Kyōdo Shiryō Kankōkai, 1936–1938.

Okada Akio 岡田章雄. "Kirishitan shinkō to hōken shakai dōtoku" キリシタン信仰と封建社会道徳 (Kirishitan belief and feudal social morality), *Nihon bunka kenkyū* 日本文化研究 (Studies in Japanese culture), no. 5. Tokyo, Shinchōsha 新潮社, 1959.

Okamoto Yoshitomo 岡本良知. *Jūroku-seiki Nichiō kōtsūshi no kenkyū* 十六世紀日歐交通史の研究 (Studies in the history of intercourse between Japan and Europe in the sixteenth century). Rev. ed. Tokyo, Rokkō Shobō 六甲書房, 1942.

―― *Tenshō 14nen Ōsaka-jō ekkenki* 天正十四年大坂城謁見記 (Accounts of the 1586 audience in Osaka Castle). Tokyo, Kasahara Shoten 笠原書店, 1942.

―― *Toyotomi Hideyoshi: Nanbanjin no kiroku ni yoru* 豊臣秀吉・南蛮人の記録による (Toyotomi Hideyoshi: according to Southern Barbarian accounts). Chūkō Shinsho 28. Tokyo, Chūō Kōron-sha, 1963.

Ōkubo Hikozaemon 大久保彦左衛門. *Genpon Mikawa monogatari* 原本三河物語 (Mikawa monogatari, the original text), ed. Nakada Norio 中田祝夫. 2 vols. Tokyo, Benseisha 勉誠社, 1970.

Ōmura-ke hiroku 大村家秘録 (Confidential records of the house of Ōmura), in *Shiseki zassan* 史籍雜纂 (Historical miscellanea), I, 162–173. Tokyo, Kokusho Kankōkai, 1911.

Ōmura-ki 大村記 (Ōmura chronicle), in *Shiseki zassan*, I, 142–162.

Oranda-ryū geka shinan 阿蘭陀流外科指南 (Introduction into the Dutch style of surgery). 5 *kan* in 4 vols. Kyoto, Izumoji Izumi no Jō 出雲寺和泉掾, Hōei 寶永2 (1705), Kyoto University Library copy.

Orfanel, Jacinto, OP. *Historia de la Iglesia del Japón*, Archivo de la Provincia del Santisimo Rosario (Manila), Division de MSS., Seccion: Japón, Tomo 1; dated 24 May 1621.

Ōtomo-kō oie oboegaki 大友公御家覺書 (Memoranda on the princely house of Ōtomo), in *Kokushi sōsho* 國史叢書 (Library of Japanese history), ed. Kurokawa Masamichi 黑川眞道, XXIV, 285–348. Tokyo, Kokushi Kenkyūkai 國史研究會, 1916.

Ōtsuka Mitsunobu 大塚光信, ed. *Kirishitan-ban Esopo monogatari* キリシタン版エソポ 物語 (The Kirishitan press Tales of Aesop). Kadokawa Bunko 2632. Tokyo, Kadokawa, 1971.

Pacheco, Diego, SJ. "Nihon Nijūroku Sei Junkyōsha no tabiji ni kansuru oboegaki" 日本二十六聖殉教者の旅路に関する覚え書 (Memorial on the journey of the Twenty-Six Holy Martyrs of Japan), *Kirishitan kenkyū* 8:40–86 (1963).

———"Hoan Baputisuta de Baeza Shinpu no nishokan ni tsuite" ホアン・バプティスタ・デ・バエザ神父の二書翰について (Concerning two letters of Padre Joan Baptista de Baeza), *Kirishitan kenkyū* 10:67–99 (1965).

Pagés, Léon. *Histoire de la Religion Chrétienne au Japon depuis 1598 jusqu'a 1651.* 2 vols. Paris, Charles Douniol, 1869–1870.

———*Histoire de la Religion Chrétienne au Japon*, tr. Yoshida Kogorō 吉田小五郎 assisted by Joseph Krischer SJ, *Nihon Kirishitan shūmon shi* 日本切支丹宗門史. 3 vols. Iwanami Bunko 1637–46. 8th printing. Tokyo, Iwanami, 1968.

Paske-Smith, M. *Japanese Traditions of Christianity.* Kobe, J.L. Thompson & Co., 1930.

Pérez, Lorenzo, OFM. "Cartas y relaciones del Japón," *Archivo Ibero-Americano* 4:388–418 (1915); 6:197–309 (1916); 9:55–142, 168–263 (1918); 10:26–70 (1918); 11:232–292 (1919); 13:29–60, 145–197, 321–375 (1920); 14:161–206 (1920); 15:166–208, 332–359 (1921); 16:54–105, 163–219 (1921); 17:29–78 (1922); 19:145–194 (1923).

———"Fray Juan Pobre de Zamora: su relación sobre la pérdida del Galeón 'San Felipe', y martirio de San Pedro Bautista y compañeros," *Erudición Ibero-Vltramarina* 2:217–[235] (1931).

P'o-hsieh chi [*Hajashū*] 破邪集 (Collection countering perniciousness), comp. Hsü Ch'ang-chih 徐昌治 (1640). 8 vols. Mito reissue with a preface by Tokugawa Nariaki 德川齊昭, Ansei 安政 2 (1855).

Pound, Ezra, tr. *The Classic Anthology Defined by Confucius.* Cambridge, Mass., Harvard University Press, 1954.

Radhakrishnan, S. *Indian Philosophy*, vol. 2. Rev. 2nd ed. London, George Allen & Unwin, 1931.

Relacion del insigne martyrio, qve padecio por la Fe de Christo el Milagroso P. Marcelo Francisco Mastrilli de la Compañia de IESVS en la Ciudad de Nangasaqui de los Reynos del Iapō a 17. dias del mes de Octubre deste año pasado de 1637. [Manila, Colegio de la Compañia de Jesus, por Tomás Pinpín, 1638?]

Ribadeneira, Marcelo de, OFM. *Historia de las islas del Archipiélago filipino y reinos de la Gran China, Tartaria, Cochinchina, Malaca, Siam, Cambodge y Japón*, ed. Juan R. de Legísima OFM. Colección España Misionera, vol. 3. Madrid, La Editorial Católica, 1947.

Rinzairoku 臨濟錄, ed. Asahina Sōgen 朝比奈宗源. Iwanami Bunko 1202. 4th printing. Tokyo, Iwanami, 1938.

Rodriguez Tçuzzu, João, SJ. *ARTE DA LINGOA DE IAPAM* COMPOSTA

PELLO Padre Ioão Rodriguez Portugues da Cõpanhia de IESV diuidida em tres LIVROS. COM LICENÇA DO ORDINARIO, E SVPERIORES EM Nangasaqui no Collegio de Iapão da Companhia de IESV Anno. 1604. (colophon dated 1608); facsimile published by Shima Shōzō 島正三, Rodorigesu Nihon daibunten ロドリゲス日本大文典. Tokyo, Bunka Shobō Hakubunsha 文化書房博文祉, 1969.

Rodriguez Tçuzzu, João, SJ. ARTE DA LINGOA DE IAPAM, annotated Japanese translation by Doi Tadao, Nihon daibunten 日本大文典. Tokyo, Sanseidō, 1955.

————História da Igreja do Japão, ed. João do Amaral Abranches Pinto. 2 vols. Macao, Noticias de Macau, 1954–1955.

————História da Igreja do Japão, annotated Japanese translation by Doi Tadao et al., Nihon kyōkai shi 日本教会史. 2 vols. Dai Kōkai Jidai Sōsho 9–10. Tokyo, Iwanami, 1967–1970.

Romani, Ulderico, SDB. Un Samurai Senza Macchia e Senza Paura. Rome, Officium Libri Catholici, 1959.

ROYEI. ZAFIT. (Wakan rōeishū, maki no jō 倭漢朗詠集卷之上, Keichō 5nen 慶長五年) IN COLLEGIO IAPONICO SOCIETATIS IESV. Cum facultate Ordinarij, & Superiorum. ANNO 1600. Facsimile, transcription, and commentary by Doi Tadao: Keichō 5nen Yasokai-ban Wakan rōeishū 慶長五年耶蘇會板倭漢朗詠集// ROYEI ZAFIT 朗詠雜筆: A Japanese Anthology (Poems for Recital), A Collection of Words Used in Letters etc., ed. Kyōto Daigaku Bungakubu Kokugogaku Kokubungaku Kenkyūshitsu 京都大學文學部國語學國文學研究室. Kyoto, Kyōto Daigaku Kokubungakkai 京都大學國文學會, 1964.

Rupp, Gordon. Luther's Progress to the Diet of Worms. New York, Harper & Row, 1964; Harper Torchbook TB 120.

Rzepkowski, Horst, SVD. Thomas von Aquin und Japan. Studia Instituti Missiologici Societatis Verbi Divini Nr. 9. St. Augustin/Siegburg, Steyler Verlag, 1967.

————"Thomas von Aquin und der Zen-Buddhismus," Neue Zeitschrift für Missionswissenschaft 24.2:146–150 (1968).

Satō Shōsuke 佐藤昌介. Yōgakushi kenkyū josetsu 洋学史研究序說 (Introductory study of the history of the Western Learning). Tokyo, Iwanami, 1964.

Schurhammer, Georg, SJ. Das Kirchliche Sprachproblem in der Japanischen Jesuitenmission des 16. und 17. Jahrhunderts. Tokyo, Deutsche Gesellschaft für Natur- und Völkerkunde Ostasiens, 1928; "Mitteilungen," Band 23.

Schütte, Josef Franz, SJ. "Drei Unterrichtsbücher für Japanische Jesuitenprediger aus dem XVI. Jahrhundert," Archivum Historicum Societatis Iesu 8.2:223–256 (1939).

————Valignanos Missionsgrundsätze für Japan. Rome, Edizioni di Storia e Letteratura. I. Band I. Teil: Das Problem (1573–1580), 1951. I. Band II. Teil: Die Lösung (1580–1582), 1958.

————El "Archivo del Japon": Vicisitudes del Archivo Jesuítico del Extremo Oriente y Descripción del Fondo Existente en la Real Academia de la Historia de Madrid. Archivo Documental Español, vol. 20. Madrid, Real Academia de la Historia, 1964.

————"Wichtige Japandokumente in einem Band der Propaganda-Kongregation im Staatsarchiv von Florenz," Archivum Historicum Societatis Iesu 35.69:232–241 (1966).

————Introductio ad Historiam Societatis Jesu in Japonia, 1549–1650. Rome, Institutum Historicum Soc. Jesu, 1968.

Schwade, Arcadio, SJ. "Saisho no Furanshisuko-kaishi no raichō ni kansuru hōkoku hosoku" 最初のフランシスコ会士の来朝に関する報告補足 (Supplementary report concerning the advent to Japan of the first Franciscans), Kirishitan kenkyū 8:266–271 (1963).

————"Funai no korejiyo ni tsuite" 府內のコレジョについて (On the Funai collegio), Kirishitan kenkyū 10:56–66 (1965).

Sengoku jinmei jiten 戦国人名辞典 (Sengoku biographical dictionary), ed. Takayanagi Mitsutoshi 高柳光壽 and Matsudaira Toshikazu 松平年一. Tokyo, Yoshikawa Kōbunkan, 1963.

Shasekishū 沙石集 (A sand pebble collection), comp. Mujū 無住, ed. Watanabe Tsunaya 渡邊綱也. Nihon Koten Bungaku Taikei 85. Tokyo, Iwanami, 1966.

Shih-pa shih lüeh 十八史略, comp. Tseng Hsien-chih 曾先之, ed. Nakayama Kyūshirō 中山久四郎 and Shiono Shinjirō 鹽野新次郎, *Jūhachi-shi ryaku shinshaku* 十八史略 新釋 (Epitome of the eighteen histories, with new commentary), vol. 1, Shōwa Kanbun Sōsho 昭和漢文叢書. Tokyo, Kōdōkan 弘道館, 1930.

Shimada Kenji 島田虔次. *Shushigaku to Yōmeigaku* 朱子学と陽明学 (The Chu Hsi Learning and the Wang Yang-ming Learning). Iwanami Shinsho 637. Tokyo, Iwanami, 1967.

Shimoda Kyokusui 下田曲水. *Zantei Amakusa Kirishitan shi* 暫定天草切支丹史 (A tentative history of the Amakusa Kirishitans). Kumamoto, Kumamoto Toshokan Kan'yūkai 熊本圖書館館友會, 1941.

Shinmura Izuru 新村出. *Nanban kōki* 南蠻廣記 (Tidings of the Southern Barbarians). Tokyo, Iwanami, 1925.

Shiryō ni yoru Nihon no ayumi: Kinsei-hen 史料による日本の歩み—近世編 (The course of Japan according to its historical sources: the Early Modern period), ed. Ōkubo Toshiaki 大久保利謙, Kodama Kōta 児玉幸多, Yanai Kenji 箭内健次, and Inoue Mitsusada 井上光貞. 9th printing. Tokyo, Yoshikawa Kōbunkan, 1963.

Shuo yüan 說苑, Ssu-pu ts'ung-k'an.

Smith, Bruce L. "Propaganda," in *International Encyclopedia of the Social Sciences*, ed. David L. Sills, XII, 579–589. New York, The Macmillan Co. and The Free Press, 1968.

Sōgō chihōshi dainenpyō 総合地方史大年表 (Comprehensive chronology of provincial history), ed. Kodama Kōta 児玉幸多, Okayama Yasushi 岡山泰四, and Kanai Madoka 金井圓. Tokyo, Jinbutsu Ōrai-sha, 1967.

Sources of Japanese Tradition, ed. Ryusaku Tsunoda, Wm. Theodore DeBary, and Donald Keene. 2nd printing. New York, Columbia University Press, 1959.

Sukeno Kentarō 助野健太郎. *Kirishitan no shinkō seikatsu* キリシタンの信仰生活 (Kirishitan religious life). Tokyo, Chūō Shuppansha 中央出版社, 1957.

Suzuki, Daisetz (Suzuki Daisetsu 鈴木大拙). *Zen Buddhism: Selected Writings of D. T. Suzuki*, ed. William Barrett. Garden City, N.Y., Doubleday, 1956; Anchor Books A 90.

——— *Essays in Zen Buddhism*, 3rd series. 3rd ed. London, Rider, 1958.

——— *Manual of Zen Buddhism*. New York, Grove Press, 1960; Evergreen Original E-231.

Suzuki Ryōichi 鈴木良一. *Toyotomi Hideyoshi* 豊臣秀吉. Iwanami Shinsho 171. Tokyo, Iwanami, 1954.

——— *Oda Nobunaga* 織田信長. Iwanami Shinsho 649. Tokyo, Iwanami, 1967.

Suzuki Shōsan 鈴木正三. *Ha Kirishitan* 破鬼理死端 (interior title 破吉利支丹; Christians Countered), woodblock printed by Ogawa Tazaemon 小川多左衞門. Kyoto, Zenke Shorin Ryūshiken 禪家書林柳枝軒. Kanbun 2 (1662), Kyōto Furitsu Sōgō Shiryōkan copy.

——— *Roankyō* 驢鞍橋 (The donkey's saddle-bone), comp. Echū 惠中, ed. Suzuki Daisetsu. Iwanami Bunko 3767–69. Tokyo, Iwanami, 1948.

——— *Suzuki Shōsan Dōnin zenshū* 鈴木正三道人全集 (Complete works of Suzuki Shōsan), ed. Suzuki Tesshin 鈴木鐵心. Tokyo, Sankibō Busshorin 山喜房佛書林, 1962.

Tagita Kōya 田北耕也. *Shōwa jidai no senpuku Kirishitan* 昭和時代の潜伏キリシタン (The underground Kirishitans of the Shōwa period). Tokyo, Nippon Gakujutsu Shinkōkai 日本学術振興会, 1954.

Taikō shiryōshū 太閤史料集 (Collected sources on Hideyoshi), ed. Kuwata Tadachika. Sengoku Shiryō Sōsho 戦国史料叢書 1. Tokyo, Jinbutsu Ōrai-sha, 1965.

Taishō shinshū daizōkyō 大正新修大藏經 // *The Tripitaka in Chinese*, ed. Takakusu Junjirō 高楠順次郎. 85 vols. Tokyo, Taishō Issaikyō Kankōkai 大正一切經刊行會, 1924–1932.

Takakusu Junjirō. *The Essentials of Buddhist Philosophy*, ed. Wing-tsit Chan and Charles A. Moore. 3rd ed. Honolulu, Office Appliance Co., 1956.

Takeda Shingen kahō 武田信玄家法 (The house laws of Takeda Shingen), in *Nihon kyōiku bunko* 日本教育文庫 (Library of Japanese education), *Kakun-hen* 家訓篇 (House regulations), pp. 220–236. Tokyo, Dōbunkan, 1910.

Takita Manabu 田北學, ed. *Ōtomo shiryō* 大友史料 (Ōtomo sources). 2 vols. Ōita: Kin'yōdō Shoten 金洋堂書店, 1937–1938.

———, ed. *Hennen Ōtomo shiryō* 編年大友史料 (Ōtomo sources: chronological compilation). 2 vols. Tokyo, Fuzanbō, 1942–1946.

———ed. *Zoku Ōtomo shiryō* 續大友史料 (Ōtomo sources: continued). 6 vols. Vol. 1, Beppu Daigaku-kai 別府大学会, 1955; the rest privately published, Ōita, 1955–1956.

———ed. *Zoku hennen Ōtomo shiryō* 續編年大友史料 (Ōtomo sources: chronological compilation, continued). 10 vols. Ōita, privately published, 1956–1959.

———, ed. *Zōho teisei hennen Ōtomo shiryō* 増補訂正編年大友史料 (Ōtomo sources: enlarged and revised chronological compilation). 30 vols. Ōita, privately published, 1962–1969.

Tanaka Tomoe 田中智枝. "Shimazu Takahisa no Kirishitan kinsei ni tsuite" 島津貴久のキリシタン禁制について (On Shimazu Takahisa's prohibition of Christianity), *Kirishitan Bunka Kenkyūkai kaihō* 10.1:1–22 (September 1967).

Tao shu ch'üan chi 道書全集 (Collected Taoist texts). Ch'ing K'ang-hsi 淸康熙 21 (1682) edition in the Harvard-Yenching Library.

The Cloud of Unknowing, translated into Modern English with an Introduction by Clifton Wolters. Harmondsworth, Middlesex, Penguin Books, 1961.

Tokugawa jikki 德川實紀 (True record of the Tokugawa), vols. 2–4, ed. Kuroita Katsumi 黑板勝美. Kokushi Taikei 國史大系 39–41. Tokyo, Yoshikawa Kōbunkan, 1964.

Toyama Mikio 外山幹夫. "Kyūshū ni okeru daimyō ryōkoku no keisei: Ōtomo-uji o chūshin to shite" 九州に於ける大名領国の形成―大友氏を中心として (The composition of the daimyo domain in Kyushu: with the focus on the Ōtomo family), *Nihon rekishi* 101:27–34 (November 1956).

——— "Shugo daimyō to shite no Ōtomo-uji no seikaku ni tsuite: kashindan hensei katei o shu to shite mitaru" 守護大名としての大友氏の性格について―家臣団編成過程を主としてみたる (On the Ōtomo family's character as *shugo daimyō*: viewed chiefly through the process of the organization of the vassalage structure), *Hisutoria* ヒストリア 18:40–55 (June 1957).

Tseng-pu Sung-Yüan hsüeh-an 增補宋元學案 (Critical anthology of the Sung and Yüan Learning, with supplements), comp. Huang Tsung-hsi 黃宗羲 et al., Ssu-pu pei-yao.

Tsuchihashi Yachita 土橋八千太, Paul, SJ. *Japanese Chronological Tables*. Tokyo, Sophia University Press, 1952.

Tsuji Zennosuke 辻善之助. *Kaigai kōtsū shiwa* 海外交通史話 (Talks on the history of overseas commerce). Tokyo, Tōadō Shobō 東亞堂書房, 1917.

——— *Zōtei Kaigai kōtsū shiwa* 增訂海外交通史話 (Talks on the history of overseas commerce, revised expanded edition). Tokyo, Naigai Shoseki Kabushiki Kaisha 內外書籍株式會社, 1930.

Tsuruta Yasunari 鶴田八洲成. "Shijitsu Amakusa Shirō no kenkyū: sono keireki to kazoku-ensha soshite rekishiteki igi" 史實天草四郎の研究―その經歷と家族・緣者そして歷史的意義 (A study of the historical Amakusa Shirō: his career, his family and relations, and his historical significance), *Kirishitan Bunka Kenkyūkai kaihō* 10.3/4:1–60 (October 1968).

Tsuruya Nanboku zenshū 鶴屋南北全集 (Complete works of Tsuruya Nanboku), vol. 1, ed. Gunji Masakatsu 郡司正勝. Tokyo, San'ichi Shobō 三一書房, 1971.

Uchida Ginzō 內田銀藏. *Kinsei no Nihon* 近世の日本 (Early Modern Japan). Tokyo, Fuzanbō, 1919.

Valignano, Alexandro, SJ. *CATECHISMVS CHRISTIANAE FIDEI, IN QVO VERITAS nostrae religionis ostenditur, & sectae Iaponenses confutantur, editus à Patre Alexandro Valignano societatis IESV . . . Olyssipone, excudebat Antonius Riberius.* 1586. *CATECHISMI CHRISTIANAE FIDEI, in quo veritas nostrę religionis ostenditur, & sectę Iaponenses confutantur, LIBER SECVNDVS.* Authore Alexandro Valignano societatis IESV. Olyssipone excudebat Emmanuel de Lyra, Typog. 1586. Photographic copy in the Kirishitan Bunko, Sophia University, Tokyo.

———*CATECHISMVS*, Japanese translation by Ieiri Toshimitsu 家入敏光, *Nihon no katekizumo* 日本のカテキズモ. Tenri Toshokan Sankō Shiryō 天理図書館参考資料 7. Tenri, Tenri Toshokan 天理図書館, 1969.

———*Historia del Principio y Progresso de la Compañía de Jesús en las Indias Orientales (1542–64)*, ed. Josef Wicki SJ. Bibliotheca Instituti Historici S.I. 2. Rome, Institutum Historicum S.I., 1944.

———*Advertimentos e Avisos acerca dos Costumes e Catangues de Jappão (1581)*, critical edition and Italian translation by Josef Franz Schütte SJ, *Il Cerimoniale per i Missionari del Giappone.* Rome, Edizioni di Storia e Letteratura, 1946.

———*Sumario de las Cosas de Japon (1583)*, ed. José Luis Alvarez-Taladriz. *Monumenta Nipponica* Monographs 9. Tokyo, Sophia University Press, 1954.

———*Sumario*, Japanese translation by Matsuda Kiichi and Sakuma Tadashi 佐久間正, *Nihon junsatsuki* 日本巡察記. Tōzai Kōshō Ryokōki Zenshū 東西交渉旅行記全集 5. Tokyo, Tōgensha, 1965.

VOCABVLARIO DA LINGOA DE IAPAM com adeclaração em Portugues, feito por ALGVNS PADRES, E IRMAÕS DA COMPANHIA DE IESV COM LICENÇA DO ORDINARIO, & Superiores em Nangasaqui no Collegio de IaPAM DA COMPANHIA DE IESVS. ANNO M.D.CIII. SVPPLEMENTO DESTE VOcabulario impresso no mesmo Collegio da CōPANHIA DE JESV COM a sobredita licença, & approuação. Anno. 1604. Facsimile published by Doi Tadao, *Nippo jisho* 日葡辞書. Tokyo, Iwanami, 1960.

Wajima Yoshio 和島芳男. *Chūsei no jugaku* 中世の儒学 (Mediaeval Confucianism). Nihon Rekishi Sōsho 日本歴史叢書 11. Tokyo, Yoshikawa Kōbunkan, 1965.

Waley, Arthur, tr. *The Analects of Confucius.* New York, Random House; Modern Library Paperbacks P 66.

Watson, Burton, tr. *Basic Writings of Mo Tzu, Hsün Tzu, and Han Fei Tzu.* New York, Columbia University Press, 1967.

———, tr. *The Complete Works of Chuang Tzu.* New York, Columbia University Press, 1968.

Watsuji Tetsurō 和辻哲郎. *Sakoku: Nihon no higeki* 鎖國―日本の悲劇 (Sakoku: a tragedy for Japan). Tokyo, Chikuma Shobō, 1950.

Weber, Max. *From Max Weber: Essays in Sociology*, ed. H.H. Gerth and C. Wright Mills. New York, Oxford University Press, 1958; Galaxy Book 13.

Willeke, Bernward, OFM. "Saisho no Furanshisuko-kaishi no raichō" 最初のフランシスコ会士の来朝 (The advent to Japan of the first Franciscans), *Kirishitan kenkyū* 8:249–265 (1963).

Xavier, Saint Francis. *Epistolae S. Francisci Xaverii aliaque eius scripta*, ed. Georg Schurhammer SJ and Josef Wicki SJ. 2 vols. Monumenta Historica Societatis Iesu 67–68. Rome, Monumenta Historica Soc. Iesu, 1944–1945.

Yabuuchi Genzui 藪內彥端, comp. *Chion'in shi* 知恩院史 (History of the Chion'in). Kyoto, Chion'in, 1937.

Yamaga Sokō 山鹿素行. *Shinpen buke jiki* 新編武家事記 (Accounts of military houses, newly edited). Tokyo, Shin Jinbutsu Ōrai-sha 新人物往来社, 1969.

Yamaguchi Osamu 山口修. *Amakusa* 天草. Rev. ed. Kumamoto, Kinryūdō 金龍堂, 1968.

Yasokaishi Nihon tsūshin 耶蘇會士日本通信 (Jesuit relations from Japan), ed. and tr. Murakami Naojirō and Watanabe Yosuke 渡邊世祐. 2 vols. Ikoku Sōsho 異國叢書. Rev. reprint. Tokyo, Yūshōdō, 1966.

Yasokaishi Nihon tsūshin: Bungo-hen 耶蘇會士日本通信・豐後編 (Jesuit relations from Japan: Bungo collection), ed. and tr. Murakami Naojirō. 2 vols. Zoku Ikoku Sōsho 續異國叢書. Tokyo, Teikoku Kyōikukai Shuppanbu 帝國敎育會出版部, 1936.

Yokomichi Mario 橫道萬里雄 and Omote Akira 表章, eds. *Yōkyokushū* 謠曲集 (Collected Nō chants), vol. 1. Nihon Koten Bungaku Taikei 40. Tokyo, Iwanami, 1960.

Yoshida Sumio 吉田澄夫. *Amakusa-ban Kinkushū no kenkyū* 天草版金句集の研究 // *On the Qincuxú (Kinku-syu) Published in 1593 by the Amakusa Collegio of the Jesuit Mission in Japan*. Tôyô Bunko Ronsô Series A, vol. 24. Tokyo, Tôyô Bunko, 1938. Includes a photographic reproduction of the original: *XIXO, XIXXO nadono vchiyori nuqi idaxi, qincuxúto nasu mono nari* (Compilation of Golden Words, selected from among the Four Books, Seven [Military] Texts, and others).

Zengo ji-i 禪語字彙 (Dictionary of Zen phrases), comp. Nakagawa Jūan 中川渋庵 and Imai Fukuzan 今井福山. 2nd printing. Tokyo, Morie Shoten 森江書店, 1956.

Zenrin sego shū 禅林世語集 (Collection of popular Zen sayings), ed. Tsuchiya Etsudō 土屋悅堂. Kyoto, Kichūdō 其中堂, 1957.

Zokuzoku gunsho ruijū 續々群書類從 (Classified textual corpus; second continuation), vol. 12. (*Shūkyō-bu* 宗敎部 2); Tokyo, Kokusho Kankōkai, 1907.

Glossary

*Chinese readings are marked with one star.
**Archaic romanizations are marked with two stars.

A 阿
Abidatsuma kusha-ron 阿毘達磨俱舎論
Ai Gozaemon 安威五左衞門
Aizawa Seishisai 會澤正志齋
Akashi 明石
Akashi Kamon 明石掃部
Akechi Mitsuhide 明智光秀
Akizuki 秋月
amaboshi dangi アマボシ談議
Amakusa 天草
Amakusa Shirō Tokisada 天草四郎時貞
Amano Shirō 天野四郎
Amaterasu 天照
Amaterasu Ōmikami 天照大神
Amida 阿彌陀
Amida-kyō 阿彌陀經
Amida Nyorai 阿彌陀如來
anatsurushi 穴吊し
anjo 安女，安助，安如
aragoto 荒事
Arai Hakuseki 新井白石
Arai Toshi 新井トシ
araiya-shiki 阿頼耶識
Araki Murashige 荒木村重
Arima 有馬
Arima Genba no Jō Toyouji 有馬玄蕃
允豊氏
Arima Harunobu 有馬晴信
Arima Haruzumi 有馬晴純
Arima kiroku 有馬記錄
Arima Yoshisada 有馬義貞
Arioka 在岡
Asai 淺井
Asaka Tanpaku 安積澹泊
Asakura 朝倉
Asakura Kageakira 朝倉景鏡
Asakura Sōteki Norikage 朝倉宗滴
教景
Asakusa 淺草
Ashikaga 足利
Ashikaga Gakkō 足利學校

Ashikaga no Shō 足利莊
Ashikaga Yoshiaki 足利義昭
Ashikaga Yoshimitsu 足利義滿
Ashikaga Yoshiteru 足利義輝
ashura 阿修羅
Aso 阿蘇
Asuka 飛鳥
Awa 阿波
Awaji 淡路
**Ayamatteua aratamuruni, fabacaru-
coto nacare. 過則勿憚改
Azuchi 安土
Azuchi-Momoyama 安土桃山

Baba Saburōzaemon 馬場三郎左衞門
Baian 梅庵
Bakufu 幕府
bakuhan 幕藩
Bakumatsu 幕末
Bandō 坂東
Banmin tokuyō 萬民德用
Banzuii Chiyo 幡随意智譽
Bateren 伴天連，罰天連，破天連
Baterenki 伴天連記
Bingo 備後
Bishamon 毘沙門
biwa hōshi 琵琶法師
Bizen 備前
Bojutsu no hōji 戊戌の封事
Bon 盆
bonnō gosshō 煩惱業障
Bosatsu shotaikyō 菩薩處胎經
Bosatsuji jikyō 菩薩地持經
bugyō 奉行
Bungo 豊後
Bunroku 文祿
Bunsei 文政
Buppō no shidai ryaku nukigaki 佛法の
次第略拔書
Buppō sōron 佛法總論
bushi 武士

515

bushidō 武士道
Busse funi 佛世不二
Butsuzen Butsugo 佛前佛後
Buzen 豊前
byōbu 屏風

**Cambaco 關白
**Cami 上
**Canon 觀音
**canzusa 加津佐
**Catangues 氣質
**catçŭua cotoba qeicono tame, catçŭua
    yono tocu no tame 且うは言葉稽古の
    爲 且うは世の得の爲
*Chang Lu 張魯
*Chang Tsai 張載
*Chao-ming 昭明
*Ch'eng I (I-ch'uan) 程頤 (伊川)
*Chhi 氣
*ch'i 氣
*Ch'iao 蹻
Chie Izu 智惠伊豆
*Chih 跖
*chih 質
chihōshin 知法身
Chikugo 筑後
Chikugo no Kami 筑後守
chikushō 畜生
Chikuzen 筑前
*Ch'in 秦
*Ch'in Shih Huang-ti 秦始皇帝
*Ch'ing-ching ching 清靜經
Chion'in 知恩院
*Ch'iu-shui 秋水
chō 町
chōjuten 長壽天
chōrō 長老
Chōsogabe 長宗我部
Chōsogabe Motochika 長宗我部元親
*Chou 周
*Chou Lien-hsi 周濂溪
chū 忠
*Chu Hsi 朱熹
*Chu-Tsai 主宰
Chūai Tennō 仲哀天皇 , 仲愛天皇
*Chuang Shan 莊山
*Chuang Tzu 莊子
Chūgoku 中國
chūkō 中劫
*Chung Yung 中庸
*Chün tao 君道
**Conzuquedono 上野殿
**Cubo 公方

**Cūgues 公家

dai geki 大外記
**Dai ichi, go ittai no Deus uo vyamai,
    tattomi tatematçurubexi. 第一御一体
    のてうすをうやまひたつとミ奉るへし
Dai Iō 大醫王
Dai Muryōju-kyō 大無量壽經
dai nichi 大日
dai sen-sekai 大千世界
dai uso 大嘘
Daibenzaiten 大辯才天
Daihatsu nehankyō 大般涅槃經
daijō daijin 太政大臣
Daijō endon 大乘圓頓
Daijō gishō 大乘義章
**Daijodono 彈正殿
daikan 代官
daikō 大劫
daimoku 題目
daimyō-bun 大名分
Dainichi 大日
Dainichi Daishō Fudō Myōō 大日大聖
不動明王
Dainichi Nyorai 大日如來
Dainippon-koku 大日本國
Daitokuji 大德寺
Daitsūchishō Butsu 大通智勝佛
Daiusu 提宇子
Daiusu-chō だいうす町
Daiusu monto 提宇子門徒
**daiuzo 大嘘
dakuten 濁點
Dandoku 檀特
danmari だんまり
**Dayri 内裏
Dengyō 傳教
Denshin hōyō 傳心法要
Deshima 出島
🈡 goittai o banji ni koe taisetsu ni
    uyamai tatematsurubeshi 🈡 御一體ヲ
    萬事ニ越へ大切ニ敬ヒ奉ルヘシ
Dōgen 道元
dōjō 道塲
dōjuku 同宿
dōka 道歌
dōmonshū 同紋衆
dōri 道理
dōshin 同心
Dōshun 道春

Echigo 越後
Echizen 越前

Echū 惠中
Eiroku 永祿
endon 圓頓
Endon-shū 圓頓宗
Engi 延喜
enkyō 圓教
Enma-ō 閻魔王
enman 圓滿
ennyū 圓融
Enō dankyō 惠能壇經
Enryakuji 延曆寺
Eshun 惠春, 惠俊
eta 穢多

★Fei-hsiu 斐休
★★Fitotçu niua, tada go ittai no Deus uo
banji ni coyete, go taixet ni vyamai-
tatematçurubexi. Futatçu niua, vaga
mi no gotoqu, Proximo uo vomoye
toyŭ coto core nari. 一にはたゝ御一体
のてうすを万事にこえて御大切にうや
まひ奉るへし. 二には我身のことくほ
ろしもをおもへと云事是也.
★Fu Hsi 伏羲
Fu-u 不于
Fuchi 淵
Fuchū 府中
Fudō 不動
Fujita Tōko 藤田東湖
Fujiwara no Sumitomo 藤原純友
Fujiwara Seika 藤原惺窩
fujōkan 不淨觀
Fukahori Sumikata 深堀純賢
Fukan 不干
★Fukien 福建
Fukuda 福田
Fukuda Kanechika 福田兼親
Fukuoka 福岡
Fukuyama 福山
fumie 踏繪
Fumoto no kusawake 麓草分
Funai 府內
funi 不二
funnu 忿怒
Furaten ふらてん
Furaten Bateren 不羅手無伴天連, 浮羅
天破天連
furigana 振り假名
Furukomu 普留考務
Furuna 富留那
fuse 布施
Fushimi 伏見
futaiten 不退轉

Futo 浮屠

Gaikotsu 骸骨
gaki 餓鬼
Gamō Ujisato 蒲生氏鄉
gekokujō 下尅上
Gengi 玄義
Genki 元龜
Genna [Genwa] 元和
Gerigori 計里故離
geten 外典
Gifu 岐阜
Gion 祇園
go fukyūzai 五不救罪
go gyakuzai 五逆罪
Go-Nara no In 後奈良院
Go-Toba 後鳥羽
★★Goin. Itçutçu no coye. 五音. 五ツノ音
Goittai no Ｄ o taisetsu ni uyamai
tatematsurubeshi 御一体ノＤ ヲ大切ニ
敬イ奉ルベシ
★★Goittaino Deusuo vyamai tattomi
tatematçurubexi. 御一たいのＤ
をうやまひたつとミ奉るべし
Gojŏ 五條
Gojō Horikawa 五條堀川
★★Gojŏ. Iin, Gui, Rei, Chi, Xin. 五常.
仁義禮智信
gokai 五戒
gokei 五刑
gokenin 御家人
Gōko no yasu 江湖野子
goma 護摩
gomi 五味
gonge 權化
gongen 權現
goningumi 五人組
gonjitsu 權實
gonke no shinsei 權化ノ神聖
gonkyō 權敎
★★Gonrocu 權六
★★Goquinay 五畿內
Gosan 五山
Gosan Bungaku 五山文學
gosanke 御三家
gotai 五體
Gotō (islands) 五島
Gotō (family) 後藤
Gotō Takaaki 後藤貴明
goyō gakusha 御用學者
gozō 五臟
Gōzumo がうずも
guchi 愚痴

Ha Daiusu 破提宇子
Ha Kirishitan 破吉利支丹
Hachiman 八幡
Hachiman Daibosatsu 八幡大菩薩
hachinan 八難
Hachiya Daizen Daibu Kennyū 蜂屋
大膳大夫謙入
Hai Yaso 排耶蘇
haikai 俳諧
hakase 博士
Hakata 博多
Hakuō Koji 伯翁居士
hakyaku 破却
★Han 漢
han 藩
Hanazono 花園
Hannya shingyō 般若心經
Hara 原
Harima 播磨
Hasegawa Gonroku 長谷川權六
Hasegawa Sahyōe no Jō Fujihiro 長谷
川左兵衞尉藤廣
Hashiba Chikuzen 羽柴筑前
Hashimoto Tahyōe 橋本多兵衞
hassō 八相
hatamoto 旗本
Hayashi 林
Hayashi Eiki 林永喜
Hayashi Razan 林羅山
Hayashi Shunsai 林春齋
Hayashi Zōsu 林藏主
Heiji no Ran 平治ノ亂
Heike 平家
Heike monogatari 平家物語
Hekiganroku 碧巖錄
Hekki Akitsura (Tachibana Dōsetsu)
戸次鑑連 (立花道雪)
Hekki Tachibana 戸次立花
Hiei 比叡
Higo 肥後
Higoroya [Hibiya] 日比屋
hijō 非情
hikari o yawarage chiri ni majiwari-
tamau 光ヲ和ケ塵ニ交リ玉フ
Hiko-nagisa-take-u-gaya-fuki-aezu no
Mikoto 彦波瀲武鸕鶿草葺不合尊
Himeji 姬路
hinoe ne 丙子
hinoe uma 丙午
Hirado 平戸
hiragana ひらがな
Hirakata 枚方
Hisōjiyō 比佐宇志也宇
Hitachi obi 常陸帯

Hitoyoshi 人吉
Hizen 肥前
hōben hosshin 方便法身
Hōei 寶永
Hogen no Ran 保元ノ亂
Hogoshū 反故集
hōjin 報身
Hōjō Awa no Kami Ujinaga 北條安房
守氏長
Hōjō Sagami Tarō Tokimune 北條
相模太郎時宗
Hōjō Yoshitoki 北條義時
Hokekyō 法華經
Hokekyō gengi 法華經玄義
Hokekyō mongu 法華經文句
Hokke 法華
hōkō sunawachi shugyō nari 奉公則
修行ナリ
Hōkōji 法廣寺
Honda Kōzuke no Suke Masazumi
本田上野介正純
Honda Sado no Kami Masanobu
本多佐渡守正信
Hondo 本渡
Hōnen Shōnin 法然上人
hongaku 本覺
Honganji 本願寺
honji 本地
honji suijaku 本地垂迹
honji suijaku no iware 本地垂迹ノ謂レ
Honnōji 本能寺
honshō 本性
hōō-koku 法王國
Hōrengekyō 法蓮華經
Hōryūji 法隆寺
Hosokawa 細川
Hosokawa Etchū no Kami Tadatoshi
細川越中守忠利
Hosokawa Tadaoki 細川忠興
hosshin 法身
hosshō 法性
hosshō hosshin no honbutsu 法性法身
ノ本佛
Hossō 法相
hossu 法主
hotoke 佛
★Hou Ching 侯景
Hōzō Biku 法藏比丘
★hsi 希
★Hsia 夏
★*Hsien-t'ien kua-wei t'u* 先天卦位圖
★Hsien Yang 咸陽
★Huang T'ing-chien 黃庭堅
★Hui 回

*Hui-neng 惠能
*Hui Tzu 惠子
*hun 魂
*Hunan 湖南
Hyakumanben Chionji 百萬遍知恩寺
hyakushō-bun 百姓分
hyakushō-mochi 百姓持
hyō 俵
hyōjōsho 評定所
Hyūga 日向

*i 夷
*I-ching 易經
*I-hsing 一行
Ibukiyama 伊吹山
Ichijō 一條
Ichijō Abura no Kōji 一條油小路
Ichijō Kanesada 一條兼定
Ichiku 市來
ichinen sanzen 一念三千
ichinyo 一如
Igarashi 五十嵐
Ikitsuki 生月
ikki 一揆
Ikkō 一向
Ikkō ikki 一向一揆
Ikkōshū 一向宗
Ikkōshū metsuke 一向宗目付
Imatomi 今富
in-i 因位
Inasa 稲佐
Inoue Chikugo no Kami Masashige
井上筑後守正重
Inoue Han'emon no Jō Kiyohide 井上
半右衞門尉清秀
**Inovii Sicungodonne 井上筑後殿
Iruman 伊留滿, 伊留慢, 以妻慢
Iruman kokoroe no koto 伊留滿心得ノ事
Isahaya 諫早
Ise 伊勢
Ise Daimyōjin 伊勢大明神
Ise Jingū Bunko 伊勢神宮文庫
Ise Nagashima 伊勢長島
Ishida 石田 Antonio
Ishida Jibu no Shōyū Mitsunari 石田
治部少輔三成
Ishigae Jūzō no Suke Sadakiyo 石谷十
藏介貞清
Ishikawa Jōzan 石川丈山
Ishiyama Honganji 石山本願寺
issai shujō shitsu u busshō 一切衆生悉
有佛性
isshin 一心
isshō no kikai 一生の奇會

Itakura Iga no Kami Katsushige 板倉
伊賀守勝重
Itakura Naizen no Kami Shigemasa
板倉內膳正重昌
Itō 伊東 Mancio
itomaki no tachi 糸卷の太刀
itomakimono 糸卷物
Iwakura 岩倉
Iwami Ginzan Bugyō 石見銀山奉行
Iyo 伊豫
Izanagi no Mikoto 伊弉諾尊
Izanami no Mikoto 伊弉冊尊
Izu Kinzan Bugyō 伊豆金山奉行
Izumi 和泉
Izumo 出雲
Izumo Taisha 出雲大社

Jakkōdo 寂光土
Jakyō taii 邪敎大意
jashūmon 邪宗門
*jen hsin 人心
jigoku 地獄
jijū 侍從
jikkyō 實敎
Jimmu Tennō 神武天皇
Jimon 寺門
jinai 寺內
Jingū Kōgō 神功皇后
jinshin 仁心
jiryō 寺領
jisha 侍者
jishō 自性
jissō musō 實相無相
jitō 地頭
jitsu-u 實有
jitsuaku 實惡
jiyū 自由
jiyū jizai 自由自在
Jizo Bosatsu 地藏菩薩
Jō-yuishiki-ron 成唯識論
Jōbon Daiō 淨飯大王
Jōdo 淨土
Jōdo Shinshū 淨土眞宗
jōi 攘夷
Jōjakkōdo 常寂光土
Jōjitsu 成實
jōjū-ekū no shidai 成住壞空ノ次第
jōkamachi 城下町
Jōshū 趙州
jūaku 十惡
Judō no koto 儒道之事
jūkai 十戒
junshi 殉死
jusha 儒者

Kaga 加賀
Kagazume Minbu no Shōshō Tada-
zumi 加々爪民部少輔忠澄
Kagoshima 鹿兒島
kahō 果報
★Kai-t'ien 蓋天
Kaikyō 戒經
kaishaku 介錯
Kaiten shishi 回天詩史
kaji 加持
kakon 嫁婚
Kakuban 覺鑁
kakubutsu kyūri 格物究理
Kakure 隱れ
Kakure monto 隱れ門徒
Kamachi Shigenami 蒲池鎭並, 鎭蓮
kami 神
"Kamigami no bishō" 神神の微笑
Kamigyō 上京
kan 貫
Kan Muryōju-kyō 觀無量壽經
Kan Shōjō 菅相丞
kana 假名
Kana shōri 假名性理
Kanazawa 金澤
kanbun 漢文
Kan'ei 寬永
kanme 貫目
Kannon 觀音
kanoe saru 庚申
kanpaku 關白
kansō 官僧
Kanzan 關山
Kanzeon 觀世音
Karatsu 唐津
Kariya 苅谷
Kasuga 春日
katakana カタカナ
katakiuchi 仇討
Katō Higo no Kami Kiyomasa 加藤
肥後守清正
Kawachi 河內
Kawachiura 河內浦
Kawara Jūrōbei 河原十郎兵衞
Kawazumi Saburōemon 川角三郎
右衞門
Kawazumi Taikōki 川角太閤記
kazoetoshi 數え年
Kazusa (province) 上總
Kazusa (town) 加津佐
Kegon 華嚴
Kegon-kyō 華嚴經
Keichō 慶長

kekyō 化境
kendan funyūken 檢斷不入權
Kengiroku 顯僞錄
Kengyō no Bō 檢校の坊
Kenninji 建仁寺
Kennyo Kōsa 顯如光佐
keshin 化身
ki 氣
★Kiangsi 江西
Kibe 岐部 Casui Pedro
kihō ni wa orazu 危邦ニハ不居
Kii 紀伊
Kiichi Kengyō 喜一檢校
Kikkawa Motoharu 吉川元春
Kikuchi 菊池
Kikyōya 桔梗屋 Juan
Kimura 木村 Sebastião
Kinkakuji 金閣寺
kinsei daimyō 近世大名
Kinuya 絹屋 Juan
Kirishitan 吉利支丹, 切支丹, 貴利支丹,
鬼理志端
Kirishitan bungaku 吉利支丹文學
Kirishitan Buppō no koto 吉利支丹佛法の事
Kirishitan daimyō 切支丹大名
Kirishitan-kan 切支丹館
Kirishitan monogatari 切支丹物語
Kirishitan ōrai 貴理師端往來
Kirishitan Yashiki 切支丹屋敷
Kirishito-ki 契利斯督記
Kiso 木曾
Kita no Mandokoro 北政所
Kitano Tenmangū 北野天滿宮
Kiyohara Geki Ekata (Dōhaku) 清原
外記枝賢(道白)
Kiyomori 清盛
Kizu 木津
kō 孝
Kobayakawa Takakage 小早川隆景
Kobinata 小日向
Kōbō 弘法
Kōchi 高知
kōdan 講談
Kōdōkanki jutsugi 弘道館記述義
Kōfukuji 興福寺
Kohachiya Nyūdō 古蜂屋入道
koji 居士
Kōji 弘治
Kojima 戶島
kokka ankō 國家安康
Kokonoe Masazane 九戶政實
kokoro oba urasaji ga tame nari 心ヲバ
ウラサジカ爲也

koku 石
kokū hokkai 虛空法界
kokudo o osamen 國土を治めん
kokujin 國人
Kokura 小倉
kokutai 國體
komushin 虛無身
Konchiin Sūden 金地院崇傳
Kongōkai Dainichi Nyorai 金剛界大日
如來
kongōken 金剛拳
Kongōkyō 金剛經
Konishi Ryūsa 小西隆佐，立佐
Konishi Settsu no Kami Yukinaga
小西攝津守行長
Konoye コノェ Bartholomeo
kontai ryōbu no mandara 金胎兩部
曼荼羅
Koretō muhonki 惟任謀叛記
Korobi Kirishitan 轉び切支丹
korobu 轉ぶ
Kōsa 光佐
Kōshinpi 加字志牟比
kōtan senrō 荒誕淺陋
Kōyasan 高野山
Kozasa 小佐々
kū wa tadachi ni mu ni shite naki
mono nareba 空ハ直ニ無ニシテナキ
物ナレバ
Kuchinotsu 口之津
*kuei 鬼
*kuei-shen 鬼神
*kuei-shen che erh-ch'i chih liang-neng
yeh 鬼神者二氣之良能也
Kumamoto 熊本
Kumazawa Banzan 熊澤蕃山
kumi 組
Kunaikyō Hōin 宮內卿法印
Kuni-sazuchi no Mikoto 國狹槌尊
Kuni-tokotachi no Mikoto 國常立尊
kunishū 國衆
Kunōzan 久能山
kurobōzu 黑坊主
Kuroda Josui Yoshitaka (Kodera
Kanbei) 黑田如水孝高 (小寺官兵衛)
Kuroda Naoyuki 黑田直之
Kuroda Uemon no Suke Tadayuki
黑田右衞門佐忠之
Kurume 久留米
Kusha 俱舍
Kusha-ron 俱舍論
Kushi-inada Hime 奇稻田姬
kusō 九相

kusugurimono 擽物
Kusunoki 楠
kusurimono くすりもの
Kuzōshi 句双紙
kyo 虛
kyōdan 教團
Kyōgoku 京極 Maria
Kyōhō 享保
Kyōnyo 教如
kyorei fumai 虛靈不昧
kyōryō rinshin 教令輪身
Kyōto Shoshidai 京都所司代
Kyozen キョゼン Paul
Kyūshū godōza ki 九州御動座記
Kyūshū Tandai 九州探題

*li 理
*Li chi 禮記
*Liang 梁
*Lü hsing 呂刑
*Lü Tzu-yüeh 呂子約

Maeda 前田
Maeda Toshiie 前田利家
Magoroku 孫六
Maka shikan 摩訶止觀
manbō ze shinnyo shinnyo ze manbō
萬法是眞如眞如是萬法
Manji 萬治
Manjuji 萬壽寺
mappō 末法
Marishi-ten 摩利支天
Marubashi Chūya 丸橋忠彌
Maruchiriyo no shiori マルチリヨの栞
Maruchiru no michi 丸血留の道
Marugame 丸龜
Masamune 正宗
Masatsune 正常
Mashita Moritsugu 增田盛次
Mashita Uemon no Jō Nagamori
增田右衞門尉長盛
masse 末世
**Matsodairo Ysossama 松平伊豆様
Matsudaira Izu no Kami Nobutsuna
松平伊豆守信綱
Matsudaira Kai no Kami Terutsuna
松平甲斐守輝綱
Matsudaira Sadamasa 松平定政
Matsukura Bungo no Kami Shige-
masa 松倉豐後守重政
Matsukura Nagato no Kami Katsuie
(Shigeharu, Shigetsugu) 松倉長門守
勝家(重治，重次)

Matsumura 松村
Matsunaga Danjō Hisahide (Sōtai)
松永彈正久秀 (霜臺)
Matsunaga Teitoku 松永貞德
Matsuo 松尾
Matsuura 松浦
Matsuura Shiryō Hakubutsukan
松浦史料博物館
Matsuura Takanobu 松浦隆信
Maya 摩耶
**Meaco 都
Meakashi Chūan 目明忠庵
meikun 明君
Meireki 明暦
meitoku 明德
meiyo 名譽
metsuke 目付
**Miaco/Miacö 都
Mida 彌蛇
Miidera 三井寺
Mikawa 三河
Mikoshi Nyūdō 見越入道
Mimigawa 耳川
Mimizugawa 美々津川
Minamoto 源
Minamoto no Yoritomo 源賴朝
*Ming 明
*Ming Ti 明帝
Mino 美濃
mino 簑
Miroku 彌勒
Mito 水戸
Miwa 三輪
Miwa monogatari 三輪物語
Miyako 都
Miyoshi 三好
Miyoshi Shūri no Daibu Chōkei
[Nagayoshi] 三好修理大夫長慶
Miyoshi Yoshitsugu 三好義繼
Mizuno Hyūga no Kami Katsunari
水野日向守勝成
Mōanjō 盲安杖
Mogi 茂木
Momoyama 桃山
Mongu 文句
monme 匁
monshu 門主
monto 門徒
Monzen 文選
monzen-machi 門前町
Mōri 毛利
Mōri Motonari 毛利元就
Mōri Terumoto 毛利輝元

mōryō onna 盲聾瘖痘
mu 無
mu-i hō 無爲法
muchi yaku mutoku (Fabian) 無智亦無德
muchi yaku mutoku (Hannya) 無智亦無得
muga 無我
muji mubetsu 無二無別
mujishō 無自性
mujō 無常
Mukai Genshō 向井元升, 玄松
mura hachibu 村八分
Murasakino 紫野
Murayama Shūan 村山秋安
Murayama Tōan Antonio 村山当安
安当仁与, 等安, 東安
Murayama Tokuan 村山德安
Muromachi 室町
Muryōju 無量壽
mushikkai 無色界
musō 無相
Musō Soseki 夢窓疎石
myō 妙
Myōhō rengekyō 妙法蓮華經
myōkai 冥界
Myōkakuji 妙覺寺
Myōon Bosatsu 妙音菩薩
Myōshinji 妙心寺
myōshu 名主
Myōshū 妙秀
myōtai 冥諦
Myōtei mondō 妙貞問答

Nabeshima 鍋島
Nabeshima Shinano no Kami Katsu-
shige 鍋島信濃守勝茂
Nagasaki Bugyō 長崎奉行
Nagasaki Daikan 長崎代官
Nagasaki itsuji 長崎逸事
Nagasaki Jinzaemon Sumikage
長崎甚左衞門純景
Nagashino 長篠
Nagatani 長谷
Naidaijin 內大臣
naiten 內典
Nakagawa Sebyōe no Jō Kiyohide
中川瀬兵衞尉清秀
Nakamiya 中宮
Nakane Iki no Kami 中根壹岐守
Namu Amida Butsu 南無阿彌陀佛
namu = minami nashi 南無＝ミナミ
ナシ
Nanban byōbu 南蠻屏風
Nanbanji 南蠻寺

Nanbanryū 南蠻流
**nanguinata 長刀
Naniwa 難波
Nanzenji 南禪寺
Negoro 根來
Nenbutsu 念佛
Niabara ニアバラ Luis
Nichiren 日蓮
Nichiren Shōnin 日蓮聖人
Nihongi 日本紀
Nihonshi tanpō 日本史探訪
Nijō 二條
nijū-go tai 二十五諦
nijū naru kokoro 二重ナル心
nijū-yo nen 二重餘年
Nikan 二官 Donatus
niku zōka 肉造化
ningen no hakku 人間ノ八苦
Ninin bikuni 二人比丘尼
Niō 二王, 仁王
Nishi Kichibei 西吉兵衞
nisōgi 二僧祇
Nizōgi 二藏義
Nobuzumi 信澄
nyūdō 入道

**O 皇
Ō-mononushi no Mikoto 大物主命
Ōbaku Kiun 黃檗希運
Oda 織田
Oda Nobunaga 織田信長
Oda Nobutada 織田信忠
Oda Nobutaka 織田信孝
Ōe 大江
Ōe no Masafusa 大江匡房
Ōgaki 大垣
Ogasawara Ukon no Daibu Tadazane 小笠原右近大夫忠眞
ōge hosshin 應化法身
ōge no Nyorai 應化ノ如來
Ogino 荻野
Ōhara 大原
ōjin 應身
Ōjin Tennō 應神天皇
Okamoto San'emon 岡本三右衞門
Okayama 岡山
Okitanawate 沖田畷
Ōkōchi 大河內
Ōkubo Hikozaemon 大久保彥左衞門
Ōkubo Iwami no Kami Nagayasu [Chōan] 大久保石見守長安
Ōkubo Sagami no Kami Tadachika 大久保相模守忠隣

ōmetsuke 大目付
Ōmi 近江
Ōmura 大村
Ōmura Naozumi 大村直澄
Ōmura Sumisaki 大村純前
Ōmura Sumitada 大村純忠
Ōmura Sumiyoshi 大村純伊
Ōmura Yoshisaki 大村喜前
Ōmura Yūko 大村由己
**Omurandono 大村殿
on mo shirazu 恩モ知ラス
Ōnin 應仁
Onjōji 園城寺
onma no sakite 御馬先手
Onmyōryō 陰陽寮
Onshinji 恩眞寺
on'yashiki 御屋敷
Oranjin o miru no ki 觀和蘭人記
osa byakushō 長百姓
Ōsumi 大隅
Ōtaki 大多喜
otogi-shū 御伽衆
Ōtomabe no Mikoto 大苫邊尊
Ōtomo 大友
Ōtomo kōhaiki 大友興廢記
Ōtomo shichikakoku no zei 大友七ケ國の勢
Ōtomo Sōrin Yoshishige 大友宗麟義鎭
Ōtomo Yoshiaki 大友義鑑
Ōtomo Yoshimune 大友義統
otona 乙名
Ōtonoji no Mikoto 大戶之道尊
Ōtsu 大津
Ōtsu Denjūrō 大津傳十郎
Ōuchi Teruhiro 大內輝弘
Ōuchi Yoshitaka 大內義隆
Owari 尾張
Ōyano 大矢野

*P'an-kuWang 盤古王
*p'o 魄

**Qifŏniua irazu, rampŏniua vorazu: tenca michi aru toqimba mamiye: michi naqi toqimba cacuru. 危邦不入亂邦不居. 天下有道則見無道則隱
**Qimi qimi tarazu, xin motte xin tarazumba arubecarazu. 君不爲君臣以不可有不爲臣
**Qincuxŭ 金句集
**Quambacudono 關白殿

Raichō jikki 來朝實記

Rangakusha 蘭學者
Rennyo 蓮如
rikugō 六合
Rikyū shittetsu 利休七哲
Rinzai 臨濟
Risen 理仙，理專
Ritsu 律
Roankyō 驢鞍橋
rōgatsu yōka 蠟月八日
rōjū 老中
Rokkaku 六角
Rokuhara 六波羅
Rokuso dankyō 六祖壇經
Rōmajin shochi kengi 羅馬人處置献議
rōnin 牢人
roppu 六腑
Rorensu ろれんす
**Rŏxite cô naxi 勞而無功
"Rushiheru" るしへる
rusui 留守居
ruten 流轉
Ryōbu Shintō 兩部神道
Ryōgankō 兩眼考
Ryōhōki 兩豐記
Ryōyo Shōkei 了譽聖冏
Ryūzōji 龍造寺
Ryūzōji Takanobu 龍造寺隆信

**Sackay Sammoccysame 酒井讚岐樣
**Sacuma 薩摩
Sadamune 貞宗
Sado Kinzan Bugyō 佐渡金山奉行
Saga 佐賀
Saigō 西鄉
Saigō Sumitaka 西鄉純堯
Saihō Jōdo 西方淨土
Saitō Gonnai 齋藤權內
Sakai 堺
Sakai Sanuki no Kami Tadakatsu
酒井讚岐守忠勝
Sakitsu 崎津
Sakoku 鎖國
Sakuma Morimasa 佐久間盛政
Sakuma Uemon 佐久間右衞門
samurai-bun 侍分
sanbukyō 三部經
sandoku 三毒
Sanga Hōki no Kami Yoriteru 三箇
伯耆守賴照
sangai 三界
Sangan yokō 三眼餘考
Sanja takusen 三社託宣
sanjin 三身

sanjū-ni sō 卅二相
Sankoku 山谷
Sanmon 山門
sanmyō o sagaitaru koto 三冥ヲサカイ
タル事
Sannō 山王
Sanron 三論
sanshō 三障
Sanuki 讚岐
sanze 三世
sanzen dai sen-sekai 三千大千世界
Sanzu no Kawa 三途の川
sarugaku 猿樂
Satsuma 薩摩
Sawa 澤
Sawano Chūan 澤野忠庵
Sayō yoroku 查祅餘錄
sechi bensō 世智辯聰
seidaku dōjō no ki 清濁動靜ノ氣
Seika sensei no gyōjō 惺窩先生ノ行狀
seimei no keishi 生命の輕視
seisatsu 制札
Seiyō kibun 西洋紀聞
seken o ri-sen 世間を利せん
Sekigahara 關ヶ原
Sekihei Dōnin gyōgōki 石平道人行業記
Sekihei Dōnin gyōgōki bengi 石平道人
行業記辯疑
Sekihei Dōnin shisō 石平道人四相
Sen no Rikyū 千利休
Senchaku hongan nenbutsushū 選擇本願
念佛集
Senchakushū 選擇集
Sendai 仙臺
Sengoku 戰國
sengoku bushi 戰國武士
sengoku daimyō 戰國大名
Sennan no Tsu 泉南ノ津
seppuku 切腹
Seson 世尊
Sessō 雪窓
Settsu 攝津
Shaka 釋迦
Shaka Nyorai 釋迦如來
Shaku jōdo nizōgi 釋淨土二藏義
shami 沙彌
*Shan ch'üan shu 山權數
*Shang 商
*Shang shu 尙書
*Shang Ti 上帝
*Shao Yung 邵雍
Sharajurin 娑羅樹林
*shen 神

★Shen Kua 沈括
★*Shen shih* 審時
shi, nō, kō, shō 士農工商
Shibata kassenki 柴田合戰記
Shibata Katsuie 柴田勝家
Shichi-kan Ryōga-kyō 七卷楞伽經
shidai 四大
Shide no Yama 死出の山
shido 四土
Shiga 志賀
Shigi 信貴
Shigo Shōten Haraizō Zensu Maro
死後生天破羅韋增善主摩呂
Shijō 四條
Shijō no Bōmon Ubayanagi 四條坊門
姥柳
shikaku 始覺
shikaku hongaku no satori 始覺本覺の
悟り
shikan 止觀
Shiki 志岐
Shikimi Ichizaemon 式見市左衛門
shikkai 色界
shikō 四劫
Shimabara 島原
Shimazu 島津
Shimazu Takahisa 島津貴久
Shimazu Yoshihisa 島津義久
Shimo 下
Shimogyō 下京
Shimon しもん
Shimonoseki 下關
Shimōsa 下總
Shimotsuke 下野
shin-i-shiki 心意識
shin, sō, gyō 眞草行
Shinano 信濃
Shin'en Shōnin 眞緣上人
shingatai 神我諦
Shingen 信玄
Shingon 眞言
shin'i 順恚
shinjo 心所
shinnō 心王
Shinnō Fudō 心王不動
shinnyo 眞如
Shinran 親鸞
shinsanshū 新參衆
Shinshū 眞宗
Shintō no koto 神道之事
shippō 七寶
shishi 志士
Shizu ga Take 賤ヶ嶽

Shizu no Hara 靜原
Shizuoka 靜岡
shōbō 正法
Shōdoshima 小豆島
shōen 莊園
Shōhei 承平
Shōhei-Tengyō no Ran 承平・天慶
ノ亂
shōjōhi 猩猩緋
shoke 庶家
shōkō 小劫
Shōkōkan 彰考館
Shōkokuji 相國寺
shokuhō daimyō 織豐大名
Shōkyū no Hen 承久ノ變
shōnagon 少納言
Shōtai 承兌
Shōtoku 正德
Shōtoku Taishi 聖德太子
Shōyū 頌遊
Shūgi gaisho 集義外書
shugo 守護
shugo daimyō 守護大名
shuinjō 朱印狀
shujō 衆生
shukke 出家
shūkyō daimyō 宗教大名
Shūkyōroku 宗鏡錄
shūmon-aratame yaku 宗門改役
★Shun 舜
★*Shun tien* 舜典
shunban 蠢蠻
Shuron gedō 數論外道
Shuryōgon-kyō 首楞嚴經
shuryōgon sanmai 首楞嚴三昧
shuso 首座
shusse 出世
★★Singok 地獄
sō 相
Soga Hisasuke 曾我古祐
sōki 惣櫃
Sokkyohen 息距篇
sōmei eichi 聰明叡智
sōmetsuke 惣目付
sōmoku kokudo shikkai jōbutsu 草木
國土悉皆成佛
sonnō jōi 尊王攘夷
Sonogi 彼杵
sōsū 惣樞
Sōtō 曹洞
Sotome 外海
Sōzoku ki 草賊記
★Su Shih 蘇軾

Suetsugu Heizō Masanao 末次平藏政直
Suetsugu Kōzen 末次興善
Suganoya Kuemon no Jō Nagayori
菅谷九右衛門尉長頼
Sugawara Michizane 菅原道眞
suijaku 垂迹
Suijini 沙土煮
Sumiyoshi 住吉
★Sun En 孫恩
★Sung 宋
Sunpu 駿府
Suō 周防
Suruga 駿河
Susanoo 素戔鳴
Suzuki Jinja 鈴木神社
Suzuki Saburō-Kurō Shigenari 鈴木
三郎九郎重成
Suzuki Shigetatsu 鈴木重辰
Suzuki Shōsan 鈴木正三

★Ta-hsüeh chih tao tsai ming ming-te
大學之道在明明德
★Ta Yü mo 大禹謨
Tachibana 立花
Tachibana Hida no Kami Muneshige
立花飛驒守宗茂
tachikaeri 立ち歸り
Tafukuji 多福寺
★T'ai-ch'eng 臺城
★T'ai-chi t'u 太極圖
★T'ai-chi t'u chieh-i 太極圖解義
taigi meibun 大義名分
Taiheiji 泰平寺
Taiheiki 太平記
Taiheiki nukigaki 太平記拔書
Taiji jashūron 對治邪宗論
Taikō 太閤
Taikōki 太閤記
Taira 平
Taira no Ason 平朝臣
Taira no Masakado 平將門
Tairō 大老
taisetsu 大切
Taitokuin-den 臺德院殿
Taiyūin-sama 大猷院樣
Takai 高井 Cosme
Takaku 高來
Takaoka 高岡
Takatsuki 高槻
Takayama 高山
Takayama Hida no Kami Zusho
(Dario) 高山飛驒守厨書（大慮）
Takayama Ukon 高山右近

Hikogorō 彥五郎
Minami no Bō 南坊
Nagafusa 長房
Shigetomo 重友
Tōhaku 等伯
Ukon no Daibu 右近大夫
Ukon no Jō 右近允，右近尉
Ukon no Shōgen 右近將監
Ukon no Suke 右近亮，右近助
Yūshō 友祥
(Justo) 壽須，壽子
Takeda 武田
Takeda Katsuyori 武田勝頼
Takeda Shingen 武田信玄
Takenaka Uneme no Kami Shige-
yoshi 竹中采女正重義
Takoyakushi Muromachi nishi-iru
蛸藥師室町西入ル
Takuan 澤庵
Takushima 度島
tameshigiri 試し斬り
Tamura 田村
★T'ang (dynasty) 唐
★T'ang (of Shang) 湯
★tao hsin 道心
Tatsu no Kuchi no hōnan 龍口法難
Tawara 田原
tegara 手柄
Tenchi hajimari no koto 天地始りの事
Tendai 天臺
Tendai sandaibu 天臺三大部
Tendō 天童
tengu 天狗
Tengyō 天慶
Tenjiku Tokubei ikoku banashi 天竺
德兵衛韓噺
Tenka 天下
Tenka fubu 天下布武
Tenka no Sōdaikan 天下の惣代官
tenkō 轉向
Tenman Daijizai Tenjin 天滿大自在天神
Tenman Tenjin 天滿天神
Tenmei 天命
Tenmon 天文
tennen no gedō 天然の外道
tennin no gosui 天人の五衰
Tenpō 天保
Tenri 天理
Tenryūji 天龍寺
Tenshō 天正
Tenshōki 天正記
Tenshu 天主
Tenshukyō taii 天主教大意

Tentaishaku 天帝釋
Tentō 天道
Tentō no garasa 天道之加羅佐
Terazawa 寺澤
Terazawa Hyōgo no Kami Katataka
寺澤兵庫頭堅高
Terazawa Shima no Kami Masanari
(Hirotaka) 寺澤志摩守正成（廣高）
Tetchisen 鐵圍山
★t'i 體
Tōba 東坡
★★Tocuã 德安
Toda Saemon no Kami (Samon
Ujikane) 戸田左衛門督（左門氏鐵）
Tōdaiji 東大寺
tōdō 東堂
Tōfukuji 東福寺
Togashi 富樫
Togashi Masachika 富樫政親
Tōji 東寺
tōken 唐犬
Tokubei 德兵衞
Tokugawa 德川
Tokugawa Hidetada 德川秀忠
Tokugawa Iemitsu 德川家光
Tokugawa Ienobu (Kōfu Tsunatoyo)
德川家宣（甲府綱豐）
Tokugawa Ietsuna 德川家綱
Tokugawa Ieyasu 德川家康
Tokugawa Nariaki 德川齋昭
Tokugawa Tsunayoshi 德川綱吉
Tokugawa Yorinobu 德川賴宣
tono 殿
ton'yoku 貪慾
Tōriten 忉利天
Tōru 融
Tosa 土佐
Tōshōgū 東照宮
Tosotsuten 兜率天
Toyokunnu no Mikoto 豐斟渟尊
Toyotomi 豐臣
Toyotomi Hidetsugu 豐臣秀次
Toyotomi Hideyori 豐臣秀頼
Toyotomi Hideyoshi 豐臣秀吉
★Tsa hsüeh-pien: Su-shih I chieh
雜學辨蘇氏易解
Tsu 津
tsū 通
tsuchinoto u 己卯
Tsukushi 筑紫
Tsukushi shoke kōhaiki 筑紫諸家興廢記
Tsushima 對馬
Tsutsui Junkei 筒井順慶

Tsutsui Sadatsugu 筒井定次
Tsutsumi Rokuzaemon 堤六左衞門

u 有
U-gaya-fuki-awasezu no Mikoto
鸕鶿草葺不合尊
u-i hō 有爲法
u-konoe 右近衞
u-sō sekai 有相世界
Uesugi Norizane 上杉憲實
Uijini 渥土煮
ujō 有情
Ukita Hideie 宇喜多秀家
Uma no Jō 右馬之允
Un 吽
Unko Keyō 雲居希膺
★★Unquio 雲居 [?]
Unzen 雲仙
Urado 浦戸
Urakami 浦上
Urugan Bateren 宇流加武伴天連，宇留
龕伴天連
Usa 宇佐
Usa mondō 宇佐問答
Usuki 臼杵
Uto 宇土
Uttan'otsu 鬱單越

★★Vcondono 右近殿
★★Vozàca 大坂
★★Vso uo fuqu 嘯を吹く

Wada Koremasa 和田惟政
Wada Korenaga 和田惟長
wakō dōjin 和光同塵
★Wang chih 王制
★Wang Yang-ming 王陽明
★wei 微
★Wen 文
★Wu 武
★Wu Ti 武帝
★Wu tu 五蠹

★★Xaca 釋迦
★★Ximoguio 下京
★★Xireranuoba xirerito xeyo: xirezaranuoba xirazuto xeyo: core xireru
nari. 知之爲知之不知爲不知是知也
★★xogun/xōgun 將軍

yaburu ヤブル
Yagyū Tajima no Kami 柳生但馬守
Yajirō ヤジロウ

yakata 屋形
Yakuin Zensō (Tokuun) 施藥院全宗
(德雲)
yakunin 役人
Yakushi 藥師
yakushu no iritaru hitotsu no hitsu
藥種ノ入タルーツノ櫃
yamabushi 山伏
Yamaga Sokō 山鹿素行
Yamaguchi 山口
Yamanba 山姥
Yamato 大和
Yamato Kōriyama 大和郡山
Yamazaki 山崎
Yamazaki Kai no Kami Ieharu 山崎
甲斐守家治
Yamazato 山里
Yanagawa 柳川
★Yao 堯
Yariisu 彌理居須
Yasaka 八坂
Yase 八瀬
Yaso 耶蘇，耶蘇
Yaso Tenchūki 耶蘇天誅記
★★yaxiqi 屋敷
★★Yedo/Yendo 江戶
★Yen-shou 延壽
★★YO VO ITOI, IESV CHRIStono
gocŏxeqiuo manabi tatematçuru
世をいとひꝑの御かうせきをまなひ奉る

Yodogimi 淀君
Yōhōken 養方軒 Paulo
yokkai 欲界
Yokoseura 橫瀬浦
Yōkyoku 謠曲
yoriki 與力
Yoshino 芳野
★Yu 由
Yui Shōsetsu 由井正雪
Yuishiki-ron 唯識論
Yūki Yamashiro no Kami Shinsai
Tadamasa 結城山城守進齋忠正
yūmyō 勇猛
★yung 用
Yūsan 幽山
Yūtei 幽貞
★Yü 禹
★Yüan-wu 圜悟

zangi sange 慚愧懺悔
zashiki 座敷
zazen 坐禪
zen'aku funi, jashō ichinyo 善惡不二
邪正一如
Zenmon no ippiki ōkami 禪門の一匹狼
Zensu [Zesu] 善主
Zensumaru ぜんす丸
Zō agongyō 雜阿含經
zōhō 像法
zōsu 藏主

Index

A (Guardian of the Law), 225
Acapulco, 135
Adam and Eve, 36, 168, 273–7, 278, 297, 301–2
Advertimentos e Avisos acerca dos Costumes e Catangues de Jappão by Alexandro Valignano SJ, 58–9, 61, 62, 427
Aesop, 20, 68, 148, 248
Ai Gozaemon (Dom Simão), 112, 114, 124, 420
Aida Yūji, 127, 129
Aizawa Seishisai, 242, 245–6
Akashi, 110, 125–6, 129–30
Akashi Kamon (Dom João), 264, 436, 466–7
Akechi Mitsuhide, 82–3, 109, 128, 424, 488
Akizuki, daimyo house, 22
Akutagawa Ryūnosuke, 142, 179, 254
Albrecht von Brandenburg, 474
Albuquerque, João de, OFM, 402
Alcazar Quivir, Battle of, 425
Alexander VI, Pope, 135, 425
Almeida, Luis de, SJ, 31, 62, 93; in Amakusa, 218, 221; in Arima, 28; in Bungo (Funai), 77, 208, 414; in Cabral's estimate, 414–5; in Ōmura, 27, 87–8; in popular imagination, 215, 477; in Satsuma, 33
Almeida, Pedro de, 415
Alvarez, Gonçalo, SJ, 104
Amakusa, 31, 252; *collegio* of, 145, 148, 169, 222, 478; daimyo of, 103; *Kakure* in, 222–3; mission press of, 148; and Shimabara Uprising, 218–23, 363, 488; Suzuki Shōsan's activities in, 7, 229–30, 232
Amakusa Sea, 38
Amakusa Shirō Tokisada (Amano Shirō), 3, 220–1, 363, 368, 452–3
Amaterasu Ōmikami, 180–1, 246, 254, 283, 347, 483
Ambrose, Saint, 67
Amida, 39, 120, 122, 182, 201–2, 219, 339, 344, 377, 384, 440, 442, 467, 482, 497; and Amidism, 41; invocation of (*nenbutsu*), 43, 79, 338, 351, 443; *see also* Pure Land, True Pure Land
anatsurushi (suspension in the pit), 186, 187, 191, 203, 205; Ferreira said to have died by, 211; Mastrilli subjected to, 198–9
Anesaki Masaharu, 166, 181–2
Angelis, Jeronymo de, SJ, 137
anjo (angels), 231, 272–3; *see also* Lucifer
Antichrist, 221
Antonio of Crato (pretender to Portuguese crown), 135, 138–9, 425, 426

Aquaviva, Claudio, General SJ, 104
Aquinas, Saint Thomas, 40–1, 251
Arabia, 303, 311
Arai Hakuseki: and Sidotti, 237–9; *Seiyō kibun*, 238–41, 245; on War of the Spanish Succession, 239–40; defines the Christian poison, 241
Arai Toshi, 403
Araki Murashige, 49–51, 127–8, 130, 405
Arima: daimyo house and domain, 27–8, 90, 94, 98, 103, 111, 132, 218, 418; *seminario* of, 28, 64, 70, 81
Arima Genba no Jō Toyouji, 364
Arima Harunobu (Dom Protasio), 28, 56, 64, 110, 425, 435
Arima Haruzumi, 90
Arima Yoshisada (Dom André), 27–8
Arioka, 51
Aristotle, 65, 66, 251, 252, 298, 460
Arroyo, Alonzo de, SJ, 199
ARTE DA LINGOA DE IAPAM by João Rodriguez Tçuzzu SJ, 20
Asai, daimyo house, 123
Asai Ryōi, 489
Asaka Tanpaku, 238
Asakura, daimyo house, 123
Asakura Kageakira, 123
Asakura Sōteki Norikage, 75
Asakusa, leprosarium of, 479
Ashikaga Bakufu (shogunate), 22, 75
Ashikaga Gakkō ("huniversidade de Bandou"), 37, 402
Ashikaga no Shō (in Shimotsuke), 402
Ashikaga Yoshiaki, 25, 127, 400
Ashikaga Yoshimitsu, 482
Ashikaga Yoshiteru, 127, 423, 476, 478
Aso family, 23
Asuka, 132
asuras, 46, 381, 490
Atlas Japannensis by Arnoldus Montanus, 200–2
Augustinians in Japan, 161, 437
Avila Girón, Bernardino de, 427; on 1614 persecution in Kyoto, 216–7, 487; on Murayama Tōan, 160–1
Awaji, 177
Azuchi: Bateren entertained by Nobunaga in, 325–7, 476–7; mission consultation of, 57, 61; *seminario* of, 19, 64, 69, 81, 403, 408
Azuchi-Momoyama period, 2, 26; literature of, 184, 248

Harvard East Asian Series